Introduction to Governmental and Not-for-Profit Accounting

Seventh Edition

Introduction to Governmental and Not-for-Profit Accounting

Martin Ives
New York University (retired)

Terry K. Patton
Midwestern State University

Suesan R. Patton
UHY LLP

PEARSON

Boston   Columbus   Indianapolis   New York   San Francisco   Upper Saddle River
Amsterdam   Cape Town   Dubai   London   Madrid   Milan   Munich   Paris   Montreal   Toronto
Delhi   Mexico City   São Paulo   Sydney   Hong Kong   Seoul   Singapore   Taipei   Tokyo

Editor in Chief: Donna Battista
Editorial Project Manager: Christina
 Rumbaugh
Editorial Assistants: Jane Avery and
 Lauren Zanedis
Director of Marketing: Maggie
 Moylan Leen
Marketing Assistants: Kimberly Lovato
Director of Production: Nancy Fenton
Production Project Manager:
 Clara Bartunek

Creative Art Director: Jayne Cor
Cover Designer: Bruce Kenselaar
Cover Art: Fotolia
Full-Service Project Managemer
 Munesh Kumar/Aptara®, Inc.
Printer/Binder: Courier Compar
 Westford
Cover Printer: Lehigh/Phoenix–
 Hagerstown
Text Font: Minion Pro Regular

Credits and acknowledgments borrowed from other sources and reproduced, wit
permission, in this textbook appear on the appropriate page within text.

Library of Congress Cataloging-in-Publication Data

Ives, Martin.
 Introduction to governmental and not-for-profit accounting / Martin I
Patton, Suesan Patton.—7th ed.
  p. cm.
 Rev. ed. of: Introduction to governmental and not-for-profit accounting / Martin Ives . . .
[et al.]. 6th ed.
 ISBN-13: 978-0-13-277601-1
 ISBN-10: 0-13-277601-4
 1. Fund accounting. 2. Finance, Public—Accounting. 3. Nonprofit
organizations—Accounting.
I. Patton, Terry K. II. Patton, Suesan R. III. Introduction to governmental and not-
for-profit accounting. IV. Title.
 HF5681.F84R39 2013
 657′.835—dc23

                                                         2012020546

10 9 8 7 6 5 4 3 2 1

ISBN 10:   0-13-277601-4
ISBN 13: 978-0-13-277601-1

BRIEF CONTENTS

CONTENTS

PREFACE

We have had extensive experience in teaching, in working at all three levels of government, in setting accounting standards, and in auditing financial statements. We know that accounting standards have become increasingly complex in an increasingly complex world. Therefore, we wrote this basic-level text on governmental and not-for-profit financial accounting and reporting with one key objective: to make it easy to read and understand. To accomplish this objective, we followed this general approach: discuss the accounting principle, show the journal entry, provide an illustration.

Given that the text is designated as an "introduction" to the subject, we tried to cover the basic accounting and financial reporting principles in as comprehensive a manner as possible. To keep the text practical and of the "real world," we enhanced the discussion of the principles with numerous illustrations drawn from financial reports prepared by actual governments and not-for-profit organizations. We updated the material to cover the latest accounting standards issued by the standards-setting bodies. Finally, we designed the end-of-chapter questions, discussion scenarios, exercises, and problems specifically to help students better understand the material covered in the text.

This text is written for college students (both accounting and public administration majors) and for practitioners. To permit use by different types of readers, its 15 chapters cover not only the specialized financial accounting and reporting standards applicable to the governmental and not-for-profit sectors, but also the basic processes of business-type accounting. Those who have not had a course in basic accounting or who need a brief refresher can start with Chapter 15 (Fundamentals of Accounting) and draw selectively on the governmental, not-for-profit, health care, and financial statement analysis chapters. Because of its flexibility, this text can be used by all of the following:

1. Accounting majors who wish to learn the fundamentals of governmental and not-for-profit accounting in either a full semester or less than a full semester
2. Public administration majors who have had no previous accounting training but who need a basic understanding of general, governmental, not-for-profit, and health care accounting; financial reporting; and financial statement analysis
3. Persons employed by governments and not-for-profit organizations, including the federal government, health care entities, colleges and universities, and voluntary health and welfare organizations
4. Persons preparing for the Uniform Certified Public Accountant (CPA) examination, Certified Government Financial Manager (CGFM) examination, and civil service examinations
5. Persons who wish, on their own, to learn about the financial accounting and reporting practices of governments and not-for-profit organizations

FEATURES OF THIS EDITION

Real Situations Illustrate the Application of Theory

To prepare for the practice of accounting, auditing, and financial management, students must be able to visualize the application of accounting theory to real-world situations. In preparing this seventh edition, we made a particular effort to increase the use of illustrations based on financial statements issued by actual governments and not-for-profit organizations. For example,

1. Throughout the text we used the financial statements of Mt. Lebanon, Pennsylvania, a relatively small governmental entity outside Pittsburgh, to illustrate governmental transactions,

events, use of funds, and financial reporting. Mt. Lebanon is small enough to allow students to readily visualize the transactions leading to its financial statements. To show how financial statements are used in the real world, we added our own analysis of Mt. Lebanon's financial position in Chapter 14.

2. To supplement the data provided by Mt. Lebanon's statements, we used the financial statements of many other entities, both governmental and not-for-profit. For example, we used the notes to the financial statements of the American Museum of Natural History to illustrate accounting for collections held by museums; the financial statements of New York's Metropolitan Transportation Authority to illustrate how various types of subsidies are reported by governmental enterprises; and the notes to Fordham University's financial statements to show how colleges and universities account for some of the more complex contributions they receive.

3. To enliven the text, we significantly increased the special feature that we call Governmental (or Not-for-Profit) Accounting in Practice. For example, our detailed discussion of the financial status of Social Security helps illustrate the extensive amount of detail provided in the annual financial report prepared by the United States government; and our discussion of the procedures used by Charity Navigator to assess the financial performance of not-for-profit entities helps illustrate the nature of the data provided in not-for-profit financial statements.

Discussion of Modified Accrual Basis of Accounting Improved

Governmental accounting is taught after students have learned the theory of accrual accounting and the journal entries needed to record accrual-related transactions and events. Because of this, some students have difficulty grasping both the concepts underlying the modified accrual basis/financial resources measurement focus used in governmental-type funds and the accounting and financial reporting implications. Therefore, we completely rewrote Chapter 5 for this edition.

Chapter 5 now contains extensive discussion of why modified accrual accounting is used, the basic principles of modified accrual accounting, and—in a Governmental Accounting in Practice illustration—a discussion of how financial statements prepared using modified accrual accounting can mislead the unwary reader because modified accrual does not always measure the economic substance of transactions and events. We believe our frank coverage of the subject—and the classroom discussion it should engender—will help the student better understand it. Chapter 5 also includes more detailed discussion of the accounting entries needed to record transactions and events under modified accrual accounting, a comprehensive end-of-chapter illustration that covers the entire accounting and financial reporting cycle, and many new discussion scenarios, exercises, and problems. We also rewrote Chapter 4 to better set the stage for the material covered in later chapters.

Text Updated for New Accounting Standards

Keeping an accounting text up-to-date can be challenging because accounting standards-setters are invariably working on new standards while the text is being written. This edition takes account of all standards issued by the Governmental Accounting Standards Board through GASB Statement No. 63 and even refers to several statements and concepts statements in progress while the text was being written. Chapter 5 of the text was updated to incorporate the requirements of

GASB Statement No. 54, which has had a major effect on fund balance reporting. All other chapters were also updated to incorporate relevant new standards (and GASB Implementation Guides) issued after the sixth edition of this text was prepared. We will keep instructors informed of relevant new standards through the Pearson web site.

Coverage of Other Types of Entities Expanded

Although most of this text (Chapters 2 through 10) is devoted to state and local government accounting, we have continued to provide extensive coverage of the unique aspects of accounting and financial reporting for the federal government and not-for-profit entities, including not-for-profit hospitals. We expanded Chapter 11 (federal government) to cite specific references to the government's Standard General Ledger. Exploring the citations included in this chapter will give students greater insight into federal government finances; our new Federal Financial Reporting in Practice provides an accounting perspective on the growth of the federal deficit.

We also added new illustrations to the material covered in the chapters on not-for-profit organizations. All references to FASB standards and AICPA documents were changed to the FASB's new Accounting Standards Codification (ASC). Recognizing some of the more complex financial instruments held by not-for-profit entities as a result of the contributions they receive, we added a section on split-interest agreements.

Actual Financial Statements Analyzed

Accounting and public administration students need to understand not only how accounting information is gathered and reported, but also how it is used. Therefore, we continued the chapter on financial statement analysis (Chapter 14), which was included in previous editions. Our discussion of the principles of financial statement analysis is supplemented with our own analysis of a real government (Mt. Lebanon) and a real hospital (unnamed). As a basis for analyzing the financial position of the hospital, we used "indicators" and "norms" taken from data on actual hospitals, available at various web sites. Our objective here was to provide the inquisitive student with sufficient data to "do it yourself."

Continuing Problems

This text has three "continuing problems" for instructors who like to reinforce the discussion of accounting principles with problems that carry throughout the text. One problem, called Leisure City, is designed to emphasize fund accounting. It starts at the end of Chapter 5 and covers fund level accounting and financial reporting in Chapters 5 through 8. The other two, called CoCo City and Croton Village, also cover fund-level accounting transactions but are designed primarily to emphasize fund-level and government-wide financial reporting. They are presented at the end of Chapters 9 and 10 and are developed so that portions of each problem can be assigned, as appropriate, with Chapters 2 through 10.

Ancillary Package

To assist instructors in the classroom, the solutions manual and test item file are available for download by registered faculty at the Instructor Resource Center www.pearsonhighered.com. Updates on new standards, prepared by the authors of this text, are also available at that site.

ACKNOWLEDGMENTS

We sincerely appreciate the help of the many members of the professional community, students, and faculty in preparing this edition and previous editions of this text. In particular, we thank the following:

Joseph R. Razek and Gordon A. Hosch, who wrote the original text and who set the tone for the content and presentation of the material in the subsequent editions. We have tried to continue on the path they set.

Those who assisted us in obtaining the financial statements and other material we used to make governmental and not-for-profit accounting and financial reporting come alive. They are Ms. Marcia Taylor, Assistant Manager of the Municipality of Mt. Lebanon, Pennsylvania, and a member of the Governmental Accounting Standards Board, and Mr. John Lordan, Chief Financial Officer and Treasurer of Fordham University, New York. Marcia went beyond the call of duty to answer the questions we raised to ensure that our many references to Mt. Lebanon's financial data were complete, accurate, and up-to-date.

Those who answered the questions we raised during the writing of this edition regarding accounting standards and procedures. They include Mr. David Bean, Director of Research and Technical Activities, and Mr. Kenneth Schermann, Senior Technical Advisor, of the Governmental Accounting Standards Board; and Ms. Wendy Comes, Executive Director, and Ms. Eileen Parlow, Assistant Director, of the Federal Accounting Standards Advisory Board.

The people at Pearson, Donna Battista, Editor-in-Chief; Christina Rumbaugh, Editorial Project Manager; Nancy Fenton, Senior Managing Editor; Clara Bartunek, Production Project Manager.

Mr. Ives also thanks his wife, Eunice, whose encouragement in writing this text (and reminding him when it was time to eat) helped make the project a joy. As new authors on the book, Mr. and Mrs. Patton thank their coauthor, Mr. Ives, for his guidance and patience while working together on the seventh edition.

ABOUT THE AUTHORS

Martin Ives, MBA, CPA (inactive), CGFM (retired), CIA, served for 16 years as Distinguished Adjunct Professor of Public Administration at New York University's Wagner Graduate School of Public Service. Before entering the academic world, Mr. Ives was Vice Chair and Director of Research of the Governmental Accounting Standards Board, First Deputy Comptroller of the City of New York, Deputy Comptroller of the State of New York, and a member of the Federal Accounting Standards Advisory Board.

In addition to this text, Mr. Ives is the author of the textbook *Assessing Municipal Financial Condition*, coauthor of the textbook *Government Performance Audit in Action*, and coauthor of *Program Control and Audit* and *Financial Condition Analysis and Management*. He has also written chapters for books on auditing and municipal finance, has authored about 30 articles for *the Journal of Government Financial Management, the Journal of Accountancy, the Internal Auditor*, and other professional journals, and has spoken to numerous professional and civic organizations.

Mr. Ives was founding president of the Albany chapter of the Institute of Internal Auditors, president of the Capitol District Chapter of the American Society for Public Administration, and a member of the founding board of the Association of Government Accountants' Certified Government Financial Manager program. He has received many honors and awards, including the Public Service Award (Fund for the City of New York); the Governor Charles Evans Hughes Award (Capitol District chapter of the American Society for Public Administration); and the S. Kenneth Howard Award (Association for Budgeting and Financial Management). He has also been voted Adjunct of the Year by the students at NYU's Wagner Graduate School.

Terry K. Patton, PhD, CPA, CGFM, is the Robert Madera Distinguished Professor of Accounting and Dean of the Dillard College of Business Administration at Midwestern State University in Wichita Falls, Texas. He teaches governmental accounting, auditing, and accounting research and communications. He received his Bachelor's degree from Midwestern State University, a Master's degree from the University of North Texas, and a PhD from Texas Tech University.

Dr. Patton began his career in public accounting, where he audited local governments. Later, he served as a Project Manager and as the Research Manager for the Governmental Accounting Standards Board. He has coauthored a governmental accounting book for practitioners, *Guide to Governmental Financial Reporting Model: Implementing GASBS No. 34*, and another governmental accounting textbook published by Pearson Prentice Hall. He has published articles in the *Accounting Review, Accounting Horizons*, the *Journal of Accounting and Public Policy*, and the *Journal of Public Budgeting, Accounting, and Financial Management*, among others. Dr. Patton regularly speaks to accounting professionals on state and local governmental accounting topics.

Suesan R. Patton is the National Director of Quality Initiatives for UHY LLP in Dallas, Texas, as well as the principal author of two PPC Thomson practitioner guides on governmental accounting and financial reporting—*Preparing Governmental Financial Statements under GASBS No. 34* and *Governmental Financial Statement Illustrations and Trends*. Mrs. Patton also currently serves as a member of the Association of Government Accountants Financial Management Standards Board and as a reviewer for the Government Finance Officers Association's Certificate of Excellence in Financial Reporting Program.

Most of Mrs. Patton's career has been spent in standards-setting, beginning as a Manager with the American Institute of CPAs Accounting Standards Division and continuing with a 15-year stint with the Governmental Accounting Standards Board as a Senior Project Manager. She received a Bachelor of Arts degree in English Literature with a Concentration in Accounting from the University of Cincinnati.

Chapter 1

Governmental and Not-for-Profit Accounting Environment and Characteristics

Chapter Outline

After completing this chapter, you should be able to do the following:

- Their distinguishing characteristics
- Their operating environment
- The needs of users of their accounting information
- The objectives of their financial reporting
- The distinctive characteristics of their accounting and financial reporting
- The jurisdiction of their accounting standards-setting bodies

The entities covered in this textbook—state and local governments, the federal government, and not-for-profit organizations—represent a significant portion of our total economic activity. Government consumption expenditures account for more than 20 percent of gross domestic product, some $2.9 trillion of the $14.1 trillion of gross domestic product in 2009. But consumption data alone do not measure total government expenditures because they exclude significant payments to individuals for Social Security, Medicare, and Medicaid. When payments to individuals are included, total state and local government current expenditures were more than $2.0 trillion, and total federal government outlays were nearly $3.0 trillion in 2008. To give you an idea of the financial scope of not-for-profit entities, the Internal Revenue Service reports that the total expenses of Internal Revenue Code 501(c)(3) organizations (religious, educational, charitable, scientific, and literary entities) were $1.3 trillion in 2007.

Why is governmental and not-for-profit accounting covered separately from business enterprise accounting? In fact, many aspects of governmental accounting and most aspects of not-for-profit accounting are no different from those of business enterprise accounting. Governments and not-for-profit entities do have some unique transactions—governments are financed primarily by taxes, and not-for-profit entities receive significant amounts of contributions. But the answer to the question lies deeper than that. Governmental and not-for-profit entities operate in an environment different from that of business enterprises, and the users of their accounting data have somewhat different information needs. For example, the legally adopted budget plays a particularly significant role in governmental financial activities. Legal restrictions and resource-provider restrictions on the use of resources play a greater role in governmental and not-for-profit entities than in business enterprises. As a result, both internal accounting systems and external financial reporting for governmental and not-for-profit entity users are designed to provide certain types of data that differ from the data reported by business enterprises.

This chapter discusses the characteristics of governmental and not-for-profit entities, the major differences between their environments and that of business enterprises, and the distinctive accounting and financial reporting resulting from those differences. This chapter also describes the accounting and financial reporting standards-setting process for governmental and not-for-profit entities.

GOVERNMENTAL AND NOT-FOR-PROFIT ORGANIZATIONS

It is not always easy to distinguish among governmental, not-for-profit, and for-profit organizations. The distinction lies less in the functions these entities perform than in the details of how the entities are organized, governed, and financed. For example, hospitals may be for-profit, not-for-profit, or governmental organizations. A hospital is not necessarily a governmental one just because it was financed partly with tax-exempt debt issued by a governmental agency. An entity is not necessarily a not-for-profit one just because it was created under a state's not-for-profit corporation law.

Governmental entities include the following:

- Federal government
- General-purpose political subdivisions (such as states, counties, cities, and towns)
- Special-purpose political subdivisions (such as school districts)
- Public corporations and bodies corporate and politic (such as state-operated toll roads and toll bridges)

Other organizations created by governments by statute or under not-for-profit corporation laws are governmental if they possess one or more of the following characteristics: (1) their officers are popularly elected, or a controlling majority of their governing body is appointed or approved by governmental officials; (2) they possess the power to enact and enforce a tax levy; (3) they hold the power to directly issue debt whose interest is exempt from federal taxation; or (4) they face the potential that a government might dissolve them unilaterally and assume their assets and liabilities.[1]

Not-for-profit organizations exhibit certain basic characteristics that distinguish them from business enterprises. Not-for-profit entities (1) receive contributions of significant amounts of resources from resource providers who do not expect equivalent value in return; (2) operate for purposes other than to provide goods and services at a profit; and (3) lack ownership interests like those of a business enterprise.[2] As a result, not-for-profit organizations may obtain contributions and grants not normally received by business enterprises. On the other hand, not-for-profit organizations do not engage in ownership-type transactions, such as issuing stock and paying dividends. Four broad categories of not-for-profit organizations are discussed in this text: voluntary health and welfare organizations, health care organizations, colleges and universities, and other not-for-profit organizations.

THE OPERATING ENVIRONMENT

Governmental and not-for-profit organizations operate in a social, legal, and political environment different from the environment of for-profit business enterprises. As a result, users of governmental and not-for-profit financial statements have somewhat different needs than do users of business enterprise financial statements. These environmental differences have caused accounting standards-setters to develop accounting and financial reporting requirements for governmental and not-for-profit entities that sometimes differ from requirements for business enterprises.

The Governmental Accounting Standards Board (GASB), the accounting standards-setting body for state and local governments, suggests that the major environmental differences between governments and business enterprises relate to organizational purpose, sources of revenue, potential for longevity, relationship with stakeholders, and role of the budget.[3] Some of these

---

[1]For further discussion, see American Institute of Certified Public Accountants, *AICPA Audit and Accounting Guide, Health Care Organizations* (New York: AICPA, 2006), p. 2; and Martin Ives, "What Is a Government?" *The Government Accountants Journal* (Spring 1994), pp. 25–33.

[2]Statement of Financial Accounting Concepts No. 4, "Objectives of Financial Reporting by Nonbusiness Organizations" (Stamford, CT: Financial Accounting Standards Board, 1980), par. 6.

[3]"Why Governmental Accounting and Financial Reporting Is—and Should Be—Different," Governmental Accounting Standards Board (2006).

factors apply as well to differences between the environments of not-for-profit entities and business enterprises. In the discussion that follows, we combine some of these factors and add another to show their potential consequences for accounting and financial reporting.

Organizational Purposes

Business enterprises exist to enhance the wealth of their owners. Because income is quantifiable and can be measured in monetary terms, business enterprise financial reporting focuses primarily on earnings and its components. A corporation might be considered an attractive investment if its revenues have exceeded its expenses consistently, and investors can look forward to continued growth in the bottom line.

In sharp contrast, governmental and not-for-profit entities exist to provide services to their constituents. They generally try to accumulate a reasonable surplus of financial resources to cushion against economic contraction and to provide for emergency needs. But these entities do not operate to maximize inflows over outflows. Indeed, if a local government were to accumulate large operating surpluses, many taxpayers would soon complain that they were being overtaxed.

For governmental and not-for-profit organizations, reporting whether inflows exceeded outflows is only part of the picture. The challenge to financial reporting lies also in demonstrating *accountability* for the resources entrusted to these organizations. When used in the broad sense of the term, *accountability* embraces not only probity and legal compliance, but also efficiency in delivering services and effectiveness in accomplishing program results. The GASB encourages state and local governments to report on outputs (including cost per unit of service) and outcomes (program results) to supplement their annual financial reporting. The federal government already requires federal agencies to prepare an annual *Performance and Accountability Report,* which encompasses both financial and performance reporting.

Sources of Revenue and Relationship with Stakeholders

Business enterprises derive virtually all their revenues from exchange transactions, generally involving specific products or services, between willing buyers and sellers. Governments, on the other hand, obtain most of their revenues from taxation—wherein taxpayers involuntarily transfer resources for a basket of services that may or may not bear a direct relationship to what the taxpayer wants or needs. Many not-for-profit entities obtain significant resources from voluntary donors who expect no product or service in exchange, but who are nevertheless concerned with whether their donations are achieving their intended purposes.

Taxes and donations are unique to governmental and not-for-profit entities and hence require special accounting standards appropriate to those transactions. Equally important, the nature of taxes and donations creates relationships with the providers of those resources that emphasize the accountability aspects of financial reporting, discussed in the preceding section.

Financial reporting for business enterprises means reporting to owners and lenders who can divest themselves quickly of their investments if they choose to do so. Also, for business enterprises, accountability to their customers is direct and immediate: A consumer who doesn't like the product or service simply will not buy it again. In contrast, taxpayers are unlikely to be able to move from the jurisdictions where they reside as readily as investors can sell securities, and taxpayers may not benefit directly from the services provided by the taxes they pay. Similarly, donors often cannot see for themselves the results of their contributions. The need for and means of demonstrating accountability take on added significance because of the nature of the relationship between these entities and their stakeholders.

Potential for Longevity

Business enterprises are at risk of going out of business for many reasons, such as global competition, emerging products, changing consumer tastes, inefficiencies, and recession. Not-for-profit organizations face similar risks. Business enterprises may also go out of business by being bought out by other enterprises. However, because of the power to tax and the nature of their services, general-purpose governments rarely go out of business and are not bought and sold like business enterprises.

As a result, governmental accounting standards-setters have tended to take a longer-term perspective than their business enterprise counterparts in developing accounting measurements for certain types of transactions. One notable difference concerns the standards for pensions and other postemployment benefits.

Role of the Budget and Legal Requirements

Business enterprises are free to provide only those goods and services they believe will enhance their profits. They usually cannot be required to provide goods and services against their will, and if they cannot cope with the legal or social environment, they are free to leave the market. Their spending decisions may or may not be subject to budgets, but if they are, the budgetary amendment process is relatively simple. Commercial organizations also can borrow money when convenient, subject only to requirements of lenders and investors.

Governmental entities, on the other hand, are required by law (constitution, charter, or statute) to provide certain services. For example, most city charters provide for police and fire protection. Managers cannot refuse to provide these services because of cost or because they believe their residents do not deserve them. Indeed, local government managers often complain about "unfunded mandates" from higher-level governments—requirements to perform specific services without an equal amount of resources being provided.

Most of the resources obtained by governmental entities come from taxes, higher-level government grants, and borrowing. Some special-purpose governments, such as colleges and universities, also receive significant resources in the form of donor contributions. Spending decisions made by the federal government, states, and general-purpose local governments are based on budgets that have the force of law. Budgetary appropriations typically cannot be exceeded without specific legislative approval. Generally, resources provided by higher-level governments must be used only for the specific *purposes* designated by those governments. Most governmental borrowings are constrained by law as to purpose, quantity, and timing. Amounts borrowed may be subject to specific limits, such as value of real property in the jurisdiction. New bond issues may require approval by the electorate or by a higher-level government.

Many not-for-profit organizations derive most of their resources from donor contributions, which may be subject to restrictions as to what they can be used for, when they can be used, or whether they must be maintained in perpetuity. Recipient organizations are legally bound to adhere to these donor restrictions.

Because of these factors, internal accounting for governmental and not-for-profit organizations generally focuses on the controls needed to ensure compliance with laws and donor restrictions. Accounting records and internal reports for governmental entities are designed to ensure adherence to spending limitations contained in legally adopted budgets and other legal documents. Accounting records for not-for-profit entities are designed to ensure that purpose and time restrictions imposed by donors are heeded. Further, external reports prepared by both governmental and not-for-profit entities are designed to inform users of the amount of available resources that may be used without restriction for the general purposes of the entity as well as the extent and nature of any restrictions.

USERS AND USES OF ACCOUNTING INFORMATION

Persons both internal and external to entities use accounting information. It is important to understand that internal users of information usually can specify the kinds of information they need to fulfill their duties. Hence, accounting systems and most reports derived from those systems are designed primarily to meet the needs of internal users. For example, governmental managers need accounting information to keep day-to-day control over spending to ensure that amounts authorized by the budget are not exceeded and that sufficient resources will be available to cover the full year's operations. Managers of not-for-profit entities need accounting data to help keep expenses in line with budgets and within limitations imposed by donors and grantors. Managers of both governmental and not-for-profit entities need to monitor the day-to-day availability of cash. Boards of trustees require reports derived from accounting systems to help them perform their governance responsibilities.

In establishing financial reporting standards, however, accounting standards-setters emphasize the needs of *external* users—those not directly involved in the operations of the reporting entity—because they do not have ready access to the entity's information. The major external users of governmental and not-for-profit entity financial reports are resource providers, oversight bodies, and service recipients. Resource providers include taxpayers, donors and potential donors, investors and potential investors, bond-rating agencies (which provide data to investors), and grant-providing organizations, such as higher-level governments and foundations. External oversight bodies include higher-level governments and regulatory agencies. Service recipients include citizen advocate groups. Because of the wide array of external users of financial reporting, the statements and related notes that comprise external reporting are often referred to as "general purpose" reporting.

Users of governmental and not-for-profit financial reporting might seek answers to the following types of questions:

- Does the entity have sufficient financial resources to provide a reasonable cushion against near-term revenue shortfalls caused by economic contraction?
- What is the likelihood of the entity's ability to pay its short-term and long-term financial obligations?
- What is the entity's ability to continue to provide a particular level of services?
- Does the entity use its resources consistent with budgetary limitations, donor restrictions, and legal and regulatory requirements?
- Do restrictions on use of resources appear to be reducing flexibility in meeting program goals?
- Do financial data show evidence of inefficiency, such as excessive administrative and fund-raising costs or slow collection of taxes receivable?
- Is there evidence of excessive financial risk taking?

External financial reporting by governmental and not-for-profit organizations provides information to help answer these questions.

OBJECTIVES OF FINANCIAL REPORTING

As previously mentioned, the GASB establishes accounting standards for state and local governments. The Federal Accounting Standards Advisory Board (FASAB) sets standards for the federal government, and the Financial Accounting Standards Board (FASB) sets them for not-for-profit entities. All three have issued *concepts statements* on financial reporting objectives for the entities in their jurisdictions. Concepts statements are not standards; instead, they articulate the framework within which the standards are developed. The individual concepts statements on objectives of financial reporting have both similarities and differences based on the differing environments within which the entities operate. The governmental standards-setting bodies, in particular, emphasize the need for data to help financial report users assess accountability.

State and Local Government Financial Reporting

The GASB statement of reporting objectives for state and local governments calls for financial reporting to assist in fulfilling government's duty to be publicly accountable and to help users assess that accountability. To meet those objectives, financial reporting needs to provide data to show whether current-year revenues were sufficient to pay for current-year services, to demonstrate whether resources were obtained and used in accordance with the legally adopted budget, and to help users assess the entity's service efforts, costs, and accomplishments.

In addition to helping users evaluate the entity's operating results for the year and assess the level of services that can be provided by the entity, financial reporting that follows GASB objectives also discloses an entity's ability to meet its obligations as they come due. Financial reporting should accomplish the latter objective by providing information about financial position and condition and about physical and other nonfinancial resources with useful lives that extend beyond the current year, and by disclosing restrictions on resources and risk of potential loss of resources. (The GASB's financial reporting objectives are discussed in more detail in Chapter 9.)

Federal Government Financial Reporting

FASAB objectives for federal financial reporting cover budgetary integrity, operating performance, stewardship, and systems and controls. The objectives state that financial reporting should assist in fulfilling the government's duty to be publicly accountable for money raised through taxes and other means and for their expenditure in accordance with the government's budget. Financial reporting also should assist report users in (1) evaluating the entity's service efforts, costs, and accomplishments and its management of assets and liabilities; (2) assessing the impact on the nation of the government's operations and investments and how, as a result, the nation's financial condition has changed and may change in the future; and (3) understanding whether financial management systems and internal accounting and administrative controls are adequate.

Not-for-Profit Organization Financial Reporting

The FASB's financial reporting objectives for not-for-profit organizations focus on information useful to present and potential resource providers, as well as other users, in making rational decisions about allocating resources to those organizations. Such information helps in assessing (1) the services provided by the entity and its ability to continue to provide them, (2) how the entity's managers discharged their stewardship responsibilities, and (3) the entity's performance, including its service efforts and accomplishments. Not-for-profit entities should provide information about their economic resources, obligations, net resources, restrictions on the use of resources, and liquidity.

DISTINCTIVE ACCOUNTING AND FINANCIAL REPORTING CHARACTERISTICS

Several characteristics of governmental and not-for-profit organization accounting and financial reporting are unique or distinctive when compared with those of business enterprises. These characteristics, which flow primarily from the environmental factors discussed earlier, are introduced here and described in greater detail in other chapters of this text.

Use of Fund Accounting

Fund accounting is perhaps the most distinctive feature of governmental and not-for-profit organization accounting. Fund accounting segregates an entity's assets, liabilities, and net assets into separate accounting entities based on legal requirements, donor-imposed restrictions, or special regulations. Fund accounting is a convenient control mechanism to help ensure that resources are spent for the intended purposes—like using separate cookie jars for food, rent, clothing, and so on.

Because each fund is a separate accounting entity, each must have a set of *self-balancing accounts;* that is, the total assets of a particular fund must equal the total of its liabilities and fund balance (or net assets or net position). Thus, the accounting records of a particular fund must identify the unique resources of that fund and the claims to those resources, as distinguished from all other funds.

Entities that use fund accounting generally maintain a General Fund or an Unrestricted Current Fund, whose resources can be used for any purpose designated by the governing body. In addition, these entities use separate funds to account for the acquisition and disposition of resources whose use is restricted in some manner (generally by law, regulation, or donor requirement) to specific purposes.

For many years, fund accounting provided the foundation both for internal accounting control purposes and for external financial reporting by governmental and not-for-profit entities. In response to concerns expressed by external financial reporting users about the complexity of fund-based financial reporting, however, the reporting emphasis shifted away from funds and to the entity as a whole. Nevertheless, general-purpose governments continue to use fund accounting for internal purposes, and the GASB requires both government-wide and fund-based reporting for external reporting purposes. The FASB does not require not-for-profit entities to use fund-based reporting but does not preclude such reporting, provided the entity complies with the FASB's financial reporting requirements.

Incorporation of Budgets into Accounting Systems

A unique feature in governmental fund accounting is the use of *budgetary accounts* in the accounting system for certain types of funds. Budgetary accounting is particularly pervasive in the federal government, where budgetary and financial accounting tracks operate side by side. State and local governments incorporate budgetary accounting to a somewhat lesser extent, but it is nevertheless significant. The requirement for incorporating budgetary accounting into governmental fund accounting systems highlights the importance of ensuring that legally adopted budgets are not exceeded.

Measurement Focus and Basis of Accounting

Business enterprises use the *accrual basis of accounting*, as distinguished from the cash basis of accounting, when they prepare financial statements. *Basis of accounting* is a term that refers to *when* assets, liabilities, revenues, and expenses are recognized as such in an entity's financial statements. Under the accrual basis of accounting, revenues are recognized when they are earned, not necessarily when cash is received; and expenses are recognized when they are incurred, not necessarily when cash is paid. Not-for-profit organizations, including not-for-profit hospitals, and the federal government also use the accrual basis of accounting in financial reporting.

State and local governments also use the accrual basis of accounting when they report on their business-type activities. For their basic governmental functions, however, state and local governments use a unique, hybrid-type basis of accounting called the *modified accrual basis of accounting*. When using this basis of accounting, they measure only inflows and outflows of *current financial resources*, rather than all economic resources. The accounting implications of this measurement method and focus are discussed in Chapters 2 through 6, and the financial reporting implications are covered in Chapters 9 and 10.

Entity-Wide and Fund-Level Reporting

Does the use of funds in governmental and not-for-profit internal accounting have a major effect on external financial reporting? For many years, the answer to this question was yes. Recently, however, the financial reporting focus has turned toward the entity as a whole. The change in emphasis came about for practical reasons. Entities having many types of funds and reporting on a fund basis often issued financial statements that looked complex and were not readily comprehensible because of the extensive details. State and local governments issued financial statements with 10 or more columns, and many not-for-profit organizations issued statements showing each group of funds layered one atop another in a "pancake" format.

To make financial reporting more useful, accounting standards-setters now emphasize the need for financial reporting on the entity as a whole, specifically as follows:

- State and local governments report on two levels: a government-wide level that distinguishes only between governmental and business-type activities, and a fund level that reports on individual funds. Although the fund-level financial statements are prepared on the same basis of accounting used within the funds, the government-wide financial statements are prepared using the full accrual basis of accounting.
- Not-for-profit organization financial statements are required to focus on the organization as a whole. Within those statements, the organizations need to report on three classes of net assets: those that are unrestricted and those that are either temporarily restricted or permanently restricted by donors.

Financial Reporting of Restricted Resources

Reporting on restricted resources is much more pervasive in governmental and not-for-profit entity financial reporting than it is in business enterprise reporting. For state and local governments, reporting by funds facilitates the reporting of restricted resources. In addition, the fund balances within each fund must be reported in up to five classifications depicting the different levels of constraints on the use of resources. And as previously noted, not-for-profit entities must show the extent to which resources are unrestricted, temporarily restricted, or permanently restricted as to use.

ACCOUNTING PRINCIPLES AND STANDARDS

Rules guiding accounting and financial reporting are referred to as *generally accepted accounting principles* (GAAP). The American Institute of Certified Public Accountants (AICPA) defines this term as follows:

> [T]he consensus at a particular time as to which economic resources and obligations should be recorded as assets and liabilities by financial accounting, which changes in assets and liabilities should be recorded, when these changes should be recorded, how the assets and liabilities and changes in them should be measured, what information should be disclosed and how it should be disclosed, and which financial statements should be prepared.
>
> Generally accepted accounting principles encompass the conventions, rules, and procedures necessary to define accepted accounting practice at a particular time. The standard of "generally accepted accounting principles" includes not only broad guidelines of general application, but also detailed practices and procedures.[4]

Establishing Generally Accepted Accounting Principles

The origins of GAAP can be traced back to the period just after the 1929 stock market crash, when attempts were made to formulate accounting principles. Many criticized the earliest statement of principles as being little more than a codification of the then-current accounting practices. Continued concerns with the way in which accounting principles were being established led to the formulation of the FASB in 1973 and then to the GASB in 1984. Seven members are appointed to each of these bodies by the Financial Accounting Foundation (FAF), an entity whose members are appointed by certain professional accounting and financial organizations. Advisory councils to both the FASB and the GASB are composed of individuals representing organizations concerned with the activities of the standards-setting bodies. The FASB–GASB structure is shown in Exhibit 1-1.

The FASB and the GASB are charged with establishing and improving standards of accounting and financial reporting within their respective areas of jurisdiction. The GASB's jurisdiction includes all state and local governmental entities, including government-sponsored colleges and universities, health care providers, and utilities. The FASB establishes standards for all nongovernmental entities, including not-for-profit colleges and universities and health care providers. Under this arrangement, it is possible for the two boards to establish different accounting and reporting standards for similar transactions of similar entities, such as hospitals. Although this situation occurs sometimes, the two boards cooperate with each other to keep differences to a minimum.

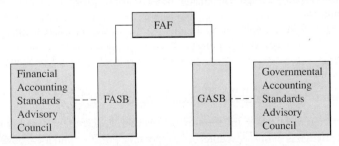

EXHIBIT 1-1 Relationship Between the FASB, the GASB, and the FAF

---

[4]Statement No. 4, "Basic Concepts and Accounting Principles Underlying Financial Statements of Business Enterprises" (New York: AICPA, 1970), pars. 137 and 138.

The FASAB was established in 1990 to develop accounting standards and principles for the federal government. Its nine members include six public (nonfederal) members and representatives of the offices of the three officials who have prime responsibility for federal accounting and financial management—the U.S. comptroller general, the director of the Office of Management and Budget (OMB), and the secretary of the Treasury. FASAB proposals become GAAP for federal agencies if neither the comptroller general nor the director of OMB objects.

Standards promulgated by the three boards are GAAP by virtue of the due process used by the boards in developing them and the authority accorded them by the Code of Professional Conduct of the AICPA. The due process used in developing the standards includes using task forces, holding public hearings, issuing "exposure drafts" of proposals for comment by interested parties, and carefully considering those comments before issuing the standards. Auditors may not express unqualified opinions on financial statements that violate standards issued by the applicable board.

Standards are identified by Statement Number and in Codifications issued by the Boards. Individual Statements also contain the basis for the conclusions reached by the Boards. "Basis for Conclusions" sections tend to be detailed and are helpful to the student desiring more detailed understanding of issues underlying a particular standard as well as the matters considered by the Board in reaching conclusions. Throughout this text, we identify applicable standards either by Statement Number or by Codification section.

Governmental Accounting in Practice

Establishing Standards in a Political Environment

The GASB establishes accounting standards, but it has no enforcement powers. Several institutions, however, play a major role in enforcing GASB standards, including the governments themselves, the accounting profession, and the credit-rating agencies. Recent experience in Connecticut and Texas illustrates this point.

The state of Connecticut passed a law in the early 1990s requiring that its budget be balanced in accordance with generally accepted accounting principles. (This is unusual because GASB standards apply to financial reporting, not budgeting.) Each year, however, the state legislature delayed implementing the law because it chose not to raise the taxes or to cut the expenditures needed to achieve GAAP balance. As a result, the state ran up annual deficits when measured in accordance with GAAP. Then, in 2007, the legislature passed a bill giving the *state comptroller* the authority to establish GAAP for *financial reporting*. Someone had the bright idea that, if the standards don't fit the situation, all you need to do is change the standards!

Governor M. Jodi Rell, deeply concerned that the bill would jeopardize Connecticut's credit rating, promptly vetoed it. The governor felt that credit analysts and municipal bond buyers wanted to see financial statements that followed uniform accounting standards set by an independent standards-setting body. Right on, Madam Governor!

But not everyone thinks the way Governor Rell thinks. Some officials in Texas were bothered by the implications of a new GASB standard that requires financial statement recognition of expenses and liabilities for employee postemployment health care benefits. (We discuss this standard in Chapter 8.) So Texas enacted a law in 2007 giving the state and its local governments the option to ignore the standard. Because governments feared that auditors and creditors would take a dim view of those who chose to ignore the standard, the state and most Texas local governments decided to follow the standard anyway.

Source: New York Times, articles by Mary Williams Walsh, May 18, June 2, and July 8, 2007.

Hierarchy of Generally Accepted Accounting Principles

As business practices and new financial instruments continue to evolve, financial statement preparers may encounter transactions not specifically addressed by their standards-setting body. To deal with these situations, practitioners may be helped by documents issued by the staff of the standards-setting body or by other organizations that issue relevant professional guidance. They, therefore, need to know the relationships various sources of professional guidance have with each other. For this reason, a hierarchy of GAAP has been established to guide financial statement preparers and auditors for each type of entity. For example, GASB standards recognize the following hierarchy of pronouncements for state and local governments, ranked from most authoritative to least authoritative:

a. Officially established accounting principles; that is, GASB Statements and Interpretations. These Statements and Interpretations are periodically incorporated into the GASB's Codification of Governmental Accounting and Financial Reporting Standards.
b. GASB Technical Bulletins. Also, AICPA Industry Audit and Accounting Guides and AICPA Statements of Position, provided they are specifically made applicable to state and local government entities by the AICPA and cleared by the GASB.
c. AICPA Practice Bulletins, provided they are specifically made applicable to state and local government entities and cleared by the GASB. Also, consensus positions of a group of accountants organized by the GASB that attempts to reach consensus positions on accounting issues applicable to state and local government.
d. Implementation guides published by the GASB staff. Also, practices that are widely recognized and prevalent in state and local government.

If the accounting treatment for a transaction or event is not specified in any of the foregoing sources, a financial statement preparer may consider other accounting literature, such as GASB Concepts Statements; pronouncements within the GAAP hierarchy for nongovernmental entities if not specifically made applicable by the GASB to state and local government entities; FASB Concepts Statements; FASAB Statements, Interpretations, Technical Bulletins, and Concepts Statements; AICPA Issues Papers; International Public Sector Accounting Standards of the International Public Sector Accounting Standards Board; and certain other enumerated sources.

ORGANIZATION OF TEXTBOOK

Chapters 2 through 10 of the textbook cover state and local government accounting and financial reporting. The chapters move from the recording of budgetary and financial accounting information to the preparation of financial statements. Chapters 2 and 3 introduce you to some of the unique aspects of governmental accounting—the use of fund accounting, the accounting measurements used in each fund, and the way budgetary accounting is integrated into the accounting system. Chapters 4 through 8 discuss the nature of the transactions generally encountered in each fund and describe the applicable accounting procedures and measurements. Accounting within the funds provides the basis for preparing fund-level financial statements, discussed in Chapter 9. Adjustments are then made to the fund financial statements to prepare the government-wide financial statements, discussed in Chapter 10.

Separate chapters are presented on federal government accounting (Chapter 11), not-for-profit accounting (Chapter 12), and hospital accounting (Chapter 13). Chapter 14 shows how an analyst would review an entity's financial statements to help draw conclusions about some of the factors that affect the financial health of governments and hospitals. Chapter 15 provides an introduction to general accounting; it can be used as a refresher for the accounting student or as a basic introduction to accounting for the public administration student.

Review Questions

Q1-1   Describe the characteristics that distinguish not-for-profit organizations from business enterprises.

Q1-2   Identify the various types of entities that constitute governmental organizations, and describe the characteristics of other organizations that, when created by governments, are also considered to be governmental entities.

Q1-3   Identify and briefly explain three major environmental characteristics of governmental and not-for-profit organizations.

Q1-4   Illustrate the kinds of restrictions placed by laws on the ability of governments to use resources, and by donors on the ability of not-for-profit entities to use resources.

Q1-5   Who are the users of governmental and not-for-profit entity accounting information, and for what purposes might they use that information?

Q1-6   List the three ways identified by the GASB in which financial reporting can help users assess governmental accountability.

Q1-7   List three unique characteristics of state and local governmental accounting as contrasted with business enterprise accounting.

Q1-8   What are the jurisdictions of the accounting standards-setting bodies: GASB, FASAB, and FASB?

Q1-9   Why is a hierarchy of generally accepted accounting principles needed?

Discussion Scenarios and Issues

D1-1   Croton Hospital was a not-for-profit entity. Because it experienced financial difficulties, the county in which the hospital was located assumed control of Croton's assets and liabilities. The county executive appointed all five members of the hospital's new board of trustees. The hospital's chief accountant, who was not replaced, continued to use the same accounting principles and financial reporting used before the county takeover. Explain the position the county comptroller should take regarding Croton's accounting and financial reporting.

D1-2   State law provides that all cash not immediately needed by school districts to finance current operations be forwarded to the counties in which the school districts are located. The law also requires that county treasurers place these resources in a separate fund and invest them on behalf of the school districts. Because Contra County is experiencing financial problems and to provide resources to the county, the county treasurer tells the county administrator that he plans to invest the school district funds in "junk bonds" yielding 9 percent interest. He will credit the "normal" rate of return (5 percent) to the school districts and the remaining 4 percent to the county itself. Explain the position the county administrator should take on the treasurer's proposal.

D1-3   A city ordinance provides that "no money shall be spent for any purpose without the prior approval of the city council." In approving the budget for the year, the council had authorized spending $1,300,000 for road maintenance. Late in the year, after the city had spent virtually the entire $1,300,000, a major storm washed out portions of several roads leading to the elementary school. The school was inaccessible, and the mayor wanted to enter into an emergency contract to repair the roads. City engineers estimated that the cost of the repairs would be about $350,000. If the city entered into such a contract, the total amount spent on road maintenance for the year would be greater than the amount authorized. Recognizing the need for prompt action, the mayor immediately entered into the contract without seeking prior city council approval. Comment on the legal, financial, and accounting systems implications of this scenario.

Exercises

E1-1   (Characteristics of not-for-profit and governmental entities)
The mayor of a large city approaches a group of citizens and suggests that they form an organization to provide social, educational, and recreational programs for local youth. The group agrees and forms an entity called the Community Youth Organization (CYO). The group also chooses a board of directors, and the board hires an executive director and several staff members. CYO's activities are financed entirely by grants from the city, and many of CYO's programs are held after school hours in the high school. Is the CYO a not-for-profit or a government organization? Why? What changes in characteristics would be needed to change it from one type of entity to the other?

E1-2   (Accounting standards-setting bodies)
Three accountants started talking about hospitals. One said he was treated at a not-for-profit hospital, another said she was treated at a county hospital, and the third said he had just returned from the hospital run by the U.S. Veterans Administration. They wondered why three different bodies established accounting standards for hospitals. Give reasons for and against the existence of three accounting standards-setting bodies.

E1-3   (Accounting standards-setting procedures)
Several not-for-profit organizations use television campaigns to obtain pledges to contribute cash. Some people think that not-for-profit entities should recognize pledges as revenues when the cash is actually received. Others would recognize revenues when the pledges are made, subject to a provision for amounts not likely to be collected. Based on that scenario, discuss (a) the need for an accounting standards-setting body, (b) the qualifications that members of that body should possess, and (c) the procedures that body should adopt in establishing accounting standards.

E1-4   (Objectives of financial reporting)
An objective of business enterprise financial reporting is to provide "information about an enterprise's performance provided by measures of earnings and its components." City governments, however, are not concerned with "earnings." One of the financial reporting objectives cited by the GASB regarding governments is that reporting should show whether current-year revenues were sufficient to pay for current-year services. Based on these objectives, comment on the following assertions:
a. Accrual accounting is not necessary in governmental financial reporting.
b. Financial reporting alone is insufficient for measuring governmental performance; there is also a need for reporting on program efficiency and effectiveness.

E1-5   (Use of funds in governmental accounting)
On Election Day, the citizens of a small village voted affirmatively on the following proposition: "To authorize the sale of $3,000,000 in bonds for the purpose of constructing a new firehouse." The village manager then told the finance commissioner: "Put the entire proceeds from the bond sale into the General Fund. That way, we can hire more firefighters with any proceeds from the bond sale that were not used to build the firehouse." Comment on the village manager's instructions to the finance commissioner.

Chapter 2

The Use of Funds in Governmental Accounting

Chapter Outline

After completing this chapter, you should be able to do the following:

- Understand the nature and purpose of fund accounting and identify the major fund categories used in governmental accounting

- Compare and contrast the current financial resources measurement focus and modified accrual basis of accounting with the economic resources measurement focus and accrual basis of accounting

- Understand the relationship between governmental budgeting and accounting within governmental-type funds

- Identify the fund types used within each of the major fund categories, describe the function of each fund type, and give examples of when each fund type is used

- Understand the measurement focus and basis of accounting used by each fund type

- Identify the financial statements used by each fund type

INTRODUCTION

As noted in Chapter 1, state and local governmental accounting differs from business enterprise accounting in three major respects. State and local governmental accounting (a) uses separate funds to account for its financial activities, (b) focuses on flows of current financial resources and uses a modified accrual basis of accounting in some funds, and (c) incorporates budgetary accounts into the financial accounting system for some funds. This chapter provides an overview of the material that will be discussed in detail in Chapters 3 through 10. We discuss the nature of fund accounting, describe the purposes of the various funds used in state and local governmental accounting, and introduce the concept of the current financial resources measurement focus and modified accrual basis of accounting.

To better understand the unique aspects of state and local governmental accounting, it is necessary to consider the types of activities performed by governments, how the activities are financed, and how governments are organized to perform them. It is also necessary to grasp the important role played by laws and budgets. State constitutions and statutes and local laws determine what governments do, how their activities are financed, and how they are organized. Most day-to-day governmental activities are driven by budgets that, once enacted, have the force of law. Accounting systems must be designed not only to help provide accountability for resources entrusted to the government, but also to help ensure compliance with budgetary requirements and limitations.

There are several ways to characterize governmental activities. One is to distinguish them as either governmental, business, or fiduciary in nature. The distinction among the three lies primarily in their purposes and in how the activities are financed.

- Governmental-type: General-purpose governments (such as states, counties, and cities) provide a range of basic, day-to-day services, including police and fire protection, sanitation, parks and recreation, and transportation. The operating costs of these services are financed mostly by tax revenues, intergovernmental grants, and general fees. Capital assets (such as buildings and roads) used in providing these services are financed primarily by long-term borrowing, which is ultimately paid off primarily from tax revenues.
- Business-type: General-purpose and, often, special-purpose governments provide other specific services—such as mass transit and water and electric utility services—financed not by taxes, but instead by user fees or charges that cover both operating and capital costs. Because of how they are financed and administered, these activities are often referred to as business-type or proprietary-type activities.
- Fiduciary-type: Many governmental entities also perform certain fiduciary-type services, holding segregated resources on behalf of others. For example, a government may perform investing or tax collection services on behalf of other governments. Also, governments may hold and invest resources on behalf of their employees and those of other governments to pay pensions when the employees retire.

Not all governments are organized similarly, nor are their activities financed the same way. For example, one municipality may finance its trash and garbage collection from general tax revenues, another may create a legally separate governmental corporation to provide these services through user charges, and a third may leave trash collection to private-sector carters. Similarly, electricity may be provided to the citizenry through the legally constituted governmental entity, a separate specially created governmental corporation, or private enterprise. One municipality may finance all aspects of highway maintenance through general tax revenues, while another may impose a special gasoline tax just to finance a particular aspect of highway maintenance. Therefore, care needs to be taken when comparing the finances of one government with those of another.

Governmental-type activities are controlled by a legally adopted budget—perhaps the single most important financial document prepared by governments. The revenue side of the budget shows estimates of how much will be raised from each revenue source. On the spending side, the budget both authorizes and limits how much may be spent for each activity or purpose. Internal accounting systems are designed to, among other things, meet the needs of the central government budget manager (to help monitor actual results in relation to the budget), the departmental budget manager (to show resources available for spending), and the cash manager (to help in preparing day-to-day cash forecasts).

State constitutions and statutes and local ordinances generally require "balanced budgets;" even where not specifically required, the balanced budget is the norm for prudent fiscal behavior. But what is a balanced budget? Does it mean balanced on the accrual basis, the cash basis, or some other basis of accounting? In fact, governmental budgets tend to be balanced more on the cash basis than the accrual basis of accounting. Terms like *expenditures* are not defined in the laws, and major obligations resulting from current-year activities may not be financed fully in the budget. Some balanced budget laws permit current-year operations to be financed with long-term borrowing. As a result, governmental budgets may be balanced in form, but not in economic substance. (See the box "Form versus Substance in Budgeting" later in this chapter.) If the accounting system needs to be responsive to budgetary needs, what are the accounting measurement and financial reporting implications of budgetary practices? This is one of the issues discussed here and in later chapters.

FUND ACCOUNTING

Funds as Subdivisions of an Entity

You are already familiar with the *entity* concept. As you know, the *reporting entity* defines the boundaries of a particular financial reporting unit by describing *whose* assets, liabilities, revenues, expenses, and equities are included in its financial report. If a parent corporate business enterprise exercises control over its legally separate subsidiaries, the financial activities of all those units are consolidated for financial reporting purposes.

Although it is defined in a somewhat different manner, this notion of reporting entity applies as well to state and local governments. New York City's 2010 financial report, for example, covered not only the activities of the legally constituted government of New York City, but also the activities of about 20 separate legal organizations (such as the Health and Hospitals Corporation) for which New York City is financially accountable. In this context, New York City is called the *primary government;* its constituent legally separate entities, which are public authorities or public benefit corporations, are called *component units*. We will return to this aspect of the reporting entity in Chapter 9.

In state and local governmental accounting, however, there is an additional dimension to the reporting entity. For internal accounting purposes, the primary government itself is disaggregated—subdivided—into separate fiscal and accounting entities, called funds. Each fund accounts for particular assets, liabilities, net assets, and inflows and outflows of resources. Funds are the basic building blocks of governmental accounting and financial reporting.

The formal definition of a fund is:

> . . . a fiscal and accounting entity with a self-balancing set of accounts recording cash and other financial resources, together with all related liabilities and residual equities or balances, and changes therein, which are segregated for the purpose of carrying on specific activities or attaining certain objectives in accordance with special regulations, restrictions or limitations.[1]

In this definition, the term *fiscal entity* refers to the separate budgetary nature of funds that have only spendable financial resources, and the term *accounting entity* refers to a separate unit that is treated as an entity for accounting purposes. Some types of funds also have capital assets.

The accounting equation within the funds is similar to that used in commercial accounting. In the absence of owners' equity, however, the equity aspect of the governmental accounting equation becomes either fund balance or net position, depending on the type of fund involved.

Why Governments Use Fund Accounting

Governmental entities must comply with legal requirements set forth in constitutions, city charters, statutes, local ordinances, and so forth. Because their day-to-day activities are guided by budgets proposed by the executive branch and enacted into law by the legislative branch, internal accounting systems are needed to ensure compliance with budgetary spending limits. Funds have traditionally provided a basic control mechanism for ensuring compliance with legal restrictions on the use of governmental resources. Indeed, most funds are established based on specific legal requirements.

---

[1]*GASB Codification of Governmental Accounting and Financial Reporting Standards* (GASB Cod.) Sec. 1300, "Statement of Principle—Fund Accounting Systems" (Norwalk, CT: GASB, 2010).

To illustrate, if the legislature wants to segregate gasoline taxes from other revenues to ensure a steady flow of resources that can be used only to repair roads, it may establish a dedicated fund to record receipt of the taxes and their subsequent expenditure. If the citizens vote to approve a bond issue for a new firehouse, segregating the bond proceeds in a dedicated fund helps ensure that the proceeds are used for no other purpose. If the legislature wishes to demonstrate its intent to dedicate resources to the repayment of the debt, it may create a fund for that purpose. A dedicated pension trust fund that accumulates employer and employee contributions and the related earnings helps ensure that the resources will be used to pay pension benefits when employees retire.

Is fund accounting absolutely necessary? Not to the extent it is used in practice. Many governments can readily accomplish the purposes of fund accounting by establishing separate accounts for restricted resources within a single accounting and fiscal entity. In fact, there is no consistency among governments in the extent to which they create funds. Some governments use many more funds than others, even though they perform the same functions. Further, excessive use of funds—for example, earmarking a particular type of tax to finance one purpose, a particular fee for another purpose, and so on—is considered a poor financial management practice because it reduces a government's flexibility in providing for citizen needs as priorities change. Finally, fund accounting provides no *absolute* assurance that dedicated resources will be used only for authorized purposes—a simple coding error can result in a charge to the wrong fund; hence, we used the phrase "helps ensure" in the preceding paragraph.

On the other hand, some governments are quite complex because they are engaged in various business-type activities. Creating separate funds (and legally separate component units) helps provide the control mechanisms, the financing tools, and the administrative structures needed to manage those activities.

Fund Categories

As noted earlier, the activities performed by governments can be categorized as either governmental, business (or proprietary), or fiduciary, depending on their purpose and/or how they are financed. The funds used by state and local governments can be similarly categorized. Within each *category* are several specific *fund types*. The categories are described next, and the fund types within each category are described later. As we will see in the next section, there is a major difference between the accounting measurements made in the governmental fund category and those in the other two fund categories.

Governmental-type funds are used to account for most of the day-to-day public services provided by state and local governments. Depending on the type of government, these services may include public safety (policing and fire suppression), elementary and secondary education, health and mental health, sanitation, environmental protection, parks and recreation, transportation, and so forth. Governments finance these services primarily by levying taxes on various revenue bases, such as real property values, general sales and specific types of sales (such as cigarettes and motor fuel), and personal incomes. They may also receive grants from other levels of government in addition to other revenues such as fines, fees, investment income, and concession income.

Capital assets used to provide these services (such as police stations and office buildings) are often financed through the proceeds of debt, which are accounted for in a separate governmental-type fund. To repay the debt sold to finance capital assets, funds are accumulated, primarily from tax revenues, in yet another governmental-type fund.

One of the characteristics of governmental-type funds is that their expenditures are likely to be controlled by budgets proposed by the executive branch of government and legally adopted by the legislative branch in the form of *appropriations*—authorizations to spend. The way governments prepare budgets and the legal status afforded them profoundly affect accounting within the governmental-type funds, as we shall see in the next section of this chapter and in later chapters. Although well-run governments do long-range planning, their annual budgets for day-to-day operations are short run in nature. They generally cover activities for only one year.

Proprietary-type (or business-type) funds are used to account for governmental activities that operate in a manner similar to that of private-sector businesses in the sense that they charge fees for services and measure whether their revenues will cover their expenses. Examples of such activities are municipal hospitals, electric and water utilities, mass transit facilities, lotteries, and central motor pools. Many of these activities are self-supporting because their fees are sufficient to cover their costs. Others (such as mass transit facilities) may receive subsidies from their parent government, while some (such as lotteries) provide net revenues for the parent. When these business-type activities are performed by agencies within the legally constituted government, a separate proprietary fund is established. When the activities are performed by legally separate component units, these entities use what is called "proprietary fund accounting."

Fiduciary-type funds are used to account for resources that governments hold in a trust or agency capacity for others. "Others" might be individuals, other governments, or private organizations. Because they are held for others, the resources in these funds cannot be used to support the government's own programs. Examples of situations in which a government might be acting in a trust or agency capacity include investment pools operated by a sponsoring government on behalf of other governments and sales taxes collected by a state on behalf of county and city governments.

Financial Reporting with the Use of Funds

External financial reporting is guided by the requirements of GASB Statement No. 34, "Basic Financial Statements—and Management's Discussion and Analysis—for State and Local Governments" (1999), as amended. GASB Statement No. 34 requires two sets of financial statements, *fund statements* and *government-wide statements*. Two sets of statements are prepared for several reasons:

- The measurement focus and basis of accounting used in the governmental-type fund category is different from that in the other two categories, as discussed in the next section.
- The information provided by the fund statements for the governmental-type fund category is incomplete (and may be misleading because it is incomplete).
- While reporting on each fund serves a purpose, there is also a need for an overview of the finances of the government as a whole.

The fund set of financial statements consists of three groupings—by fund category—of individual sets of statements prepared for each fund. For the governmental-type fund category, the statements report resource inflows and outflows (which we will sometimes refer to as "operating statements") and financial position (balance sheets). Financial statements for proprietary-type funds are operating statements, statements of net position, and statements of cash flows. Statements of net position and changes in net position are prepared for fiduciary-type funds.

The government-wide set of financial statements consolidates the individual funds into two groups of activities, governmental- and business-type. In preparing the government-wide statements, adjustments are made to the fund statements so that all activities use the same measurement focus and basis of accounting. In addition, the fiduciary-type funds are excluded from the consolidation because they do not support the government's own programs. (As you read Chapters 4, 5, and 6, keep in mind that certain adjustments will be needed to prepare the government-wide financial statements.) Chapters 9 and 10 describe how the financial statements are prepared.

MEASUREMENT FOCUS AND BASIS OF ACCOUNTING

In addition to the use of funds, another distinctive feature of state and local governmental accounting lies in the way inflows and outflows are measured in one of the fund categories—governmental-type funds. To grasp the implications of this notion, we first need to discuss the terms *measurement focus* and *basis of accounting*.

- *Measurement focus* refers to *what* is being expressed and *which resources* are being measured in reporting an organization's financial performance and position. For example, when a business enterprise focuses on measuring its net profit for the year, it takes account of transactions and events affecting both its financial and capital resources. If it wants to know how its activities affected its cash balance, it considers only the transactions that increase or decrease cash.
- *Basis of accounting* is a *timing* concept. It relates to *when* the assets, liabilities, revenues, and expenses (or expenditures) are recognized (recorded) in financial statements.

Measurement focus and basis of accounting are considered together because timing of recognition helps achieve what one is trying to measure. For example, using the accrual basis of accounting provides the most accurate measure of the change in an organization's net assets and liabilities.

Application to Proprietary-Type and Fiduciary-Type Funds

Proprietary-type funds are used to account for governmental activities that operate in a manner similar to that of commercial business enterprises. Although not motivated to make a profit, managers of governmental business activities are concerned with whether the revenues derived from user charges are sufficient to cover all costs of doing business. Therefore, just like that for commercial business entities, the accounting system for governmental business activities must take account of transactions and events that affect *all* the economic resources available to the activity—financial and capital. GASB literature refers to this measurement focus as the *economic resources measurement focus*.

To determine whether revenues are sufficient to cover costs, accounting measurements in proprietary-type funds are made using the *accrual basis* of accounting. This means that, in the proprietary-type funds, revenues are recognized in the period they are earned, even if the cash has not been received. Expenses are recognized when assets are consumed (or costs have expired) or when liabilities are incurred, even if the cash has not been paid. Capital outlays, for example, are initially recorded as assets and then depreciated to allocate their costs over their estimated useful lives. Also, because of the passage of time, unpaid interest on borrowed capital is accrued when financial statements are prepared even if it is not yet due to be paid.

The economic resources measurement focus and accrual basis of accounting are also used for accounting and reporting on fiduciary-type funds.

Application to Governmental-Type Funds

Accounting within the governmental-type funds has evolved historically as an accommodation to budgetary needs. To manage the basic day-to-day activities accounted for in the governmental-type funds, departmental budget officers and the government's central budget office need to know the amount of *financial resources* available for *current* spending. The central budget office also needs data to help monitor actual performance against the current year's budget and to plan future years' budgets.

Let's look at the big picture first, taking the perspective of the central budget office. The governmental budget process is spending oriented, cash oriented, and short run in nature. The thinking used in preparing the annual budget runs something like this:

- If a government needs to acquire capital assets, its budget may provide for raising financial resources by selling long-term bonds. When the financial resources are spent, the acquired capital assets are not available for future spending, unless they are sold and converted to cash.
- The government needs cash to pay principal and interest on the bonds, but depreciating assets does not produce cash. Instead, financial resources to pay the principal and interest must be raised primarily through taxation.
- Taxes will produce cash for the current budget period only to the extent the taxpayers pay in a timely manner. Taxpayers that don't pay in time to pay the government's bills don't produce budgetary revenues.
- On the other hand, if liabilities are incurred during a year because employees earn, say, vacation pay, but the accrued vacation pay will be paid in the form of cash only on retirement, the current year's budget need not raise taxes to finance it.

Now let's look at budget management from the perspective of the city police department's budget officer. Assume the police department is authorized to spend $60,000 to acquire supplies and $80,000 to acquire police sedans. If the department has spent $50,000 to acquire supplies, it has only $10,000 left to buy additional supplies. If it has spent $60,000 to buy two police sedans, it has only $20,000 left to buy another sedan. For *budgetary management* purposes, the relevant information is not the inventory of supplies or the depreciated value of the sedans; rather, what is relevant is the fact that the police department has $10,000 of financial resources left to acquire more materials and $20,000 of financial resources left to buy another sedan.

To provide data on the amount of *financial resources available for current spending*, the *current financial resources* measurement focus is used in governmental-type funds. Using this measurement focus involves recording *inflows and outflows of liquid assets* and, as such, has a distinctly budgetary orientation. When the current financial resources measurement focus is used, resource inflows are classified broadly as "revenues" and "other financing sources." Resource outflows are classified broadly as "expenditures" and "other financing uses."

Governmental-type funds use a *modified accrual basis of accounting*, rather than the accrual basis of accounting, because the modified basis focuses on flows of current financial resources. The effect of the difference in measurement focus is that neither capital assets nor long-term liabilities are recorded in the governmental-type funds. Further, the combined effect of the differences in measurement focus and basis of accounting is that accrual accounting is *modified* in the governmental-type funds to record only those accruals that affect near-term financial resource inflows and outflows.

We will discuss the accounting measurement implications of the current financial resources measurement focus and modified accrual basis of accounting in the governmental-type funds at length in Chapters 4 through 6. For now, here are a few basic concepts:

- **Revenue recognition.** When accrual accounting is used, revenues are recognized when they are earned. When governments modify accrual accounting for purposes of recognizing revenue in governmental-type funds, tax revenues such as property taxes must also be "measurable and available" to be recognized. *Measurable* refers to the ability to state the amount of revenue in terms of dollars. *Available* means collectible within the current period or soon enough thereafter so it can be used to pay the bills of the current period. For property tax revenues, "soon enough thereafter" is interpreted in the accounting standards to mean no more than 60 days after the accounting period ends. So, for example, property taxes levied for the year ended December 31, 2012, are recognized as revenue for 2012 if they are expected to be collected by the end of February 2013.
- **Expenditure recognition.** Expenditure recognition in governmental-type funds is influenced by the budgetary nature of those funds; that is, the funds are designed to have only current financial resources and to exclude long-term liabilities. As a result, three types of expenditures (decreases in financial resources) appear in operating statements prepared for governmental-type funds: current operating items; capital asset acquisitions; and debt service (interest and repayment of principal on long-term borrowing). Exclusion of long-term liabilities from governmental-type funds causes the amounts recognized for operating expenditures to be modified from the amounts that would be recognized under full accrual accounting.

  For many items (such as salaries, supplies, and utilities) *operating expenditures* are recognized in the period in which the related liabilities are incurred because the liabilities are payable from financial resources shortly after they are incurred. Some liabilities, however, do not require liquidation with currently available financial resources and are generally not provided for in the current budget. Such liabilities and the related operating expenditures are recognized when the liabilities *mature.* So, for example, if employees are allowed to accumulate vacation leave until they separate or retire from service, related expenditures and liabilities are not recognized until they come due for payment (mature) on employee separation. Expenditures and liabilities for pensions and retiree health care benefits earned by the employees during an accounting period are recognized for that period *only to the extent the government finances them.* These modifications (or exceptions) to the accrual basis of accounting, discussed in detail in Chapter 5, can significantly affect the amounts reported as expenditures in a particular year compared with the amounts that are recognized under full accrual accounting. In short, excluding long-term liabilities also results in excluding the related expenditures.

  When fund financial resources are spent to acquire capital assets, financial resources are consumed and cannot be spent for anything else. Accordingly, *capital outlay expenditures* equal to the amount spent are reported in the governmental fund operating statement because available financial resources have decreased. (Records are kept of the acquired capital asset, but those records are not part of the fund financial accounting system; they are used only for the government-wide statements.) Similarly, *debt service expenditures* are reported when debt principal is repaid because financial resources have decreased. Interest on long-term debt is also a debt service expenditure, but is recognized as an expenditure in the period the interest is *due for payment*, similar to the way interest is treated in the budget. This is yet another modification to the accrual basis of accounting.

Governmental Accounting in Practice

Form versus Substance in Budgeting

In exchange for providing services, governmental and private-sector employees generally receive compensation in the form of salaries and benefits. Benefits may include pensions and retiree health care. Employees receive the salary portion of their compensation shortly after they perform the work. The employees earn the *right* to the benefits during the periods they work but don't receive the cash (or whatever form the benefit may take) until after they retire. The employer, however, receives the full value of the employment exchange during the periods the employees work; therefore, the employer's *obligation* for paying both salaries and benefits arises during those working periods.

But what if the government budgets for those benefits on a purely cash basis; that is, by not budgeting for the benefits until the years the actual payments are due, after the employees retire? Is the budget "balanced" if the government fails to set aside money for the benefits in the years the benefits are earned? We suggest such budgets are balanced in form—on a cash flow basis—but not in economic substance.

In fact, some governments consistently do not budget in the current year for the full amount of pension benefits earned by employees in the current year, and virtually every government budgets for retiree health care benefits in the year they are paid, not when the employees earn the benefit. In a 2011 report, the Pew Center for the States pegged the cumulative unfunded obligation for employee benefits at more than $1.2 trillion, just for states and localities that participate in state plans. Part of the unfunded obligation resulted from declines in equity security values, but most of it was caused by not budgeting for the benefits when earned by the employees.

- *Bond Proceeds.* A further distinguishing characteristic of the current financial resources measurement focus is the accounting treatment of general obligation bond proceeds. When a business enterprise obtains resources from the sale of bonds, it credits the long-term liability account "bonds payable" to offset the debit to cash. But bond proceeds provide current financial resources available for spending and governmental-type funds do not report long-term liabilities; therefore, the recipient fund recognizes an inflow of financial resources in its *operating statement*, reporting the inflow as an "other financing source." (As with capital assets, records are kept of the long-term bond liabilities, but those records are not part of the *fund* financial accounting system.)

As the foregoing concepts indicate, the current financial resources measurement focus/ modified accrual accounting basis is *generally* consistent with the way governments budget. (Budgets are not prepared in a uniform manner among state and local governments; some are prepared on a cash basis, and some are modified just slightly from the cash basis.) However, accounting and financial reporting to accommodate budgetary needs does not mean that capital assets and longer-term obligations are ignored. If they were ignored, there would be a potential for misrepresentation. Therefore, as previously noted, governmental financial reporting standards require two sets of financial statements. The fund-level statements are based on the standards for accounting *within* the funds, so statements prepared for governmental-type funds use the current financial resources measurement focus and modified accrual basis of accounting. For government-wide financial reporting, the data reported for governmental-type funds are aggregated and adjusted to the economic resources measurement focus and accrual basis of accounting. Capital assets and bonds payable are reported in the government-wide statements.

Tables 2-1 and 2-2 summarize the measurement focus, basis of accounting, and broad category of activities embraced within the three fund categories. Table 2-3 lists the specific fund types within each category and shows the measurement focus and basis of accounting applicable to each fund type. An overview of these funds and examples of individual fund financial statements are presented in the remainder of this chapter.

TABLE 2-1 Fund Categories

	Governmental-Type Funds	Proprietary-Type Funds	Fiduciary-Type Funds
Focus	Current financial resources	Economic resources	Economic resources
Activity	General government activities	Activities financed by user fees	Resources held for others
	Legally dedicated resources		

TABLE 2-2 Cash, Accrual, and Modified Accrual Bases of Accounting

	Cash Basis	Accrual Basis	Modified Accrual Basis
Record revenue	When cash is received	When revenue is earned	When measurable and available
Record expenses (expenditures)	When cash is paid	When asset is consumed or expense is incurred	Generally when liability is incurred (with specific exceptions)
Applicable fund category		Proprietary, Fiduciary	Governmental

TABLE 2-3 Summary of Accounting Procedures within Funds

Fund Type	Category	Measurement Focus	Basis of Accounting
General	Governmental	Current financial resources	Modified accrual
Special Revenue	Governmental	Current financial resources	Modified accrual
Debt Service	Governmental	Current financial resources	Modified accrual
Capital Projects	Governmental	Current financial resources	Modified accrual
Permanent	Governmental	Current financial resources	Modified accrual
Enterprise	Proprietary	Economic resources	Accrual
Internal Service	Proprietary	Economic resources	Accrual
Pension Trust	Fiduciary	Economic resources	Accrual
Investment Trust	Fiduciary	Economic resources	Accrual
Private-Purpose Trust	Fiduciary	Economic resources	Accrual
Agency	Fiduciary	Economic resources	Accrual

Source: Adapted from GASB Statement No. 34, "Basic Financial Statements—and Management's Discussion and Analysis—for State and Local Governments" (Norwalk, CT: GASB, 1999), Table B-2, p. 151.

Governmental Accounting in Practice

Current Financial Resources versus Economic Resources

As already discussed, the GASB requires preparation of two sets of financial statements: a fund set and a government-wide set. The required reconciliation of the net change in fund balances for governmental-type funds (fund set) with the change in net assets for governmental activities (government-wide set) explains the effect on the operating statements of using different measurement focuses and bases of accounting in each set. To illustrate, as a result of its fiscal year 2010 operations, fund balances of New York City's governmental-type funds declined by $1,582 million. But net assets of the governmental activities reported in the government-wide set declined by $11,702 million. So the bottom line reported in the fund set was better than that reported in the government-wide set. Here are some of the reconciling items from the fund operating statement to the government-wide operating statement. (Numbers are in millions of dollars.)

Capital outlays are reported as expenditures in governmental-type funds. However, in the government-wide operating statement, the cost of those assets is allocated over their estimated useful lives and reported as depreciation expense. Because capital outlays exceeded depreciation expense in the current period, the bottom line of the fund statements is worse than that of the government-wide statements by

Purchases of capital assets	$5,783	
Depreciation expense	(2,139)	$3,644

Issuing long-term debt provides current financial resources to governmental-type funds, while repaying long-term debt consumes those resources. Neither transaction has any effect on the operating results reported in the government-wide statements. But because bond proceeds exceeded principal repayments, the bottom line of the fund statements is better than that of the government-wide statements by

Proceeds from sales of bonds	$(10,818)	
Repayment of bond principal	5,886	
Other	(78)	(5,010)

The City does not finance retiree health care benefits as earned by employees. Instead, benefits are paid on behalf of employees after they retire. The resulting accrual, made for purposes of preparing the government-wide statements, does not require expenditure of current financial resources. Therefore, the bottom line of the fund statements is better than that of the government-wide statements by   (9,440)

Source: Based on the Comprehensive Annual Financial Report, City of New York, NY, for the fiscal year ended June 30, 2010.

GOVERNMENTAL-TYPE FUNDS

Five types of governmental funds are used to account for the day-to-day operating services provided by state and local governments: the General Fund, Special Revenue Funds, Debt Service Funds, Capital Projects Funds, and Permanent Funds. All governments have one General Fund; most governments use one or more Special Revenue Funds, Capital Projects Funds, and Debt Service Funds; and some have Permanent Funds. Table 2-4 summarizes the purposes of each fund type and gives examples of their use.

The financial statements of Mt. Lebanon, Pennsylvania, for the year ended December 31, 2009, illustrate the types of revenues, expenditures, assets, liabilities, and other accounting elements encountered within governmental-type funds. The statements also help introduce the reporting implications of the measurement focus and basis of accounting used in those funds. Mt. Lebanon, a suburb of Pittsburgh, has a population of about 33,000. It has received the Certificate for Excellence in Financial Reporting, awarded by the Government Finance Officers Association, for 33 consecutive years. Table 2-5 presents the statements of revenues, expenditures, and changes in fund balances (operating statements) for four of Mt. Lebanon's governmental-type funds, and Table 2-6 presents the balance sheets. We will return to these statements in later chapters.

Following is a skeletal outline of the governmental-type fund operating statements. Notice in particular the caption "Other financing sources and uses, including transfers" and the items listed under that caption in Table 2-5. This caption is needed to accommodate the financial resources measurement focus used in the governmental-type funds; it is also used to report the relatively large number of interfund resource transfers caused by the use of fund accounting. Also, notice the types of revenues, expenditures, and other financing sources for each of the fund types in Table 2-5.

Revenues (detailed)
− Expenditures (detailed)
= Excess (deficiency) of revenues over expenditures
± Other financing sources and uses, including transfers (detailed)
± Special and extraordinary items (detailed)
= Net change in fund balances
+ Fund balances—beginning of period
= Fund balances—end of period[2]

Next, notice the general format of the governmental fund balance sheets in Table 2-6: assets = liabilities + deferred inflows of resources + fund balances. Mt. Lebanon, like most governments, reports deferred inflows of resources as a result of applying the measurable and available

---

[2]GASB Cod. Sec. 2200.159. For accounting in governmental-type funds, the GASB defines *revenues* essentially as increases in fund financial resources other than from interfund transfers and debt issue proceeds, and *expenditures* as decreases in fund financial resources other than through interfund transfers (GASB COD Sec 1800.114). The GASB provides no specific definition of *other financing sources or uses*. Although inconsistencies in standards regarding fund accounting make it difficult to develop precise definitions, we suggest the following for working purposes: (a) *Revenues* are inflows of fund financial resources related to the current reporting period, resulting from transactions (such as taxes and intergovernmental grants) that generally produce increases in the net assets of the entity as a whole. (b) *Other financing sources* are increases in the assets of a fund that generally do not increase net assets of the entity as a whole. They include debt issue proceeds and interfund transfers (which do not increase net assets of the entity as a whole) and the sale of capital assets (which may increase them). (c) *Expenditures* are outflows of financial resources related to the current reporting period, for current operations, capital outlay, and payment of debt service on long-term debt, subject to the measurement issues discussed in Chapter 5.

criteria for recognizing revenues in governmental-type funds. Governmental-type funds might also have deferred outflows of resources.

The General Fund

All general-purpose governments and certain special-purpose governments, such as school districts, use a *General Fund*. By definition, the General Fund is a residual fund; that is, it is used to account for and report all financial resources not accounted for and reported in some other fund. In reality, however, the General Fund is the single most important fund because it encompasses government's basic day-to-day operations. It is the fund that politicians and citizens alike focus on during the budget adoption period.

General Funds obtain most of their resources from taxes on real property, general sales or specific types of sales, and personal and corporate incomes. They may also obtain intergovernmental grants for specific programs such as education and public assistance. Licenses, fees, and fines also are generally recorded in the General Fund. These resources are expended for basic operating programs, such as police and fire suppression services, trash removal, parks and cultural activities, traffic control, road maintenance, and the general administrative functions of government. The General Fund may also be used to acquire nonmajor items of equipment, including police sedans. In addition, financial resources may be transferred from the General Fund to other funds to fully or partially finance the activities of those funds.

Assets found in the General Fund are primarily *current financial resources* and usually include cash, investments, receivables (such as unpaid property taxes), and receivables from other funds. In governmental accounting terminology, short-term receivables from other funds are

TABLE 2-4	Purposes of Governmental-Type Funds
Fund Type	**To Account For**
General	All financial resources not accounted for in some other fund; includes most day-to-day activities of government
	Examples: Operations of police, fire, and sanitation departments
Special Revenue	Specific revenue items restricted or otherwise limited to spending for specific purposes other than debt service or capital projects
	Examples: Dedicated tax on motor fuel for highway paving and care or on hotel occupancy for business district maintenance
Capital Projects	Financial resources restricted or otherwise limited to spending for capital outlays, including facilities and other capital assets
	Examples: Construction of firehouse, office buildings, roads
Debt Service	Financial resources restricted or otherwise limited to spending for principal and interest on general long-term debt
	Examples: Property taxes and transfers of financial resources from other funds to pay debt service on long-term debt sold to acquire capital assets
Permanent	Resources restricted to the extent that only earnings (not principal) may be used to support the government's programs
	Examples: Public cemetery perpetual-care fund; endowment fund for acquiring library books

TABLE 2-5 Governmental-Type Funds—Statements of Revenues, Expenditures, and Changes in Fund Balances

Mt. Lebanon, Pennsylvania
Selected Governmental-Type Funds
Statements of Revenues, Expenditures, and Changes in Fund Balances
For the Year Ended December 31, 2009
(in thousands of dollars)

	General Fund	Special Revenue Fund	Capital Projects Fund	Debt Service Fund
Revenues				
Taxes	$22,761			
Licenses, permits, fees	832	$ 7,043		
Intergovernmental grants	1,241			
Other	4,413	41	$ 6	$
Total revenues	29,247	7,084	6	0
Expenditures				
Current:				
General government	4,216		71	
Public works	6,216	3,734		
Culture, recreation	2,594			
Public safety	9,846			
Other current	1,681			
Debt service:				
Principal				1,640
Interest				870
Capital outlay	280		4,425	
Total expenditures	24,833	3,734	4,496	2,510
Excess of revenues over expenditures	4,414	3,350	(4,490)	(2,510)
Other Financing Sources (Uses)				
Transfers in	369		2,555	2,510
Transfers out	(3,364)	(2,992)		
Proceeds—bond issuance			2,115	
Bond issuance premium			3	
Total other financing sources (uses)	(2,995)	(2,992)	4,673	2,510
Net change in fund balance	1,419	358	183	0
Fund balance, beginning of year	6,348	1,894	80	0
Fund balance, end of year	$ 7,767	$ 2,252	$ 263	$ 0

Source: Adapted from the Comprehensive Annual Financial Report, Mt. Lebanon, Pennsylvania, December 31, 2009.

TABLE 2-6   Governmental-Type Funds—Balance Sheets

Mt. Lebanon, Pennsylvania
Selected Governmental-Type Funds
Balance Sheets
December 31, 2009
(in thousands of dollars)

	General Fund	Special Revenue Fund	Capital Projects Fund	Debt Service Fund
Assets				
Cash and cash equivalents	$ 5,641	$ 3,698	$ 447	$
Receivables:				
Taxes	3,751			
Assessments	16	672		
Accounts	565		17	
Due from other funds	630		520	
Due from other governments	472			
Advance to other funds	760			
Other	468			
Total assets	$12,303	$ 4,370	$ 984	$ 0
Liabilities				
Accounts payable	$ 595	$ 941	$ 590	$
Advance deposits	480			
Due to other funds		875	114	
Accrued payroll	848			
Total liabilities	1,923	1,816	704	0
Deferred Inflows of Resources				
~~Deferred~~ revenue	2,613	302	17	
Fund Balances				
Nonspendable	760			
Restricted		2,252	263	
Assigned for subsequent year's budget	1,896			
Assigned for other purposes	1,426			
Unassigned	3,685			
Total fund balances	7,767	2,252	263	0
Total liabilities, deferred inflows of resources, and fund balances	$12,303	$ 4,370	$ 984	$ 0

Source: Adapted from the Comprehensive Annual Financial Report, Mt. Lebanon, Pennsylvania, December 31, 2009. (We made some format changes to enable this illustration to show the effect of changes in accounting standards after this statement was prepared.)

referred to as *due from other funds;* if they result from loans not currently due, they are referred to as loans receivable or *advances to other funds.* Liabilities found in the General Fund are also primarily currently due to be paid. They typically include salaries and accounts payable and payables to other funds. The latter items are referred to as *due to other funds;* as in the case of receivables, if these liabilities are not currently due, they are referred to as loans payable or *advances from other funds.* (Inclusion of long-term loans between funds is an exception to the general rule regarding current financial resources. The special treatment required in this case is discussed in Chapter 5.)

As noted earlier, the General Fund is also likely to have deferred inflows of resources, primarily because application of the measurable and available criteria for recognizing property taxes results in recording property taxes receivable for revenues that will not be recognized until a future accounting period. Accounting for property taxes is discussed in detail in Chapter 5.[3]

The excess of assets over liabilities and deferred inflows of resources in the General Fund is called fund balance. Fund balance results from the cumulative excess of revenue and other sources of financing over expenditures and other uses of fund resources. The fund balance is of major concern both in the budget process and in analyzing financial condition because it shows—subject to various constraints—the net assets available for future spending. Fund balance is expressed in up to five classifications, based on the extent to which the government is required to honor those constraints. The classifications—nonspendable, restricted, committed, assigned, and unassigned—are discussed in Chapter 5.

Scan the format and the captions shown for the numbers in the General Fund column of Mt. Lebanon's financial statements. In the operating statement (Table 2-5) notice that expenditures are reported by major function. Each function may cover salaries, supplies, and other expenditures incurred by several departments. Notice also the section "Other Financing Sources (Uses)." These increases and decreases in General Fund financial resources (which include transfers in and out of funds) are neither revenues nor expenditures, but they nevertheless affect the net change in fund balance. In the balance sheet (Table 2-6) notice the current nature of the assets and liabilities, as well as the various components of fund balance. Also notice that, because the $760 (thousand) loan receivable is not currently available for spending, an equivalent amount is classified as nonspendable fund balance.

COMPARISON WITH BUSINESS ENTERPRISE REPORTING—OPERATING STATEMENT   Before discussing the purposes of the other four governmental-fund types, it is useful to better understand the financial reporting implications of the accounting measurements in governmental-type funds. We can accomplish this to some extent by exploring the major differences between financial statements prepared for governmental-type funds and the statements prepared for business enterprises. We will refer again to Tables 2-5 and 2-6, looking at the data in all four fund types.

As previously stated, governmental fund operating statements focus not on measurement of net profit, but rather on increases and decreases of current financial resources, leading to balance sheets that measure the amount of *financial resources available for spending.* Thus, when a governmental-type fund spends current financial resources to acquire capital assets, the result—in terms of the effect on current financial resources—is to reduce the amount of financial resources available for spending. The fact that it acquired capital assets is relevant to the entity's

---

[3]Until recently, deferred inflows of resources were reported as liabilities. GASB Statement No. 63, "Financial Reporting of Deferred Outflows of Resources, Deferred Inflows of Resources, and Net Position" (June 2011) and related standards reclassified the reporting effects of certain specific transactions from assets and liabilities to deferred outflows and deferred inflows of resources, respectively.

ability to perform its mission, but not to the measurement focus of the fund financial statements. Similarly, long-term borrowing results in an inflow of financial resources available for current spending. Increasing its long-term debt is relevant to the entity's long-term financial position, but not to the measurement focus of the governmental fund financial statements.

This difference in measurement focus causes governmental fund operating statements to use a format different from that used by business enterprises. To accommodate the current financial resources measurement focus, the governmental-type fund operating statement takes on aspects of a cash flows statement. (Conceiving of these statements as modified cash flows statements helps you understand both the elements reported and the measurements made in them.) Notice, for example, that Mt. Lebanon's operating statement (Table 2-5) shows capital outlays and repayment of long-term debt principal as expenditures in several of the funds; it also shows proceeds from the sale of long-term debt as inflows of financial resources in the Capital Projects Fund. Business enterprises would report these items in the statement of cash flows and the effect of the transactions in their balance sheets.

Another significant difference between governmental fund and business enterprise operating statements lies in the appearance of transfers among funds in the governmental statements. Table 2-5 shows transfers among all four governmental-type funds. Transfers cause increases or decreases in the financial resources of the affected funds and therefore need to be reported in the individual fund financial statements. Although transfers among related companies occur in business enterprises, they are eliminated when financial statements are prepared because they do not affect the enterprise as a whole. (When governmental entities prepare government-wide financial statements, interfund transfers offset each other and are eliminated, as discussed in Chapter 10.)

The other important difference between governmental fund and business enterprise operating statements is not apparent from Table 2-5. This difference results from the accounting measurements made in the governmental-type funds, which use the modified accrual basis of accounting. (Recall the discussion earlier in the chapter regarding pension and retiree health care benefits.) We will discuss this difference in detail in later chapters.

COMPARISON WITH BUSINESS ENTERPRISE REPORTING—BALANCE SHEET   Significant differences between balance sheets prepared for governmental-type funds and business enterprises also result from the current financial resources measurement focus used by governmental-type funds. Notice that the balance sheets (Table 2-6) prepared for Mt. Lebanon's governmental-type funds consist almost entirely of currently spendable financial resources. The governmental-type funds do not report any capital assets, such as buildings and equipment, even though it is clear from the fund operating statements that Mt. Lebanon acquired capital assets during the current year and it is reasonable to assume it still has capital assets acquired in previous years. Similarly, notice that the liabilities sections of Mt. Lebanon's governmental fund balance sheets report only short-term liabilities, even though it is clear from the operating statements that Mt. Lebanon had proceeds from the sale of bonds during the year. Business corporations that have capital assets and long-term bonds payable report them on their balance sheets.

Another significant difference between the balance sheets prepared for governmental-type funds and for business enterprises concerns the difference between assets and liabilities. This net difference is called owners' equity for business enterprises and fund balance for government. In business corporations, owners' equity consists of contributed capital and retained earnings. No attempt is made to show how much of the equity is available for spending. Both internal and external users of governmental-type fund statements, however, are very concerned with the fund balances—the amounts available for spending either for general purposes or for specific purposes.

Therefore, the fund balances on governmental fund balance sheets are expressed in up to five classifications, depending on the level of constraint regarding the use of the net financial resources. Four of those levels are shown in Table 2-6. The five levels are discussed in detail in Chapter 5.

After considering the types of assets, liabilities, and equity reported in Mt. Lebanon's financial statements, it is apparent that the accounting equation for governmental-type funds differs from the traditional business-type accounting equation. Governmental funds report *only a portion* of the assets and liabilities reported by business enterprises. The governmental fund accounting equation covers *only financial assets and certain matured liabilities that it expects to pay shortly after the end of the reporting period*. From a practical standpoint, the governmental fund accounting equation may be expressed as follows:

financial assets = matured short-term liabilities + deferred resource inflows + fund balance

In that equation "financial assets" include primarily cash, investments, and receivables; "matured short-term liabilities" include primarily accounts payable, salaries payable, amounts payable to other funds, and other matured liabilities due for payment and expected to be paid shortly after the accounting period ends; and "deferred resource inflows" are net assets acquired by the government that apply to, and will be recognized as revenues in, a future reporting period. Further, "short-term" in governmental funds has a shorter time frame than the 1 year period that defines *current* in business enterprise accounting.

Special Revenue Funds

Special Revenue Funds are used to account for the proceeds of specific revenue sources that are restricted or committed to spending for specified purposes other than debt service or capital projects. (Resources obtained for debt service and capital projects are accounted for in other fund types, as discussed later.) The foundation for establishing a Special Revenue Fund lies in the decision, generally based in law or contract, to restrict or commit the proceeds of one or more *specific sources of revenue* for specified purposes.

Generally, the sources of revenue for Special Revenue Funds are specific taxes and fees. Many states also account for specific-purpose federal grants in Special Revenue Funds. Governments may supplement the specific sources of revenue with transfers from the General Fund, so long as those resources must be used for the specified purpose of the Special Revenue Fund. However, proceeds of the specific revenue sources should comprise a substantial portion of the fund's resource inflows. If the government no longer expects the specific revenue sources to be a substantial portion of the fund's resources, the special revenue designation should be discontinued. (The GASB does not define "substantial;" one of the definitions in our dictionary is "considerable in importance, degree, value, amount or extent.")

Following are some illustrations of Special Revenue Funds:

- A city enacts a tax on the occupancy of hotels and motels for the specific purpose of improving the appearance of its downtown business area. A Special Revenue Fund accounts for the proceeds and spending of the tax.
- A state enacts a law requiring that parks admissions or parking fees be used solely for seasonal planting in the parks. A Special Revenue Fund accounts for the collection of the fees and the expenditures for the plantings.

A government may have more than one Special Revenue Fund, each of which is a separate accounting and fiscal entity. Using a Special Revenue Fund enables greater transparency in reporting on the dollars collected from the specific revenue source and how those dollars were used. As noted earlier in this chapter, however, creating Special Revenue Funds reduces budgetary flexibility. Governments are required to disclose in the notes to the financial statements the purpose for each Special Revenue Fund, as well as which revenues and other resources are reported in those funds.

The Special Revenue Fund used by Mt. Lebanon (Tables 2-5 and 2-6) is a Sewage Fund, which accounts for a specific revenue source—a sewer service surcharge to water bills, assessed against properties in the municipality for sewage activities. Notice the large transfer out from the Special Revenue Fund in Table 2-5. Most of that transfer went to the Capital Projects Fund for construction needed to meet federal requirements.

The types of assets, liabilities, revenues, expenditures, and transfers found in Special Revenue Funds generally are similar to those found in the General Fund. However, only the General Fund can have Unassigned fund balance; by its nature, Special Revenue Funds have limitations on how their resources may be spent. Because accounting and financial reporting for Special Revenue Funds is virtually identical to that of the General Fund (both fund types use the current financial resources measurement focus and modified accrual basis of accounting), Chapters 4 and 5 cover both fund types.

Capital Projects Funds

Capital Projects Funds are used to account for and report on financial resources that are restricted or otherwise limited to spending for capital outlays, including the acquisition or construction of capital facilities and other capital assets. The term *capital facilities* includes buildings (such as office buildings and firehouses), building improvements, and infrastructure assets (such as roads and bridges). "Other capital assets" covers items such as buses, fire trucks, and computer workstation equipment. Capital Projects Funds are not used to account for capital-related outflows financed by proprietary funds or assets held in trust for individuals, private organizations, or other governments.

Capital Projects Funds should always be used when capital outlays are financed from general obligation bond proceeds.[4] Indeed, separate funds should be used for each bond issue to ensure transparency regarding use of the bond proceeds, including appropriate disposition of resources not needed to complete the project for which debt was issued.

Financial resources flowing through Capital Projects Funds generally include proceeds of long-term borrowing and intergovernmental grants. Some governments make it a practice to finance part of their capital asset needs from taxes and fees, so it is not uncommon to find transfers from the General Fund or a Special Revenue Fund into a Capital Projects Fund. Also, some governments have a policy of financing smaller items of equipment, such as police sedans and furniture, directly from the General Fund. Some key the use of Capital Projects Funds to their capital asset capitalization policy, and some do not. For example, an entity may decide that assets with a useful life of more than 1 year and costing more than $10,000 are capitalized; therefore, acquisitions of such assets are accounted for in a Capital Projects Fund, but acquisitions of assets not meeting those criteria are accounted for in the General Fund. In short, practices regarding use of Capital Projects Funds are not uniform, a factor the GASB considered in defining when they are used.

Long-term borrowing and transfers from other funds are reported as other financing sources in the operating statement. Intergovernmental grants are reported as revenues. Capital Projects Funds may also obtain revenues from the temporary investment of financial resources.

---

[4]General obligation bonds are secured by the municipality's *full faith, credit, and taxing power*. They are distinguished from revenue bonds, which are secured solely by the *revenues generated by the project being financed*. See section on Enterprise Funds later in this chapter.

Often, the amount reported as other financing sources will be greater than the amount of revenues shown in the operating statement.

Assets normally found on the balance sheet of a Capital Projects Fund include cash, temporary investments, receivables, and amounts due from other funds or governments. Liabilities include accounts payable (including amounts retained from contractors pending completion and acceptance of projects) and amounts due to other funds or governments. But because it uses a current financial resources measurement focus, a Capital Projects Fund balance sheet shows neither the capital assets nor the long-term debt sold to acquire those assets. Capital assets and bonds payable are, however, reported in the government-wide financial statements, which are prepared using the economic resources measurement focus and accrual basis of accounting. To accumulate such data for government-wide reporting, this text (Chapter 10) suggests using a memorandum set of accounts, called a Capital Investment Account Group.

Turn to the Capital Projects Fund columns in Mt. Lebanon's operating statement and balance sheet (Tables 2-5 and 2-6). Notice that Mt. Lebanon makes capital outlays primarily from its Capital Projects Fund, but also from its General Fund. These outlays are reported as fund expenditures. Its Capital Projects Fund obtains significant resources from long-term borrowing and transfers from other funds, which are reported as other financing sources. Also, notice the absence of capital asset and bonds payable accounts in the balance sheet.

Debt Service Funds

Debt Service Funds are used to account for and report on financial resources that are restricted or otherwise limited to spending for principal and interest on *general* long-term debt. (The term *general* here refers to debt other than that related to and expected to be paid from proprietary-type or fiduciary type funds.) Debt Service Funds also may be used to accumulate resources for paying long term liabilities resulting from debt like commitments, such as lease purchase agreements and installment purchase contracts. Debt serviced by proprietary or fiduciary fund resources is not *general* long-term debt, so resources accumulated for that purpose should be reported in a proprietary or fiduciary fund.

Debt Service Funds should be used if legally mandated or if financial resources are being accumulated for principal and interest that comes due in future years. The latter situation arises, for example, if the bond agreement requires accumulation of resources in a sinking fund. In fact, governments may use several Debt Service Funds because each bond agreement requires establishing a separate fund. Although—in the absence of such requirements—debt service payments may be made directly from general revenues and accounted for in the General Fund, using Debt Service Funds is a desirable financial management practice.

Debt Service Fund resources come most often from transfers from the General Fund or other funds, income from investment of resources held by the fund, and taxes assessed specifically to service the debt. Fund resources may also come from a portion of bond issue proceeds (sold to finance capital projects) that is set aside specifically as a reserve to ensure payment of future debt service. Also, bond agreements may require that debt proceeds not used—because bond-financed capital projects cost less than originally estimated—be transferred from the Capital Projects Fund to the Debt Service Fund when the project is completed. Debt service expenditures generally result from payment of principal and interest on the debt.

The assets of Debt Service Funds most often consist of cash and investments, and sometimes receivables. Liabilities are generally for interest and principal that have matured (i.e., come due for payment) but have not yet been paid. Because these funds use the current financial resources measurement focus, the long-term liability for principal that has not yet matured is not reported in the fund balance sheet.

For an illustration of Debt Service Fund transactions and balances, turn to the Debt Service Fund columns in Tables 2-5 and 2-6. Notice that Mt. Lebanon's debt service expenditures were financed entirely from interfund transfers. Its balance sheet shows no account balances because Mt. Lebanon made transfers to the Debt Service Fund in the exact amount of the expenditures and all payments were made as required. Although this occurs occasionally, Debt Service Funds more often report some assets and liabilities.

Permanent Funds

Permanent Funds are used to report resources that are legally restricted so that only the earnings generated by the principal, and not the principal itself, may be used to support programs that benefit the government or its citizens. Permanent Funds do not include private-purpose trust funds, which are fiduciary-type funds, discussed later in this chapter.

An example of a Permanent Fund is a perpetual-care public cemetery fund, whose resources generate revenues to maintain the cemetery. Another example is an endowment made to a public library, in which the endowment must be maintained in perpetuity and the income generated by the endowment must be used to purchase library books.

Financial statements prepared for Permanent Funds are similar to those shown in Tables 2-5 and 2-6. Assets of Permanent Funds generally include cash and investments. Liabilities might include amounts due to other funds. Permanent Fund revenues generally include investment income (interest, dividends, and net increase or decrease in the fair value of investments). Distributions of assets to the fund designated as the beneficiary of Permanent Fund earnings—usually a Special Revenue Fund—are reported as transfers out.

PROPRIETARY-TYPE FUNDS

Proprietary-type funds are used when a governmental unit handles its financial operations in a manner generally similar to that of business enterprises. Activities that use proprietary fund accounting and reporting charge user fees for their services and focus on determining operating income (or cost recovery) and changes in net position. Examples of such activities include operation of electric and water utilities, airports, mass transit facilities, and central motor pools. Although sometimes subsidized by transfers (often from the General Fund), these activities are financed by user charges that at least partially cover operating and capital costs. As a result, accounting principles followed by proprietary-type funds are similar to those followed by commercial entities; that is, they use an economic resources measurement focus and the accrual basis of accounting. Accrual-basis accounting provides governmental units with accurate measures of revenues and expenses to help in developing user charges; cash flows information is also provided to help determine user charges and any subsidy needed to run an activity.

The two types of proprietary funds are Enterprise Funds and Internal Service Funds. Table 2-7 summarizes the purposes of these funds and gives examples of their use.

Enterprise Funds

Enterprise Funds may be used to account for any activity whose products or services are sold for a fee to external users, such as the general public. Enterprise Funds may also sell to the government

TABLE 2-7	Purposes of Proprietary-Type Funds
Fund Type	**To Account For**
Enterprise	Resources used to supply goods and services, for a fee, to users who are entirely or primarily external to the governmental unit
	Examples: Municipal airport, municipal electric utility
Internal Service	Resources used to supply goods or services, based on cost reimbursement, within the governmental unit and to other governments
	Examples: Central motor pool, central purchasing function

itself, but those sales represent only a small part of the total fund revenues. Enterprise Funds *must* be used if any one of the following criteria is met:

- The activity is financed with debt that is secured solely by a pledge of the net revenues from the activity's fees and charges. (This type of debt is referred to as revenue bonds.)
- Laws or regulations require that the costs of providing services, including capital costs (such as depreciation or debt service), be recovered through fees and charges, rather than with taxes.
- The activity's pricing policies set fees and charges that are designed to recover its costs, including capital costs (such as depreciation or debt service).

As noted previously, operations accounted for in Enterprise Funds may include municipally owned utilities, mass transit facilities, toll roads and toll bridges, airports, parking facilities, and lotteries. Generally, a separate fund is established for each type of activity. As discussed in Chapter 9, many of these business-type activities are organized as public authorities or public benefit organizations, legally separate from the parent government. When that happens, they use enterprise-type accounting, but are reported as separate "component units" rather than as Enterprise Funds of the parent government.

Internal Service Funds

Internal Service Funds are used to account for providing goods or services within the reporting governmental unit (including its agencies and departments, other funds, and component units) or to other governments, on a user-charge, cost-reimbursement basis. Internal Service Funds should be used only if the reporting government is the *predominant participant* in its activity; otherwise, the activity should be reported as an Enterprise Fund. Activities typically performed by Internal Service Funds (a separate fund is established for each activity) are motor pool operations, data processing, printing services, and supplies acquisition and distribution.

Internal Service Funds are established primarily to achieve cost savings by means of (1) consolidating similar support-type activities performed by several agencies into a single unit and (2) purchasing in volume. The accounting system used for Internal Service Funds is designed to accumulate the total cost of goods or services provided, leading to the calculation of user charges based on the cost per unit of service or product or total cost for a specific job. For example, depreciation of machinery is part of the cost of providing printing services. Therefore, as with Enterprise Funds, the economic resources measurement focus and full accrual basis of accounting are used.

Internal Service Funds bill the funds receiving the goods or services (often the General Fund). The amounts billed are reported as revenues of the Internal Service Fund and as expenditures (expenses) of the recipient fund. As discussed in Chapter 10, these interfund billings are eliminated when the government-wide financial statements are prepared.

Reporting on Proprietary-Type Funds

Three financial statements are prepared for proprietary-type funds: an operating statement (called a statement of revenues, expenses, and changes in fund net position), a statement of net position, and a statement of cash flows. To illustrate them (see Tables 2-8, 2-9, and 2-10), we use the statements prepared by the Mt. Lebanon Parking Authority, a legally separate component unit of Mt. Lebanon that accounts for and reports on its activities in the same manner as an Enterprise Fund. (After these statements were issued, the Mt. Lebanon Commissioners "folded" the authority into the municipality, which now operates the activity as an Enterprise Fund.)

TABLE 2-8	Enterprise Fund—Statement of Revenues, Expenses, and Changes in Net Position

Mt. Lebanon Parking Authority
Statement of Revenues, Expenses, and Changes in Net Position
Year Ended June 30, 2010
(in thousands of dollars)

Operating Revenues		
Vehicle space rental	$ 835	
Meter collections	378	
Fine collections	203	
Rental income	159	
Total operating revenues		$ 1,575
Operating Expenses		
Personnel	531	
Insurance	58	
Contracted services	104	
Utilities	78	
Repair and maintenance supplies	54	
Depreciation and amortization	452	
Total operating expenses		1,277
Operating income		298
Nonoperating Revenues (Expenses)		
Intergovernmental revenues	5	
Interest income	4	
Interest expense	(161)	
Total nonoperating revenues (expenses)		(152)
Net income		146
Net position, beginning of year		5,430
Net position, end of year		$ 5,576

Source: Adapted from the Financial Statements, Mt. Lebanon Parking Authority, for the years ended June 30, 2010 and June 30, 2009, and presented here as an Enterprise Fund.

TABLE 2-9   Enterprise Fund—Statement of Net Position

Mt. Lebanon Parking Authority
Statement of Net Position
June 30, 2010
(in thousands of dollars)

Assets

Current assets:

Cash and cash equivalents—unrestricted	$ 820	
Cash and cash equivalents—restricted	335	
Investments	204	
Accounts receivable	8	
Due from Municipality of Mt. Lebanon	2	
Prepaid expenses	112	
Total current assets		$ 1,481
Capital assets not being depreciated		2,727
Capital assets, net of accumulated depreciation of $6,571		5,990
Total assets		10,198

Liabilities

Current liabilities:

Current portion of long-term debt	545	
Accrued interest payable	73	
Accounts payable and accrued payroll	60	
Unearned income	33	
Current portion of note due to Mt. Lebanon	34	
Total current liabilities		745
Noncurrent liabilities:		
Long-term debt	3,285	
Note due to Municipality of Mt. Lebanon	592	
Total noncurrent liabilities		3,877
Total liabilities		4,622

Net Position

Invested in capital assets, net of related debt	4,317	
Restricted	334	
Unrestricted	925	
Total net position		$ 5,576

Source: Adapted from the Financial Statements, Mt. Lebanon Parking Authority, for the years ended June 30, 2010 and June 30, 2009, and presented here as an Enterprise Fund. (We changed the format to show the effects of accounting standards issued after this statement was prepared.)

TABLE 2-10   Enterprise Fund—Statement of Cash Flows

Mt. Lebanon Parking Authority
Statement of Cash Flows
Year Ended June 30, 2010
(in thousands of dollars)

Cash Flows from Operating Activities		
Receipts from customers	$1,573	
Payments for goods and services	(393)	
Payments to employees	(419)	
Net cash provided by operating activities		$ 761
Cash Flows from Investing Activities		
Purchase of investments	(204)	
Sale of investments	203	
Interest income	4	
Net cash provided by investing activities		3
Cash Flows from Capital and Related Financing Activities		
Payment of long-term debt	(564)	
Payment of interest on long-term debt	(169)	
Acquisition of property and equipment	(217)	
Net cash (used in) capital, related financing activities		(950)
Net decrease in cash and cash equivalents		(186)
Cash and cash equivalents (restricted plus unrestricted):		
Beginning of year		1,341
End of year		$1,155
Reconciliation of Operating Income to Net Cash Provided by Operating Activities		
Operating income		$ 298
Adjustments to reconcile to net cash provided by operating activities:		
Depreciation and amortization	$ 452	
Change in operating assets and liabilities:		
Accounts receivable	0	
Prepaid expenses	9	
Accounts payable and accrued payroll	4	
Unearned income	(2)	
Total adjustments		463
Net cash provided by operating activities		$ 761

Note: End of year cash ($1,155) is the total of unrestricted cash ($820) and restricted cash ($335) shown in the balance sheet.

Source: Adapted from the Financial Statements, Mt. Lebanon Parking Authority, for the years ended June 30, 2010 and June 30, 2009, and presented here as an Enterprise Fund. (We changed the format to show the effects of accounting standards issued after this statement was prepared.)

The operating statement for Enterprise Funds is presented in multistep format, with separate captions for operating income (or loss), nonoperating revenues and expenses, and other items. The general format for this statement is as follows:

Operating revenues (detailed)
    Total operating revenues
Operating expenses (detailed)
    Total operating expenses
        Operating income (loss)
Nonoperating revenues and expenses (detailed)
        Income before other revenues, expenses, gains, losses, and transfers
Capital contributions (grant, developer, and others), additions to endowments,
special and extraordinary items (detailed), and transfers
        Increase (decrease) in net position
Net position—beginning of period
Net position—end of period[5]

Operating revenues earned by Enterprise Funds usually result primarily from user charges. Enterprise Fund operating expenses depend on the type of operations but usually include the cost of services, supplies used, utilities, depreciation, and so forth. Notice the charge for depreciation in Table 2-8. Because Enterprise Funds use the economic resources measurement focus and accrual basis of accounting, depreciation must be included as an expense. Nonoperating revenues and expenses include investment revenue and interest expense. Capital contributions include grants from higher-level governments to acquire capital assets and contributions from developers. *Extraordinary items* are transactions and events that are unusual in nature and occur infrequently, such as a municipal bankruptcy. *Special items* refer to transactions and events within the control of management that are either unusual in nature or occur infrequently, such as a large one-time revenue from the sale of capital assets. Transfers include subsidies received from another fund.

Notice that the illustrative statement of net position (Table 2-9) is prepared in classified form. A *classified statement of net position* presents the assets and liabilities so as to distinguish between those that are current and those that are noncurrent (or long term). *Current assets* include cash and items that will be converted to cash or used up in operations within 1 year. *Noncurrent assets* include capital assets like land, buildings, and equipment. A parking facility, such as the one illustrated here, is also likely to include significant site improvements. *Current liabilities* are debts that are due to be paid within 1 year, while *noncurrent liabilities* are debts that will be paid more than 1 year in the future.

Notice also that the statement of net position in Table 2-9 is presented in this format: assets − liabilities = net position. The statement may also be presented in the traditional balance sheet format: assets − liabilities + net position. The Mt. Lebanon Parking Authority has no items that the GASB has identified as deferred outflows or deferred inflows of resources; if it did, the statement of net position would be presented in this format: (assets + deferred outflows of resources) − (liabilities + deferred inflows of resources) = net position. The net position is displayed in three major components: invested in capital assets, net of related debt; restricted; and unrestricted. Financial statement formats and the details of net position (as well as related calculations) are discussed in detail in Chapter 7.

Finally, notice the presence of *restricted* cash and cash equivalents in Table 2-9. Restricted resources generally result from a contractual, legal, or regulatory requirement, such as a debt covenant requiring that cash be set aside to pay debt service on a bond. The restricted designation signifies that the resources are not available for general purposes. The restricted assets shown here are being held to pay currently due debt service, as required by a debt covenant.

---

[5]GASB Cod. Sec. 2200.170, as amended.

Because Enterprise Funds use the economic resources measurement focus, their operating statements do not report financing transactions and capital asset acquisitions. Therefore, a statement of cash flows, illustrated in Table 2-10, is prepared for Enterprise Funds. Cash flow statements prepared for governmental Enterprise Funds differ from their commercial counterparts in two ways: (a) they report four classifications of cash flows (operating, investing, noncapital financing, and capital and related financing activities) rather than three; and (b) they are prepared on the direct method (showing, for example, the purposes of cash flows for operating purposes), rather than the indirect method. In Table 2-10, notice particularly the section on cash flows from capital and related financing activities. (Noncapital financing activities are not shown here because there were none.)

FIDUCIARY-TYPE FUNDS

Fiduciary-type funds are used to account for assets held by a government in a trust or agency capacity for others (individuals, other governments, or private organizations). Because they are held for others, these resources cannot be used to support the government's own programs. The fiduciary fund category includes Pension (and other employee benefit) Trust Funds, Investment Trust Funds, Private-Purpose Trust Funds, and Agency Funds. Trust Funds are distinguished from Agency Funds generally by the existence of a trust agreement that affects the degree of management involvement and the length of time the resources are held. Table 2-11 presents a summary of the fiduciary-type funds, showing the purpose and examples of each.

Pension (and Other Employee Benefit) Trust Funds

The most widely used and often the most significant Trust Funds are *Pension (and other employee benefit) Trust Funds*. These funds account for resources required to be held in trust for members and beneficiaries of public employee defined benefit and defined contribution pension plans, health care and other postemployment benefit plans, and other employee benefit plans. *Defined benefit pension plans* guarantee specific benefits on retirement. *Defined contribution plans* do not guarantee

TABLE 2-11 Purposes of Fiduciary-Type Funds	
Fund Type	**To Account For**
Pension Trust	Resources held in trust for employee retirement plans and other employee benefit plans
	Examples: Defined benefit pension plan, retiree health benefit plan
Investment Trust	Resources of an external investment pool managed by a sponsoring government
	Examples: The portion of an external investment pool that belongs to other governments
Private-Purpose Trust	Resources of all other trust arrangements maintained for benefit of individuals, other governments, and private organizations
	Examples: Unclaimed (escheat) property, such as bank accounts, investment accounts, and other property held pending claim by rightful owners
Agency	Resources held in a custodial capacity that must be disbursed according to law or contractual agreement
	Examples: Sales or property taxes collected by a government on behalf of another government, Social Security taxes withheld from employees and kept separately pending distribution to the federal government

specific benefits; instead, benefits are based on periodic contributions to the plans and the earnings on those contributions. Many state governments maintain pension plans that cover not only state employees, but also one or more classes of local government employees, such as teachers.

Investment Trust Funds

Some governments sponsor investment pools, wherein they invest and manage resources belonging both to the sponsoring government (the *internal* portion of the pool) and to governments that are external to the sponsoring government (the *external* portion of the pool). The internal portion of these investment pools is reported as assets of the funds for which the investments were made. The external portions, however, are reported in *Investment Trust Funds,* another type of fiduciary fund.

Private-Purpose Trust Funds

Private-Purpose Trust Funds are used to report all other trust arrangements under which the principal and income are held for the benefit of individuals, other governments, and private organizations. An example of a Private-Purpose Trust Fund is an Escheat Property Fund. *Escheat property* is private property that reverts to a governmental entity in the absence of legal claimants or heirs. Many governments have laws that enable a rightful owner or heir to reclaim such property into perpetuity if the claimant can establish a right to it.

Agency Funds

Agency Funds are used to account for resources held by governmental units in a purely custodial capacity. These funds generally involve only the receipt and subsequent disbursement (after a short period of time) of assets held for individuals, private organizations, or other governments. Agency Funds may be used also to account for resources belonging both to other governments and the custodial government. For financial reporting purposes, however, only the resources belonging to other governments are reported in an Agency Fund. Assets held for the reporting government, pending distribution within the reporting government, should be reported in the appropriate governmental or proprietary fund.

An example of an Agency Fund is a *Tax Agency Fund,* wherein the reporting government collects taxes (such as sales taxes or property taxes) both for itself and as agent for other governments. The resources are held for a short period of time in an Agency Fund, which serves as a clearing account, pending distribution to the appropriate government. Agency Funds are also used to account for deposits made by contractors when submitting bids on general government construction contracts.

It is possible to use one Agency Fund to account for several agency relationships, provided there are no legal restrictions. However, due to the legal problems that exist in situations involving trusts, a separate fund generally is used for each individual trust.

Reporting on Fiduciary-Type Funds

For all fiduciary-type funds other than Agency Funds, governmental entities are required to prepare a statement of changes in fiduciary net position and a statement of fiduciary net position. These funds are reported using the economic resources measurement focus and the full accrual basis of accounting. Agency Funds have no "net position" because their resources are equal to the liabilities to be paid from the resources. A statement of fiduciary net position is prepared for Agency Funds, but not a statement of changes in fiduciary net position.

For an example of the financial statements prepared for fiduciary-type funds, see Tables 2-12 and 2-13 relating to Mt. Lebanon's Pension Trust Fund. Notice that, in the statement of changes in plan net position (Table 2-12), the major headings are called *additions* and *deductions,* rather

TABLE 2-12   Pension Trust Fund—Statement of Changes in Fiduciary Net Position

Mt. Lebanon, Pennsylvania
Pension Trust Fund
Statement of Changes in Plan Net Position
Year Ended December 31, 2009
(in thousands of dollars)

Additions		
Contributions:		
Employer, including state aid	$ 1,375	
Employee	222	
Total contributions		$ 1,597
Investment income:		
Net appreciation in fair value of investments	8,773	
Interest and dividends	1,624	
Total investment income	10,397	
Less, investment expense	140	
Net investment income		10,257
Total additions		11,854
Deductions		
Benefits	2,902	
Administrative expenses	94	
Total deductions		2,996
Increase in plan net position		8,858
Net Position Held in Trust for Benefits		
Beginning of year		45,468
End of year		$54,326

Source: Adapted from the Comprehensive Annual Financial Report, Mt. Lebanon, Pennsylvania, December 31, 2009.

than revenues and expenses. Notice also that the additions to plan net position are from two basic sources—contributions to the plan and investment income. Investment income is derived not only from interest and dividends, but also from changes (appreciation or decline) in the fair value of the investments held by the plan. The most significant deduction from plan net position during the year results from the payment of benefits to retirees and their beneficiaries.

The statement of plan net position (Table 2-13) is simply a statement of the net assets held in trust for the beneficiaries. Investments represent the most significant asset. Other assets generally shown in this statement are cash and receivables. Liabilities generally consist only of accounts payable (related to the administrative expenses) and refunds payable. Notice that the liability regarding the employer's pension promise—the present value of amounts due to current and retired employees for services rendered in the past—is not reported here. Therefore, the reader cannot discern from this statement what may be the most important aspect of the employer's pension promise; namely, the extent to which the employer's obligation for benefits is covered by the assets held in the plan. As discussed in Chapter 8, those data are provided in notes to the employer's financial statements and in other supplemental information.

| **TABLE 2-13** | Pension Trust Fund—Statement of Fiduciary Net Position |

Mt. Lebanon, Pennsylvania
Pension Trust Fund
Statement of Plan Net Position
Year Ended December 31, 2009
(in thousands of dollars)

Assets		
Accrued income receivable		$ 101
Accrued contributions		8
Investments, at fair value:		
Equity funds	$36,091	
Fixed income funds	15,624	
Short-term funds	2,591	54,306
Total assets		54,415
Liabilities		
Accounts payable		89
Net Position		
Held in trust for benefits		$54,326

Source: Adapted from the Comprehensive Annual Financial Report, Mt. Lebanon, Pennsylvania, December 31, 2009.

Governmental Accounting in Practice

How Many Funds Are Enough?

The numbers and types of funds used by municipal governments have nothing to do with the size of the government. Rather, the fund structure depends on how the government is organized, how it is financed, and how many funds its officials decide to establish.

New York City has a population of more than 8.3 million, and the total expenses of its governmental activities were $67.4 billion in 2009. Yet its fund structure is relatively simple. It has a General Fund, a New York City Capital Projects Fund, and a General Debt Service Fund. New York accomplishes some of its capital construction and financing activities through specially created public benefit corporations, resulting in the establishment of 5 other Capital Projects Funds and 8 other Debt Service Funds. New York City has its own pension systems, and its complex labor negotiations have resulted in the establishment of 5 large Pension Trust Funds and 13 other labor benefit Trust Funds. But New York has no Special Revenue, Enterprise, on Internal Service Funds.

Akron, Ohio, has a population of 217,000, and the total expenses of its governmental activities were only $345 million in 2009. To account for these activities, Akron uses 48 individual governmental-type funds, including more than 25 Special Revenue Funds! Akron also has 6 Enterprise Funds and 8 Internal Service Funds. Akron provides pension and other retiree benefits through plans operated by the State of Ohio, so it has no Pension Trust Funds. Nevertheless, it has 5 fiduciary-type funds for other purposes.

So New York City's population may be almost 40 times that of Akron, but when it comes to creating funds, Akron wins in a walk.

Review Questions

Q2-1   Define *fund* as the term is used in governmental accounting.

Q2-2   What is the purpose of fund accounting?

Q2-3   List the three categories of funds used in governmental accounting, and describe the types of activities accounted for in each category.

Q2-4   Describe the difference between *economic resources measurement focus* and *current financial resources measurement focus*. Which measurement focus is used in each fund category?

Q2-5   How has governmental budgeting influenced the measurement focus and basis of accounting used in the governmental funds category?

Q2-6   Compare the timing of revenue and expense (or expenditure) recognition using the *accrual basis of accounting* with that using the *modified accrual basis of accounting*. Which basis of accounting is used in each fund category?

Q2-7   List the governmental-type funds, and briefly describe the use of each.

Q2-8   The controller for the City of Walla Walla recently made the following comment: "At a minimum, we could run city government with the use of only one fund." Do you agree with this statement? Why or why not?

Q2-9   Why are there no capital assets in governmental-type funds?

Q2-10 List the proprietary-type funds, and briefly describe the use of each.

Q2-11 Why do proprietary-type funds use full accrual accounting?

Q2-12 List the fiduciary-type funds, and briefly describe the use of each.

Q2-13 Discuss why Agency Funds do not have a fund balance.

Discussion Scenarios and Issues

D2-1   A large city has been financing all of its services through property taxes and sales taxes. As the cost of services has been increasing, the city has found it necessary to raise its tax rates. A special commission appointed by the mayor suggests that it would be possible to reduce the property tax rate by charging residents a monthly fee to cover the costs of collecting and disposing of trash and garbage. The mayor likes the suggestion and wants to run the sanitation activity like a commercial business. Describe the fund accounting implications of adopting that suggestion.

D2-2   Each department in a large city maintains its own fleet of vehicles. The cost of purchasing and maintaining the vehicles is financed through the General Fund. One day, the mayor walks past the parking lot of the Parks Department and notices that many vehicles are not being used. The mayor calls her finance commissioner into the office and says: "Couldn't we save money by setting up a central motor pool and requiring each department to use a pool vehicle whenever they need one?" The finance commissioner replies: "Yes, that will save us lots of money, but we will need to change our accounting system a bit to handle it." Discuss the fund accounting implications of the finance commissioner's reply.

D2-3   During a heated campaign for mayor of Hoschkosh, an unsuccessful candidate said: "I will do away with all the special interests in government. I will abolish all the Special Revenue Funds and merge that money with the general operating resources of the city." You are the successful candidate in that race, and now the local press is pressuring you to respond to the campaign promise of the other candidate. How would you respond to the press?

D2-4   To fulfill a campaign promise, the new mayor of Cordelia is looking for ways to finance an increase in the level of police protection without raising the city's property tax rate. He reads the city's financial report and notices that the Capital Projects Fund has a large fund balance. He discusses the fund balance with his finance commissioner, who says: "The fund balance is high because the city voted to sell bonds last year to finance construction of a new firehouse. The architect just finished the design of the firehouse, and we are about to award a constructon contract." The mayor responds: "Forget the firehouse. I promised to put more police patrols on the street. Let's use the bond proceeds to hire more police officers." How should the finance commissioner respond to the mayor?

Exercises

E2-1   (Fund categories)
State which category of funds (governmental-type, proprietary-type, or fiduciary-type) would be used by a state government for each of the following purposes:
1. To construct a new highway
2. To pay salaries of personnel who maintain state parks
3. To accumulate resources to pay pension benefits for its employees
4. To collect sales taxes on behalf of local governments that impose such a tax
5. To operate a central printing department that prints forms and reports for all state departments

E2-2   (Identification of funds, measurement focus, and basis of accounting)
For each scenario shown in Exercise E2-1, state which fund type would be used and which measurement focus and basis of accounting would be used for each fund type.

E2-3   (Identification of funds used by a large city)
This information is extracted from or based on the notes to the financial statements issued by New York City. For each item described, identify the fund used by New York City.
1. "This is the general operating fund of the City. Substantially all tax revenues, Federal and State Aid (except aid for capital projects) and other operating revenues are accounted for in |this fund|."
2. "This fund . . . accounts for resources used to construct or acquire fixed assets and make capital improvements."
3. "This fund, required by State legislation . . . into which payments of real estate taxes and other revenues are deposited in advance of debt service payment dates. Debt service on all City . . . bonds is paid from this fund."

4. These funds account for assets held on behalf of the City's employees to pay pension benefits.

E2-4   (Nature of governmental-type funds)
State whether the following sentences are true or false regarding the nature and uses of *governmental-type funds*. If the sentence is false, state why.
1. Debt service expenditures and capital outlays are never made directly from the General Fund.
2. Special Revenue Funds are used if the law restricts one or more specific sources of revenue, rather than general tax revenues, for specific purposes.
3. Special Revenue Funds cannot be used if a portion of the revenues are derived from transfers from the General Fund.
4. Capital Projects Funds are used to account for and report on all capital assets, whether they are financed from the proceeds of general obligation bonds or from revenue bonds sold by proprietary funds.
5. Debt Service Funds are used to accumulate resources for paying debt service in the current year, but not in future years.

E2-5   (Measurement focus and basis of accounting in governmental-type funds)
State whether the following sentences are true or false regarding accounting measurements within *governmental-type funds*. If the sentence is false, state why.
1. Capital assets are recognized as assets and depreciated over their estimated useful lives.
2. Repayments of bond principal are recorded as expenditures.
3. Liabilities for compensated absences are not accrued unless they are required to be liquidated with current financial resources.
4. As a general rule, property taxes are recognized as revenue and reported in the operating statement, provided they are expected to be collected at a future date.

E2-6   (Nature of proprietary-type funds and measurements within them)
State whether the following sentences are true or false regarding *proprietary-type funds* and the accounting measurements made within them. If the sentence is false, state why.

1. Enterprise Funds are used when a governmental entity sells products or services primarily to external parties (such as the general public) for a fee or user charge.
2. An Enterprise Fund may not be used if the entity, such as a provider of mass transit services, receives subsidies from the General Fund.
3. To ascertain the amount of capital assets acquired by an Enterprise Fund during the year, you should read the statement of revenue, expenses, and changes in net position.
4. When Enterprise Funds are used, expenses are accrued only if they are expected to be paid within 60 days after the end of the year.
5. When Enterprise Funds are used, revenues are recognized in the period they are earned, even if cash has not been received.

E2-7   (Nature of fiduciary-type funds and measurements within them)
State whether the following sentences are true or false regarding the nature of *fiduciary-type funds* and the accounting measurements within them. If the sentence is false, state why.

1. Governments may access the resources of fiduciary funds to help support their own programs.
2. When a government sponsors an Investment Trust Fund, the portion that belongs to other governments is reported as assets of the Fund, but the portion belonging to the sponsoring government is not.
3. The statement of net position for a typical Agency Fund shows assets and liabilities, but no fund balance.
4. When reporting on the resources of Pension Trust Funds, equity securities held by the Funds are reported at original cost.

E2-8   (Measurement focus and basis of accounting for different fund types)
Several new city council members asked you to explain why the financial statements for the Water Enterprise Fund "seem to look different" than the financial statements for the General Fund. "For example," says one, "the captions are different, and some accounts in the Water Enterprise Fund statements don't appear in the General Fund statements." Write the explanation that you would provide for these council members.

E2-9   (Nature of governmental fund types and fund balances)
J. J. Peachum is running for election as a commissioner of the municipality of Mt. Lebanon. He examines Table 2-6 in the text and calculates the total of the fund balances to be $10,282,000. Then, in a major campaign speech, he announces: "We have a surplus of more than $10 million. If elected, I will use this entire slush fund to reduce your property taxes." Comment on Peachum's assertion, based solely on your analysis of Table 2-6, your understanding of the nature of governmental-type funds, and your general knowledge of governmental finance. (Fund balances will be discussed in Chapter 5, and financial statement analysis will be covered in Chapter 14.)

E2-10   (Effect of different measurement focuses and bases of accounting)
Following are some of Friendly Village's transactions during the calendar year 2013. For each transaction, state (a) the amount the Village would report as expenditures for the year 2013 if the transaction occurred in a governmental-type fund and (b) the amount it would report as expenses for the year if the transaction occurred in an Enterprise Fund.

1. Friendly paid $600,000 in salaries during the year. In addition, during the last pay period, Friendly's employees earned $5,000 by December 31, but that amount was not paid until January 7, 2014.
2. Friendly used the proceeds of long-term bonds to buy a sanitation truck. The truck was delivered on July 1, 2013, and immediately placed into service. The truck cost $100,000 and had an estimated useful life of 10 years.
3. Friendly had agreed to pay off the $100,000 used to buy the sanitation truck (see previous transaction) over a 5-year period, starting December 31, 2013. On that date, Friendly paid the first installment on the debt, $10,000 in principal and $3,000 in interest.

E2-11 (Identification of funds through examples)

For each of the following situations, indicate which fund would be used to report the transaction.

1. A city made payments to a contractor on a major bridge project.
2. The Department of Streets purchased materials to be used to repair potholes.
3. A city paid salaries to the employees of its Fire Department.
4. The state Tax Department collected sales taxes on behalf of several large cities in the state.
5. A city accumulated resources in a fund to pay principal and interest on its general obligation bonds.
6. A city acquired land for bridge approaches as part of the project mentioned in the first situation.

E2-12 (Identification of funds through examples)

For each of the following situations, indicate which fund would be used to report the transaction. Note: Several of the transactions require using more than one fund.

1. A city-owned water utility sent bills to the city for water provided to city departments.
2. The city's mass transit facility received an operating subsidy from the city and a construction grant from the federal government.
3. The city sent out property tax bills to finance day-to-day city operating activities.
4. The city sold bonds to construct new roads—a major capital project.
5. The city used tax resources to pay for new police sedans. (The city classifies the purchase of all sedans as "minor capital items," to be paid from tax resources rather than the sale of bonds.)
6. The city paid principal and interest on a bond issue from resources accumulated for that purpose.
7. The city's centralized printing facility billed the city's Tax Department for printing tax forms.
8. The city levied a special hotel tax dedicated to beautifying its downtown shopping area.

E2-13 (Identification of funds through examples)

For each of the following situations, indicate which fund would be used to report the transaction. Note: Several of the transactions require using more than one fund.

1. A city owned airport sent bills for landing fees to various airlines.
2. The fund that operates a central motor pool sent bills at the end of the month to all city agencies that used the motor pool.
3. A county received cash from three school districts in accordance with a state law that requires counties to invest temporarily idle cash on behalf of all school districts in the county.
4. A state collected a special fee of $75 from each resident who owned a motor vehicle. The revenues were dedicated to financing a special road improvement program.
5. A city sent a check for $3 million to a fund that accumulates resources for the purpose of paying postemployment health care benefits to its employees.

E2-14 (Use of funds)

The mayor of New West Norwalk wants to simplify the accounting system used by the town. He approached you with the following task: Reduce the number of individual funds used in our governmental-type funds. How might you achieve this purpose?

E2-15 (Use of funds)

For each of the following situations, write a short paragraph describing a specific set of circumstances that would require use of the fund listed.

1. An Investment Trust Fund
2. An Agency Fund
3. A Special Revenue Fund
4. A Capital Projects Fund
5. An Internal Service Fund
6. An Enterprise Fund

E2-16 (Matching—use of funds)

Using the following codes, indicate which listed fund best fits each description by placing the appropriate code in the space provided.

GF   General Fund
SRF   Special Revenue Fund

CPF   Capital Projects Fund
DSF   Debt Service Fund
EF   Enterprise Fund
ISF   Internal Service Fund

____ 1. Services are provided to the general public, and the costs of providing the services are financed by user charges.

____ 2. Resources are accumulated to pay principal and interest on general long-term debt.

____ 3. Salaries are paid to police officers.

____ 4. Goods or services are furnished to other segments of the governmental unit on a user charge basis.

____ 5. Specific revenue sources are dedicated to a particular purpose other than capital projects or debt service.

____ 6. Expenditures are made by the city's streets department.

____ 7. An "operating income" figure is computed.

Problems

P2-1   (Discussion of the nature of the three fund categories)
Identify and describe the three fund categories used in governmental accounting. For each category, discuss the broad purposes, and illustrate the purposes by identifying several specific fund types. Also, describe the measurement focus and basis of accounting used in making accounting measurements within each category.

P2-2   (Identification of activities with funds and identifying funds with the appropriate measurement focus and basis of accounting)
Jasmin City is a small city on the Canadian border of the United States. Because of its colorful history and fine restaurants, it is a tourist destination. Jasmin uses separate funds to account for the following activities. For each of the activities listed, state (a) the type of fund that Jasmin City will use, (b) the measurement focus and basis of accounting of each fund, and (c) the fund-level financial statements required for each fund.

1. The city's day-to-day operating activities.
2. Sources of financing and expenditures related to the construction of an office building.
3. Payment of debt service on long-term bonds issued to build the office building.
4. A central activity that acquires supplies and sells them to the various city agencies.
5. A city-owned utility that buys and sells electricity to its residents.
6. A fund that accumulates resources to pay pensions to city employees.
7. An activity that invests funds on behalf of two small neighboring cities.
8. Disposition of sales taxes collected by the city on behalf of the county where it is located.

P2-3   (Discussion of concepts)
Answer each of the following questions.

1. A city operates a municipal health clinic that provides outpatient care for children. The city charges fees for services from those who can afford to pay, bills the state for Medicaid-eligible patients, and subsidizes the clinic to the extent necessary. What type of fund is most suitable for this activity? Why?

2. A state maintains a central printing activity that provides services to all departments. For example, it prints the state budget document, the annual financial report, all the tax forms, and all license documents. What type of fund is most suitable for this activity? Why?

3. Several small governmental units decided to pool their resources to build and operate a regional airport. What type of fund would you recommend for the airport? Why?

4. A city decides to dedicate resources to improving the appearance of its downtown business area. Among other things, it adds 2 percent to its hotel occupancy tax and earmarks it for that purpose. What type of fund is most suitable for this activity? Why?

P2-4   (Identification of activities with particular governmental-type funds)
Using only the governmental-type funds, indicate which would be used to record each of the following transactions and events:

GF   General Fund
SRF   Special Revenue Fund
DSF   Debt Service Fund
CPF   Capital Projects Fund
PF   Permanent Fund

____ 1. The city transferred cash to the fund used to accumulate resources to pay bond principal and interest.
____ 2. The city received its share of a state sales tax that is legally required to be used to finance library operations.
____ 3. The city sent property tax bills to homeowners to help pay for day-to-day operating costs.
____ 4. The city paid for five fire engines, using resources accumulated in a fund to pay for capital assets.
____ 5. The city received a grant from the state to build an addition to the city hall.
____ 6. The city received the proceeds of general obligation bonds to finance the construction of a new police station.
____ 7. The mayor was paid his monthly salary.
____ 8. Expenditures for the operation of the Police Department were recorded.
____ 9. Parks admissions fees, dedicated for use in day-to-day maintenance of the city park system, were collected.
____ 10. The city paid a contractor who had completed a report on the potential for improving police deployment as a way to reduce the crime rate.
____ 11. The city workers were paid their weekly salaries.
____ 12. The city retired some of its outstanding bonds, using money accumulated for that purpose.
____ 13. A federal grant was received to help pay for the cost of constructing the new city hall.
____ 14. The city received a donation from a taxpayer with the stipulation that it be invested and kept in perpetuity, so that the income from the investments could be used to buy library books.
____ 15. The city received income from the investments made in the previous activity.

P2-5   (Identification of activities with particular governmental- and proprietary-type funds)
Using the governmental- and proprietary-type funds, indicate which would be used to record each of the following events.

GF   General Fund
SRF   Special Revenue Fund
DSF   Debt Service Fund
CPF   Capital Projects Fund
PF   Permanent Fund
EF   Enterprise Fund
ISF   Internal Service Fund

____ 1. Bonds were issued by the fund used to account for providing water to the residents of a municipality.
____ 2. The fund that finances the city's basic day-to-day operating activities lent $50,000 to the fund that will provide city agencies with supplies on a user charge basis.
____ 3. The city-operated utility that provides electricity to the residents of a municipality billed the city for electricity provided to city agencies.
____ 4. The city charter requires all hotel taxes to be accounted for in a separate fund dedicated to maintaining the downtown business district. Hotel tax collections for the period were $500,000.
____ 5. Salaries were paid to the city's police officers and firefighters.
____ 6. The state lottery, which operates like a business entity, sent a check for its net revenues (after paying lottery prizes) to the state. The state will add these revenues to general state revenues as part of the state's program for financing elementary and secondary education.

       ___ 7. Interest and principal on the city's general obligation debt were paid, using resources accumulated specifically for that purpose.

       ___ 8. The fund that finances the city's day-to-day operating activities transferred cash to the fund that pays principal and interest on outstanding debt.

       ___ 9. The city sold general obligation bonds to buy land as part of a city hall expansion program.

       ___ 10. The city's central motor pool billed each city department for use of vehicles.

       ___ 11. The state established a highway beautification program, to be financed by dedicating a new motor vehicle license fee to that purpose.

       ___ 12. A wealthy taxpayer donated securities to a village, stipulating that the donation be kept in perpetuity and that the resulting investment income be used solely to help support the activities of the village library.

       ___ 13. The state-operated toll road collected tolls of $1 million.

       ___ 14. The village maintains a perpetual-care public cemetery fund. Income from that fund was transferred to the fund that accumulates resources dedicated to maintaining the cemetery.

P2-6   (Identification of funds when there are interfund transactions)

Each of these transactions affects two funds. Use the following codes to identify the types of funds needed to record the transactions.

GF   General Fund
CPF   Capital Projects Fund
DSF   Debt Service Fund
SRF   Special Revenue Fund
EF   Enterprise Fund
ISF   Internal Service Fund
PTF   Pension Trust Fund

       ___ 1. The fund that finances the city's day-to-day activities makes a payment to the fund that invests money pending payment of pensions to city employees.

       ___ 2. The city's electric utility fund sends bills to the fund that serves as a central purchasing, storage, and supply agency for all city departments.

       ___ 3. The fund that operates a central motor pool for all village departments on a cost-reimbursement basis sends a bill to several departments for services.

       ___ 4. After completing a large capital project, the city had $75,000 left in the fund. As required by city charter, the fund transferred the $75,000 to the fund that accumulates resources to pay off the bonds sold to finance the capital project.

       ___ 5. To reduce the need for borrowing, the city transferred $500,000 from the fund that pays for day-to-day operating expenditures to the fund that accumulates resources to pay for acquiring capital assets.

       ___ 6. A city ordinance decreed that all parking fines, wherever collected, be placed in a separate fund and used to maintain the city zoo. Although the fines covered virtually all operating expenditures, the fund that finances day-to-day operating expenditures transferred $30,000 to the separate fund so it could acquire several new animals.

P2-7   (Transactions involving all funds)

Indicate which fund(s) would be used to record each of the following actions performed by the city, county, or state referred to in the transaction. Use the following codes:

GF   General Fund
SRF   Special Revenue Fund
DSF   Debt Service Fund
CPF   Capital Projects Fund
PF   Permanent Fund
EF   Enterprise Fund
ISF   Internal Service Fund
PTF   Pension Trust Fund

ITF   Investment Trust Fund

PPTF   Private-Purpose Trust Fund

AF   Agency Fund

___ 1. The city made a contribution to the employees' retirement fund.

___ 2. Taxes that are dedicated to street repairs were collected. The ordinance establishing the tax requires a separate accounting for these resources.

___ 3. The contractors who were building a bridge were paid.

___ 4. General governmental revenues were transferred to the fund that accumulates resources to retire general long-term debt.

___ 5. The salary of the chief of police was paid.

___ 6. The central supplies fund sent out bills (covering the cost of the supplies plus overhead) for supplies provided to the Police and Fire Departments and to the city airport.

___ 7. The city received from a citizen a gift to be held in perpetuity. The investment income must be used to provide free concerts in city parks.

___ 8. Bonds were issued to finance construction of an office building.

___ 9. The Police Department purchased three police sedans, using general tax revenues.

___ 10. Sales taxes were collected by the state Tax Department. One-half of what was collected was deposited in the fund that accumulates resources to finance day-to-day operating activities, and one-half was held for remitting to other governments on whose behalf the state collects taxes.

___ 11. The city sold some of its excess office equipment. The proceeds were to be used for general city operations.

___ 12. General obligation bonds were retired, using resources accumulated in a fund used solely for that purpose.

___ 13. The county bus system, accounted for as a separate fund, sold bonds to finance a bus depot.

___ 14. The city uses a separate fund to account for its central purchasing function. Supplies were purchased by this fund.

___ 15. A citizen donated securities to the city, stipulating that the principal amount must remain intact and that the income must be spent to provide free food to the elderly at the city-operated senior citizen centers.

___ 16. The county treasurer distributed to school districts the school districts' shares of the earnings from investments made by the county-operated investment pool.

P2-8 (Implications of differences in measurement focus and basis of accounting)

1. Explain the meaning of *measurement focus* and *basis of accounting*.

2. Discuss the difference between the *economic resources measurement focus* and the *current financial resources measurement focus*. Describe how using the two measurement focuses results in different accounting treatments for the acquisition and subsequent use of capital assets.

3. Discuss the difference between the *accrual basis of accounting* and the *modified accrual basis of accounting*. Describe how using the two bases of accounting result in different accounting treatments for the recognition and measurement of property tax revenues.

P2-9 (Justification for using different measurement focuses and bases of accounting)

1. Discuss the justification for using the economic resources measurement focus and accrual basis of accounting by a municipally operated water utility.

2. Discuss the justification for using the current financial resources measurement focus and the modified accrual basis of accounting in the General Fund.

3. Discuss the advantages and disadvantages of using the current financial measurement focus and the modified accrual basis of accounting in the General Fund.

P2-10 (Statement preparation—General Fund)

Using the following data, prepare a statement of revenues, expenditures, and changes in fund balance for the General Fund of Jasmin City for the year ended December 31, 2013.

Miscellaneous revenues	$ 180,000
Licenses and permits revenues	1,000,000
Education program expenditures	2,000,000
Public safety expenditures	4,000,000
Transfers to other funds	1,500,000
Property tax revenues	7,000,000
State and federal grants	2,000,000
Parks program expenditures	750,000
Highways program expenditures	900,000
Transfers from other funds	700,000
Fund balance at beginning of year	1,500,000

P2-11   (Multiple choice)

1. Which of the following fund types of a governmental unit has/have current financial resources as a measurement focus?

	General Fund	Enterprise Fund
a.	Yes	Yes
b.	Yes	No
c.	No	No
d.	No	Yes

2. Which fund should record the proceeds of a federal grant made to assist in financing the future construction of a police training facility?
   a. General Fund
   b. Special Revenue Fund
   c. Capital Projects Fund
   d. Enterprise Fund

3. Which fund should record the receipts from a special tax levied to pay principal and interest on general obligation bonds issued to finance the construction of a city hall?
   a. Debt Service Fund
   b. Capital Projects Fund
   c. Enterprise Fund
   d. Special Revenue Fund

4. Several years ago, a city established a fund to retire general obligation bonds issued for the purpose of constructing a new police station. This year the city made a $50,000 contribution to that fund from its general revenues. The fund also realized $15,000 in revenue from its investments. The bonds due this year were retired. This year's transactions require accounting recognition in which funds?
   a. General Fund and Internal Service Fund
   b. Debt Service Fund and Special Revenue Fund
   c. Debt Service Fund and General Fund
   d. Capital Projects Fund and Debt Service Fund

5. Which fund would recognize a transaction in which a municipal electric utility paid $150,000 for new equipment out of its earnings?
   a. Enterprise Fund
   b. General Fund
   c. Capital Projects Fund
   d. Special Revenue Fund

6. Which of the following funds of a governmental unit records the acquisition of a fixed asset as an expenditure rather than as an asset?
   a. Internal Service Fund
   b. Pension Trust Fund

    c. Enterprise Fund

    d. General Fund

7. Which of the following funds of a governmental unit uses the modified accrual basis of accounting?

    a. Internal Service Fund

    b. Enterprise Fund

    c. Pension Trust Fund

    d. Debt Service Fund

8. Under the modified accrual basis of accounting for a governmental unit, revenues should be recognized in the accounting period in which they _____.

    a. are earned

    b. are earned or levied and become available and measurable

    c. are earned and collectible

    d. are collected

P2-12   (Multiple choice)

1. Which fund should record the fixed assets of a central purchasing and stores department organized to serve all municipal departments?

    a. Enterprise Fund

    b. Internal Service Fund

    c. General Fund

    d. Capital Projects Fund

2. Which fund would a city use if it had a separate fund to hold and then remit to an insurance company the lump sum of hospital-surgical insurance premiums collected as payroll deductions from employees?

    a. Agency Fund

    b. Special Revenue Fund

    c. Internal Service Fund

    d. Private-Purpose Trust Fund

3. Which fund would be used to account for the activities of a municipal employee retirement plan that is financed by equal employer and employee contributions?

    a. Agency Fund

    b. Internal Service Fund

    c. Pension Trust Fund

    d. Private-Purpose Trust Fund

4. A transaction in which a municipal electric utility issues bonds (to be repaid from its own operations) requires accounting recognition in which fund?

    a. General Fund

    b. Debt Service Fund

    c. Capital Projects Fund

    d. Enterprise Fund

5. Which fund should be used to account for a special tax on business district properties to finance the cost of decorations and special lighting during a holiday season?

    a. General Fund

    b. Special Revenue Fund

    c. Enterprise Fund

    d. Internal Service Fund

6. Which fund should record the liability for general obligation bonds issued for constructing a city hall and serviced from tax revenues?

    a. Enterprise Fund

    b. General Fund

    c. Capital Projects Fund

    d. None of the above

7. To provide for the retirement of general obligation bonds, a city transfers a portion of its general revenue receipts to a separate fund. In which fund should the city account for receipt of the transfer?
   a. Debt Service Fund
   b. Internal Service Fund
   c. Capital Projects Fund
   d. Special Revenue Fund
8. Which fund should be used to account for the operations of a municipal swimming pool receiving the majority of its support from charges to users?
   a. Special Revenue Fund
   b. General Fund
   c. Internal Service Fund
   d. Enterprise Fund
9. A city collects property taxes for the benefit of sanitary, park, and school districts (all of which are legally separate governmental units) and periodically remits collections to these units. Which fund is used to account for this activity?
   a. Agency Fund
   b. General Fund
   c. Internal Service Fund
   d. Private-Purpose Trust Fund
10. Bay Creek's municipal motor pool maintains all city-owned vehicles and charges the various departments for the cost of rendering those services. In which of the following funds should Bay Creek account for the cost of such maintenance?
    a. General Fund
    b. Internal Service Fund
    c. Special Revenue Fund
    d. Enterprise Fund

P2-13 (Multiple choice)

1. Which of the following funds is likely to have the caption "long-term bonds payable" in its fund balance sheet/statement of net position?
   a. Capital Projects Fund
   b. Enterprise Fund
   c. General Fund
   d. Debt Service Fund
2. Which of the following funds is likely to have the caption "equipment" in its fund balance sheet/statement of net position?
   a. Capital Projects Fund
   b. Agency Fund
   c. Enterprise Fund
   d. General Fund
3. A state government collects sales taxes both for the state and for all counties within the state that levy a sales tax. In which fund should the state record the liability for sales taxes it holds on behalf of the counties?
   a. Agency Fund
   b. Special Revenue Fund
   c. General Fund
   d. Enterprise Fund
4. Which of the following statements is true regarding accounting for capital assets by state and local governments?
   a. Capital outlays are recorded as expenditures in Internal Service Funds.
   b. Capital outlays are recorded as assets in Enterprise Funds, but the depreciation on those assets is recorded in the General Fund.

   c. Capital outlays are recorded as assets in Special Revenue Funds and are depreciated in those
       funds.
   d. Capital outlays are recorded as capital outlay expenditures in the General Fund.
5. Which of the following statements is true regarding the accounting measurement implications
    of the current financial resources measurement focus and modified accrual basis of accounting?
    a. Capital assets are recorded as assets when they are acquired.
    b. Revenues are recognized when they are earned.
    c. Expenditures and liabilities for compensated absences are recognized when the liabilities
        come due for payment as employees resign or retire.
    d. A fund liability is recorded upon the receipt of proceeds from the sale of bonds.
6. A city maintains a motor pool for all city-owned vehicles. It charges city agencies as the vehicles
    are used, so that the charges cover the cost of operating and maintaining the vehicles. Which
    fund should the city use to account for pool revenues and expenses?
    a. General Fund
    b. Internal Service Fund
    c. Special Revenue Fund
    d. Enterprise Fund
7. A county is responsible for holding temporarily idle funds owned by school districts and
    investing the funds until needed. Which type of fund should the county use to report the activ-
    ities and balances held for the school districts?
    a. Enterprise type
    b. Fiduciary type
    c. Governmental type
    d. Special Purpose type
8. When a municipal electric utility bills the municipal Police Department for electric services,
    two funds are needed to record the transaction. Which two are needed?
    a. Enterprise Fund and Internal Service Fund
    b. Enterprise Fund and General Fund
    c. Internal Service Fund and General Fund
    d. Special Revenue Fund and Agency Fund

P2-14 (Difference between expenditures and expenses)
       Based on the information shown below, calculate for the year ended December 31, 2012, (a) the
       total amount of expenditures that would be recognized when using the current financial resources
       measurement focus and modified accrual basis of accounting, and (b) the total amount of expenses
       that would be recognized using the economic resources measurement focus and accrual basis of
       accounting.

Salaries paid in cash during 2012	$3,000,000
Salaries applicable to 2012, due to be paid January 5, 2013	20,000
Utility bill applicable to 2012, due to be paid January 10, 2013	10,000
Equipment acquired at the beginning of 2012 and having an estimated useful life of 10 years	200,000
Payment of principal on long-term debt on December 31, 2012	100,000
Payment of interest on long-term debt on December 31, 2012	40,000

Chapter 3

Budgetary Considerations in Governmental Accounting

Chapter Outline

Learning Objectives

Budget Laws

Budgetary Types and Approaches
   General Fund and Special Revenue Fund Budgets
   Capital Budgets and Plans
   Cash Forecasts
   Budgetary Approaches
      Governmental Budgeting in Practice: Mt. Lebanon Uses Zero-Based Budgeting

The Budget Process
   Budgetary Policy Guidelines
   Budget Calendar
   Budget Instructions
   Revenue Estimates
   Departmental Expenditure Requests
    Preparing a Budgetary Worksheet
   Nondepartmental Expenditure and Interfund Transfer Requests

Service Efforts and Accomplishments

Budgetary Review
      Governmental Budgeting in Practice: Using Sound Budgetary Policies
      and Practices

The Budget Document

Legislative Consideration and Adoption of the Budget

Property Tax Levy

Using Budgetary Information

Classifying Revenues and Expenditures
   Revenue Classification
   Expenditure Classification

Budgetary Accounting
　Recording the Adopted Budget
　Recording Encumbrances
　Detailed Illustration

Other Aspects of Budgetary Accounting
　Budgetary Interchanges and Other Revisions
　Encumbrance Accounting Details
　Allotment Systems

Review Questions

Discussion Scenarios and Issues

Exercises

Problems

After completing this chapter, you should be able to do the following:

- Identify the types of budgets and budgetary approaches used by governmental units
- Understand the steps involved in preparing a budget
- Calculate the millage rate used by a governmental unit
- Understand the legal nature of the appropriation act
- Explain how budgets are used to help monitor financial performance
- Understand the purpose of budgetary accounting
- Understand how budgetary accounting is incorporated into financial accounting systems
- Prepare budgetary general journal entries
- Prepare revenues and appropriations subsidiary ledgers

Governments exist to provide a variety of services to their constituents. Most of the resources available to a particular governmental unit are derived from those who pay taxes to that unit, and most taxpayers do not particularly enjoy paying taxes. Therefore, it can be said that the various services provided by governments must compete with each other for scarce resources. For example, if the constituency believes an enhanced economic development program is needed, a decision may need to be made as to whether the resources to finance that program will be obtained by reducing police protection, reducing street maintenance, or increasing the property tax rate. If economic contraction indicates a likely decline in sales tax revenues, a decision may need to be made as to which services provided by government will need to be reduced and by how much.

　Budgeting is the process that provides for accumulating resources and for allocating them among competing programs. A budget is a formal estimate of the resources that an organization plans to spend for specified purposes during a specified time period (typically, a fiscal year) and the proposed means of acquiring these resources. The budget sets forth the activities the organization plans to undertake and how the organization expects to finance them. Once approved, the budget represents public policy in that its adoption implies certain objectives, as well as the means of accomplishing those objectives, as determined by the legislative body. In addition to serving as a framework for operations, the budget has the force of law in most local governments. This means that revenues can be raised only from authorized sources and that expenditures can be incurred only for authorized purposes and in amounts not to exceed authorized maximums. The authority to spend up to a maximum amount is called an "appropriation."

Even if not required by law, the use of a budget is strongly recommended. The GASB expresses the following general principles regarding budgets and budgetary accounting:

1. An annual budget(s) should be adopted by every governmental unit.
2. The accounting system should provide the basis for appropriate budgetary control.
3. Budgetary comparisons should be presented as required supplementary information for the General Fund and for each major Special Revenue Fund that has a legally adopted annual budget.[1]

In this chapter we concentrate on the budget process and budgetary accounting.

BUDGET LAWS

States usually have constitutional and/or statutory requirements governing both their own budgets and the budgets of local governmental units located within their borders. These laws may cover such matters as the types of budgets to be prepared, funds required to have budgets, public input into the budgetary process, and the means of putting the budget into effect.

To encourage fiscal responsibility, the laws of nearly all states require a "balanced budget." Generally, a budget is considered balanced if proposed expenditures do not exceed estimated resources available for the year. For example, the state of North Carolina requires that "each local government and public authority shall operate under an annual balanced budget ordinance adopted and administered in accordance with this Article. A budget ordinance is balanced when the sum of estimated net revenues and appropriated fund balances is equal to appropriations." Georgia requires all its local governments to "adopt and operate under an annual balanced budget for the general fund, each special revenue fund, and each debt service fund."

Studies have shown, however, that state and local government requirements for balanced budgets are not very rigorous. For example, in some states the chief executive may be required to submit a balanced budget, but the legislative body is not required to adopt a balanced budget; in some states, budgets are required to be in balance at the start of the year, but not at the end. In addition, under virtually all the laws, budgets may be balanced in form, but not in substance; budgetary balance can be achieved by not budgeting for certain expenditures attributable to the current period, but not required to be paid in cash until subsequent years, such as pensions and postemployment health care benefits. (We return to this issue in Chapter 5.) Nonetheless, balanced budget requirements, even if imperfect, undoubtedly benefit taxpayers.

BUDGETARY TYPES AND APPROACHES

There are basically two types of budgets: operating and capital. Operating budgets are concerned with spending on and financing of day-to-day activities, such as public safety, education, and recreation; capital budgets focus on the acquisition of long-lived resources, such as buildings, roads, and equipment. Although both types of budgets are prepared generally for periods of 1 year (a few governments prepare biennial budgets), they are often prepared within the context

---

[1]GASB Cod. Sec. 1100.111.

of longer-range financial plans (4 or 5 years). Governments also prepare monthly (and even daily) cash forecasts to ensure that sufficient cash is on hand to pay bills as they come due.

General Fund and Special Revenue Fund Budgets

Virtually all governments prepare annual operating budgets for the General Fund and the more significant Special Revenue Funds. The budget document typically shows actual revenues and expenditures for the previous year and for the current year to date, as well as anticipated revenues and proposed expenditures for the forthcoming budget year. Mt. Lebanon's budget summary for 2010 shows actual revenues and expenditures for 2007 and 2008 and the budgets for 2009 and 2010.

The expenditure side of an operating budget generally provides information on the specific purpose of services performed by each operating unit. It also provides object-of-expenditure details, such as amounts estimated to be spent on personnel and supplies. The revenue side of an operating budget shows the estimated amounts to be received from each revenue source, such as various types of taxes and nontax revenues.

To illustrate, Mt. Lebanon's budget summary for 2010 shows proposed expenditures of $2,700,400 for recreation programs. The detail supporting the budget request describes all the recreation programs. For example, the budget line for the Tennis Center program shows the 2008 actual expenditures, the 2009 budget, and the 2010 budget. The narrative accompanying the budget request describes the Tennis Center operation, stating that the center is open from 7:30 a.m. to 10:30 p.m. daily for 23 weeks and that it provides instructional and competitive tennis programming. Another section of the budget request shows the detailed object-of-expenditure budgets. The details for the Tennis Center budget request of $187,710 include part time and temporary wages of $67,580, contractual services of $50,840, utilities of $29,050, and so on.

Capital Budgets and Plans

Capital budgets articulate the plans of expenditures for long-lived assets and the means of financing them. Mt. Lebanon's Capital Projects Fund budget is keyed to its 5-year capital improvement program, a "rolling" or continuous capital plan that adds a future year and drops the earliest year as annual revisions are made. Mt. Lebanon's 2012 capital improvement program runs about 100 pages and describes each proposed capital project, its estimated cost over the years 2012 through 2016, and the proposed means of financing it. For example, the Large Truck Replacement project for the department of public works shows planned expenditures for 2012, 2014, and 2016. It also proposes that the expenditures be financed by a combination of proceeds from the sale of older equipment and taxes.

Cash Forecasts

Cash forecasts estimate the amounts of cash to be received and expended during a particular period. Governmental units are likely to receive a large percentage of their revenues in an uneven manner during the year while their expenditures are generally spread out ratably over the year, possibly leading to cash shortages and surpluses at various times. Governments make cash forecasts to anticipate such cash shortages and surpluses so that plans can be made for orderly short-term borrowing and investing. A cash forecast is shown in Table 3-1.

Budgetary Approaches

Various approaches to budgeting have evolved over the years, changing with the gradual improvement of managerial techniques. The National Advisory Council on State and Local

TABLE 3-1	Illustrative Cash Forecast

Sample City
General Fund
Cash Forecast
Second Quarter, 2012

	April	May	June	Quarter
Beginning cash balance	$ 12,000	$ 10,500	$ 16,350	$ 12,000
Cash receipts:				
Property taxes	$ 13,000	$ 28,000	$ 230,500	$ 271,500
Sales taxes	95,000	97,000	96,000	288,000
Fixed asset sales	500	1,000	3,000	4,500
Fines and penalties	15,000	15,000	18,000	48,000
License fees	5,500	3,000	1,600	10,100
Total cash receipts	$ 129,000	$ 144,000	$ 349,100	$ 622,100
Cash available[a]	$ 141,000	$ 154,500	$ 365,450	$ 634,100
Cash disbursements:				
Personal services	$ 56,000	$ 58,000	$ 57,500	$ 171,500
Travel	2,500	4,000	11,000	17,500
Operating expenses	32,000	36,000	35,500	103,500
Equipment	10,000	30,000	25,000	65,000
Transfers to Capital Projects Funds	130,000	—	82,000	212,000
Transfers to Debt Services Funds	—	—	50,000	50,000
Total disbursements	$ 230,500	$ 128,000	$ 261,000	$ 619,500
Minimum cash balance	10,000	10,000	10,000	$ 10,000
Total cash required	$ 240,500	$ 138,000	$ 271,000	$ 629,500
Excess (deficiency) of cash available over cash required	$ (99,500)	$ 16,500	$ 94,450	$ 4,600
Financing:				
Tax anticipation notes	$ 100,000	—	—	$ 100,000
Repayment of notes	—	$ (10,000)	$ (90,000)	(100,000)
Interest	—	(150)	(800)	(950)
Net financing	$ 100,000	$ (10,150)	$ (90,800)	$ (950)
Ending cash balance	$ 10,500	$ 16,350	$ 13,650	$ 13,650

[a]Before financing.

Budgeting, an organization created by the Government Finance Officers Association, suggests that the budget process should incorporate a long-term perspective, establish linkages to broad organizational goals, focus budget decisions on results and outcomes, and promote effective communication with stakeholders.

Budgets can be prepared under one of several approaches, generally referred to as object-of-expenditure; performance; program and planning-programming budgeting; and zero-based budgeting. These approaches differ to some extent as to type of information presented

Governmental Budgeting in Practice

Mt. Lebanon Uses Zero-Based Budgeting

Mt. Lebanon's approach to budgeting—the zero-based budget (ZBB)—is more sophisticated than the object-of-expenditure approach illustrated in this text. When the object-of-expenditure approach is used, there is a tendency to consider a department's current budget as a starting point (or base), from which requests are made for additional expenditures. Under ZBB, however, each year's budget starts from scratch (or zero), with each activity justified as if it were new. ZBB got its start in the United States with the Carter administration. Like all other budget approaches, it has both supporters and critics.

A key feature of the ZBB approach is the identification of "decision packages"—programs for which separate cost figures can be maintained. Service levels are described for each package, with each successive level providing for increased service with its incremental cost. The various levels are ranked in order of importance to the municipality, giving decision makers the opportunity to choose the level of service to be provided.

The proposed budget for Mt. Lebanon's Tennis Center provides a simple illustration. As noted in the text, Mt. Lebanon proposed spending $187,710 in 2010 on its Tennis Center program, enabling the center to operate from 7:30 a.m. to 10:30 p.m. daily for 23 weeks. As a result, the center will generate revenues (included in the revenue estimates) of $200,600, creating an estimated "net profit" of $12,890. The budget also shows, for consideration by Mt. Lebanon's commissioners, an incremental service level, providing for repairs to the grounds at a cost of $11,020. But this expenditure will not generate revenues, so if adopted, the profit would be reduced to $1,870.

and as to how expenditures are aggregated. The simplest—the object-of-expenditure approach—is illustrated in this text. Under the object-of-expenditure approach (also known as the traditional or line-item approach), budgets are prepared to show, as line items, every category of expenditure to be made during the year, described in terms of the physical good or service to be obtained by the government. Performance or program data may be included with an object-of-expenditure budget to support the various appropriation requests. The object-of-expenditure budget is suited to the typical method of budget preparation—by governmental department.

All departments are likely to need the services of their employees, utilities, and operating supplies, so at a minimum, departmental budgets will require appropriations for those *current operating* items. Additionally, appropriations may need to include payments for temporary employees and contractual services. Some departments may need motor vehicles and other special equipment for daily operations. Automobiles, fire trucks, dump trucks, and the like ordinarily last for several years. In any given year, however, a department might need to purchase vehicles to replace those that have worn out and/or to expand operations. Thus, departmental budgets often include *capital outlay* appropriations for vehicle and equipment purchases. In short, a departmental budget always includes appropriations for a variety of current operating items and might also have appropriations for capital expenditures.

THE BUDGET PROCESS

The budget process is a continuous cycle, wherein evaluation of this year's performance significantly influences next year's budget. The process described here focuses on the detailed procedures within a budget year. (It should be recognized, however, that well-managed governments manage for results. To accomplish this purpose, they identify their missions, goals, and objectives; prepare long-term operating plans to establish policies and operating strategies to achieve goals and objectives efficiently and effectively; prepare long-term financial plans; and prepare annual budgets containing measurable goals and performance objectives.) The typical annual budget process can be broken down into the following steps:

1. Prepare budgetary policy guidelines.
2. Prepare the budget calendar.
3. Prepare and distribute budget instructions.
4. Prepare revenue estimates.
5. Prepare departmental (or program) expenditure requests.
6. Prepare nondepartmental expenditure and interfund transfer requests.
7. Prepare a capital outlay request summary, if appropriate.
8. Consolidate departmental expenditure requests, nondepartmental expenditure and interfund transfer requests, capital outlay requests, and revenue estimates, and submit them to the chief executive officer (CEO) for review and revision.
9. Prepare the budget document.
10. Present the budget document to the legislative body.
11. Hold public hearings on the budget.
12. Record the approved budget in the accounts.
13. Determine the property tax (millage) rate.

Budgetary Policy Guidelines

At the outset of the budgetary process, the CEO, the budget officer, and members of the legislative body may discuss the policies to be followed when preparing the budget. During these discussions, fiscal conditions of the current year are reviewed, along with the prospects for the following year. In addition, the following points might be considered:

1. The level of revenues collected to date and the level of revenues likely to be collected during the remainder of the year
2. Possible increases or decreases in current taxes and fees, and ideas for new taxes and fees
3. Current and future economic conditions, as well as any possible developments that might affect the revenues or expenditures of the following year (e.g., a plant closing or the loss of a federal grant)
4. Items due the following fiscal year that might require an unusually large expenditure, such as repayment of a bond issue
5. The status of current-year revenues and expenditures and the possibility of a surplus (or deficit)

Analysis of these issues provides insight into potential financial problems a government may face during the following year. From the discussions of these issues, budgetary policies satisfactory to the CEO, the legislative body, and other affected parties should emerge. Resulting *budgetary policy guidelines* should be disseminated to all persons responsible for preparing and reviewing various segments of the budget. The policies might cover, for example;

1. Types of programs and services to be emphasized and deemphasized
2. Changes in capital requirements

3. Legally permissible increases or decreases in taxes and fees
4. Contractually required salary adjustments
5. Inflationary adjustments

Budget Calendar

For the budgetary process to proceed in an organized manner, certain deadlines must be met. A budget calendar formalizes all key dates in the budgetary process and often is specified by a government's laws. The calendar itself can be a simple listing of dates. At a minimum, it should list the steps of the budgetary process and the dates on which each of the various steps must be finished. More elaborate calendars often list who is responsible for each step and what data must be provided by whom and to whom. A sample budget calendar is shown in Table 3-2.

Budget Instructions

To disseminate the budgetary policy guidelines and to assist the various subunits in preparing expenditure requests, a set of budget instructions should be prepared and sent to each person responsible for a segment of the budget. Budget instructions should contain the following:

1. A budget calendar
2. A copy of the budgetary policy guidelines
3. A statement summarizing the organization's anticipated fiscal condition for the year
4. A statement of specific policies to be followed when preparing expenditure requests
5. A set of inflationary guidelines to be used in estimating future expenditures
6. Specific instructions on how each form and worksheet should be completed
7. Instructions on where to seek help and clarification of any ambiguities

TABLE 3-2	Illustrative Budget Calendar for a December 31 Fiscal Year
July 6	Departments receive instructions for the preparation of the budget.
August 15	Departmental expenditure requests are returned to the budget officer.
September 6–21	Departmental hearings are held with the mayor.
October 1–8	Review and preliminary presentation is made to the city council.
October 9–31	Budget is reviewed and finalized by the mayor.
November 5–18	Budget printing and production take place.
November 20	Mayor formally presents the budget to the city council.
November 21–December 15	City council conducts public hearings.
December 18	City council formally votes on the budget.
December 20–30	Budgetary information is entered into the computer.
January 1	New fiscal year begins.

Revenue Estimates

A key part of the budgetary process is determining the total amount of resources available for spending in the coming fiscal year. This determination requires the responsible individuals to

1. Estimate probable fund balance in each fund at the end of the current year.
2. Project revenues expected to be realized during the budget year.
3. Summarize the estimates in a statement of estimated revenues (and transfers-in), such as the one illustrated in Table 3-3.

Departmental Expenditure Requests

Expenditure requests should be prepared by each department, agency, or other subunit of the government. These documents show the total expenditures of the prior year, the total estimated expenditures for the current year, and the proposed amounts of expenditures for the budget year. Detailed supporting schedules for each major object-of-expenditure should accompany these requests. Expenditure requests force department heads and other managers to examine the objectives, current levels of activity, and accomplishments of their subunits and to determine whether operational improvements are possible. If managers wish to expand the scope of the activities of their subunits, they must be able to justify the additional expenditures.

Expenditure requests often serve as the basis for departmental budgetary hearings, held by the central budget office, enabling those who make budget decisions to raise questions regarding the reasonableness of the requests in terms of program goals and past performance. Expenditure requests also help budgetary decision makers evaluate the departmental requests in light of the missions, goals, and objectives of the entire government and allocate resources to those activities that best serve the objectives of the government as a whole.

The following process should be applied to each line item when preparing departmental expenditure requests:

1. Determine total expenditures for the past year, and project expenditures for the current year.
2. Apply inflation and cost-of-living factors and other allowances for "uncontrollable" factors to each current-year expenditure. This will result in a "baseline" expenditure request.
3. Identify those activities to be expanded, scaled back, or discontinued. Identify any new activities that, if funded, will commence the following year.
4. Adjust each proposed expenditure for the changes in the type and level of activities identified in step 3.
5. Prepare a justification for each new activity or each increase in the level of an existing activity. Include in this justification the effect that not adopting or increasing the level of the activity will have on the organization.
6. Prepare a budgetary worksheet for each type of expenditure (personal services, contractual services, materials and supplies, etc.). The formats of the worksheets will vary with the type of expenditure being projected, although each worksheet should show the prior-year, current-year, and projected budget-year level of expenditures for each line item.
7. Summarize the information from each worksheet on the expenditure request.

PREPARING A BUDGETARY WORKSHEET Let's look at the steps involved in preparing a budgetary worksheet using the personal services (payroll) object-of-expenditure as an example. The heart of a personal services budget is the *position classification plan,* which lists all authorized

TABLE 3-3 Statement of Actual and Estimated Revenues (and Transfers In)

Fund: General
Date: September 15, 2012

Prepared by _PNW_
Approved by _LVT_

Acct. #	Source	2011 Actual	Jan.–Aug. 2012 Actual	Sept.–Dec. 2012 Est. Act.	Total 2012 Est. Act.	2012 Budget	2013 Budget	Remarks
1110	Property tax	$3,246,575	$1,384,300	$1,940,700	$3,325,000	$3,325,000	$3,550,000	Reassessment of property
1112	Liquor tax	355,240	235,650	124,350	360,000	354,000	480,000	International Exposition
1114	Sales tax	1,864,680	1,252,840	857,160	2,110,000	2,200,000	2,650,000	Same as above
1116	Royalty payments	385,000	245,000	120,000	365,000	375,000	300,000	Decline in gas production
1119	Fines and penalties	84,610	63,450	30,000	93,450	92,000	100,000	International Exposition
1121	Rental charges	8,500	6,500	3,500	10,000	9,500	11,000	Same as above
	Subtotal	$5,944,605	$3,187,740	$3,075,710	$6,263,450	$6,355,500	$7,091,000	
2010	Transfer from Enterprise Fund	122,000	—	145,000	145,000	145,000	50,000	Major events
	Total	$5,066,605	$3,187,740	$3,220,710	$5,408,450	$6,500,500	$7,241,000	

67

position titles within a department and their corresponding salaries. From the plan, past and current personnel costs can be identified. The positions expected to be occupied during the budget year should be recorded on the personal services worksheet, along with the past, current, and projected rate or salary attached to each position.

Some governments budget for employee (fringe) benefits as a separate item for each departmental activity; other governments budget for them as nondepartmental items, discussed in the next section. Because the cost of fringe benefits may differ by activity (police and fire department fringe benefits are likely to be more costly than general government employee fringe benefits), budgeting for them separately for each activity produces more accurate data for making budget decisions.

Other personal service costs that must be considered are overtime, shift differentials, and requests for temporary help. For example, on certain holidays it is sometimes necessary to ask police officers to work overtime to handle the crowds of parade watchers. In addition, some cities hire students to perform special tasks, such as street repairs, during the summer. These costs are usually known well in advance and can easily be determined by multiplying projected hours by appropriate pay and fringe benefit rates.

Another factor that warrants consideration in budgeting for personal services is the likelihood of vacancies from retirement or termination and the speed with which the vacancies are likely to be filled. The potential for vacancies provides opportunities for cost savings that cannot be ignored either by the department or the central budget office.

Table 3-4 shows a personal services budgetary worksheet for a police department. Notice that the worksheet explains the calculations made to develop requested amounts and justifies certain increases on the basis of expanded operational responsibilities.

When the worksheets for the various objects-of-expenditure are complete, summary information is transferred from these forms to the departmental expenditure request document. This schedule contains, at a minimum, the title of each object-of-expenditure, the level of prior- and current-year expenditures, and the requested level of expenditures for the budget year.

Some organizations summarize the requested level of expenditures by activity (e.g., vice squad, juvenile control, traffic control, and so on). Such information helps the CEO and members of the legislative body make judgments on the costs and benefits of specific activities. An expenditure request for a police department is shown in Table 3-5.

Nondepartmental Expenditure and Interfund Transfer Requests

Nondepartmental expenditures are expenditures that do not relate to any one specific department or activity. Instead, they relate to the organization as a whole. They are, therefore, budgeted by the central budget office. Examples of nondepartmental expenditures include utility and maintenance costs of buildings used by several departments or programs (such as a city hall), interest on long-term debt, and liability insurance premiums for city-owned vehicles. Some expenditures, such as judgments and claims and employee benefits, may be budgeted either by each department or by the central budget office. In addition, many organizations budget an amount to cover possible revenue shortfalls, emergencies, or contingencies. An interfund transfer is a movement of existing resources from one fund to another as necessary for operating purposes. Interfund transfers are classified separately from revenues and expenditures. Table 3-6 provides an example of a nondepartmental expenditure and interfund transfer request.

TABLE 3-4 Personal Services Worksheet

Fund: General
Function: Public Safety
Department: Police

Prepared by _PE_
Approved by _PRT_
Date: _September 15, 2012_

Code	Position Title	Prior-Year Actual			Current-Year Est. Actual			Budget Request[b]			Remarks
		No.	Rate[a]	Amount	No.	Rate[a]	Amount	No.	Rate[a]	Amount	
101	Chief	1	$51,300	$ 51,300	1	$54,000	$ 54,000	1	$59,474	$ 59,474	
102	Captain	2	44,888	89,775	2	47,250	94,500	2	52,324	104,648	
104	Lieutenant	4	38,475	153,900	4	40,500	162,000	4	42,903	171,612	
105	Detective	2	32,063	64,125	2	33,750	67,500	2	35,753	71,506	
106	Sergeant	5	29,925	149,625	5	31,500	157,500	5	33,369	166,845	
108	Police Officer	12	25,650	307,800	12	27,000	324,000	14	28,602	400,428	Two new positions[c]
	Total	26		$816,525	26		$859,500	28		$974,513	

[a]Includes employee benefits, which are budgeted at 13.5% of salaries and wages. This rate is 1% higher than the current rate because of an expected increase in the cost of pension and health care benefits.

[b]Includes a cost-of-living factor of 5.0% plus an additional merit increase of $2,000 each for the chief and captains.

[c]Justification for new positions: In the latter part of the current year, an area of 4 square miles was annexed. To provide an adequate level of protection in this area and the original parts of the city, an additional patrol unit is necessary. If this additional unit is denied, the annexed area, containing 562 residents, will receive inadequate police protection, or the entire city will receive a lower level of protection due to the overextending of available personnel and equipment. In either case the level of crime can be expected to rise significantly if the additional unit is not approved.

TABLE 3-5	Departmental Expenditure Request

Fund: General
Function: Public Safety
Department: Police

Prepared by ___**BER**___
Approved by ___**PRT**___
Date: September 15, 2012

Code	Object	Prior-Year Actual	Current-Year Budget	Current-Year Est. Actual	Budget Request
100	Personal services	$816,525	$859,500	$859,500	$ 974,513
200	Travel	4,600	4,800	4,800	5,350
300–600	Operating	60,500	61,600	61,450	62,350
700	Equipment	62,470	66,500	65,800	87,100
	Total	$944,095	$992,400	$991,550	$1,129,313

Narrative: The Police Department maintains law and order in the community. Major departmental expenditures are for personnel, operating, and equipment. Because of the increased area of the city, the department must add two police officers and an additional police cruiser. In addition, it must replace three police cruisers that have reached the end of their useful lives. Finally, the department must upgrade its communication system because of a recently passed law requiring that police departments throughout the state maintain comprehensive networks that are integrated into the state system.

SERVICE EFFORTS AND ACCOMPLISHMENTS

Many organizations supplement their budget requests with data showing what they expect to accomplish during the year. These kinds of data are consistent with the current trend toward managing for results and reporting service efforts and accomplishments. The following data are typically provided for each of the major functions performed by a department:

1. Description of the function
2. Inputs (service efforts)—numbers of personnel (and dollar amounts) and amounts of materials, supplies, and equipment needed to accomplish the function
3. Outputs—quantities of services expected to be performed (e.g., number of lane miles of road expected to be maintained during the budget year)
4. Outcomes—the results expected to be achieved during the budget year (e.g., 85 percent of the lane miles will be rated as "very good" or better as a result of efforts made during the budget year)

Information presented on service efforts and accomplishments should cover the past year, current year, and budget year. The performance measures (i.e., anticipated outputs and outcomes) should be used by departmental managers and the chief executive of the governmental unit to help assess budget priorities, to monitor performance during the year, and to report to the public at year-end.

BUDGETARY REVIEW

Departmental expenditure request documents are submitted to the central budget office, together with the worksheets and other supporting materials. The chief budget officer or a member of the staff assesses each request and contacts departmental officials to help resolve

TABLE 3-6 Nondepartmental Expenditure and Interfund Transfer Request

Fund: General
Date: September 15, 2012

Prepared by ___CCW___
Approved by ___LVT___

Code	Object	Prior-Year Actual	Current-Year Budget	Current-Year Est. Actual	Budget Request	Remarks
730	City dues	$ 1,500	$ 1,500	$ 1,500	$ 1,500	
810	Repairs	—	—	3,000	20,000	Damage to city hall from dust storm
850	Legal settlements	150,000	120,000	210,000	200,000	Uninsured portion of damage claims
925	Audit fees	12,000	15,000	15,500	18,000	Inflation
930	Legal services	35,000	35,000	40,000	40,000	Inflation
950	Advertising	2,000	2,500	2,450	8,000	Promote International Exposition
970	Res. for contingencies	205,000	180,000	180,000	165,000	
980	Transfer to Debt Service Fund	500,000	500,000	500,000	1,300,000	Bond issue
	Total	$905,500	$854,000	$952,450	$1,752,500	

Governmental Budgeting in Practice

Using Sound Budgetary Policies and Practices

The way in which a government prepares and manages its annual budgets can affect its financial condition significantly. Indeed, the financial condition of some governments has deteriorated, and their credit ratings have been downgraded because of poor budgeting policies and practices, such as deliberately overestimating revenues or underestimating expenditures, borrowing long term to finance day-to-day operating expenditures, and "balancing" budgets through nonrecurring resource enhancements (e.g., selling assets or future revenue streams).

Credit-rating agencies consider four basic factors when rating state and local obligations: economic, financial, debt, and management/administrative. Here are some of the budgetary practices considered by Fitch when examining the management and administrative factors affecting a government's credit rating:

- Preparation of revenue and expenditure estimates, including key assumptions used in making the estimates (conservatism in estimating is viewed favorably)
- Consideration of current economic, political, and financial conditions in the preparation of budgets
- Regular review of budget status *during the year*, enabling the government to control future spending through timely identification of "underperforming revenues or overspending"

Fitch also likes to see governments adopt sound budgetary policies regarding such matters as multiyear revenue and expenditure forecasting, restrictions on the use of nonrecurring revenues, and maintenance of fund balances (or "rainy day" funds) as a cushion against potential revenue and expenditure volatility.

Source: FitchRatings, Public Finance, "U.S. Local Government Tax-Supported Rating Criteria," October 8, 2010.

---

questions raised during the review process. The governmental budget process may also provide for holding hearings on departmental budget requests. Assessing each request requires consideration of many factors, including compliance with budgetary guidelines, validity of assumptions underlying the request, likely level of service needed or demanded by the public, efficiency of the department in providing services with existing resources, and relative priority accorded each activity.

In most governments, the chief budget officer is responsible for ensuring that the total proposed expenditures do not exceed total budgeted resources (the sum of estimated revenues plus fund balance expected at the end of the current year). Because the total expenditure requests often exceed budgeted resources, even after the screening process discussed in the preceding paragraph, and because of legal requirements to submit balanced budgets, the budget officer may need to decide which requests should be included in the budget document without modification and which requests should be reduced or eliminated. These judgments often involve political considerations involving both taxation policies and activity priorities and are likely to require consultation with the CEO.

The final review of the expenditure requests is made by the CEO. The purposes of the final review are (1) to obtain the CEO's input into the budgetary process, (2) to act as a court of last resort for disputes between the budget officer and departmental officials, and (3) to enable the CEO to prepare specific budget recommendations to the legislative body.

THE BUDGET DOCUMENT

After completion of the final review, the budget officer assembles the budget requests, the revenue projections, and the CEO's recommendations into a comprehensive budget document, which is presented to the legislative body. The budget document may contain the following elements:

1. A *budget message,* which, in general terms, discusses the following:
   a. The fiscal experience of the current year
   b. The present financial position of the organization
   c. Major financial issues faced during the past year and expected during the budget year
   d. Assumptions used when preparing budget requests
   e. Significant revenue and expenditure changes from the current year's budget
   f. New program initiatives and anticipated accomplishments during the year
   g. Significant budgetary changes resulting from the proposed new program initiatives, such as increased numbers of personnel and new debt issues
   h. The future economic outlook of the organization
2. A *budget summary,* which lists the total estimated revenues by source and the total budgeted expenditures by program or department and for the organization as a whole
3. *Detailed supporting schedules,* including estimated revenues by source and object-of-expenditure data
4. A *capital projects schedule*
5. *Detailed justifications of the budgetary recommendations*
6. *Supplementary information,* such as departmental budget request worksheets, performance reports showing program outputs and outcomes, and a cash forecast
7. Drafts of appropriation and tax levy ordinances or acts

Table 3-7 contains excerpts from Mt. Lebanon's 2010 budget document. Part A of the table presents the General Fund column of the "2010 Budget Recap," a summary that shows expenditures at the broad *program* level. Part B provides some detail, showing the proposed expenditures for the *activities* within one of the *departments* (Police Department) included within one of the programs. (Each activity is discussed in detail in this part of the budget document.) Part C provides more detail, showing proposed expenditures for one of the Police Department activities (police field services) at the *object-of-expenditure* level. The related numbers in Parts A, B, and C are shown in boldface. As you review Part A, notice that the budget is balanced partly with the use of existing fund balance of $1,614,540. Although shown with revenues for budgetary purposes, existing fund balance does not provide revenues in the accounting sense. The amount shown for debt service ($2,520,960) will be transferred to the Debt Service Fund.

LEGISLATIVE CONSIDERATION AND ADOPTION OF THE BUDGET

The completed budget document is sent to the legislative body, which reviews, modifies, approves, and adopts it. Before approving the budget document, the legislative body usually conducts administrative hearings. In some cases, the budget document is furnished to a legislative finance or ways-and-means committee for review and comment.

TABLE 3-7	Illustration of Portions of a Budget Document

Part A. 2010 Budget Recap (General Fund of Mt. Lebanon's 2010 Budget Document)

Revenues	
Taxes:	
Real estate	$10,241,710
Earned income	9,293,610
Local services	324,000
Real estate transfer	1,150,000
County sales	645,000
Utility	27,850
Total taxes	21,682,170
Nontax Revenues:	
Licenses, permits, and fees	881,400
Fines, forfeitures, and penalties	146,460
Investment and rental	12,000
Intergovernmental	1,745,140
Recreation	2,479,580
Charges for service and other revenue	1,719,080
Transfers between funds	100,000
Use of surplus/fund balance	1,614,540
Total nontax revenues	8,698,200
Total revenues	$30,380,370
Expenditures	
Operating:	
General government	$ 4,345,490
Community development	868,730
Public works	6,318,700
Human services	1,294,960
Recreation	2,700,400
Public safety	**11,150,920**
Total operating	26,679,200
Capital Improvements	1,180,210
Debt Service	2,520,960
Total expenditures	$30,380,370

Part B. Excerpt from Public Safety Section of Detailed Budget Justification by Activity

Public Safety	
Fire Department	$ 3,185,360
Police Department:	
Police administration	602,600
Police field services	**4,693,160**
Police support services	251,040

TABLE 3-7	*(continued)*	
Investigative services		708,960
Traffic safety		644,420
School crossing protection		466,680
Crime prevention unit		293,580
Animal control		305,120
Total Police Department		7,965,560
Total public safety program		**$11,150,920**

Part C. Police Field Services Section of Line Item (Object-of-Expenditure) Part of Budget

Police Field Services	
Regular salaries and wages	$ 2,480,240
Overtime wages	308,000
Fringe benefits	1,784,380
Professional and consulting services	2,500
Office supplies	700
Books and periodicals	50
Equipment and furniture	117,290
Total police field services	**$ 4,693,160**

Many governmental entities are required by law to hold public hearings on the budget. Citizen input into budgetary decisions is obtained by allowing interested parties to offer their views on the budget to the legislative body. When the budget hearings conclude, the legislative body completes its deliberations, makes any modifications to the budget document it believes are necessary, and enacts a final appropriation ordinance or, in the case of a state, appropriation act. The budget ordinance or act provides legal authorization to make the expenditures listed in the budget. After the appropriation ordinance or act has been passed, the budgeted amounts are entered into the accounts, as discussed later in this chapter.

PROPERTY TAX LEVY

After approval of the budget, the legislative body must raise revenues necessary to finance the budgeted expenditures. The collection of many types of revenues does not require frequent action on the part of the legislative body. These revenues usually result from previous actions, such as established license fees and sales tax rates. Other revenue measures, however, require legal action more frequently, the most common example being property taxes.

Two approaches are used to determine the taxes to be assessed on each piece of property. Under one approach, the assessed value of the property (less any exemptions) is multiplied by a flat rate, which is "permanently" fixed by law. More commonly, property taxes are assessed on the basis of a government's fiscal need (subject to legal limits). When the latter approach is used, the government must first determine a tax (millage) rate that, when applied to the assessed value of the property, will provide the desired amount of revenue. This calculation requires consideration of (1) uncollectible or delinquent taxes and (2) property exempt from taxation (such as land belonging to religious organizations) and exemptions due to military service, age, physical condition, and other factors. If a village needed to raise property taxes in the amount of $3,550,000, it would compute its tax (millage) rate as follows:

Amount to be collected	$ 3,550,000
Estimated uncollectible property taxes (assumed)	4%
Required tax levy ($3,550,000/.96)	$ 3,697,917
Total assessed value of property (assumed)	$ 80,000,000
Less, property not taxable (assumed)	(2,000,000)
	$ 78,000,000
Less, exemptions (assumed)	
Homestead	$ (1,000,000)
Veterans	(500,000)
Old age, blindness, etc.	(900,000)
	(2,400,000)
Net assessed value of property	$ 75,600,000

Tax (millage) rate = required tax levy / net assessed value of property
= $3,697,917 / $75,600,000
= .0489

In this example, the property tax will be levied at the rate of $4.89 per $100 of net assessed valuation. If the tax rate is expressed in mills (thousandths of a dollar), it will be 48.90 mills. Thus, the owner of a piece of property with a net (after exemptions) assessed value of $200,000 will be required to pay property taxes of $9,780 ($200,000 × .0489).

USING BUDGETARY INFORMATION

Budgets provide an important control mechanism, both for the department and activity heads and for the central budget office. If, for example, a department has spent 50 percent of its personal services budget after only 4 months have elapsed, it may lack sufficient budget authority to complete the year. Why did this occur, and what action needs to be taken? By comparing actual expenditures with budgeted appropriations, managers, legislators, and other decision makers can judge the organization's financial performance and can take corrective action when necessary. If revenue collections are lagging behind estimates, knowledge of departmental spending to date can help the central budget office determine where savings can be achieved to bring expenditures in line with projected revenues for the year.

Well-managed governments produce monthly statements for internal use that detail budgeted and actual expenditures, by object, and the remaining amount available for spending. This information is particularly important to organizations that are subject to antideficiency laws (laws that make the overspending of one's budget an act subject to civil and/or criminal penalties), as well as to those managers whose performance is judged by whether they meet their objectives within their budgets. In addition, knowledge of amounts available for spending is helpful to organizational personnel when planning activities for the rest of the fiscal year. If the spending rate is greater than originally planned, their unit must curtail its activities or ask for a supplemental appropriation from the legislative body. If the remaining amount available for spending is higher than originally planned, the unit can expand its activities.

Table 3-8 provides an illustration of a budgetary control report. In addition to showing the budget for the current month and the year to date, it shows (1) actual expenditures incurred for

TABLE 3-8 Budgetary Control Report

Fund: General
Function: Public Safety
Department: Police

Prepared by: RGS
Date: September 30, 2012

	Year to Date					Object-of-Expenditure	Current Month				
Budget	Actual	Variance	% Budget	Code			Budget	Actual	Variance	% Budget	Available for Spending
						Contractual Services					
$ 75	$ 60	$ 15(F)	20	301	Advertising		$ 8	$ 10	$ 2(U)	25	$ 40
1,200	1,300	100(U)	8	310	Printing		133	120	13(F)	10	300
6,000	6,200	200(U)	3	320	Vehicle maintenance		667	645	22(F)	3	1,800
4,200	3,900	300(F)	7	330	Communication		467	378	89(F)	19	1,700
150	180	30(U)	20	350	Dues and subscriptions		17	21	4(U)	24	20
225	200	25(F)	11	360	Postage		25	30	5(U)	20	100
450	550	100(U)	22	370	Telephone		50	35	15(F)	30	50
300	300	—	—	380	Professional services		33	0	33(F)	100	100
$ 12,600	$ 12,690	$ 90(U)	1		Subtotal		$ 1,400	$ 1,239	$ 161(F)	12	$ 4,110
						Supplies and Materials					
$ 825	$ 850	$ 25(U)	3	401	Office supplies		$ 92	$ 97	$ 5(U)	5	$ 250
3,525	3,595	70(U)	2	410	Building maintenance		392	370	22(F)	6	1,105
7,875	7,750	125(F)	2	420	Fuel		875	825	50(F)	6	2,750
$546,375	$563,430	$17,055(U)	3		Grand total		$60,708	$63,386	$2,678(U)	4	$165,070

these periods; (2) differences between budgeted and actual expenditures (called variances) in both absolute numbers and as a percentage of budget; and (3) amounts that can be spent for the remainder of the year without exceeding the budget. If the amount spent is less than the amount budgeted, a favorable (F) variance is shown. If the amount spent is more than the amount budgeted, an unfavorable (U) variance is shown.

To control program performance, budgetary control reports should be supplemented with budgetary performance reports. Anticipated performance set forth in the submitted budget should be used to develop measures of actual performance. When this is done, anticipated performance (expressed in terms of expected quantities of outputs and outcomes) becomes a benchmark for measuring what actually happens during the year. The resulting monthly or quarterly reports help department managers and the chief executive to manage for results. When also used to report to the public, these performance reports help governmental managers demonstrate accountability.

Budgetary comparisons also appear in external annual financial reports. The GASB requires that annual financial reports include budgetary comparison schedules or statements for the General Fund and each major Special Revenue Fund with a legally adopted budget. These schedules should show (1) the original adopted budget, (2) the final appropriated budget, and (3) actual revenues and expenditures on the budgetary basis of accounting.[2] We discuss these schedules in subsequent chapters.

CLASSIFYING REVENUES AND EXPENDITURES

The budget significantly influences government finances and accounting practices. A basic principle of government accounting is that budgetary and accounting systems should be integrated and use common classifications and terminology as much as possible. In this section, we introduce the classification system widely used by governments for both budgeting and accounting. The classification scheme for revenues is fairly simple; the classification scheme for expenditures is more complex because of the need for accountability and control over spending.

Revenue Classification

Revenues should be budgeted and accounted for at a minimum by (1) fund and (2) source within the fund. Typical sources of revenues include various types of taxes, charges for services, fines and forfeits, fees for licenses and permits, interest on investments, and intergovernmental revenues (grants received from other governments). Notice, for example, the types of revenues budgeted by Mt. Lebanon in Table 3-7.

The total amount of any particular revenue source may be accounted for in a single fund or in several funds. For instance, most of the property taxes may be used to finance the General Fund, but a portion may be earmarked for a Special Revenue Fund or the Debt Service Fund. Charges for services may also be earmarked for several funds. Practice varies as to the mechanics of recording revenues apportioned among funds. In some governments, the General Fund initially accounts for all property tax receipts and subsequently transfers the appropriate share to other funds. In other governments, the General Fund and other funds each account directly for their respective shares of total property tax revenue.

Expenditure Classification

Governments are accountable to their citizens for resources spent to achieve governmental objectives. The need both to be accountable and to demonstrate accountability leads governments to

---

[2]GASB Cod. Sec. 2400.102.

use up to five levels of subclassification in budgeting and accounting for expenditures. This detail provides structure for budget development and enables accumulation of expenditure data in various combinations to facilitate reporting and analysis. Turn back to Table 3-7 and notice that, within the General Fund, Mt. Lebanon's budget summary shows amounts for each broad program. The program total may cover expenditures for one or more departments (public safety includes the Police and Fire Departments); each department may perform one or more major activities (the Police Department performs eight activities); and expenditures within each activity are classified by object, such as "regular salaries and wages" and "fringe benefits."

The five expenditure classification levels and an example of each are as follows:

Fund	General Fund
Function/program	Public safety
Organizational unit	Police Department
Activity	Police field services
Object	Overtime wages

The *fund* classification level is obvious and needs no further explanation. *Functions* and *programs* are almost synonymous from a practical standpoint. A function is a group of related activities intended to accomplish a major government responsibility; a program is a group of activities directed toward attaining specific objectives. *Organizational unit* refers to specific departments of the government (fire, police, public works, etc.). Additional examples of the *activity* subclassification within the Police Department are shown in Table 3-7.

Finally, the *object* (object-of-expenditure) classification refers to the physical description of items purchased or services received; for example, regular salaries and wages or personal services (payroll), contractual services such as rent payments, materials and supplies, and equipment. The object-of-expenditure classification is particularly important from a budgetary standpoint because objects are the building blocks of a budget. Also, individual expenditures usually are made at the object level, so comparing budgeted amounts with actual expenditures in terms of objects-of-expenditure is useful for departmental control of expenditures. Governments sometimes classify objects-of-expenditure in two broad classifications—personal services (PS) and other-than-personal services (OTPS)—and identify subclassifications within each of them.

Although this multilevel classification system may appear complex, it is not difficult to work with because the lower-level subclassifications "roll up" into higher-level subclassifications. For example, all the object-of-expenditure amounts within any specified activity will define the budget for that activity. The sum of the budgeted amounts for all the activities within a department defines that department's total budget, and so forth. Table 3-9 presents a diagram of the expenditure classification roll-ups.

Particular reporting situations rarely require that all five classifications be shown simultaneously. External financial reporting requires only that governmental fund expenditures be classified "at a minimum by function."[3] Similarly, internal reporting on a department would focus on expenditures by organizational unit, activity, and object-of-expenditure.

Finally, we need to discuss the concept of *level of budgetary control*. This refers to the level of subclassification within the expenditures budget at which expenditures cannot legally exceed

---

[3]GASB Cod. Sec. 2200.160. In their external fund-level operating statements, many governments (including Mt. Lebanon) classify expenditures by "character", that is, whether they are *current operating, capital outlay,* or *debt service* in nature. Current operating expenditures are shown by program or function, and separate captions are provided for debt service and capital outlay. Classifying by character is readily accomplished by aggregating capital outlay and debt service expenditures according to object code.

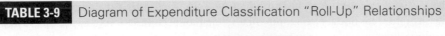

TABLE 3-9   Diagram of Expenditure Classification "Roll-Up" Relationships

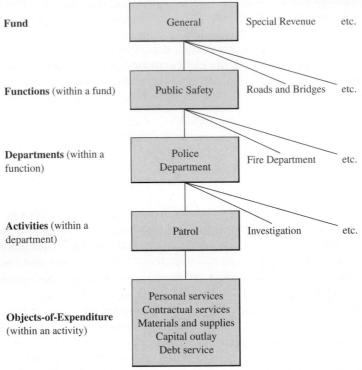

budgeted amounts. The level of control is defined in budgetary or organizational terms, for example, by fund (the highest level), by government department or activity (intermediate levels), or by object-of-expenditure (a low level). Should it become necessary for a department to spend more than the total appropriation at the legal level of control, permission to do so must be obtained. Governments differ as to both the level at which approval must be obtained and the branch of government (e.g., city manager or city council) that may grant approval. Generally, approvals take the form of an amendment to the budget.

A practical consequence of the legal level of budgetary control is that it determines the extent to which department heads and CEOs may use discretion in determining the amounts and purposes for which expenditures are incurred. A high level of budgetary control affords a manager considerable spending discretion, while a low level grants the manager minimum flexibility in making spending decisions.

Thus, if a government has defined the legal level of control at the fund level, the CEO has the authority to allocate the fund's total appropriation as he or she sees fit among the various operations (e.g., functions and departments) accounted for within that fund. If the legal level of budgetary control is established at, say, the department level, the department head has the authority to allocate the department appropriation to various activities as he or she sees fit, but may not incur expenditures in excess of the department appropriation. If a government establishes the legal level of budgetary control at the object-of-expenditure level within each specified activity, a department manager has minimal flexibility to redirect spending.

Mt. Lebanon, for example, does not maintain control at the object-of-expenditure (line item) level. Therefore, if the police chief requires additional police officer overtime, he or she may do so—without approval—by using resources originally budgeted for, say, regular salaries and wages (see Part C of Table 3-7). On the other hand, the police chief may spend additional resources on an activity within the department—say, investigative services—only if (a) he or she identifies another activity in which sufficient funds are available (perhaps police field services) and (b) approval is obtained from the CEO and the finance director (see Part B of Table 3-7).

BUDGETARY ACCOUNTING

The importance of the budget in government accounting is epitomized by *budgetary accounting*. Budgetary accounting has several elements designed to help both the central budget office and departmental managers monitor actual financial performance against the budget. Recording appropriations and spending against the appropriations provides accountability and helps ensure that appropriation limitations are not exceeded. Recording budgeted and actual revenues in the accounting system, as well as appropriations and charges against them, gives the central budget office the data needed to curtail expenditures in response to looming revenue shortfalls.

From the general ledger perspective, it is best to consider the budgetary accounting journal entries separate from the financial accounting entries. Actually, there are only a few types of budgetary journal entries: (a) to record the budget; (b) to record changes to the budget; (c) to record the placing of purchase orders or contracts; and (d) to reverse the entry when items ordered are received. Budgetary controls are facilitated by maintaining subsidiary revenues and appropriations ledgers, and preparing periodic reports comparing budgeted with actual revenues and budgeted appropriations with charges against the appropriations.

Recording the Adopted Budget

To illustrate the budgetary journal entries, assume an entity called Tiny Town performs a single function (public safety) within a single department (the Police Department). The legal level of budgetary control is at object-of-expenditure level. The town council makes appropriations for three objects-of-expenditure. Table 3-10 shows the approved budget for the General Fund for 2012.

TABLE 3-10 General Fund Budget

Tiny Town
General Fund Budget
Calendar Year 2012

Estimated Revenues		
Property taxes	$900,000	
Miscellaneous	100,000	$1,000,000
Appropriations		
Salaries	$700,000	
Materials	190,000	
Police cars	100,000	990,000
Budgeted Increase in Fund Balance		$ 10,000

At the beginning of the fiscal year, Tiny Town makes the following budgetary accounting entry in the General Fund to record the adopted budget.

Estimated revenues	1,000,000	
Appropriations		990,000
Budgetary fund balance		10,000
To record the 2012 budget.		

To best understand this entry, it is useful to decompose it into two parts. First, Tiny Town could record estimated revenues in this manner:

Estimated revenues	1,000,000	
Budgetary fund balance		1,000,000
To record estimated revenues for 2012.		

The debit to Estimated revenues predicts the effect, in isolation, that *actual* revenues will have on the fund balance at the end of the year—that is, actual revenues are predicted to be $1,000,000 and, by themselves, would increase the fund balance by $1,000,000. Likewise, Tiny Town could record its planned expenditures—that is, its budget appropriations—as follows:

Budgetary fund balance	990,000	
Appropriations		990,000
To record appropriations for 2012.		

This entry, in essence, identifies the amount of fund net assets (fund balance) that Tiny Town plans to spend during 2012. That is, expenditures are predicted (authorized) to be $990,000 and, by themselves, would reduce the fund balance by that amount.

The $10,000 credit balance in the Budgetary fund balance account—from the original entry or from the combined effect of its two parts—indicates that Tiny Town expects a budget surplus for the year.[4] That is, if actual revenues and expenditures prove to be exactly as budgeted, the ending actual fund balance will increase by $10,000 (actual revenues of $1,000,000 less expenditures of $990,000 = $10,000). Conversely, if Tiny Town had appropriated an amount greater than estimated revenue, the resulting *debit* balance in the Budgetary fund balance account would signal that Tiny Town anticipates a budget deficit for the year.

In practice, the journal entry to record the budget is prepared in compound form (debiting the two estimated revenue accounts and crediting the three appropriations accounts), as shown later in the chapter. Our purpose in using single estimated revenues and appropriations accounts here was to make it easier to understand the nature of the journal entry.

The purpose of recording estimated revenues and appropriations is to establish reference points for budgetary controls. At any time during the year, government officials can compare the estimated revenues with actual revenues to see if the estimates are being met. Similarly, as charges are being made against the various appropriations accounts, officials can see whether sufficient balances are available for additional spending.

---

[4]Some writers and practitioners prefer to credit Unassigned fund balance (a financial account) rather than Budgetary fund balance (a budgetary account) when recording the budget. We do not recommend this practice because it (a) creates the appearance of increases or decreases in actual fund balance before changes actually occur; (b) may mislead unsophisticated preparers and users of financial reports; and (c) needlessly confuses budgetary accounting with financial accounting.

Recording Encumbrances

The other basic element of budgetary accounting involves recording *encumbrances* against the amounts available for appropriation. Encumbrances reduce the amounts available for appropriation for items *ordered* by a government but not yet received. Recall that a business entity ordinarily makes three entries related to the purchase and use of supplies: one to record the liability for the purchase, a second to record payment of the liability, and a third (or series of entries) to record supplies used. Businesses do not make formal accounting entries to record items on order. In contrast, from the budgetary perspective, a portion of the appropriation effectively is "used up," or *encumbered,* at the point a government orders supplies—even though the supplies have not yet been received. Thus, a government may make four entries related to the purchase and use of supplies: The first entry encumbers the appropriation for the cost of an order placed with a supplier, a second records the liability for the purchase, and a third records payment of the liability. Depending on the nature of the accounting system, a fourth entry (or series of entries) may be made to record supplies used.

At the point it issues a purchase order, a government expresses its *intent* to incur an expenditure (a reduction of net assets). From a financial accounting standpoint, the expenditure is not recognized until the related liability is incurred, typically when the ordered materials are received. From a budgetary accounting standpoint, however, the purchase order uses up a portion of the appropriation. The government gives formal accounting recognition to the order by recording an *encumbrance* equal to the purchase order amount. If Tiny Town were to issue a purchase order for $1,000, the entry to record the encumbrance would be this:

Encumbrances	1,000	
Budgetary fund balance reserved for encumbrances		1,000
To record encumbrance for purchase order.		

The encumbrance (debit) reduces the net available appropriation. The "budgetary fund balance reserved for encumbrances" is, in effect, a placeholder for the ensuing liability. When the open purchase order is fulfilled (i.e., ordered items are received), the encumbrance entry is reversed, and an expenditure is recorded. Assuming that the cost of goods received equals the cost of goods ordered, Tiny Town would make the following two entries:

Budgetary fund balance reserved for encumbrances	1,000	
Encumbrances		1,000
To reverse encumbrances.		
Expenditures	1,000	
Vouchers payable (or Cash)		1,000
To record expenditure for purchased materials.		

Thus, at any time, the available appropriation equals the amount appropriated minus the total of the outstanding encumbrances (for purchase orders placed but not received) and the expenditures. Note that the purpose of recording encumbrances is to provide control over an appropriation characterized by expenditures that are unpredictable as to timing and/or amount, or in cases in which a single appropriation supports geographically dispersed activities. In contrast, some appropriations are drawn down by expenditures in predictable patterns, (e.g., monthly payments on a photocopier lease). For such appropriations, encumbrances serve no control purpose and need not be recorded; the amount available for spending is reduced directly by recording the expenditure.

Detailed Illustration

We are now ready to illustrate the budgetary accounting entries within the context of an example that contains both budgetary and financial accounting entries. This will help you see how budgetary accounting helps maintain budgetary control. Budgetary control—through budget-to-actual comparisons—is facilitated by maintaining *subsidiary revenues and appropriations ledgers* to which postings are made from both the financial accounting entries and the budgetary accounting entries. We will start with the Tiny Town budget from Table 3-10 and add some budgetary and financial accounting transactions. (To simplify the illustration, the financial accounting transactions shown here are cash-based; modified accrual accounting is introduced in Chapter 4.) We will also post the transactions to the subsidiary ledgers. The events and transactions for January 2012 are as follows:

Date

January 2	The budget is recorded.
3	Property taxes of $500,000 are received in cash.
8	Two police cars are ordered at an estimated total cost of $46,000.
12	Police cars ordered Jan. 8 are received at an invoiced cost of $45,000.
15	Miscellaneous revenues totaling $13,000 are received in cash.
16	Two more police cars are ordered at an estimated total cost of $54,000.
21	Police cars ordered Jan. 16 are received with an invoice for $55,000.
22	Property taxes of $399,500 are received in cash.
25	Materials are ordered with an expected cost of $15,000.
28	The ordered materials are received along with an invoice for $16,000.
31	Payday for Tiny Town's employees is the last day of the month; salaries of $60,000 are paid.

Here is how the Tiny Town transactions are recorded in general journal form and how the entries affect the revenues ledger (Table 3-11) and appropriations ledger (Table 3-12):

Jan. 2	Estimated revenues—property taxes	900,000	
	Estimated revenues—miscellaneous	100,000	
	Appropriations—salaries		700,000
	Appropriations—materials		190,000
	Appropriations—police cars		100,000
	Budgetary fund balance		10,000
	To record the budget in the general ledger.		

Notice that the debit items in the above entry are posted for each revenue source in the estimated revenues columns of the revenues ledger, and the credits to appropriations are posted for each appropriation in the appropriations columns of the appropriations ledger. The balance column of the revenues ledger now shows debit balances of $900,000 for property taxes and $100,000 for miscellaneous revenue, indicating that no actual revenues have yet been recorded. In the appropriations ledger, the available appropriations columns show the full amounts appropriated as available for spending because there have not yet been any encumbrances or expenditures.

Jan. 3	Cash	500,000	
	Revenues—property taxes		500,000
	To record receipt of property taxes in the general ledger.		

| **TABLE 3-11** | Illustrative Revenues Ledger |

Tiny Town
General Fund
Revenues Ledger
January 2012

Source: Property Taxes

Date	Item	Estimated Revenues Dr	Actual Revenues Cr	Difference Dr (Cr)
2	Budget	900,000		900,000
3	Cash receipts		500,000	400,000
22	Cash receipts		399,500	500

Source: Miscellaneous

Date	Item	Estimated Revenues Dr	Actual Revenues Cr	Difference Dr (Cr)
2	Budget	100,000		100,000
15	Cash receipts		13,000	87,000

The credit to Revenues from this entry is posted by source to the *actual* revenues column of the revenues ledger; the resulting $400,000 balance indicates that this amount of property tax revenues remains to be realized to meet the budget estimate.

Jan. 8	Encumbrances—police cars	46,000	
	Budgetary fund balance reserved for encumbrances		46,000
	To record encumbrance for purchase of police cars.		

The debit to Encumbrances from the January 8 entry is posted to the encumbrances column of the appropriations ledger for the police cars appropriation. The resulting $54,000 balance in the available appropriation column shows that this is the amount of the police car appropriation remaining available for future spending.

Jan. 12	Budgetary fund balance reserved for encumbrances	46,000	
	Encumbrances—police cars		46,000
	To reverse encumbrance for purchase of police cars.		
	Expenditures—police cars	45,000	
	Vouchers payable		45,000
	To record purchase of police cars.		

Notice that the credit to Encumbrances in the first January 12 entry, when posted to the encumbrances column in the appropriations ledger for police cars, reverses the encumbrance previously posted. Reversing the encumbrance restores—momentarily—the available police car appropriation to the original $100,000 amount. The debit to Expenditures from the second January 12 entry, when posted to the expenditures column, reduces the available police car appropriation to $55,000. The net effect of posting the two journal entries is that the encumbrance for $46,000 has been replaced with an expenditure for $45,000. Hence, whereas the available

| TABLE 3-12 | Illustrative Appropriations Ledger |

Tiny Town
General Fund
Appropriations Ledger
January 2012

Object Code: Salaries

Date	Item	Appropriation Cr	Encumbrances Dr	Encumbrances Cr	Expenditures Dr	Available Appropriation Cr
2	Budget	700,000				700,000
31	Payroll				60,000	640,000

Object Code: Materials

Date	Item	Appropriation Cr	Encumbrances Dr	Encumbrances Cr	Expenditures Dr	Available Appropriation Cr
2	Budget	190,000				190,000
25	Order materials		15,000			175,000
28	Receive materials			15,000		190,000
28	Record expenditure				16,000	174,000

Object Code: Police Cars

Date	Item	Appropriation Cr	Encumbrances Dr	Encumbrances Cr	Expenditures Dr	Available Appropriation Cr
2	Budget	100,000				100,000
8	Order 2 vehicles		46,000			54,000
12	Receive 2 vehicles			46,000		100,000
12	Record expenditure				45,000	55,000
16	Order 2 vehicles		54,000			1,000
21	Receive 2 vehicles			54,000		55,000
21	Record expenditure				55,000	0

appropriation balance was $54,000 on January 8 after the encumbrance was recorded, the available appropriation balance on January 12—after the invoice was received—is $55,000 because the actual cost of this purchase was $1,000 less than anticipated.

Jan. 15	Cash	13,000	
	Revenues—miscellaneous		13,000
	To record collection of miscellaneous revenue.		

The credit to miscellaneous revenue, when posted to the actual revenues column of the revenues ledger, reduces the estimated revenues to be received to $87,000. Year-to-date comparisons of amounts collected with amounts normally collected in comparable periods helps budget officials determine if the estimate for the year is likely to be achieved.

Jan. 16	Encumbrances—police cars	54,000	
	Budgetary fund balance reserved for encumbrances		54,000
	To record encumbrance for purchase of police cars.		

The debit to Encumbrances from the January 16 entry is posted to the encumbrances column of the appropriations ledger appropriation for police cars. The resulting $1,000 credit balance in the available appropriation column shows that, at the time the second police car order is encumbered, Tiny Town still has $1,000 of police car appropriation available for future spending.

Jan. 21	Budgetary fund balance reserved for encumbrances	54,000	
	Encumbrances—police cars		54,000
	To reverse encumbrance for purchase of police cars.		
	Expenditures—police cars	55,000	
	Vouchers payable		55,000
	To record purchase of police cars.		

Similar to the January 12 entries, the credit to Encumbrances from the first January 21 entry reverses the encumbrance previously posted in the appropriations ledger. Reversing the encumbrance raises the available police car appropriation temporarily to $55,000. The debit to Expenditures from the second January 21 entry zeroes out the available appropriation for police cars. The unanticipated $1,000 extra cost of the second order of police cars absorbed the remaining appropriation in its entirety. If the invoice had been for an amount greater than $55,000, the police cars could not have been accepted without an increase in the police cars appropriation by the town council.

Jan. 22	Cash	399,500	
	Revenues—property taxes		399,500
	To record receipt of property tax revenue.		

Similar to the January 3 entry, the credit to Revenues in the January 22 entry is posted to the actual column of the revenues ledger account for property taxes. The resulting $500 debit amount in the balance column shows that, to this point, actual property tax revenues are less than estimated property tax revenues by $500.

Jan. 25	Encumbrances—materials	15,000	
	Budgetary fund balance reserved for encumbrances		15,000
	To record encumbrance for purchase of materials.		

The debit to Encumbrances in the January 25 entry, $15,000, is posted to the encumbrances column of the appropriations ledger account for the materials object. As a result, $175,000 of the appropriation remains available for spending.

Jan. 28	Budgetary fund balance reserved for encumbrances	15,000	
	Encumbrances—materials		15,000
	To reverse encumbrance for materials purchased.		
	Expenditures—materials	16,000	
	Vouchers payable		16,000
	To record receipt of materials ordered Jan. 25.		

Posting the credit to Encumbrances in the first of the January 28 entries to the appropriations ledger reverses the encumbrance of January 25, resulting in the temporary restoration of the available materials appropriation to $190,000. The $16,000 debit to Expenditures in the second January 28 entry, when posted to the expenditures column of the appropriations ledger, reduces the available appropriation to $174,000. (One might expect that the invoice would be for the same amount as the purchase order. However, a purchase order might permit a supplier to ship a quantity that is, say, 10 percent more than the amount ordered.)

Jan. 30 Expenditures—salaries	60,000	
Cash		60,000
To record disbursement of payroll at month end.		

The end-of-month payroll entry is posted to the expenditures column of the appropriations ledger in the salaries account, leaving an available balance of $640,000. First, notice that this expenditure was not preceded by an encumbrance. Salaries generally are not encumbered because budgetary control is maintained through a separate "vacancy control" procedure, whereby all the positions covered by the budget are listed (see the personal services worksheet in Table 3-4 on page 69), showing the name of the individual occupying the position. Vacancies may be filled, not filled, or delayed in being filled, depending on operational needs and how much of the appropriation remains available. Second, notice that the $60,000 expenditure is slightly more than 1/12 of $700,000. This might raise a "red flag" for budget officials. But an efficient police chief will know that several officers will retire shortly and that hiring replacements at lower pay levels will ensure that sufficient funds will be available to meet the payroll for the rest of the year.

We see from this illustration how the revenues and appropriations ledgers provide useful information about actual account balances compared with budgeted amounts. For instance, after Tiny Town received the first two police cars, the appropriations ledger showed that the remaining available appropriation was $55,000. As a result, the town was able to buy better-equipped cars when it placed the second order. Close monitoring of encumbrance and expenditure *rates* on the materials and personal services appropriations enables budget officials to ensure there will be sufficient amounts available to finance operations for the full year. Similarly, a report based on the data provided by the revenues ledger will enable budget officials to determine promptly the likelihood of a shortfall from budgeted amounts.

OTHER ASPECTS OF BUDGETARY ACCOUNTING

Budgetary Interchanges and Other Revisions

Events may occur during the year that warrant changes to the originally adopted budget. For example, unforeseen events or conditions may arise that require increasing a particular appropriation. Or an economic contraction may occur that warrants reducing the estimated sales tax revenues or some other revenue source; in that event, the government may also decide to reduce several appropriations to keep the budget in balance. The type of budgetary action to be taken in these circumstances depends on such factors as the budgetary condition of the department requiring an appropriation increase and the financial condition of the government itself.

Returning to the Tiny Town illustration, suppose an unforeseen event occurs that requires an $8,000 increase in overtime, which is paid for from the salaries appropriation. Analysis of the expenditure rate for the other appropriations might show that the Police Department will not need to spend the entire amount appropriated for materials. A *budgetary interchange* will autho-rize the department to spend an additional $8,000 for salaries and simultaneously reduce the spending authorization for materials. The journal entry is this:

Appropriations—materials	8,000	
Appropriations—salaries		8,000
To record budgetary interchange as a result of unforeseen event.		

Notice that, as a result of the interchange, the total amount budgeted by Tiny Town does not change. But, if the Police Department were unable to finance its additional salary needs by reducing one of its other appropriations, the town might need to make a *budgetary revision.* Tiny Town's original budget for 2012 estimated a $10,000 increase in fund balance. It could use that planned "surplus" to finance the increase in the salaries appropriation. The journal entry would be this:

Budgetary fund balance	8,000	
Appropriations—salaries		8,000
To record budgetary revision as a result of unforeseen event.		

For another illustration, suppose Tiny Town's budget officer were to make a mid year review of the budgetary situation. She finds that, because of a sluggish economy, miscellaneous revenues are coming in at a rate lower than anticipated and that, for the full year, they will prob-ably be $15,000 less than originally budgeted. The town had budgeted for a $10,000 surplus, so another $5,000 must be found to ensure the town will maintain a balanced budget for the year. Therefore, the mayor may order the police chief to "hold the line" on spending from the materials appropriation or to stop hiring police officers when vacancies arise. When the council authorizes a *budget revision*, the following journal entry is made to reduce the estimated miscellaneous rev-enues by $15,000 and, say, the materials appropriation by $5,000:

Appropriations—materials	5,000	
Budgetary fund balance	10,000	
Estimated revenues—miscellaneous		15,000
To record budgetary revision.		

The original budget, adjusted by all legally authorized legislative and executive changes applicable to the fiscal year (including budgetary interchanges and other budget revisions) is called the *final budget.*

Encumbrance Accounting Details

As noted earlier in the chapter, the amount of an invoice may be more or less than the amount of the purchase order. This may occur for various reasons; for example, the purchase order may be based on an estimate; or the purchase order may permit the supplier to ship a quantity greater than the amount ordered, up to a specified percentage; or the final price of the item(s) may depend on the cost of a specific component.

If the amount of the invoice differs from the amount of the purchase order, the expenditure obviously will be either greater or smaller than the amount encumbered when the order was placed. The key thing to remember is that the journal entry to reverse the encumbrance must be *in the same amount as the amount originally encumbered*; the expenditure must be recorded for the actual invoice amount. As a result of the journal entries, the unencumbered balance of the appropriation is automatically adjusted because the original encumbrance in the appropriations ledger is replaced with an expenditure for the actual amount of the purchase.

But what if a department receives only a portion of the items ordered, with the remaining items back-ordered by the supplier for later delivery? In that event, the encumbrance should be reversed only in the proportion that the quantity of items received bears to the total quantity ordered. For example, if a department orders 10 chairs at a cost of $150 per chair, it will record an encumbrance for $1,500 (10 × $150). If it receives only 4 chairs, with the other 6 to be delivered at a later date, it will reverse the encumbrance in the amount of $600 (4 × $150). The remainder of the encumbrance will be reversed when the department receives the other 6 chairs. If the supplier continues to delay delivery and the department decides to cancel the remaining 6 chairs, it will reverse the encumbrance at the time of cancellation.

On occasion, the amount available for an appropriation that is normally subject to encumbrance accounting may be reduced directly by an expenditure without recording an encumbrance. This may occur, for example, if an unforeseen emergency requires immediate acquisition of an item without issuing a purchase order.

Allotment Systems

Some governments use allotment systems to help control departmental expenditure rates. When allotment systems are used, the central budget office subdivides the appropriations into *time-based allotments*, usually for a quarter-year at a time. Because the allotment system permits departments to spend no more than the amount of the quarterly allotment, the central budget office is in a position to react rapidly to changing economic conditions by reducing the amount the agencies may spend in the latter part of the year.

When an allotment system is used, the appropriations accounts are retitled "Unallotted appropriations." The budgetary journal entry is this (amounts assumed):

Estimated revenues—various sources	5,000,000	
Unalloted appropriations—various functions		4,900,000
Budgetary fund balance		100,000
To record 2013 budget.		

Each time the central budget office makes allotments to the departments, the Unallotted appropriations accounts are debited and the Allotments accounts are credited. If, for example, the first quarter's allotments total $1,225,000, the following journal entry is made:

Unallotted appropriations—various functions	1,225,000	
Allotments—various functions		1,225,000
To record first quarter's allotments.		

The government may maintain either a combined appropriations/allotments ledger or a separate allotments ledger. In either case, the individual departments may spend (or encumber) no more than the amounts allotted to them. The final column of the ledger is headed *Available*

Allotment, and encumbrances and expenditures are posted to the ledger in the same way they are made to the appropriations ledger, previously illustrated.

Review Questions

Q3-1   What is a budget? What purposes does it serve?

Q3-2   Identify the types of budgets prepared by state and local governments.

Q3-3   Identify various approaches to budget preparation. Which approach is most common in practice?

Q3-4   What is the purpose of cash forecasting, and how does it assist in the smooth functioning of a government?

Q3-5   List the steps involved in preparing a budget.

Q3-6   What information should be included in a set of budgetary instructions?

Q3-7   What is the purpose of a budget calendar?

Q3-8   What is a capital budget? Why should it be prepared for a period greater than one year?

Q3-9   What is a millage rate? How is it determined?

Q3-10   What is an *appropriation*?

Q3-11   What is meant by the term *legal level of budgetary control*? Cite some examples.

Q3-12   Does the balance in the Estimated revenues account represent an asset? Why or why not?

Q3-13   What information is conveyed by the Budgetary fund balance account?

Q3-14   Identify five typical sources of revenues received by local governments.

Q3-15   Identify the various subclassifications of expenditures used in governmental budgeting and accounting.

Q3-16   What is the purpose of encumbrance accounting?

Discussion Scenarios and Issues

D3-1   The City of Toth produces monthly budgetary control reports. The amount shown in the budget column is $1/12$ of the annual budget. Over lunch, two department heads were discussing this report. The first manager said, "I like the idea of using $1/12$ of my annual budget each month. My costs are constant throughout the year. I can usually find small savings and show favorable variances each month." The second manager disagreed. "I don't like it. Most of my costs are incurred during Carnival and around Christmas. As a result, I always have unfavorable variances in March and December regardless of what I do. It is especially upsetting because employee performance appraisals are made in April, and the council looks especially hard at our March results." What is the problem with the way these control reports are prepared? What should be done to make the reports more reflective of the actual performance of the departments?

D3-2   Your state legislature is considering a balanced budget amendment. One proposed approach defines balanced budgets as ones in which estimated revenues for the year equal that year's appropriations. A second defines balanced budgets as ones in which expected resources available at the beginning of a fiscal year (beginning fund balance plus estimated revenues) equal that year's appropriations. A third defines balanced budgets similarly to the second, but would require that the beginning fund balance be maintained at a particular level (e.g., 5 percent of revenues) except in specifically defined circumstances, such as a recession that lasts more than 18 months. Which approach would you prefer and why?

D3-3   During lunch, the director of the Streets and Parkways Department of Thor City made the following comment: "For the past 10 years, I have deliberately overstated my labor and equipment needs by 20 percent when preparing my budget request. I figure that the city council will cut it by 10 percent, and I can use the other 10 percent as slack. If there is money left over, I can always find a way to spend it." Do you consider this behavior to be ethical? If not, what steps might you, as budget director, take to cut down on this "padding"?

D3-4   Rex, a budget officer, conducted a class for nonaccounting managers and program directors on the subject of budgets. Rex began the class discussion by asking, "What are some of the uses of a budget?" One manager replied, "Planning." Another said, "Evaluating performance." Still another suggested, "Coordinating activities." "What about implementing plans?" inquired another. "Or communicating them?" added still another. "Don't forget motivation," one manager warned from the rear of the room. "I'm on the school board," commented another, "and we use it to authorize actions." Finally, one manager asked, "Can budgets do all that?" "Yes," Rex responded, "all that and more." Select four of the uses suggested by the mangers, and explain how budgets accomplish those uses.

Exercises

E3-1   (Budgeting cash disbursements)
A city is preparing its cash forecast for the month of July. Based on the following information, compute the estimated cash disbursements for July.

Items vouchered in July	$650,000
Estimated payments in July for items vouchered in July	50%
Items vouchered in June	$400,000
Estimated payments in July for all items vouchered in June	70%
Estimated payments in July for items vouchered prior to June	$50,000
Items vouchered in June but returned in July before payment was made	$20,000

E3-2   (Budgeting cash receipts)
A city is preparing its cash forecast for the month of May. Using the following information, compute the estimated cash receipts from sales tax collections in May.

Sales tax rate	5%
Estimated retail sales in May	$2,000,000
Actual retail sales in April	$1,500,000
Estimated percentage of May sales resulting in sales taxes remitted by merchants to city in May	20%
Estimated percentage of April sales resulting in sales taxes remitted by merchants to city in May	70%

E3-3   (Determination of property tax rate)
The county legislature approved the budget for 2013. Revenues from property taxes are budgeted at $800,000. According to the county assessor, the assessed valuation of all of the property in the county is $50 million. Of this amount, property worth $10 million belongs to the federal government or to religious organizations and, therefore, is not subject to property taxes. In addition, certificates for the following exemptions have been filed:

Homestead	$2,500,000
Veterans	1,000,000
Old age, blindness, etc.	500,000

In the past, uncollectible property taxes averaged about 3 percent of the levy. This rate is not expected to change in the foreseeable future. Using all of this information, determine (a) the property tax rate that must be used to collect the desired revenues from property taxes and (b) the levy on a piece of property that was assessed for $100,000 (after exemptions).

E3-4   (Estimating the fund balance at the end of the year)
At the end of the preceding year, the General Fund of the Atlas Township School Board had a fund balance of $800,000. General Fund revenues and expenditures for the current year are expected to be as shown here. Determine the projected year-end fund balance for this fund.

	Year-to-Date Actual	Remainder of Year Estimated
Revenues		
Property taxes	$1,250,000	$500,000
Out-of-township tuition	50,000	20,000
Share of lottery receipts	100,000	50,000
State grants	500,000	—
Expenditures		
Salaries	$ 875,000	$450,000
Fringe benefits	90,000	40,000
Operating expenses	588,000	240,000
Equipment	110,000	50,000
Transportation	15,000	10,000
Debt service	100,000	100,000

E3-5   (Multiple choice)
1. What is a key difference between budgets prepared by governmental units and by commercial organizations?
    a. Budgets prepared by commercial organizations must be approved by a governing body, whereas those prepared by governmental units need no approvals.
    b. Budgets prepared by governmental units are legal documents, whereas those prepared by commercial organizations are not.
    c. Operating and capital budgets and cash forecasts are prepared by governmental units, but only operating budgets are prepared by commercial organizations.
    d. Budgets prepared by commercial organizations are formally recorded in the organizations' operating accounts, whereas those prepared by governmental units are not.
2. Which of the following is not included when preparing cash forecasts?
    a. Personal services
    b. Redemption of bonds
    c. Utilities
    d. Depreciation
3. Who prepares a nondepartmental expenditures request?
    a. The department heads as a group
    b. The auditor
    c. The city council
    d. The CEO or the budget director
4. When the city's budget is approved, the total amount appropriated is greater than the estimated revenues. What are the implications of that budget?
    a. The city anticipates a budget surplus for the year.
    b. The city anticipates a budget deficit for the year.
    c. The city anticipates neither a budget surplus nor a deficit for the year.
    d. The city will need to credit the account Budgetary fund balance.
5. Which of the following events results in a debit to the Encumbrances account?
    a. The budget is approved.
    b. Supplies are received.
    c. A purchase order is placed.
    d. An invoice is paid.
6. In the appropriations ledger, the amount available for appropriation is equal to
    a. the total appropriation minus total invoices paid.
    b. the total appropriation minus outstanding encumbrances.

      c. the total appropriation minus expenditures.

      d. the total appropriation minus both outstanding encumbrances and expenditures.

    7. A city places a purchase order for police sedans at an estimated price of $100,000. The purchase order allows the supplier to increase the price by up to 5 percent if the price of steel increases. The city receives the sedans along with an invoice for $104,000. With what amount should the city credit the Encumbrances account?

      a. $1,000

      b. $4,000

      c. $100,000

      d. $104,000

E3-6   (Budget laws)

Every state has a law(s) regulating its own budgetary practices and those of its local governmental units. Check the law(s) of your state to determine the following:

    1. Are budgets legally required by local governmental units, such as cities and counties, in your state?

    2. For what funds must budgets be prepared?

    3. Must governmental budgets prepared in your state be "balanced"? If so, what does your state law consider to be a balanced budget?

    4. What legal provisions are made for public input into the budgetary process in your state?

E3-7   (Budgetary fund balance)

Compute the debit or credit, if any, to be made to the Budgetary fund balance for a county's General Fund under each of the following assumptions:

    a. Budgeted revenues and expenditures each are $30,000,000.

    b. Budgeted revenues are $30,000,000, and budgeted expenditures are $31,500,000.

    c. Budgeted revenues are $33,000,000, and budgeted expenditures are $32,600,000.

E3-8   (Budgetary accounting)

Sleepy Hollow's General Fund budget for fiscal 2013 is based on the following estimated revenues and appropriations. Is Sleepy Hollow projecting a budgetary surplus or a deficit for 2013? Prepare the journal entry to record the 2013 budget.

Estimated Revenue		**Appropriations**	
Property taxes	$2,000,000	Administration	$ 425,000
Sales taxes	720,000	Public safety	1,500,000
Licenses and permits	120,000	Streets	630,000
Fines and forfeits	8,500	Parks and recreation	367,000

E3-9   (Relationship between budgetary fund balance and actual fund balance)

The Village of Albert's Alley recorded the following budgetary journal entry at the beginning of fiscal 2013:

Estimated revenue	5,000,000	
Appropriations		4,950,000
Budgetary fund balance		50,000

At the end of fiscal 2013, what would be the effect on the ending *actual* fund balance, assuming the following:

    a. Actual revenues are equal to estimated revenues, and actual expenditures are $7,000 less than appropriations.

    b. Actual revenues are equal to estimated revenues, and actual expenditures are equal to appropriations.

    c. Actual revenues exceed estimated revenues by $4,000, and actual expenditures are equal to appropriations.

    d. Actual revenues are $3,000 less than estimated revenues, and actual expenditures are $2,000 less than appropriations.

E3-10   (Encumbrance journal entries)

A village ordered supplies for its Fire Department at an estimated cost of $16,700. The supplies were received with an invoice for $16,800. The village accepted the shipment and the invoice. Prepare journal entries to record these transactions in the General Fund.

Note: Credit Vouchers payable when the expenditure is recorded; classify the expenditure as Public safety.

E3-11   (Encumbrance journal entries)

Prepare journal entries to record the following transactions for the Village of Radnor. Classify the expenditures as Parks supplies.

1. Placed purchase order 960 for supplies in the amount of $8,000 and purchase order 961 for supplies in the amount of $6,000. The purchase orders allowed the suppliers to ship and bill for additional quantities, up to 5 percent of the order.

2. Received the supplies ordered on purchase order 960, together with an invoice for $8,300. The supplies, including the additional quantities, were accepted, and a voucher was prepared for $8,300.

3. Received all the supplies ordered on purchase order 961, together with an invoice for $5,800. The supplier said that production costs were less than anticipated, and it was passing the lower cost on to Radnor. A voucher for $5,800 was prepared.

4. The voucher for $8,300 was paid.

E3-12   (Effect of transactions on balance of appropriation available for spending)

Assume the Parks Department in E3-11 had received an appropriation for supplies in the amount of $35,000. After processing the journal entries in E3-11, calculate the balance left in the appropriation for spending.

E3-13   (Encumbrances and partial orders)

On October 1, 2013, the City of Highland placed an order with Ajax Sand & Gravel Co. for 1,000 tons of cinders to be spread upon Highland's streets during winter storms. The estimated cost of the cinders was $10 per ton, delivered. Ajax delivered 800 tons of cinders to Highland's road maintenance yard on October 20, along with an invoice for $8,000. Ajax delivered the remaining 200 tons of cinders on November 1, along with an invoice for $2,000. Prepare the General Fund journal entries necessary on October 1, October 20, and November 1, 2013. Classify the expenditures as Road maintenance.

E3-14   (Budget revision)

The town council received an increasing number of complaints from citizens about the poor condition of some of the streets following an exceptionally harsh winter. In response, the town council directed that the public safety appropriation be reduced by $500,000 to support an increase in the town's streets and bridges appropriation. Prepare the journal entry to record this event.

Problems

P3-1   (Budgeting revenues)

The following information relates to the prior- and current-year revenues of the Jeter Village General Fund.

	2011 Actual	Jan.–Sept. 2012 Actual	Oct.–Dec. 2012 Est. Act.	2012 Budget
Property taxes	$5,436,720	$4,084,000	$1,400,000	$5,504,000
Interest and penalties	38,486	22,800	15,000	38,000
Sales taxes	872,680	454,500	445,000	900,000
Fines and penalties	64,842	39,240	30,000	70,000
Share of lottery receipts	—	54,250	175,750	225,000
License fees	9,650	7,540	2,460	10,000

Additional information:

1. Because of a reassessment of commercial property, property taxes are expected to increase by $400,000 in 2013.
2. Interest and penalties and license fees are expected to remain constant over the next several years.
3. Because of an increase in the sales tax from 4 percent to 5 percent and the expected hosting of several large conventions in 2013, sales tax revenues are expected to increase by 20 percent.
4. Because of the conventions just mentioned, fines and penalties should rise by 10 percent in 2013.
5. Because of the lottery's success in its first few months of operation, city officials expect the village's share of the lottery receipts to double in 2013.

Using Table 3-3 as a guide, prepare a statement of actual and estimated revenues for 2012 and budgeted revenues for 2013. Prepare the 2013 budgeted revenues by applying the additional information to the estimated actual revenues for the full calendar year 2012 and rounding the result to the nearest $1,000.

P3-2   (Budget summary)
Using your answers from the preceding problem and the following information, prepare a budget summary for the General Fund of Jeter Village for fiscal year 2013. Assume that the fund balance at the beginning of 2013 is $2,607,241.

1. The Village has three departments: Public Safety, Administration, Streets and Parkways.
2. Budgeted appropriations for the three departments for fiscal year 2013 are as follows:

	Public Safety	Administration	Streets and Parkways
Personal services	$1,115,000	$1,450,000	$1,846,285
Travel	10,000	20,000	1,850
Equipment	650,000	100,000	80,900
Operating expenses	85,000	60,000	36,450

3. Budgeted nondepartmental items include a $1 million transfer to the Debt Service Fund and a $50,000 transfer to the Derek Park Fund.

P3-3   (Budgetary journal entry)
If the Jeter Village council adopts the budget as submitted, prepare the journal entry to record the adopted budget.

P3-4   (Budgetary journal entry)
A city adopted the following budget for its General Fund for 2013. Prepare the journal entry to record the budget.

Estimated Revenues

Property taxes	$ 9,500,000
Sales taxes	1,835,000
Fines and forfeits	65,500
Intergovernmental	1,455,250
	$12,855,750

Appropriations

Administration	$ 2,250,000
Public safety	4,770,500
Parks and recreation	1,150,000
Streets	3,435,000
Libraries	900,000
	$12,505,500

P3-5   (Budgetary accounting)
Prepare journal entries to record the following transactions and events affecting the General Fund of the Village of Kowitt Gorge during fiscal 2013.

1. The annual budget was adopted as follows:

    Estimated Revenues

Property taxes	$1,600,000
Fines and forfeits	150,000
Intergovernmental	475,000
	$2,225,000

    Appropriations

General government	$ 210,000
Public safety	1,580,000
Streets	395,000
	$2,185,000

2. Purchase orders were issued for supplies with the following estimated costs:

General government	$ 210,000
Public safety	1,450,000
Streets	395,000
	$2,055,000

3. Revenues were received in cash as follows:

Property taxes	$ 855,000
Fines and forfeits	117,000
Intergovernmental	295,000
	$1,267,000

4. Items on order were received and accepted, and vouchers were prepared, as follows. (Amounts shown as "Estimated" are the purchase order amounts; amounts shown as "Actual" are the approved invoice amounts.)

	Estimated	Actual
General government	$ 165,000	$ 163,500
Public safety	719,000	720,100
Streets	135,000	134,000
	$1,019,000	$1,017,600

5. The Kowitt Gorge village council revised the budget, reducing the public safety appropriation by $120,000 and increasing the streets appropriation by a similar amount.
6. Additional revenues were received in cash as follows:

Property taxes	$742,000
Fines and forfeits	37,000
Intergovernmental	181,000
	$960,000

7. Items on order were received and accepted, and vouchers were prepared, as follows:

	Estimated	Actual
General government	$ 45,000	$ 45,000
Public safety	693,700	691,250
Streets	234,800	235,350
	$973,500	$971,600

P3-6   (Revenues and appropriations subsidiary ledgers)
Prepare the revenues and expenditures subsidiary ledgers for the 2013 Village of Kowitt Gorge transactions and events listed in P3-5. What are the balances for each individual source of revenues after the final transaction? What are the available appropriations for each function after the final transaction?

P3-7   (Journal entries and subsidiary ledgers)
The events and transactions listed below took place in the General Fund of Lawton City during fiscal 2013. Prepare the necessary general journal entries.

1. The General Fund annual operating budget was adopted as follows:

Estimated Revenues

Property taxes	$2,550,000
Charges for services	400,000
Miscellaneous	175,000
	$3,125,000

Appropriations

Administration	$ 465,000
Public safety	1,860,000
Roads and bridges	930,000
	$3,255,000

2. Purchase orders were issued for supplies with the following estimated costs:

Administration	$ 465,000
Public safety	1,860,000
Roads and bridges	930,000
	$3,255,000

3. Revenues were received in cash as follows:

Property taxes	$2,005,000
Charges for services	248,000
Miscellaneous	65,000
	$2,318,000

4. Some of the supplies ordered in transaction 2 were received and accepted, and vouchers were approved for payment, as follows. (Amounts shown in the "Estimated" column are the purchase order amounts; amounts shown in the "Actual" column are the approved invoice amounts.)

	Estimated	Actual
Administration	$ 265,000	$ 263,500
Public safety	902,000	902,000
Roads and bridges	776,000	776,000
	$1,943,000	$1,941,500

5. Additional revenues were received in cash as follows:

Property taxes	$535,000
Charges for services	155,000
Miscellaneous	111,000
	$801,000

6. Additional purchase orders from transaction 2 were fulfilled with the following estimated and actual costs:

	Estimated	Actual
Administration	$ 200,000	$ 201,000
Public safety	948,000	947,000
Roads and bridges	154,000	153,500
	$1,302,000	$1,301,500

P3-8   (Revenues and appropriations subsidiary ledgers)

Prepare the revenues and expenditures subsidiary ledgers for the 2013 events and transactions of Lawton City listed in P3-7. What is the balance for each revenue source after the final transaction? What is the available appropriation for each function after the final transaction?

P3-9   (Budgetary revisions)

The following budgetary events occurred in Marilyn County during calendar year 2013:

1. The legislature approved the following budget:

Estimated Revenues	
Property taxes	$1,000,000
Sales taxes	2,900,000
Appropriations	
General government—salaries	$ 800,000
General government—all other	400,000
Parks—salaries	2,000,000
Parks—all other	600,000

2. Because a special event necessitated hiring temporary personnel, the legislature approved a budgetary interchange, authorizing the Parks Department to spend an additional $60,000 in salaries and reducing the Parks Department appropriation for "all other" by an equal amount.

3. Based on a mid-year review of the impact of the economy on tax revenues, the finance commissioner estimated that sales tax collections would be $125,000 less than the estimate used in preparing the original budget. The legislature revised the budget by reducing estimated sales tax revenues by $125,000 and reducing the appropriation for General government—all other by $75,000.

Prepare journal entries to record these events. Also, prepare a two-column schedule showing the original adopted budget and the final budget. (The final budget will show the effects of the two budget revisions. The line showing the difference between estimated revenues and appropriations should be captioned "Excess of estimated revenues over appropriations.")

Chapter 4

The Governmental Fund Accounting Cycle

An Introduction to General and Special Revenue Funds

Chapter Outline

Learning Objectives

Background
    The General Fund
    Special Revenue Funds
    Revenue and Expenditure Recognition
    Short-Term Financing and Investing

Basic Entries in General and Special Revenue Funds
    The Scenario and the Budgets
    Transactions and Events and Resulting Journal Entries

Fund Financial Statements

Closing the Accounts

Control Accounts and Subsidiary Ledgers

Other Matters and Concluding Comments

Review Questions

Discussion Scenarios and Issues

Exercises

Problems

After completing this chapter, you should be able to do the following:

- Understand the nature of transactions and events that are recorded in the General Fund and Special Revenue Funds
- Understand the relationship between budgetary accounting and financial accounting
- Prepare the journal entry to record the budget at the beginning of the fiscal year
- Identify transactions and events to the General Fund and Special Revenue Funds
- Prepare basic operating entries for revenues and expenditures during the fiscal year
- Prepare entries to record short-term borrowing and repayment

- Prepare year-end budgetary and financial accounting closing entries
- Describe and prepare financial statements for the General Fund and Special Revenue Funds

This chapter applies the principles set forth in Chapters 2 and 3 to certain transactions and events that occur routinely in two governmental-type funds—the General Fund and Special Revenue Funds. We discuss these fund types together because they experience similar transactions and events and because they are subject to similar accounting and financial reporting principles.

Governmental entities always adopt budgets for transactions and events affecting the General Fund and often adopt them for Special Revenue Funds. Therefore, one objective of this chapter is to demonstrate the relationship between budgetary accounting and financial accounting and reporting. Another is to illustrate how accounting for General Fund transactions and events is separated from accounting for Special Revenue Fund transactions and events. A third objective is to describe the full accounting and financial reporting cycle—from recording transactions and events to preparing financial statements, and ultimately to closing the books. This chapter is introductory in nature, so the transactions and events illustrated here are basic. The details, the complexities, and the modifications to accrual basis accounting are covered in Chapter 5.

BACKGROUND

The General Fund

The General Fund is the most significant single fund maintained by state and local governments. Although formally defined as the fund used to account for and report on all *financial resources* not accounted for in another fund, the General Fund is much more than a catchall fund. In fact, the General Fund is used to account for and report on the basic day-to-day operating services provided by governments. States, counties, cities, towns, villages, and other general-purpose governments perform different types of activities; in fact, some cities provide the types of services provided at the county level in other states and even in the same state. But each local government has one General Fund to account for its basic operating activities.

General Fund activities are financed by three major types of revenue: taxes, intergovernmental grants, and a host of miscellaneous items. Taxes on real property provide most of the tax revenues raised by local governments; general sales taxes, individual income taxes, and sales taxes on selected items like cigarettes and motor fuel provide the bulk of the tax revenues raised by state governments. Grants from higher-level governments also provide a relatively large share of the revenues obtained by many state and local governments. In addition, revenues are obtained from interest on short-term investments, licenses to operate facilities and permits to perform services, fees from admission to parks and other facilities, fines from parking and other violations, and many other sources.

For example, Mt. Lebanon's General Fund operating statement (see Table 2-5 on page 29) shows four revenue categories, but this statement is highly aggregated. Mt. Lebanon's 2011 detailed General Fund budget shows numerous revenue sources: six types of taxes; eight types of licenses, permits, and fees; three types of fines, forfeitures, and penalties; one source of investment income; four intergovernmental grants; eight types of recreation revenues; and ten types of charges for services and other items. For budgeting and accountability purposes, separate accounts are needed for each of these items.

When reporting on the General Fund, general-purpose governments often classify their current operating expenditures in about five to ten broad programs, depending on the scope of their activities. These broad programs might include general government, public safety, social services, education, environmental protection, culture and recreation, transportation services, public works, and health. Depending on its budgetary and accounting procedures, a government may also choose to report certain types of expenditures (such as pensions, fringe benefits, and judgments and claims) either as part of each function or as separate items.

Each broad program may include several organizational units, and each organizational unit may be responsible for several identifiable activities. Thus, Mt. Lebanon's public safety program covers Police Department and Fire Department expenditures. The Police Department budget contains separate amounts for eight activities, including field services, support services, investigative services, school crossing protection, and crime prevention. And each activity contains amounts for various objects of account, such as regular salaries and wages, overtime wages, fringe benefits, utilities, and training. Again, for budgeting and accountability purposes, separate accounts are maintained for each object of account within each activity.

Special Revenue Funds

As discussed in Chapter 2, Special Revenue Funds are used to account for the proceeds of specific revenue sources that are restricted or committed to spending for specified purposes other than debt service or capital projects. To establish a Special Revenue Fund, one or more *specific* sources of revenue (rather than general tax revenues) are dedicated for a *specified* purpose. A particular government may have no Special Revenue Funds or as many as deemed appropriate by its governing body or as required by a higher-level government. Theoretically, use of Special Revenue Funds provides elected officials, resource providers, and the citizenry a greater degree of assurance that the resources provided for specified purposes are used only for those purposes.

To illustrate the use of Special Revenue Funds, Mt. Lebanon maintains three such funds: a Sewage Fund, a State Highway Aid Fund, and a Library Operating Fund. The Sewage Fund operates under annual legally adopted budgets and is financed by a special sewer service fee assessed against real property. Those resources are used solely to meet operating expenditures and to finance infrastructure needs in accordance with federal Environmental Protection Agency requirements. The State Highway Aid Fund, required by state law and dedicated to road maintenance, is financed by state grants. The Library Operating Fund obtains most of its resources from intergovernmental grants and transfers from the General Fund.

In another example, Oneida County, New York, maintains two Special Revenue Funds, a County Road Fund and a Special Grant Fund. The relatively large County Road Fund, dedicated in accordance with state law to the repair and maintenance of roads, is financed primarily with state grants and transfers from the General Fund. The Special Grant Fund accounts for federal grants received under the Workforce Investment Act. Yet another example of the use of Special Revenue Funds concerns the use of proceeds from the Colorado state lottery. By law, these revenues are shared among Colorado towns and cities and must be spent for open-space preservation, such as land acquisition. The state operates the lottery and distributes the local governments' shares of the proceeds. The local governments, in turn, account for receipt and expenditure of these resources in Special Revenue Funds to help ensure they are spent only as intended.

Revenue and Expenditure Recognition

The modified accrual basis of accounting is used to recognize and measure revenues and expenditures in the General and Special Revenue Funds, as discussed in Chapter 2. The modified accrual basis of accounting is generally consistent with governmental budgeting practices, which focus on near-term liquidity. The accrual basis of accounting is modified in recognizing and measuring both revenues and expenditures. Under the modified accrual basis of accounting, revenues are recognized when they become *susceptible to accrual*; that is, when they are *measurable* and *available*. Expenditures are recognized in the period the related liabilities are incurred, subject to certain significant exceptions for liabilities that do not require liquidation with current financial resources. Indeed, the liabilities reported in General and Special Revenue Funds are only those that represent claims against the funds' *current* financial resources.

- *Regarding the "measurable and available" criteria for revenue recognition:* The major revenue source in the illustration used in this chapter is the real property tax. Revenues from property taxes are reasonably measurable before the cash is received because the property tax levy is based on a known amount needed to balance the budget. Further, the illustration in this chapter assumes the entire property tax levy will be "available"; that is, the entire receivable resulting from the levy will be converted to cash in the current period or soon enough thereafter to pay the bills of the current period. The transactions and events that create the miscellaneous revenues illustrated in this chapter are all assumed to produce cash in the current period.
- *Regarding the exceptions for expenditure recognition:* The transactions and events that create the expenditures illustrated in this chapter are all assumed to require cash payment either in the current period or shortly thereafter (say, within 30 to 60 days) from current financial resources. GASB standards provide that, when modified accrual accounting is used, expenditures that should be accrued include those that "once incurred, normally are paid in a timely manner and in full from current financial resources—for example, salaries, professional services, supplies, utilities, and travel."[1]

Because this chapter has limited objectives, the modifications and exceptions to the accrual basis of accounting will *not* be discussed. They will be covered instead in Chapter 5.

Short-Term Financing and Investing

Governments may need to borrow short term because of how their cash flows are structured. Revenue inflows tend to be "lumpy," particularly for local governments, while expenditure outflows tend to occur in relatively even amounts throughout the year. The difference between cash inflows and outflows is caused by the fact that many local governments require property taxes to be paid either once a year or twice a year (6 months apart), while payments for salaries, supplies, and the like occur ratably during the year. Property tax calendars vary among governments—the first payment may occur before the year begins, during the first month of the year, at some time during the first 6 months, or in some unusual situations, not until the start of the year after the year for which the tax was levied. The net result of the cash flow situation is that governments either need to borrow short term, have resources to invest short term, or both.

Short-term financing generally takes three forms: tax-anticipation notes (TANs), issued in anticipation of tax receipts (generally, property taxes) and payable from those receipts; revenue

---

[1]GASB Cod. Sec. 1600.119.

anticipation notes (RANs), issued in anticipation of other revenue sources, usually from higher-level governments; and bond anticipation notes (BANs), issued in anticipation of a future bond issue. BANs are generally issued to provide interim financing of capital projects and are discussed in Chapter 6. TANs and RANs are issued to meet temporary operating cash flow requirements. Proceeds from TANs and RANs are recorded as liabilities in the General Fund or a Special Revenue Fund. When the obligations mature, generally within 12 months, they are paid (with interest) from the tax receipts or other revenues in anticipation of which they had been issued. TANs and RANs may mature early in the year after the borrowing; in that event, interest on the outstanding obligation needs to be accrued at year-end.

State and local governments may also have "idle" cash in their General Fund or Special Revenue Funds, which is available for investment in short-term financial instruments. This situation generally results from the accumulation of cash resources in previous years and from receipt of property taxes or other revenues early in the fiscal year. Such investments result in investment income. Interest earned on short-term investments held at year-end should be accrued, provided it meets the criterion of availability; that is, collectible soon enough after the end of the year to pay current-period liabilities.

BASIC ENTRIES IN GENERAL AND SPECIAL REVENUE FUNDS

The Scenario and the Budgets

The Village of Kaatskill, which operates on a calendar year basis, is governed by an elected board of trustees. Its day-to-day activities are administered by an appointed village manager. The village has a General Fund, which is financed primarily by taxes on real property, and a Training Special Revenue Fund, which is financed by an annual grant from the state. The village manager is responsible for preparing annual budgets for activities accounted for in both funds; the budgets become law after review and approval by the board of trustees.

The General Fund balance sheet at January 1, 2013, showed cash of $70,000, no liabilities, and a fund balance (Unassigned) of $70,000. The approved budget for calendar year 2013 is as follows:

Estimated Revenues		
Real property taxes	$2,000,000	
Licenses and fees	70,000	
Fines and forfeits	50,000	$2,120,000
Appropriations		
General government salaries	$ 300,000	
Public Safety Department:		
Salaries	1,200,000	
Supplies	100,000	
Street Maintenance Department:		
Salaries	400,000	
Supplies	95,000	
Debt service	5,000	2,100,000
Budgeted Increase in Fund Balance		$ 20,000

Kaatskill maintains off-line budgetary control over the salaries appropriations by listing all the positions (e.g., police detectives, sergeants, and so on) that comprise the appropriation, as well as the names and salaries of the personnel who are filling the positions. As vacancies arise, the village manager must approve the department heads' decisions to fill them. Budgetary control over the supplies appropriations is maintained through an encumbrance system. Department heads are authorized to make budgetary interchanges between the salaries and supplies appropriations within a department, but requests for additional appropriations for a department as a whole require formal approval by the village trustees.

Kaatskill uses a *voucher system* for authorizing payments. In addition to documenting approval for payment, the voucher shows which account will be debited. The credit is always to *vouchers payable*, an account that has the same meaning as *accounts payable* in business enterprise accounting. (Most governments use vouchers for all payments, including salaries; however, to avoid cluttering the text with journal entries, we use vouchers only where the situation dictates the need to record a liability before payment.)

Kaatskill established the Training Special Revenue Fund based on state law. The state gives all municipalities that have law enforcement units an annual grant that may be used only for paying police officers while in training status. In accordance with state law, any balance remaining in the Special Revenue Fund at year-end is carried over to the following year. On January 1, 2013, Kaatskill's Training Special Revenue Fund had cash of $10,000, no liabilities, and a fund balance (Restricted) of $10,000. (The designation of fund balance as unassigned or restricted will be discussed in Chapter 5.) Based on preliminary data received from the state, the village trustees adopt the following budget for the Training Special Revenue Fund for 2013.

Estimated Revenues	
Intergovernmental revenue	$ 45,000
Appropriations	
Public Safety Department—salaries	$ 50,000
Budgeted (Decrease) in Fund Balance	($ 5,000)

Transactions and Events and Resulting Journal Entries

1. To record the adopted budgets at the beginning of the fiscal year, the following *budgetary* journal entries are made in the General Fund and the Training Special Revenue Fund:

In the General Fund:

Estimated revenues—real property taxes	2,000,000	
Estimated revenues—licenses and fees	70,000	
Estimated revenues—fines and forfeits	50,000	
Appropriations—general government		300,000
Appropriations—public safety salaries		1,200,000
Appropriations—public safety supplies		100,000
Appropriations—street maintenance salaries		400,000
Appropriations—street maintenance supplies		95,000
Appropriations—debt service		5,000
Budgetary fund balance		20,000

To record adopted General Fund budget for 2013.

In the Special Revenue Fund:

Estimated revenues—intergovernmental revenues	45,000	
Budgetary fund balance	5,000	
Appropriations—public safety salaries		50,000

To record adopted Special Revenue Fund budget for 2013.

Notice that the account Budgetary fund balance is credited when estimated revenues exceed approropriations and is debited when estimated revenues are less than appropriations. Kaatskill apparently anticipates using a portion of the opening fund balance of the Special Revenue Fund to pay for the 2013 expenditures.

Table 4-1 illustrates the revenues ledger for real property taxes, and Table 4-2 illustrates the appropriations ledger for the street maintenance supplies appropriation maintained by Kaatskill. Trace the journal entries for estimated real property tax revenues and the street maintenance supplies appropriation to the ledgers.

TABLE 4-1   Illustrative Revenues Ledger

Village of Kaatskill
General Fund
Revenues Ledger
Calendar Year 2013

Source: Real property taxes

Entry no.	Item	Estimated Revenue Dr	Actual Revenue Cr	Difference Dr (Cr)
1	Budget	2,000,000		2,000,000
2	Property tax levy		2,000,000	0

TABLE 4-2   Illustrative Budgetary Appropriations Ledger

Village of Kaatskill
General Fund
Appropriations Ledger
Calendar Year 2013

Function: Street maintenance supplies

Entry no.	Item	Appropriation Cr	Encumbrances Dr	Encumbrances Cr	Expenditures Dr	Available Appropriation
1	Budget	95,000				95,000
6	Place PO 3		70,000			25,000
6	Place PO 4		20,000			5,000
7	Receive PO 3			70,000		75,000
7	Expend PO 3				70,000	5,000
7	Receive PO 4			20,000		25,000
7	Expend PO 4				21,000	4,000

2. Kaatskill levies the real property taxes provided for in the budget. Property taxes are payable in two equal installments, during March and September of 2013. Based on past experience, Kaatskill assumes all taxes will be paid either during 2013 or soon enough thereafter to pay expenditures attributable to 2013. Therefore, it makes no provision for uncollectible taxes. The following financial journal entry records the tax levy.

In the General Fund:

Property taxes receivable	2,000,000	
Revenues—property taxes		2,000,000

To record the 2013 property tax levy.

Trace the journal entry to the revenues ledger.

3. Because of the timing of the two property tax installments, Kaatskill's cash flow projections indicate that it needs to borrow $400,000. On January 3, Kaatskill sells tax anticipation notes in the amount of $400,000 to a local bank, payable with interest of $4,000 on October 3. Because the liability is short term, the borrowing is recorded as a liability of the General Fund. The financial journal entry to record the borrowing is as follows:

In the General Fund:

Cash	400,000	
Tax anticipation notes payable		400,000

To record borrowing on tax anticipation note.

4. Kaatskill receives cash of $980,000 from real property tax collections during the year. Because the property tax revenues had been accrued previously, the property taxes receivable account is credited, as shown in the following financial journal entry:

In the General Fund:

Cash	980,000	
Property taxes receivable		980,000

To record property tax collections.

5. Kaatskill receives a check from the state for $30,000 as a police officer training grant. The state also advises Kaatskill that, as a result of budget difficulties, no further grant will be made available in 2013. To ensure its training expenditures do not exceed available resources, the village trustees amend the Training Special Revenue Fund budget, reducing both the estimated revenues and the appropriation by $15,000. Recording the check and the village trustees' budgetary action requires the following financial and budgetary entries:

In the Special Revenue Fund:

Cash	30,000	
Revenues—intergovernmental revenues		30,000
To record state grant for police training.		
Appropriations—public safety salaries	15,000	
Estimated revenues—intergovernmental revenues		15,000
To record budgetary adjustment.		

6. Kaatskill places purchase orders for supplies, chargeable to the following appropriations:

   PO 1—Public safety supplies: $45,000 for weapons and ammunition

   PO 2—Public safety supplies: $52,000 for radio equipment

   PO 3—Street maintenance supplies: $70,000 for pothole patching aggregate

   PO 4—Street maintenance supplies: $20,000 for small tools

   The budgetary journal entry to record the placing of the purchase orders is as follows:

   In the General Fund:

Encumbrances—public safety supplies	97,000	
Encumbrances—street maintenance supplies	90,000	
Budgetary fund balance reserved for encumbrances		187,000
To record encumbrances for purchase orders 1, 2, 3, 4.		

   Trace the posting of the budgetary journal entry for street maintenance supplies to the appropriations ledger in Table 4-2; notice how the two encumbrances reduce the amount of the appropriation available for spending from $95,000 to $5,000.

7. The supplies ordered in all four purchase orders are received and inspected. The invoices for PO 1, 2, and 3 are for the same amounts as shown in the purchase orders: $45,000 for PO 1, $52,000 for PO 2, and $70,000 for PO 3. However, the invoice for PO 4 is for $21,000 because the order allowed the supplier to ship and bill for additional quantities up to 5 percent. All the invoices are approved for payment, and vouchers are prepared. The first journal entry reverses the budgetary entry made in transaction 6 for the encumbrances; the second (a financial journal entry) records the expenditures and the liability. Notice that the amounts shown in the budgetary entry to reverse the encumbrances are the same as the amounts shown to record the encumbrances, but the amounts shown in the financial entry are greater by $1,000.

   In the General Fund:

Budgetary fund balance reserved for encumbrances	187,000	
Encumbrances—public safety supplies		97,000
Encumbrances—street maintenance supplies		90,000
To reverse encumbrances for ordered items received.		
Expenditures—public safety supplies	97,000	
Expenditures—street maintenance supplies	91,000	
Vouchers payable		188,000
To record expenditures and liability.		

   Trace the posting of the journal entries for street maintenance supplies to the appropriations ledger in Table 4-2; notice how the difference between the amount ordered and the amount expended reduces the amount available for spending by an additional $1,000, to $4,000.

8. The vouchers prepared in the previous transaction are paid, resulting in the following financial journal entry:

   In the General Fund:

Vouchers payable	188,000	
Cash		188,000
To record payment of vouchers for supplies.		

9. During the year, Kaatskill receives additional cash from the following sources:

Real property taxes	1,000,000
Licenses and fees	63,000
Fines and forfeits	47,000
	1,110,000

Kaatskill considers revenues from licenses and fees and from fines and forfeits to be immaterial and, therefore, accounts for them on the cash basis. The following financial journal entry is made to record the cash receipts:

In the General Fund:

Cash	1,110,000	
Property taxes receivable		1,000,000
Revenues—licenses and fees		63,000
Revenues—fines and forfeits		47,000

To record cash receipts.

10. On October 3, Kaatskill repays the $400,000 borrowed on a tax anticipation note earlier in the year, together with interest of $4,000 (see transaction 3). The following financial journal entry is needed to record the payment:

In the General Fund:

Tax anticipation notes payable	400,000	
Expenditures—debt service	4,000	
Cash		404,000

To record repayment of borrowing, with interest.

11. During the year, Kaatskill pays salaries to its employees, chargeable to the following appropriations:

General Fund—general government salaries	290,000
General Fund public safety salaries	1,175,000
General Fund—street maintenance salaries	380,000
Training Special Revenue Fund—public safety salaries	33,000

The following financial journal entries record the cash payments:

In the General Fund:

Expenditures—general government salaries	290,000	
Expenditures—public safety salaries	1,175,000	
Expenditures—street maintenance salaries	380,000	
Cash		1,845,000

To record payment of salaries.

In the Special Revenue Fund:

Expenditures—public safety salaries	33,000	
Cash		33,000

To record payment of salaries under state training grant.

12. The last payment for salaries in 2013 covered the pay period ended Friday, December 27. Payment for the period December 28–31 will not be made until 2014. As noted earlier in the chapter, GASB standards require that salary expenditures for the stub period must be accrued in governmental funds because "once incurred, [they] normally are paid in a timely manner and in full from current financial resources." Governments generally budget for stub period salaries each year because failure to accumulate resources for them will result, periodically, in the need for budgeting for an additional pay period, which may create budget problems. The accrual is chargeable to the following appropriations:

General Fund—general government salaries	4,000
General Fund—public safety salaries	15,000
General Fund—street maintenance salaries	6,000

To record the accrual, the following financial journal entry is needed:

In the General Fund:

Expenditures—general government salaries	4,000	
Expenditures—public safety salaries	15,000	
Expenditures—street maintenance salaries	6,000	
Accrued salaries payable		25,000
To record accrual of salaries at year-end.		

Based on the opening balances in the funds and the foregoing journal entries, preclosing trial balances, shown in Table 4-3, are prepared.

TABLE 4-3	Year-End Preclosing Trial Balances

For the General Fund:

Village of Kaatskill
General Fund
Preclosing Trial Balance
December 31, 2013

Account	Dr	Cr
Budgetary Accounts		
Estimated revenues—real property taxes	$2,000,000	
Estimated revenues—licenses and fees	70,000	
Estimated revenues—fines and forfeits	50,000	
Appropriations—general government		$ 300,000
Appropriations—public safety salaries		1,200,000
Appropriations—public safety supplies		100,000
Appropriations—street maintenance salaries		400,000
Appropriations—street maintenance supplies		95,000
Appropriations—debt service		5,000
Budgetary fund balance		20,000

TABLE 4-3	(continued)		

Account	Dr	Cr
Financial Accounts		
Cash	123,000	
Property taxes receivable	20,000	
Accrued salaries payable		25,000
Fund balance (unassigned)		70,000
Revenues—property taxes		2,000,000
Revenues—licenses and fees		63,000
Revenues—fines and forfeits		47,000
Expenditures—general government salaries	294,000	
Expenditures—public safety salaries	1,190,000	
Expenditures—public safety supplies	97,000	
Expenditures—street maintenance salaries	386,000	
Expenditures—street maintenance supplies	91,000	
Expenditures—debt service	4,000	
	$4,325,000	$4,325,000

For the Training Special Revenue Fund:

Village of Kaatskill
Training Special Revenue Fund
Preclosing Trial Balance
December 31, 2013

Account	Dr	Cr
Budgetary Accounts		
Estimated revenues—intergovernmental revenues	$ 30,000	
Budgetary fund balance	5,000	
Appropriations—public safety salaries		$ 35,000
Financial Accounts		
Cash	7,000	
Fund balance (restricted)		10,000
Revenues—intergovernmental revenues		30,000
Expenditures—public safety salaries	33,000	
	$ 75,000	$ 75,000

FUND FINANCIAL STATEMENTS

Financial statements for the General Fund and the Training Special Revenue Fund can be prepared from the preclosing trial balances in Table 4-3. For governmental-type funds, GASB standards require preparation of two basic statements: a balance sheet and a statement of revenues, expenditures, and changes in fund balances. GASB standards also require preparation of

TABLE 4-4   Illustrative Statements of Revenues, Expenditures, and Changes in Fund Balances

Village of Kaatskill
Governmental Funds
Statements of Revenues, Expenditures, and Changes in Fund Balances
For the Year Ended December 31, 2013

	General Fund	Training Special Revenue Fund
Revenues		
Property taxes	$2,000,000	
Licenses and fees	63,000	
Fines and forfeits	47,000	
Intergovernmental		$ 30,000
Total revenues	2,110,000	30,000
Expenditures		
General government salaries	294,000	
Public safety salaries	1,190,000	33,000
Public safety supplies	97,000	
Street maintenance salaries	386,000	
Street maintenance supplies	91,000	
Debt service	4,000	
Total expenditures	2,062,000	33,000
Excess (deficiency) of revenues over expenditures	48,000	(3,000)
Fund balances, beginning of year	70,000	10,000
Fund balances, end of year	$ 118,000	$ 7,000

a budgetary comparison report, which may be presented either as a basic statement or a supplementary schedule. (Financial reporting is discussed in detail in Chapter 9 and Chapter 10; for now, we are introducing financial reporting to show the complete accounting and financial reporting cycle.)

Kaatskill's General Fund and Training Special Revenue Fund statements of revenues, expenditures, and changes in fund balances are presented in Table 4-4 in columnar form, side by side, similar to the way Mt. Lebanon's fund financial statements are shown in Chapter 2 and Chapter 9. The major sections of Kaatskill's operating statements are revenues and expenditures; another major section generally found in operating statements—other financing sources and uses—is not shown here because Kaatskill had none.

Because Kaatskill has relatively few appropriations, we show *all* the individual expenditure accounts in these statements. Generally, however, the separate object accounts (in this case, salaries and supplies) within departments or functions are combined in the basic statements, similar to the way Mt. Lebanon does it, as shown in Table 2-5 on page 29. These object-of-account details are presented generally in separate schedules. Notice that none of the budgetary accounts are shown in this statement.

| **TABLE 4-5** | Illustrative Balance Sheets |

Village of Kaatskill
Governmental Funds
Balance Sheets
December 31, 2013

	General Fund	Training Special Revenue Fund
Assets		
Cash	$ 123,000	$ 7,000
Property taxes receivable	20,000	
Total assets	$ 143,000	$ 7,000
Liabilities		
Accrued salaries payable	$ 25,000	
Total liabilities	25,000	
Fund Balances		
Restricted		$ 7,000
Unassigned	118,000	
Total fund balances	118,000	7,000
Total liabilities and fund balances	$ 143,000	$ 7,000

Kaatskill's General Fund and Training Special Revenue Fund balance sheets, prepared from the trial balances, are presented in columnar form in Table 4-5. Notice that the fund balance in the General Fund is reported as Unassigned; this is because the opening balance and transactions and events during the year indicated no constraints on the future use of the net resources. The fund balance in the Training Special Revenue Fund is classified as Restricted because, as stated earlier in the chapter, state law requires that the grant be used only for paying police officers while in training status. Fund balance classifications are discussed in detail in Chapter 5.

The budgetary comparison report may be presented either with the basic financial statements or as a required supplementary schedule. Kaatskill's budgetary comparison schedules are presented in Table 4-6. The budgetary comparison schedule compares the original and final budgets (recall that Kaatskill amended its budget for the Training Special Revenue Fund in transaction 5) with the actual revenues and expenditures on the *budgetary* basis of accounting. In the simple illustration used in this chapter, the budgetary basis and modified accrual basis of accounting produce the same results, but the results on a budgetary basis might have been different if, for example, Kaatskill had budgeted on the cash basis of accounting.

A variance column, showing favorable and unfavorable variances from the final budget, may also be presented. Notice, for example, that Kaatskill's General Fund ended the year with a fund balance $28,000 greater than budgeted. This occurred because, although actual revenues were $10,000 below budget, expenditures were $38,000 below budget.

TABLE 4-6   Illustrative Budgetary Comparison Schedules

Village of Kaatskill
General Fund
Budgetary Comparison Schedule
For the Year Ended December 31, 2013

	Original and Final Budgets	Actual	Variance
Revenues			
Property taxes	$2,000,000	$2,000,000	$ —
Licenses and fees	70,000	63,000	(7,000)
Fines and forfeits	50,000	47,000	(3,000)
Total revenues	2,120,000	2,110,000	(10,000)
Expenditures			
General government salaries	300,000	294,000	6,000
Public safety salaries	1,200,000	1,190,000	10,000
Public safety supplies	100,000	97,000	3,000
Street maintenance salaries	400,000	386,000	14,000
Street maintenance supplies	95,000	91,000	4,000
Debt service	5,000	4,000	1,000
Total expenditures	2,100,000	2,062,000	38,000
Excess of revenues over expenditures	20,000	48,000	28,000
Fund balance, beginning of year	70,000	70,000	—
Fund balance, end of year	$ 90,000	$ 118,000	$ 28,000

Village of Kaatskill
Training Special Revenue Fund
Budgetary Comparison Schedule
For the Year Ended December 31, 2013

	Original Budget	Final Budget	Actual	Variance
Revenues				
Intergovernmental grant	$ 45,000	$ 30,000	$ 30,000	$ —
Expenditures				
Public safety salaries	50,000	35,000	33,000	2,000
Excess of revenues over expenditures	(5,000)	(5,000)	(3,000)	2,000
Fund balance, beginning of year	10,000	10,000	10,000	—
Fund balance, end of year	$ 5,000	$ 5,000	$ 7,000	$ 2,000

CLOSING THE ACCOUNTS

Closing the accounts for the year can be accomplished with two journal entries for each fund. Using the preclosing trial balances in Table 4-3, first close the self-balancing budgetary accounts against each other. Then, close the nominal financial accounts into fund balance. The closing journal entries are as follows:[2]

In the General Fund:

Appropriations—general government salaries	300,000	
Appropriations—public safety salaries	1,200,000	
Appropriations—public safety supplies	100,000	
Appropriations—street maintenance salaries	400,000	
Appropriations—street maintenance supplies	95,000	
Appropriations—debt service	5,000	
Budgetary fund balance	20,000	
Estimated revenues—property taxes		2,000,000
Estimated revenues—licenses and fees		70,000
Estimated revenues—fines and forfeitures		50,000
To close budgetary accounts.		
Revenues—property taxes	2,000,000	
Revenues—licenses and fees	63,000	
Revenues—fines and forfeits	47,000	
Expenditures—general government salaries		294,000
Expenditures—public safety salaries		1,190,000
Expenditures—public safety supplies		97,000
Expenditures—street maintenance salaries		386,000
Expenditures—street maintenance supplies		91,000
Expenditures—debt service		4,000
Fund balance		48,000
To close financial accounts.		

In the Special Revenue Fund:

Appropriations—public safety salaries	35,000	
Estimated revenues—intergovernmental grants		30,000
Budgetary fund balance		5,000
To close budgetary accounts.		
Revenues—intergovernmental grants	30,000	
Fund balance	3,000	
Expenditures—public safety salaries		33,000
To close financial accounts.		

---

[2]Mechanically, the closing process can be achieved through any of several combinations of closing entries. For example, some accountants prefer to close actual revenues against estimated revenues with any difference being debited or credited to fund balance. Similarly, expenditures can be closed against appropriations, again, with any difference debited or credited to fund balance. However, closing the accounts in such a manner can create confusion. Accordingly, we recommend the simple, straightforward practice of first reversing the budgetary accounts and then closing actual revenues against expenditures with any difference between revenues and expenditures being debited or credited to fund balance.

CONTROL ACCOUNTS AND SUBSIDIARY LEDGERS

Return to transactions 2, 4, and 9, and notice that the Village of Kaatskill debited the asset account Property taxes receivable for the full amount of the 2013 tax levy and credited that account when the taxes were collected. The balance in the Property taxes receivable account, of course, consists of many smaller amounts receivable from individual property owners. In practice, governments maintain records of the specific property taxes levied on—and paid by—individual property owners so they can identify those who are in arrears on their tax liabilities.

To avoid the problem of maintaining thousands of separate general ledger accounts to cover each piece of taxable property, governments maintain a general ledger *control account* supported by a *subsidiary ledger* similar to that maintained for accounts receivable in business enterprises. The control account records *aggregate* increases and decreases in property taxes receivable, while the subsidiary ledger captures the increases and decreases in taxes receivable by individual taxpayer in what are called "subsidiary accounts," or "subaccounts." The subsidiary ledger for property taxes receivable often is called a "tax roll."

In practice, a tax roll will include, for each piece of taxable property, details such as the legal description of the property, address of the property, type of property (in cases in which, for example, undeveloped property is taxed at a rate different from that for developed property), name of property owner, and assessed value.

Table 4-7 illustrates a simplified tax roll. Individual amounts are posted to this subsidiary ledger to correspond to the totals for the entries in transactions 2 (property tax levy) and 4 and 9 (cash receipts) in the Kaatskill illustration. The ledger shows the property taxes receivable from individual property owners constituting the total property tax levy of $2,000,000

TABLE 4-7   Village of Kaatskill Tax Roll

Village of Kaatskill
Tax Roll 2013

Taxpayer	Item #	Levied	Collected	Dr (Cr) Balance Due
A. Ruddigore	2	$ 2,500		$ 2,500
	4		$ 1,250	1,250
	9		1,250	0
P. Penzance	2	3,000		3,000
	4		1,500	1,500
	9		1,500	0
T. Mikado	2	4,000		4,000
	4		2,000	2,000
	9		0	2,000
Etc.		etc.	etc.	etc.
Totals		$2,000,000	$1,980,000	$20,000

and the property tax collections from individuals for the year, which aggregate $1,980,000. It also identifies T. Mikado as one of the delinquent taxpayers. As explained in Chapter 5, Kaatskill may impose interest and/or penalties on property owners who are in arrears on property tax payments. Ultimately, Kaatskill may foreclose on property for which taxes have not been paid.

OTHER MATTERS AND CONCLUDING COMMENTS

Earlier in this chapter we referred to potential investment transactions in the General Fund. If an entity uses cash to make a short-term investment in, say, a certificate of deposit (CD), it will debit Investments and credit Cash. Income on the CD should be recognized on the modified accrual basis of accounting; thus, investment income should be accrued at year-end if collectible soon enough after the end of the period to be used to pay liabilities of the current period.

We also referred to the need for accruing liabilities and expenditures for "liabilities that, once incurred, normally are paid in a timely manner and in full from current financial resources— for example, salaries, professional services, supplies, utilities, and travel." We illustrated the journal entries needed to accrue for salaries and to record vouchers payable on receipt of supplies. Accruals for items like utilities, professional services, and travel should be made in the same manner, with a debit to Expenditures and a credit to Accrued expenditures payable.

It should be recognized, however, that the transactions and events discussed in this chapter were chosen primarily to illustrate the basic elements of fund accounting and financial reporting and the relationship between budgetary and financial accounting. We did not describe the nuances of the modified accrual basis of accounting, nor did we illustrate accounting for the various types of interfund transfers resulting from the use of fund accounting. Consider these examples:

- The entire $20,000 of Property taxes receivable in the Kaatskill illustration is delinquent because the second installment was due to be paid in September. The illustration assumes that delinquent taxes will be collected early enough in 2014 to pay expenditures attributable to 2013. But suppose analysis as of December 31 shows that the delinquent taxpayers are not likely to make payment early in 2014. What adjustment, if any, is needed under the modified accrual basis of accounting?
- The training grant had a purpose restriction, but no other requirements. But what if the state had required Kaatskill to pay part of the cost of the training? How would Kaatskill account for the transfer of resources from the General Fund to the Special Revenue Fund, and how would the transfer be reported in the financial statements?
- On the expenditure side of the ledger, the illustration showed the accounting for unpaid salaries due to be paid shortly after the beginning of the year. But suppose Kaatskill, like most other governments, permits its employees to accumulate vacation pay and "cash out" a portion of the unused leave at retirement. What, if any, accrual must be made in the funds? Also, what if Kaatskill provides pension and other postemployment benefits to its employees, but does not finance the benefits as they are earned or finances them only partially as they are earned? What, if any, accrual must be made in the funds?

The *modifications* to the accrual basis of accounting in governmental-type funds and the interfund transfers will be discussed in Chapter 5.

Review Questions

Q4-1   The General Fund is defined as the fund used to account for all financial resources not accounted for in another fund, but it is actually much more than that. Explain why.

Q4-2   What is the minimum number of Special Revenue Funds you would expect a local government to have?

Q4-3   What are some similarities and differences between a General Fund and a Special Revenue Fund?

Q4-4   What are the financial implications of a situation in which the debits to aggregated Estimated revenues are less than the aggregated credits to Appropriations?

Q4-5   Do the differences between full accrual accounting and modified accrual accounting apply to revenues, expenditures, or both? Explain.

Q4-6   Give an example of a revenue source that, when the modified accrual basis of accounting is used, can be accrued before cash is received, and explain why the accrual can be made.

Q4-7   Give examples of liabilities that must be accrued under the modified accrual basis of accounting, and explain why those accruals must be made.

Q4-8   What is a voucher? What purpose does a voucher serve?

Q4-9   Which financial statements or schedules must be prepared for General Funds?

Q4-10   For a General Fund or a Special Revenue Fund, what does a credit balance in the fund balance account(s) at the end of the year signify? What does a debit balance signify?

Q4-11   Does a credit balance in the fund balance account(s) at the end of the year necessarily mean the fund has sufficient cash to pay its liabilities in a timely manner? Explain.

Discussion Scenarios and Issues

D4-1   The county of Edvic is facing a General Fund deficit in 2013 because actual tax collections are lagging behind estimates. At a staff meeting, the village manager tells the chief of public works that the chief will need to terminate one employee in April to help keep the budget in balance. The chief of public works says: "I have a better idea. You know that state grant the finance commissioner put into a Special Revenue Fund because it could be used only for planting trees along the highways? Why don't I just tell one of my boys to fill out his time sheets so that the time he spends changing street light bulbs is charged against the Special Revenue Fund. Neither our finance commissioner nor the state will ever know the difference." How should the village manager respond?

D4-2   The newly elected mayor of Oksford noticed that in the recently enacted budget of that city's General Fund, revenues exceed expenditures by $15,000. Later that year, after a hurricane caused a large amount of damage, she ordered the city's finance officer to write a check for $15,000 from the General Fund to an emergency relief fund. Because of the unexpected nature of the hurricane, no appropriation had been made to cover this transaction. When confronted by the press, she pointed out that the state's balanced budget laws require only that the General Fund "break even" and that she could not, in good conscience, allow the city to retain idle resources when people needed help. What, if anything, did the mayor do wrong?

D4-3   The State of York operates on a calendar year basis. Rocky Feller, the governor, is particularly proud of his reputation for making sure the state lives within its means. He knows that revenues in 2012 are coming in at a slower pace than anticipated, and he fears that expenditures may exceed revenues for the first time in his tenure as governor. He seeks advice from his budget director, who says: "No problem. I'll just tell the agencies not to send invoices for utilities, travel expenses, and professional services to the comptroller during November and December for payment. Because the state uses the modified accrual basis of accounting, the comptroller won't charge the bills to 2012." The elected state comptroller is responsible not only for paying the bills, but also for preparing financial statements in accordance with GAAP. What should the comptroller do when he learns about the budget director's idea?

Exercises

E4-1   (Budgetary entries)

The following budget was approved by a small village. Prepare the journal entry to record the budget.

Estimated Revenues		
Property taxes	$200,000	
Licenses	25,000	
Parking fines	10,000	$235,000
Appropriations		
General government	$ 50,000	
Public safety	130,000	
Parks and recreation	40,000	220,000
Budgeted Increase in Fund Balance		$ 15,000

E4-2   (Budgetary entries)

Harmon School District's General Fund accounts for all revenues and expenditures. At the start of school year 2013 (which runs from July 1, 2012, to June 30, 2013) the fund balance is $350,000. The approved budget for 2013 follows. Prepare the journal entry to record the approved budget. What will be the size of the fund balance at the end of the year if actual revenues and expenditures are exactly as budgeted?

Estimated Revenues	
Property taxes	$3,600,000
Investment income	100,000
Miscellaneous income	50,000
Appropriations	
Administration	$ 300,000
Instruction	2,400,000
Pensions, other benefits	350,000
Transportation	200,000
Building maintenance	150,000
School supplies	180,000
Debt service	160,000
All other expenditures	70,000

E4-3   (Encumbrances and payment)

On August 10, 2012, the school district in exercise E4-2 issued a purchase order for school supplies in the amount of $50,000. On August 20 the school supplies arrived, together with an invoice for $51,000. The invoice was approved for payment because the purchase order allowed for price increases up to 5 percent. The invoice was paid on August 30. Prepare the entries necessary to record the encumbrance, approval for payment of the invoice, and payment of the invoice.

E4-4   (Salary payment and accrual)

During the fiscal year ended June 30, 2013, Harmon School District (see exercise E4-2) paid salaries of $2,160,000, chargeable to the instruction appropriation. Instruction salaries for the last biweekly pay period in June 2013, amounting to $120,000, will be paid on July 5, 2013. Prepare entries to record instruction salary expenditures for fiscal year 2013.

E4-5   (Encumbrances and approval for payment)

The sheriff's office in the village of Katoonah had a General Fund appropriation of $85,000 for public safety supplies. On April 25 the sheriff ordered supplies with a quoted price of $80,000. On May 15 one-half of the supplies arrived, along with an invoice for $40,000. On June 6 the other half of the supplies arrived, accompanied by an invoice for $42,000. Both invoices were approved for payment. Prepare journal entries to record the encumbrance and acceptance of the supplies. Also, state the balance available for spending in the public safety supplies appropriation after acceptance of the second delivery of supplies.

E4-6   (Short-term borrowing and investing transactions)

A local government operates on a calendar year basis. Prepare journal entries to record the following transactions and events for calendar year 2012:

1. On February 1, 2012, borrowed $100,000 on tax anticipation notes (TANs). The TANs will be repaid with 1.0 percent interest on January 31, 2013.
2. To prepare for issuing financial statements for 2012, accrued interest on the TANs through December 31, 2012.
3. Invested $50,000 in a CD on April 1, 2012. The CD, which pays interest of 1.5 percent, will mature on September 30, 2012.
4. The CD matured on September 30, 2012.

E4-7   (Journal entries to record miscellaneous transactions and events)

A city's Parks Department has these two General Fund appropriations: Parks Department salaries and Parks Department other than salaries. Prepare journal entries to record the following transactions and events applicable to calendar year 2013; identify the appropriation to be charged:

1. Salaries of $7,000 were paid in October 2013.
2. A purchase order for trees was placed at an estimated cost of $1,000.
3. The trees ordered in the previous transaction were received and accepted. The invoice was approved for payment.
4. The invoice received in the previous transaction was paid.
5. An invoice for $2,000 for November electricity services was approved for payment in early December 2013.
6. Parks Department employees worked during the last week of December 2013 and earned $4,000. They will be paid in early January 2014.
7. An invoice for $3,000 for December electricity services was received in early January 2014.

E4-8   (Journal entries to record miscellaneous transactions and events)

Prepare journal entries to record the following transactions and events applicable to the calendar year 2013 operations of Lily City:

1. The approved budget for the year follows:

Estimated Revenues	
Property tax revenues	$600,000
Licenses and fees	30,000
Appropriations	
Public safety salaries	$550,000
Public safety, other expenditures	90,000

2. Property taxes of $600,000 were levied, and bills totaling that amount were mailed at the beginning of the year. During the year, $590,000 of property taxes were collected. Licenses and fees collected amounted to $28,000.
3. Salaries paid during the year amounted to $580,000; police officers earned an additional $12,000 during December that will be paid in January.
4. Purchase orders for supplies were placed in the amount of $60,000. The entire amount ordered was received during the year, together with invoices totaling $56,000. The invoices were approved for payment.

E4-9   (Closing entries)

The ledger of the General Fund of the City of New Elisa shows the following balances at the end of the fiscal year. Prepare closing journal entries for these budgetary and financial accounts.

Estimated revenues	$300,000
Appropriations	305,000
Budgetary fund balance	5,000
Revenues	300,000
Expenditures	285,000

E4-10 (Closing entries)

At the end of calendar year 2013, the following balances were found in the ledger of the Old Elias Library Fund. Prepare closing journal entries for these budgetary and financial accounts. Also, state the effect of the year's operating results on the library's fund balance.

Estimated revenues	$800,000
Appropriations	750,000
Budgetary fund balance	50,000
Revenues	780,000
Expenditures	760,000

(handwritten: } budgetary ; } financial)

Problems

P4-1 (Accounting and financial reporting cycle)

In an effort to improve its recreation facilities and to provide employment during the recession, Empire State created a Trails Special Revenue Fund. By law, all traffic fines collected by the state police were directed to be placed in the Trails Special Revenue Fund and used to pay only the salaries of individuals employed to create new hiking trails in Placid State Park. The Special Revenue Fund had the following transactions and events during calendar year 2013. Prepare journal entries to record these transactions and events, and prepare a statement of revenues, expenditures, and changes in fund balance for the Trails Special Revenue Fund for 2013.

1. The legislature adopted and the governor approved a budget with estimated traffic fine revenues of $900,000 and parks and recreation program salaries of $880,000.
2. Received parking fine revenues of $890,000 during the year.
3. Paid salaries of $870,000 during the year.
4. Incurred a liability of $7,000 for salaries earned by employees on December 30 and 31 that will be paid in early January 2014.

P4-2 (Transactions and financial statements)

The trustees of the Ketzel Park Special Revenue Fund approved the following budget for calendar year 2013:

Estimated Revenues		
General admissions fees	$260,000	
Admissions fees (big cat zoo)	140,000	$400,000
Appropriations		
Parks and recreation salaries	$280,000	
Parks and recreation supplies	40,000	
Parks and recreation cat food	60,000	380,000
Budgeted Increase in Fund Balance		$ 20,000

Transactions and events for calendar year 2013 were as follows:

1. Recorded the approved budget for the year.
2. Collected $250,000 in general admissions fees and $160,000 in big cat zoo admissions fees during the year.
3. Ordered supplies for $38,000.
4. All supplies ordered in previous transaction arrived, together with an invoice for $37,000. The invoice was approved for payment, but was not paid during the year.
5. The Ketzel Park trustees approved a $10,000 increase in the cat food appropriation.
6. During the year, salaries were paid in the amount of $270,000. Also, at year-end, an accrual of $9,000 was made for salaries earned but not paid.

7. Cat food in the amount of $68,000 was purchased, paid for, and consumed. (Purchase orders for cat food are not prepared. Record the liability for receipt of the food and the payment.)

Use the preceding information to do the following:
   a. Prepare journal entries to record the foregoing transactions and events.
   b. Prepare a statement of revenues, expenditures, and changes in fund balance.
   c. Prepare a balance sheet. Assume that the fund balance is classified as Committed.
   d. Prepare a budgetary comparison schedule.

P4-3   (Transactions and financial statements)

The City of Senasqua started calendar year 2013 with General Fund cash of $50,000 and fund balance (unassigned) of $50,000. The Senasqua council approved the following General Fund budget for 2013:

Estimated Revenues
Property taxes	$850,000	
Licenses and fees	70,000	
Investment income	5,000	$925,000
Appropriations		
Salaries	$800,000	
Utilities	50,000	
Equipment	85,000	935,000
Budgeted Decrease in Fund Balance		$ 10,000

The following transactions and events occurred in 2013:
   1. Recorded the approved budget for the year.
   2. Levied property taxes of $850,000. (The council assumed all property taxes would be collected in time to pay the year's expenditures.)
   3. Collected property taxes in the amount of $840,000 and licenses and fees of $70,000.
   4. Invested $50,000 of available cash in a CD. Later in the year, redeemed the CD in full with interest of $2,000.
   5. Ordered police sedans for $80,000.
   6. Received police sedans (with some extra bells and whistles) and an invoice for $82,000. (The police chief liked the bells and whistles and approved the invoice for $82,000.) The invoice was subsequently paid. (Note: Record this purchase as a capital outlay expenditure.)
   7. Paid salaries of $770,000 and utility bills of $45,000.
   8. During the last few days in December, Senasqua employees earned $25,000, which will be paid at the end of the pay period in early January 2014. Also, Senasqua received a utility bill for $4,000 for December 2013, which will be paid in January 2014.

Use the preceding information to do the following:
   a. Prepare journal entries to record the foregoing transactions and events.
   b. Prepare a statement of revenues, expenditures, and changes in fund balance.
   c. Prepare balance sheet. Assume the fund balance is classified as Unassigned.
   d. Prepare a budgetary comparison schedule.

P4-4   (Multiple choice)
   1. Under the modified accrual basis of accounting, when are revenues considered to be *available*?
      a. When earned
      b. When cash is received
      c. When measurable with reasonable accuracy
      d. When collectible in the current period or soon enough thereafter to pay current-period bills
   2. In budgetary accounting, what is the net effect of receiving all the items ordered together with an invoice for an amount less than the amount encumbered?

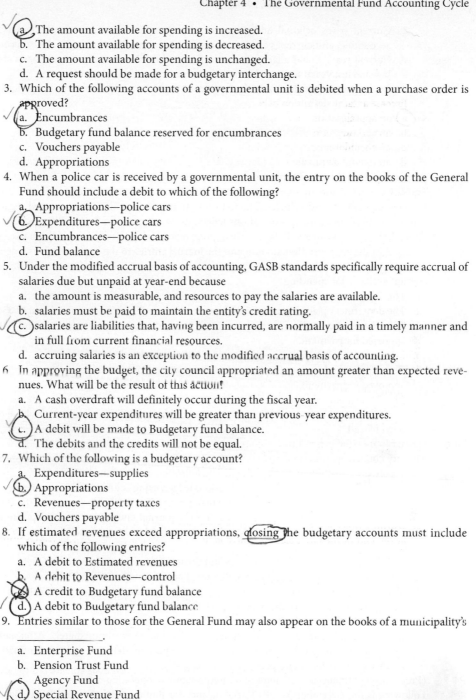

a. The amount available for spending is increased.

b. The amount available for spending is decreased.

c. The amount available for spending is unchanged.

d. A request should be made for a budgetary interchange.

3. Which of the following accounts of a governmental unit is debited when a purchase order is approved?

a. Encumbrances

b. Budgetary fund balance reserved for encumbrances

c. Vouchers payable

d. Appropriations

4. When a police car is received by a governmental unit, the entry on the books of the General Fund should include a debit to which of the following?

a. Appropriations—police cars

b. Expenditures—police cars

c. Encumbrances—police cars

d. Fund balance

5. Under the modified accrual basis of accounting, GASB standards specifically require accrual of salaries due but unpaid at year-end because

a. the amount is measurable, and resources to pay the salaries are available.

b. salaries must be paid to maintain the entity's credit rating.

c. salaries are liabilities that, having been incurred, are normally paid in a timely manner and in full from current financial resources.

d. accruing salaries is an exception to the modified accrual basis of accounting.

6. In approving the budget, the city council appropriated an amount greater than expected revenues. What will be the result of this action?

a. A cash overdraft will definitely occur during the fiscal year.

b. Current-year expenditures will be greater than previous-year expenditures.

c. A debit will be made to Budgetary fund balance.

d. The debits and the credits will not be equal.

7. Which of the following is a budgetary account?

a. Expenditures—supplies

b. Appropriations

c. Revenues—property taxes

d. Vouchers payable

8. If estimated revenues exceed appropriations, closing the budgetary accounts must include which of the following entries?

a. A debit to Estimated revenues

b. A debit to Revenues—control

c. A credit to Budgetary fund balance

d. A debit to Budgetary fund balance

9. Entries similar to those for the General Fund may also appear on the books of a municipality's _____.

a. Enterprise Fund

b. Pension Trust Fund

c. Agency Fund

d. Special Revenue Fund

10. When a budgetary comparison schedule is prepared, columns are needed for

a. Last year's budget, current year's budget, and current year's actual results on the budgetary basis of accounting

b. Current year's original budget, current year's final budget, and current year's actual results on the budgetary basis of accounting

   c. Current year's original budget, current year's actual results on the budgetary basis of accounting, and current year's actual results on the modified accrual basis of accounting

   d. Current year's final budget, current year's actual results on the budgetary basis of accounting, and last year's actual results on the budgetary basis of accounting

  11. Authority granted by a legislative body to make expenditures and to incur obligations during a fiscal year is the definition of _____.

   a. an appropriation
   b. an authorization
   c. an encumbrance
   d. an interfund transfer

P4-5 (Encumbrance and expenditure accounting)

The city council made an appropriation of $95,000 to the Police Department for the purchase of supplies, equipment, and vehicles. The following transactions and events occurred regarding this appropriation. Prepare an appropriations ledger, using columns for Encumbrances (Dr. and Cr.), Expenditures, and Available Balance. Then, prepare journal entries to record the transactions and events. Post the appropriation amount and the journal entries to the appropriations ledger. Charge all expenditures to Supplies and equipment. Make sure your final posting shows the remaining amount available for spending.

 1. The department placed PO 1 for five motorcycles, estimated to cost $10,000 each.
 2. The department placed PO 2 for crime prevention supplies at an estimated cost of $30,000.
 3. The motorcycles ordered in PO 1 arrived in good condition. The invoice of $50,000 was approved for payment.
 4. PO 3 was placed for radio equipment at an estimated cost of $10,000.
 5. The supplies ordered in PO 2 arrived, along with an invoice for $32,000. The invoice was approved for payment.
 6. The department obtained a check from the finance director for $250, made out to a local supplier, to purchase a new firearm for $250 on an emergency basis; no purchase order had been placed.

P4-6 (Encumbrance and expenditure accounting)

The city council appropriated $80,000 to the Parks Department for the purchase of shrubs, trees, small tools, and small items of equipment. The following transactions and events occurred regarding this appropriation. Prepare an appropriations ledger, using columns for Encumbrances (Dr. and Cr.), Expenditures, and Available Balance. Then, prepare journal entries to record the transactions and events. Post the amount appropriated and the journal entries to the appropriations ledger. Charge all expenditures to Supplies. Make sure your final posting shows the remaining amount available for spending.

 1. The department placed PO 1 for trees and shrubs at an estimated cost of $25,000.
 2. The department placed PO 2 for small tools at an estimated cost of $30,000.
 3. The items in PO 1 arrived in good condition, along with an invoice for $27,000. The invoice was forwarded to the comptroller for payment.
 4. The comptroller paid the invoice for $27,000.
 5. An emergency made it necessary to acquire two chain saws immediately. After calling three local suppliers to get the best price, the parks superintendent got a check for $450 from the finance commissioner and picked up the chain saws.

P4-7 (Preparation of financial statements and interpretation of operating results)

Following is the December 31, 2013, trial balance for Radnor City's General Fund. Based on this information, prepare (a) a statement of revenues, expenditures, and changes in fund balance, (b) a balance sheet, and (c) a budgetary comparison schedule. Classify the fund balance as Unassigned. Then, examine the budgetary comparison schedule, and write a short paragraph explaining the results of the year's operations in relation to the budget.

Account	Dr	Cr
Estimated revenues—property taxes	$ 500,000	
Estimated revenues—intergovernmental	150,000	
Estimated revenues—licenses and fees	100,000	
Estimated revenues—fines	50,000	
Budgetary fund balance	10,000	
Appropriations—general government		159,000
Appropriations—parks and recreation		175,000
Appropriations—public safety		446,000
Appropriations—social services		30,000
Expenditures—public safety	441,000	
Expenditures—general government	150,500	
Expenditures—parks and recreation	170,500	
Expenditures—social services	27,000	
Cash	35,600	
Property taxes receivable	67,200	
Tax anticipation notes payable		10,000
Accrued interest payable		800
Revenues—property taxes		497,000
Revenues—intergovernmental		154,000
Revenues—licenses and fees		99,000
Revenues—fines		48,000
Fund balance		62,000
Vouchers payable		21,000
	$1,701,800	$1,701,800

P4-8   (Miscellaneous scenarios requiring journal entries)
The following transactions and events pertain to Bean County's General Fund for the calendar year 2013. Prepare the journal entries needed to record the transactions and events (including year-end accruals where appropriate). If a journal entry requires a charge to expenditures, debit the account Expenditures—other than salaries.

1. The entity receives invoices in early January 2014 for $25,000 for professional services obtained in 2013, and $32,000 for December 2013 utility services.
2. The entity borrows $500,000 on August 1, 2013, in anticipation of the collection of property taxes. The borrowed amount is due to be repaid on January 31, 2014, with interest at the rate of 1.5 percent per annum.
3. The entity invests $300,000 cash in a CD on November 1, 2013, at an interest rate of 1 percent per annum. The CD will mature on January 31, 2014.
4. In September 2013 the entity receives and accepts supplies that had been ordered in August. The amount that had been encumbered was $40,000, but the amount of the approved invoice was $42,000.

P4-9   (Complete accounting cycle and financial statements)
The city council of E. Staatsboro approved the following budget for the General Fund for fiscal year 2013:

Revenues

Property taxes	$335,000	
License fees	40,000	
Fines and penalties	15,000	
Total revenues		$390,000
Appropriations		
Salaries	$350,000	
Supplies and utilities	30,000	
Debt service	3,000	
Total appropriations		383,000
Budgeted Increase in Fund Balance		$ 7,000

The postclosing trial balance for the fund, as of December 31, 2012, was as follows:

	Debits	Credits
Cash	$ 15,000	
Vouchers payable		$ 8,000
Fund balance (unassigned)		7,000
	$15,000	$15,000

The following transactions and events occurred during FY 2013:
1. Levied property taxes of $335,000 and mailed tax bills to property owners.
2. Borrowed $300,000 on tax anticipation notes at an interest rate of 1 percent per annum.
3. Ordered supplies expected to cost $18,000.
4. Received the supplies along with an invoice for $19,000; paid the invoice immediately.
5. Received cash ($383,000) from the following sources: property taxes ($330,000), licenses and fees ($38,000), fines and penalties ($15,000).
6. Paid cash for the following purposes: unpaid vouchers at the start of year ($8,000), salaries ($340,000), utility bills ($11,000).
7. Repaid the tax anticipation notes 6 months after the date of borrowing, with interest.
8. Processed a budgetary interchange, increasing the appropriation for supplies and utilities by $2,000 and reducing the appropriation for salaries by a like amount.
9. Will pay salaries for the last few days in December, amounting to $2,000, at the end of the first pay period in January 2014; also, received in early January 2014 a utilities invoice for $1,000 applicable to December 2013.

Use the preceding information to do the following:
a. Prepare journal entries to record the budget and the listed transactions and events.
b. Prepare a preclosing trial balance.
c. Prepare a balance sheet; a statement of revenues, expenditures, and changes in fund balance; and a budgetary comparison schedule.
d. Prepare closing journal entries.

Chapter 5

The Governmental Fund Accounting Cycle

General and Special Revenue Funds (Continued)

After completing this chapter, you should be able to do the following:

- Understand the implications of the basic principles of recognition and measurement on financial data reported in governmental-type funds

- Prepare journal entries to record property tax revenues and receivables

- Prepare journal entries to record revenues and receivables from sales taxes, income taxes, intergovernmental grants, and other revenue sources

- Understand the nature of liabilities in governmental-type funds

- Apply the recognition and measurement principles to record expenditures and liabilities in governmental-type funds

- Account for the four types of interfund transactions

- Account for the acquisition and disposition of capital assets and supplies in governmental-type funds

- Understand and report the five classifications of fund balance

- Account for and report on year-end open encumbrances

- Prepare financial statements for the General Fund and Special Revenue Funds

This chapter expands on the material presented in Chapter 4 regarding accounting in the General Fund and Special Revenue Funds. The transactions and events described in Chapter 4 were simplified to meet the learning objectives of that chapter; thus, all property taxes levied were "available" to pay current-period liabilities; expenditures were of a type that required accrual under the modified accrual basis of accounting; and all supplies ordered were received before the year ended. Chapter 4, however, did not describe the transactions and events that trigger modifications to the accrual basis of accounting, nor did it cover the complexities inherent in the transactions and events related to governmental activities.

This chapter explains the theory behind the current financial resources measurement focus and modified accrual basis of accounting, and illustrates the theory's application to General and

Special Revenue Fund transactions and events.[1] Real property tax transactions are discussed in detail, and accounting for sales and personal income tax revenues, intergovernmental grants, and other revenues is described. We also cover salary-related expenditures (such as vacation pay, pensions, and postemployment health care benefits), judgments and claims, inventories and prepayments, acquisition and disposition of long-lived assets, the four types of interfund transactions, and other transactions.

Several aspects of financial reporting for governmental-type funds are discussed in this chapter. A recent change in financial reporting standards, regarding display of the fund balance section of the balance sheet, is described and illustrated. Also, the chapter illustrates (a) how the format of the statement of revenues, expenditures, and changes in fund balance (discussed in Chapter 4) is modified to report interfund transfers and other financing sources and uses and (b) how deferred resource inflows and outflows are displayed on the balance sheet.

A detailed illustrative series of transactions and events for the General Fund is presented at the end of the chapter. The illustration starts with opening fund balances and an adopted budget and includes preparation of a statement of revenues, expenditures, and changes in fund balance; a balance sheet; and a budgetary comparison statement.

RECOGNITION AND MEASUREMENT—GENERAL PRINCIPLES

Governmental-type funds are basically budgetary devices. For internal purposes, the accounting records need to provide data to manage the current budget and prepare future budgets. But governmental budgets have a short-term horizon, and standards developed for accounting within the governmental-type funds have been influenced significantly by a budgetary perspective. To grasp the details of accounting recognition and measurement in the governmental-type funds, we need to look at the accounting standards in light of some budgetary thinking.

- *Focus on spendable resources.* From the perspective of the budget maker, resources held in governmental-type funds have utility only to the extent they can be spent to meet current budgetary needs. Resources that can be spent currently are financial resources, like cash and resources convertible to cash in the near term, such as investments, taxes receivable, and amounts due from other funds and other governments. So if a fund's resources are used to acquire capital assets, the assets are available to meet program needs, but they are not available for *current spending* unless sold and converted to financial resources. Capital assets are not recorded in governmental-type funds because they are not financial resources available for current spending. Most governments also account for the acquisition of supplies as if consumed when purchased.
- *Revenues recognized if resources are "available."* The conservative budget maker is concerned with the ability to convert taxes receivable to cash soon enough to pay current bills. Hence, from a revenue perspective, the word *current* (in the term *current financial resources*) generally covers a shorter time frame than the 1-year period used in private enterprise to

---

[1]As this edition of the text was being prepared, the GASB was in the early stages of developing a Concepts Statement on recognition and measurement. (Concepts Statements are road maps for future standards setting.) Because of inconsistencies in the current financial resources measurement focus model, some of which are noted in this chapter, the GASB was considering replacing the model with a "near-term financial resources measurement focus." The outcome of the due process and resulting GASB deliberations is unknown. Conceivably, some of the inconsistencies may be eliminated in future accounting standards without dealing with the more fundamental issues inherent in the modifications to accrual accounting resulting from the measurement focus.

distinguish current from noncurrent. Under GASB standards, governments recognize revenues only to the extent that they are "*measurable* and *available* to finance expenditures of the fiscal period;" the standards define *available* to mean "collectible within the current period or soon enough thereafter to be used to pay liabilities of the current period."[2] As we will see shortly, there is some inconsistency in the revenue recognition standards because the period of time "soon enough thereafter" is explicitly defined for real property tax revenues, but not for other revenues.

- *Expenditure budgeting on a cash or near-cash basis.* If you are familiar with the governmental budget process, you are aware of the problems encountered in balancing budgets, particularly in times of economic contraction. It is not uncommon to hear about balancing the budget through gimmicks, such as budgeting for revenues that are not likely to materialize or anticipating delayed payment of bills. Depending on the fiscal circumstances, a government may choose not to finance certain types of expenditures, such as pensions and retiree health care benefits, in the years the benefits are earned by the employees. This is possible because there is a long time lapse between the earning of the benefits and the actual payment to or on behalf of the employees. When that occurs, the governments are not budgeting for all expenditures attributable to the budget period.

- *Expenditures accrued if liabilities are incurred and "normally" paid from current financial resources.* GASB standards state that "in the absence of an explicit requirement to do otherwise, a government should accrue a governmental fund liability in the period in which the government incurs the liability."[3] Depending on the circumstances, however, the "requirement to do otherwise" can be significant. As a result, the liabilities reported in the General Fund and Special Revenue Funds are generally those that will be paid shortly after the start of the next year. Major expenditures and corresponding liabilities may not be recognized simply *because the government chooses not to budget for them and finance them* in the year the obligation is incurred.

The modifications to accrual accounting relate to the manner in which long-term debt is accounted for in the funds. GASB standards declare that, except for long-term debt expected to be paid from proprietary and fiduciary funds, the "unmatured long-term indebtedness of the government . . . is *general long-term debt* and should not be reported as liabilities in governmental funds." "General long-term debt" is then defined to include not only debt arising from the issuance of general obligation bonds, but also "noncurrent liabilities on . . . compensated absences, claims and judgments, pensions . . . and other commitments that are not current liabilities properly recorded in governmental funds."[4] In short, certain liabilities—and the expenditures creating those liabilities—are omitted from the funds. (As we will see in Chapter 10, those liabilities are reported in a separate set of financial statements called government-wide financial statements.)

What types of liabilities are recorded in the funds? According to the standards, (1) those that "once incurred, normally are paid in a timely manner and in full from current financial resources—for example, salaries, professional services, supplies, utilities, and travel"[5] and (2) those that have "matured" and are "normally expected to be liquidated with expendable available financial resources."[6]

---

[2]GASB Cod. Sec. 1600.106.
[3]GASB Cod. Sec. 1600.119.
[4]GASB Cod. Sec. 1500.103.
[5]GASB Cod. Sec. 1600.119.
[6]GASB Cod. Sec. 1600.122.

We covered the accruals resulting from the first type in Chapter 4. But the second type creates exceptions to accrual accounting, and as a result, significant expenditures and liabilities that would be reported on the accrual basis of accounting are not reported under the modified accrual basis of accounting. We will discuss this matter in greater detail shortly, when we deal with the specifics.

PROPERTY TAX REVENUES AND RECEIVABLES

U.S. Census Bureau statistics show that real property taxes represent about 72 percent of the tax revenues and 28 percent of total general revenues raised by all local governments in the United States. For any single local government, however, the proportion of tax revenues provided by property taxes may vary considerably from the overall average. Only a few states levy taxes on real property.

Laws regarding the administration of real property taxes also vary among taxing jurisdictions. Tax calendars generally require that property taxes be paid once or twice during the year for which the tax is levied, but some governments require payment before the year, and some even permit payment *after* the year for which the tax is levied. Tax calendars may also provide taxpayer discounts for payment before the due date and penalties for payment after the due date. Property tax laws also typically provide for taxpayer rights to appeal their property tax assessments and for government rights to seize and foreclose on properties for which taxes have not been paid. Property tax accounting procedures need to provide for all these eventualities.

Basic Principles and Journal Entries

Under the modified accrual basis of accounting, property tax *revenues* are recognized in the fiscal period *for which* the tax is levied, provided the taxes are available. *Available* means the taxes must be collected within the current period or soon enough thereafter to be used to pay liabilities of the current period; the time period "soon enough thereafter" cannot exceed 60 days, unless unusual circumstances justify a greater period.[7] (Studies show that most governments use a 60-day period, but a few use a shorter period, and a few use a longer period.) At year-end, revenues expected to be collected after the 60-day period are deferred and recognized in the next year.

On the other hand, *assets* (cash or taxes receivable) from property tax transactions are recognized "in the period when an enforceable legal claim arises or when the resources are received, whichever occurs first." Hence, for most governments that levy property taxes, *receivables* are reported at year-end (reduced by an allowance for estimated uncollectible taxes) regardless of when they are expected to be converted to cash. If property taxes are collected before the period for which the taxes are levied, the revenues are deferred and recognized in the period for which they are levied.[8]

Many local governments require homeowners to pay real property taxes during the year for which the taxes are levied. However, the full amount levied may not be collected because taxpayers successfully appeal the assessed values on which the taxes are based or because the taxes are otherwise deemed uncollectible. So, assume a town needs to raise a net of $1,000,000 from

---

[7]GASB COD Sec. P70.104.
[8]GASB COD Sec. P70.105, P70.106, and P70.107.

property taxes in 2012, but experience shows that about 3 percent of the tax levy is either refunded or deemed uncollectible. The town, therefore, decides to levy property taxes of $1,030,000 to obtain net tax collections of $1,000,000. The following journal entry is made to record the levy:

Property taxes receivable	1,030,000	
Allowance for refunds and uncollectible taxes		30,000
Revenues—property taxes		1,000,000
To record levy of 2012 property taxes, net of 3 percent allowance for refunds and uncollectible taxes.		

Assume actual cash collections during the year are $990,000. This journal entry records the collection:

Cash	990,000	
Property taxes receivable		990,000
To record collection of property taxes in fiscal 2012.		

Assume several taxpayers appeal their tax assessments, and the appeals are upheld. As a result, cash refunds of $15,000 are made to taxpayers who had already paid their taxes, and tax bills are reduced by $10,000 for taxpayers who had not yet paid. The following journal entry records those transactions:

Allowance for refunds and uncollectible taxes	25,000	
Cash		15,000
Property taxes receivable		10,000
To record results of successful property tax appeals.		

Governmental Accounting in Practice

Financing Property Tax Refunds

Governments may encounter financial problems if they fail to take account—during the budgeting and tax-levying processes—of the consequences of taxpayer appeals of property tax assessments. The illustration in the text shows how governments can provide for loss of anticipated revenues by establishing an allowance account for refunds and uncollectible taxes. Establishing an allowance account causes the government to raise additional revenues in the year of the tax levy to offset revenue shortfalls resulting from the appeals process. Failure to follow this procedure may keep tax rates down in one year, but can have serious consequences for future years.

For example, the *New York Times* (December 11, 2010) carried an article titled "Nassau Caught in Fiscal Crisis Despite Wealth." According to the *Times*, "As the economy faltered in 2007, [the County Executive] . . . began relying heavily on one-shot revenue generators . . . He resorted to *borrowing* [italics added] to pay one of the county's always onerous bills: the refunds given to residents who appeal their property tax assessments." This is one of the factors listed as contributing to the county's "full-fledged fiscal crisis."

The lesson: Governments should consider the potential revenue loss from property tax assessment appeals by budgeting for it *in the fiscal year for which the property tax is levied*. Unless that is done, there may be both cash and revenue shortfalls in the year of the tax levy or in subsequent years, depending on when property tax assessment appeals are adjudicated and refunds are paid.

Year-End Adjustments

At the end of the year, the town's finance director needs to review the unpaid tax bills to see if the balance of the Allowance for refunds and uncollectible taxes account is sufficient to cover potential uncollectible accounts. Assume she believes only one taxpayer (who owes $3,000) will be unable to pay. The Allowance account has a balance of $5,000 ($30,000 – $25,000), so she decides to reduce it to $3,000.[9] The following journal entry reduces the account balance by $2,000 and simultaneously increases 2012 revenues:

Allowance for refunds and uncollectible taxes	2,000	
Revenues—property taxes		2,000
To reduce the balance of the Allowance for refunds and uncollectible taxes account to current estimate.		

Assume the laws provide that uncollected taxes become delinquent on November 30. To record that fact for financial reporting purposes, the word *delinquent* needs to be added to the titles of the affected accounts—Property taxes receivable and Allowance for refunds and uncollectible taxes. Based on the year's transactions, the receivables account has a balance of $30,000 ($1,030,000 – [$990,000 + $10,000]), and the allowance account has a balance of $3,000 ($5,000 – $2,000). The following journal entries reclassify the accounts from current to delinquent:

Property taxes receivable—delinquent	30,000	
Property taxes receivable		30,000
To reclassify receivables to delinquent.		
Allowance for refunds and uncollectible taxes	3,000	
Allowance for refunds and uncollectible taxes—delinquent		3,000
To reclassify allowance account to delinquent.		

As a result of the foregoing journal entries, the net realizable value of the delinquent receivables is $27,000 (gross receivables of $30,000 less allowance of $3,000). Before closing the books, the finance director needs to comply with the "available" principle by estimating how much of the delinquent property taxes will be collected during the first 60 days of the next year. Revenue recognition related to receivables *not expected to be collected in 60 days* needs to be deferred until 2013. In practice, it is easy to make this estimate because actual collections during the first 60 days are likely to be known before the financial statements are issued. If the finance director estimates that $18,000 of the net receivables will be collected in the first 60 days of 2013, the journal entry needed to defer revenues related to the remaining $9,000 follows:

Revenues—property taxes	9,000	
Deferred revenues—property taxes		9,000
To record deferral of property taxes expected to be collected after the first 60 days of 2013.		

---

[9]You may question why the town should establish an allowance account if it can foreclose on the property and sell it to obtain the taxes owed. One answer is that several years may elapse before foreclosure proceedings are completed. Increasing the original tax levy to provide for the allowance helps ensure availability of sufficient cash to meet the expenditures of the budget year. Another answer is that the town may realize less than the taxes owed because the property is destroyed, or loses value, or because of some other reason.

Summary Results and Following Year's Transactions

Based on these transactions, the town will realize $1,002,000 ($1,000,000 + $2,000) from the 2012 tax levy. Of this amount, $993,000 ($1,000,000 + $2,000 − $9,000) is recognized in 2012. At the beginning of 2013, the journal entry to record the deferral is reversed, causing $9,000 to be recognized as revenues in 2013. (If a similar journal entry had been made at the beginning of 2012 to recognize revenues deferred from 2011, the actual revenues recognized in 2012 would be greater than $993,000.)

   If future transactions occur as anticipated, delinquent property taxes of $27,000 will be collected in 2013, and $3,000 will be written off against the allowance account. But what if the $3,000 is actually collected in cash in a later year, because the taxpayer is able to pay the delinquent taxes or because foreclosure on the property produces sufficient cash to pay the balance due? In either event, the credit balance in the allowance account for delinquent taxes can be reduced to zero, and $3,000 can be recognized as property tax revenues of the later year; or the $3,000 balance in the allowance account for delinquent taxes can be considered in establishing the size of the allowance account in the later year. Either treatment produces the same accounting result.

Tax Discounts

Sometimes governments allow taxpayers to take cash discounts for early payment of property taxes. Discounts should be treated as a reduction of revenue in the same manner as uncollectible accounts. To illustrate, assume a government levies property taxes of $600,000. To encourage early payment of taxes, it offers a 2 percent discount for payment within the discount period. Based on past experience, the government estimates that actual discounts taken will be, say, $10,000. The following journal entry is needed when taxes are levied:

Property taxes receivable	600,000	
Allowance for discounts on property taxes		10,000
Revenues—property taxes		590,000
To record property tax levy, net of estimated discount for prompt payment.		

   Any difference between the estimated amount to be collected and actual collections during the discount period requires an adjustment to revenues. If actual discounts taken are only $9,000, the journal entry to record the cash collected is this:

Cash	591,000	
Allowance for discounts on property taxes	10,000	
Property taxes receivable		600,000
Revenues—property taxes		1,000
To record collection of property taxes, net of discounts.		

Interest on Delinquent Taxes and Tax Liens

Many governments charge penalties against delinquent taxpayers in the form of interest on the amount of taxes owed. Interest rates may increase with the length of the payment delay. If interest totaling $2,000 is charged to delinquent taxpayers (and the resulting revenue is considered "available"), the following journal entry records the receivable and recognizes the revenue:

Interest and penalties receivable	2,000	
Revenues—interest and penalties		2,000
To record assessment of late-payment penalties.		

Governments may establish an Allowance for uncollectible interest and penalties when making the preceding journal entry. The amount involved, however, is generally too small to warrant the effort. Further, as a practical matter, many governments do not accrue interest and penalties receivable in the accounting records at all. Instead, they calculate the interest and penalties owed and charge the taxpayer for them when the taxpayer pays the delinquent taxes. This is a matter of convenience and is justified on the basis of materiality.

When back taxes are owed, a government may place a lien against the property. A *lien* is the legal right to prevent sale of a piece of property in order to satisfy a claim against the property owner; the property cannot be sold or transferred by the owner until the lien is removed. When a lien is placed against a piece of property, existing receivables accounts are reclassified to an account called Tax liens receivable. To illustrate, assume a lien is placed against a piece of property for which delinquent taxes are $8,000 and accrued interest and penalties are $500. The entry to recognize the lien follows:

Tax liens receivable	8,500	
Property taxes receivable—delinquent		8,000
Interest and penalties receivable		500
To reclassify property taxes, interest, and penalties receivable as a tax lien receivable.		

If it costs $300 to process and advertise the lien, this cost will be added to the lien receivable (increasing the receivable to $8,800), with the following journal entry:

Tax liens receivable	300	
Cash		300
To record cost of processing and advertising a tax lien.		

In extreme cases, if the property owner does not pay the lien, the government will exercise its right to seize the property and sell it to the highest bidder. After the taxes, penalties, and costs of the sale have been deducted, any remaining proceeds from selling the property will be sent to the now-former property owner. Assume the property in this illustration is sold at auction for $12,000 and the auctioneer is owed $1,500 for his services. In that event, the net proceeds of the auction are $10,500, an amount more than enough to settle the $8,800 lien receivable. The following entry records the receipt of cash from sale of the property ($12,000), the settlement of the lien receivable ($8,800), and the amounts due to the auctioneer ($1,500) and former property owner ($1,700):

Cash	12,000	
Tax liens receivable		8,800
Vouchers payable		3,200
To record forced sale of property to satisfy lien and amounts due auctioneer ($1,500) and former property owner ($1,700).		

SALES TAX AND INCOME TAX REVENUES AND RECEIVABLES

State governments obtain most of their tax revenues from personal income taxes, general sales taxes, and taxes on specific items, such as motor fuel. These taxes are derived from the application of tax rates to underlying exchange transactions wherein, for example, a merchant sells clothing or an individual earns wages. The government obtains sales tax revenues by requiring the merchant to remit periodically the taxes collected from the customer on the government's behalf. Personal income taxes are collected by a combination of employer withholding of taxes from employee-taxpayer earnings and taxpayer submission of periodic payments based on estimates and annual "settlements."

The standards regarding these "derived" tax revenues are expressed in a different manner than property taxes because of differences in the nature of the taxes and how they are collected, but the effect of the standards is generally the same. According to GASB Statement No. 33, assets from derived tax revenues are recognized in the period the underlying exchange occurs, and revenues are recognized (net of refunds and estimated uncollectible amounts) in the period the underlying exchange occurs *and* the resources are available.[10] *Available* means the same for these taxes as it does for property taxes (i.e., collected in the current period or soon enough thereafter to pay liabilities of the current period), but the GASB, in an apparent inconsistency, does not require that the "60-day" property tax rule be applied to sales taxes and income taxes. The GASB does, however, require note disclosure of the length of time the government uses to define *available* for purposes of revenue recognition.[11]

Governments generally require merchants to remit sales tax collections shortly after the reporting period, which may be monthly or quarterly. As a practical matter, governments record sales taxes when they receive the taxes, regardless of whether they collect the taxes directly or another government collects the taxes for them. At year-end, an accrual is made to record taxes collected by the merchants during the fiscal year but not received by the government until after the end of the year.

To illustrate, assume a city "piggybacks" its 2 percent sales tax on top of the state's 4 percent tax. The state collects the combined 6 percent tax from the merchants and later remits the city's portion of the collections to the city. If the city receives sales taxes of $300,000 from the state during calendar year 2012, it will make the following entry:

Cash	300,000	
Revenues—sales taxes		300,000
To record receipts from sales taxes during 2012.		

At year-end, the city needs to make an accrual for uncollected taxes. Assume that, in January 2013, the state advises the city that it will remit, by February 28, 2013, an additional $125,000 for taxes collected during the last quarter of 2012. Further, based on past experience with late filers of tax returns, the city expects to receive in April an additional $35,000 applicable to 2012. The city has a policy of considering sales taxes applicable to a particular year as "available" if

---

[10]GASB Cod. Sec. N50. 113 and N50.127a.

[11]GASB Statement No. 38, par. 7. In its basis for conclusions on this standard, the GASB notes (par. 42) that, in practice, the time period typically falls between 30 days and 1 year.

received by February 28 of the following year; hence, $35,000 of the $160,000 receivable is not "available." The following entry is needed:

Sales taxes receivable	160,000	
Revenues—sales taxes		125,000
Deferred sales tax revenues		35,000
To record receivable for fiscal 2012 sales taxes to be collected during 2013.		

Accounting for personal income taxes is similar to that for sales taxes, but administration is more complex, and a greater degree of estimation is required. Personal income taxes may be collected during the year by means of employer tax withholdings and periodic taxpayer estimates. Additional payments on withholdings and estimates may be received after the end of the fiscal year. Individuals then have several months to file final returns and either claim refunds for overpaid taxes or pay additional taxes.

For an example of the year-end accrual of personal income taxes in the General Fund, assume the following three-part scenario: (1) A state reporting on a calendar year basis for the year ended December 31, 2012, receives withheld taxes and estimated tax payments totaling $2,000,000 during January 2013, applicable to taxpayer earnings during 2012. (2) In addition, based on final tax returns applicable to calendar year 2012 (due by April 15, 2013), the state anticipates receiving additional tax receipts of $300,000 and refund claims amounting to $500,000. (3) It also expects to receive an additional $100,000 from late filers of final returns.

In the note disclosures to its financial statements, the state describes its accounting policy regarding "available" resources as follows: If final personal income tax returns are received by April 15, refund claims are recognized as liabilities, and payments received with final returns are considered "available"; if final returns are received after April 15, payments received with the returns are reported as deferred revenues. The journal entries, keyed to each item in the scenario, are as follows:

(1) Income taxes receivable	2,000,000	
Revenues—income taxes		2,000,000
To accrue tax revenues applicable to 2012, received in January 2013.		
(2) Income taxes receivable	300,000	
Revenues—income taxes	200,000	
Income tax refunds payable		500,000
To accrue income taxes receivable and tax refunds applicable to 2012, based on final tax returns expected to be received by April 15.		
(3) Income taxes receivable	100,000	
Deferred income taxes		100,000
To accrue income taxes receivable and deferred, applicable to 2012, based on final returns expected to be received after April 15.		

> **Governmental Accounting in Practice**
>
> **Accounting for Personal Income Taxes**
>
> As noted in the text, the complexities inherent in the administration of the personal income tax may result in reporting not only taxes receivable, but also a liability for tax refunds and deferred revenues. For example, as detailed in the notes to its financial statements, New York State's General Fund balance sheet for the fiscal year ended March 31, 2010, shows both an asset of $5.797 billion for personal income taxes receivable and a liability of $5.418 billion for personal income tax refunds. The state also reports deferred revenue from personal income taxes.
>
> New York State's personal income tax receivable at March 31, 2010, results from (a) uncollected estimated taxpayer payments with final returns (due April 15, 2010) for the 2009 calendar year, (b) uncollected estimates and withholdings applicable to the first quarter of calendar year 2010, and (c) audit assessments for additional amounts related to prior periods. The liability for personal income tax refunds results from estimated taxpayer overpayments related to calendar year 2009 and the first quarter of calendar year 2010.

INTERGOVERNMENTAL GRANTS AND OTHER REVENUES

Intergovernmental Grants

State and local governments generally receive about 30 percent to 40 percent of their revenues from intergovernmental grants. These grants generally come with "strings" attached; that is, they may contain *time requirements* (specifying the period during which the resources must be used or when use may begin), *purpose restrictions* (specifying what activities the grant may be used for), or both.

GASB standards require that grant recipients recognize revenues in governmental-type funds in the period that all applicable *eligibility requirements* have been met *and* the resources are available.[12] For example, a grant provider may require that, to be eligible for a grant, the recipient must be a particular type of government (say, a school district), that a grant application be approved, and that allowable costs be incurred. (Grantors often provide resources on a reimbursement basis, requiring grantees to bill for allowable costs; these grants are called "expenditure-driven" grants.) If a grantor provides a cash advance, the revenue should be deferred until the eligibility requirements have been met. Again, "available" means collected in the current period or expected to be collected soon enough thereafter to pay liabilities of the current period, but the "60-day" rule was not made applicable to grants.

Although time requirements affect the accounting period in which grant revenues are recognized, purpose restrictions do not.[13] Thus, if a grant has purpose restrictions but no time requirements, the entire grant amount should be recognized when all eligibility requirements are met. Any unspent revenues remaining at year-end should be reported as Restricted fund balance[14] until the resources are used for the specified purpose. The following scenarios show how to apply the accounting standards.

Grant with purpose restrictions, but no time requirements: A state appropriation provides grants to cities with populations over 75,000 to train police officers. Cities must apply for the grants, describing the need for training and the training methodology to be used. When the state approves the grant, it places no time limit on use of the resources. In this situation, the eligibility requirements

---

[12]GASB Cod. Sec. N50.127d.

[13]GASB Cod. Sec. N50.110 and N50.111.

[14]In several instances, this text refers to particular classifications of fund balance, such as Restricted fund balance. Fund balance classifications are discussed in detail toward the end of this chapter in a section entitled "Fund Balance Presentation."

for the grant relate only to the size of the city and to state approval of the application. The requirement to use the resources for training police officers is a purpose restriction, but the grant contains no time requirement. When the state advises a city that it has been awarded a grant of $100,000, the city will make the following journal entry, recognizing both the receivable and the revenue:

Due from state government	100,000	
Intergovernmental revenues—grants		100,000
To record receipt of grant award for police training.		

At year-end, as discussed in Chapter 4, the revenue account will be closed out to Unassigned fund balance. But what if the city spent only $75,000 of the grant in the year it received the grant? In that situation, the city would need to reclassify $25,000 of the Unassigned fund balance to Restricted fund balance to signify that a portion of the fund balance must be used for a specified purpose.

Grant with expenditure incurrence and time requirements: A state provides grants to school districts for 75 percent of teacher salaries incurred in a special education program, up to a maximum amount set forth in a grant agreement. To be eligible for the grant, the school district must have begun the applicable school year and must have incurred teacher salary costs. Although the state makes advance payments to school districts before the school year starts, the district must file quarterly expenditure reports to receive subsequent advances. The state agrees to pay a school district a maximum of $1,000,000 under this program for the full 2012 school year, at the rate of no more than $250,000 each quarter. If the state makes an advance payment to the school district of $200,000 before the school year starts, the school district has not yet met the eligibility requirements, because the school year has not begun and costs have not been incurred. Hence, the school district records a liability on receipt of the advance, as follows:

Cash	200,000	
Advance received on grant		200,000
To record receipt of advance on grant.		

If the school district spends $300,000 on teacher salaries (covering both its share and the state's share of expenditures) in the first quarter of 2012, it makes the following entry:

Expenditures—special education teacher salaries	300,000	
Cash		300,000
To record payment of special education program teacher salaries.		

Having met the time and expenditure eligibility requirements, the school district will recognize grant revenues of $225,000 (75 percent of $300,000) and record a receivable for the difference between the $200,000 advance and the recognized revenues, as follows:

Advance received on grant	200,000	
Due from state government	25,000	
Intergovernmental revenues—grants		225,000
To recognize grant revenue at 75 percent of costs.		

Pass-through grants: Governments often receive so-called "pass-through grants" that they can transfer to or spend on behalf of a secondary government. For example, a state might receive from the federal government a grant for security activities that it disburses to various cities. As a general rule, pass-through grants should be recognized as revenues and expenditures in the primary recipient's governmental-type funds, provided it has administrative involvement with the program. "Administrative involvement" includes, for example, monitoring secondary recipients for compliance with program requirements, determining eligible secondary recipients or projects, or having the ability to exercise discretion over how the funds are allocated to secondary recipients. If the primary recipient serves merely as a "cash conduit" and has no administrative involvement, it should account for the grant in an Agency Fund.[15]

Fines, Fees, Licenses, and Miscellaneous Revenues

The GASB classifies fines and penalties as "imposed nonexchange revenues." It requires that *assets* from such events be recognized in the period an enforceable legal claim arises and *revenues* be recognized in the period an enforceable legal claim arises and the resources are available.[16] Fines may be imposed for various reasons, including motor vehicle violations and violations resulting from inspection of certain facilities. There may be a lengthy time period between issuance of the notice of violation, the end of the appeals process (when an enforceable legal claim arises), and collection of fines. Some fines may be "settled" for a lower amount or may not be collected at all. When receivables are recognized, experience may dictate both deferring recognition of some revenues (because the availability criterion is not met) and establishing an allowance for uncollectible receivables (because the amount collected may be less than the amount of the fines).

By contrast, GASB standards say that "golf and swimming fees, inspection charges, parking fees and parking meter receipts, and the vast multitude of miscellaneous exchange revenues are best recognized when cash is received" and that "business licenses are generally not susceptible to accrual."[17] From a financial reporting perspective, none of these items may generate sufficient revenues to warrant accrual-basis accounting. Revenues from motor vehicle fines, however, may be significant. Also, issuance of licenses and assessments of fines may be important aspects of program management, particularly in activities involving the inspection of facilities, such as restaurants and nursing homes. Hence, receivables and revenues from fines *and* issuance of licenses may be recognized (net of an allowance for uncollectible amounts) if records are such that receivables and revenues are susceptible to accrual.

Payments in Lieu of Taxes

Governments often receive payments from other entities (governments, not-for-profit entities, and even their enterprise funds and component units) to cover revenues lost because the entities are legally exempt from paying property taxes. Such payments are called *payments in lieu of taxes* (PILOTs). The amounts may be based on what the government would have received had the entities been required to pay property taxes or may be negotiated based on the cost of certain specific activities (such as police protection and fire suppression services) that enter into the property tax rate.

PILOTs received from the federal government have the characteristics of grants, and revenues should be recognized when eligibility requirements have been met and the revenues are available. PILOTs received from not-for-profit entities have characteristics of both grants and fees for services; in the absence of specific GASB standards, it appears appropriate to recognize receivables and revenues in the period the services are provided, subject to the availability criterion.

---

[15]GASB Cod. Sec. N50.104b and N50.128.

[16]GASB Cod. Sec. N50.104, N50.114, and N50.127.

[17]GASB Cod. Sec. 1600.110 and 1600.112.

PILOTs received from a government's enterprise fund would be reported as revenues in the period the services are provided (subject to the availability criterion), provided the payments are reasonably equivalent in value to the services provided; if not, the receipts would be reported as interfund transfers (see section on "Interfund Transactions" later in this chapter).

EXPENDITURES AND FUND LIABILITIES

Nature of Liabilities in Governmental-Type Funds

As previously noted, GASB standards distinguish between *governmental fund liabilities* (which are claims against current financial resources) and *general long-term liabilities* (which include liabilities resulting not only from issuance of general obligation bonds, but also from current operating transactions and events that create obligations not currently payable). Because general long-term liabilities are not reported in the funds, the related expenditures also are not reported in the funds until they become due and payable from current financial resources. To implement this distinction between fund liabilities and general long-term liabilities, GASB standards identify three categories of transactions and events that create liabilities and expenditures:

1. Items that, "once incurred, normally are paid in a timely manner and in full from current financial resources—for example, salaries, professional services, supplies, utilities, and travel."[18] Such liabilities are considered as claims against current financial resources, and if not paid at year-end, expenditures are accrued and liabilities are reported in the governmental funds, as discussed in Chapter 4.

2. Items that create liabilities that governments "normally" expect to liquidate over future time periods with financial resources that are available in those future periods.[19] GASB standards identify the following items as falling within this category: claims and judgments, compensated absences, special termination benefits, and landfill closure and postclosure care costs. Expenditures and liabilities for these items are recognized as *the liabilities mature (i.e., as they come due for payment) each year on the occurrence of relevant events*, such as the settlement of claims or the resignation of employees. The portion of the liability that has not matured is considered general long-term debt, rather than fund debt.

3. Liabilities resulting from promises to pay pensions, retiree health care, and other postemployment benefits. As will be discussed shortly, there are wide variations—among both governments and types of benefits—in how and to what extent these promises are financed. The obligations may be financed through annual contributions to a trust fund as the benefits are earned (called "advance-funded"), partially advance-funded, or financed as benefits are actually paid to or on behalf of the retirees (called "pay-as you go" financing) GASB standards say expenditures from governmental funds for these salary-related items should be "equal to the amount contributed to the plan or expected to be liquidated with expendable available financial resources."[20] Hence, these benefits are accounted for as expenditures and liabilities in the period they are financed. Liabilities resulting from differences between amounts calculated on the accrual basis of accounting and amounts financed are considered general long-term debt.

---

[18]GASB Interpretation No. 6, par. 12.

[19]Ibid., pars. 11 and 14. In describing this category, GASB standards refer to the liabilities as those that are "normally expected to be liquidated with expendable available financial resources."

[20]GASB Statement No. 27, par. 16 and GASB Statement No. 45, par. 19.

Before reading on, reflect for a moment on the departures from accrual-basis accounting in categories 2 and 3. The measurements produced by these principles clearly are more closely related to cash-basis accounting than to accrual-basis accounting. Of particular concern is the potential for lack of accounting uniformity among governments in measuring expenditures within category 3.

Application of Standards to Specific Transactions and Events

How do these general principles translate to specific measurements for transactions and events that occur in the General Fund and Special Revenue Funds? Let us examine some transactions and events for each of the transaction categories just enumerated. In these illustrations, assume the government's fiscal year ends December 31, 2012.

SALARIES, SUPPLIES, AND UTILITIES   Salaries, supplies, and utilities paid from the General Fund and Special Revenue Funds fall in category 1. Therefore, salaries, supplies, and utility services that are unpaid at year-end would be accrued in those funds in a manner similar to the accrual that would be made in business enterprise accounting, as discussed in Chapter 4. For example, assume a government pays salaries biweekly and the last payment made in 2012 was for the period ended December 24, 2012. An accrual must be made for salaries in the amount of, say, $150,000 earned during the period December 25 to December 31, even though payment is not made until January 2013. Also, assume the government received an electric bill of $12,000 for the month ended December 31, 2012, and paid the bill in January 2013. The following adjusting journal entry must be made in the funds for the year ended December 31, 2012:

Expenditures—salaries	150,000	
Expenditures—utilities	12,000	
Accrued liabilities		162,000
To record accrued liabilities for salaries and utilities applicable to 2012.		

CLAIMS AND JUDGMENTS   Claims and judgments paid from governmental-type funds fall in category 2. Governments that do not transfer risk to third parties by means of insurance are subject to claims for damages for various torts, such as damages to vehicles caused by a government's sanitation truck operators. These claims may not be settled or adjudicated for several years. Assume a government receives three claims for events that occurred in 2012. The government agrees to settle one claim for $10,000 in late 2012 and schedules it for payment on January 10, 2013. A second case is being negotiated, and government attorneys believe it can be settled sometime in 2013 at a probable cost of $30,000. A third case is in litigation, and government attorneys believe the government will probably be required to pay at least $45,000 in damages.

If accrual basis accounting were used, the government would need to recognize an expense and a liability of $85,000 ($10,000 + $30,000 + $45,000), the total probable loss on the three cases.[21] Under modified accrual accounting, however, an accrual is made only for the *matured* liability; that is, the $10,000 settled claim that is coming due for payment. In this

---

[21]GASB Cod. Sec. C50.110.

scenario, $10,000 is the "amount normally expected to be liquidated with expendable available financial resources." If the claim is paid from the General Fund, the entry for the December 31, 2012, accrual is this:

Expenditures—claims and judgments	10,000	
Accrued liabilities		10,000
To record liability for settled claim to be paid in January 2013.		

The remaining $75,000 (a general long-term liability) would be recorded as an expense and a liability in the 2012 *government-wide* financial statements, as explained in Chapter 10. The actual amount of the settlements on those cases would be reported as *General Fund expenditures* in the years the liabilities mature, perhaps 2013 or 2014.

COMPENSATED ABSENCES Compensated absences also fall within category 2. Under GASB standards for government-wide reporting, vacation leave and other compensated absences with similar characteristics should be accrued as an expense and a liability as those benefits are earned by employees if (a) the employees' rights to receive compensation are attributable to services already performed *and* (b) it is probable that the employer will compensate the employees through paid time off or some other means, such as cash payments at termination or retirement.[22] Under the modified accrual basis of accounting, however, an accrual is made only for the *matured* liability, that is, amounts coming due for accumulated compensated absences because employees have been terminated or have retired as of December 31, 2012, but have not yet received payment.

To illustrate, assume a village allows its employees to accumulate vacation pay up to 30 days. It has two employees, each of whom earns $200 a day. Employee A has accumulated 25 days of unused vacation pay as of December 31, 2012, and has no plans to retire. Employee B retired on December 15, having accumulated 20 days of unused vacation pay. The village will pay employee B $4,000 (20 × $200) on January 10, 2013, for the unused vacation pay. If these employees are paid from the General Fund, the village will need to make an accrual on December 31, 2012, only for the vacation pay earned by and due to employee B because the liability for that employee has *matured*. The liability for both employees' vacation pay will appear in the government-wide financial statements.

PENSION, RETIREE HEALTH CARE, AND OTHER POSTEMPLOYMENT BENEFITS Category 3 embraces pension, retiree health care, and other postemployment benefits. Most governmental employers that provide pension benefits do so through defined benefit pension plans, as described in Chapter 8. Historically, many governmental employers have budgeted for and financed these plans through annual contributions to the plans in accordance with actuarial calculations, *as the benefits are earned by the employees.* Indeed, that is the norm for financing pension benefits. The intent of such financing is that the amounts contributed annually to the pension plan, together with the earnings on the investments made with the contributions, will be sufficient to pay the promised pension benefits from date of retirement to date of death.

Regarding these benefits, there is a long time lapse between the earning of the benefits and the actual payout. The question then is this: from the accounting perspective, when does the employer's obligation arise? And the answer is, as the GASB notes: "The cost associated with an

---

[22]GASB Cod. Sec. C60.104.

employee's postemployment benefit is deemed to be incurred, and conceptually should be recognized, in the years during which the employer receives services rather than during the postemployment period when payments are made."[23]

When pension benefits are financed as earned, they are in essence being financed using accrual accounting principles. But many employers contribute less to the plans than the amount recommended by their actuaries or the amount calculated in accordance with the accrual-basis standards established by the GASB for *government-wide* financial reporting. Further, virtually all employers that provide retiree health care benefits finance them based on amounts actually paid out on behalf of retired employees. As a result, across the spectrum of state and local governments, there is a wide range in the levels to which pension and retiree health care benefits are financed.

The GASB's standard for recognizing and measuring these expenditures *within the funds* (i.e., "the amount contributed to the plan or expected to be liquidated with expendable available financial resources") basically mirrors the financing procedures. As a result, the same lack of uniformity that exists among governments in financing also exists in accounting for the benefits within the governmental-type funds.

To illustrate, assume that the actuaries recommend, using accrual-basis accounting standards, that states A and B each contribute $1,000,000 to their pension plans and $800,000 to their retiree health care plans in 2012. State A contributes to its pension plan the full amount

---

Governmental Accounting in Practice

What Do General Fund Operating Statements Measure?

The General Fund statement of revenues, expenditures, and changes in net assets is derived from financial data using the current financial resources measurement focus and the modified accrual basis of accounting. For some governments, this statement has the potential for misleading the unwary reader because *it does not measure the economic substance* of the year's transactions and events. Instead, it is more in the nature of a modified statement of cash flows.

What the statement measures depends primarily on how the government chooses to budget for and finance certain operating costs, particularly its pension and retiree health care benefit obligations. For a good example of the limitations of the fund financial statements, visit the State of Illinois web site, and examine its General Fund statement of revenues, expenditures, and changes in net assets for the fiscal year ended June 30, 2009. The state's expenditures ($34.133 billion) exceeded revenues ($32.162 billion) by $1.971 billion. After deducting net other financing uses, the state's net assets were reduced by $3.643 billion as a result of the year's operations.

A "loss" of $3.643 billion sounds bad enough. But if you delve further into the financial report, you will find that Illinois underfinanced its employee pension and retiree health care benefits by more than $3 billion, when computed in accordance with the GASB's accrual accounting standards. Its five pension systems are only 50.6 percent funded, and its retiree health care systems have zero assets to cover $27 billion in obligations. You won't find that information in the *fund* financial statements.

To understand the results of operations and financial position of a governmental entity, the financial statement reader must read *beyond* the fund financial statements—which, as previously discussed, have a *budgetary focus on financial resources and claims upon them*. The reader must also analyze the government-wide statements, the reconciliation between the fund statements and the government-wide statements, the notes, and the supplementary information. We discuss this further in Chapters 9 and 10.

---

[23]GASB Statement No. 45, par. 75.a.

recommended by its actuary and contributes $350,000 to its retiree health care plan, slightly more than the $300,000 it expects to pay out on behalf of its retirees. State B contributes to its pension plan only 60 percent of the amount recommended by its actuary and contributes to its retiree health care plan only the $300,000 it expects to pay out on behalf of its retirees. Accrual accounting dictates that each state report expenses of $1,800,000. As a result of modified accrual accounting standards, however, state A will report expenditures of only $1,350,000 ($1,000,000 for pensions and $350,000 for retiree health care), and state B will report expenditures of only $900,000 ($600,000 for pensions and $300,000 for retiree health care). For an example of an actual situation, see the box "Government Accounting in Practice: What Do General Fund Operating Statements Measure?"

INTERFUND TRANSACTIONS

Transactions between individual funds of a government tend to occur relatively often. One fund might (a) sell services or goods to another fund in an ordinary exchange transaction; (b) make an outright transfer of cash or goods to another fund with no expectation of repayment; (c) make a loan to another fund (and expect repayment), and (d) accommodate another fund by paying the other's share of an invoice pertaining to both funds (and expect reimbursement). All four types of transactions require journal entries in each fund, but because the transactions are different in nature, the entries take different forms.

Interfund Services Provided and Used

As the name implies, *interfund services provided and used* transactions occur when one fund sells goods to or performs services for another fund for a price approximating their external exchange value. These transactions occur typically when an Enterprise Fund or an Internal Service Fund provides goods or services to governmental departments that receive appropriations through the General Fund. Such transactions result in the recognition of revenues and expenditures (or expenses) by the participating funds in the same manner as if an exchange transaction occurred between the government and a commercial entity.

To illustrate, although a government's Electric and Water Enterprise Funds exist primarily to provide services to the jurisdiction's residents, governmental departments financed through the General Fund also require electric and water services. Therefore, they purchase the services from the Enterprise Funds in the same way they would purchase them from a commercial enterprise if the Enterprise Funds did not exist. Thus, if the General Fund receives a bill for $50,000 from the Water Utility Fund for water supplied to city departments, the transaction would be recorded as follows:

In the General Fund (the purchaser of services):

Expenditures—water services	50,000	
Due to Water Utility Fund		50,000
To record billing from Water Utility Fund.		

In the Water Utility Fund (the seller of services):

Due from General Fund	50,000	
Revenues—water services		50,000
To record billing to General Fund.		

Interfund Transfers

Interfund transfers record flows of assets (such as cash or goods) without equivalent flows of assets in return and without a requirement for repayment. Interfund transfers account for the largest part of the interfund activity of many governments. A typical interfund transfer is a periodic cash transfer from the General Fund to a Debt Service Fund so the latter fund can pay for debt service. Other examples are (1) an operating subsidy from the General Fund to an Electric Utility Fund (Enterprise Fund); (2) a payment made by the General Fund to a Capital Projects Fund for part of the cost of constructing a capital project that is financed also with an intergovernmental grant; and (3) a transfer of the residual fund balance of a Debt Service Fund to the General Fund after the principal and interest have been paid in full.

Unlike interfund services provided and used (which are exchange-type transactions), interfund transfers should not be accounted for as revenues and expenditures/expenses of either fund involved in the transaction. Instead, interfund transfers in and out are reported in governmental fund operating statements as Other financing sources (uses) after the caption "Excess (deficiency) of revenues over expenditures." (For illustration, see Table 5-2 later in this chapter.) In proprietary fund operating statements, interfund transfers in and out are reported separately after the caption "Income (loss) before transfers" and other items, if any, as illustrated on page 41 and in Chapter 7.

To illustrate, if a city council directs the General Fund to transfer $100,000 to the Debt Service Fund, the following entries are made in the respective funds:

In the General Fund (the transferor):

Transfer out to the Debt Service Fund	100,000	
Cash		100,000
To record transfer to Debt Service Fund.		

In the Debt Service Fund (the transferee):

Cash	100,000	
Transfer in from General Fund		100,000
To record transfer from General Fund.		

Transfers out and in can be accrued before cash is paid. If that had occurred in the preceding illustration, the General Fund would have credited the liability account Due to Debt Service Fund (rather than Cash), and the Debt Service Fund would have debited the asset account Due from General Fund (rather than Cash). Interfund transfers should net to zero among all funds within a government; that is, for every transfer in reported in a fund, an equal transfer out should be reported in another fund.

Interfund Loans

Interfund loans arise when one fund lends cash to another with a requirement for repayment. When the loan is made, the lender fund records a receivable, and the borrower records a payable. Although there is no authoritative requirement to do so, practitioners generally distinguish between short-term and long-term interfund loans.[24] To illustrate accounting for a short-term

---

[24]A distinction is made because, in theory, governmental-type funds have only *current* financial resources. Therefore, if a governmental fund makes a long-term loan, it will acquire a noncurrent resource. GASB standards do not define *short-term* and *long-term*. Some practitioners consider a loan long-term if it is due to be paid more than 1 year after the financial statement date, but consistency with fund accounting theory suggests that the asset is long-term if it is not *available to liquidate current fund liabilities.*

interfund loan, assume a General Fund (that operates on a calendar year basis) lends $75,000 to a Proprietary Fund on January 15, 2013, requiring repayment by January 15, 2014. When the loan is made, the transaction is recorded in each fund as follows:

In the General Fund (the lender):

Due from Proprietary Fund	75,000	
Cash		75,000
To record short-term loan.		

In the Proprietary Fund (the borrower):

Cash	75,000	
Due to General Fund		75,000
To record short-term borrowing.		

For financial reporting purposes, if there were several interfund loans, the broader captions Due from other funds and Due to other funds would be used. Notice that loan transactions are the only ones among the four types of interfund transactions that affect only balance sheet accounts.

If a long-term loan were to be made, the receivables and payables captions would be changed to "Advance to . . ." and "Advance from . . .," respectively. Notice, however, that making a long-term loan causes an anomaly—the existence of a noncurrent asset in a fund that is supposed to have only current financial resources. To deal with that issue, an additional journal entry is needed to enable the balance sheet of the lending fund to signify that a portion of its fund balance (i.e., the portion represented by the long-term advance) is not currently available for spending.[25] The journal entries needed to record a long-term advance (say, for 5 years) of $75,000 from the General Fund to a Proprietary Fund would be as follows:

In the General Fund (the lender):

Advance to Proprietary Fund	75,000	
Cash		75,000
To record long-term loan to Proprietary Fund.		
Unassigned fund balance	75,000	
Nonspendable fund balance		75,000
To record reclassification of fund balance to nonspendable as a result of long-term loan.		

In the Proprietary Fund (the borrower):

Cash	75,000	
Advance from General Fund		75,000
To record long-term loan from General Fund.		

Interfund Reimbursements

Sometimes expediency may require that an expenditure be paid entirely or partly by a fund other than the one that should be charged for the transaction. Subsequent repayment to the paying fund by the fund properly chargeable for the expenditure is called an *interfund reimbursement*. For example, assume the General Fund receives and pays an invoice of $25,000 for professional

---

[25]The journal entry to accomplish this result is the second of the two General Fund entries. Fund balance presentation is discussed in detail later in this chapter.

services, but the invoice covers $18,000 of services received by the General Fund and $7,000 of services received by a Capital Projects Fund. As a result, the Capital Projects Fund owes the General Fund $7,000. The following entries have the effect of (a) shifting $7,000 of the expenditure from the books of the General Fund to the books of the Capital Projects Fund and (b) recording an interfund receivable and payable:

In the General Fund (the fund requiring reimbursement):

Due from Capital Projects Fund	7,000	
Expenditures—professional services		7,000
To record reimbursement due from Capital Projects Fund for services paid for by General Fund.		

In the Capital Projects Fund (the fund properly chargeable):

Expenditures—professional services	7,000	
Due to General Fund		7,000
To record expenditure for services initially paid for by General Fund.		

At a later date, when the Capital Projects Fund pays cash to the General Fund to settle the interfund liability, the "due from" and "due to" balances are eliminated.

Governmental Accounting in Practice

An Analytical Perspective on Interfund Transfers and "One-Shots"

Readers of business enterprise financial statements are concerned with transactions that affect the "quality" of reported net profits. Similarly, readers of governmental financial statements need to be concerned with the nature of *all* transactions that affect the net change in fund balance of the General Fund and other governmental-type funds.

Financial analysts are particularly concerned with interfund transfers and certain other items appearing in the General Fund statement of revenues, expenditures, and changes in fund balance. To see where these items appear in this statement, turn to the financial reporting format for governmental-type funds on page 28, and notice the captions between the "Excess (deficiency) of revenues over expenditures" and "Net change in fund balances." The captions are "Other financing sources and uses, including transfers" and "Special and extraordinary items." The transactions and events reported in these captions, particularly within the General Fund, may have significant implications for the financial health of the government.

Both transfers in and transfers out may be either recurring or occasional. For example, the transfer in to the General Fund of net proceeds from lottery ticket sales provides a recurring source of resources. But the transfer in to the General Fund of balances remaining in closed-out funds may represent a nonrecurring inflow intended to shore up the finances of the General Fund in times of fiscal stress. Analysts refer to these nonrecurring inflows as "one-shots." A subsidy to a mass transit facility operated by a component unit of the government, reported as a transfer out of the General Fund, may represent a recurring but *increasing* drain on the parent government's resources.

The "Other financing sources and uses" section also includes items such as proceeds from the issuance of long-term debt and proceeds from the sale of capital assets. When such items appear in the General Fund statement of revenues, expenditures, and changes in fund balance, they may also represent one-shot inflows designed to help "balance" the budget. Significant transactions or events *within the control of management* that are *either* unusual in nature *or* infrequent in occurrence are captioned "special items." They may include the sale and leaseback of a government facility—a transaction that produces a one-shot financial resource inflow, but creates long-term debt.

OTHER ACCOUNTING MATTERS

Acquisition and Disposition of Long-Lived Assets

The acquisition or construction of capital facilities and other capital assets is generally accounted for through the Capital Projects Fund, particularly when financed by the issuance of debt. However, some governments have a policy of financing smaller items of capital equipment, such as sedans used by police and fire departments, with tax and other resources. As a result, the acquisition of long-lived assets is accounted for, to some extent, in the General Fund and Special Revenue Funds.

Under the *current financial resources* measurement focus used in governmental-type funds, purchases of capital assets are accounted for as immediate expenditures, rather than as depreciable balance sheet assets. This is because—from the perspective of the governmental-type fund—using the fund's resources to buy capital assets is no different from using its resources to pay for salaries, utilities, or anything else: They all decrease the available spendable financial resources of the fund.

To illustrate, if the government purchases police sedans for $40,000 using the resources of the General Fund, the journal entry in the General Fund is this:

Expenditures—capital outlay	40,000	
Vouchers payable		40,000
To record capital outlay in General Fund.		

Having been recorded as immediate expenditures, it follows that capital assets acquired with General Fund resources cannot appear in the General Fund balance sheet. Further, having been immediately "written off" (because they were recorded as expenditures) on acquisition, there are no capital assets to depreciate in the General Fund. It is possible, however, that the assets will be sold when they are no longer needed. Because the General Fund shows no "book value" for the assets, the entire proceeds from the sale are recorded as an inflow of resources. If, for example, the police sedans in the preceding illustration are sold at auction for $3,000, the journal entry to record the sale is this:

Cash	3,000	
Other financing sources—proceeds from the sale of general		3,000
fixed assets		
To record sale of sedans at auction.		

To summarize from the perspective of the theory of accounting for governmental-type funds, under the current financial resources measurement focus, the General Fund has only financial resources. Like other governmental-type funds, the General Fund accounts for inflows and outflows of spendable financial resources; once financial resources are spent, they are gone and cannot be spent again. Therefore, when financial resources are used to acquire capital assets, the accounting effect is the same as it is when financial resources are used to pay for operating expenditures. Further, because the General Fund does not try to measure net income, depreciation is neither necessary nor appropriate within that fund. But records do need to be kept of capital assets, and government-wide financial reporting uses the economic resources measurement focus for *all* governmental activities, regardless of the funds used to do the accounting. Treatment of the acquisition and disposition of capital assets and use of depreciation in the government-wide set of financial statements are discussed in Chapter 10.

Inventories and Prepayments

Governments generally do not acquire materials and supplies for resale. For the most part, they acquire materials and supplies for near-term use in operations (such as road, water main, and vehicle maintenance). The well-run governmental repair shop will keep inventory records, maintaining a base stock of supplies to ensure timely delivery of service. However, inventories of materials and supplies tend not to be significant in relation to total assets.

GASB standards provide a rather strange option regarding expenditure recognition for materials and supplies in governmental-type funds. Materials and supplies "may be considered expenditures either when purchased (purchases method) or when used (consumption method), but significant amounts of inventory should be reported in the balance sheet."[26] The consumption method of inventory accounting inherently produces a balance sheet amount, but—assuming the inventory is significant in amount—the purchases method requires a special journal entry, as discussed below.

CONSUMPTION METHOD The consumption method of inventory accounting requires recording materials and supplies as assets when purchased and as expenditures when consumed. Thus, when the consumption method is used, the acquisition of supplies is considered an exchange of one financial asset (cash) for another (supplies inventory), and the expenditure occurs on consumption of the inventory. If supplies costing $100,000 are purchased during the year and $85,000 of that amount is consumed, the journal entries to record the purchase and use are as follows:

Supplies inventory	100,000	
Vouchers payable		100,000
To record purchase of supplies.		
Expenditures—supplies	85,000	
Supplies inventory		85,000
To record usage of supplies.		

PURCHASES METHOD The purchases method of inventory accounting records purchases of supplies as expenditures immediately on acquisition. Therefore, in contrast to the entries made in the foregoing illustration, the following entry is made when $100,000 of supplies is bought:

Expenditures—supplies	100,000	
Vouchers payable		100,000
To record acquisition of supplies.		

The purchases method of accounting for materials and supplies is consistent with the way most governments budget for supplies and is also consistent with governmental-type fund accounting for capital assets; that is, supplies are "written off" as expenditures when acquired. (Conceptually, this method does not view inventory as a financial asset.) As previously mentioned, however, GASB standards require that significant amounts of inventory should be reported in the balance

---

[26]GASB Cod. Sec. 1600.127.

sheet. Therefore, if the year-end inventory is $15,000 and that amount is considered significant, the following journal entry is made:[27]

Supplies inventory	15,000	
Nonspendable fund balance		15,000
To record year-end inventory under purchases method.		

At the end of the following year, to report any change in the inventory balance, the inventory account and the fund balance account should be adjusted upward or downward with a similar journal entry. Use of the term "nonspendable" fund balance is explained in the next section on "Fund Balance Presentation."

GASB standards provide the same accounting option for recording prepayments (such as prepaid insurance and prepaid rent) as they do for materials and supplies. Thus, if expenditures for insurance and similar services cover more than one accounting period, they may be allocated among the affected accounting periods (the consumption method), or they may be accounted for as expenditures in the year of acquisition (the purchases method). Unlike the approach to year-end inventories, the standards are silent regarding the need for reporting significant amounts of unexpired insurance and other prepayments as assets; nevertheless, the preparer may choose to do so if prepayments are considered material.

Although the consumption method may be used, General Fund and Special Revenue Fund expenditures for insurance and rent that cover more than one accounting period typically are charged to the accounting period in which the services are acquired (the purchases method), and prepaid amounts are not considered significant. Thus, if resources of $60,000 are used to acquire a 3-year insurance policy in 2013 for General Fund activities, the following journal entry is made in the General Fund in 2013, and no year-end adjustment is made:

Expenditures—insurance	60,000	
Vouchers payable		60,000
To record acquisition of 3-year insurance policy.		

Warrants

Some governments require that, before a check can be written and payment made, a warrant be prepared. A warrant is an order, drawn by the appropriate authority, requesting the treasurer (or someone designated by that person) to pay a specified sum of money to a particular person or organization. Its purpose is to assist in preventing unauthorized payments. No journal entries are needed when warrants are prepared.

FUND BALANCE PRESENTATION

As noted previously, the net assets of a governmental-type fund—the difference between the total assets and the total liabilities—is called "fund balance." Several references to fund balance in this chapter were preceded by terms like Restricted, Nonspendable, and Unassigned. For example,

[27] As a practical matter, many governments use the purchases method and do not consider the year-end inventory to be significant. Note that we record significant inventory amounts with a direct credit to fund balance. Some writers prefer recording the inventory with a credit to Other financing sources. We suggest the latter method is inconsistent with the purchases method because it changes the year's operating results and effectively converts the purchases method to the consumption method.

when discussing intergovernmental grants, we said that unspent resources on grants with purpose restrictions should be classified as "restricted" fund balance. We now discuss all the classifications of fund balance used in financial reporting and the implications the reader of financial statements may draw from them.

As shown in Table 2-4 of Chapter 2, all governmental-type funds other than the General Fund are used to account for resources that are restricted or otherwise limited to spending for *specific purposes or functions*. But even within the purpose or function limitations, there are varying degrees of constraint; for example, a constitutional or contractual requirement regarding the use of resources is far more constraining on a government than an expression of intent by the government's legislature. Further, use of some of the General Fund resources also may be constrained in varying degrees by the requirements of a higher-level government or by actions of local governmental officials. Users of General Fund financial statements, in particular, need to know the extent and the nature of these constraints so they can determine how much of the fund balance is available for future *general-purpose* spending.

To provide information on the availability of fund balances, GASB Statement No. 54 requires the fund balance sections of governmental-type fund balance sheets to be reported in five potential classifications, based on the extent to which the entity is bound to honor constraints on the purposes for which fund balances may be spent. The classifications, in descending order of constraint, are Nonspendable, Restricted, Committed, Assigned, and Unassigned.

Not all governments are likely to have all five fund balance classifications in a given year. Only the General Fund can have a *positive* Unassigned fund balance. Also, by definition, the fund balances of Special Revenue Funds, Capital Projects Funds, Debt Service Funds, and Permanent Funds have been assigned for some specific purpose or function; hence, the fund balances for those funds are classified *at least* as Assigned. Descriptions and illustrations of the five fund balance classifications follow.

Fund Balance Classifications

NONSPENDABLE FUND BALANCE   Fund balances classified as nonspendable are amounts that are not available for appropriation because they are either (a) not in spendable form or (b) legally or contractually required to be maintained intact. For example,

- Resources are reported in governmental-type fund balance sheets when the government accounts for supplies on the purchases method and has significant amounts of inventory at year-end. A government may also report prepaid items in this manner. As shown on page 151, recording the inventory asset or the prepayment results in a corresponding credit to Nonspendable fund balance.
- Longer-term interfund loans result in receivables that are not currently available for spending. Therefore, when such loans are recorded, there also needs to be a reclassification of the amount loaned from Unassigned to Nonspendable fund balance. Notice the interfund loan ($760,000) made by the Mt. Lebanon General Fund (page 30) and the related Nonspendable fund balance.
- The corpus of a Permanent Fund is legally or contractually required to be maintained intact and is reported as Nonspendable fund balance, as shown in Table 6-11 on page 212.

RESTRICTED FUND BALANCE   Fund balances classified as restricted have the most binding degree of constraint because the related resources can be used for no purpose other than that specified in the constitutional provision, enabling legislation, or contractual provision creating the restriction. Specifically, such constraints may be either

a. Externally imposed by creditors (such as through debt covenants), grantors, contributors, or laws or regulations of other governments; or

b. Imposed by law through constitutional provisions or enabling legislation.[28]

GASB Statement No. 54 defines "enabling legislation" as legislation that authorizes the government to mandate payment of resources (from external resource providers) and includes a legally enforceable requirement that the resources be used only for the purposes stipulated in the legislation. A "legally enforceable requirement" is one whereby the government can be compelled by external parties (such as citizens and the judiciary) to use the resources only as stipulated in the legislation.

Examples of transactions and events creating Restricted fund balance follows:

- The government receives an intergovernmental grant that contains a purpose restriction, as discussed in the earlier section on "Intergovernmental Grants."
- A local government statute authorizes a specific tax or fee for a specified purpose (such as a hotel occupancy tax, levied specifically for beautifying the downtown business district), and legal enforceability regarding use of the tax is established by case law or discussion with governmental counsel.
- Based on a voter-approved proposition, a bond agreement states the specific purpose for which the proceeds of debt will be used.
- A bond agreement requires that 1 year's debt service be maintained with a trustee until the debt from a particular bond issue is fully redeemed.

COMMITTED FUND BALANCE   Fund balances classified as committed are amounts that are constrained as to use as a result of formal action (legislation, resolution, or ordinance) of the government's *highest level of decision-making authority*. These actions require consent of both the legislative and executive branches of government, where applicable.

Amounts classified as committed are distinguished from amounts classified as "restricted by enabling legislation" in that (a) amounts committed may be deployed to other uses through the same types of due process action (legislation, resolution, or ordinance) that created the commitment and (b) constraints on the use of committed amounts are imposed by the government *separately* from the authorization to raise the underlying revenue. Therefore, compliance with the commitment of resources to specific purposes is not considered "legally enforceable," as previously defined.

To illustrate, refer to the previous illustration of restricted resources regarding the hotel occupancy tax. If legal enforceability regarding the decision to use the resources to beautify the downtown area has not been established, then the fund balance should be classified as committed, rather than restricted.

ASSIGNED FUND BALANCE   Amounts constrained by a government's *intent* to spend resources for specific purposes are classified as assigned. The intent to spend may be expressed either by the government's governing body or a body (such as a budget committee) or official to which the governing body has delegated that authority. Constraints imposed on assigned amounts can be

---

[28]GASB Cod. Sec. 1800.134.

more easily removed than those imposed on restricted or committed amounts because (a) assigned constraints are not imposed externally and (b) internal authority to impose the constraint need not be at the highest level of decision making. In no event can the amounts assigned be so great as to create a deficit in Unassigned fund balance.

Any fund balance in a governmental-type fund other than the General Fund that is not classified as nonspendable, restricted, or committed should be classified as assigned. Classifying these amounts as assigned reinforces the point that net assets reported in Special Revenue Funds, Capital Projects Funds, and Debt Service Funds cannot be used for the government's general purposes.

Here are some illustrations of Assigned fund balances:

- The city council's Finance Committee expresses written intent to use part of the General Fund balance for future spending on street lighting, but no appropriation has been made as yet for that purpose. Notice that the General Fund column of Mt. Lebanon's balance sheet on page 30 contains such assignments; they are intended for future pension obligations and winter storm costs.
- The governing body appropriates a portion of the government's year-end fund balance to eliminate an anticipated budgetary deficit in the subsequent year's budget equal to the projected excess of expected expenditures over expected revenues. Notice that the General Fund column of Mt. Lebanon's balance sheet on page 30 contains such an assignment.

UNASSIGNED FUND BALANCE   Unassigned fund balance is the residual classification for the General Fund only. The amount reported as unassigned is available for spending for any legal purpose. From the perspective of both internal financial statement users and external analysts, the Unassigned fund balance is available as a cushion against revenue shortfalls caused by economic contraction and as a means of financing any future needs. It should also be noted that, because of the ease in removing the constraints, much of the Assigned fund balance probably can be accessed readily for general purposes, if needed.

Accounting for and Reporting on Fund Balance Classifications

The composition of governmental fund balance is essentially a year-end financial reporting process; that is, data accumulated within the accounting system should enable the financial statement preparer to make the appropriate classifications for financial reporting purposes. In fact, the original journal entries made to record some transactions, such as Advances to other funds, result in recording Nonspendable fund balances.

If a government has restricted resources from grants, internal records are generally needed for billing and for determining how much has been spent on the grant. If a government uses both restricted and unrestricted resources to finance a particular program, it should compute the composition of year-end fund balances by applying its accounting policies regarding the order in which expenditures were incurred during the year.

Judgment may be needed in making some classifications. For example, suppose a government receives a grant with a requirement that it match the grant with its own resources. It accounts for the grant in a Special Revenue Fund and classifies the resources as Restricted fund balance. If it transfers General Fund resources to that fund to make the match, year-end balances of the transferred resources also would be classified as Restricted fund balance.[29]

---

[29]GASB Comprehensive Implementation Guide, 2010–2011, Q and A Z54.8, p. Z-41.

Effect of Year-End Encumbrances on Fund Balance Classification

In Chapters 3 and 4, we assumed all materials and services ordered (and encumbered) during the fiscal year are received on or before the year's end. In reality, however, not all items ordered during the year are received in the same year, particularly when the orders are placed toward the end of the year. As discussed in Chapter 3, encumbrances are a constraint on the amount available for spending. What happens to encumbrances that are still open at year-end, and how does that affect the classification of fund balance?

Laws differ among jurisdictions regarding unexpended appropriations at year-end. Some governments allow the encumbered portions of their unexpended appropriations at year-end to remain open. When the supplies or services are received, they are charged against the open appropriation of the year for which they were budgeted. More often, the appropriations lapse at the end of the year and become void as spending authority. In that case, expenditures relating to the open encumbrances will be charged to the following year's appropriations. Regardless of how they are handled for budget purposes, however, year-end open encumbrances are not expenditures, and liabilities for financial accounting purposes are not recorded until the year the supplies or services are received.

To the extent that the entity's fund balances have been classified as restricted, committed, or assigned, amounts encumbered within those classifications should not be displayed separately in the fund balance section of the balance sheet because the classification itself adequately describes the constraint. However, amounts encumbered from *unassigned resources should be reported as Assigned fund balance* because the authority given to the person that places the order results in that amount meeting the criteria for classification as assigned. Because the revenue, expenditure, and transfer accounts are closed to Unassigned fund balance when the books are closed, as described in Chapter 4, the following journal entry is needed to reclassify open encumbrances at year-end (if not previously classified as restricted, committed, or assigned) from Unassigned fund balance to Assigned fund balance (amounts assumed):

Unassigned fund balance	100,000	
Assigned fund balance		100,000
To classify year-end open encumbrances as assigned.		

This journal entry will be reversed at the start of the next year.

In addition, because all budgetary account balances need to be closed at year-end, the following entry is needed:

Budgetary fund balance reserved for encumbrances	100,000	
Encumbrances		100,000
To close year-end outstanding encumbrances.		

At the start of the next year, the encumbrances are reestablished by means of a debit to Encumbrances and a credit to Budgetary fund balance reserved for encumbrances.

REVIEW OF YEAR-END FINANCIAL STATEMENTS

As noted in Chapters 2 and 4, the year-end financial statements prepared for the General Fund and each Special Revenue Fund are a balance sheet and a statement of revenues, expenditures, and changes in fund balance. In addition to these statements, a budgetary comparison schedule (or statement) must be prepared for the General Fund and for each major Special Revenue Fund that has a legally adopted annual budget.

The financial statements described in Chapter 4 were based on the illustration contained in that chapter. Therefore, they did not illustrate the financial reporting effects of certain transactions described in this chapter—specifically, interfund transfers and deferred revenues.

Governmental fund statements of revenues, expenditures, and changes in fund balance have three major sections: Revenues, Expenditures, and—where applicable—Other financing sources and uses. Transfers in from other funds are common Other financing sources, and Transfers out to other funds are common Other financing uses reported in governmental-type funds. The financial resources measurement focus of governmental-type funds also results in Other financing sources. For example, significant sales of capital assets often produce Other financing sources in the General Fund, and proceeds from the sale of long-term obligations often result in Other financing sources in the Capital Projects Fund. See Table 5-2 on page 165 for an illustration of how Other financing sources and uses are displayed in the General Fund.

The illustration in Chapter 4 assumed that the entire property tax levy would meet the "available" criterion. In actual practice, however, a portion of the property tax levy is not likely to be available, and revenue recognition will be deferred to a subsequent accounting period. Table 5-3 on page 166 shows how deferred inflows of resources are displayed on the General Fund balance sheet. Mt. Lebanon's financial statements in Table 2-5 and Table 2-6 (pages 29 and 30) provide additional illustrations.

Table 5-4 on page 167 presents the budgetary comparison schedule in a slightly different format from that shown in Chapter 4. Both formats are acceptable methods of display.

REVIEW PROBLEM ON THE GENERAL FUND

The Problem

The following problem summarizes the material in this chapter from the recording of transactions and events to the preparation of year-end financial statements and closing the books. Read each transaction, prepare the journal entry, and compare it with the solution shown after the problem. Then, trace the trial balance to the financial statements.

Jazzmin County's annual budget becomes law after the budget submitted by the elected county manager is reviewed and approved by the county legislature and the appropriation act is signed by the county manager. The postclosing trial balance of the General Fund of Jazzmin County, as of December 31, 2011, is as follows:

	Debits	Credits
Cash	$ 82,000	
Property taxes receivable—delinquent	35,000	
Deferred property tax revenues		$ 15,000
Assigned fund balance		5,000
Unassigned fund balance		97,000
	$117,000	$117,000

inflow (handwritten annotation next to "Deferred property tax revenues")

Following are some of the county's accounting policies:

- A control account for property taxes is used.
- Purchases of supplies and capital outlays are encumbered, but expenditures for salaries, transfers, and other items do not require encumbrances.

- Open encumbrances lapse at the end of the year, but are considered in developing the next year's budget and appropriations act.
- For consistency with property taxes, "available" for sales taxes is defined as taxes expected to be collected within the first 60 days of the next year. "Available" for intergovernmental grants is defined as amounts owed to the county and expected to be received in cash during the first 60 days of the next year.
- If the county receives a grant for a specific purpose, but with no time restriction, and both grant resources and county resources are used to perform the specific purpose, the resources expended are charged equally to each source until the restricted resources are consumed.

During the calendar year 2012, the following transactions and events take place:

Opening entries

1. The approved budget for calendar year 2012 is recorded. The budget is as follows:

   Estimated Revenues

Property taxes	$1,755,000	
Sales taxes	795,000	
Intergovermental grants	260,000	$2,810,000
Appropriations		
Public safety program—salaries	$1,300,000	
Public safety program—supplies	250,000	
Health program—salaries	500,000	
All other programs—salaries	400,000	
Vacation pay	18,000	
Capital outlays	40,000	
Pensions	77,000	
Transfer to Debt Service Fund	200,000	2,785,000
Budgeted Increase in Fund Balance		$ 25,000

2. Purchase orders outstanding at the beginning of the year, included in Assigned fund balance, are reencumbered. They are for $5,000 of public safety program supplies.

Property tax and sales tax transactions and events

3. Property taxpayers who owed $35,000 at the beginning of the year pay their delinquent taxes at various times during the year. Property taxes in the amount of $15,000 that had been recorded as deferred revenues, are recognized as revenues.
4. Property taxes are levied in the amount of $1,800,000 to raise the budgeted $1,755,000. An allowance of $45,000 is established for refunds and uncollectible taxes.
5. During the year, property taxes of $1,725,000 are collected on time and in full.
6. Several property owners protest the assessment values placed on their properties. Property owners who had paid their tax bills earlier in the year receive refunds totaling $25,000. Some other property owners have their assessments reduced before paying their tax bills; after their tax bills are reduced by $10,000, they pay the remaining $35,000.
7. Property taxes uncollected at December 31, 2012, ($30,000) are declared delinquent. Based on analysis of the delinquencies, the finance commissioner decides to reduce the allowance for uncollectible taxes to $4,000. She believes that $15,000 of the net receivable balance of $26,000 will be collected in the first 60 days of 2013, and the rest will trickle in later in the year.

8. County sales taxes are piggybacked on the state sales tax. During 2012, the state sends the county $730,000 in sales taxes collected on behalf of the county.

9. On January 20, 2013, the state tells the county that (a) the state will send $50,000 in sales taxes, applicable to 2012, on or about February 15, 2013, and (b) because some merchants have been slow in making payments, another $15,000 in collections applicable to 2012 will not be sent until April or May 2013.

Encumbrances and related payments for items received

10. Purchase orders are sent out during the year as follows:

For public safety program supplies	$240,000
For capital outlays (two sedans)	40,000

11. All supplies ordered during the year, as well as the supplies ordered in 2011 but not received as of December 31, 2011, are received. They are accepted after inspection, vouchers are prepared for $245,000, and payment is made.

12. One of the sedans, ordered for $20,000, is received. Because additional accessories were provided, the invoice is for $22,000. The sedan is accepted and a voucher for $22,000 is prepared and paid.

13. Because the first sedan cost more than anticipated (see item 12), there are insufficient funds available in the Capital outlays appropriation to pay for the second sedan. The legislature approves a $3,000 increase in the Capital outlays appropriation.

Expenditures and expenditure accruals

14. Salaries are paid as follows:

Public safety program	$1,240,000
All other programs	360,000

15. Salaries are earned as follows between December 22 and December 31, 2012. They will be paid on January 8, 2013.

Public safety program	58,000
All other programs	35,000

16. Accounting staff estimates that the county's aggregate liability for vacation days earned increased by $55,000 to $650,000 during 2012, based on the GASB's accrual accounting standards. Included in the total liability is $15,000 for unused vacation days owed to two police officers who retire on December 31, 2012. They will receive cash payment for that amount with their final paycheck on January 8, 2013.

17. When the budget was prepared, the county actuary advised the finance commissioner that the required pension contribution for the year, based on actuarial standards and GASB requirements, would be $150,000. However, the amount appropriated was only $77,000. The county does not intend to increase the appropriation. A check for $77,000 is sent to the county's Pension Trust Fund.

18. The General Fund sends $200,000 to the Debt Service Fund to provide resources for payment of principal and interest on the county's general obligation bonds.

Intergovernmental grant revenues and related expenditures

19. State law provides that the state will reimburse counties for 50 percent of salary expenditures on certain health programs. To receive the grant, the county must submit a plan

showing how it will spend the resources. The state approves the county plan, and in early January 2012, the state advises the county that it will reimburse the county a maximum of $200,000, provided the county spends at least $400,000 on the programs. During the year, the county receives advances of $180,000 based on the approved plan.

20. During the year, the county pays salaries of $420,000 on health programs covered by the grant in item 19.

21. The county advises the state that its total expenditures under the grant were $420,000 (see item 20). The county bills the state for $20,000, the difference between the maximum amount it is eligible to receive ($200,000) and the advances previously received ($180,000).

22. To encourage improvement of county programs for inspecting nursing homes, day care centers, and food establishments, the state makes grants to all counties. The county receives a cash grant of $50,000 from the state to aid the county in performing these functions. The grant contains no restrictions on when it may be used.

23. The county pays salaries of $75,000 on all other health programs. Its internal records show that $60,000 is spent on the inspection program referred to in item 22, and $15,000 is for other programs. **Note:** For use in item 25c, based on its accounting policies, the county considers $30,000 of the inspection program salaries to have been financed from the state grant and $30,000 to have been financed from county revenues.

Significant amounts of inventory at year-end

24. At year-end, before issuing financial statements, the finance commissioner concludes that the amount of public safety supplies on hand ($40,000) is significant and that it should, therefore, be reported in the financial statements.

Items affecting fund balance classification only

25. To comply with GASB Statement No. 54 regarding fund balance details, adjustments may be needed to reclassify Unassigned fund balance to other classifications. Although the adjustments do not affect the operating statement because its bottom line is the *total* fund balance, they do affect the *composition* of fund balance on the balance sheet. Items requiring reclassification of fund balance in this illustration are described here. A note to the balance sheet (see Table 5-3) shows how the adjustments affect the calculation of Unassigned fund balance.

   a. The county's budget for calendar year 2013 is enacted on December 20, 2012. Because of concerns over the economy, sales tax revenues are projected to be sluggish in 2013. To help balance the budget for 2013, the budget contains an appropriation of $25,000 from its anticipated Unassigned fund balance at December 31, 2012.

   b. There are balances of $20,000 in the Encumbrances and Budgetary fund balance reserved for encumbrances accounts. These accounts will be closed against each other in the closing process. Budgetary policies provide that 2012 appropriations will lapse, but the encumbrances will be charged to the 2013 appropriations. Therefore, an adjustment of Unassigned fund balance is needed to record the $20,000 constraint on its use.

   c. The intergovernmental grants contained purpose restrictions and other eligibility requirements. The grant in items 22 and 23 has unexpended resources, based on the county's accounting policies. Analysis of grant records (items 22 and 23) shows unexpended resources of $20,000 ($50,000 grant revenues − $30,000 expenditures). Because the financial accounts are closed to Unassigned fund balance in the closing process, an adjustment of Unassigned fund balance is needed to report $20,000 as restricted.

The Solution to the Problem

Journal entries to record the budgetary and operating transactions are as follows:

1. Estimated revenues—property taxes   1,755,000
    Estimated revenues—sales taxes   795,000
    Estimated revenues—intergovernmental grants   260,000
        Appropriations—public safety program salaries   1,300,000
        Appropriations—public safety program supplies   250,000
        Appropriations—health program salaries   500,000
        Appropriations—all other program salaries   400,000
        Appropriations—vacation pay   18,000
        Appropriations—capital outlays   40,000
        Appropriations—pensions   77,000
        Appropriations—transfer to Debt Service Fund   200,000
        Budgetary fund balance   25,000
            To record the budget for 2012.

2a. Encumbrances—public safety supplies   5,000
        Budgetary fund balance reserved for encumbrances   5,000
        To reestablish encumbrances for supplies ordered
            but not received in 2011.

2b. Assigned fund balance   5,000
        Unassigned fund balance   5,000
        To remove assignment of fund balance for
            encumbrances open at end of 2011.

3a. Cash   35,000
        Property taxes receivable—delinquent   35,000
        To record collection of delinquent property taxes.

3b. Deferred property tax revenues   15,000
        Revenues—property taxes   15,000
        To record 2011 taxes available for 2012.

4. Property taxes receivable   1,800,000
        Allowance for refunds and uncollectible taxes   45,000
        Revenues—property taxes   1,755,000
        To record property tax levy and allowance for refunds
            and uncollectible taxes.

5. Cash   1,725,000
        Property taxes receivable   1,725,000
        To record collection of 2012 property taxes.

6a. Allowance for refunds and uncollectible taxes   25,000
        Cash   25,000
        To record refunds of appealed 2012 taxes.

6 b. Cash   35,000
   Allowance for refunds and uncollectible taxes   10,000
      Property taxes receivable   45,000
    To record collection of 2012 taxes after deduction of
      upheld appeals.

7a. Property taxes receivable—delinquent   30,000
      Property taxes receivable   30,000
    To reclassify unpaid taxes as delinquent.

7b. Allowance for refunds and uncollectible taxes   10,000
      Allowance for refunds and uncollectible   4,000
       taxes—delinquent
      Revenues—property taxes   6,000
    To adjust allowance account to $4,000 and reclassify
      account to delinquent.

7c. Revenues—property taxes   11,000
    Deferred property tax revenues   11,000
    To record deferral of revenues for amount not expected
      to be collected before March 1, 2013.

8. Cash   730,000
      Revenues—sales taxes   730,000
    To record sales tax collections.

9. Sales taxes receivable   65,000
      Revenues—sales taxes   50,000
      Deferred sales tax revenues   15,000
    To record sales taxes applicable to 2012, expected to be
      collected before March 1 ($50,000) and after ($15,000).

10. Encumbrances—public safety supplies   240,000
   Encumbrances—capital equipment   40,000
      Budgetary fund balance reserved for encumbrances   280,000
    To record encumbrances for supplies and sedans.

11a. Budgetary fund balance reserved for encumbrances   245,000
      Encumbrances—public safety supplies   245,000
    To record receipt of supplies.

11b. Expenditures—public safety supplies   245,000
      Vouchers payable   245,000
    To record liability for payment of supplies.

11c. Vouchers payable   245,000
      Cash   245,000
    To record payment for supplies.

12a.	Budgetary fund balance reserved for encumbrances	20,000	
	Encumbrances—capital equipment		20,000
	To record receipt of sedans		

12b.	Expenditures—capital outlay	22,000	
	Vouchers payable		22,000
	To record liability for payment of sedan.		

12c.	Vouchers payable	22,000	
	Cash		22,000
	To record payment for sedan.		

13.	Budgetary fund balance	3,000	
	Appropriations—capital outlays		3,000
	To record increase in appropriation.		

14.	Expenditures—public safety program salaries	1,240,000	
	Expenditures—all other program salaries	360,000	
	Cash		1,600,000
	To record payment of salaries in 2012.		

15.	Expenditures—public safety program salaries	58,000	
	Expenditures—all other program salaries	35,000	
	Accrued salaries and other payables		93,000
	To accrue unpaid salaries due and payable.		

16.	Expenditures—vacation pay	15,000	
	Accrued salaries and other payables		15,000
	To accrue vacation pay due to be paid to retirees in January 2013.		

(Note: No accrual is made for vacation pay that is earned but not due for payment.)

17.	Expenditures—pensions	77,000	
	Cash		77,000
	To record payment to Pension Trust Fund.		

(Note: No accrual is made for the difference between pension benefits earned by the employees and the amount paid to the trust fund.)

18.	Transfer out to Debt Service Fund	200,000	
	Cash		200,000
	To record transfer to Debt Service Fund.		

19.	Cash	180,000	
	Advance received on grants		180,000
	To record advances received under health grant.		

(Note: This entry is needed each time an advance is received, which might be quarterly.)

20. Expenditures—health program salaries 420,000

      Cash 420,000

    To record payment of health program salaries.

21. Advance received on grants 180,000

Due from state government 20,000

      Revenues—intergovernmental grants 200,000

    To record revenues earned on grant and balance due
      from state.

    (Note: A state might require quarterly "settlements" of advances made at the start of the quarter. If so,
    the "earning" of the grant revenues and the amount due on the "settlement" would be recorded
    quarterly; a single settlement is shown here for simplicity.)

22. Cash 50,000

      Revenues—intergovernmental grants 50,000

    To record grant that must be used only for inspection
      purposes but has no time restrictions.

23. Expenditures—health program salaries 75,000

      Cash 75,000

    To record health program salaries for 2012.

    (Note: In actual practice, separate appropriations may be made for major programs. Records may be kept
    in various ways to show how much of the inspection program expenditures applies to the grant. Among
    other things, such data can be used to report the Restricted fund balance.)

24. Supplies inventory 40,000

      Nonspendable fund balance 40,000

    To record supplies inventory at December 31, 2012.

25a. Unassigned fund balance 25,000

      Assigned fund balance 25,000

    To record assignment of fund balance based on
      appropriation made to balance 2013 budget.

25b. Unassigned fund balance 20,000

      Assigned fund balance 20,000

    To record assignment of fund balance based on open
      encumbrances on December 31, 2012.

25c. Unassigned fund balance 20,000

      Restricted fund balance 20,000

    To record restriction of fund balance based on
      unexpended grant resources.

To develop the trial balance shown in Table 5-1, we posted all the journal entries, except those shown for items 25a, 25b, and 25c. Those three journal entries were considered in preparing the fund balance section of the balance sheet.

| **TABLE 5-1** | General Fund—Preclosing Trial Balance for Jazzmin County |

Jazzmin County
General Fund
Preclosing Trial Balance
December 31, 2012

	Debits	Credits
Estimated revenues—property taxes	$1,755,000	
Estimated revenues—sales taxes	795,000	
Estimated revenues—intergovernmental grants	260,000	
Appropriations—public safety program salaries		$1,300,000
Appropriations—public safety program supplies		250,000
Appropriations—health program salaries		500,000
Appropriations—all other program salaries		400,000
Appropriations—vacation pay		18,000
Appropriations—capital outlays		43,000
Appropriations—pensions		77,000
Appropriations—transfer to Debt Service Fund		200,000
Budgetary fund balance		22,000
Encumbrances—capital outlays	20,000	
Budgetary fund balance reserved for encumbrances		20,000
Cash	173,000	
Property taxes receivable—delinquent	30,000	
Allowance for refunds and uncollectible taxes—delinquent		4,000
Sales taxes receivable	65,000	
Due from state government	20,000	
Supplies inventory	40,000	
Accrued salaries and other payables		108,000
Deferred property tax revenues		11,000
Deferred sales tax revenues		15,000
Nonspendable fund balance		40,000
Unassigned fund balance		102,000
Revenues—property taxes		1,765,000
Revenues—sales taxes		780,000
Revenues—intergovernmental grants		250,000
Expenditures—public safety program salaries	1,298,000	
Expenditures—public safety program supplies	245,000	
Expenditures—health program salaries	495,000	
Expenditures—all other program salaries	395,000	
Expenditures—vacation pay	15,000	
Expenditures—capital outlays	22,000	
Expenditures—pensions	77,000	
Transfer out to Debt Service Fund	200,000	
	$5,905,000	$5,905,000

Budget

TABLE 5-2 General Fund—Statement of Revenues, Expenditures, and Changes in Fund Balance

Jazzmin County
General Fund
Statement of Revenues, Expenditures, and Changes in Fund Balance
Year Ended December 31, 2012

Revenues

Property taxes	$1,765,000	
Sales taxes	780,000	
Intergovernmental grants	250,000	$2,795,000

Expenditures

Public safety program salaries	1,298,000	
Public safety program supplies	245,000	
Health program salaries	495,000	
All other program salaries	395,000	
Vacation pay	15,000	
Capital outlays	22,000	
Pensions	77,000	2,547,000
Excess of Revenues over Expenditures		248,000

Other Financing Sources (Uses)

Transfer out to Debt Service Fund	(200,000)
Increase in fund balance	48,000
Fund balance, January 1, 2012	102,000
Increase in nonspendable fund balance	40,000
Fund balance, December 31, 2012	$ 190,000

Note: Journal entry 24 increased the supplies inventory with a direct credit to fund balance. The line "Increase in nonspendable fund balance" is needed in this statement to arrive at the total fund balance shown in the balance sheet.

TABLE 5-3	Balance Sheet

Jazzmin County
General Fund
Balance Sheet
December 31, 2012

Assets		
Cash		$ 173,000
Property taxes receivable—delinquent	$ 30,000	
Less, allowance for refunds and uncollectible taxes	4,000	26,000
Sales taxes receivable		65,000
Due from state government		20,000
Supplies inventory		40,000
Total assets		$ 324,000
Liabilities		
Accrued salaries and other payables	$ 108,000	
Total liabilities		$ 108,000
Deferred Inflows of Resources		
Deferred property tax revenues	11,000	
Deferred sales tax revenues	15,000	
Total deferred inflows of resources		26,000
Fund Balance		
Nonspendable supplies inventory	40,000	
Restricted for grant	20,000	
Assigned for 2013 budget	25,000	
Assigned for capital outlays	20,000	
Unassigned	85,000	
Total fund balance		190,000
Total liabilities, deferred inflows of resources, and fund balance		$ 324,000

Note: The Unassigned fund balance of $85,000 represents the total fund balance of $190,000 shown in the statement of revenues, expenditures, and changes in fund balance, minus the Nonspendable fund balance of $40,000 and the effect of the three reclassifications shown in journal entries 25a ($25,000), 25b ($20,000), and 25c (20,000). If we had posted the three journal entries before preparing the trial balance (Table 5-1), the Unassigned fund balance shown in the trial balance would have been $37,000. That amount plus the increase in fund balance shown in the operating statement (Table 5-2) equals $85,000.

TABLE 5-4	Budgetary Comparison Schedule

Jazzmin County
General Fund
Budgetary Comparison Schedule
Year Ended December 31, 2012

	Budgeted Amounts		Actual Amounts
	Original	Final	(Budgetary Basis)
Budgetary fund balance, beginning	$ 102,000	$ 102,000	$ 102,000
Resource inflows			
Property taxes	1,755,000	1,755,000	1,765,000
Sales taxes	795,000	795,000	780,000
Intergovernmental grants	260,000	260,000	250,000
Amount available for appropriation	2,912,000	2,912,000	2,897,000
Charges to appropriations (outflows)			
Public safety program salaries	1,300,000	1,300,000	1,298,000
Public safety program supplies	250,000	250,000	245,000
Health program salaries	500,000	500,000	495,000
All other program salaries	400,000	400,000	395,000
Vacation pay	18,000	18,000	15,000
Capital outlays	40,000	43,000	22,000
Pensions	77,000	77,000	77,000
Transfer to Debt Service Fund	200,000	200,000	200,000
Total charges to appropriations	2,785,000	2,788.000	2,747,000
Budgetary fund balance, end	$ 127,000	$ 124,000	$ 150,000

Note: The budgetary comparison schedule (or statement), a required element of financial reporting, is discussed further in Chapter 9. The schedule may be prepared using various formats. The "original" budget comes from the journal entry recording the adopted budget. The "final" column comes from the preclosing trial balance. The actual column is prepared using the budgetary basis of accounting, which may be the cash basis, the modified accrual basis used in financial accounting, or some other hybrid basis.

We assumed, for purposes of preparing this schedule, that Jazzmin's budgetary basis is the modified accrual basis used for financial reporting purposes, except that supplies inventory is not spendable for budgetary purposes. In this instance, the Budgetary fund balance is the total of the Restricted, Assigned, and Unassigned fund balances on the balance sheet ($150,000) because that amount is available for appropriation in 2013. (The amount "Assigned for 2013 budget" was appropriated to help balance the 2013 budget, and the amount "Assigned for capital outlays" represents the encumbered item that lapsed for expenditure in 2012 and will be appropriated in 2013.)

Closing Journal Entries

The simplest way to close the books is to (1) close budgetary account debits and credits to each other (see the following journal entries 1 and 2), (2) close revenue, expenditure, and other financing sources (uses) accounts to Unassigned fund balance (see journal entry 3), and (3) make the entries shown for item 25 in the Jazzmin County illustration. Those entries remove restricted and assigned amounts from Unassigned fund balance. The preclosing trial balance gives the amounts for the journal entries, which are shown here:

1.	Appropriations—public safety program salaries	1,300,000	
	Appropriations—public safety program supplies	250,000	
	Appropriations—health program salaries	500,000	
	Appropriations—all other program salaries	400,000	
	Appropriations—vacation pay	18,000	
	Appropriations—capital outlays	43,000	
	Appropriations—pensions	77,000	
	Appropriations—transfer to Debt Service Fund	200,000	
	Budgetary fund balance	22,000	
	Estimated revenues—property taxes		1,755,000
	Estimated revenues—sales taxes		795,000
	Estimated revenues—intergovernmental grants		260,000
	To close budgetary accounts.		
2.	Budgetary fund balance reserved for encumbrances	20,000	
	Encumbrances—capital outlays		20,000
	To close budgetary encumbrance accounts.		
3.	Revenues—property taxes	1,765,000	
	Revenues—sales taxes	780,000	
	Revenues—intergovernmental grants	250,000	
	Expenditures—public safety program salaries		1,298,000
	Expenditures—public safety program supplies		245,000
	Expenditures—health program salaries		495,000
	Expenditures—all other program salaries		395,000
	Expenditures—vacation pay		15,000
	Expenditures—capital outlays		22,000
	Expenditures—pensions		77,000
	Transfer out to Debt Service Fund		200,000
	Unassigned fund balance		48,000
	To close operating accounts to Unassigned fund balance.		

Notice that the year's increase in Unassigned fund balance ($48,000) shown in the last journal entry plus the beginning-of-year Unassigned fund balance in the trial balance ($102,000) equals $150,000. The three adjustments from the journal entries for item 25 total $65,000. The resulting Unassigned fund balance is $85,000, the amount shown in the balance sheet.

Review Questions

Q5-1 What is the purpose of establishing an allowance for uncollectible property taxes at the time the property tax levy is recorded?

Q5-2 What is the basic rule for recognizing property tax revenues in governmental-type funds?

Q5-3 What is a property tax lien?

Q5-4 What is the basic rule for recognizing sales tax and personal income tax revenues in governmental-type funds?

Q5-5 Cite two examples of circumstances in which a government may find it necessary to record deferred revenues in governmental-type funds?

Q5-6 What is the basic rule for recognizing intergovernmental grant revenues in governmental-type funds?

Q5-7 Describe the implications of the phrase "normally expected to be liquidated with expendable available financial resources" as applied to accruing liabilities for compensated absences in governmental-type funds?

Q5-8 Identify the four categories of interfund transactions. Which of the four results in the recognition of revenues and expenditures (expenses)?

Q5-9 Why is depreciation not recorded in governmental-type funds?

Q5-10 What is the accounting treatment for supplies inventories if the purchases method is used to record their acquisition?

Q5-11 What is an allotment? What is the purpose of an allotment system?

Q5-12 What is the purpose of reporting fund balance in five classifications? What is the difference between Restricted fund balance and Assigned fund balance?

Q5-13 How are open encumbrances at year-end reported in the financial statements?

Discussion Scenarios and Issues

D5-1 The governor and his college-age daughter are talking after dinner. The governor has had a tough day at the office discussing the state's budget problems. The daughter is home on vacation after having completed a course in municipal accounting. She has just told her dad about the substance of this chapter in this text. "That's great," says the governor, "you just solved my problem. I'll tell my budget director to prepare the budget using those wonderful GAAP rules you just described. We'll save money by firing our actuary because his ideas about financing pension and retiree benefits cost too much. We'll save more money by budgeting zero dollars for pensions because the pension plan has enough resources to pay benefits to retirees for several years. And we'll save even more by budgeting just enough for retiree health care benefits to pay the bills of our retirees, rather than putting money into a fund to pay for those currently working." The governor's daughter looks at him and says: "Hold on a sec, Dad, you're getting me a bit worried." What did his daughter say about "those wonderful GAAP rules" that caused the governor to reach his conclusion? Why is his daughter worried?

D5-2 As this text was being written, the GASB web site indicated that one of its agenda projects was called "Conceptual Framework—Recognition and Measurement Attributes." One question covered by the project was "What messages are financial statements conceptually attempting to convey?" In discussing the history of the project, the web site noted that, at one meeting, the board focused on the specific meaning of the term *current financial resources* so that it might explain with greater specificity the message conveyed by statements prepared using that measurement focus, but the board "did not reach a conclusion on the issue." This project has been on the agenda for about 5 years. After studying this chapter, comment on the issues troubling the GASB by discussing any inconsistencies or other problems you perceive in the standards regarding recognition and measurement of revenues, receivables, expenditures, and liabilities.

D5-3   When reviewing the financial statements of Crescent City, Councilwoman Peggy Doubleton noticed that the city uses an Allowance for uncollectible property taxes. This seemed odd to her because the city had recently sold several acres of land that had been seized for nonpayment of property taxes. At the next council meeting, she moved that the city no longer provide for uncollectible property taxes because the city had the right to seize property for nonpayment of taxes. As a result, it could eventually recover any lost revenue. Further, by eliminating this allowance, revenues could be increased immediately, and additional services could be provided without incurring a deficit. Would you vote for Councilwoman Doubleton's motion if you were a council member? Why or why not?

D5-4   Joe Babitt, a former executive of T-Mart, just started a term as mayor of Saulk Center. For the past several days he has been looking for a way to keep his campaign promise to increase services without raising taxes or service charges. While lunching at the country club with the treasurer of T-Mart, the subject of a recent sale and leaseback of one of T-Mart's stores came up. Following a common practice in retailing, T-Mart had erected a building and sold it to an investor. It then signed a long-term lease on the building. "Bingo! That's it," thought Mayor Babitt. "We can sell several of the city's buildings—as well as police cars, fire engines, and other vehicles—to investors and lease them back. That will give us the revenues we desperately need. Now I can concentrate on fighting crime." Do you agree with Mayor Babitt? If not, what are the flaws in his reasoning?

D5-5   River City requires not-for-profit organizations owning real property and personal property, like vehicles and construction equipment, to make payments in lieu of property taxes. Homes for People, a large, not-for-profit organization, owns several rental properties in the city's central business district and operates a large fleet of trucks and bulldozers. Sy Sutter, the city's assessor, is an active member of this organization. Recently, Sutter informed the director of Homes for People that the organization would no longer be required to make payments in lieu of property taxes because of the assistance it had provided the city in cleaning up after a recent hurricane, thus saving the city a large sum of money. Sutter did not notify the city council of this action, reasoning that "in the end, it will all balance out." Was this action ethical? Why or why not? How could such an action be prevented in the future?

Exercises

E5-1   (Accounting for property taxes)

Orinoco City's General Fund had the following transactions regarding property taxes during calendar year 2012. Prepare journal entries to record the transactions.

1. Orinoco levies property taxes in the amount of $2,000,000. Experience shows that 3 percent of the amount levied will not be collected for various reasons, including appeals of tax assessments.
2. Based on tax assessment appeals, Orinoco reduces taxes for several taxpayers by a total of $60,000.
3. Orinoco collects cash of $1,800,000 on the property tax levy.
4. Orinoco declares as delinquent all taxes unpaid as of December 31.
5. For financial reporting purposes, the Orinoco comptroller determines that all unpaid taxes will be collected in 2013, but that only $115,000 of the amount due will be collected in the first 60 days of 2013.

E5-2   (Accounting for property taxes)

The General Fund of the City of Snake River operates on a calendar year basis. It sends bills to property owners on January 2. Taxes are due March 1, but taxpayers are allowed until March 31 to make payment without penalty. Taxpayers who pay before March 1 are allowed to deduct a 1 percent discount. Taxpayers who fail to pay by April 1 are declared delinquent, and notice is sent to them that they owe a penalty of 4 percent of the unpaid taxes. Prepare journal entries to record the following Snake River transactions:

1. Levies property taxes in the amount of $1,000,000. Past experience shows that about $6,000 of that amount will not be collected because taxpayers take advantage of the 1 percent discount.

2. Collects cash of $693,000 before March 1 from taxpayers who had been billed $700,000, but who deducted the 1 percent early payment discount.

3. Collects cash of $275,000 from taxpayers in the month of March.

4. Declares all unpaid taxes to be delinquent and sends notices to delinquent taxpayers that they owe a 4 percent penalty. Snake River's accounting policy calls for accruing the penalty at the time taxes are declared delinquent.

E5-3   (Grant accounting)

Harmon School District accounts for all activities in its General Fund. The school district receives the following grants:

1. Grant A: Harmon is reimbursed by the state for costs incurred in teaching students with disabilities. To receive reimbursement, the district must submit quarterly reports showing its expenditures. Its expenditures for the quarter September through November 2012 were $450,000.

   Prepare separate journal entries to record its expenditures under the grant and its billing to the state.

2. Grant B: Harmon receives a grant in the amount of $100,000 from the federal government for the sole purpose of teaching students with disabilities. The grant contains no time limits and may be used any time after the school district receives the grant.

   Prepare three separate journal entries to record receipt of the $100,000 grant, expenditure of $65,000 on the grant during school year 2013, and year-end classification of fund balance.

E5-4   (Expenditure accruals)

A state whose fiscal year ends June 30, 2013, had the following transactions and events. For each item, compute how much total expenditures the state will report in the General Fund Statement of revenues, expenditures, and changes in fund balance for the year ended June 30, 2013. Also, state the accounting principle that governs calculation of the amount to be accrued at the end of the accounting period.

1. During the year, the state paid salaries of $3,600,000. Its employees also earned $150,000 during the period June 23–30, but the payroll for that period will be paid on July 12.

2. The state permits its employees to accumulate up to 30 days of vacation leave. The employees are entitled to be paid on termination or retirement for any unused vacation days. At the beginning of the fiscal year, the state's liability for unused vacation pay was $720,000. By the end of the fiscal year, the vacation pay liability had increased to $810,000. The latter amount includes $16,000 owed to employees who retired as of June 30, 2013 with unused vacation pay. That amount will be paid on July 12, 2013.

3. At the beginning of the fiscal year, the state's actuary advised the budget director that a total of $430,000 would have to be paid into a Retiree Health Care Trust Fund if the state were to contribute to the fund based on the benefits earned by its active employees during fiscal 2013. The adopted budget, however, contained an appropriation for $115,000, the amount of benefits the state expected to pay on behalf of retired employees. During the year, actual payments on behalf of retired employees were $96,000. An additional $12,000 was scheduled to be paid in July 2013 for health care benefits claimed in June 2013.

E5-5   (Judgments and claims)

A citizen sued a city because he was accidentally shot by a police officer. The city acknowledges responsibility for the accident, and based on ongoing negotiations, the city's attorney believes the citizen's claim will probably be settled for about $75,000. The accident occurred on March 14, 2013; the government's fiscal year ends June 30, 2013; and the city's attorney believes settlement will be reached in about January 2014. Prepare the journal entry, if any, the city should make regarding this event when it closes its General Fund books for fiscal year 2013. To support your answer, state the principle that governs the accounting for this event in the General Fund.

E5-6   (Year-end accounting for encumbrances)

A local government's budget policy allows open encumbrances to lapse at the end of the year. Its budget for the following year takes the open encumbrances into account, and expenditures resulting from those encumbrances are charged against the following year's appropriations. Its General Fund has open encumbrances of $75,000 at the end of fiscal year 2012. There are no restrictions or commitments on the use of these resources. What journal entry or entries should be made at the end of fiscal 2012? What journal entry or entries should be made at the start of fiscal 2013?

E5-7   (Interfund transactions)

The following interfund transactions occurred in Becca City's General Fund during the year ended December 31, 2012. For each transaction, describe its nature (e.g., is it an interfund transfer, an interfund loan, etc), prepare the journal entry in the General Fund, and prepare the journal entry in the other affected fund.

1. Received an invoice for $15,000 from the City's Electric Utility Fund for electricity service in October.
2. Loaned $30,000 to the Parks Special Revenue Fund in May (the Special Revenue Fund was to repay the loan in September 2012).
3. Gave $50,000 to the City's Mass Transit Authority as a subsidy because transit fares were insufficient to pay the authority's operating expenses.

E5-8   (Treatment of inventories—purchases method)

The City of Nickston uses the purchases method to account for the acquisition of supplies by its General Fund. At the end of fiscal 2012, the supplies inventory was valued at $63,000. At the end of fiscal 2013, the supplies inventory was valued at $71,000. Prepare the journal entry that needs to be made at the end of fiscal 2013 to adjust the amount of the supplies inventory.

E5-9   (Classification of fund balance)

The General Fund of Attmore County has a total fund balance of $850,000 at December 31, 2013. Based on the following data, prepare the fund balance section of its General Fund balance sheet.

1. Attmore uses the purchases method to record supplies acquisitions. Attmore considers its year-end inventory of $112,000 to be material.
2. During the year, the General Fund loaned the Internal Service Fund $100,000. The loan will be fully repaid to the General Fund in 3 years.
3. The General Fund received a federal grant of $100,000 to help Attmore plan for anti-terrorism activities. The grant has no time restrictions. At year-end, the General Fund had unspent resources of $40,000 under the grant.
4. In accordance with the authority delegated to him, the Attmore County manager decided to set aside $75,000 of the fund balance of the General Fund for future spending to upgrade its computer systems.

E5-10 (Individual research)

Visit the web site of a state or local government to review its latest Comprehensive Annual Financial Report (CAFR). (You can generally start at www.statelocalgov.net, then select the government, then select the official or office most likely connected with the accounting activity.) Review the details of the General Fund financial statements, noting the captions, the interfund transfers, the "due from" and "due to" accounts, and the classification of fund balance. Read the notes and relate them to the subjects covered in this chapter.

E5-11 (Multiple choice—General and Special Revenue Funds)

1. The budget of Sanger County shows estimated revenues in excess of appropriations. When preparing budgetary entries at the beginning of the fiscal year, an increase will be recorded in which of the following accounts?
   a. Budgetary fund balance
   b. Encumbrances
   c. Due from other funds
   d. Surplus

2. Which of the following involves a routine movement of cash from the General Fund to a Debt Service Fund in order to provide resources to pay interest and principal on a bond issue?
   a. An interfund reimbursement
   b. An interfund loan

c. An interfund service provided and used

✓ d. An interfund transfer   ✓ GF

3. At the end of fiscal 2012, Carson City had outstanding encumbrances of $15,000. Although the city follows a policy of allowing outstanding encumbrances to lapse, it plans to honor the related purchase orders in fiscal 2013. At year-end, the city's accountant should take which of the following actions?

   a. Credit Appropriations

   b. Credit Nonspendable fund balance

✓ c. Credit Assigned fund balance

   d. Credit Budgetary fund balance

4. If the City of Castletown sells a surplus ambulance, the entry to record this sale on the books of the General Fund should include which of the following?

   a. A debit to Unassigned fund balance

   b. A debit to Encumbrances—capital equipment

✓ c. A credit to Other financing sources—proceeds from sale of general fixed assets

   d. A credit to a Vehicles fixed asset account

5. The town council of Bayou Brilleaux adopted a budget for fiscal 2013 that anticipated revenues of $750,000 and expenditures of $800,000. Which entry is used to record this budget in the accounts?

	Dr.	Cr.
a. Estimated revenues	750,000	
Reserve for deficits	50,000	
Appropriations		800,000
✓ b. Estimated revenues	750,000	
Budgetary fund balance	50,000	
Appropriations		800,000
c. Appropriations	800,000	
Budgetary fund balance	50,000	
Estimated revenues		750,000
d. Encumbrances	750,000	
Budgetary fund balance	50,000	
Appropriations		800,000

6. Which of the following best expresses the accounting standard regarding accounting for purchases and inventories in the General Fund?

   a. They must be accounted for in a manner similar to that of commercial enterprises.

   b. All purchases must be accounted for as expenditures upon acquisition.

   c. Purchases may be recorded as expenditures either when acquired or consumed; if accounted for as expenditures when acquired, year-end inventories are ignored.

✓ d. Purchases may be recorded as expenditures either when acquired or consumed; if accounted for as expenditures when acquired, year-end inventories must be reported if the amount is significant.

7. The budget of the General Fund of the City of Olde Glen shows an appropriation for capital equipment of $150,000. So far a fire engine costing $50,000 has been received and paid for. Another fire engine has been ordered, and an encumbrance for $60,000 is outstanding. How much can the city legally spend for a third fire engine this year?

✓ a. $40,000

   b. $100,000

   c. $90,000

   d. $0

Problems

P5-1   (Accounting for personal income taxes)

Saralisa's City, which operates on a calendar year basis, obtains 40 percent of its revenues from personal income taxes. Employers are required to withhold taxes from the earnings of city residents and remit them to the city monthly. City residents must also make payments, if necessary, with quarterly tax estimates. No later than April 15 of the following year, residents must file tax returns, remitting any additional taxes due to the city or claiming refunds of overpayments.

Saralisa's accounting policies call for recognizing taxes obtained from income earned during a particular calendar year provided the taxes are received during the year or before April 30 of the following year; income taxes received after April 30 are recognized as revenues of the year in which received. Prepare journal entries to record the following transactions and events related to calendar year 2012:

1. During 2012 Saralisa receives $3,250,000 from personal income taxes withheld by employers during the year and estimates filed by taxpayers during the year.
2. In January 2013, before the financial statements for 2012 are prepared, Saralisa receives $400,000 from employers and taxpayers based on taxpayer earnings during the latter part of 2012.
3. Saralisa's comptroller estimates that the city will receive $55,000 with the 2012 tax returns (due April 15, 2013), as well as requests for refunds totaling $275,000. The comptroller also estimates that $28,000 will trickle in after April 30 with tax returns filed by late filers.

P5-2   (Accounting for property taxes)

At the start of calendar year 2012, Central City's records showed the following accounts relative to prior year property taxes:

Property taxes—delinquent	52,000
Allowance for uncollectible taxes—delinquent	8,000
Deferred property tax revenues	15,000

Prepare journal entries to record the following transactions:

1. To balance its 2012 budget, which requires $1,500,000 in property taxes, Central City levies property taxes in the amount of $1,515,000, providing an allowance of $15,000 for uncollectible accounts.
2. During the year 2012, it collects property taxes as follows:

From prior year delinquent taxes	44,000
From 2012 tax levy	1,490,000

3. Central City recognizes the $15,000 deferred property tax revenues as revenues for 2012.
4. It initiates foreclosure proceedings against the delinquent taxpayer who owed the city $8,000. When it does this, it charges the taxpayer a penalty of $1,000.
5. An auctioneer sells the foreclosed property for $40,000, deducts a fee of $3,000, and remits $37,000 to the city. The city deposits the check and prepares a voucher for the net amount due to the taxpayer.
6. The city reverses the Allowance for uncollectible taxes—delinquent ($8,000) because the lien has been satisfied and all prior year delinquent taxes have been collected.
7. Central City rebates $12,000 to taxpayers who had paid their 2012 taxes, but who successfully appealed their tax assessments.
8. At year-end, the city (a) declares all unpaid 2012 taxes as delinquent; (b) concludes that there is no need for an allowance for uncollectible accounts; and (c) estimates that $15,000 of the delinquent taxes will be collected in the first 60 days of calendar year 2013.

P5-3   (Revenue accruals and other adjustments)

Sammy County is preparing financial statements for the year ended December 31, 2012. Based on the following facts, prepare journal entries to record the appropriate year-end revenue accruals and other adjustments in the county's General Fund. Also, state the accounting principle that justifies each journal entry.

1. At year-end, Sammy's delinquent property tax receivables were $60,000. The county estimated that $35,000 of those delinquencies would be collected by February 28, 2013, and the balance would trickle in during the rest of 2013.

2. Sales taxes are collected by the state on behalf of the county. On January 20, 2013, the state advised the county that (a) it would send the county a check for $150,000 before February 28, 2013, for taxes collected by merchants for the fourth quarter of 2012; and (b) based on past experience, it anticipated sending an additional check for approximately $45,000 during March or April for taxes received from late filers. Sammy's policy regarding sales taxes is to consider as "available" all taxes received before April 30, provided they were collected by merchants in the period covered by the financial statements.

3. Pursuant to state law, the county receives an annual grant from the state to inspect nursing homes and day care centers within the county. The law provides that the state will reimburse the county for 50 percent of salary and travel costs incurred by the county, but no more than the amount appropriated in the state budget for that purpose. For 2012 the amount appropriated by the state for Sammy County was $240,000. Sammy received an advance payment of $175,000 in January 2012 and was to apply for any additional amount due to the county before January 31, 2013. Sammy determined that it had spent a total of $520,000 (covering both the county's share and the state's share of the costs) on the program. (Hint: Assume Sammy had recorded both the $175,000 advance and the $520,000 of expenditures. Prepare the journal entry to record the amount due from the state.)

P5-4 (Expenditure accruals)

Nickamigo County is preparing financial statements for the fiscal year ended June 30, 2012. Based on the following facts, prepare journal entries to record the appropriate year-end expenditure accruals in the county's General Fund. Also, state the accounting principle that justifies each journal entry.

1. The work week in Nickamigo County runs from Saturday through Friday. Its employees are paid 7 days after the end of the work week. For the work week ended Friday, June 29, 2012, the employees earned $580,000. Employees who worked Saturday, June 30, earned a total of $40,000.

2. A claim for $100,000 was filed against a county health clinic for medical malpractice in March 2012. The case is scheduled to go to trial in January 2013. County attorneys believe it is probable the county will lose the case if it goes to trial and thus will try to negotiate a settlement. They believe the claim can be settled for about $40,000.

3. The county pays health care benefits on behalf of its retired employees. Nickamigo's actuary advised the county that if the plan were financed in accordance with actuarial standards, it would need to contribute $600,000 for fiscal year 2012 to its Retiree Health Care Trust Fund. Instead, the county makes monthly payments into the fund that are sufficient to pay the actual expenditures made on behalf of its retirees. The county paid $125,000 into the fund between July 1, 2011 and June 30, 2012, and will pay an additional $18,000 into the fund on July 10, 2012 for benefit claims made in June, 2012.

P5-5 (Multiple choice—General and Special Revenue Funds)

1. Which of the following sets of accounts is the General Fund likely to have?
   a. Vouchers payable, Due to other funds, and Deferred revenues—property taxes
   b. Cash, Property taxes receivable, and Capital assets
   c. Cash, Allowance for depreciation, and Allowance for uncollectible taxes
   d. Vouchers payable, Bonds payable, and Unassigned fund balance

2. Which of the following transactions results in reporting a transfer out in the General Fund statement of revenues, expenditures, and changes in fund balance?
   a. Payment to Water Enterprise Fund for use of water by county departments.
   b. Payment to Motor Pool Internal Service Fund for use of automobiles by county departments.
   c. Payment to Debt Service Fund for debt service on general obligation debt.
   d. Payment to Sewage Special Revenue Fund as a short-term loan to that fund.

3. A village levied property taxes of $910,000 on January 1, 2012, for calendar year 2012 and immediately set up an allowance of $10,000 for uncollectible taxes. The village collected

$870,000 in cash during 2012. It expected to collect $22,000 of the unpaid taxes during the first 60 days of 2013 and an additional $8,000 during the rest of 2013. How much should the village recognize as property tax revenues in its 2012 General Fund financial statements?

a. $870,000
b. $892,000
c. $900,000
d. $910,000

4. Based on the information in the previous scenario, how much should the village report as Deferred inflows—property taxes in its 2012 General Fund financial statements?

a. $0
b. $8,000
c. $18,000
d. $30,000

5. These two events occurred in the same city toward the end of calendar year 2012:

- City employees earned $85,000 during the last week of December 2012, but were not paid until January 5, 2013.
- A city sanitation vehicle accidentally sideswiped a parked car during November 2012. The city acknowledged that it was at fault, and its attorneys expect to pay $10,000 to settle the claim. However, the city is slow in settling claims, so it probably won't pay the claim until early 2014.

Based on only these two events, how much should the city report as expenditures for calendar year 2012?

a. $0
b. $10,000
c. $85,000
d. $95,000

6. A state provides pension benefits to retired employees who have worked at least 5 years for the state. Based on employee salaries during 2012, the state actuary calculated that the employees earned pension benefits totaling $14 million. The state appropriated $10 million to the General Fund for payment to its Pension Trust Fund. However, the state encountered financial problems during 2012 and sent its pension system a check for $8 million in October 2012, saying that it would pay no more for the year. The Pension Trust Fund actually paid pension benefits of $5 million during 2012. How much should the General Fund recognize as pension expenditures for 2012?

a. $5 million
b. $8 million
c. $10 million
d. $14 million

7. Pursuant to the law, a city authorizes imposition of a hotel occupancy tax for the sole purpose of beautifying the downtown area. During the year the city collects hotel occupancy taxes of $800,000, deposits that amount in a Downtown Redevelopment Special Revenue Fund, and spends $450,000 of it. How should the remaining $350,000 of net assets be classified in the Special Revenue Fund's balance sheet?

a. As Nonspendable fund balance
b. As Reserved fund balance
c. As Assigned fund balance
d. As Restricted fund balance

8. Which of the following transactions or events best describes when a grant recipient may recognize revenues from intergovernmental grants in governmental-type funds?

a. The recipient must receive cash from the grant provider.
b. The recipient must enter into a contract with the grant provider.

c. The recipient must spend all the resources made available in the grant.

d. The recipient must comply with all grant eligibility requirements, and the resources must be "available."

P5-6 (Interfund transactions)

Prepare journal entries to record these interfund transactions in each affected fund:

1. The General Fund makes a short-term loan of $75,000 to a Special Revenue Fund.

2. The General Fund sends $100,000 cash to the Debt Service Fund so the latter fund can pay the debt service on general obligation bonds.

3. The General Fund receives a bill for $45,000 from the Motor Pool Internal Service Fund for motor vehicle services provided to city agencies in April.

4. The General Fund had previously paid $34,000 for consulting services and recorded the entire amount as expenditures. It now bills the Capital Projects Fund $10,000 for that fund's share of the consulting services.

P5-7 (Correction of errors)

A city's General Fund received cash from the following sources during fiscal year 2012. All the receipts were credited to revenue accounts. Identify the incorrect credits (some may be correct), and make journal entries to correct them.

1. The General Fund received $10,000 from the Debt Service Fund when the Debt Service Fund was closed out after a bond issue was fully paid.

2. The General Fund received $15,000 from the Parks Special Revenue Fund for that fund's share of the cost of an electric bill previously paid by the General Fund. The receipt was in response to a billing from the General Fund to the Parks Special Revenue Fund.

3. After meeting all eligibility requirements, the General Fund received $20,000 from the state as a grant that could be used at any time.

4. The General Fund received $25,000 from the state as an advance on a grant. The state required the city to use the grant for expenditures to be incurred during 2013.

5. The General Fund received $30,000 from the collection of parking meter fees.

P5-8 (Preparation of financial statements)

The commissioners of the Regents Park Commission Special Revenue Fund approved the following budget for calendar year 2012. Assume that the Unassigned fund balance at the beginning of the year was $10,000. Also, assume that no encumbrances were outstanding and no supplies were on hand at the beginning or the end of the year. Prepare a statement of revenues, expenditures, and changes in fund balance. In addition, prepare a budgetary comparison schedule, assuming the originally approved budget and the final budget are identical.

Estimated Revenues

Property taxes	$300,000	
Concession rentals	100,000	
User charges	200,000	$600,000
Appropriations		
Wages and salaries	$200,000	
Capital equipment	300,000	
Supplies	50,000	550,000
Budgeted Increase in Fund Balance		$ 50,000

During the year, actual revenues were as follows:

Property taxes	$300,000
Concession rentals	120,000
User charges	185,000

Actual expenditures were as follows:

Wages and salaries	$199,000
Capital equipment	296,000
Supplies	48,000

P5-9   (Journal entries for selected events and transactions)
Prepare the general journal entries necessary to record the following *selected* transactions of the General Fund of the City of Roxyville.

1. Property taxes of $4,000,000 were levied. The city estimates that 1.5 percent of the total levy will prove uncollectible and that $2,000,000 (gross) of the $4,000,000 tax levy will be collected soon enough to qualify for a 2 percent discount.
2. Property taxes of $1,800,000 (gross receivable) were collected within the 2 percent discount period. The remaining taxes are now past due and are declared delinquent.
3. Property taxes of $1,550,000 (gross receivable) were collected after the discount period expired, together with late penalties of $3,400.
4. The city's Building Inspection Department, accounted for through the General Fund, did work for an expansion of the city's water utility operation, accounted for through an Enterprise Fund. The Building Inspection Department billed the water utility $10,250.
5. A $220,000 3-year loan was authorized and made from the General Fund to the Water Utility Enterprise Fund to provide interim financing for an expansion project.
6. A new paving machine for the Street Department (accounted for through the General Fund) was ordered at a price of $32,000.
7. Payment of $600,000 of General Fund cash was authorized and made to provide permanent capital for a new Internal Service Fund.
8. The city council reviewed budget-to-actual operating results to date with the Finance Director and reduced the estimate of sales tax revenue by $24,000; correspondingly, the council decided to reduce the appropriation for street maintenance by $20,000.
9. The paving machine ordered in item 6 was received along with an invoice for $31,700. The invoice was vouchered for payment.
10. A property owner is withholding payment of property taxes pending appeal of the assessed valuation of the property for the current year. The city's attorney believes the appeal will be denied. However, the appeal action means that property taxes that would normally already have been collected, $42,000, will probably not be received until well into the next fiscal year.
11. Delinquent taxes receivable of $9,500 were written off as uncollectible.
12. It was discovered that the purchase of a copy machine for $3,850, previously recorded as a capital outlay expenditure of the mayor's office (General Fund), was actually made to benefit the public library (Special Revenue Fund). The General Fund and the Special Revenue Fund maintain their cash accounts at separate banks. The date to transfer the cash has not yet been set.

P5-10   (Journal entries for selected transactions and events)
The General Fund postclosing trial balance of the City of Harlan Heights showed the following balances on December 31, 2012:

	Debits	Credits
Cash	$ 65,000	
Property taxes receivable—delinquent	45,000	
Allowance for uncollectible taxes—delinquent		$ 8,000
Vouchers payable		25,000
Deferred property tax revenues		15,000
Assigned fund balance		12,000
Unassigned fund balance		50,000
	$110,000	$110,000

Prepare entries to record the following transactions and events for calendar year 2013:

1. Harlan collected $40,000 of delinquent property taxes during 2013. The balance of the delinquent property taxes outstanding at the beginning of the year was written off as uncollectible.

2. The Assigned fund balance at the beginning of the year represented outstanding encumbrances that were allowed to lapse at year-end. The purchase orders that had been encumbered will be honored and charged against 2013 appropriations.

3. Harlan adopted the following budget at the beginning of 2013:

Estimated Revenues:

Property taxes	$550,000	
Miscellaneous	50,000	$600,000
Appropriations:		
Public safety personal services (PS)	$400,000	
Public safety other than PS (OTPS)	100,000	
Pensions	60,000	
Transfer to Mass Transit Authority	20,000	580,000
Budgeted Increase in Fund Balance		$ 20,000

4. Property taxes were levied in the amount of $575,000 to provide revenues of $550,000 after allowing $25,000 for estimated uncollectible taxes.

5. As a result of appealing their assessments, taxpayers received reductions in their tax bills of $20,000. Harlan collected property taxes of $530,000 during 2013.

6. All remaining unpaid taxes were declared delinquent. The comptroller concluded that all delinquencies would be paid and that no allowance for uncollectible taxes would be needed. The comptroller also estimated that $15,000 of the delinquencies would be collected during the first 60 days of 2014.

7. The pension appropriation was based on the actuary's estimate, but the mayor, after conferring with the council, paid only $40,000 to the Pension Trust Fund.

8. In accordance with policy regarding bus fares, a subsidy of $20,000 was paid to the Mass Transit Authority.

9. To balance the budget for 2014, the approved budget contained an appropriation of $35,000 from the anticipated fund balance at December 31, 2013.

Summary Problem—Complete Accounting Cycle of General Fund

Following is the postclosing trial balance of the General Fund of Leisure City as at December 31, 2012.

	Debits	Credits
Cash	$300,000	
Property taxes receivable—delinquent	50,000	
Due from state government	80,000	
Supplies and materials	30,000	
Salaries payable		$ 25,000
Deferred revenues—property taxes		20,000
Nonspendable fund balance		30,000
Assigned fund balance		15,000
Unassigned fund balance		370,000
	$460,000	$460,000

The following additional information is provided regarding the city's accounting policies and other matters:

1. Only items charged to the appropriation "Supplies and materials—other programs" are encumbered. Encumbrances lapse if they are outstanding at the close of a fiscal year. They are,

however, included in the following year's appropriation. Outstanding encumbrances at the end of 2012 ($15,000) are reported as Assigned fund balance.

2. The appropriation "Other program costs" covers vacation pay, pension and retiree health care benefits, and all other program expenditures.
3. The city uses the purchases method to record the acquisition of supplies. The year-end supplies inventory is considered to be material and is reported in the city's financial statements.
4. The city's accounting policy regarding income taxes is to recognize income taxes as revenue of the tax year provided they are expected to be received by April 15 of the following year, the due date for filing tax returns.
5. The city maintains tight controls over licensing fees and fines from its inspection program and considers them susceptible to accrual.

The following transactions and events occurred in 2013:

1. The city council of Leisure City approves the following budget for fiscal 2013:

Estimated Revenues

Property taxes	$3,200,000	
Income taxes	2,400,000	
Intergovernmental grants	300,000	
Licensing fees and fines	100,000	$6,000,000

Appropriations

Food inspection program	$ 600,000	
Salaries—other programs	$4,000,000	
Supplies and materials—other programs	300,000	
Other program costs	600,000	
Transfer to Debt Service Fund	400,000	5,900.000

Budgeted Increase in Fund Balance $ 100,000

2. Open encumbrances at the end of 2012 are restored.
3. All delinquent property taxes outstanding at the end of 2012 are collected between January and May of 2013, together with late payment penalties of $2,000.
4. The state pays the $80,000 it owes the city.
5. The city levies property taxes in the amount of $3,300,000 in anticipation of realizing net cash of $3,200,000. It establishes a $100,000 allowance for uncollectible taxes and discounts.
6. The city reduces tax bills by $60,000 based on taxpayer appeals of property value assessments, and taxpayers deduct $30,000 in discounts for early payment of bills. As a result, the city's net collection of property taxes in 2013 against the 2013 tax levy is $3,150,000.
7. All remaining unpaid taxes are declared delinquent. The city comptroller concludes that no allowance for uncollectible taxes is needed. He believes that $45,000 of the delinquent taxes will be collected in the first 60 days of 2014.
8. During 2013, the city collects $2,300,000 in personal income taxes as a result of withholdings by employers and payments made by taxpayers based on estimates for calendar year 2013.
9. At year-end, the comptroller estimates that, based on past experience, it is likely that taxpayers who file timely (that is, by April 15, 2014) will request refunds of $120,000 and will make payments of $50,000 with their returns. The comptroller also estimates that about $25,000 of additional taxes probably will be received later in 2014 from late filers of tax returns.
10. At the beginning of the year, the city receives an advance of $200,000 from the state on a grant for inspecting food establishments. The grant is for a maximum amount of $300,000, subject to the following requirements: (a) the state will reimburse the city for 50 percent of all expenditures paid by the city on the food inspection program, up to the maximum

amount of the grant; and (b) the city must file a claim for the balance due to the city by no later than December 31, 2013.

11. The city pays $580,000 to operate the inspection program referenced in the previous transaction. It also files a claim on December 31 for the balance due from the state for the program.

12. The city bills a total of $95,000 in licensing fees and inspection fines (through violation notices). It collects $85,000 cash during the year and expects to collect the rest during the first 60 days of 2014.

13. In addition to the item recorded in transaction 2, purchase orders for supplies and materials are placed in the amount of $280,000 and charged to the appropriation "Supplies and materials—other programs."

14. The following transactions occur regarding the total amount encumbered:
    a. Invoices of $260,000 are received, vouchered for payment, and paid against encumbrances totaling $265,000.
    b. Encumbrances totaling $10,000 are cancelled.
    c. Encumbrances of $20,000 remain open at year-end. The appropriation lapses, but the purchase orders will be honored against the following year's appropriation.

15. Salaries of $3,925,000 are paid during the year. Of this amount, $3,900,000 is charged to the appropriation for salaries—other programs, and $25,000 is charged to salaries payable at the beginning of the year.

16. At year-end, salaries owed to employees for the last week in December total $80,000. They will be paid with the first payroll in 2014.

17. Long-term general obligation debt is sold early in 2013, causing an increase in debt service requirements for the year. As a result the General Fund budget is amended; the appropriation for "Transfer to Debt Service Fund" is increased by $40,000.

18. A cash transfer of $440,000 is made to the Debt Service Fund.

19. The following transactions and events occur regarding the appropriation for "Other program costs":
    a. Analysis of vacation leave records shows that the total liability to employees for unused vacation days increases by $25,000 as a result of the year's activity. The total liability includes $10,000 due to employees who retire December 31; they will receive that amount in January 2014.
    b. The retirement system actuary advises the city that the increase in liability for retiree health care benefits as a result of employees who have worked in 2013 is $75,000. The city's policy, however, is to finance only the health care benefits of its retirees. For the year, those expenditures are $50,000, of which $45,000 is paid during the year, and the rest will be paid in January 2014.
    c. During the year, other payments of $500,000 are charged to the appropriation.

20. The year-end inventory of supplies and materials totals $35,000.

21. To avoid an increase in property tax rates, Leisure City's budget for 2014 includes a formal appropriation of $50,000 to finance the difference between estimated revenues and appropriations.

Use the preceding information to do the following:
  a. Prepare journal entries to record the foregoing transactions and events.
  b. Prepare a trial balance for 2013 after recording the journal entries.
  c. Prepare a balance sheet and a statement of revenues, expenditures, and changes in fund balance.
  d. Prepare a budgetary comparison schedule for 2013.

Chapter 6

The Governmental Fund Accounting Cycle

Capital Projects Funds, Debt Service Funds, and Permanent Funds

Leased Assets
Permanent Funds
   Control of Fund Activities
   Accounting for Fund Activities
Concluding Comment
Review Questions
Discussion Scenarios and Issues
Exercises
Problems
Summary Problem

After completing this chapter, you should be able to do the following:

- Explain why and how Capital Projects Funds are used in governmental accounting
- Prepare the journal entries normally made within Capital Projects Funds
- Prepare fund financial statements for Capital Projects Funds
- Explain why and how Debt Service Funds are used in governmental accounting
- Prepare the journal entries normally made within Debt Service Funds
- Prepare fund financial statements for Debt Service Funds
- Prepare journal entries pertaining to leased assets
- Explain why and how Permanent Funds are used in governmental accounting
- Prepare the journal entries normally made within Permanent Funds
- Prepare fund financial statements for Permanent Funds

There are five types of governmental funds: the General Fund, Special Revenue Funds, Capital Projects Funds, Debt Service Funds, and Permanent Funds. In Chapters 4 and 5, we focused on accounting for the General Fund and Special Revenue Funds. Because accounting for all governmental funds is similar—they all have the same current financial resources measurement focus and use the modified accrual basis of accounting—accounting for Capital Projects Funds, Debt Service Funds, and Permanent Funds should seem familiar. The difference lies primarily in the types of transactions that are commonly accounted for in these funds, because they can be used only when financial resources are restricted or limited for a specific purpose.

Capital Projects Funds and Debt Service Funds commonly are used to track the construction of and debt repayment for large-scale public works projects. *Capital Projects Funds* are used to account for and report on financial resources that are restricted or otherwise limited to spending for capital outlays—typically the acquisition or construction of major capital assets. *Debt Service Funds* are used to account for and report on financial resources that are restricted or otherwise limited to spending for principal and interest on *general* long-term debt. That debt, which is typically backed by the "full faith and credit" of a government, is generally issued for capital asset acquisition purposes, but it can be issued also for operating purposes.

Typically, governments finance large capital acquisitions or construction projects, such as buildings and bridges, with the proceeds from the sale of general obligation bonds. The related debt covenants often include two important requirements. First, the bond proceeds can be expended only for the purpose for which the bonds were sold, that is, the construction and/ or purchase of a particular capital asset. Second, the borrowing government must set aside financial resources for the express purpose of "servicing"—making interest and principal payments on—the debt. Capital projects may be financed also with intergovernmental grants and tax resources.

These debt covenant requirements make it prudent for a government to establish a Capital Projects Fund to account for the *construction* of the capital asset and a Debt Service Fund to account for accumulating resources to repay the debt and to make interest and bond principal payments as they come due. Governmental GAAP actually *require* that a government use a Capital Projects Fund if the project is financed wholly or partly by general obligation bond proceeds.[1] Also, under governmental GAAP, "Debt service funds are required if they are legally mandated and/or if financial resources are being accumulated for principal and interest payments maturing in future years."[2]

In the simplest case, a government undertakes a single capital construction project that is to be paid for by issuing general obligation bonds. A Capital Projects Fund will be established to account for issuance of the bonds and expenditures related to the construction until the project is completed in 2 or 3 years. When the project is completed, the Capital Projects Fund is closed, with any remaining assets being transferred to another fund. The Debt Service Fund, on the other hand, will have a "life" equivalent to the duration of the financing bond issue—for example, 20, 25, or 30 years.[3]

In practice, there is little consistency among governments with respect to the number of Capital Projects Funds and Debt Service Funds they maintain, and the number often is the result of local law or custom. If convenience dictates and legal requirements allow, governments may use the same Capital Projects Fund to account for a series of specific projects over several years. Governments also may establish separate Capital Projects Funds for each major project and terminate them when the related projects are completed. Indeed, the authoritative guidance does not provide rigid rules regarding the number of funds that must be used. On one hand, governmental GAAP[4] require governments to use the minimum number of funds practicable, suggesting that individual projects should be accounted for in a single Capital Projects Fund whenever possible. However, careful attention must be paid to bond indenture provisions or restrictions placed on the use of certain types of resources. Often, such restrictions will prevent accounting for multiple projects in the same fund. The same facts and arguments apply to Debt Service Funds.[5]

Permanent Funds are different from other governmental funds because they are used to report resources that are legally restricted so that only the earnings generated by investing the principal (or corpus of a gift), and not the principal itself, may be used to support the government's own programs. In other types of governmental funds, both the principal and the earnings on the principal can be used for the purpose of the fund. A common type of Permanent Fund is a

---

[1]GASB Cod. Sec. 1300.106.

[2]GASB Cod. Sec. 1500.113.

[3]Financing large capital projects with bond proceeds is traditional in local governments. On the assumption that a capital asset has a physical life of 30 years, financing the assets with a 30-year bond issue means that the cost of the assets will be borne by approximately the generations of citizens (taxpayers) who will benefit from using the asset.

[4]GASB Cod. Sec. 1100.104.

[5]Some governmental accountants differentiate between the demands of *accounting* versus *financial reporting* when discussing the number of funds that should be used. They suggest that a single Capital Projects Fund or Debt Service Fund may be sufficient in many cases for the purpose of financial reporting in compliance with GAAP, provided information pertaining to individual capital projects or bond issues is maintained internally within a government's accounting system.

perpetual-care government-owned cemetery fund. Individuals donate money to the Cemetery Permanent Fund with the provision that only the earnings from these resources can be used to maintain the cemetery.

MEASUREMENT FOCUS AND BASIS OF ACCOUNTING

As with all governmental-type funds, the measurement focus of Capital Projects Funds, Debt Service Funds, and Permanent Funds is on current financial resources, which means that these funds account only for the accumulation of financial resources and the expenditure of those resources. As a result, long-lived assets are not accounted for in Capital Projects Funds, Debt Service Funds, and Permanent Funds, nor are any long-term liabilities accounted for within these funds. The current financial resources criterion focuses on assets currently available—financial assets—and the claims due and payable against those assets—short-term liabilities.

The basis of accounting for Capital Projects Funds, Debt Service Funds, and Permanent Funds is the same as for the other governmental-type funds—modified accrual. Therefore, the recognition and measurement principles discussed in Chapter 5 apply to these fund types. In general, revenues are recorded when they are measurable and available, and expenditures are recorded when the related liability is incurred, subject to the exceptions discussed in Chapter 5. (Another exception to the liability recognition principle under modified accrual accounting involves the treatment of interest on long-term debt, discussed later in this chapter.)

This chapter first discusses and illustrates Capital Projects Fund accounting and financial reporting for the transactions that normally occur during construction of a large-scale public works project. The chapter then focuses on accounting and reporting for the operations of a Debt Service Fund. The chapter concludes by considering the accounting and financial reporting of transactions in a Permanent Fund.

CAPITAL PROJECTS FUNDS

Overview

Acquisition or construction of major capital facilities and other capital assets (other than those financed by proprietary and trust funds) typically is accounted for in Capital Projects Funds. Examples of capital facilities include a new city hall and infrastructure assets, such as a bridge; other capital assets include buses and fire trucks. The resources used to finance Capital Projects Funds usually come from general obligation debt, transfers from other funds, intergovernmental revenues, and private donations.

Capital assets of a relatively minor nature, such as furniture and automobiles, usually are financed through the General Fund or a Special Revenue Fund, although they may be financed through a Capital Projects Fund. For example, purchases of a new police car or a desk for the mayor's office are recorded as expenditures in the fund that made the acquisition, which is more often the General Fund than a Capital Projects Fund (see Chapters 2 and 5).

Capital Budgets

Capital projects normally are controlled by capital budgets. A typical capital budget is illustrated in Table 6-1. Notice that a description of each project is given in addition to the amount requested and the source of financing. In the illustration, the city has been given an early settler and businessman's house, which it intends to restore and turn into a museum. In addition, the

Governmental Accounting in Practice

Capital Asset Financing and Fund Accounting

When New York City emerged from a severe fiscal crisis in the late 1970s, it adopted a policy of issuing debt primarily for "brick and mortar" expenditures. Unless the capital asset had a unit cost of $15,000 or more (there has, of course, been some inflation since then) and had an economic life of more than 5 years, it had to be charged as an expenditure of the tax-financed General Fund. Other governments, such as Mt. Lebanon, PA, and Tempe, AZ, also make it a practice of financing a portion of their capital budgets from tax revenues. Fitch Ratings—Public Finance issued a paper in June 2005, entitled "To Bond or Not to Bond," stating: "The presence of a pay-as-you-go [tax-financed] program [for acquiring capital assets] not only reduces the amount of debt needed, but provides budgetary flexibility in years when expenditure cuts are necessary."

The way in which capital assets are financed affects the fund types used to record the transactions. Notice, for example, that Mt. Lebanon charges a portion ($280,000) of its capital outlay expenditures directly to its General Fund and a portion ($4,425,000) directly to its Capital Projects Fund (see Table 2-5 on page 29). Further, because a major capital project is financed by sewage charges, there is a transfer out (most of the $2,992,000 item) from the Sewage Special Revenue Fund to the Capital Projects Fund.

city is planning to remodel a fire station, repair two streets, and renovate its events center (a 3-year project).

Many governments supplement their current-year capital budgets with long-term capital programs. A long-term capital program presents information on the capital improvements desired over a multiyear period of time—often for 5 to 10 years. It lists the projects planned, the estimated cost of each project, and the proposed sources of financing for each project. Generally, it is prepared on a "continuous" basis, with a future year added, the past year dropped, and the other years updated for new cost estimates.

Although some people may regard long-term capital programs as wish lists and some projects may never materialize, long-term capital programs are good organizing, planning, and communicating tools. They enable users to see at a glance what is needed, what is desired, and what the government may be able to afford. Such information is particularly valuable to legislators who must prioritize projects to allocate limited resources. Having a comprehensive long-term capital budget is also helpful when considering whether some capital needs could be financed with intergovernmental grants or tax resources.

TABLE 6-1	Capital Budget		
Date: September 30, 2012			**Prepared by <u>JEM</u>**
Project Description		**Budget Request**	**Source of Funding**
Restore Kell house			
Purchase furniture		$ 200,000	Federal and state grants
Fire station—1001 Bluff Street		300,000	Bond proceeds
Repair streets			
Indiana and Scott		700,000	Bond proceeds and federal grant
Kay Yeager Event Center renovation		300,000	Tax revenues
Total		$1,500,000	

Summary of Fund Activities

The nature and order of events involving capital projects may vary according to local ordinances and procedures, the relative size of the project, and the type of financing involved; however, this section illustrates the typical sequence of project activities. After a project is approved, financing arrangements are made, and contracts are let as applicable.

To finance projects, governmental units usually issue general obligation bonds and solicit federal and/or state grants. Bond and grant proceeds are not always spent immediately upon receipt. In such cases, the Capital Projects Fund will be used to account for some short-term investment activity. As construction work progresses, investments are liquidated, and payments are made to the contractor until the project is completed and finally accepted. Any financial resources remaining in the fund after the final payments are made on a project are transferred to another fund or returned to the grantors, as applicable.

Control of Fund Activities

The operations of a Capital Projects Fund are generally controlled through provisions of bond indentures, provisions of grant agreements, and so forth. Therefore, formal budgetary integration into the accounts, as used in the General Fund and Special Revenue Funds, is not always necessary. For consistency within this text, though, we will assume that a budget is recorded and used for control purposes in the Capital Projects Fund. Such accounting procedures are especially helpful if a single fund is being used to account for more than one project.

Encumbrance accounting is ordinarily used for these funds because of the extent of involvement with contracts and purchase orders and because of the need to control the related expenditures. Thus, in our example of a construction project, a regular encumbrance entry is made when the contract is signed. Expenditures on the contract are treated in the manner previously illustrated for encumbered purchase orders.

Accounting for Fund Activities

OPERATING ENTRIES   For illustrative purposes, assume that the City of Rubyville decides to build a sports complex at a cost of $18,000,000 and includes the project in its 2012 capital budget. Financing for the project consists of a general obligation bond issue for $10,000,000, which is restricted by debt covenant for expenditures associated with constructing the sports complex, and an $8,000,000 expenditure-driven grant from the state. The state grant proceeds are recognized as revenue to the Capital Projects Fund when qualifying expenditures are made, and the proceeds from the bond issue are classified as other financing sources when received. Accordingly, the following entry is made to record the budget:

Estimated revenues	8,000,000	
Estimated other financing sources	10,000,000	
Appropriations		18,000,000
To record the budget.		

If the bonds are sold at par (face) value, the following entry is made:

Cash	10,000,000	
Other financing source—long-term debt issued		10,000,000
To record the issuance of bonds.		

Because Capital Projects Funds follow a current financial resources measurement focus, bonded-debt principal is not recorded as a liability of a Capital Projects Fund.

If grant proceeds are received from the state before project costs are incurred, receipt of the cash is recorded as follows:

Cash	8,000,000	
Advance on construction grant		8,000,000
To record receipt of state grant proceeds.		

As qualifying construction expenditures occur, revenue from the state grant is recognized, and the advance account is reduced.

This government will retain an architectural firm to prepare plans for the project and to serve as project adviser for a $400,000 fee. When the contract with the architectural firm is signed, an encumbrance entry is made as follows:

Encumbrances—capital project	400,000	
Budgetary fund balance reserved for encumbrances		400,000
To record encumbrance of architect's fee.		

(For purposes of simplicity, a single encumbrance control account will be used in the remainder of this chapter.) The contract with the architectural firm requires the city to pay 90 percent of the fee when the plans are completed; the remainder of the fee will be paid upon completion of the project. The following entries are made when the plans for the sports complex are accepted:

Budgetary fund balance reserved for encumbrances	360,000	
Encumbrances—capital project		360,000
To reverse encumbrance prior to recording expenditure.		
Expenditures—architect's fees	360,000	
Vouchers payable		360,000
To record the liability for architect's fees.		
Vouchers payable	360,000	
Cash		360,000
To record payment of vouchers payable.		

After evaluating bids for the project submitted by various contractors, the city accepts the bid by TKP Construction Company of $17,600,000. After the contract is signed, the following entry is made:

Encumbrances—capital project	17,600,000	
Budgetary fund balance reserved for encumbrances		17,600,000
To record encumbrance of construction contract.		

Only part of the cash on hand is needed immediately, so the city invests $9,000,000 in short-term securities:

Investments	9,000,000	
Cash		9,000,000
To record investment of idle cash.		

As the project advances, the contractor sends a progress billing report to the city, requesting payment of $5,500,000 on the project. The payment is approved, less a 10 percent *retained percentage*. Retaining (holding back) a certain amount from each payment to a contractor provides an incentive for the contractor to timely and satisfactorily complete the job. If the contractor does not perform, the retained amount can be used to pay another contractor to complete the project. (The retained percentage procedure, also commonly called "retainage," is standard practice in the construction industry.) The following entries are made for the billing:

Budgetary fund balance reserved for encumbrances	5,500,000	
Encumbrances—capital project		5,500,000
To reverse part of the encumbrance for the construction contract.		
Expenditures—construction costs	5,500,000	
Retainage payable		550,000
Construction contracts payable		4,950,000
To record construction expenditure and related liabilities.		

Note the use of the Retainage payable account. Because the retainage is owed to the contractor, it is reported as a liability in the balance sheet of the Capital Projects Fund. The following entry is made to record payment of the construction voucher:

Construction contracts payable	4,950,000	
Cash		4,950,000
To record payment of amount currently due to contractor		

Assuming the state agreed that the grant money would be used before the bond proceeds, recording the $5,500,000 construction expenditure drives the recognition of construction grant revenue, so the following entry is needed:

Advance on construction grant	5,500,000	
Revenues—construction grant		5,500,000
To record revenues from state construction grant.		

Interest earned—but not yet received—on the investments to this point is $300,000. (Recall that interest earned on short-term investments held at year-end by governmental-type funds should be accrued provided it meets the available criterion.) Assume that the local laws permit Capital Projects Funds to use any interest earned through the investment of idle funds to help finance the project.[6] The entry to record this interest is as follows:

Interest receivable on investments	300,000	
Revenues—investments		300,000
To record interest earned on investments.		

Notice that during the year, all costs incurred in constructing the sports complex are charged (debited) to expenditures. At the end of the year, the Expenditures—construction costs

---

[6]In some jurisdictions, interest earned on Capital Projects Fund investments must be used for debt service rather than being available to finance capital construction.

account will be closed into Restricted fund balance.[7] Consistent with the current financial resources measurement focus used for governmental-type funds, the asset's cost is not capitalized in the Capital Projects Fund. As mentioned in Chapter 5, general capital assets are reported only in the government-wide financial statements. Financial reporting of these assets is explained in more detail in the concluding comments for this chapter and in Chapters 9 and 10.

The city's Cash account has a balance of more than $3,000,000. Management decides that $3,000,000 should be invested in short-term securities. The entry to record the investment is this:

Investments	3,000,000	
Cash		3,000,000
To record investment of excess cash.		

Investments held by governments generally are reported at current fair value.[8] Changes in the fair value of most governmental investments are reported in the operating statement, along with interest and dividends received. Investments that are not reported at fair value include debt instruments purchased with a maturity date of 1 year or less; for example, commercial paper and U.S. Treasury obligations. These investments are reported at amortized cost. Because the construction of the sports complex is a short-term project, management decided that all of the government's investments should be short term; for instance, CDs or Treasury notes. As a result, no year-end fair value adjustment is needed. The only entry needed pertaining to investments is the interest revenue accrual, recorded in an earlier journal entry.

At this point, all entries for the year have been recorded, so a trial balance can be prepared (see Table 6-2).

CLOSING ENTRIES, FIRST YEAR   The budgetary entries made at the beginning of the year for Estimated revenues, Estimated other financing sources, and Appropriations are reversed at year-end. Likewise, the year-end remaining balances in Encumbrances—capital project and the related Budgetary fund balance reserved for encumbrances are reversed. These accounts are not needed for financial reporting purposes because they are budgetary entries, and all of the fund balance that remains at year-end is already restricted for the sports complex. Revenues, other financing sources, and expenditures are closed to Restricted fund balance, because the grant revenues and other financing sources (i.e., the general obligation bond proceeds) recognized in the fund were restricted by the grantor state or the debt covenant, respectively.[9]

---

[7]In this case, both the bond proceeds received and the grant received by the city are legally restricted for the construction of the sports complex, so all of the fund balance in this fund is restricted.

[8]GASB Cod. I50.

[9]Two common reasons why fund balance is classified as restricted are stipulations in bond covenants that permit bond proceeds to be used only for a restricted purpose (such as a capital project) and provisions in grant agreements that limit use of grant proceeds to a particular program or a specific capital project. In contrast to Restricted fund balance, Assigned fund balance results only from internal constraints on resources that can be easily removed by the government. Thus, for example, if debt covenants do not specify how *investment earnings* from unspent bond proceeds accounted for in a Capital Projects Fund are to be used and the government's management expresses the intent to use them for a particular purpose, such earnings generally are classified as Assigned fund balance.

TABLE 6-2	Trial Balance—Capital Projects Fund

City of Rubyville
Capital Projects Fund
Sports Complex Fund
Preclosing Trial Balance
December 31, 2012

	Debits	Credits
Cash	$ 690,000	
Investments	12,000,000	
Interest receivable	300,000	
Retainage payable		$ 550,000
Advance on construction grant		2,500,000
Revenues—construction grant		5,500,000
Revenues—investment interest		300,000
Other financing source—long-term debt issued		10,000,000
Expenditures—architect's fees	360,000	
Expenditures—construction costs	5,500,000	
Estimated revenues	8,000,000	
Estimated other financing sources	10,000,000	
Appropriations		18,000,000
Encumbrances—capital project	12,140,000	
Budgetary fund balance reserved for encumbrances		12,140,000
	$48,990,000	$48,990,000

At the end of the accounting period, December 31, 2012, the following entries are necessary to close the books:

Appropriations	18,000,000	
Estimated revenues		8,000,000
Estimated other financing sources		10,000,000
To close the budgetary accounts.		
Revenues—state construction grant	5,500,000	
Revenues—investment interest	300,000	
Other financing source—long-term debt issued	10,000,000	
Expenditures—architect's fees		360,000
Expenditures—construction costs		5,500,000
Restricted fund balance		9,940,000
To close the operating accounts.		
Budgetary fund balance reserved for encumbrances	12,140,000	
Encumbrances—capital project		12,140,000
To close encumbrance accounts.		

Financial Statements Illustration

Individual financial statements prepared for Capital Projects Funds include an operating statement and a balance sheet. The fiscal-year ending 2012 financial statements for the Sports Complex Fund are illustrated in Tables 6-3 and 6-4. Notice that the entire fund balance is reported as restricted; because the encumbrance of $12,140,000 is significant—indeed, the amount encumbered exceeds the fund balance—its existence should be disclosed in the notes to the financial statements. The overall reporting process is discussed in Chapters 9 and 10.

Completing the Project: The Following Year

Although most governmental units use the fiscal year as their accounting period, authorization and control of capital projects are related to the projects' entire lives. In our illustration, therefore, at the beginning of 2013, the city needs to reestablish the budgetary accounts for encumbrances ($12,140,000). The city should also record the budget for the estimated project revenues for 2013—the unrecognized portion of the state grant ($2,500,000) and the earnings on the investments (estimated to be $150,000). The entries to record these items are as follows:

Encumbrances—capital project	12,140,000	
Budgetary fund balance reserved for encumbrances		12,140,000
To establish the encumbrances account.		
Estimated revenues	2,650,000	
Budgetary fund balance	9,490,000	
Appropriations		12,140,000
To record the remainder of the budget for the sports complex project.		

When the project is completed, the contractor submits a final bill for the amount due—$12,100,000 (assume, for simplicity, that only one billing is made in 2013)—and the architect submits a final bill for $40,000. Because the project has not yet been inspected and accepted, the city retains 10 percent from the payment to the contractor. The entries to record these events are as follows:

Budgetary fund balance reserved for encumbrances	12,140,000	
Encumbrances—capital project		12,140,000
To remove the encumbrances for the remaining cost of the contracts.		
Expenditures—architect's fees	40,000	
Vouchers payable		40,000
To record the balance due to the architect.		
Expenditures—construction costs	12,100,000	
Retainage payable		1,210,000
Construction contracts payable		10,890,000
To record the balance due to the contractor.		

To pay these liabilities, the city liquidates all the investments held by the Capital Projects Fund and recognizes the related investment interest income for the year of $130,000. Assuming

TABLE 6-3	Statement of Revenues, Expenditures, and Changes in Fund Balance

City of Rubyville
Capital Projects Fund
Sports Complex Fund
Statement of Revenues, Expenditures, and Changes in Fund Balance
For the Year Ended December 31, 2012

Revenues	
Construction grant	$ 5,500,000
Investments	300,000
Total revenues	5,800,000
Expenditures	
Construction costs	5,500,000
Architect's fees	360,000
Total expenditures	5,860,000
Excess of expenditures over revenues	(60,000)
Other Financing Sources	
Other financing source—long-term debt issued	10,000,000
Net change in fund balance	9,940,000
Fund balance at beginning of year	0
Fund balance at end of year	$ 9,940,000

TABLE 6-4	Balance Sheet—Capital Projects Fund

City of Rubyville
Capital Projects Fund
Sports Complex Fund
Balance Sheet
December 31, 2012

Assets	
Cash	$ 690,000
Investments	12,000,000
Interest receivable	300,000
Total assets	$12,990,000
Liabilities	
Retainage payable	$ 550,000
Advance on construction grant	2,500,000
Total liabilities	3,050,000
Fund Balance	
Restricted for capital project	9,940,000
Total liabilities and fund balance	$12,990,000

$12,430,000 of cash is received (covering the $12,000,000 investment, the $300,000 of interest previously accrued, and the $130,000 of interest earned in 2013), the entry is as follows:

Cash	12,430,000	
Interest receivable on investments		300,000
Revenues—investment interest		130,000
Investments		12,000,000
To record liquidation of investments and related revenues.		

The entry to record the payment of the architect and contractor liabilities is this:

Construction contracts payable	10,890,000	
Vouchers payable	40,000	
Cash		10,930,000
To record payment of vouchers to contractor and architect.		

The balance in the Retainage payable account is $1,760,000, representing the balance at the beginning of 2013 ($550,000) plus the amount retained during 2013 ($1,210,000). Assume that, upon final inspection, the project manager finds some defects that need to be remedied before the project can be accepted. The construction company already has removed its equipment and employees, so it authorizes the city to have the repairs made by a local contractor. The repairs cost $450,000, so the following entry is made:

Retainage payable	450,000	
Cash		450,000
To record payments to contractor to repair building defects.		

All of the expenditures related to the sports complex have been incurred, so the city recognizes the remainder of the state grant as revenue, as follows:

Advance on construction grant	2,500,000	
Revenues—construction grant		2,500,000
To record revenue from state construction grant.		

After the building has been accepted, the contractor will be paid the remaining retainage of $1,310,000 ($1,760,000 − $450,000). This payment will be recorded as follows:

Retainage payable	1,310,000	
Cash		1,310,000
To record the final payment to the contractor for sports complex construction.		

CLOSING ENTRIES, SECOND YEAR   On completion and acceptance of the project, the Sports Complex Fund will no longer be needed, and therefore, the temporary or nominal accounts will be closed. This process first involves reversing the budgetary entry and then closing the operating accounts to Restricted fund balance. The necessary entries are as follows:

Appropriations	12,140,000	
Estimated revenues		2,650,000
Budgetary fund balance		9,490,000
To close the budgetary accounts for 2013.		

Revenues—investment interest	130,000	
Revenues—construction grant	2,500,000	
Restricted fund balance	9,510,000	
Expenditures—architect's fees		40,000
Expenditures—construction costs		12,100,000
To close the operating accounts for 2013.		

After the preceding entries are posted, the sports complex Capital Projects Fund has two "residual" account balances: Cash, $430,000, and Restricted fund balance, $430,000, representing the earnings on the investments. Disposition of these resources will depend on the provisions of the state grant and the bond issue. For illustrative purposes, assume these amounts must be used for eventual retirement of the bonds sold to finance the project (a typical provision in practice). This requires the following entries in the Capital Projects Fund:

Transfer out to Debt Service Fund	430,000	
Cash		430,000
To record transfer to the Debt Service Fund.		
Restricted fund balance	430,000	
Transfer out to Debt Service Fund		430,000
To close the transfer account.		

At this point, all the Capital Projects Fund's balance sheet accounts have zero balances. The Debt Service Fund will record its "side" of the interfund transfer as follows:

Cash	430,000	
Transfer in from Capital Projects Fund		430,000
To record transfer from the Capital Projects Fund.		

Issuance of Bonds at a Premium or Discount

The bonds issued for construction of the City of Rubyville's sports complex were sold at face value. Often, government bonds are sold at a price above or below face value because the prevailing interest rates when the bonds are issued are below or above the stated interest rate on the face of the bonds. When the bond price is different from the face value of the bonds, the difference should be recorded separately from the face value.

To illustrate, assume that the bonds issued by the City of Rubyville were sold for $11,000,000. The face value of these bonds (or the amount paid to the bondholders at maturity) is $10,000,000, and the city receives an extra $1,000,000 as a bond premium. Whether bonds are issued at a premium or discount, an account, Other financing source—long-term debt issued, is credited for the face value of the bonds. If the bonds are sold at a premium, an account, Other financing source—bond issue premium, is credited for the excess of cash received over the face value of the bonds. In such a case, the following entry is made in the Capital Projects Fund when the bonds are issued:

Cash	11,000,000	
Other financing source—long-term debt issued		10,000,000
Other financing source—bond issue premium		1,000,000
To record the issuance of bonds.		

Bond covenants determine how the premium can be used. In some instances, a premium may be used for the purpose for which the bonds were issued—for example, kept in the Capital Projects Fund for construction of a capital asset. In other instances, a premium is required to be used to repay the debt. If the premium must be used to repay the bonds, the following entry is made in the Capital Projects fund to transfer the amount of the premium to a Debt Service Fund:

Transfer out to Debt Service Fund	1,000,000	
Cash		1,000,000
To record transfer of bond premium to Debt Service Fund.		

This entry is made in the Debt Service Fund to record the receipt of cash from the Capital Projects Fund:

Cash	1,000,000	
Transfer in from Capital Projects Fund		1,000,000
To record transfer of bond premium from Capital Projects Fund.		

If bonds are issued for less than face value (at a discount), the total proceeds are recorded in the Capital Projects Fund, and Other financing source—long-term debt issued is credited for the face amount of the bonds, as indicated previously. Another account, Other financing use—bond issue discount, is debited for the amount of the discount. This lower bond price may cause a problem, however, if the bonds do not provide enough resources to complete the project. At this point, the project manager must either scale down the project or seek additional resources.

Regardless of whether bonds are issued at a premium or discount, the government will incur issuance costs. Bond issue costs include legal, financial advisor, accounting, underwriting, and registration fees. Issue costs are reported as expenditures in the fund that pays them. For example, if the City of Rubyville incurred and paid $6,000 of issue costs when the sports complex bonds were issued, the following entry would be made in the Capital Projects Fund:

Expenditures—bond issue costs	6,000	
Cash		6,000
To record payment of bond issue costs.		

Issuance of Bonds between Interest Payment Dates

If bonds are issued between interest payment dates, the interest accrued to the date of sale must be paid to the issuing government by the buyer. Because this amount will be used to pay interest on the next interest date, it is recorded directly in the Debt Service Fund instead of in the Capital Projects Fund.

Arbitrage

As we have seen, Capital Projects Fund activities often involve the short-term investment of idle cash. Making such investments is sound practice; however, government officials need to exercise care to avoid running afoul of arbitrage regulations. In simple terms, *arbitrage* refers to borrowing money at a certain interest rate while investing the money at a higher interest rate. Governments often have the opportunity to earn arbitrage by issuing lower interest rate tax-exempt debt, but earning a higher interest rate on taxable investments.

The Internal Revenue Code (the Code) has strict rules regarding the amount of interest that can be earned without penalty from the proceeds of tax-exempt debt issued by a government. These rules generally provide that interest earned on the investment of tax-exempt debt proceeds cannot be greater than interest paid. If the interest earned is higher, then the government is subject to the arbitrage provisions of the Code. Excess interest earned by a state or local government must be paid to the federal government, or it will be subject to either an excise tax on the excess earnings or revocation of the tax-exempt status of its debt. Revocation of the tax-exempt status of its debt would result in a government paying higher interest rates on future debt issues.

Governmental Accounting in Practice

Mt. Lebanon's Capital Projects Funds

Mt. Lebanon, Pennsylvania, maintains only two Capital Projects Funds. The majority of its capital project activities are accounted for in one Capital Projects Fund. Construction or capital acquisition activities accounted for in this fund include sewage infrastructure, street reconstruction, sidewalk improvements, lighting improvements at a park, and recreation center improvements. Some governments might have separate Capital Projects Funds for each of these activities, but the accounting personnel at Mt. Lebanon are able to maintain adequate accounting controls by using one fund for multiple activities—most of which are small construction projects. The balance sheet and statement of revenues, expenditures, and changes in fund balance for Mt. Lebanon's primary Capital Projects Fund are presented in Tables 6-5 and 6-6.

Notice that this fund contains some of the same types of assets and liabilities described in this chapter as common to Capital Projects Funds—cash, interfund receivables and payables, and accounts payable. (The other Capital Projects Fund used by Mt. Lebanon shows similar assets and liabilities.) Mt. Lebanon's major sources of funding for its capital projects are bond proceeds and transfers from the Sewage Special Revenue Fund. The external restrictions imposed on the use of these resources warrant classifying the entire fund balance of Mt. Lebanon's Capital Projects Fund as restricted.

TABLE 6-5 Balance Sheet—Capital Projects Fund—Mt. Lebanon, Pennsylvania

Mt. Lebanon, Pennsylvania
Capital Projects Fund
Balance Sheet
December 31, 2009

Assets	
Cash and cash equivalents with treasurer	$446,802
Accounts receivable	17,351
Due from other governments	520,190
Total assets	$984,343
Liabilities	
Accounts payable	$590,277
Due to other funds	113,494
Total liabilities	703,771
Deferred Inflows of Resources	
Deferred revenues	17,351
Fund Balance	
Restricted	263,221
Total liabilities, deferred inflows of resources, and fund balance	$984,343

Source: Adapted from Comprehensive Annual Financial Report, Mt. Lebanon, Pennsylvania, December 31, 2009.

TABLE 6-6	Statement of Revenues, Expenditures, and Changes in Fund Balance— Capital Projects Fund—Mt. Lebanon, Pennsylvania

Mt. Lebanon, Pennsylvania
Capital Projects Fund
Statement of Revenues, Expenditures, and Changes in Fund Balance
For the Year Ended December 31, 2009

Revenues	
Investments	$ 5,855
Expenditures	
Capital outlays	4,496,067
Excess of expenditures over revenues	(4,490,212)
Other Financing Sources	
Transfers in	2,555,316
Proceeds from bond issuance	2,117,770
Total financing sources	4,673,086
Net change in fund balance	182,874
Beginning fund balance	80,347
Ending fund balance	$ 263,221

Source: Adapted from Comprehensive Annual Financial Report, Mt. Lebanon, Pennsylvania, December 31, 2009.

The arbitrage provisions of the Code are complex, and a complete discussion is beyond the scope of this text. Because of the complexity of the laws regulating the types of securities in which a governmental unit may invest and the arbitrage regulations, governmental units usually seek the aid of their accountants and attorneys whenever tax-exempt debt proceeds are invested.

DEBT SERVICE FUNDS

Overview

Many governments issue *general obligation* debt, typically to finance capital projects, as we have seen. General obligation debt also may be sold for other purposes, such as financing operating deficits. By definition, general obligation debt (usually bonds) is secured by the "full faith and credit" of the government; that is, repayment of principal and payment of interest on the debt are supported by a pledge of the entity's property tax collections and any other resources. The payment of principal and interest on a debt is referred to as *servicing* the debt. Thus, Debt Service Funds are used to accumulate resources that will be used to pay principal and interest on general obligation long-term debt. General obligation debt does not include debt that will be serviced from resources accumulated in Enterprise Funds or Internal Service Funds.[10]

---

[10]Although it is possible to have general obligation debt that will be serviced by an Enterprise Fund, a discussion of such debt is beyond the scope of this section. It is also possible, but not likely, that a Permanent Fund could contain long-term debt that is serviced in that fund. That discussion, too, is beyond the scope of this section.

In many instances debt that becomes due in installments, such as serial bonds, can be serviced directly by the General Fund. However, if a legal requirement dictates a separate Debt Service Fund, such a fund must be established. In addition, a separate Debt Service Fund must be established if the governmental unit is accumulating resources currently for the future servicing of debt, such as term bonds. (These accumulated resources are generally referred to as a sinking fund.) Although this section will concentrate on the accounting for bonds, it is important to remember that any form of long-term obligation, such as installment purchases or notes, may require the establishment of a Debt Service Fund.

Types of Government Debt

Before discussing the accounting for a Debt Service Fund, the types of debt governments may have and the governmental funds used to account for them should be considered.

Chapters 4 and 5 included a discussion of the liabilities that are reported in governmental funds. Governmental funds are not used to account for general long-term liabilities because the current financial resources measurement focus dictates that only financial assets and short-term liabilities be reported. Therefore, only short-term liabilities—such as accounts payable, salaries payable, and vouchers payable—commonly are reported in the General Fund, Special Revenue Funds, and Capital Projects Funds.

Long-term liabilities, such as general obligation bonds and interest on them, generally are not reported in governmental funds until they are *due and payable*. This means that governmental fund balance sheets do not show a liability for even the current portion of long-term bonds and related interest unless it becomes due before year-end and is not paid (making it "past due"), or unless it meets an exception to the due and payable rule. (The exception, which allows for accruing bond payments due early in the next fiscal year, is discussed later in this chapter.) To illustrate the past-due scenario, assume the City of Rubyville failed to make a required principal and interest payment on its 20-year general obligation serial bond. The required amount would be recorded as expenditures and liabilities in the governmental fund that services the debt. This is an unusual occurrence because governments seldom fail to make timely debt service payments.

The most common types of general obligation debt are *term* and *serial* general obligation bonds. The principal portion of *term* bonds matures at one specified future date. The principal portion of *serial* bonds matures over a period of time—often over 10 or more years. Serial bonds are more common because they allow for more constant debt service payments over a period of years. That is, some principal and interest comes due each year over a period of years, rather than having the entire principal come due in a single period, as occurs with term bonds. (As previously noted, using sinking funds when term bonds are issued accomplishes the same financial effect as issuing serial bonds.) Relatively smooth debt service payments generally are better for budgeting cash flows and for causing taxpayers to pay for the services they receive.

As discussed in Chapter 4, governments also borrow short term to provide cash for operating or capital purposes. For example, they may sell tax or revenue anticipation notes, backed by future near-term taxes or revenues, to help support current operations. Some notes mature in less than 1 year and, because of their short-term nature, generally are reported as liabilities in governmental funds.[11] At year-end, unpaid interest on short-term notes is accrued as a governmental

---

[11]Bond anticipation notes are issued in anticipation of issuing bonds. They are used to allow a government to begin a capital project before receiving bond proceeds. If certain conditions are met, they can be accounted for as long-term liabilities even though they have a maturity of less than 1 year.

Governmental Accounting in Practice

If It Smells like Debt, It Must Be Debt

As discussed in the text, when governments borrow to finance capital projects, they may do so through a variety of techniques. They may borrow *directly* through the sale of general obligation bonds. Or they may borrow through the *"back door"* by entering into lease-purchase arrangements with private businesses, specially created public benefit corporations, and even other governments. Accounting for acquisition of equipment by means of a lease-purchase agreement with a private business is illustrated on page 209. Instead of crediting Other financing sources—long-term debt issued, you credit the account Other financing sources—capital leases in the fund that receives the resources and report the resulting debt in the government-wide financial statements.

But what if a state builds a prison by creating a fully controlled public benefit corporation that issues bonds, turns the proceeds over to the state, and then pays off the debt over 30 years by obtaining annual "rents" from the state equal to the debt service on the bonds? Or what if the state builds an office building by entering into a similar arrangement with the county in which the state builds the building? From the accounting perspective, the answer is the same as that shown later in the text when equipment is financed with lease-purchase debt. In short, if the arrangement smells like debt, you account for it as if it were debt.

New York State makes heavy use of this type of financing arrangement, though it is hardly alone. In its fund financial statements for the period ended March 31, 2011, New York State reported the following amounts as other financing sources: General obligation bonds issued—$500 million; *Financing arrangements issued—$2.253 billion*. In its government-wide statement of net position at March 31, 2011, the state reported these amounts due in more than 1 year: Bonds payable—$3.258 billion; *Obligations under lease-purchase and other financing arrangements—$39.597 billion*. Failure to account for these "other financing arrangements" as debt would clearly understate a government's long-term obligations.

---

fund liability. Long-term notes—including bank notes, certificates of obligation, and commercial paper—are not reported in governmental funds until the principal and interest on them are due and payable. Hence, accounting for long-term notes is similar to accounting for bonds.

Governments also finance capital acquisitions by using leases or lease-purchase agreements. A discussion of the types of leases commonly used by governments and the accounting for a capital lease are illustrated later in this chapter.

Finally, some governments now are financing the construction of major capital assets, such as roads or bridges, by entering into "service concession" arrangements with an operator, which may be a private company or another governmental entity. In this arrangement, the operator finances and builds a facility, such as a road. The government owns the road (and reports it in its government-wide financial statements), but it transfers the right to use the road to the operator for a defined number of years. The operator has the right to charge and collect fees from those using the road. At the end of the arrangement, the right to operate the road, which has been maintained at a condition level defined in the arrangement, reverts to the government.

Summary of Fund Activities

In practice, the sequence of events recorded in Debt Service Funds will vary according to the specific requirements of the bond indenture or the ordinance authorizing the bond issue. The following general summary of activity reflects the types of events that normally occur in Debt Service Funds. First, assets are received by the fund. They are recorded as revenues or transfers in from other funds—usually the General Fund, sometimes a Special Revenue Fund—depending on their nature. During the time between receipt of the resources and payment of principal and interest, the government may invest the assets. The investing activities also are recorded in the Debt Service Fund. Finally, as the principal and interest come due, they are paid from Debt Service Fund assets.

As a reminder, the proceeds from issuing debt are not recorded in a Debt Service Fund, but rather in the fund that will use the proceeds—often a Capital Projects Fund. Any assets remaining in a Capital Projects Fund after the project is completed may be transferred to a Debt Service Fund, as discussed earlier in this chapter.

Control of Fund Activities

The operations of Debt Service Funds generally are controlled by bond indentures and budgetary authorizations. Many governmental units do not record a formal budget for these funds. For purposes of uniformity, however, we will assume a budget is recorded and used for control purposes.

Encumbrance accounting is seldom applied in Debt Service Funds because of the absence of purchase orders, contracts, and so forth. The expenditures of these funds consist primarily of payments of bond principal and interest and fiscal agent fees. Because these expenditures are made according to the terms prescribed in the bond indenture, encumbrance accounting in Debt Service Funds serves no meaningful control purpose.

Accounting for Fund Activities

OPERATING ENTRIES   Recall that the City of Rubyville issued $10,000,000 of serial bonds on March 1, 2012, for construction of its sports complex, illustrated in the discussion of Capital Projects Funds. The bond indenture provides for semiannual interest payments of 5 percent on March 1 and September 1 (the annual interest rate is 10 percent on the outstanding debt), starting September 1, 2012, with $1,000,000 of principal to be repaid on March 1, 2014, and every year thereafter until the bonds mature on March 1, 2023 (10 payments later). Further, assume the city desires to spread the taxpayers' burden of servicing the debt evenly throughout the life of the bonds. To meet this goal, the voters approved a special addition to the local property tax for servicing the bonds. This tax is estimated to provide $1,250,000 of revenue in 2012. In addition, the city's budget provides for a transfer of $250,000 from the General Fund to the Debt Service Fund. (Entries involved in the actual issuance of the bonds are illustrated in the preceding section on Capital Projects Funds.)

The entry to record the Debt Service Fund budget for the fiscal year beginning January 1, 2012, is as follows:

Estimated revenues	1,250,000	
Estimated other financing sources	250,000	
Appropriations		505,000
Budgetary fund balance		995,000
To record the budget.		

The Estimated other financing sources account is the budgetary account used to record the anticipated transfer from the General Fund. Appropriations for the year include one interest payment of $500,000 that will be made on September 1, 2012, and the *fiscal agent's* fee of $5,000. The fiscal agent will keep records of the sale of the bonds and will make semiannual interest payments and payments of principal as they come due. Usually, a fiscal agent is a local bank or other financial institution. Notice that only one interest payment is required in 2012; therefore, only that amount is included in the current year's annual budget.

Assuming a $6,000 allowance for uncollectible taxes, the government will need to bill $1,256,000 to collect property tax revenues of $1,250,000. Recording the tax levy requires the following entry:

Property taxes receivable	1,256,000	
Allowance for uncollectible property taxes		6,000
Revenues—property taxes		1,250,000
To record the tax levy.		

Collection of $1,150,000 of the taxes results in the same entry as that illustrated in Chapters 4 and 5 for the General Fund and Special Revenue Funds.

Cash	1,150,000	
Property taxes receivable		1,150,000
To record collection of current taxes.		

If $2,500 of uncollectible taxes is written off, the following entry is made:

Allowance for uncollectible property taxes	2,500	
Property taxes receivable		2,500
To write off uncollectible accounts.		

If $1,000,000 of the cash is invested in short-term marketable securities, the following entry is made:

Investments	1,000,000	
Cash		1,000,000
To record the investment of cash.		

When a portion of the investments ($450,000) matures and interest of $20,000 on the investments is earned and received, the following entry is made:

Cash	470,000	
Investments		450,000
Revenues—interest earned on investments		20,000
To record investments liquidated and related income.		

The interest due to the city's bondholders on September 1, 2012, is recorded as follows:

Expenditures—interest	500,000	
Matured interest payable		500,000
To record matured interest.		

In practice, governments often do not record the matured interest payable, but instead credit Cash directly, because the payable likely will be reversed the same day the cash payment is made to the fiscal agent. We are including it here to illustrate *that the liability for interest in Debt Service Funds is not recorded until it becomes due and payable;* we will return to this issue shortly.

When cash is disbursed to the fiscal agent for the September 1 interest payment, the following entry is made:

Matured interest payable	500,000	
Cash		500,000
To record the payment of cash to the fiscal agent.		

The transfer from the General Fund to the Debt Service Fund is recorded in the Debt Service Fund as follows:

Cash	250,000	
Transfer in from General Fund		250,000
To record transfer in from General Fund.		

The corresponding entry to record the transfer in the General Fund is this:

Transfer out to Debt Service Fund	250,000	
Cash		250,000
To record transfer out to Debt Service Fund.		

When the fiscal agent submits a bill for $5,000 to the fund for servicing the debt and it is paid, the following entry is made:

Expenditures— fiscal agent fees	5,000	
Cash		5,000
To record fiscal agent fees.		

Assume now that Rubyville's year 2012 has ended. The next payment of debt service is due on March 1, 2013. What about the interest on the bonds for the "stub period" from September 1 to December 31, 2012? One of the most notable aspects of the modified accrual basis of accounting pertains to interest on long-term debt. Under modified accrual accounting, interest on long-term debt is not recorded as an expenditure until it becomes legally due (matures), rather than being accrued based on the passage of time, as is the case in full accrual accounting. The reason for this practice is that most governments' budgetary appropriations provide only for bond principal and interest that come *due* during the fiscal year. Accruing a liability before payment is legally due could result in a debit balance (a deficit) in the fund balance account. An accrual is not made because the liability is not yet due to be paid, and hence resources are not required to be available. (This line of reasoning is budgetary in nature and demonstrates the budgetary orientation of governmental-type funds.) An accrual for interest is made when the governmental fund financial statements are converted to government-wide statements, as discussed in Chapter 10.

When resources are available for Debt Service Fund payments and those payments will be made within the first month of the next accounting period, governmental units have the option, under GAAP, of recording the liability and the associated expenditure at the end of the year before the payments are due.

In contrast to the treatment of bond interest payable, an end-of-year entry is needed to accrue interest earned but not received on the investments, provided the "available" criterion is met:

Interest receivable on investments	55,000	
Revenues—interest earned on investments		55,000
To record the interest earned on investments.		

TABLE 6-7   Trial Balance—Debt Service Fund

City of Rubyville
Debt Service Fund
Sports Complex Bond Fund
Preclosing Trial Balance
December 31, 2012

	Debits	Credits
Cash	$ 365,000	
Property taxes receivable	103,500	
Allowance for uncollectible property taxes		$ 3,500
Investments	575,000	
Interest receivable	55,000	
Revenues—property taxes		1,250,000
Revenues—interest earned on investments		75,000
Revenues—net increase in fair value of investments		25,000
Transfer in from General Fund		250,000
Expenditures—interest	500,000	
Expenditures—fiscal agent fees	5,000	
Estimated revenues	1,250,000	
Estimated other financing sources	250,000	
Appropriations		505,000
Budgetary fund balance		995,000
	$3,103,500	$3,103,500

Recall that investments held by governments generally are reported at fair value. If the remaining $550,000 of marketable securities previously acquired and still held at December 31, 2012, had a fair value of $575,000, the following journal entry would be made to record the increase in value:

Investments	25,000	
Revenues—net increase in fair value of investments		25,000
To record the increase in the fair value of investments.		

A preclosing trial balance for Rubyville's Debt Service Fund at the end of the year is shown in Table 6-7.

CLOSING ENTRIES   At the end of the accounting period, December 31, 2012, closing entries are needed. In our example, entries are made to close the budgetary accounts and to close the revenues, expenditures, and transfer in. Pending further consideration of the facts regarding classification of the fund balance (discussed in the next paragraph), the latter entries are closed to the Assigned fund balance account because any positive fund balance remaining in governmental funds other than the General Fund are considered to be at least *assigned*, as noted in Chapter 5 under "Fund Balance Presentation."

A portion of the $1,095,000 fund balance of the Debt Service Fund needs to be classified as restricted because the resources generated by the voter-approved property tax can be used only for paying debt service on the sports complex bonds. Another portion needs to be classified as assigned because the $250,000 transfer arises from a budgetary decision and lacks the characteristics warranting higher classification. When governments have both restricted and unrestricted resources available for spending in a particular governmental-type fund, a policy is needed as to which resources have been spent from the fund. (The GASB requires that this policy be disclosed in the notes to the financial statements.) Most governments have a policy of first using the resources having the greater degree of constraint. Assume Rubyville's policy is to charge restricted resources before charging assigned resources, because it could more easily transfer to another fund any assets remaining in the Debt Service Fund after the sports complex bonds have been fully repaid. We can apply this policy by subtracting the total Debt Service Fund expenditures ($505,000) from property taxes (a restricted resource) and related revenues ($1,350,000)—see Table 6-8 later in the chapter—leaving $845,000 to be classified as Restricted fund balance. As a result, the entire $250,000 transfer from the General Fund is classified as Assigned fund balance.

Appropriations	505,000	
Budgetary fund balance	995,000	
Estimated revenues		1,250,000
Estimated other financing sources		250,000
To close the budgetary accounts for 2012.		
Revenues—property taxes	1,250,000	
Revenues— interest earned on investments	75,000	
Revenues—net increase in fair value of investments	25,000	
Transfer in from General Fund	250,000	
Expenditures—interest		500,000
Expenditures—fiscal agent fees		5,000
Assigned fund balance		1,095,000
To close the operating accounts for 2012.		
Assigned fund balance	845,000	
Restricted fund balance		845,000
To reclassify fund balance from assigned to restricted at fiscal year-end.		

ENTRY NECESSARY FOR INTEREST PAYMENT IN SUBSEQUENT YEAR As already mentioned, interest on long-term debt generally is not accrued at the end of the year under the modified accrual basis of accounting. Thus, when the March interest payment is made in 2013, the following entries are necessary:

Expenditures—interest	500,000	
Matured interest payable		500,000
To record matured interest.		
Matured interest payable	500,000	
Cash		500,000
To record disbursement of cash to fiscal agent for bond interest payable.		

The remaining entries for payment of interest over the life of the debt are the same as this entry, except, of course, that interest amounts will decrease as the outstanding principal balance decreases.

SELECTED ENTRIES FOR PAYMENT OF PRINCIPAL   When all or a portion of the principal of the bond issue is *due to be paid*, the liability is recorded in the Debt Service Fund. The following entries are made for this purpose (assume we are recording the first principal payment in 2014):

Expenditures—bond principal	1,000,000	
Matured serial bonds payable		1,000,000
To record matured bond principal.		
Matured serial bonds payable	1,000,000	
Cash		1,000,000
To record disbursement of cash to fiscal agent for matured principal.		

As with Matured interest payable, governments often do not record an entry for the Matured serial bonds payable, but instead debit Expenditures—bond principal and credit Cash when the cash payment is made to the fiscal agent for the principal portion of the bonds. We included the additional journal entry here to illustrate the need for recognizing the liability in Debt Service Funds only as the debt matures.

Financial Statements Illustration

The fund financial statements for the Debt Service Funds are a statement of revenues, expenditures, and changes in fund balance and a balance sheet. These are illustrated for 2012 in Tables 6-8 and 6-9. The overall reporting process is discussed in Chapters 9 and 10.

TABLE 6-8	Statement of Revenues, Expenditures, and Changes in Fund Balance

City of Rubyville
Debt Service Fund
Sports Complex Bond Fund
Statement of Revenues, Expenditures,
and Changes in Fund Balance
For the Year Ended December 31, 2012

Revenues	
Property taxes	$1,250,000
Interest earned on investments	75,000
Net increase in fair value of investments	25,000
Total revenues	1,350,000
Expenditures	
Interest	500,000
Fiscal agent fees	5,000
Total expenditures	505,000
Excess of revenues over expenditures	845,000
Other Financing Sources	
Transfer in	250,000
Net change in fund balance	1,095,000
Fund balance at beginning of year	0
Fund balance at end of year	$1,095,000

TABLE 6-9	Balance Sheet—Debt Service Fund

City of Rubyville
Debt Service Fund
Sports Complex Bond Fund
Balance Sheet
December 31, 2012

Assets	
Cash	$ 365,000
Property taxes receivable (net of allowance for uncollectibles of $3,500)	100,000
Interest receivable	55,000
Investments	575,000
Total assets	$1,095,000
Fund Balances	
Restricted	$ 845,000
Assigned	250,000
Total fund balance	$1,095,000

Governmental Accounting in Practice

Mt. Lebanon's Debt Service Fund

Table 6-10 shows the statement of revenues, expenditures, and changes in fund balance for the one Debt Service Fund used by Mt. Lebanon. The expenditures reported here are the ones that are common in Debt Service Funds—debt service principal and interest. The debt service payments are financed by transfers from the General Fund and the Sewage Special Revenue Fund. Mt. Lebanon had no assets or liabilities in its Debt Service Fund at the end of its fiscal year (and, therefore, prepared no balance sheet) because it apparently transferred the exact amount needed to pay the debt service.

As noted earlier in the text, Debt Service Funds should be used if legally mandated or if financial resources are being accumulated for paying debt service in future years. A balance sheet would be needed, for example, to report resources accumulated in a sinking fund—pursuant to a bond agreement—to make future debt service payments. If an entity is not legally required to have a Debt Service Fund or is not accumulating resources to pay debt service in future years, it could make debt service payments directly from the General Fund.

LEASED ASSETS

Governmental units often lease assets rather than purchase them. Because governmental-type funds report only spendable resources, a lease presents problems beyond those found in commercial accounting. The illustration presented in this section is not intended to be all-inclusive with respect to leased assets. Complications like residual values and bargain purchase options are omitted in favor of a straightforward general lease model.

As in commercial accounting, governmental units enter into operating leases and capital leases in their everyday operations. A lease is classified as an operating lease if the lessee does not acquire any property rights through the contract. These leases are generally short-term and are recorded by a debit to an expenditure account and a credit to Cash when rental payments are made.

TABLE 6-10	Statement of Revenues, Expenditures, and Changes in Fund Balance— Debt Service Fund—Mt. Lebanon, Pennsylvania

Mt. Lebanon, Pennsylvania
Debt Service Fund
Statement of Revenues, Expenditures, and Changes in Fund Balance
Year Ended December 31, 2009

Revenues	
Investment earnings	$ 1,000
Total revenues	1,000
Expenditures	
Debt Service	
Principal	1,641,000
Interest	869,618
Total expenditures	2,510,618
Excess of expenditures over revenues	(2,509,618)
Other Financing Sources	
Transfers in	2,509,618
Net change in fund balance	0
Fund balance at beginning of year	0
Fund balance at end of year	$ 0

Source: Adapted from Comprehensive Annual Financial Report, Mt. Lebanon, Pennsylvania, December 31, 2009.

A lease is classified as a capital lease by the lessee if the lessee acquires property rights through the contract, the lease is noncancellable, and it meets at least one of the following tests. (Items 2 and 3 are not considered if, at its outset, the lease term is in the last 25 percent of the economic life of the asset.)

1. The lessee owns the property at the conclusion of the lease, through either a transfer of title or a bargain purchase option.
2. The life of the lease is 75 percent or more of the expected economic life of the asset.
3. The present value of the minimum lease payments is 90 percent or more of the fair market value of the leased asset.

If a government enters into a capital lease as a lessee, the government records a debit to a capital expenditure and a credit to an Other financing source. In effect, a capital lease is reported as if the government had financed the acquisition of a capital asset through long-term borrowing. Remember, a debit to capital outlay expenditures is recorded in a governmental fund when a capital asset is purchased, and a credit is made to an Other financing source when a government receives proceeds from long-term borrowings. This entry "nets out" the receipt and disbursement of cash that would take place if money actually were first borrowed and then expended.[12]

---

[12]If instead of leasing the capital asset, the government had borrowed money long term and used the borrowed money to acquire a capital asset, a governmental-type fund would have recorded (a) a debit to Cash and a credit to an Other financing source for the borrowing and (b) a debit to Capital expenditures and a credit to Cash for the acquisition of the capital asset.

To illustrate, assume the City of Rubyville leases a new computer having a fair market value of $862,426 and an economic life of 5 years. Assume further that the relevant interest rate is 8 percent. Based on this information, the government (lessee) must record the present value of the minimum lease payments as an expenditure. If these payments are $200,000 per year, payable on January 1 of each year, the present value of the rental payments is $862,426 ($200,000 × 4.31213) or ($200,000 × [1 + 3.31213]). If the computer is acquired by a department accounted for in the General Fund, the entry to record the transaction is as follows:

Expenditures—capital outlay	862,426	
Other financing sources—capital leases		862,426
To record a capital lease.		

Notice that the initial recording of the lease has no effect on the fund balance of the General Fund. The expenditure is offset by the other financing source.

Because the capital lease is recorded initially at the present value of the lease payments, each lease payment technically consists of both an interest component and a principal payment component. However, because the first lease payment of $200,000 is due at the time the lease is signed, that payment has no interest component. The second payment on the lease obligation occurs 1 year after the lease is signed, so a portion of that $200,000 lease expenditure represents interest. Thus, when the initial lease payment is made at the inception of the lease, the following entry is made in the General Fund:

Expenditures—capital lease principal	200,000	
Cash		200,000
To record lease payment due.		

When the second lease payment comes due 1 year later, the following entry is made:

Expenditures—capital lease principal	147,006	
Expenditures—interest on capital lease	52,994	
Vouchers payable		200,000
Interest calculation:		
Initial debt	$862,426	
Less, first payment	200,000	
Book value of obligation during first year	$662,426	
Interest rate	×.08	
Interest portion of the second payment	$ 52,994	

Governmental leases usually contain a fiscal funding clause, which is a provision in the lease that permits the government to cancel the lease if resources are not appropriated to make lease payments. If the possibility of actual cancellation is remote, a fiscal funding clause does not affect the noncancellable test. In other words, the lease is still capitalized.

PERMANENT FUNDS

Permanent Funds are used to account for resources that are legally restricted in a manner that (1) only earnings on the principal of these resources can be expended and (2) the earnings must be used to support the programs that benefit the government or its citizens in general. For example, a donor gives $1,000,000 to a city to support the city library. The donor, however, states that only the earnings from investing the gift may be used to purchase library books and electronic media. A Permanent Fund would be used to account for these activities.

A distinction should be made between Permanent Funds and Fiduciary Funds. Permanent Funds are used to report nonexpendable gifts that must benefit a government's own programs, as opposed to specific individuals, organizations, or other governments. Fiduciary Funds are used to hold assets in a trustee capacity for the benefit of entities or individuals outside the government. For example, a Pension Trust Fund—one type of Fiduciary Fund—benefits individual employees of a government by accumulating resources for their pensions, investing those resources, and eventually providing retiree pension benefits, but the fund itself does not support the government's own programs. (Fiduciary Fund accounting and financial reporting are discussed in Chapter 8.)

Permanent Funds should be established only when required by legal trust agreement or by law. When such legal agreements do not exist, the General Fund or a Special Revenue Fund should be used, depending on the type of restrictions placed on the resources.

Control of Fund Activities

The operations of Permanent Funds are controlled through applicable state laws and individual trust agreements. Therefore, the accounting system must be designed to provide information and reports that permit a review of this stewardship role. Unless legally stipulated, formal integration of the budget into the accounting system is not usually required. Activities financed by Permanent Funds typically are budgeted in the fund that receives the Permanent Funds' earnings (usually Special Revenue Funds).

Accounting for Fund Activities

Assume the estate of John Cash makes a bequest to Tech City of $5,000,000. The bequest provides that the corpus of the gift is to remain intact permanently, that all realized and unrealized investment gains and losses shall become part of the corpus, and that all other investment income (net of operating expenses) shall be transferred to the city's Museum Special Revenue Fund. Because only the net investment income can be expended and these expenditures must support programs that benefit the city, a Permanent Fund, the Cash Bequest Fund, is used to account for the bequest and its activities. Shortly after the bequest is received, the entire amount is invested in securities. The entries to record the bequest and the purchase of securities are as follows:

Cash	5,000,000	
Revenues—bequest		5,000,000
To record bequest from estate of John Cash.		
Investments	5,000,000	
Cash		5,000,000
To record investment of fund resources.		

During the year, the fund earns $200,000 on its investments. It also pays operating expenditures of $7,000. The following journal entries are made:

Cash	200,000	
Revenues—investment income		200,000
To record investment income for the year.		
Operating expenditures	7,000	
Cash		7,000
To record fund operating expenditures.		

The fund trustee distributes $175,000 to the Museum Special Revenue Fund in accordance with the terms of the bequest and makes the following journal entry:

Transfer to Museum Special Revenue Fund	175,000	
Cash		175,000
To record transfer to Museum Special Revenue Fund.		

GASB standards require that investments be reported at fair value. The fund trustee determines that the fund's investments have a fair value of $5,125,000 at year-end. The following entry records the $125,000 increase in fair value.

Investments	125,000	
Revenues—net appreciation in fair value		125,000
To record increase in fair value of investments.		

Based on the year's transactions, the account balances are as follows:

	Debits	**Credits**
Cash	$ 18,000	
Investments	5,125,000	
Revenues—bequest		$ 5,000,000
Revenues—investment income		200,000
Revenues—net appreciation in fair value		125,000
Transfer to Museum Special Revenue Fund	175,000	
Operating expenditures	7,000	
	$ 5,325,000	$ 5,325,000

You can tell from inspection of the account balances that the net assets (or fund balance) of the Permanent Fund at year-end are $5,143,000. The fund balance consists of two parts: (a) Nonspendable fund balance of $5,125,000, representing the increase in the corpus of the Cash Bequest Fund ($5,000,000 + $125,000) and (b) Restricted fund balance of $18,000, representing the remaining amount of the net investment income that will ultimately be transferred to the Museum Special Revenue Fund ($200,000 − [$175,000 + $7,000]). As discussed in Chapter 5, the fund corpus is Nonspendable fund balance because it is legally required to be maintained intact; and the amount remaining to be transferred to the Special Revenue Fund is Restricted fund balance because the restriction was externally imposed by a donor.

Financial statements for a Permanent Fund are a balance sheet and a statement of revenues, expenditures, and changes in fund balance. The statements of Tech City's Cash Bequest Fund, shown in Tables 6-11 and 6-12, are based on the foregoing account balances and the data regarding the classifications of fund balance.

CONCLUDING COMMENT

Recall that under governmental fund GAAP, neither capital assets nor long-term debt are reported in fund-level financial statements. However, capital assets are required to be reported in the government-wide financial statements. In any event, all governments should keep detailed records of their capital assets and periodically verify their physical existence with these records.

TABLE 6-11 Permanent Fund—Balance Sheet

Tech City
Permanent Fund
Cash Bequest Fund
Balance Sheet
December 31, 2012

Assets	
Cash	$ 18,000
Investments, at fair value	5,125,000
Total assets	$ 5,143,000
Fund Balance	
Nonspendable	$ 5,125,000
Restricted for Museum Special Revenue Fund	18,000
Total fund balance	$ 5,143,000

Capital asset adjustments needed for preparing government-wide financial statements generally can be made by analyzing capital asset expenditures and sales during the year. However, not all transactions affecting capital assets flow through the financial accounting records; for example, assets may be written off because of expiration of useful life or theft. To improve internal controls over capital assets and to facilitate preparation of the government-wide financial statements, we suggest that governments establish a memorandum set of records. These records can be called the Capital Investment Account Group (CIAG). Chapter 10 contains a description of the workings of the CIAG.

TABLE 6-12 Permanent Fund—Statement of Revenues, Expenditures, and Changes in Fund Balance

Tech City
Permanent Fund
Cash Bequest Fund
Statement of Revenues, Expenditures, and Changes in Fund Balance
December 31, 2012

Revenues		
Bequest	$ 5,000,000	
Investment income	200,000	
Net appreciation in fair value of investments	125,000	$ 5,325,000
Expenditures		
Operating expenditures		7,000
Excess of revenues over expenditures		5,318,000
Other Financing Sources (Uses)		
Transfer out to Museum Special Revenue Fund		(175,000)
Net change in fund balance		5,143,000
Fund balance, beginning of year		0
Fund balance, end of year		$ 5,143,000

Review Questions

Q6-1   Explain the relationship between Debt Service Funds and Capital Projects Funds.

Q6-2   Are acquisitions of capital assets always accounted for through Capital Projects Funds? Explain.

Q6-3   Under what circumstances are Capital Projects Funds used?

Q6-4   How are Capital Projects Funds controlled?

Q6-5   Why is encumbrance accounting generally used for Capital Projects Funds?

Q6-6   Are closing entries necessary in the accounting records for a capital project that is not completed in the first year?

Q6-7   Are capital assets recorded in Capital Projects Funds? Why or why not?

Q6-8   Under what circumstances are Debt Service Funds used?

Q6-9   How are the activities of Debt Service Funds controlled?

Q6-10   Are budgets typically recorded in Debt Service Funds?

Q6-11   When is interest recorded as an expenditure in Debt Service Funds?

Q6-12   When is general long-term debt principal recorded in Debt Service Funds?

Q6-13   What information can a city oversight body obtain from a Debt Service Fund?

Q6-14   On what bases are investments valued on governmental fund balance sheets?

Q6-15   Bonds that finance capital projects sometimes are issued at a premium or a discount. How might a bond premium be accounted for? A bond discount?

Q6-16   What is *arbitrage,* and what is its significance in government financial management?

Q6-17   Under what circumstances are Permanent Funds used?

Q6-18   How are the activities of Permanent Funds controlled?

Q6-19   Are budgets typically recorded in Permanent Funds?

Q6-20   How are Permanent Funds different from Fiduciary Funds?

Discussion Scenarios and Issues

D6-1   Julius I. Tornado is the chief operating officer of Green Valley. One day last week he came to your office to discuss the terms of a new bond issue the city plans to sell. The proceeds from these bonds will be used to construct a new city hall and courthouse building. The total estimated cost of the project is $100,000,000. Tornado believes that as chief finance officer, you should have some input into the terms included in the bond indenture and how to account for the bond issue. The bonds will be redeemed in a lump sum at the end of 25 years. The city is barely balancing its budget now, so Tornado is concerned that there will not be enough resources available to pay the interest for the next 25 years and redeem the principal when it comes due. What recommendations do you have for Tornado?

D6-2   Liz Figgie, the chief financial officer for Pine City, is involved in the planning process for an arena. The city is trying to attract a professional basketball team, and to do so, it must have a first-class arena available. If you were Figgie, what suggestions would you bring to the first committee meeting regarding financing and construction of the arena?

D6-3   Assume you are the accounting supervisor for the City of Secret Valley, and you discover a violation the city made regarding its bond indentures. The city has four bond issues outstanding, and the bond indenture for each requires a separate accounting. In error, a new entry-level accounting clerk did not set up separate Debt Service Funds for each bond issue. It is the end of the current year, and you are responsible for preparing the annual report. In desperation, you go to your superior, Janet Well, the chief financial officer of the city, and ask her for guidance. She suggests you not worry about such a petty thing—"No one reads these reports anyway." What would you do?

D6-4   Reginald Canary, the mayor of the City of Bloomerville, is trying to locate available resources in the governmental-type funds to help "bail out" the General Fund. The General Fund expenditures currently exceed budgetary amounts by $10 million with 2 months remaining in the fiscal year. Canary feels some unused resources in a Capital Projects Fund or a Debt Service Fund could be transferred to the General Fund to alleviate the impending budget deficit. Each of these funds has a fund balance of at least $50 million. If Canary cannot locate the needed resources, he will have to borrow money using tax anticipation notes based on an emergency tax levy. This prospect is a major problem for him because the current year is an election year. Is Canary's plan ethical? If you were the chief financial officer of Bloomerville, how would you respond to Canary? How could such a situation be prevented?

Exercises

E6-1   (Fill in the blanks—general terminology)
1. Encumbrance accounting usually (is or is not) _____ used in Capital Projects Funds.
2. The entry to record the budget of a Capital Projects Fund would include a (debit or credit) _____ to Appropriations.
3. A contractor recently completed a bridge for the City of Paige. After the contractor removed his workers and equipment, several deficiencies were noticed. Another contractor was hired to repair these deficiencies. The cost of the repairs should be charged to _____.
4. Long-term bonds issued by a Capital Projects Fund (are or are not) _____ reported as a liability of that fund.
5. During the year, a city acquired furniture for the mayor's office, land for a parking garage, and a fire truck. The furniture was financed from general city revenues; the land and the cost of the parking garage were financed primarily from general obligation bond proceeds; and the fire truck was financed from general tax revenues. Which of these projects would require the use of a Capital Projects Fund?

E6-2   (Use of Capital Projects Funds)
The City of New Falls is planning to acquire furniture and fixtures for the mayor's office and the council chambers. One of the council members, Ryan Cannedy, sent you a memo asking whether a Capital Projects Fund is needed to record the acquisition of the furniture. Write a memo in response to Council Member Cannedy.

E6-3   (Multiple choice)
1. The resources used to finance Capital Projects Funds may come from which of the following sources?
   a. Private donations
   b. General obligation debt
   c. Intergovernmental revenues
   d. All of the above
2. The issuance of bonds to provide resources to construct a new courthouse should be recorded in a Capital Projects Fund by crediting which of the following accounts?
   a. Bonds payable
   b. Revenues—bonds
   c. Fund balance
   d. Other financing source—long-term debt issued
3. What entry must be made at the beginning of the new period when encumbrance accounting is used for a construction project that continues beyond the end of an accounting period?
   a. A credit to Revenues
   b. A debit to Cash
   c. A debit to Expenditures
   d. A debit to Encumbrances
4. What is done with resources that remain in a Capital Projects Fund after the project is completed?
   a. Always transferred to a Debt Service Fund
   b. Always returned to the provider(s) of the resources
   c. Disbursed according to the directives of the resource provider
   d. Always transferred to the General Fund

5. What journal entry is made in the Capital Projects Fund when a contract is signed and encumbrance accounting is used?

   a. Encumbrances   xxxx
      Budgetary fund balance reserved for encumbrances   xxxx
   b. Vouchers payable   xxxx
      Reserve for encumbrances   xxxx
   c. Expenditures—construction costs   xxxx
      Vouchers payable   xxxx
   d. Budgetary fund balance reserved for encumbrances   xxxx
      Fund balance   xxxx

6. The principal amount of bonds issued to finance the cost of a new city hall would be recorded as a liability in which of the following funds?

   a. General Fund
   b. Special Revenue Fund
   c. Capital Projects Fund
   d. Debt Service Fund
   e. None of the above

7. Why is encumbrance accounting usually used in Capital Projects Funds?

   a. Long-term debt is not recorded in these funds.
   b. The budget must be recorded in these funds.
   c. It helps the government control the expenditures.
   d. The modified accrual basis of accounting is used.

8. The City of New Easton constructed a convention center. After completion of the project, the convention center should be recorded as an asset in which of the following funds?

   a. General Fund
   b. Capital Projects Fund
   c. Debt Service Fund
   d. Both b and c
   e. None of the above

9. The City of Matthews has been given a $1,000,000 gift that is restricted by the donor, Rebecca Smith. Ms. Smith's gift agreement mandates that only the earnings from the gift may be used to maintain or improve athletic facilities owned by the city. Which fund should be used to account for the gift?

   a. Special Revenue Fund
   b. Permanent Fund
   c. Capital Projects Fund
   d. Private Purpose Trust Fund

10. The gift from Rebecca Smith (see previous question) earned $50,000 this year. The city council decides that these resources should be used to construct new sand volleyball courts for public use. Which fund should be used to account for the construction of the courts?

    a. Capital Projects Fund
    b. General Fund
    c. Special Revenue Fund
    d. Enterprise Fund

E6-4   (Use of a Capital Projects Fund)
Explain why a separate fund generally is used to account for the construction and acquisition of major general capital assets.

E6-5   (Comparison of commercial and governmental accounting)
Both Waste, Inc. (a private trash collector) and Croton Falls Village will acquire new sanitation trucks. Both will borrow long term, making similar financial arrangements to finance the trucks, and both will pay the same amount to acquire the trucks. Waste, Inc. uses normal commercial GAAP to account for its activities. Croton Falls Village maintains a Capital Projects Fund and a

Debt Service Fund for its accounting. The following transactions and events will occur in calendar year 2013. Make journal entries to record these transactions and events, as applicable, first for Waste, Inc. and then for Croton Falls Village. For Croton Falls Village, indicate the appropriate fund in which the transactions are recorded.

1. April 1. Sells bonds for $300,000. The bonds are payable in 20 semiannual installments of $15,000 each, with interest of 5 percent per annum on the unpaid balance, starting October 1, 2013.
2. April 1. Acquires sanitation trucks at a total cost of $300,000. The trucks have an estimated useful life of 10 years. (Make journal entry only to record payment of cash.)
3. October 1. Pays the first installment of principal and interest on the long-term debt. (Ignore entry to record the source of cash to make payment.)
4. December 31. Makes adjusting journal entries, as necessary, to prepare financial statements.

E6-6   (Fill in the blanks—general terminology)
1. Payment of principal and interest on debt is referred to as _____.
2. A periodic transfer of resources from the General Fund to a Debt Service Fund is reported as a(n) _____ on the operating statement of the funds.
3. Payment of principal is reported as a(n) _____ on the _____ of a Debt Service Fund.
4. A financial institution that makes principal and interest payments in the name of a governmental unit is called a(n) _____.
5. A debit balance in Fund balance is called a(n) _____.

E6-7   (Use of a Debt Service Fund)
The City of Crestview has only one Debt Service Fund for all of its bond issues. Is the city in compliance with GAAP for governmental units? Explain.

E6-8   (Multiple choice)
1. Several years ago a city established a sinking fund to retire an issue of general obligation bonds. This year the city made a $50,000 contribution to the sinking fund from general revenues and realized $15,000 in revenue from securities in the sinking fund. The bonds due this year were retired. These transactions require accounting recognition in which of the following funds? (AICPA adapted)
   a. General Fund
   b. Debt Service Fund
   c. Debt Service Fund and General Fund
   d. Capital Projects Fund, Debt Service Fund, and General Fund
   e. None of the above
2. To provide for the retirement of general obligation bonds, a city invests a portion of its general revenue receipts in marketable securities. This investment activity should be accounted for in which of the following funds? (AICPA adapted)
   a. Trust Fund
   b. Enterprise Fund
   c. Special Assessment Fund
   d. Special Revenue Fund
   e. None of the above
3. As part of its process to legally adopt Brockton City's General Fund budget for the year beginning January 1, 2013, the city council includes a portion of its existing fund balance as a budgetary resource to eliminate a projected excess of expected expenditures over estimated revenues. What will be the effect of the council's action on Brockton City's financial statements for the year ended December 31, 2012?
   a. A cash overdraft
   b. An increase in encumbrances
   c. An increase in Assigned fund balance
   d. A decrease in revenues
   e. None of the above

4. Which of the following funds is used to account for the operations of a public library receiving the majority of its support from property taxes levied specifically for that purpose? (AICPA adapted)
   a. General Fund
   b. Special Revenue Fund
   c. Enterprise Fund
   d. Internal Service Fund
   e. None of the above

5. A special tax was levied by Downtown City to retire and pay interest on general obligation bonds that were issued to finance the construction of a new city hall. Where are the receipts from the tax recorded?
   a. Capital Projects Fund
   b. Special Revenue Fund
   c. Debt Service Fund
   d. General Fund
   e. None of the above

6. Which of the following funds use(s) modified accrual accounting?
   a. All governmental-type funds
   b. General Fund and Special Revenue Funds only
   c. Only the General Fund
   d. Only Debt Service Funds
   e. None of the above

7. The current financial resources measurement is used to account for which of these?
   a. All assets and liabilities
   b. Financial assets and short-term liabilities in governmental-type funds
   c. Capital assets and long term liabilities recorded in governmental funds
   d. The timing of the recognition of revenues and expenses
   e. None of the above

E6-9   (Discussion of control in the General Fund and in Debt Service Funds)
Compare and contrast the methods used to control expenditures in the General Fund and in Debt Service Funds. Be sure to explain the reasons for any differences.

E6-10   (Journal entries in a Debt Service Fund)
Green Valley issued $20,000,000 of general obligation bonds to construct a multipurpose arena. These bonds will be serviced by a tax on the revenue from events held in the arena and will mature in 2017. During 2012, Green Valley budgeted $2,500,000 of tax revenues and $2,000,000 for interest on the bonds in its Debt Service Fund. Prepare the journal entries necessary to record (a) the budget and (b) the expenditure when the interest comes due for payment.

E6-11   (Leases)
Plymouthville leased equipment with a fair market value of $905,863. The life of the noncancellable lease is 10 years, and the economic life of the property is 10 years. Using an 8 percent interest rate, the present value of the minimum lease payments is $905,863. The first payment of $125,000 is due January 1 of the current year. Each additional payment is due on the first of January in the next 9 years. What is the amount of the asset to be recorded in Plymouthville's Capital Projects Fund? If no asset will be recorded, explain why.

Problems

P6-1   (Journal entries and financial statements—Capital Projects Fund)
The following transactions occurred during 2012:
   1. The City of Watersville approved the construction of an enclosed concert arena for a total cost of $75,000,000 in order to attract professional events. On the same day, a contract with a 6 percent

retainage clause was signed with V.P. Construction Company for the arena. The arena will be financed by a $75,000,000 general obligation bond issue. Investment revenue of $4,000,000 was also included in the budget. (Assume that the budget is recorded in the accounts and encumbrance accounting is used.)

2. Watersville received $76,000,000 from the sale of bonds, which included a premium of $1,000,000 over the $75,000,000 face value. The $1,000,000 premium was transferred immediately to the appropriate Debt Service Fund.

3. The city invested $74,900,000 in securities.

4. The contract signed with V.P. stipulated that the contract price included the architect fees. The architects were paid their fee of $25,000 by Watersville. (Assume that a vouchers payable account was not used.)

5. The contractor submitted a progress billing of $3,000,000; the billing (less a 6 percent retainage) was approved.

6. Investments that cost $3,000,000 were redeemed for $3,000,000 plus $50,000 interest.

7. V. P. was paid the amount due in transaction 5.

8. Income totaling $3,700,000 was received on the investments.

9. V. P. submitted another progress billing of $8,000,000. The billing, less the retainage, was approved.

10. Investments originally costing $7,800,000 were redeemed to make the payment to V.P. Cash proceeds of $8,100,000 were received.

11. The contractor was paid the amount due in transaction 9.

12. Investment income of $60,000 was accrued.

13. Investment income of $10,000 was received in cash.

Use the preceding information to do the following:

a. Prepare the journal entries necessary to record these transactions in the Capital Projects Fund. Assume that the city operates on a calendar year.

b. Prepare a trial balance for the Capital Projects Fund as of December 31, 2012, before closing.

c. Prepare any necessary closing entries. The debt covenant for the general obligation bonds states that the bond proceeds and any earnings from investing the proceeds must be used for the construction of the arena. If any unused bond proceeds or related investment earnings remain at completion of the project, they will be transferred to the Debt Service Fund.

d. Prepare a statement of revenues, expenditures, and changes in fund balance for 2012 and a balance sheet as of December 31, 2012.

e. Prepare the journal entries necessary to record the remainder of the budget and to reestablish the budgetary accounts for encumbrances on January 1, 2013. Assume that investment revenue expected to be earned in 2013 is $2,000,000.

P6-2   (Journal entries, financial statements, and closing entries for a Capital Projects Fund)
The following transactions occurred during the fiscal year July 1, 2012, to June 30, 2013:

1. The City of Spainville approved the construction of a city hall complex for a total cost of $120,000,000. A few days later, a contract with a 5 percent retainage clause was signed with Paltrow Construction for the complex. The buildings will be financed by a federal grant of $25,000,000 and a general obligation bond issue of $100,000,000. During the current year, investment revenue of $4,000,000 is budgeted. (Assume the budget is recorded in the accounts and encumbrance accounting is used.)

2. The bonds were issued for $90,000,000 (the face amount of the bonds was $100,000,000). The difference between the actual cost of the project and the bond and grant proceeds was expected to be generated by investing the excess cash during the construction period.

3. The city collected the grant from the government.

4. The city invested $90,000,000.

5. The contract signed with Paltrow stipulated that the contract price included architect fees. The architects were paid their fee of $45,000 by Spainville. (Assume a Vouchers payable account is used.)

6. Paltrow submitted a progress billing for $25,000,000. The billing, less 5 percent retainage, was approved. Assume that the city will use resources from the federal grant to make this payment.

7. Investments that cost $5,000,000 were redeemed for a total of $5,020,000.

8. Investment income totaling $3,500,000 was received in cash.
9. The contractor was paid the amount billed in transaction 6, less a 5 percent retainage.
10. The contractor submitted another progress billing for $25,000,000. The billing, less retainage, was approved.
11. Investments totaling $14,600,000 were redeemed, together with additional investment income of $1,400,000.
12. The contractor was paid the amount billed in transaction 10, less a 5 percent retainage.
13. Investment income of $250,000 was accrued.
14. Bond interest totaling $10,000,000 was paid.

Use the preceding information to do the following:
   a. Prepare the journal entries necessary to record these transactions in a Capital Projects Fund for the City of Spainville.
   b. Prepare a trial balance for the fund as of June 30, 2013, before closing.
   c. Prepare any necessary closing entries. The general obligation bond proceeds and federal grant revenues are restricted by the debt covenant and the federal government for construction of the city hall complex. Neither the debt covenant nor the federal grant makes any mention of how investment earnings on their money should be used. Based on authority granted it by the city council, the City of Spainville's management has decided to use the investment earnings for construction of the city hall complex or, if not needed for construction, for debt service.
   d. Prepare a statement of revenues, expenditures, and changes in fund balance for the year ended June 30, 2013, and a balance sheet as of June 30, 2013.
   e. Prepare the journal entry or entries necessary to record the remainder of the budget and to reestablish the budgetary accounts for encumbrances as of July 1, 2013. Assume investment revenues of $2,000,000 are expected in the 2013 fiscal year.

P6-3   (Journal entries regarding a bond issue and accounting for a premium)
Archambault Township authorized a bond issue for a parking garage wish an estimated cost of $4,000,000. The garage would be financed through a $2,500,000 bond issue and a $1,500,000 contribution from the General Fund. The General Fund made its contribution, and the bonds were sold for $2,700,000, which included a $200,000 premium over the face amount of the bonds. Prepare journal entries to record the budget for the parking garage, the payment and receipt of the General Fund's contribution, and the issuance of the bonds, assuming the premium remained in the Capital Projects Fund. Identify the fund(s) used to record the transactions. Also, identify alternate methods of disposing of the bond premium.

P6-4   (Journal entries for several funds and financial statements for a Capital Projects Fund)
Following is a trial balance for the Tilker Falls Boat Marina Capital Projects Fund and the transactions that relate to the 2012–2013 fiscal year. Prepare all the journal entries necessary to record these transactions and close the Capital Projects Fund. In addition, identify the fund(s) used (a Vouchers payable account is not used). Also, prepare a statement of revenues, expenditures, and changes in fund balance for the Boat Marina Capital Projects Fund for the 2012–2013 fiscal year.

Tilker Falls
Boat Marina Capital Projects Fund
Trial Balance
July 1, 2012

	Debits	Credits
Cash	$ 30,000	
Investments	500,000	
Retainage payable		$ 10,000
Restricted fund balance		520,000
	$530,000	$530,000

1. The budget for the marina project provided for a remaining appropriation of $500,000. Record the budget, and reestablish the budgetary accounts for encumbrances, which totaled $500,000 on June 30, 2012. Assume $30,000 of investment income (dividends and interest) is budgeted.
2. The contractor, Martinez Construction, submitted a progress billing on the marina for $300,000. The billing, less retainage of 10 percent, was approved.
3. Investments were redeemed for $320,000. This amount included $20,000 of investment income.
4. Martinez Construction was paid the amount billed in transaction 2, less the 10 percent retainage.
5. Investment income of $15,000 was received in cash.
6. The final billing was received from Martinez Construction for $200,000. The billing, less the retainage of 10 percent, was approved.
7. All remaining investments were redeemed for $205,000. This amount included $5,000 of investment income.
8. Martinez Construction was paid the amount billed in transaction 6, less a 10 percent retainage.
9. During final inspection of the project, prior to official acceptance, several construction defects were noted by the city engineer. Because Martinez Construction had already relocated its workers and equipment, the city was authorized to have the repairs made by a local contractor at a cost not to exceed $40,000. The actual cost of the repairs totaled $32,000. The remainder of the retainage was sent to Martinez Construction.
10. After the repairs, the project was formally approved, and the accounting records were closed. The remaining cash was transferred to the Debt Service Fund.

P6-5   (Budgetary journal entries for a capital project and the related bond issue)

Watson Township plans to build an auditorium. The plans were drawn for $100,000 by an architect who will complete the plans and bill the city after the bonds are issued. The township accepted a bid from Forrester Contractors for $8,000,000 for the entire project, which should take 2 years to build. It will not be started until October 1, 2012, so the projected completion date is September 30, 2014. The township's accounting supervisor plans to establish a Debt Service Fund to accumulate resources for repaying the bonds that will be issued to finance the project. These bonds will be serviced from property tax revenues and are expected to be issued at a face amount of $8,000,000. During 2012, $100,000 of investment revenue earned on the bond proceeds is expected to be available for construction purposes. The bonds will pay interest on April 1 and October 1 of each year, beginning in 2013. Prepare the journal entries needed to record the budget and the encumbrance in the appropriate funds for calendar year 2012, based on the preceding budgetary information.

P6-6   (Journal entries, financial statements, and closing entries for a Debt Service Fund)

The following are a trial balance and several transactions that relate to Lewisville's Concert Hall Bond Fund:

Lewisville		
Debt Service Fund		
Concert Hall Bond Fund		
Trial Balance		
July 1, 2012		
Cash	$ 60,000	
Investments	40,000	
Restricted fund balance		$100,000
	$100,000	$100,000

The following transactions took place between July 1, 2012, and June 30, 2013:

1. The city council of Lewisville adopted the budget for the Concert Hall Bond Fund for the fiscal year. The estimated revenues totaled $100,000, the estimated other financing sources totaled $50,000, and the appropriations totaled $125,000.

2. The General Fund transferred $50,000 to the fund.
3. To provide additional resources to service the bond issue, a property tax was levied upon the citizens. The total levy was $100,000, of which $95,000 was expected to be collected.
4. Property taxes of $60,000 were collected.
5. Revenue received in cash from the investments totaled $1,000.
6. Property taxes of $30,000 were collected.
7. The fund liability of $37,500 for interest was recorded, and that amount of cash was transferred to the fiscal agent.
8. A fee of $500 was paid to the fiscal agent.
9. Investment revenue totaling $1,000 was received in cash.
10. The fund liabilities for interest in the amount of $37,500 and principal in the amount of $50,000 were recorded, and cash for the total amount was transferred to the fiscal agent.
11. Investment revenue of $500 was accrued.

Use the preceding information to do the following:
   a. Prepare all the journal entries necessary to record the preceding transactions for the Concert Hall Bond Fund.
   b. Prepare a trial balance for the Concert Hall Bond Fund as of June 30, 2013.
   c. Prepare a statement of revenues, expenditures, and changes in fund balance and a balance sheet for the Concert Hall Bond Fund (assume all fund balance is restricted).
   d. Prepare closing entries for the Concert Hall Bond Fund.

P6-7 (Journal entries, financial statements, and closing entries for a Debt Service Fund)
Following are a trial balance and the transactions that relate to the City of Patin Heights' Debt Service Fund:

City of Patin Heights
Bridge Bonds Debt Service Fund
Trial Balance
December 31, 2012

	Debit	Credit
Cash	$60,000	
Investments	30,000	
Restricted fund balance		$90,000
	$90,000	$90,000

1. The city council of Patin Heights adopted the budget for the Debt Service Fund for 2013. The estimated revenues totaled $1,000,000, the estimated other financing sources (a transfer from the General Fund) totaled $500,000, and the appropriations totaled $202,000.
2. The $500,000 transfer from the General Fund was recorded although it had not yet been paid to the Debt Service Fund.
3. To provide additional resources to service the bond issue, a property tax was levied upon the citizens. The total levy was $1,000,000, of which $975,000 was expected to be collected.
4. Property taxes of $780,000 were collected.
5. Property tax receivables of $5,000 were written off.
6. Income received in cash from investments totaled $5,000.
7. Property taxes of $150,000 were collected.
8. The fund liability of $50,000 for interest on bonds was recorded, and that amount of cash was transferred to the fiscal agent.
9. Investment income of $3,000 was received in cash.
10. The fund liabilities for interest on bonds in the amount of $50,000 and principal in the amount of $100,000 were recorded, and cash for the total amount was transferred to the fiscal agent.

11. The fiscal agent's fee of $1,000 was accrued (credit Vouchers payable).
12. Investment revenue of $1,500 was accrued.
13. The transfer accrued in transaction 2 was collected.
14. Investments totaling $1,000,000 were purchased.

Use the preceding information to do the following:
   a. Prepare all the journal entries necessary to record these transactions for the Debt Service Fund.
   b. Prepare a trial balance for the Debt Service Fund as of December 31, 2013.
   c. Prepare a statement of revenues, expenditures, and changes in fund balance for 2013 and a balance sheet as of December 31, 2013, for the Debt Service Fund (assume all fund balance is restricted).
   d. Prepare closing entries for the Debt Service Fund.

P6-8   (Journal entries for several funds)
Following are several transactions that relate to Bultena Township for the fiscal year 2012 (assume a voucher system is not used). Prepare all the journal entries necessary to record these transactions in the appropriate governmental-type fund(s), and identify the fund(s) used.

1. The General Fund operating budget was approved. It included estimated revenues of $1,200,000, estimated other financing sources of $300,000, appropriations of $1,150,000, and estimated other financing uses of $100,000.
2. The Police Department paid its salaries of $50,000.
3. The General Fund made a transfer to a Debt Service Fund of $100,000.
4. Office furniture previously ordered for $45,000 was received, and the bill was paid. Old furniture that cost $23,000 was sold for $500; the proceeds could be used in any manner by the city.
5. The fire chief ordered $1,000 of supplies.
6. General obligation long-term debt principal matured, and the final interest payment became due. These amounts were $75,000 and $7,500, respectively. Assume a Debt Service Fund and a fiscal agent are used.
7. The appropriate amount of cash was sent to the fiscal agent to process the debt service payments described in the previous transaction.
8. The supplies ordered in transaction 5 arrived, along with an invoice for $1,025. The excess amount was approved, and a check was sent to the supplier.
9. The property tax for the year was levied by the General Fund. The total amount of the tax was $500,000. City officials estimated that 99 percent would be collected.
10. Collections of property taxes during the year totaled $490,000.
11. The remaining property taxes were classified as delinquent after $2,000 was written off as uncollectible.
12. The General Fund received a $1,000 interfund transfer from an Enterprise Fund (record only the General Fund portion).

P6-9   (Journal entries for several funds and a trial balance for a Debt Service Fund)
Following are several transactions that relate to the Village of Brooks Haven in 2012. Prepare all the journal entries necessary to record these transactions. In addition, identify the fund(s) in which each entry is recorded. Also, prepare a trial balance for the Debt Service Fund as of December 31, 2012.

1. The General Fund operating budget was approved. It included estimated revenues of $500,000, appropriations of $400,000, and estimated other financing uses of $90,000.
2. Encumbrances of $50,000 were recorded in the General Fund.
3. The budget for the Parks Special Revenue Fund was approved. It included estimated revenues of $60,000 and appropriations of $59,000.
4. The General Fund made its annual transfer of $100,000 to a Debt Service Fund.
5. The Debt Service Fund recorded the liability for principal and interest, $20,000 and $40,000, respectively.
6. The Debt Service Fund invested $10,000 of Debt Service Fund cash in securities.

7. The salaries of the general governmental administrative staff were paid: $15,000. Assume that salaries were not encumbered.
8. The fiscal agent who manages the investment activities of the Debt Service Fund was paid a fee of $1,000.
9. The property tax used to service the bond issue was levied. The total levy was $30,000, of which $29,000 is expected to be collected.
10. A cash expenditure for office supplies for the mayor's office was made: $900. The amount that had been encumbered was $1,000.
11. Debt Service Fund cash of $60,000 was paid to the fiscal agent to pay interest and principal (see transaction 5).

P6-10 (Journal entries for several funds)

Prepare journal entries for each of the following transactions. In addition, identify the fund in which each entry would be recorded.

1. The General Fund made its annual contribution of $1,500,000 to the fund that will pay $1,000,000 principal and $500,000 interest on outstanding general obligation debt.
2. The city paid $1,000,000 of principal and $500,000 of interest on outstanding general obligation bonds from resources previously accumulated.
3. A Debt Service Fund previously retired the total principal and the interest in full on an outstanding bond issue. Currently the fund carries a balance of $300,000. These resources can be spent by the General Fund in any way the city manager considers appropriate.
4. The Police Department paid $300,000 for equipment. This equipment was ordered 3 months prior to delivery at an estimated cost of $295,000 (assume a voucher system is used and the excess expenditure is approved and paid).
5. The fiscal agent for the city was paid its annual $10,000 fee from resources accumulated in the only Debt Service Fund used by the city.

P6-11 (Journal entries for several funds)

The following transactions and events occurred in East Fritzsch Township. Record these transactions in journal form. Also, indicate the fund in which each transaction amount is recorded.

1. The township paid cash for four police cars. Each car cost $18,000. They were originally ordered at $20,000 each.
2. The township issued bonds for the purpose of constructing playgrounds in the city. The bonds had a face value of $20,000,000 and were sold for $19,900,000.
3. The mayor of the township signed a contract with Dumas Office Furniture Company to buy furniture for his office. The total cost of the furniture was $8,900. The furniture will be delivered next month.
4. Two additional police officers were hired to help patrol the new playgrounds; each of them will receive $50,000 a year.
5. The Fire Department sold several pieces of used equipment, which originally cost the township $20,000. The fire chief negotiated a selling price of $3,000 for the equipment.
6. The township made its annual payment of principal and interest on its outstanding debt. A total of $5,000,000 was paid: $1,000,000 of principal and $4,000,000 of interest.
7. The township levied a property tax to service the outstanding debt. The total amount of the tax was $4,000,000, of which $3,900,000 was expected to be collected. (Assume the use of a separate fund.)
8. The city hall construction project started in the prior year was completed this year. This year $1,500,000 of costs were incurred. In the prior year a total of $7,500,000 was incurred. Financing for the project came from a bond issue that was sold at the time the project was started.
9. The township's board of supervisors approved a budget amendment for the General Fund. An extra $300,000 appropriation was included in the budget for the current year.
10. The township made payments on outstanding leases totaling $300,000. This amount included $175,000 for interest. The leases are accounted for in the General Fund, and encumbrance accounting is used.

P6-12   (Leased assets)

On January 1, 2012, the chief operating officer of New Belgium, Jeff Stambaugh, signed a noncancellable lease for street equipment. The lease was for 10 years, the economic life of the property. The fair market value of the equipment (and present value of the minimum rentals) is $75,152. The township's incremental borrowing rate is 7 percent. The $10,000 annual lease payment is due on the first day of each year beginning in 2012.

Prepare all journal entries necessary to record the lease transaction for 2012 and the payment made in 2013. (Assume the government uses a voucher system.)

P6-13   (Journal entries for several funds)

The following transactions took place during 2012. Record these transactions in journal form. Also, indicate the fund in which each transaction is recorded.

1. The city sold some of its street repair equipment. The equipment originally cost $50,000, but it was sold for $500.

2. A $2,000,000 bond issue was sold at par. The bonds were general obligation debt issued to finance the cost of an addition to the local court system building.

3. Nondedicated property taxes totaling $100,000 were collected.

4. Construction of a bridge across the Mississippi River was completed at a total cost of $8,000,000. The bridge had been under construction since 2010. Costs incurred in previous years totaled $7,000,000. (Prepare the closing entry, assuming the only transaction during 2012 was the expenditure necessary to complete the bridge. Also, assume fund balance is restricted.)

5. A Debt Service Fund paid the interest on outstanding debt: $800,000.

6. A Debt Service Fund retired bonds with a face value of $3,000,000.

7. The General Fund made its annual transfer of $6,000,000 to a Debt Service Fund.

8. Old office equipment in the mayor's office was discarded. The original cost of the equipment was $900.

9. A contract was signed with Legal, Inc. to construct an addition to the court building. The amount of the contract was $5,000,000.

10. The construction costs paid on the court addition during the year were $500,000.

11. The Fire Department acquired a fire engine. The vehicle had been ordered earlier in the year. The order was encumbered for $140,000. The actual cost of $138,000 was paid when the fire engine was received.

P6-14   (Leased assets)

The Police Department of Ramser Falls signed a noncancellable lease for computer equipment on January 1, 2012. The lease was for 5 years, the economic life of the property. The fair market value of the equipment (and present value of the minimum rentals) is $21,198, and the city's incremental borrowing rate is 9 percent. The annual lease payments are $5,000 and are due on the first day of the year, beginning on January 1, 2012. Assuming the equipment is delivered when the lease is signed, prepare all journal entries necessary to record the lease transaction for 2012 and the payment made in 2013.

P6-15   (Journal entries and correcting entries for several funds)

Following is a selection of improperly recorded transactions that occurred during 2012 and a description of how each transaction was recorded by a township. Prepare the necessary entries to correct these mistakes. Also, identify the fund(s) involved. Closing entries are not required. If no entry is required, indicate "None." The books for the current year, 2012, have not been closed.

1. The governing board adopted a budget for the General Fund for 2012 that included estimated revenues of $900,000, estimated other financing sources of $200,000, appropriations of $800,000, and estimated other financing uses of $150,000. The budget was not recorded in the books.

2. The township purchased a fire truck in February. The bookkeeper made the following entry in the General Fund:

Fire truck	125,000	
Vouchers payable		125,000

The voucher was paid, but the payment was not recorded.

3. A property tax was levied in March. The total levy was $500,000. Approximately 3 percent was expected to be uncollectible. By the end of the year $390,000 had been collected, and the remainder was delinquent. The only entries made during the year were for the collections as a debit to Cash and credit to Revenues—property taxes.

4. Bonds were retired in June 2012. The township accumulated $505,000 in a Debt Service Fund by the end of 2012. Part of these resources ($500,000) was used to retire the bonds. The remainder was available to be used by the township in any way it desired. The only entries recorded in the Debt Service Fund during the year were as follows:

Bonds payable	500,000	
Vouchers payable		500,000
Vouchers payable	500,000	
Cash		500,000

5. Some surplus equipment was sold in September for $20,000 (with no restrictions on the use of these resources). The equipment was originally purchased for $245,000 several years ago. The following entry was made in the General Fund:

Cash	20,000	
Loss on sale of equipment	225,000	
Equipment		245,000

6. The General Fund made its annual contribution to a Debt Service Fund. These resources will be used to pay interest. The only entry made was in the General Fund:

Bonds payable	100,000	
Cash		100,000

7. The interest paid out of the Debt Service Fund during 2012 on the debt mentioned in transaction 6 was mistakenly recorded in the General Fund as follows:

Interest expense	100,000	
Cash		100,000

P6-16   (Complete cycle—Permanent Fund)

Dr. Theodore Dough made a $500,000 gift to the Village of Radnor. Dr. Dough stipulated that the corpus of the gift (together with all investment gains and losses) was to remain intact in perpetuity and that all earnings on the investments (after paying expenses for administering the gift) were to be used solely for the purchase of books by the Teddy Library Special Revenue Fund. Record the following transactions in the Dough Permanent Fund, and prepare the required fund financial statements for the year ended December 31, 2012.

1. Dough donated $500,000 to the Village of Radnor.
2. The entire gift was immediately invested in various securities.
3. The investments earned $30,000 in dividends and interest during the year.
4. The Permanent Fund paid the village $2,000 for administrative expenses.
5. In accordance with the terms of the gift, $25,000 was sent to the Teddy Library Special Revenue Fund.
6. At year-end, the investments held by the Permanent Fund had a fair market value of $508,000.

Summary Problem

Leisure City had sold bonds in the amount of $4,000,000 during the latter part of 2012 to improve its water delivery system. As a result, on December 31, 2012, its Capital Projects Fund reported cash of $4,000,000 and fund balance (restricted) of $4,000,000. Leisure City anticipated completing the project during 2013. It also anticipated receiving a $1,000,000 grant from the federal government to aid in the construction project. Leisure City's Debt Service Fund had neither assets nor liabilities at December 31, 2012.

The city adopted a budget for its Capital Projects Fund but not for its Debt Service Fund. It uses encumbrance accounting in the Capital Projects Fund. The Leisure City ordinance provides that all amounts remaining in the Capital Projects Fund on completion of a construction project must be transferred to the Debt Service Fund. The following transactions and events affecting the two funds occurred in 2013:

1. The city council adopted the following budget for the Capital Projects Fund for 2013:

Estimated revenues—federal grant	$1,000,000
Estimated revenues—investment income	20,000
Appropriations—water system upgrade	5,000,000

2. The Capital Projects Fund invested $3,000,000 in a 6-month CD bearing interest at the rate of 1 percent per annum.

3. Because of budgetary problems experienced by the federal government, the city received a cash grant in the amount of only $600,000. A letter attached to the grant said that no additional grant would be forthcoming; further, the grant stipulated that city resources had to be used before the grant could be used and that, if the city did not spend at least $4,600,000 on the project, a proportionate share of the grant must be returned to the federal government.

4. After reviewing construction cost estimates, the city decided to sell additional bonds in the amount of $400,000 face value. The city realized cash of $425,000 from the sale (which included a $25,000 premium), all of which was deposited in the Capital Projects Fund.

5. The city council amended the Capital Projects Fund budget, reducing the estimated revenues from federal grants by $400,000 and adding a line item for Estimated other financing sources— bond issue in the amount of $400,000.

6. The city entered into two contracts: (a) one with the Leveille Construction Co. in the amount of $4,600,000 for construction services and (b) the other with Elisa Engineering in the amount of $400,000 for construction supervision.

7. The CD in transaction 2 matured. Leisure City received $3,015,000 cash, which included interest on the CD.

8. Leveille completed construction work on the water delivery system upgrade and submitted an invoice for $4,600,000. Leisure City approved and paid the bill, less 5 percent retainage pending final approval of the work by Elisa Engineering.

9. Elisa Engineering gave final approval to Leveille's work. As a result, Leisure City paid the retainage to Leveille (see transaction 8). Elisa also submitted an invoice for $400,000, which Leisure City approved and paid.

10. Based on the provisions of the federal grant (see transaction 3), Leisure City recognized the entire amount of the grant as revenue.

11. The construction contract having been completed, Leisure City transferred all the resources remaining in the Capital Projects Fund to the Debt Service Fund.

12. The Debt Service Fund recognized the debt service liability for 2013, based on the following debt service requirement:
    a. $4,000,000 of debt, issued December 1, 2012, and due in equal *annual* installments of principal over 20 years, starting November 30, 2013, with interest of 5 percent per annum on the unpaid principal
    b. $400,000 of debt, issued June 1, 2013, and due in equal *semiannual* installments of principal over 20 years, starting November 30, 2013, with interest of 5 percent per annum on the unpaid principal

13. The Debt Service Fund received $440,000 cash from the General Fund to pay debt service (see Chapter 5, Summary Problem, transaction 18, on page 181).

14. The Debt Service Fund paid the debt service amount due for the year.

Use the preceding information to do the following:

a. Prepare journal entries to record the foregoing transactions and events in the appropriate funds.

b. Prepare preclosing trial balances as of December 31, 2013, for the Capital Projects Fund and the Debt Service Fund.

c. Prepare balance sheets and statements of revenues, expenditures, and changes in fund balances for the Capital Projects Fund and the Debt Service Fund.

d. Prepare a budgetary comparison statement for the Capital Projects Fund.

Chapter 7

The Governmental Fund Accounting Cycle

Proprietary-Type Funds

After completing this chapter, you should be able to do the following:

- Understand the similarities between Internal Service Funds and Enterprise Funds
- Explain why and how Internal Service Funds are used in governmental accounting
- Prepare the journal entries normally recorded in Internal Service Funds
- Prepare fund financial statements for Internal Service Funds
- Explain why and how Enterprise Funds are used in governmental accounting
- Prepare the journal entries normally recorded in Enterprise Funds
- Prepare fund financial statements for Enterprise Funds

This chapter discusses fund-level financial accounting and reporting for proprietary funds, that is, Internal Service Funds and Enterprise Funds. Government-wide financial reporting of these funds is discussed in Chapters 9 and 10.

OVERVIEW

Proprietary funds in state and local government are used to account for certain government-operated activities in essentially a private-sector, or business, fashion. There are two types of proprietary funds: Internal Service Funds and Enterprise Funds. The basic difference between the two fund types is the nature of the customer base. The customers of Internal Service Fund activities are various departments within the same government and, occasionally, other nearby governments. The customers of Enterprise Funds, on the other hand, are primarily individual citizens, but can include government departments as well.

Proprietary funds account for activities involved in providing goods and/or services to paying customers *on an exchange basis.* Thus, the operating cycle of a proprietary fund is similar to that of a business organization: During the fiscal period, the fund acquires assets such as supplies, property, and equipment. Goods or services are provided to paying customers, and revenues from user charges are recorded. The cost of assets used is recorded along with other operating and nonoperating expenses. Revenues earned are compared with expenses incurred, and the resulting profit or loss increases or decreases net position.

Some Internal Service Funds price goods and services above cost to provide financing for expansion or to cover anticipated inflation when equipment must be replaced. Sometimes the services provided by Enterprise Funds (such as mass transit, discussed later in the chapter) are "underpriced" and subsidized by General Fund revenues as a matter of public policy. And some activities accounted for in Enterprise Funds (such as lotteries) produce "profits" that are transferred to the General Fund. By computing the activity's full cost of operations and comparing these costs with the revenues earned, the extent of the subsidy needed is determined.

Because of the need to measure all costs, proprietary funds use the total economic resources measurement focus. Accordingly, fixed assets (and depreciation thereof) are accounted for within proprietary funds, as is any long-term debt serviced exclusively by proprietary fund revenues. Also, proprietary funds use the full accrual basis of accounting, so revenues are recognized when they are earned (without regard to the "measurable and available" considerations found in governmental-type funds), and expenses, not expenditures, are recognized in the period in which they are incurred. Because the focus of this type of fund is to provide information to evaluate the cost-recovery of its operations, governments often report individual activities in separate funds.

What Determines Whether a Proprietary Fund Is an Enterprise Fund or an Internal Service Fund?

As we have mentioned, the deciding factor in whether a proprietary fund is classified as an Enterprise Fund or an Internal Service Fund is the customer base. In this regard, the GASB states, "Internal service funds should be used only if the reporting government is the predominant participant [customer] in the activity. Otherwise, the activity should be reported as an enterprise fund."[1] Thus, the GASB Codification discusses proprietary fund accounting primarily in terms of Enterprise Funds. According to the GASB, Enterprise Funds *may* be used to report any activity for which a fee is charged to external users for goods or services. Activities *are required* to be accounted for as Enterprise Funds if any one of the following criteria is met:

   a. The activity is financed with debt that is secured solely by a pledge of the net revenues from fees and charges of the activity [debt of this kind usually is in the form of *revenue bonds*]. . . .
   b. Laws or regulations require that the activity's costs of providing services including capital costs (such as depreciation or debt service) be recovered with fees and charges, rather than with taxes or similar revenues.
   c. The pricing policies of the activity establish fees and charges designed to recover its costs, including capital costs (such as depreciation or debt service).[2]

Governments should apply each of these criteria in the context of the activity's principal revenue sources. Governments are not required to use Enterprise Funds for insignificant activities that are financed by user charges.

Although some of the services provided by proprietary funds are the same as those provided by private-sector profit and not-for-profit entities—such as water utilities, bus companies, and colleges—proprietary funds apply only GASB pronouncements, not FASB pronouncements. This requirement is relatively recent; in GASB Statement 62, "Codification of Accounting and Financial Reporting Guidance Contained in Pre-November 30, 1989, FASB and AICPA Pronouncements," issued in December 2010, the GASB adopted all pre-1989 FASB and AICPA pronouncements that it considered applicable to proprietary funds. The financial statements for individual proprietary funds are a statement of revenues, expenses, and changes in fund net position; a statement of net position (or balance sheet); and a statement of cash flows.

Proprietary fund statements of net position should be prepared using a classified format. Under this format, assets are classified as *current* assets if they are reasonably expected to be realized in cash or sold or consumed within a year. All other assets are classified as *noncurrent*. Liabilities are classified as *current* based on whether their liquidation is reasonably expected to require the use of current assets or the creation of other current liabilities. All other liabilities are *noncurrent*. Deferred outflows and inflows are classified in the same manner.

---

[1]GASB Cod. Sec. 1300.110.
[2]GASB Cod. Sec. 1300.109.

The general format for the statement of revenues, expenses, and changes in fund net position is presented as follows:

Operating revenues (detailed)
   Total operating revenues
Operating expenses (detailed)
   Total operating expenses
   Operating income (loss)
Nonoperating revenues and expenses (detailed)
   Income before other revenues, expenses, gains, losses, and transfers
Capital contributions, special and extraordinary items, and transfers (detailed)
   Increase (decrease) in net assets
Net position—beginning of period
Net position—end of period[3]

The proprietary fund statement of net position reports all assets, deferred outflows of resources, liabilities, deferred inflows of resources, and net position. Deferred outflows of resources and deferred inflows of resources are defined in GASB Concepts Statement 4, "Elements of Financial Statements." Deferred outflows represent a use of net assets by the government that is applicable to a future reporting period—and, therefore, deferred. Deferred inflows are an acquisition of net assets by the government that is applicable to a future reporting period. Deferred outflows and inflows are limited to items specifically identified as such by the GASB; they are required to be reported separately from proprietary fund assets and liabilities. The GASB requires the net position section of the statement of net position to be reported in three components: (1) net investment in capital assets; (2) restricted; and (3) unrestricted.

SPECIFIC ASPECTS OF INTERNAL SERVICE FUNDS

Summary of Fund Activities

Governments establish Internal Service Funds to account for the operations of providing goods or services in-house to departments in circumstances where it can be done at a lower cost, or perhaps more conveniently, than if the same goods or services were obtained externally. Internal Service Funds typically are used to account for activities such as central data-processing services, motor pools, risk management, and inventory and supply (central stores) functions. In this chapter we focus on the activities of a central motor pool. This type of service is typical for governments and is illustrative of the general operations of Internal Service Funds.

When a central motor pool is established, the first step is to acquire capital from the General Fund or some other fund. This money is used to acquire automobiles, trucks, and so forth. As the vehicles are used, each fund or department using them is billed based on the number of miles driven. Revenue from the billings is used to pay for the operating costs of the vehicles and, possibly, for their replacement.

---

[3]GASB Statement 34, "Basic Financial Statements—and Management's Discussion and Analysis—for State and Local Governments," par. 98, as amended by GASB Statement 63, "Financial Reporting of Deferred Outflows of Resources, Deferred Inflows of Resources, and Net Position."

Control of Fund Activities

The operations of Internal Service Funds are controlled indirectly by the operating budgets of the funds and departments using the goods or services and directly by means of flexible budgets. Because other funds must pay for the goods or services supplied, approval of their budgets acts as an indirect control device for Internal Service Funds.

A flexible budget is a budget in which most of the budgeted expenses are related to the level of operations. In a central motor pool, gasoline and oil costs will vary directly with the number of miles the vehicles are driven. Governmental-type funds, by contrast, operate under a fixed budget. If a department is appropriated $4,000 for supplies for the year, for example, that amount cannot be exceeded—regardless of the level of operations. In effect, the use of a fixed budget actually sets a limit on the level of operations of governmental-type funds.

The difference in budgeting practices between governmental-type funds and proprietary funds results because the revenue generated by the latter increases as the level of operations increases. Because of a general cause-and-effect relationship between the level of operations and the revenues earned and expenses incurred, a flexible budget allows higher levels of expenses at higher levels of operating activity. As previously explained, no such relationship usually exists between revenues and expenditures of governmental-type funds. For example, a Police Department usually must request an additional budget allocation if it uses all of its appropriation; such an allocation does not result automatically.

Typically we do not find the budget recorded in the accounts of Internal Service Funds, nor do we usually find the use of encumbrance accounting for these funds. Without an absolute spending limit, the use of encumbrance accounting serves no purpose. A few state or local governments are subject to laws that require the use of encumbrances for Internal Service Funds, but here we will assume that encumbrance accounting is not used.

Accounting for Fund Activities

OPERATING ENTRIES To start the central motor pool Internal Service Fund, assume the General Fund makes a transfer of $500,000 to the Motor Pool Fund. The entries to record this transfer are as follows:

In the General Fund:

Transfer out to Motor Pool Fund	500,000	
Cash		500,000
To record transfer of initial capital to Motor Pool Fund.		

In the Internal Service Fund:

Cash	500,000	
Transfer in from General Fund—capital contribution		500,000
To record transfer of initial capital from General Fund.		

If the Internal Service Fund acquires a fleet of vehicles for $400,000, the following entry is made:

Automobiles	300,000	
Trucks	100,000	
Cash		400,000
To record the acquisition of vehicles.		

Billings of $57,000 to various General Fund departments for use of the vehicles are recorded as follows:

In the Internal Service Fund:

Due from General Fund	57,000	
Revenues—vehicle charges		57,000
To record charges to departments for use of vehicles.		

In the General Fund, charged to department that received $8,000 worth of services:

Expenditures—vehicle usage	8,000	
Due to Motor Pool Fund		8,000
To record the use of vehicles during the period.		

Collections of $45,000 from the user departments accounted for within the General Fund are recorded in the Internal Service Fund as follows:

Cash	45,000	
Due from General Fund		45,000
To record payments received from departments using vehicles.		

The corresponding disbursement entry in a user fund (amount assumed) would be as follows:

Due to Motor Pool Fund	8,000	
Cash		8,000
To record payment to Motor Pool Fund.		

During the year, gasoline, oil, and maintenance expenses totaling $14,000 are incurred, of which $10,000 are paid in cash. These expenses are recorded in the Motor Pool Fund as follows:

Gasoline and oil expense	9,500	
Maintenance expense	4,500	
Cash		10,000
Accounts payable		4,000
To record the gasoline, oil and maintenance expenses for the period.		

Payment of salaries of $10,000, ignoring withholdings, is recorded as follows:

Salaries expense	10,000	
Cash		10,000
To record salaries expense.		

If the motor pool rents warehouse space from the government for $2,000 per year, the entry to record the rental will be this:

Rent expense	2,000	
Cash		2,000
To record the rent for the year.		

The General Fund will record the receipt of the rent as follows:

Cash	2,000	
Revenues—rental of warehouse space		2,000
To record the receipt of the rent from the Motor Pool Fund.		

As previously indicated, depreciation is an expense that is recognized in Internal Service Funds. Assuming the amounts given, the entry to record depreciation for the year follows:

Depreciation expense—automobiles	20,000	
Depreciation expense—trucks	10,000	
Accumulated depreciation—automobiles		20,000
Accumulated depreciation—trucks		10,000
To record depreciation for the year.		

Although additional entries can be made, these summary journal entries are sufficient to illustrate the activities of Internal Service Funds and the recognition of related revenues and expenses. A trial balance for the Motor Pool Fund at the end of the year is shown in Table 7-1.

CLOSING ENTRY   The closing process for Internal Service Funds is similar to the one used for commercial enterprises. Each of the revenue, expense, and other temporary accounts is closed,

TABLE 7-1   Trial Balance—Motor Pool Fund

City of Fort Chessie
Internal Service Fund
Motor Pool Fund
Trial Balance
December 31, 2013

	Debits	Credits
Cash	$123,000	
Due from General Fund	12,000	
Automobiles	300,000	
Accumulated depreciation—automobiles		$ 20,000
Trucks	100,000	
Accumulated depreciation—trucks		10,000
Accounts payable		4,000
Transfer in from General Fund—capital contribution		500,000
Revenues—vehicle charges		57,000
Gasoline and oil expense	9,500	
Maintenance expense	4,500	
Salaries expense	10,000	
Rent expense	2,000	
Depreciation expense—automobiles	20,000	
Depreciation expense—trucks	10,000	
	$591,000	$591,000

and the change in position is recorded in the Net position account. The following entry relates to the previous illustration:

Revenues—vehicle charges	57,000	
Transfer in from General Fund—capital contribution	500,000	
Gasoline and oil expense		9,500
Maintenance expense		4,500
Salaries expense		10,000
Rent expense		2,000
Depreciation expense—automobiles		20,000
Depreciation expense—trucks		10,000
Net position		501,000

To close the revenue, expense, and transfer accounts for the period.

Financial Statements Illustration

As indicated earlier, the individual financial statements for Internal Service Funds are a statement of revenues, expenses, and changes in fund net position; a statement of net position (or balance sheet); and a statement of cash flows. The general format for the statement of revenues, expenses, and changes in fund net position was introduced in the "Overview" section and is applied here in Table 7-2. A statement

TABLE 7-2	Statement of Revenues, Expenses, and Changes in Fund Net Position—Internal Service Fund

City of Fort Chessie
Internal Service Fund
Motor Pool Fund
Statement of Revenues, Expenses, and Changes in Fund Net Position
For the Year Ended December 31, 2013

Operating Revenues		
Vehicle charges		$ 57,000
Operating Expenses		
Gas and oil expense	$ 9,500	
Maintenance expense	4,500	
Salaries expense	10,000	
Rent expense	2,000	
Depreciation expense—automobiles	20,000	
Depreciation expense—trucks	10,000	
Total operating expenses		56,000
Operating income		1,000
Transfer in from General Fund		500,000
Change in net position		501,000
Net Position at Beginning of Year		0
Net Position at End of Year		$501,000

TABLE 7-3	Statement of Net Position—Internal Service Fund

City of Fort Chessie
Internal Service Fund
Motor Pool Fund
Statement of Net Position
December 31, 2013

Assets

Current assets:		
Cash	$123,000	
Due from General Fund	12,000	
Total current assets		$135,000
Noncurrent assets:		
Automobiles (net of accumulated depreciation of $20,000)	280,000	
Trucks (net of accumulated depreciation of $10,000)	90,000	
Total noncurrent assets		370,000
Total assets		505,000
Liabilities		
Current liabilities:		
Accounts payable		4,000
Net Position		
Net investment in capital assets	370,000	
Unrestricted	131,000	
Total net position		$501,000

of net position format is preferred by the GASB. It presents assets, plus deferred outflows of resources, less liabilities, less deferred inflows of resources, to equal net position. Or a balance sheet format (assets plus deferred outflows of resources equals liabilities plus deferred inflows of resources, plus net position) may be used. The statement of net position format is illustrated in Table 7-3.

Recall that on a statement of net position, the GASB requires that the net position section be reported in three components: (1) net investment in capital assets; (2) restricted; and (3) unrestricted. One way to derive the balances of the three net position classifications is to close all nominal accounts to a Net position account and then analyze that account to determine its components for financial reporting purposes. Notice that in the statement of net position for the Motor Pool Fund (Table 7-3), only components 1 and 3 are reported, because the fund has no restricted net position. Restricted position results from contractual and other restrictions placed on the use of the assets by outside parties or by law. Restricted assets are discussed in greater detail in the next section of this chapter.

For the Motor Pool Fund, the net investment in capital assets is equal to $370,000 − 0, or $370,000. Nothing is deducted from the capital (noncurrent) asset balances because the fund has no related debt. The remainder of the net position, $131,000 ($501,000 − $370,000), is reported as unrestricted.

The example of a cash flows statement appears in Table 7-4 and completes the illustration of financial statements for Internal Service Funds. The statement of cash flows required by the GASB is different from that required in the private sector in several ways. First, use of the *direct method* is required for reporting operating cash flows. Major classes of gross operating cash receipts and

TABLE 7-4	Statement of Cash Flows—Internal Service Fund

City of Fort Chessie
Internal Service Fund
Motor Pool Fund
Statement of Cash Flows
For the Year Ended December 31, 2013

Cash Flows from Operating Activities		
Receipts from customers	$ 45,000	
Payments to suppliers	(10,000)	
Payments to employees	(10,000)	
Payments for rent	(2,000)	
Cash flows from operations		$ 23,000
Cash Flows from Capital and Related Financing Activities		
Purchase of capital assets	$(400,000)	
Capital contributed by municipality	500,000	
Cash flows from capital and related financing activities		100,000
Net increase in cash		123,000
Cash balance at beginning of year		0
Cash balance at end of year		$123,000
Reconciliation of Operating Income to Net Cash Provided by Operating Activities		
Operating income	$ 1,000	
Adjustments to reconcile operating income to net cash provided by operating activities:		
Depreciation expense	30,000	
Changes in assets and liabilities:		
Due from General Fund	(12,000)	
Accounts payable	4,000	
Net cash provided by operations		$ 23,000

gross operating cash payments are reported along with their arithmetic sum to arrive at the net cash flows from operating activities. Proprietary funds must also provide a reconciliation of operating income to net cash flows from operating activities at the bottom of the cash flows statement or in a separate schedule. This reconciliation is the equivalent of the *indirect method* used to report operating cash flows in the private sector. Although not shown in Table 7-4, cash receipts and disbursements are classified in four (instead of the FASB's three) categories: operating activities, noncapital financing activities, capital and related financing activities, and investing activities. The Motor Pool Fund did not have any noncapital financing or investing activities.

The combined totals for all Internal Service Funds should be reported in a separate column on the face of the proprietary fund financial statements, to the right of the total Enterprise Funds column.[4] This aggregate information is supported by combining statements for Internal Service Funds in the annual report.

---

[4]GASB Cod. Sec. 2200.165.

Governmental Accounting in Practice

Alpine School District, Utah

The Alpine School District in Utah uses Internal Service Funds to account for industrial insurance (self-insurance) services and school services (printing and central warehousing services). For illustrative purposes, we are using the School Services Fund. The financial statements for this fund are presented in Tables 7-5, 7-6, and 7-7. Notice that the statement of net position contains only two components of net position, like our earlier example.

TABLE 7-5	Statement of Revenues, Expenses, and Changes in Fund Net Position— Internal Service Fund—Alpine School District, Utah

Alpine School District, Utah
Internal Service Fund
School Services Fund
Statement of Revenues, Expenses, and Changes in Fund Net Position
For the Year Ended June 30, 2011
(amounts in thousands)

Operating Revenues		
Charges for services		$ 945
Operating expenses		
Salaries	$362	
Employee benefits	184	
Purchased services	56	
Supplies and materials	98	
Depreciation	74	
Total operating expenses		774
Operating income		171
Net Position at Beginning of Year		2,821
Net Position at End of Year		$2,992

Source: Adapted from a recent annual report of the Alpine School District, Utah.

TABLE 7-6	Statement of Net Position—Internal Service Fund—Alpine School District, Utah

Alpine School District, Utah
Internal Service Fund
School Services Fund
Statement of Net Position
June 30, 2011 (amounts in thousands)

Assets		
Current assets:		
Cash and investments	$1,770	
Accounts receivable	2	
Inventories	704	
Total current assets		$2,476

(continued)

TABLE 7-6 (continued)

Capital assets:		
Land	16	
Property, plant, and equipment, at cost	1,626	
Less, accumulated depreciation	(898)	
Net property, plant, and equipment		744
Total assets		3,220
Liabilities		
Current liabilities:		
Accounts payable	202	
Compensated absences payable	26	
Total current liabilities		228
Net Position		
Net investment in capital assets		744
Unrestricted		2,248
Total net position		$2,992

Source: Adapted from a recent annual report of the Alpine School District, Utah.

TABLE 7-7 Statement of Cash Flows—Internal Service Fund—Alpine School District, Utah

Alpine School District, Utah
Internal Service Fund
School Services Fund
Statement of Cash Flows
June 30, 2011 (amounts in thousands)

Cash Flows from Operating Activities		
Receipts from interfund services provided	$946	
Payments to suppliers	(80)	
Payments to employees	(553)	
Net cash provided by operating activities		$ 313
Cash Flows from Capital and Other Financing Activities		
Acquisition of capital assets		(7)
Cash Flows from Investing Activities		
Interest received		2
Increase in cash and cash equivalents		308
Cash and cash equivalents at beginning of year		1,462
Cash and cash equivalents at end of year		$1,770
Reconciliation of Operating Income to Net Cash Provided by Operating Activities		
Operating income		$ 171
Depreciation		74
Decrease (increase) in operating assets and increase (decrease) in operating liabilities:		
Inventories		(68)
Accounts payable		143
Compensated absences payable		(7)
Net cash provided by operating activities		$ 313

Source: Adapted from a recent annual report of the Alpine School District, Utah.

SPECIFIC ASPECTS OF ENTERPRISE FUNDS

Summary of Fund Activities

Enterprise Funds are used when a government provides goods or services to customers who, to a significant extent, are not part of the government. Utility operations—providing electric, water, and sewer service to the general public—are activities that normally require use of Enterprise Funds. Also, Enterprise Funds are used to account for the operations of ports, airports, public swimming pools, and golf courses.[5]

Many governments also have created business-type entities, called *public benefit corporations* or *public authorities,* that use Enterprise Fund accounting. As a result, one government may provide a service (such as electricity services) through an Enterprise Fund that is part of the legally constituted government, and another may provide the same type of service through a legally separate public benefit corporation. Depending on the circumstances, discussed in Chapter 9, the legally separate corporation may or may not be part of the government's financial reporting entity.

Control of Fund Activities

The operations of an Enterprise Fund are controlled by many means. Because the functions of this type of activity are to supply goods or services to a general market, the consumer exercises some control. Whether a consumer decides to purchase a particular good or service is true "marketplace control." However, because many Enterprise Funds are public utilities, they possess monopoly operating rights. As a result, there is no competitive market to ensure the reasonableness of the charges for services. Legislative bodies or governing boards control and approve the rates the utility can charge. These boards use operating data extensively to determine reasonable service charges, sometimes with the assistance of outside consultants. In these cases, accrual-basis accounting data are invaluable for measuring the results of operations.

Flexible budgets are used to measure and control the financial operations in Enterprise Funds in the same manner as in Internal Service Funds, and they provide an additional element of control. However, because of their nature, flexible budgets cannot be recorded in the accounts; the direct spending control found in governmental-type fund fixed budgets is not present in Enterprise Funds. Nor is encumbrance accounting generally used as a spending control for Enterprise Funds.

Accounting for Fund Activities

OPERATING ENTRIES   For illustrative purposes, assume the City of Fort Chessie owns and operates the Blanco Landfill and Recycling Center. The center operates a municipal solid waste transfer station, another transfer station for construction debris, and a recycling center for city residents. The city's own landfill was closed in 1980. A 2013 beginning trial balance for the fund is presented in Table 7-8.

The Cash—restricted for debt service account represents the amounts the activity is required to set aside each year according to a bond indenture. This amount will be held in escrow until the bonds are retired and all interest is paid.

Notice the last account, Net position. At the end of each year all nominal accounts are closed into the Net position account, and then, for reporting purposes, the total is segregated into three components (Net investment in capital assets, Restricted for debt service, and Unrestricted) for financial reporting purposes.

---

[5]Some Enterprise Funds routinely serve other departments of the government in addition to third-party customers, but the revenues obtained from governmental customers are only a small portion of the Enterprise Fund's total revenues. Prime examples are utility operations that supply water and electricity to a government's buildings and facilities as well as to the citizenry.

| **TABLE 7-8** | Trial Balance—Enterprise Fund |

City of Fort Chessie
Enterprise Fund
Blanco Landfill and Recycling Center Fund
Beginning Trial Balance
January 1, 2013

	Debits	**Credits**
Cash	$ 25,000	
Accounts receivable	15,000	
Supplies	2,000	
Cash—restricted for debt service	150,000	
Land	500,000	
Equipment	1,200,000	
Accumulated depreciation—equipment		$ 600,000
Buildings	500,000	
Accumulated depreciation—buildings		90,000
Accounts payable		20,000
Revenue bonds payable		500,000
Net position		1,182,000
	$2,392,000	$2,392,000

If waste collection billings during 2013 totaled $500,000 and $5,000 of those billings were to the city itself, the following entry should be made:

Accounts receivable	495,000	
Due from General Fund	5,000	
Revenue from waste collections		500,000
To record waste collection revenue for the year.		

Cash collections during the year total $490,000, of which $5,000 is from the General Fund. These are recorded as follows:

Cash	490,000	
Accounts receivable		485,000
Due from General Fund		5,000
To record collections from customers.		

The appropriate entries in the books of the General Fund for these two events are as follows:

Expenditures—waste collection	5,000	
Due to Blanco Landfill & Recycling Center Fund		5,000
To record cost of waste collection in 2013.		
Due to Blanco Landfill & Recycling Center Fund	5,000	
Cash		5,000
To record payment made to Blanco Landfill & Recycling Center Fund.		

Blanco Landfill & Recycling Center Fund operating expenses before depreciation are $400,000 for 2013. Of this amount, $50,000 is paid in cash, and the remainder is on credit. The entry to record this information follows:

Personal services expense	180,000	
Transfer expense	150,000	
Repairs and maintenance expense	40,000	
Other expenses	30,000	
Cash		50,000
Accounts payable		350,000
To record operating expenses for 2013.		

Because the city is measuring the full cost of operating the center, depreciation must be recorded. Assuming the appropriate amounts are as indicated in the entry, the following is recorded:

Depreciation expense—equipment	50,000	
Depreciation expense—buildings	15,000	
Accumulated depreciation—equipment		50,000
Accumulated depreciation—buildings		15,000
To record depreciation expense for 2013.		

Payments to creditors total $350,000 during the year. These payments are recorded as follows:

Accounts payable	350,000	
Cash		350,000
To record payments on accounts payable.		

Blanco Landfill & Recycling Center's long-term debt is in the form of revenue bonds payable. Revenue bonds are debt securities that are secured exclusively by the revenues generated by the fund (in contrast to general obligation bonds, which are secured by the "full faith and credit"— the general taxing power—of the government). The entry to record interest of $40,000 on the long-term debt for the current year is this:

Interest expense	40,000	
Cash		40,000
To record bond interest paid for the year.		

In this illustration, we assume the bond interest is all paid in cash; that is, $20,000 is payable on June 30 and December 31 of each year. If the interest is not due at the end of the year, a proportionate amount is accrued as an expense, just as in the private sector.

In this illustration, $50,000 of revenue bond principal is paid this year, and another $50,000 will be paid next year; the $50,000 due next year is classified as a current liability (as shown later in Table 7-11). The entry in the Center Fund to record the 2013 principal payment follows:

Revenue bonds payable	50,000	
Cash		50,000
To record payment of principal of revenue bonds due in 2013.		

Assume that during the year the center's management institutes a policy of requiring a $500 deposit from each contractor using the construction transfer station. This policy is designed to reduce the losses suffered in prior years due to contractors not paying their bills. The cash collected is considered a noncurrent asset because it must be refunded to the contractors when individual transfer agreements with the Center expire. The offsetting liability is Contractor deposits payable. If $20,000 is collected, the entry appears as follows:

Cash—contractor deposits	20,000	
Contractor deposits payable		20,000
To record amounts received for contractors' deposits.		

Also, assume that in addition to requiring deposits, management establishes a provision for uncollectible accounts. The provision for 2013 is $5,000, which is recorded as follows:

Estimated uncollectible accounts	5,000	
Allowance for uncollectible accounts		5,000
To record the estimated uncollectible accounts as of December 31, 2013.		

The Allowance for uncollectible accounts account is a contra asset and as such is reported as a deduction from Accounts receivable on the Center's statement of net position. The Estimated uncollectible accounts figure is reported in the statement of revenues, expenses, and changes in net position as a direct reduction of Revenue from waste collections to report *net* revenues.[6]

During the year the Center used $1,000 of supplies. The entry to record this use follows:

Supplies expense	1,000	
Supplies		1,000
To record supplies used during 2013.		

The preceding journal entries and trial balance reflect the typical activities of Enterprise Funds and the resulting revenues generated and expenses incurred.

The preclosing trial balance for the Blanco Landfill & Recycling Center Fund at December 31, 2013, is presented in Table 7-9.

CLOSING ENTRY The closing process for Enterprise Funds involves transferring the balances of the revenues, expenses, and other temporary accounts to the Net position account. The entry, using the data given in the example, follows:

Revenue from waste collections	500,000	
Net position	11,000	
Estimated uncollectible accounts		5,000
Personal services expense		180,000
Transfer expense		150,000
Repairs and maintenance expense		40,000
Other expenses		30,000
Depreciation expense—equipment		50,000
Depreciation expense—building		15,000
Interest expense		40,000
Supplies expense		1,000
To close the revenue and expense accounts for the period.		

---

[6]GASB 2010–2011 Comprehensive Implementation Guide, Q&A7.72.2, states that "revenues in proprietary funds should be reported net of all related allowances . . . [including] the increase or decrease in the estimate of uncollectible accounts." This treatment differs from that of private-sector accounting, which distinguishes between revenue reductions (nonrevenues, such as sales returns and allowances) and expenses of doing business (such as bad debts). We return to this issue in Chapter 13, regarding hospital accounting. Meantime, you can be the judge as to which is the more logical financial reporting treatment.

| **TABLE 7-9** | Trial Balance—Enterprise Fund |

City of Fort Chessie
Enterprise Fund
Blanco Landfill & Recycling Center Fund
Preclosing Trial Balance
December 31, 2013

	Debits	Credits
Cash	$ 25,000	
Accounts receivable	25,000	
Allowance for uncollectible accounts		$ 5,000
Supplies	1,000	
Cash—customer deposits	20,000	
Cash—restricted for debt service	150,000	
Land	500,000	
Buildings	500,000	
Accumulated depreciation—buildings		105,000
Equipment	1,200,000	
Accumulated depreciation—equipment		650,000
Accounts payable		20,000
Contractor deposits		20,000
Revenue bonds payable		450,000
Net position		1,182,000
Revenue from waste collections		500,000
Estimated uncollectible accounts	5,000	
Personal services expense	180,000	
Transfer expense	150,000	
Repairs and maintenance expense	40,000	
Other expense	30,000	
Depreciation expense—equipment	50,000	
Depreciation expense—building	15,000	
Interest expense	40,000	
Supplies expense	1,000	
	$2,932,000	$2,932,000

Notice the debit to Net position, which results from the use of one Net position account in the accounting records. For financial reporting purposes, the total in the Net position account is segregated into its three components, as discussed in the next section.

Financial Statements Illustration

Individual financial statements for Enterprise Funds are the same as those for Internal Service Funds—that is, a statement of revenues, expenses, and changes in net position; a

TABLE 7-10	Statement of Revenues, Expenses, and Changes in Fund Net Position— Enterprise Fund

City of Fort Chessie
Enterprise Fund
Blanco Landfill & Recycling Center Fund
Statement of Revenues, Expenses, and Changes in Fund Net Position
For the Year Ended December 31, 2013

Operating Revenues		
Charges for services, net		$ 495,000
Operating Expenses		
Personal services expense	$180,000	
Transfer expense	150,000	
Repairs and maintenance expense	40,000	
Depreciation expense	65,000	
Supplies expense	1,000	
Other expenses	30,000	
Total operating expenses		466,000
Operating income		29,000
Nonoperating Expenses		
Interest expense		(40,000)
Decrease in net position		(11,000)
Total Net Position at Beginning of Year		1,182,000
Total Net Position at End of Year		$1,171,000

statement of net position or balance sheet; and a statement of cash flows. These statements for the Blanco Landfill & Recycling Center Enterprise Fund are illustrated for 2013 in Tables 7-10, 7-11, and 7-12.

Refer to the statement of net postion in Table 7-11. The total balance of net position is $1,171,000. This total consists of the following three components:

1. Net investment in capital assets, $995,000. This amount is equal to the sum of the net carrying values of the land, the buildings, and the equipment ($500,000 + $395,000 + $550,000), less the related debt (current and noncurrent revenue bonds payable) of $450,000.
2. Restricted net position, $150,000. This amount represents the assets restricted for payment of revenue bonds. The $20,000 cash held as contractor deposits is not included here because it is offset by the $20,000 liability reported for contractor deposits.
3. Unrestricted net position, $26,000. This total represents the net assets that have no restrictions on their use, or the net assets not included in the previous two categories ($1,171,000 − $995,000 − $150,000).

TABLE 7-11   Statement of Net Position—Enterprise Fund

City of Fort Chessie
Enterprise Fund
Blanco Landfill & Recycling Center Fund
Statement of Net Position
December 31, 2013

Assets

Current assets:

Cash	$25,000	
Accounts receivable (net of estimated uncollectible accounts of $5,000)	20,000	
Supplies	1,000	
Total current assets		$ 46,000
Noncurrent assets:		
Cash—restricted for debt service		150,000
Cash—contractor deposits		20,000
Total noncurrent assets		170,000
Capital assets:		
Land	500,000	
Buildings (net of accumulated depreciation of $105,000)	395,000	
Equipment (net of accumulated depreciation of $650,000)	550,000	
Total capital assets		1,445,000
Total assets		1,661,000

Liabilities

Current liabilities:	
Accounts payable	20,000
Current portion of revenue bonds payable	50,000
Total current liabilities	70,000
Noncurrent liabilities:	
Contractor deposits	20,000
Revenue bonds payable	400,000
Total noncurrent liabilities	420,000
Total liabilities	490,000

Net Position

Net investment in capital assets	995,000
Restricted for debt service	150,000
Unrestricted	26,000
Total net position	$1,171,000

TABLE 7-12	Statement of Cash Flows—Enterprise Fund

City of Fort Chessie
Enterprise Fund
Blanco Landfill & Recycling Center Fund
Statement of Cash Flows
For the Year Ended December 31, 2013

Cash Flows from Operating Activities		
Receipts from customers	$490,000	
Contractor deposits	20,000	
Transfer payments	(150,000)	
Payments to suppliers	(70,000)	
Payments to employees	(180,000)	
Cash flows from operations		$110,000
Cash Flows from Capital and Related Financing Activities		
Payments for debt service		(90,000)
Net increase in cash		20,000
Unrestricted cash and restricted cash balance at beginning of year		175,000
Unrestricted cash and restricted cash balance at end of year		$195,000
Reconciliation of Operating Income to Net Cash Provided by Operating Activities		
Operating income	$ 29,000	
Adjustments to reconcile operating income to net cash provided by operating activities:		
Depreciation expense	65,000	
Changes in assets and liabilities:		
Supplies	1,000	
Accounts receivable (net)	(5,000)	
Contractor deposits	20,000	
Net cash provided by operations		$110,000

Use of Special Assessments

Special assessments are a means of financing services or capital improvements that benefit one group of citizens more than the general public. Taxpayers who receive the benefits of these activities are assessed for their share of the cost. Some special assessment activities are service special assessments, such as providing special police protection, garbage pickup, or street lighting. Service special assessments are essentially fees designed to recover the cost of these specially provided services.

If a government wishes to charge a fee to recover the entire cost of the services or wishes to know if a subsidy is being provided to certain citizens, it may use an Enterprise Fund to account for the services. Because the total economic resources measurement focus is used, this approach includes calculation of a charge for depreciation, as appropriate.

Use of an Enterprise Fund for service activities that are financed with special assessments results in entries similar to those previously presented in this chapter. The only major change is that the term *special assessment* is generally used to describe the revenues and receivables for the activity.

Governmental Accounting in Practice

The City of Ashtabula, Ohio

The City of Ashtabula, Ohio, uses a single Enterprise Fund—its Wastewater Treatment Fund—as well as several Internal Service Funds. Table 7-13 shows the statement of revenues, expenses, and changes in net position for the Wastewater Treatment Fund (all amounts are in thousands of dollars). Notice that the fund failed to recover all of its costs through charges for services. Its $466 operating loss is offset slightly by $231 in capital contributions, but increased by a $76 transfer out to other funds of the city.

Although not the case for this Wastewater Treatment Fund, some Enterprise Funds generate "profits" to be used to expand their operating plant or to replace operating plant assets when needed. Apparently, the Wastewater Treatment Fund previously issued debt (loans payable) to finance capital assets, as shown in Table 7-14—Statement of Net Position. Although that statement does not identify the Wastewater Treatment Fund's loans payable as capital debt, the net investment in capital assets reported on the Statement of Net Position makes it clear that this was the purpose of those debts. (Net investment in capital assets consists of capital assets net of depreciation of $13,959, less outstanding loans payable of $3,619, equaling the reported balance of net investment in capital assets of $10,340.)

TABLE 7-13 Statement of Revenues, Expenses, and Changes in Fund Net Position—Enterprise Fund—City of Ashtabula, Ohio

City of Ashtabula, Ohio
Enterprise Fund
Wastewater Treatment Fund
Statement of Revenues, Expenses, and Changes in Fund Net Position
For the Year Ended December 31, 2010
(amounts in thousands)

Operating Revenues		
Charges for services	$3,601	
Miscellaneous	28	
Total revenues		$3,629
Operating Expenses		
Personal services	2,112	
Contractual services	610	
Materials and supplies	837	
Depreciation	536	
Total operating expenses		4,095
Operating loss		(466)
Nonoperating Expenses		
Interest and fiscal charges		(135)
Loss Before Contributions and Transfers		(601)
Capital contributions	231	
Transfers out	(76)	155
Change in net position		(446)
Net Position Beginning of Year		12,487
Net Position End of Year		$12,041

Source: Adapted from a recent annual report of the City of Ashtabula, Ohio.

TABLE 7-14 Statement of Net Position—Enterprise Fund—City of Ashtabula, Ohio

City of Ashtabula, Ohio
Enterprise Fund
Wastewater Treatment Fund
Statement of Net Position
December 31, 2010
(amounts in thousands)

Assets

Current assets:

Equity in pooled cash and investments	$ 262	
Accounts receivable	1,891	
Materials and supplies inventory	1	
Prepaid items	42	
Total current assets		$ 2,196

Noncurrent assets:

Capital assets, nondepreciable	595	
Capital assets, depreciable, net	13,364	
Total noncurrent assets		13,959
Total assets		16,155

Liabilities

Current liabilities:

Accounts payable	86	
Accrued wages	15	
Compensated absences payable	120	
Due to other governments	2	
Accrued interest payable	38	
Loans payable	442	
Total current liabilities		703

Noncurrent liabilities:

Compensated absences payable	234	
Loans payable	3,177	
Total noncurrent liabilities		3,411
Total liabilities		4,114

Net Position

Invested in capital assets, net of related debt	10,340
Unrestricted	1,701
Total net position	$12,041

Source: Adapted from a recent annual report of the City of Ashtabula, Ohio.

The Wastewater Treatment Fund has two other sources for financing its capital assets—tap fees from customers and capital contributions from the State of Ohio. Many water and sewer utilities and other activities with operating plants charge tap fees to their customers. All or a portion of those fees are intended to provide financing for the utility, for example, when it needs to expand its capacity to meet the needs of an expanding number of customers. The Wastewater Treatment Fund reports capital contributions in the last section of its statement of revenues, expenses, and changes in net position. The fund's statement of cash flows makes it clear that $226 of the $231 represents cash payments of tap-in fees (see Table 7-15).

| **TABLE 7-15** | Statement of Cash Flows—Enterprise Fund—City of Ashtabula, Ohio |

City of Ashtabula, Ohio
Enterprise Fund
Wastewater Treatment Fund
Statement of Cash Flows
December 31, 2010
(amounts in thousands)

Increase (Decrease) in Cash and Cash Equivalents		
Cash Flows from Operating Activities		
Cash received from customers	$ 3,599	
Cash payments to suppliers for goods and services	(1,420)	
Cash payments for employee services and benefits	(2,191)	
Net cash used for operating activities		(12)
Cash Flows from Noncapital Financing Activities		
Transfers out	(76)	
Net cash used for noncapital financing activities		(76)
Cash Flows from Capital and Related Financing Activities		
Tap-in fees	226	
Proceeds of loan	272	
Acquisition of capital assets	(381)	
Principal paid on loans	(418)	
Interest paid on loans	(140)	
Net cash used for capital and related financing activities		(441)
Net decrease in cash and cash equivalents		(529)
Cash and cash equivalents beginning of year		791
Cash and cash equivalents end of year		$ 262
Reconciliation of Operating Loss to Net Cash Used for Operating Activities		
Operating loss		$(466)
Adjustments:		
Depreciation		536
(Increase)/decrease in assets:		
Accounts receivable		(2)
Materials and supplies inventory		3
Prepaid items		(5)
Increase/(decrease) in liabilities:		
Accounts payable		41
Contracts payable		(40)
Accrued wages		(54)
Compensated absences payable		(10)
Due to other governments		(15)
Net cash used for operating activities		$ (12)
Noncash Capital Financing Activities		

During 2010, the State of Ohio paid $8 directly to contractors
on behalf of the Wastewater Treatment Fund for capital assets.

Source: Adapted from a recent annual report of the City of Ashtabula, Ohio.

The balance of the capital contributions comes from direct payments made by the State of Ohio to contractors building the Wastewater Treatment Fund's capital assets (see the bottom of the cash flows statement where significant noncash transactions are required to be reported). Capital contributions can come in many forms—grants and contributions required to be used to acquire capital assets; direct payments for capital assets on behalf of the government; transfers of capital assets from governmental activities of the same government (such as our earlier illustration of contributions used to start up an Internal Service Fund); tap fees and similar customer charges (or charges to developers) that must be used to expand or replace capital assets; and contributions consisting of capital assets, such as sewer lines built by developers and then donated to the government for its use. It is up to the reporting government to review restrictions on all of its contributions to determine whether they are *capital* contributions that must be reported separately from operating and nonoperating income and expenses.

Governmental Accounting in Practice

Are All Enterprise Funds Designed to Recover Costs?

Some governmental activities accounted for in Enterprise Funds (like lotteries) make profits, which help to finance day-to-day activities accounted for in the General Fund. Others break even or make enough profit to cover the inflated cost of replacing their capital assets. And some are heavily subsidized. Principal among these are state and local transit operations. Governments that operate trains, subways, and buses depend on capital grants and large operating subsidies to keep prices down in order to encourage citizens to use public transportation or simply so that the labor force can afford to travel into the city to work. *Transit authorities often recover less than half of their costs from fare box revenues.* For example, the Washington, DC Metro recovered less than 33 percent of its operating costs from passenger fares in 2010; Atlanta's MARTA recovered only 27 percent in 2010; San Francisco's BART did better at 51 percent in 2010. New York State's Metropolitan Transportation Authority (MTA)—which runs New York City's subway and commuter rail lines affecting several counties—covered 50 percent of its operating expenses from operating revenues in 2010.

The MTA's operating statement shows that its operating expenses in 2010 were $12.7 billion, but that its operating revenues were only $6.4 billion. To partially offset its operating loss, it received $2.9 billion in operating subsidies from the state and from local governments within the state, as well as almost $1.7 billion from dedicated tax revenues. Notice how the MTA's operating statement distinguishes between subsidies that help pay for operating expenses (which it classifies as nonoperating revenues) and grants that are externally restricted for capital projects. This financial reporting is consistent with the requirements for government-wide reporting (discussed in Chapter 10), which classifies "program revenues" as either charges for services, operating grants, or capital grants.

Metropolitan Transportation Authority
(A Component Unit of the State of New York)
Consolidated Statement of Revenues, Expenses, and Changes in Net Position
Year Ended December 31, 2010
(amounts in millions)

Operating Revenues

Fare revenue	$ 4,586
Vehicle toll revenue	1,417
Rents, freight, and other revenues	416
Total operating revenues	6,419

(continued)

Operating Expenses	12,709
Operating Loss	(6,290)
Nonoperating Revenues (Expenses)	
Grants, appropriations, and taxes:	
Tax-supported subsidies—NYS	2,025
Tax-supported subsidies—NYC and local	447
Operating subsidies—NYS	194
Operating subsidies—NYC and local	191
Build America Bond subsidy	60
Mobility tax	1,662
All other, net (mostly interest expense on long-term debt)	(792)
Net nonoperating revenues	3,787
Loss Before Capital Appropriations	(2,503)
Appropriations, Grants, and Other Receipts Externally Restricted for Capital Projects	1,938
Change in Net Position	(565)
Net Position—Beginning of period	17,441
Net Position—End of period	$16,876

Source: Adapted from the 2010 annual report of the Metropolitan Transportation Authority, New York, NY. To simplify the presentation, we combined certain nonoperating revenues and expenses; the largest item, interest expense on long-term debt, was $1,299 million.

Review Questions

Q7-1   What is the cause-and-effect relationship between the revenues and the expenses of a proprietary fund?

Q7-2   Why are the revenues and expenditures of governmental-type funds "independent" of each other?

Q7-3   When should an Internal Service Fund be used?

Q7-4   What is a flexible budget?

Q7-5   How does the net position section of a balance sheet of a proprietary fund differ from the fund balance section of a governmental-type fund?

Q7-6   Why is depreciation recorded as an expense in proprietary funds, but not as an expenditure in governmental-type funds?

Q7-7   What is the difference between an Enterprise Fund and an Internal Service Fund?

Q7-8   Does the accounting guidance issued by FASB apply to proprietary funds? Explain.

Q7-9   What are revenue bonds? How do they differ from general obligation bonds?

Discussion Scenarios and Issues

D7-1   Discuss what type of fund you would use to account for the following activities:

a. A city is about to construct a new sports arena. It will use a Capital Projects Fund to account for the accumulation of resources to build the arena. The city council has passed a law calling for a special hotel–motel occupancy tax to pay the debt service on the bonds issued to build the arena. In what fund should the occupancy tax be accounted for?

b. Fed up with the poor response time in restoring power resulting from damages caused by recent storms, the city acquires the resources of a private electric power company. The city issues revenue bonds to pay for the power company's assets; the bonds are secured solely by a pledge of the net revenues resulting from the charges for supplying power to the citizens of the city and to city government offices.

c. To ensure that the city obtains the best possible price for its supplies and equipment, the city decides that all agencies within the government must obtain needed supplies through the city's purchasing department. The purchasing department will obtain a warehouse for certain items used by all departments.

D7-2   You recently agreed to make a presentation to an accounting class at your alma mater. Your topic will be governmental financial reporting. Review the financial statements for the Internal Service Funds in this chapter, and contrast them with the statements prepared for the Capital Projects Funds in Chapter 6. Identify similarities and differences between these statements as the basis for your presentation.

D7-3   The mayor asks you to help establish the pricing policy for the city's only Internal Service Fund, the Printing Fund. The mayor has decided that all city agencies must use the Printing Fund (which will have salaried personnel, equipment, and supplies) for their printing needs. However, he has not yet decided whether the General Fund should make a loan to the Internal Service Fund to acquire the equipment or whether the General Fund should make an outright grant for that purpose. Write a report to the mayor, describing the pricing options you perceive. In discussing the options, cover the implications resulting from a decision as to whether the Printing Fund will be financed with a loan or an outright grant.

D7-4   A village needs resources to finance its operations for the remainder of 2013. Poor internal control procedures under the previous administration created a serious funding problem for the new administration. The new mayor feels that if he can get through the current year, he can develop a new budget and control future expenditures to create a surplus. After reviewing the village's financial statements, the mayor wants to borrow from restricted assets in an Enterprise Fund (resources set aside, pursuant to a bond agreement, to ensure payment of debt service). The mayor is certain that future surpluses from the village's operating budget will allow him to replace the borrowed funds in 3 to 5 years. How would you respond to the mayor?

Exercises

E7-1   (Interpreting the operating statement for an Internal Service Fund)
Fort Chessie maintains a policy that its Internal Service Funds operate on a break-even basis; that is, revenues must equal expenses. Did the Motor Pool Fund illustrated in this chapter operate at a break-even level during 2013? Explain.

E7-2   (Journal entries for an Internal Service Fund)
The following transactions occurred regarding the Central Purchasing Fund, an Internal Service Fund. Record the entries for the transaction, and identify the fund(s) used.
1. The General Fund transferred $100,000 as a capital contribution to establish the fund.
2. The Purchasing Fund billed revenues of $200,000.
3. The Purchasing Fund incurred expenses of $300,000. Hint: Credit Cash for $250,000 and Accumulated depreciation for $50,000.
4. The General Fund subsidized the operations of the Purchasing Fund by transferring an additional $100,000 to the fund.

E7-3   (Relationship of a fixed asset to depreciation)
Since the Motor Pool Fund illustrated in this chapter records the acquisition of an automobile by debiting an asset account, does the cost of that automobile ever enter into the determination of income? Explain.

E7-4   (Fill in the blanks)
1. An Internal Service Fund is used when goods and/or services are provided to _____.
2. A budget that is based on the level of activity attained in a fund is called a _____.
3. The _____ basis of accounting is used in Internal Service Funds.
4. If the General Fund transfers cash to an Internal Service Fund as a permanent transfer of equity, the Internal Service Fund will credit the _____ account.
5. When an Internal Service Fund acquires a truck, the account that is debited is _____.

E7-5   (True or false)

Indicate whether the following statements are true or false. For any false statement, indicate why it is false.

1. A direct cause-and-effect relationship exists between the revenues and expenses of an Internal Service Fund.
2. Internal Service Funds are used to account for activities that involve providing services and/or products to the general public.
3. Internal Service Funds use the modified accrual basis of accounting.
4. All capital contributions received by an Internal Service Fund are credited directly to the Net position account.
5. A fixed budget is used to control an Internal Service Fund.
6. The budget is not usually recorded for an Internal Service Fund.
7. Fixed assets used in an Internal Service Fund are not reported in the fund-level statements.
8. Depreciation expense is not recorded in an Internal Service Fund that uses fixed assets.
9. An increase or decrease in Net position is calculated for Internal Service Funds.
10. Internal Service Funds do not have restricted net position accounts.

E7-6   (True or false)

Indicate whether the following statements are true or false. For any false statement, indicate why it is false.

1. Enterprise Funds are not used to account for the construction of major highways financed from tax revenues.
2. User charges must be assessed if an Enterprise Fund is to be used for accounting purposes.
3. Flexible budgets are used to control Enterprise Fund operations.
4. Depreciation is recorded in an Enterprise Fund.
5. Nonoperating expenses are separated from operating expenses in an Enterprise Fund.
6. Restricted assets are separately reported on an Enterprise Fund balance sheet.

E7-7   (Billings and collections between an Enterprise Fund and the General Fund)

A city used an Enterprise Fund to provide electricity services to the General Fund and its citizens. A total of $50,000 was billed to the General Fund and collected 30 days later. Prepare the journal entries necessary to record these transactions, and label the fund(s) used.

E7-8   (Closing entries for an Enterprise Fund)

The Municipal Park Fund for Putnam Village had the following preclosing trial balance. Prepare the closing entry necessary at June 30, 2013, and compute the components of net assets as they should be reported as of that date.

Putnam Village
Enterprise Fund
Municipal Park Fund
Preclosing Trial Balance
June 30, 2013

	Debits	Credits
Cash	$ 1,500	
Membership dues receivable	10,200	
Land	7,600	
Equipment	2,000	
Accumulated depreciation—equipment		$ 400
Accounts payable		500
Revenues from fees		14,000
Salaries expense	4,500	
Depreciation expense—equipment	300	
Utilities expense	400	
Miscellaneous expense	700	
Net position		12,300
	$27,200	$27,200

E7-9 (Comparison of accounting for long-term debt and acquisition of fixed assets, using governmental-type funds and proprietary-type funds)

The Village of Peak's Kill acquired a computer for $300,000. The computer was financed through a bond issue. Prepare the journal entries necessary to record these events, assuming the computer was acquired using (a) the General Fund and (b) an Enterprise Fund. Also, label the fund(s) used.

E7-10 (Setting prices for an Internal Service Fund)

Yorktown uses an Internal Service Fund to account for its motor pool activities. Based on the following information, calculate the price per trip that the Internal Service Fund needs to charge users of the motor pool during calendar year 2013 in order to break even:

Automobiles:

The motor pool uses two sedans, each costing $25,000 and each estimated to have a 5-year life when they were acquired in 2012.

Driver salaries:

The motor pool has a driver-administrator, who earns $45,000 a year, and a driver, who earns $35,000. The city uses a rate of 30 percent (to cover pensions and other payroll fringe benefits) for planning purposes.

Insurance:

In 2012 the city purchased a 3-year automobile accident policy at a cost of $3,000.

Fuel and maintenance costs:

Based on experience, the driver-administrator estimates that total fuel and maintenance costs for the year will be $5,000.

Billing units:

To simplify record keeping, the fund charges a fixed price per trip. Yorktown's budget office estimates that 800 trips will be taken in 2013.

E7-11 (Journal entries for an Internal Service Fund)

The Yorktown Motor Pool Internal Service Fund had the following transactions and events during January 2013. Using the data in exercise E7-10 where applicable, as well as your solution to the exercise, prepare journal entries to record the transactions.

1. Paid salaries for the month in cash (1/12 of $80,000)
2. Paid $600 cash for fuel and maintenance expenses
3. Recorded depreciation expense for the month
4. Recorded insurance expense for the month
5. Accrued fringe benefits expense for the month
6. Billed for motor vehicle services as follows: General Fund, 80 trips; Water Enterprise Fund, 10 trips

Problems

P7-1 (Journal entries and financial statements for an Internal Service Fund)

Pleasantville's Data Processing Fund, an Internal Service Fund, had the following transactions and events during calendar year 2013. The fund provides services for a fee to all departments of Pleasantville's government. Assume the fund uses a voucher system. Prepare (a) the journal entries necessary to record the transactions and events in the Data Processing Fund; (b) a statement of revenues, expenses, and changes in net position for the Data Processing Fund for 2013; and (c) a statement of net position as of December 31, 2013.

1. The General Fund made a $2,000,000 transfer of cash to establish the Data Processing Fund.
2. The Data Processing Fund paid $1,900,000 for a computer.
3. Supplies costing $4,500 were purchased on credit.
4. Bills totaling $650,000 were sent to the various city departments. If services prov. used
5. Repairs to the computer were made at a cost of $2,400. A voucher was prepared for that amount.
6. Collections from city departments for services were $629,000.

7. Salaries of $200,000 were paid to the employees.
8. Vouchers totaling $5,900 were paid.
9. As of the end of the year, $300 of supplies had not been used.
10. Depreciation on the computer for the year was $250,000.
11. The city charged the computer center $2,000 for the rental of office space and $500 for the rental of office equipment for the year. This amount was not paid at the end of the year.
12. Miscellaneous expenses not paid by the end of the year totaled $700. These amounts were owed to businesses outside the governmental unit.

P7-2   (Journal entries and financial statements for an Internal Service Fund)

Lilly County, faced with the prospect of declining revenues, decides it can save money by doing all printing in-house. The county creates the Lilly Printing Fund (an Internal Service Fund), directs departments to fulfill their bulk printing needs through that fund, and directs departments to pay the fund promptly to minimize its working capital needs. The fund had the following transactions and events during 2013. Prepare (a) journal entries to record these transactions in the Lilly Printing Fund; (b) a statement of net position as of December 31, 2013; and (c) a statement of revenues, expenses, and changes in net position for the year ended December 31, 2013.

1. Received a loan on January 2 from the county in the amount of $6,000, to be repaid in four equal annual installments of $1,500, starting December 31, 2013, with interest at the rate of 1 percent per annum on the outstanding balance. The specified purpose of the loan was to purchase equipment for $4,800 and to use the balance of $1,200 to meet working capital needs.
2. Purchased reproduction equipment for $4,800 on January 2, using cash provided in transaction 1. The equipment has an estimated useful life of 4 years and no salvage value.
3. Purchased paper and supplies for $4,500 on credit. (Because inventories are kept to a minimum, charge the purchase to Supplies expense.)
4. Sent invoices for $65,000 to departments financed by the General Fund.
5. Received cash in the amount of $63,000 as a result of transaction 4.
6. Paid the $4,500 invoice received in transaction 3.
7. Paid salaries in the amount of $50,000 and utility bills in the amount of $6,000.
8. Repaid the county $1,500 of principal on the loan, plus interest of 1 percent.
9. In preparation for year-end financial statements, recorded depreciation on the equipment for 12 months.

P7-3   (Journal entries for several funds and statements for an Internal Service Fund)

The following transactions relate to the City of Monticello for the fiscal year ended June 30, 2013. Prepare (a) all the journal entries necessary to record these transactions, and identify the fund(s) used. Also, prepare (b) a statement of revenues, expenses, and changes in net position for the Central Supplies Fund for fiscal 2012–2013 and (c) a statement of net position as of June 30, 2013.

1. The city established a Central Supplies Fund for the purpose of handling the acquisition and disbursement of supplies for the entire government. The General Fund made an initial capital contribution of $75,000 to the fund.
2. The Police Department ordered equipment at a total cost of $34,000.
3. The Central Supplies Fund purchased supplies for $29,000. This amount will be paid later.
4. The Debt Service Fund paid $120,000 of interest not previously recorded.
5. Central Supplies Fund billings to departments totaled $31,000. These supplies cost $25,000. Record the cost of the supplies as an expense: Cost of sales.
6. A Capital Projects Fund paid a contractor $100,000 for a previously submitted progress billing of $110,000. The difference between the billing and the amount paid is the retained percentage. The billing was recorded correctly when received by the fund.
7. The Central Supplies Fund acquired office equipment for $2,000. A 90-day note was signed for that amount.
8. Collections from the departments by the Central Supplies Fund totaled $27,500.

9. Salaries paid to Central Supplies Fund employees were $22,500.
10. The Police Department equipment ordered in transaction 2 was delivered at a cost of $35,000. The invoice price will be paid later. Assume the excess was approved.
11. Depreciation on the office equipment of the Central Supplies Fund was $400.
12. The Central Supplies Fund paid $25,000 to various creditors outside the governmental unit.
13. Interest expense of $50 on the note payable was accrued by the Central Supplies Fund.

P7-4   (Journal entries and financial statements for an Enterprise Fund)

The following transactions relate to the City of Arlington's Municipal Airport Fund for the fiscal year ended June 30, 2013. Prepare (a) the journal entries necessary to record these transactions in the Municipal Airport Fund; (b) a trial balance as of June 30, 2013; (c) a statement of revenues, expenses, and changes in net position for the 2012–2013 fiscal year, and (d) a statement of net position as of June 30, 2013.

1. The General Fund made a permanent contribution of $2,000,000 for working capital to start a municipal airport. The city used part of that money, together with the proceeds from a $25,000,000 revenue bond issue, to purchase an airport from a private company. The fair values of the assets and liabilities were as follows:

Accounts receivable	$ 8,000
Land	19,000,000
Buildings	5,000,000
Equipment	1,800,000
Accounts payable	(12,000)

The city purchased the airport for the fair market value of its net assets.

2. Airlines were billed $3,900,000 for rental rights to use ticket counters and landing and maintenance space. Of this amount, $3,890,000 is expected to be collectible.
3. Supplies totaling $4,500 were purchased on credit.
4. Collections from airlines totaled $3,850,000.
5. Salaries of $200,000 were paid to airport personnel employed by the city.
6. Utility bills totaling $100,000 were paid.
7. A notice was received from the Last District Bankruptcy Court. Air Chance was declared bankrupt. The airport collected only $1,000 on its bill of $3,000.
8. The airport obtained $3,000,000 of additional permanent contributions from the General Fund to help finance improvements at the airport.
9. Interest of $1,825,000 was paid to the bondholders.
10. Supplies used during the year totaled $3,600.
11. The General Fund made an advance to the airport of $1,500,000. Airport management plans to repay the advance in full in 2016.
12. A contract was signed with The Construction Company for the new facilities for a total price of $5,000,000.
13. The Municipal Airport Fund invested $2,000,000 in CDs.
14. The Municipal Airport Fund received $315,000 upon redeeming $300,000 of the CDs mentioned in transaction 13.
15. The airport purchased additional equipment for $300,000 cash.
16. Interest expense of $350,000 was accrued at the end of the year.
17. Other accrued expenses totaled $55,000.
18. Depreciation was recorded as follows:

Buildings	$500,000
Equipment	180,000

19. $12,500 of accounts payable was paid.
20. $150,000 of interest revenue was received.
21. Excess cash of $4,500,000 was invested in CDs.

P7-5   (Computation of proprietary fund net position)
Given here is the December 31, 2013, preclosing trial balance for the City of Hudson Golf Course Enterprise Fund. Compute as of December 31, 2013, (a) total net position; (b) net investment in capital assets, net of related debt; (c) restricted net position; and (d) unrestricted net position.

City of Hudson
Golf Course Enterprise Fund
Preclosing Trial Balance
December 31, 2013

	Debits	**Credits**
Cash	$ 15,045	
Accounts receivable	37,000	
Estimated uncollectible accounts		$ 5,000
Cash—restricted for debt service	150,000	
Cash—restricted for customer deposits	23,000	
Land	900,000	
Equipment	325,000	
Accumulated depreciation—equipment		105,000
Buildings	1,500,000	
Accumulated depreciation—buildings		650,000
Accounts payable		20,000
Customers' deposits payable		23,000
Interest payable on customer deposits		835
Revenue bonds payable		1,000,000
Accrued interest payable—revenue bonds		6,500
Net position, January 1, 2013		940,740
Revenue from rentals		800,000
Personal services expense	380,000	
Utilities expense	63,000	
Repairs and maintenance expense	47,000	
Depreciation expense—equipment	15,000	
Depreciation expense—building	50,000	
Interest expense	40,030	
Estimated uncollectible accounts	5,000	
Supplies expense	1,000	
	$3,551,075	$3,551,075

P7-6   (Journal entries and financial statements for an Enterprise Fund)
The Metro Central Railroad is a commuter railroad that stops at the Village of Katonah. Katonah, a growing community, decides to construct and operate a parking lot near the railroad station to accommodate the needs of its citizens. The activities of the parking lot will be accounted for in an Enterprise Fund, known as the Katonah Metro Parking Fund, because the activity will be financed with debt secured solely by pledge of the facility's net revenues from parking fees. This problem covers transactions and events during calendar years 2012 and 2013. Prepare journal entries for the following Parking Fund transactions and events during 2012:

1. Receives $5,000,000 from the sale of revenue bonds at par. The revenue bonds were sold on July 1, 2012. They mature at the rate of $250,000 a year over a period of 20 years, starting July 1, 2013. Interest on the bonds is payable annually, also starting July 1, 2013, at 4 percent per annum on the outstanding debt.
2. Pays $1,000,000 to acquire a vacant lot near the railroad station. (Note: Debit the account "Capital assets not being depreciated.")
3. Pays $4,000,000 to construct the parking lot. (Note: Debit the account "Depreciable capital assets.") The lot is completed and ready for opening as of December 31, 2012.

4. Accrues interest for 6 months on the serial bonds. (Although interest during the construction period should be capitalized in Enterprise Funds, the village considers the amount immaterial and charges it to expense.)
5. Receives an invoice for $80,000 from the Village of Katonah General Fund for all expenses incurred in financing and planning for constructing the parking lot.

Based on the foregoing transactions and events, the Katonah Metro Parking Fund starts calendar year 2013 with the following trial balance:

	Debits	Credits
Capital assets not being depreciated	$1,000,000	
Depreciable capital assets	4,000,000	
Accrued interest payable		$ 100,000
Due to Village of Katonah		80,000
Revenue bonds payable		5,000,000
Net position	180,000	
Totals	$5,180,000	$5,180,000

Prepare journal entries to record the following transactions and events of the Katonah Metro Parking Fund for calendar year 2013. Then prepare a statement of revenues, expenses, and changes in net position for the year and a statement of net position as of December 31, 2013.

1. Receives cash from parking fees in the amount of $800,000.
2. Receives cash of $60,000 in December 2013 from parking lot customers who rent space for the month of January 2014.
3. Pays the amount due at the start of the year to the Village of Katonah.
4. Pays the following expenses: salaries—$125,000; insurance—$20,000; utilities—$35,000.
5. Pays the first installment of principal and interest on the revenue bonds, due July 1, 2013.
6. Accrues interest on the revenue bonds as of December 31, 2013.
7. Records one year's depreciation on the depreciable assets. The depreciable assets are estimated to have a useful life of 20 years.

P7-7 (Explanation of basis of accounting and fixed assets for different funds)

The accounting system of the municipality of Kemp is organized and operated on a fund basis. Among the types of funds used are a General Fund, a Special Revenue Fund, and an Enterprise Fund.

1. Explain the basic differences in revenue recognition between the accrual basis of accounting and the modified accrual basis of accounting, as it relates to governmental accounting.
2. What basis of accounting should be used in fund-level accounting for each of the following funds and why?
   - General Fund
   - Special Revenue Funds
   - Enterprise Funds
3. How should fixed assets and long-term liabilities related to the General Fund and to the Enterprise Fund be accounted for in the funds? (AICPA adapted)

P7-8 (Budget for an Internal Service Fund)

The City of Oscar uses an Internal Service Fund to provide printing services to its various departments. It bills departments on the basis of an estimated rate per page of printed material, computed on the accrual basis of accounting. From the following information, compute the amount per page that the fund will charge during 2013. Based on past experience, the fund estimates that it will print 1,000,000 pages during the year. (Assume that the equipment in item 6 was contributed by the city and that the pricing objective was to recoup the cost of equipment in the rate charged over the life of the equipment.)

1. Inventory of paper on hand at beginning of year: $10,000
2. Estimated paper purchases during the year: $60,000

3. Estimated amount of paper to be consumed during the year: $55,000
4. Estimated salaries to be paid during the year: $255,000
5. Estimated salaries earned during the year, including both what was paid and what was owed at year end: $265,000
6. Cost of equipment on hand at beginning of the year (estimated life of 10 years): $1,000,000

P7-9   (Accounting for and reporting on selected transactions and events)

Rochester Rapid Transit (RRT), an Enterprise Fund of Orange County, provides bus service for county residents. Because fare revenues are insufficient to cover operating expenses, RRT—as a matter of public policy—receives operating subsidies and capital grants from Orange County, the state, and the federal government. RRT's financial reporting policies provide for distinguishing operating subsidies from capital grants in its statement of revenues, expenses, and changes in net position; the former are reported as "nonoperating revenues," while the latter are reported as capital contributions. RRT operates on a calendar year basis. Answer the questions raised regarding each of the following transactions and events that relate to RRT's calendar year 2013.

1. RRT sold revenue bonds in the amount of $2,000,000 on September 1, 2012, maturing in 10 years at the rate of $100,000 every 6 months, starting March 1, 2013, with interest at the rate of 4 percent per annum on the unpaid balance. Interest on the bonds had been accrued in RRT's financial statements for the year ended December 31, 2012. What journal entries are needed to record the debt service payments on March 1, 2013, and September 1, 2013?

2. An RRT bus accidentally sideswiped a parked vehicle in December 2013. The vehicle owner filed a claim against RRT, which does not carry insurance to cover such claims. RRT's attorneys acknowledge that the RRT bus was at fault. They believe the claim can be settled out of court for about $5,000, but the vehicle owner is seeking $7,000. The claim had not been settled at the time RRT prepared its 2013 financial statements. How should RRT report this matter in its financial statements?

3. RRT applied for a grant of $300,000 from the federal government in 2013. RRT met the eligibility requirements for the grant and received a check for $300,000. The grant was to be used solely to acquire buses, but no time requirement was imposed on RRT. As of December 31, 2013, no part of the grant had been spent. What journal entry should RRT make when it receives the cash? (Hint: See section on "Intergovernmental Grants" in Chapter 5.) How does the transaction affect financial reporting by RRT?

4. RRT received cash subsidies from Orange County ($500,000) and the state ($100,000) to help cover its operating deficits. What journal entries are needed to record each subsidy? How should each subsidy be reported in RRT's statement of revenues, expenses, and changes in net position?

P7-10   (Journal entries and financial statements for an Enterprise Fund)

The City of Paradise Falls plans to develop a golf course during 2013 and account for it as the Golf Enterprise Fund (GEF). The course will be built on a parcel of land to be purchased from a private party. The planned out-of-pocket costs for the new course and their financing are as follows:

Spending

Acquisition of land from private party	$ 500,000
Installation of sod, sprinklers, landscaping, and fencing	1,000,000
Construction of clubhouse	3,000,000
	$4,500,000

Financing

Contribution from the General Fund	$1,500,000
Term revenue bonds at 8 percent per annum, interest payable semiannually	3,000,000
	$4,500,000

The city plans to sell the bonds on February 1, 2013. Because the bonds are a term issue, bond principal matures in full on February 1, 2023. Interest is payable each August 1 and February 1, beginning August 1, 2013. The bond covenant requires that assets equal to one-tenth of the bond principal be transferred to a restricted account within the GEF on December 31 of each year. Paradise Falls observes a calendar fiscal year.

Kowitt Design and Construction, Inc. has been awarded the contract to develop the golf course. Construction will commence February 15, 2013, and be completed no later than May 31, so it can open for business during June. The contract stipulates that progress billings from Kowitt will be paid within 30 days of receipt, with 5 percent retainage held pending completion and acceptance of the project. The city engineer will inspect the contractor's work and approve progress payments.

Accounting for the GEF will be done by the city's existing accounting department (a General Fund department), which will bill the GEF for services rendered at the end of the year. To help the GEF get on its feet financially, no interfund payables will be settled in cash during 2013.

Prepare (a) journal entries (including closing entries) to record the following events and transactions for the year ended December 31, 2013, in the Golf Enterprise Fund. The corresponding entries that would be made in other funds are not required. In addition, prepare (b) the statement of net position and (c) the statement of revenues, expenses, and changes in net position for the Golf Enterprise Fund as of and for the fiscal year ending December 31, 2013.

1. January 3, 2013: Paradise Falls formally established the GEF; the fund's first transaction was the receipt, in cash, of the capital contribution from the General Fund.
2. January 24: The city acquired the adjacent parcel of land from the private owner for the planned $500,000.
3. February 1: The revenue bonds were sold at par ($3,000,000).
4. February 15: Development of the golf course itself and construction of the clubhouse commenced.
5. March 31: Kowitt submitted the first progress billing of $1,800,000. The billing was approved and vouchered after deducting the 5 percent retainage. (Because of the short duration of the construction period, no construction in progress accounts will be used.) $400,000 of the amount billed represents the cost of sod, sprinklers, landscaping, and fencing (which the city classifies as "improvements other than buildings"). The balance applies to the cost of the clubhouse ("buildings").
6. April 25: The amount currently due Kowitt was paid.
7. April 30: The second progress billing from Kowitt, $1,500,000, was approved and vouchered after deducting the 5 percent retainage; $600,000 applies to sod, sprinklers, landscaping, and fencing (which is now fully installed).
8. May 19: The amount currently due Kowitt was paid.
9. May 23: Kowitt's third and final progress billing, $700,000 (all of which represents clubhouse construction costs), was approved and vouchered after deducting the 5 percent retainage.
10. May 30: The amount currently due Kowitt was paid.
11. June 1: The new golf course was formally accepted by the city (without need for "touch-up" work), and all remaining amounts due to Kowitt were vouchered for payment.
12. June 1: Golf course maintenance equipment costing $300,000 was acquired by means of a 5-year capital lease. The lease required no down payment. Lease payments are due quarterly, beginning September 1. The amortization table for the lease for the first six payments is as follows:

Due Date	Payment	Interest	Principal Reduction	Carrying Value
				$300,000
Sept. 1, 2013	$19,244	$7,500	$11,744	288,256
Dec. 1, 2013	19,244	7,206	12,038	276,218
Mar. 1, 2014	19,244	6,905	12,339	263,879
June 1, 2014	19,244	6,597	12,647	251,232
Sept. 1, 2014	19,244	6,281	12,963	238,269
Dec. 1, 2014	19,244	5,957	13,287	224,982

13. June 2: Inventory in the amount of $12,000 was acquired for the pro shop; the purchase was vouchered for payment.
14. June 4: The course opened for business. Greens fees (charges for services) aggregated $209,000 for June. Pro shop sales (all for cash) amounted to $5,000.

15. June 30: Expenses for June were as follows. (Charge all expenses to "Operating expenses—cost of sales and services.")

Maintenance and pro shop labor (paid in cash)	48,000
Maintenance supplies, from the Parks Department—a Special Revenue Fund (invoice received, but not paid)	4,000
Water, supplied by the Paradise Falls water utility—an Enterprise Fund (invoice received, but not paid)	80,000
Cost of merchandise sold by the pro shop	2,200

16. August 1: The first debt service payment on the revenue bonds was made.
17. September 1: The first payment on the lease was made.
18. December 1: The second payment on the lease was made.
19. December 31: Greens fee revenues for the second half of 2013 totaled $370,000; pro shop sales for the same period were $21,200.
20. December 31: Second-half 2013 expenses were as follows:

Maintenance and pro shop labor (paid in cash)	$ 70,000
Maintenance supplies, from the Parks Department—a Special Revenue Fund (invoice received, but not paid)	4,000
Water, supplied by the Paradise Falls water utility—an Enterprise Fund (invoice received, but not paid)	80,000
Cost of merchandise sold by the pro shop	2,900
Accounting and administrative services provided by the accounting department—General Fund (invoice received, but not paid)	9,000
Total expenses	$165,900

21. December 31: Interest was accrued on the revenue bonds and the capital lease liability (make separate entries).
22. December 31: The GEF recorded depreciation for 2013 using the half-year convention. The building's useful life is estimated at 20 years (salvage value, $200,000) and will be depreciated straight line. Improvements other than buildings will be depreciated straight line over 10 years, with no salvage value. Equipment will be depreciated straight line over 5 years, with no salvage value.
23. The current portion of the capital lease liability was reclassified to a current liability to aid in balance sheet preparation.
24. December 31: The restricted asset account—Cash restricted for bond principal retirement—was established pursuant to the requirements of the bond covenant.

Summary Problem

Leisure City has an Electric Utility Enterprise Fund (EUEF) that provides electric power to its residents and to city agencies. Following is the EUEF opening trial balance at January 1, 2013 (all amounts are in thousands of dollars):

	Debits	Credits
Cash	$ 2,300	
Accounts receivable	960	
Short-term investments	1,000	
Capital assets	48,000	
Accumulated depreciation, capital assets		$ 14,000
Accrued interest payable		260
Serial bonds payable		26,000
Net position		12,000
Totals	$ 52,260	$ 52,260

The EUEF had the following transactions during 2013 (amounts in thousands of dollars):

1. EUEF billed residents of Leisure City $4,000 for electric power.
2. EUEF collected $4,500 of its accounts receivable.
3. EUEF established a $40 allowance for uncollectible accounts.
4. EUEF billed Leisure City's General Fund $200 for electric power provided to city departments.
5. EUEF collected the entire amount billed to the city's General Fund.
6. EUEF paid $1,300 in salaries to its employees and $400 in other operating expenses.
7. The outstanding serial bonds of $26,000 are being paid at the rate of $2,000 every year, starting October 1, 2013, with interest of 4 percent per annum on the outstanding debt. (The $260 interest payable shown in the trial balance had been accrued on December 31, 2012.) EUEF paid the debt service due on October 1, 2013.
8. The short-term investments shown in the trial balance matured. EUEF received $1,050, which included investment income of $50.
9. At year-end, EUEF accrued interest on its outstanding debt.
10. At year-end, EUEF recorded $1,600 depreciation on its capital assets.
11. At year-end, EUEF made an adjusting entry to report the current portion of its serial bonds payable as a current liability.

Use the preceding information to do the following:

a. Prepare the journal entries necessary to record these transactions in the EUEF.
b. Prepare a statement of revenues, expenses, and changes in net position.
c. Prepare a statement of net position for the EUEF.

Chapter 8

The Governmental Fund Accounting Cycle

Fiduciary Funds

Chapter Outline

After completing this chapter, you should be able to do the following:

- Distinguish between employer government pension accounting and Pension Trust Fund accounting

- Understand the basic types of pension and other postemployment benefit (OPEB) plans

- Understand the role of actuaries in pension and OPEB accounting

- Understand how pension or OPEB contributions and pension or OPEB costs are calculated

- Explain why and how Pension Trust Funds are used in governmental accounting

- Prepare the journal entries normally used in Pension Trust Fund accounting

- Prepare financial statements for Pension Trust Funds

- Explain why and how Investment Trust Funds are used in governmental accounting

- Prepare the journal entries normally used in Investment Trust Fund accounting

- Prepare financial statements for Investment Trust Funds

- Explain why and how Private Purpose Trust Funds are used in governmental accounting

- Prepare the journal entries normally used in Private Purpose Trust Fund accounting

- Prepare financial statements for Private Purpose Trust Funds

- Explain why and how Agency Funds are used in governmental accounting

- Prepare the journal entries normally used in Agency Fund accounting

- Prepare an Agency Fund statement of fiduciary net position

Governments commonly manage assets in a trustee capacity for the benefit of those outside the government. These include assets accumulated in irrevocable trusts for government employee retirement benefits; assets held in government pooled investment funds for the benefit of other governments; and assets held for the benefit of other individuals (such as a scholarship fund run by a school district to pay first-year college tuition for eligible graduating seniors).

Governments use fiduciary funds to account for assets held in a trustee or agency capacity for entities outside the government. The assets of fiduciary funds cannot be used to finance the government's own programs. The four types of funds included in this fund category are Employee Pension (and other employee benefit) Trust Funds, Investment Trust Funds, Private Purpose Trust Funds, and Agency Funds. The first three fund types involve establishing a formal (and usually long-lived) trust relationship between the government and the parties at interest. Agency funds, in contrast, are used in situations in which a government takes only custodial responsibility of resources belonging to others, usually for a comparatively short time.

The first type of fiduciary fund that we will consider is Pension (and other employee benefit) Trust Funds. Pension and other postemployment benefit (OPEB) accounting can be considered from two perspectives—that of the employer providing the benefits and that of the Pension or OPEB Trust Fund in which assets are being accumulated, invested, and ultimately paid to or for government retirees. Although the main focus of this chapter is on Pension and OPEB Trust Fund accounting and reporting, it is important to first consider pensions and OPEB from the perspective of a government employer.

OVERVIEW OF EMPLOYER GOVERNMENT PENSION AND OPEB ACCOUNTING

One of the concerns expressed in recent years by the media and politicians is the size of the retiree benefits that have been promised by state and local governments to their workers. In a November 2009 report, the Government Accountability Office noted that *unfunded* liabilities for retirement benefits other than pension benefits (primarily retiree health care) for the 50 states and 39 largest local governments exceeded $530 billion (http://www.gao.gov/new.items/d1061.pdf). In a May 2011 Economic and Budget Issue Brief (http://www.cbo.gov/ftpdocs/120xx/doc12084/05-04-Pensions.pdf), the Congressional Budget Office presented information that *unfunded* pension liabilities for state and local governments range from $700 billion to as much as $3 trillion. Given the magnitude of these *unfunded* liabilities, state and local pensions and other retiree benefits likely will continue to be in the news.

Most state and local governments provide some form of retirement benefits to their employees. These benefits can be classified in different ways. One common distinction is between defined benefit plans and defined contribution plans. Another distinction is between pension benefits and OPEB. An understanding of these terms and the distinctions between them is important.

Defined Benefit and Defined Contribution Plans

Most of us are probably familiar with the monthly retirement check that a relative receives from a former employer. In reality, the check probably does not come from the employer, but from a pension plan established by the employer. Most state and local governments have established an irrevocable pension trust fund that is used to accumulate contributions from one or more government employers for investment purposes and, ultimately, to pay benefits to retirees. Typically, governments fund their pension plans based on actuarially determined amounts, which should provide sufficient resources for future retiree benefits.

Historically, the monthly pension payments to retirees have been based on an agreement between the government and its employees before they retire. For example, a government tells its employees that the government will pay them an annual pension benefit equal to a certain percentage (say, 2 percent) of the employee's last full year of income (or average of the 3 highest-paid years, perhaps) times the number of years that the employee works. The annual pension benefit for an employee who had worked for a government for 26 years and whose last full year of salary was $68,000 would be $35,360 ($68,000 × 26 years × 2%). The employee's monthly benefit would be about $2,947, and the employee would continue to receive that amount each month until death. This type of retiree pension arrangement is called a *defined benefit plan*.

With a defined benefit arrangement, the employer promises to provide the retiree a defined future benefit over a future time period. One effect of such arrangements is that the government bears the risk associated with unknown future economic factors. The retirees are promised a certain benefit regardless of future inflation, investment returns, salary increases, and how long the retiree lives. If the stock market drops by 20 percent and the government's pension plan loses money, the employee in our example continues to receive a monthly check of $2,947 per month. The government will have to make more contributions to the pension plan to make up for the shortfall. Some defined benefit pension plans increase the employer's uncertainty by having built-in cost-of-living-adjustments. That is, pension benefits to retirees increase, for example, as the consumer price index rises.

Because of the risks associated with defined benefit plans, some governments are shifting to defined contribution plans. With a defined contribution plan, a government typically contributes a certain percentage of an employee's salary to an account in the employee's name. Often, the employee is also required to contribute a percentage of his or her salary to the plan. For example, assume a state is required to contribute 6 percent of the employee's salary of $50,000 to the plan, and the employee is required to contribute the same amount. On an annual basis, the employee's defined contribution retirement account would be increased by $3,000 for the contribution by the state ($50,000 × 6%) and another $3,000 for his or her contribution. Typically, the employee has some choice in how the money is invested—often, from an approved list of mutual funds.

At retirement, the former employee will be able to withdraw the accumulated assets from the account, generally in the form of a monthly annuity. The government's obligation to the retiree depends only on the amount it was required to contribute. Earnings on the investment of those contributions will depend on the investment choices made by the employee. Thus, in a *defined contribution* plan, the previously enumerated risks are shifted to the employees.

Pension and OPEB Plans

Although pension benefits are the most common type of postemployment benefit provided to government employees, many governments also provide OPEB, such as retiree health care benefits. OPEB may also include retiree life, dental, vision, hearing, and long-term care insurance.

One of the major differences between pension plans and OPEB plans is how they historically have been funded. For pensions, employers typically make annual contributions during the working lives of their employees to an irrevocable trust fund that should be sufficient to pay future benefits. For many government employers, this means that the amount currently held in trust for their employees is sufficient to pay benefits for several years into the future. OPEB plans, however, historically have not been advance-funded. Instead, government employers have made cash payments for retiree health care when retirees incur actual expenditures. This pay-as-you-go financing method results in governments having to find more dollars to finance retiree health care costs as the number of retirees increases. With many governments having an aging workforce, this becomes a funding problem. It is complicated by the double-digit annual increase in health care costs, which has been the norm for the past several years. (As discussed in earlier chapters, some governments also routinely underfinance their pension plans.)

Structure of Plans

Most governments that provide pension benefits to their employees make contributions to one or more pension plans; however, governments that do not *sponsor* pension plans make their contributions to external pension plans that may have dozens or hundreds of participating member governments. In practice, a pension or OPEB plan will have one of three structures: sole-employer, agent multiemployer, or cost sharing.[1]

According to the GASB, "sole and agent employers are individually responsible for the accumulation of sufficient plan net assets to pay the actuarial accrued liabilities for benefits to their employees as they come due."[2] A sole-employer plan performs the administrative and investment function for a single employer, whereas an agent multiple-employer plan pools the administrative and investment function for multiple employers in order to reduce the plan's overhead while maintaining separate accounts for each employer. Each individual employer in an agent multiple-employer plan is still liable for the benefit obligation for its retirees. Thus, the required pension contribution rates for such employers are unique to each.

In the third structure, cost-sharing plans, "the actuarial accrued liabilities of the various employers are shared, and the plan net assets are pooled and are available to pay the shared actuarial accrued liabilities as they come due."[3] This means that all employers are liable for the accumulated liabilities of the plan. As a result, the contribution rate as a percentage of payroll is the same for all employers participating in the plan.

The significance of these three plan structures is evident when determining a government's *annual pension cost* or *annual OPEB cost*. These costs are measured differently for governments participating in sole-employer or agent multiemployer plans than they are for governments participating in cost-sharing plans. Moreover, governments participating in cost-sharing plans legally are obligated to make their annual contributions in full as specified by the plan administrator; sole-employer governments and governments participating in agent multiemployer plans have flexibility to contribute less in a given year than the actuarially recommended amount—a practice that can cause the pension or OPEB plan to be severely underfunded.

The Role of Actuaries

The employer government's calculation of the annual pension cost or annual OPEB cost and related liabilities is quite complex because it requires a number of economic and demographic assumptions, such as investment returns, projected salary increases, mortality rates, and terminations

---

[1]The authoritative guidance for pension and OPEB plan accounting and reporting is found primarily in GASB Statement No. 25, "Financial Reporting for Defined Benefit Pension Plans and Note Disclosures for Defined Contribution Plans," and GASB Statement No. 43, "Financial Reporting for Postemployment Benefit Plans Other Than Pension Plans," respectively.

[2]GASB 2010–2011 Comprehensive Implementation Guide, Chapter 5—"Pensions—Employer and Plan Accounting and Reporting," answer to question 5.2.5.

[3]Ibid.

before employees obtain vested pension or OPEB rights. OPEB calculations also require making assumptions about a health care cost trend rate for several years into the future. *Actuaries* normally are called on to make these calculations. Actuaries are professionals with particular expertise in computing the costs of long-term business risks. The financial evaluations of risk provided by actuaries are essential to the successful operations of insurance companies and pension and OPEB plans. Thus, governments normally rely on the advice of actuaries in making pension- and OPEB-related decisions. Actuaries develop their recommendations, plan by plan, by performing *actuarial valuations*, usually annually or biennially. (Actuarial measures of assets and liabilities are not necessarily equivalent to accounting measures of assets and liabilities.)

Employer Accounting for Defined Benefit Contributions

As mentioned previously, governments that offer pension or OPEB benefits to their employees make pension or OPEB contributions, but pension or OPEB trust funds are used only by governments that sponsor a plan. Governments that do not sponsor a plan participate in external plans administered for several—or many—governments. Table 8-1 provides an overview of the operations of external plans and internal plans. Notice that, regardless of whether the plan is external or internal to an employer government, the government generally records its contributions to the plan as expenditures/expenses in the same funds in which other payroll-related expenditures/expenses are recorded (e.g., in the General Fund or a water utility Enterprise Fund).

All governments are required to make pension- or OPEB-related disclosures in their annual financial report. The nature and extent of these disclosures depends on the structure of the plan. When a government participates in an external plan only, financial statements for the plan are issued by the plan, not by the participating government. In contrast, when an employer government also sponsors a plan, the government typically establishes a Pension or OPEB Trust Fund to account for plan receipts, investments, and disbursements and prepares annual financial statements for that fund. Because many OPEB plans currently are financed on a pay-as-you-go basis, governments have no need to establish a trust fund.

Computing the Pension and OPEB Contribution

One of the most fundamental decisions a government faces each year is how much money it should contribute to the pension or OPEB plan. Fortunately, even though the actuary makes many assumptions and considers a variety of options, a pension or OPEB plan's actuarial valuation provides an answer, whether the plan is external to the government or sponsored by the government. That is, if a government contributes the entire amount recommended by the actuary for the year (called the "annual required contribution," or ARC), that government should be accumulating sufficient funds to pay current and future retirees.

In practice, however, governments may make annual contributions in amounts less than those recommended by actuaries. The November 2010 Public Fund Survey of large pension plans, published by the National Association of State Retirement Administrators, showed that, on average, pension plans received 88 percent of the ARC in 2009, but 4 of every 10 plans received less than 90 percent of the ARC. When a government employer contributes less than the ARC for its employees that are involved in proprietary fund activities, an amount based on the ARC is recorded in proprietary funds as the annual pension or OPEB cost (or expense). A proprietary fund also records an accrued liability for the excess of the expense over the cash contributed. In governmental-type funds, however, consistent with the current financial resources measurement focus, the amount of expenditure recorded is equal to the amount contributed to the plan or

TABLE 8-1 Defined Benefit Plan Arrangements—External versus Government-Sponsored

Plan Is External to the Employer Government

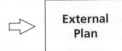

| **Funds of Employer Government** | The funds of the employer government that record payroll expenditures/expenses also make contributions to the external plan on behalf of covered employees. | **External Plan** |

The various funds account for contributions as payroll-related expenditures/expenses.

The employer government makes plan disclosures in the notes to the financial statements.

The plan issues financial statements and makes extensive disclosures.

Plan Is Sponsored by the Employer Government

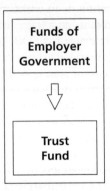

Funds of Employer Government

Trust Fund

The funds of the employer government account for contributions as payroll-related expenditures/expenses, not interfund transfers.

The employer government makes additional pension-related disclosures in the notes to the financial statements.

The trust fund receives the contributions from the various employer funds and accounts for them as "Additions—contributions from employer."

The trust fund prepares fund-level financial statements that are included in the employer government's annual financial report.

Additional arrangements found in practice include the following and combinations thereof:

- The government sponsors a pension plan for a specific employee group, such as uniformed public safety employees, and participates in an external pension plan for the remainder of the workforce eligible for pension coverage.
- The government sponsors a pension plan in which other governments participate.

expected to be liquidated with expendable available financial resources. The employer reporting for pensions and OPEB in governmental funds was discussed in more detail in Chapter 5.[4]

Regardless of the fund type involved, a government's failure to contribute the annual required amount to a pension or OPEB plan gives rise to a net pension obligation (NPO) or a net OPEB obligation (NOPEBO), which must be disclosed in the notes to the financial statements and reported as a liability in the individual government's *government-wide* statement of net position. Additionally, as we will see in the next section, the existence of an NPO or NOPEBO has a direct influence on required pension and OPEB contributions in subsequent years.

Annual Pension Cost and Annual OPEB Cost

Annual pension cost and annual OPEB cost are important concepts because they represent the economic cost to a government of providing pension and OPEB coverage for its employees in a given year. Indeed, employer governments should report pension expense (or OPEB expense) for the year equal to their annual pension cost (or annual OPEB cost) in the government-wide financial statements.[5] We discuss government-wide financial reporting in Chapters 9 and 10.

SOLE-EMPLOYER AND AGENT MULTIEMPLOYER PLANS For governments either sponsoring a sole-employer pension plan or participating in an agent multiemployer plan, *annual pension cost* or *annual OPEB cost* in the simplest case is equal to a government's *annual required contribution (ARC)*, as determined by the actuarial valuation. The ARC has two components—normal cost and amortization of the unfunded actuarially accrued liability (UAAL)—and is calculated using one of several acceptable actuarial funding methods. The normal cost is generally the present value of the pension or OPEB benefit earned by each employee for the year. The UAAL results from a variety of factors, such as previous underfunding and benefit increases attributable to earlier years of service that have not yet been fully funded. The ARC will change with each actuarial valuation because of turnover in the government's workforce, revisions to actuarial assumptions, and other factors.

If an employer government has contributed less than the ARC for a previous year, it likely will have a net pension or net OPEB obligation reported in its government-wide statement of net position. In this case, the annual pension or OPEB cost, which is reported as an expense in the government-wide statement of activities, will include three elements: (1) the ARC, (2) interest on the net pension or OPEB obligation already reported by the government, and (3) an adjustment to the ARC. Accountants typically rely on the work of actuaries to measure the amounts that are needed for financial reporting purposes, such as the annual pension or OPEB cost, the ARC, and the UAAL.

COST-SHARING PLANS The accounting for the annual pension or OPEB cost for a government participating in a cost-sharing pension or OPEB plan is much simpler. The government employer records an expenditure or expense equal to the contractually required contribution. The contractually required contribution is based on an actuarial valuation and funding policy of the plan and

---

[4]The authoritative accounting guidance for employer government pension and OPEB accounting is found, respectively, in GASB Statement No. 27, "Accounting for Pensions by State and Local Governmental Employers," and GASB Statement No. 45, "Accounting and Financial Reporting by Employers for Postemployment Benefits other than Pensions."

[5]GASB Cod. Sec. P20.115. Note, however, that the limitations of modified accrual accounting could result in reporting a smaller pension expenditure in fund financial statements should the government contribute less than the ARC.

ultimately is determined by the plan administrator. It is assessed for a period of time, which may be on a monthly or other agreed-upon basis. If assessed monthly, any unpaid contractually required contribution at the end of the month is considered a liability in the employer's fund and government-wide financial statements.

Changes to Pension Accounting

An unusual feature of current pension and OPEB accounting is that the UAAL is not reported as a liability in the government-wide financial statements of an employer. The UAAL is determined by subtracting the actuarial value of a pension or OPEB plan's assets from the actuarial present value of projected retiree pension or OPEB benefits that are related to the past service periods of current employees and retirees. The UAAL could be thought of as compensation provided to employees in previous years that has not yet been paid. It may be in the form of increases in benefits, such as cost-of-living adjustments, applicable to current workers or current retirees, but nevertheless, it is related to the past work of employees. Under the accrual basis of accounting, such costs related to the past service of employees conceptually should be expensed even if not yet paid by the government. However, as of early 2012, accounting requirements allowed these past service costs to be amortized gradually over a period of 30 years in calculating the ARC.

Also, as of early 2012, the GASB had proposed issuing a new pension accounting standard that would result in recording a net pension liability in an employer's government-wide statement of net position. This proposed pension liability would be the present value of projected benefit payments that is attributed to employees' past periods of service, less the related pension plan's net assets. The GASB had also proposed that only a portion of the change in the pension liability from one year to the next be recorded as an expense in an employer's government-wide statement of activities; the remainder would be recorded as a deferred inflow or outflow.

Other changes proposed in the pension accounting standard include changing the parameters for certain actuarial methods and assumptions and changing the accounting for cost-sharing plans. The GASB is likely to revise its OPEB accounting standards in a manner similar to its proposed revisions to the pension accounting standards. GASB proposals and standards are posted on the GASB web site (www.gasb.org).

Pension and OPEB Note Disclosures

The GASB requires extensive note disclosure by governments that provide pension benefits and OPEB to their employees. Disclosures required of all employer governments include the following:

- A detailed description of the plan, including the types of benefits it provides, and whether the plan issues a financial report.
- The authority under which obligations to contribute to the plan are established, the required contribution rates of active plan members, and the required contribution rates of employers.[6]

Additional disclosures required of employer governments participating in sole-employer or agent multiemployer plans include:

- Annual pension or OPEB cost and the dollar amount of contributions made for the current year. If the employer has a net pension or OPEB obligation, the employer also should

---

[6]GASB Cod. Sec. P20.117 and Sec. P50.120.

disclose the components of annual pension or OPEB cost (ARC, interest on the net pension or OPEB obligation, and the adjustment to the ARC), the increase or decrease in the net pension or OPEB obligation, and the net pension or OPEB obligation at the end of the year.

- Annual pension or OPEB cost, percentage of annual pension or OPEB cost contributed that year, and net pension or OPEB obligation at the end of the year—for the current year and each of the two preceding years.
- Date of the actuarial valuation and identification of the actuarial methods and significant assumptions used to determine the ARC for the current year.[7]

FIDUCIARY-TYPE FUNDS: PENSION TRUST FUNDS

Pension trust fund activities are controlled by pension agreements and local and state laws. These laws cover the operations of retirement systems in general and individual pension plans in particular. They vary in scope, ranging from laws that limit the types of investments that can be made with fund assets to laws that require specified periods of service before employees can qualify for pension benefits.

The financial statements of Pension Trust Funds include a statement of plan net position and a statement of changes in plan net position. The financial statements are prepared using the economic resources measurement focus and the full accrual basis of accounting, with the exception that plan liabilities for benefits and refunds should be recognized when due and payable in accordance with the terms of the plan. This exception does not mean that the liabilities reported are only current liabilities. It is possible for a plan to report some noncurrent liabilities such as a mortgage loan or a capital lease. Pension Trust Funds account for their Investments at fair value. Notice that a statement of cash flows is not prepared.

Operating Entries

For illustrative purposes, assume that the City of Rubyville has had a Pension Trust Fund in operation for several years. The Pension Trust Fund trial balance as of December 31, 2011, is presented in Table 8-2.

The following transactions took place during 2012. Investment income of $500,000 is received in cash. This amount includes interest income accrued at the beginning of the year: $55,000. This investment income is recorded as follows:

Cash	500,000	
Interest receivable		55,000
Additions—interest on investments		445,000
To record the receipt of interest from investments.		

When retirement benefits of $230,000 are paid, a "deduction" is recorded:

Deductions—retirement benefits	230,000	
Cash		230,000
To record retirement benefits.		

---

[7]GASB Cod. Sec. P20.118 and Sec. P50.121.

TABLE 8-2   Trial Balance—Pension Trust Fund

City of Rubyville
Pension Trust Fund
Public Employees' Retirement System
Trial Balance
December 31, 2011

	Debits	Credits
Cash	$ 15,000	
Interest receivable	55,000	
Investments—U.S. government securities	2,000,000	
Investments—corporate stocks	3,067,000	
Building	500,000	
Accumulated depreciation—building		$ 100,000
Equipment	50,000	
Accumulated depreciation—equipment		10,000
Accounts payable		65,000
Net position held in trust for pension benefits		5,512,000
	$5,687,000	$5,687,000

Some Pension Trust Funds have their own administrative staffs. In other instances the operating costs of a Pension Trust Fund are borne by the General Fund of the sponsoring government, and no operating costs appear on the financial statements of the Pension Trust Fund. In our illustration, however, we assume that employees of the City of Rubyville administer the Pension Trust Fund and that the Pension Trust Fund reimburses the General Fund for its share of the accounting and investment management costs. If accounting costs are $12,000 and investment management costs amount to $8,000, the following entries are made in the Pension Trust Fund and General Fund, respectively:

In the Pension Trust Fund (the fund properly chargeable):

Deductions—administrative costs	12,000	
Deductions—investment management costs	8,000	
Due to General Fund		20,000
To record operating costs for the current year.		

In the General Fund (the fund requiring reimbursement):

Due from Pension Trust Fund	20,000	
Expenditures—administrative costs		12,000
Expenditures—investment management costs		8,000
To record reimbursement of operating costs due from Pension Trust Fund.		

Dividends received during the year from investments are recorded as follows:

Cash	10,000	
Additions—dividends		10,000
To record dividends received during the year.		

Investment income of $50,000 earned but not received at the end of the year is recorded as follows:

Interest receivable	50,000	
Additions—interest on investments		50,000
To record interest earned but not received.		

Assume that sales of investments in corporate stocks result in a gain of $10,000 and the amount collected from these sales is $50,000.

Cash	50,000	
Investments—corporate stocks		40,000
Additions—net appreciation in fair value of investments		10,000
To record the sale of investments.		

Assuming the value of the investment portfolio increased by $25,000, the following entry is made to write up the carrying amount of fund investments:

Investments—corporate stocks	25,000	
Additions—net appreciation in fair value of investments		25,000
To record increase in fair value of investments.		

Notice that the realized gains and the unrealized gains are reported in a single account called Additions—net appreciation in fair value of investments. If losses were recorded, they would be netted with gains in the financial statements. The realized gains and losses may be separately disclosed in the notes to the financial statements, subject to certain restrictions imposed by the GASB.

During the year, the fund incurred maintenance costs on its building totaling $5,000 and purchased computer equipment at a cost of $30,000. Depreciation on all of the equipment owned by the Pension Trust Fund is $1,000, plus $10,000 for the building. These expenses are recorded as follows:

Deductions—building maintenance costs	5,000	
Cash		5,000
To record building maintenance costs.		
Equipment	30,000	
Cash		30,000
To record purchase of equipment.		
Deductions—depreciation on equipment	1,000	
Deductions—depreciation on building	10,000	
Accumulated depreciation—equipment		1,000
Accumulated depreciation—building		10,000
To record depreciation for the year.		

During the year additional administrative costs of $15,000 are incurred. These are recorded as follows:

Deductions—administrative costs	15,000	
Accounts payable		15,000
To record accrued administrative expenses.		

Payments on accounts payable during the year are recorded as follows:

Accounts payable	75,000	
Cash		75,000
To record payments on accounts payable.		

The retirement plan requires equal contributions by the employees and the government. When the amount of each contribution is determined, $200,000 in this case, the following entry is made:

Due from General Fund	400,000	
Additions—pension contributions—plan members		200,000
Additions—pension contributions—employer		200,000
To record amount due from the General Fund for pension contributions.		

8-18

In this illustration, we assume that the General Fund is the only fund that is financing pension expenditures. If any other funds were involved, a separate receivable would be established for each fund. The receipt of cash from the General Fund of $400,000 is recorded in the general journal as follows:

Cash	400,000	
Due from General Fund		400,000
To record payment received from the General Fund.		

The corresponding entries that are needed in the General Fund are shown here. In the first entry, assume that gross payroll was $997,000; of that amount, $120,000 is payroll withholding taxes owed to the federal government, and $200,000 is the amount withheld from employees for their contributions to the City of Rubyville's pension plan. The second entry records the city's contribution to the City of Rubyville's pension plan. The third entry is the payment of the amount owed from the General Fund to the Pension Trust Fund.

Expenditures—personal services	997,000	
Due to U.S. government		120,000
Due to Pension Trust Fund		200,000
Cash		677,000
To record payroll and the liability for the employees' share of pension contributions.		
Expenditures—retirement benefits	200,000	
Due to Pension Trust Fund		200,000
To record employer's pension contribution.		
Due to Pension Trust Fund	400,000	
Cash		400,000
To record payment to Pension Trust Fund.		

If cash of $600,000 is invested in corporate stocks, the entry to record this investment in the Pension Trust Fund is as follows:

Investments—corporate stocks	600,000	
Cash		600,000
To record investment.		

The preceding summary entries are sufficient to illustrate the activities typically accounted for by a Pension Trust Fund. The preclosing trial balance for the fund as of the end of the fiscal year is shown in Table 8-3.

TABLE 8-3	Preclosing Trial Balance—Pension Trust Fund

City of Rubyville
Pension Trust Fund
Public Employees' Retirement System
Preclosing Trial Balance
December 31, 2012

	Debits	**Credits**
Cash	$ 35,000	
Interest receivable	50,000	
Investments—U.S. government securities	2,000,000	
Investments—corporate stocks	3,652,000	
Building	500,000	
Accumulated depreciation—building		$ 110,000
Equipment	80,000	
Accumulated depreciation—equipment		11,000
Due to General Fund		20,000
Accounts payable		5,000
Net position held in trust for pension benefits		5,512,000
Additions—interest on investments		495,000
Additions—net appreciation in fair value of investments		35,000
Additions—dividends		10,000
Additions—pension contributions—employer		200,000
Additions—pension contributions—plan members		200,000
Deductions—retirement benefits	230,000	
Deductions—administrative costs	27,000	
Deductions—investment management costs	8,000	
Deductions—building maintenance	5,000	
Deductions—depreciation on equipment	1,000	
Deductions—depreciation on building	10,000	
	$6,598,000	$6,598,000

Closing Entry

At the end of the accounting period the books must be closed and financial statements prepared. The following closing entry is generally used for Pension Trust Funds:

Additions—interest on investments	495,000	
Additions—net appreciation in fair market value of investments	35,000	
Additions—dividends	10,000	
Additions—pension contributions—employer	200,000	
Additions—pension contributions—plan members	200,000	
Deductions—retirement benefits		230,000
Deductions—administrative costs		27,000
Deductions—investment management costs		8,000

Deductions—building maintenance	5,000
Deductions—depreciation on equipment	1,000
Deductions—depreciation on building	10,000
Net position held in trust for pension benefits	659,000

To close the nominal accounts for 2012.

Financial Statements Illustration

The individual financial statements for Pension Trust Funds are a statement of changes in plan net position and a statement of plan net position. These statements are illustrated in Tables 8-4 and 8-5. The GASB also requires two supplementary schedules for defined benefit pension plans. These two schedules are a schedule of funding progress (see Table 8-6) and a schedule of employer contributions (see Table 8-7).

TABLE 8-4   Statement of Changes in Plan Net Position—Pension Trust Fund

City of Rubyville
Pension Trust Fund
Public Employees' Retirement System
Statement of Changes in Plan Net Position
For the Year Ending December 31, 2012

Additions		
Contributions		
Employer	$200,000	
Plan members	200,000	
Total contributions		$ 400,000
Investment income		
Interest income	495,000	
Net appreciation in fair value of investments	35,000	
Dividends	10,000	
	540,000	
Less, investment expense	(8,000)	
Net investment income		532,000
Total additions		932,000
Deductions		
Benefits	230,000	
Administrative costs	27,000	
Building maintenance	5,000	
Depreciation on equipment	1,000	
Depreciation on buildings	10,000	
Total deductions		273,000
Change in net position		659,000
Net Position Held in Trust for Pension Benefits— Beginning of Year		5,512,000
Net Position Held in Trust for Pension Benefits—End of Year		$6,171,000

| **TABLE 8-5** | Statement of Plan Net Position—Pension Trust Fund |

City of Rubyville
Pension Trust Fund
Public Employees' Retirement System
Statement of Plan Net Position
December 31, 2012

Assets		
Cash	$ 35,000	
Interest receivable	50,000	
Investments, at fair value	5,652,000	
Building (net of accumulated depreciation, $110,000)	390,000	
Equipment (net of accumulated depreciation, $11,000)	69,000	
Total assets		$6,196,000
Liabilities		
Due to General Fund	20,000	
Accounts payable	5,000	
Total liabilities		25,000
Net Position Held in Trust for Pension Benefits		$6,171,000

| **TABLE 8-6** | Schedule of Funding Progress |

City of Rubyville
Pension Trust Fund
Public Employees' Retirement System
Schedule of Funding Progress
December 31, 2007–2012
(amounts in thousands)

Actuarial Valuation Date	Actuarial Value of Assets	Actuarial Accrued Liability (AAL)— Entry Age	Unfunded AAL (UAAL)	Funded Ratio	Covered Payroll	UAAL as a Percentage of Covered Payroll
12/31/07	$5,000	$5,750	$750	87.0%	$ 998	75.2%
12/31/08	5,100	5,800	700	87.9	997	70.2
12/31/09	5,350	6,100	750	87.7	995	75.4
12/31/10	5,700	6,300	600	90.5	998	60.1
12/31/11	6,000	6,400	400	93.8	1,000	40.0
12/31/12	6,200	6,500	300	95.4	997	30.1

TABLE 8-7	Schedule of Employer Contributions

City of Rubyville
Pension Trust Fund
Public Employees' Retirement System
Schedule of Employer Contributions
December 31, 2012

Year Ended	Annual Required Contribution	Percentage Contributed
2007	$197,000	100.0%
2008	193,000	100.0
2009	197,500	100.0
2010	202,000	100.0
2011	197,000	100.0
2012	200,000	100.0

The schedule of funding progress helps financial statement users determine whether the financial status of the Pension Trust Fund is improving over time. This schedule reports the trend in the funded ratio—actuarial value of assets (AVA) divided by actuarial accrued liability (AAL). The schedule also shows the trend in the UAAL as a percentage of covered payroll. (The UAAL is simply the difference between the AAL and the AVA.) As a general rule, the financial status of the pension fund is improving if the first ratio increases over time and if the second ratio decreases.

Notice that in developing these ratios, actuarial, not accounting, information is used. Actuaries generally "smooth" changes in market values of investments over periods of 3 to 5 years. The AAL is generally a by-product of the method used by the actuary to compute the funding requirement for a particular pension plan. The AAL provides a rough measure of the present value of the pension benefit earned to date by retired and active members of the plan. A key element in calculating the AAL is the investment earnings assumption (discount rate)—the plan's estimated long-term investment yield. Thus, the higher the investment earnings assumption used by the actuary, the lower the AAL. Also, the AAL is not a uniform measure of the earned pension benefit, because the AAL would be different for different actuarial funding methods. Thus, the trend in funded ratio is useful for measuring the status of the trust fund itself, but is less useful for comparing the funded status of one plan against another.

The 6-year schedule of employer contributions shows how the amounts contributed to the pension system compare each year with the ARC, calculated in accordance with the requirements discussed on page 271. The percentages will differ from 100 percent if employers do not contribute the full amount of the ARC.

The notes to the financial statements for defined benefit plans must include (1) a description of the plan, (2) a summary of significant accounting policies, (3) information about contributions and reserves, and (4) identification of concentrations of investments in certain organizations.

Financial Reporting for Defined Contribution Plans

Under defined contribution plans, the governmental employer does not commit itself to paying specified benefits to retirees, but merely to contributing to the employee's pension plan account.

The governmental employer needs to make only agreed-upon contributions, but does not have an annual pension cost, ARC, or UAAL. This makes the financial reporting for these plans much simpler. For these types of plans, the GASB requires notes disclosing the following: (1) a description of the plan, (2) a summary of significant accounting policies, and (3) identification of concentrations of investments in certain organizations.

Governmental Accounting in Practice

The Mt. Lebanon Employees' Retirement System

Mt. Lebanon, Pennsylvania, administers three sole-employer defined benefit pension plans—a general employees plan, a police officer plan, and a fire fighter plan. Tables 8-8 through 8-11 illustrate the combined financial statements for all three plans and supporting schedules for one of the plans—the police defined benefit pension plan. Notice that the format of the statement of changes in plan net position,

TABLE 8-8	Statement of Changes in Plan Net Position—Pension Trust Fund—Mt. Lebanon

Mt. Lebanon, Pennsylvania
Pension Trust Fund
Statement of Changes in Plan Net Position
Year Ended December 31, 2009
(in thousands of dollars)

Additions		
Contributions:		
Employer, including state aid	$ 1,375	
Employee	222	
Total contributions		$ 1,597
Investment income:		
Net appreciation in fair value of investments	8,773	
Interest and dividends	1,624	
Total investment income	10,397	
Less, investment expense	(140)	
Net investment income		10,257
Total additions		11,854
Deductions		
Benefits	2,902	
Administrative expenses	94	
Total deductions		2,996
Increase in plan net position		8,858
Net Position Held in Trust for Benefits		
Beginning of year		45,468
End of year		$54,326

Source: Adapted from the Comprehensive Annual Financial Report, Mt. Lebanon, Pennsylvania, December 31, 2009.

TABLE 8-9	Statement of Plan Net Position—Pension Trust Fund—Mt. Lebanon

Mt. Lebanon, Pennsylvania
Pension Trust Fund
Statement of Plan Net Position
December 31, 2009
(in thousands of dollars)

Assets		
Accrued income receivable		$ 101
Accrued contributions		8
Investments, at fair value:		
Equity funds	$36,091	
Fixed income funds	15,624	
Short-term funds	2,591	54,306
Total assets		54,415
Liabilities		
Accounts payable		89
Net Position		
Held in trust for benefits		$54,326

Source: Adapted from the Comprehensive Annual Financial Report, Mt. Lebanon, Pennsylvania, December 31, 2009.

TABLE 8-10	Schedule of Funding Progress—Police Pension Trust Fund— Mt. Lebanon

Mt. Lebanon, Pennsylvania
Schedule of Funding Progress
Police Pension Trust Fund*

Actuarial Valuation Date	Actuarial Value of Assets (a)	Actuarial Accrued Liability (AAL) (b)	UAAL (b – a)	Funded Ratio (a/b)	Annual Covered Payroll (c)	UAAL as a Percentage of Covered Payroll [(b – a)/c]
1/1/2004	$26,830,302	$26,570,578	$ (259,724)	100.9%	$3,366,121	(7.7%)
1/1/2005	28,395,320	26,136,747	(2,258,573)	108.6%	3,359,223	(67.2%)
1/1/2006	28,488,937	27,156,789	(1,332,148)	104.9%	3,046,272	(43.73%)
1/1/2007	31,028,661	29,981,657	(1,047,004)	103.5%	3,223,661	(32.5%)
1/1/2008	33,359,159	32,104,997	(1,254,162)	103.9%	3,860,497	(32.5%)
1/1/2009	28,742,491	34,832,216	6,089,725	82.5%	3,921,550	155.3%

*This is a condensed version of the schedule and does not include the funding progress information for two other Mt. Lebanon pension plans—the general employees plan and the fire fighter plan.

Source: Adapted from the Comprehensive Annual Financial Report, Mt. Lebanon, Pennsylvania, December 31, 2009.

TABLE 8-11	Schedule of Employer Contributions—Pension Trust Fund—Mt. Lebanon

Mt. Lebanon, Pennsylvania
Schedule of Employer Contributions
Police Pension Trust Fund*

Year Ended	Annual Required Contribution	Percentage Contributed
12/31/04	$ 650,111	100%
12/31/05	721,696	100%
12/31/06	1,108,395	102%
12/31/07	1,134,859	103%
12/31/08	1,037,839	102%
12/31/09	1,127,875	101%

*This is a condensed version of the schedule and does not include the contribution information for two other Mt. Lebanon pension plans—the general employees plan and the fire fighter plan.

Source: Adapted from the Comprehensive Annual Financial Report, Mt. Lebanon, Pennsylvania, December 31, 2009.

presented in Table 8-8, is much like the one presented in the text for the City of Rubyville (Table 8-4). Also, notice that three major classes of investments are identified on the statement of plan net position in Table 8-9. Mt. Lebanon maintains investment policies that limit the allowable types of investments. Generally, the plan is allowed to invest in equity securities, fixed income investments, and cash or cash equivalents. Other investment policies limit the plan to having not more than 5 percent of its total bond portfolio at the time of purchase in any one issuer and also limit the amount of bonds that it can hold in entities that have a Moody's or Standard and Poor's rating below "A" to 15 percent of the plan's total market value of fixed securities. The investment policies are described in the notes to the financial statements.

Accounts payable is the only liability reported. In accordance with accounting standards for Pension Trust Funds, liabilities do not include the present value of amounts due to current and retired employees for services rendered in the past (that is, the AAL). Information about this liability and the UAAL can be found in the schedule of funding progress presented in Table 8-10. Mt. Lebanon's police pension plan historically has been very well funded, with the actuarial value of its plan assets actually exceeding its AAL. The funded ratio for the plan on January 1, 2009, however, dropped primarily because of investment losses incurred during the 2008 economic downturn. Since then, many of these losses have been recovered. Users of governmental financial statements have commented that the schedule of funding progress and the schedule of employer contributions (presented in Tables 8-10 and 8-11) provide them with more information about the long-term health of the plan than do the fiduciary financial statements.

FIDUCIARY-TYPE FUNDS: INVESTMENT TRUST FUNDS

Fund Overview

Some governments maintain external investment pools, an arrangement that combines the resources of more than one legally separate entity and invests them on behalf of the participants to achieve economies of scale. By definition, an external investment pool can account for resources of the sponsoring government, but one or more of the participants must be a legally separate government that is not part of the same reporting entity as the sponsoring government.

External investment pools are created, for example, when state laws authorize a state treasurer to hold and invest temporarily idle cash deposited by local governments with the state treasurer, or when state laws require legally separate local school districts to deposit temporarily idle cash with a county treasurer for investment. In such instances, a fiduciary relationship develops between the government that manages the external investment pool and the participating governments.

Although the resources of external investment pools are commingled, the portion of the investment pool that belongs to the sponsoring government should be reported in an appropriate fund of the sponsoring government. The portion of the resources belonging to the other participants should be reported in a fiduciary-type fund called an Investment Trust Fund.

Summary of Fund Activities

Investment Trust Funds receive resources from participating governments. These resources are then invested in securities. Income from these securities is accounted for using the economic resources measurement focus and the full accrual basis of accounting. Gains and losses incurred in trading securities and adjusting them to fair value are recorded during the given period along with any expenses incurred. Once the income is determined for the period, it is allocated to each participant depending on the trust agreement, usually based on the amount invested.

Control of Fund Activities

Investment Trust Funds are controlled primarily by the trust agreement, which is a legal document that specifies what type of investments can be made, how the income will be measured and distributed, and how much the sponsoring government can charge for managing the fund. A key element that should be specifically identified is how much income can be distributed. Some Investment Trust Funds allow participants upon relatively short notice to withdraw the same amount as they have invested plus their net earnings to date. These Investment Trust Funds typically invest sufficient resources in short-term investments to maintain the liquidity necessary to permit withdrawals by participating governments. Other investment pools have longer time horizons and require advance notice before a withdrawal can be made. In such pools, withdrawals may be based on a participant's equity interest in a pooled net figure, such as investment income minus investment losses and expenses. The trust agreement should be specific regarding how much, if any, of the investment net income must be retained as a protection against possible future losses.

Accounting for Fund Activities

OPERATING ENTRIES   To illustrate an Investment Trust Fund, assume that two small cities (Leona and Beeville) each deposit $50,000 in the City of Rubyville's external investment pool, which is referred to as the RubyPool Investment Trust Fund. Although Rubyville could participate in the fund, we assume it does not. Leona and Beeville are seeking to use the fund management skills of Rubyville's finance staff. The City of Rubyville has agreed not to charge administrative expenses for the first year of the fund's operations. The entry to record the receipt of the money by the RubyPool Investment Trust Fund follows:

Cash	100,000	
Additions—contributions from Leona		50,000
Additions—contributions from Beeville		50,000
To record the receipt of deposits made by Leona and Beeville.		

Both Leona and Beeville would make the following entry in their general journals:

RubyPool investment	50,000	
Cash		50,000

To record investment of cash in a pool managed by the City
of Rubyville.

Investments made by Rubyville's finance staff are recorded by category of investment (e.g., U.S. government obligations, municipal obligations, etc.). If the trust fund invests $40,000 in U.S. government securities and $55,000 in corporate securities, the following journal entry should be made for the Investment Trust Fund:

Investments—U.S. government securities	40,000	
Investments—corporate securities	55,000	
Cash		95,000

To record investment of pool cash.

Notice that no entry is made on the books of either Leona or Beeville at this time.
During the year, the fund earns $5,000 of interest, of which $4,000 is received in cash. The entry to record this interest income for the RubyPool Investment Trust Fund is as follows:

Cash	4,000	
Interest receivable	1,000	
Additions—interest		5,000

To record interest earned and received during 2012.

Securities are reported at fair value in Investment Trust Funds. If the value of corporate investments increased by $3,000 during the year, the following journal entry is needed:

Investments—corporate securities	3,000	
Additions—net increase in fair value of investments		3,000

To record the increase in the fair value of investments
for 2012.

Investment expenses incurred by the fund during 2012 totaled $800. If these expenses are paid in cash, the journal entry is this:

Deductions—investment expenses	800	
Cash		800

To record investment expenses for 2012.

During 2012 corporate securities totaling $6,000 were sold for $7,000. The journal entry for this transaction is as follows:

Cash	7,000	
Investments—corporate securities		6,000
Additions—net increase in fair value of investments		1,000

To record sale of investments.

Notice that no journal entry for the preceding four events is yet necessary for the cities of Leona or Beeville. Journal entries are necessary only for the investment pool administered by the finance staff of the City of Rubyville. If $1,600 is distributed each to Leona and Beeville, the following entry is made for the RubyPool Investment Trust Fund:

Deductions—distributions to pool participants	3,200	
Cash		3,200
To record the distribution of part of the fund's resources to		
its participants.		

Leona and Beeville would each make the following journal entry to record the receipt of cash and the reduction in their investment in RubyPool:

Cash	1,600	
RubyPool investment		1,600
To record a partial distribution of cash from Rubyville's		
external investment pool.		

In practice, most Investment Trust Funds make numerous journal entries during a year. They typically have a variety of investments, which are bought and sold. They record dividends, interest, gains and losses, and changes in the fair value of investments. They have numerous deposits and withdrawals by participants in the fund. The foregoing entries provide a good, although small, sample of the types of journal entries that would be expected.

CLOSING ENTRY   The closing entry for the Investment Trust Fund is as follows:

Additions—contributions from Leona	50,000	
Additions—contributions from Beeville	50,000	
Additions—interest	5,000	
Additions—net increase in fair value of investments	4,000	
Deductions—investment expenses		800
Deductions—distributions to pool participants		3,200
Net position		105,000
To close the operating accounts of the external investment		
pool.		

In this illustration all items of revenue, expense, gain, or loss are divided based on each participant's interest in RubyPool. RubyPool had net investment earnings of $8,200 ($5,000 + $4,000 − $800) for the year, which would be divided equally between Leona and Beeville because they have an equal interest in the pool. (In reality, the accounts of each of the governments that participate in an investment pool would be updated regularly—perhaps monthly or even daily—but for simplicity they are updated only at year-end here.) The cities of Leona and Beeville would each record the following:

RubyPool investment	4,100	
Revenues—net increase in value of investments		4,100
To record a city's share of pooled investment changes		
during 2012.		

A trial balance for Rubyville's Investment Trust Fund is presented in Table 8-12.

TABLE 8-12 Trial Balance—Investment Trust Fund

City of Rubyville
Trial Balance
RubyPool Investment Trust Fund
December 31, 2012

	Debits	Credits
Cash	$ 12,000	
Interest receivable	1,000	
Investments—U.S. government securities	40,000	
Investments—corporate securities	52,000	
Additions—contributions from Leona		$ 50,000
Additions—contributions from Beeville		50,000
Additions—interest		5,000
Additions—net increase in fair value of investments		4,000
Deductions—investment expenses	800	
Deductions—distribution to pool participants	3,200	
	$109,000	$109,000

Financial Statements Illustration

The financial statements normally prepared for Investment Trust Funds are a statement of changes in fiduciary net position and a statement of fiduciary net position. These statements are illustrated in Tables 8-13 and 8-14. Notice that no cash flow statement is prepared.

TABLE 8-13 Statement of Changes in Fiduciary Net Position—Investment Trust Fund

City of Rubyville
Fiduciary Fund
Statement of Changes in Fiduciary Net Position
RubyPool Investment Trust Fund
for the Year Ending December 31, 2012

Additions		
Contributions from participating governments		$100,000
Investment earnings:		
Interest	$5,000	
Increase in fair value of investments	4,000	
Less, investment expense	(800)	
Net investment earnings		8,200
Total additions		108,200
Deductions		
Distributions to fund participants		(3,200)
Change in net position		105,000
Net Position—Beginning of the Year		0
Net Position—End of the Year		$105,000

TABLE 8-14 Statement of Fiduciary Net Position—Investment Trust Fund

City of Rubyville
Fiduciary Fund
Statement of Fiduciary Net Position
RubyPool Investment Trust Fund
December 31, 2012

Assets	
Cash	$ 12,000
Interest receivable	1,000
Investments	92,000
Total assets	$105,000
Net Position	
Held in trust	$105,000

Governmental Accounting in Practice

Wisconsin Local Government Pooled Investment Fund

The State of Wisconsin maintains a Local Government Pooled Investment Fund similar to that maintained by the City of Rubyville, but on a much larger scale as local governments throughout the state of Wisconsin invest in its fund. The statement of changes in fiduciary net position is presented in Table 8-15, and the statement of fiduciary net position is presented in Table 8-16. The State of Wisconsin follows the same accounting and measurement focus procedures as Rubyville.

TABLE 8-15 Statement of Changes in Fiduciary Net Position—Investment Trust Fund

State of Wisconsin
Statement of Changes in Fiduciary Net Position
Local Government Pooled Investment Fund
For the Fiscal Year Ended June 30, 2010
(amounts in thousands)

Additions		
Deposits		$10,124,021
Investment income of investment trust funds	$ 7,812	
Less, investment expense	(678)	
Net investment income		7,134
Total additions		10,131,155
Deductions		
Distributions	10,862,529	
Administrative expenses	344	
Total deductions		10,862,873
Net decrease in net position		(731,718)
Net Position—Beginning of Year		3,221,996
Net Position—End of Year		$ 2,490,278

Source: Adapted from the Comprehensive Annual Financial Report, State of Wisconsin, June 30, 2010.

TABLE 8-16	Statement of Fiduciary Net Position—Investment Trust Fund

State of Wisconsin
Statement of Fiduciary Net Position
Local Government Pooled Investment Fund
June 30, 2010
(amounts in thousands)

Assets	
Cash and cash equivalents	$2,490,625
Liabilities and Net Position	
Due to other funds	347
Net position held in trust for pooled participants	$2,490,278

Source: Adapted from the Comprehensive Annual Financial Report, State of Wisconsin, June 30, 2010.

FIDUCIARY-TYPE FUNDS: PRIVATE PURPOSE TRUST FUNDS

Fund Overview

Private Purpose Trust Funds are used to account for the principal and earnings of trusts maintained to benefit those outside the government—individuals, private organizations, or other governments. A typical fund of this type is one used by state governments to report escheat property.[8] These funds follow the economic resources measurement focus and the full accrual basis of accounting.

Summary of Fund Activities

The activities of Private Purpose Trust Funds are similar to those of Investment Trust Funds; they entail the receipt of resources from direct contributions made by private individuals or organizations. These resources are invested, and the income and/or principal is disbursed from the trust fund according to the trust agreement. Formal budgets and budgetary accounting are seldom used in Private Purpose Trust Funds.

Accounting for Fund Activities

OPERATING ENTRIES   Activities accounted for in Private Purpose Trust Funds generally are similar to those detailed in Chapter 6 for Permanent Funds except that Private Purpose Trust Funds benefit those outside the government rather than the government itself. Also, as noted previously, Private Purpose Trust Funds use the full accrual basis of accounting and the economic resources measurement focus. All the operating activities related to the purposes for which the trust was established are recorded within the Private Purpose Trust Fund.

As an example of the accounting procedures for Private Purpose Trust Funds, assume a prominent citizen of Rubyville establishes an educational trust fund for children of police and fire department employees killed in the performance of their duties. The trust agreement provides for an initial contribution of $2,000,000. This amount is to be invested, and income generated by the investments is to be spent on college scholarships for qualifying children.

[8]GASB Cod. Sec. 1300.113.

The entries to record receipt of the gift and the original investment of the resources are as follows:

Cash	2,000,000	
Additions—donations		2,000,000
To record the receipt of donations during 2012.		
Investments—municipal bonds	500,000	
Investments—U.S. government securities	1,500,000	
Cash		2,000,000
To record investments made during 2012.		

If the earnings on the investments amount to $60,000, the following entry would be recorded:

Cash	60,000	
Additions—investment earnings		60,000
To record investment earnings during 2012.		

During the year, scholarships totaling $55,000 are awarded and recorded with the following entry:

Deductions—scholarships	55,000	
Cash		55,000
To record scholarships for 2012.		

During 2012, operating costs of $1,000 are incurred, of which $600 is paid in cash. The entry to record these costs is as follows:

Deductions—operating costs	1,000	
Accounts payable		400
Cash		600
To record operating costs for 2012.		

Investments in municipal bonds of $200,000 are sold for $225,000, and the total proceeds are immediately reinvested in the same type of securities. The entries to record these transactions follow:

Cash	225,000	
Investments—municipal bonds		200,000
Additions—net appreciation in fair value of investments		25,000
To record redemption of investments.		
Investments—municipal bonds	225,000	
Cash		225,000
To record additional investments made in 2012.		

Additional income of $10,000 earned on investments, but not received by year-end, is recorded with the following entry:

Investment income receivable	10,000	
Additions—investment earnings		10,000
To record accrual of investment earnings at the end of 2012.		

The fair value of the municipal bonds held by the fund increased by $15,000 by the end of 2012. The entry to record this event is:

Investments—municipal bonds	15,000	
Additions—net appreciation in fair value of investments		15,000
To record the increase in fair value of investments at the end of 2012.		

CLOSING ENTRY At the end of the year, the following entry is made to close the books:

Additions—donations	2,000,000	
Additions—investment earnings	70,000	
Additions—net appreciation in fair value of investments	40,000	
Deductions—scholarships		55,000
Deductions—operating costs		1,000
Net position		2,054,000
To close the general ledger for 2012.		

Financial Statements Illustration

The financial statements for a Private Purpose Trust Fund are a statement of changes in fiduciary net position and a statement of fiduciary net position. These statements are illustrated for the City of Rubyville in Tables 8-17 and 8-18.

TABLE 8-17 Statement of Changes in Fiduciary Net Position—Private Purpose Trust Fund

City of Rubyville
Private Purpose Trust Fund
Scholarship Fund
Statement of Changes in Fiduciary Net Position
For the Year Ended December 31, 2012

Additions		
Donations		$2,000,000
Investment earnings:		
Net increase in fair value of investments	$ 40,000	
Income from investments	70,000	
Total investment earnings	110,000	
Less, investment expense	(1,000)	
Net investment earnings		109,000
Total additions		2,109,000
Deductions		
Scholarships		55,000
Change in net position		2,054,000
Net Position—Beginning of Year		0
Net Position—End of Year		$2,054,000

TABLE 8-18   Statement of Fiduciary Net Position—Private Purpose Trust Fund

City of Rubyville
Private Purpose Trust Fund
Scholarship Fund
Statement of Fiduciary Net Position
December 31, 2012

Assets		
Cash	$ 4,400	
Investments—U.S. government securities	1,500,000	
Investments—municipal bonds	540,000	
Investment income receivable	10,000	
Total assets		$2,054,400
Liabilities		
Accounts payable		400
Net Position in Trust for Scholarships		$2,054,000

Governmental Accounting in Practice

The State of Michigan Private Purpose Trust Fund

The State of Michigan maintains four Private Purpose Trust Funds: (1) Escheats Fund; (2) Gifts, Bequests, and Deposits Investment Fund; (3) Hospital Patients' Trust Fund; and (4) Michigan Education Savings Program, which is illustrated here. This fund is a college tuition savings plan, designed to collect and invest deposits made by contributors for purposes of financing tuition on behalf of future students. Investment earnings held in trust by the fund are federal and state tax-deferred until the student is ready to attend college. The federal government and the state both offer tax deductions for contributions made each year. Tables 8-19 and 8-20 show the financial statements for this fund.

TABLE 8-19   Statement of Changes in Fiduciary Net Position—
Private Purpose Trust Fund—State of Michigan

State of Michigan
Statement of Changes in Fiduciary Net Position
Private Purpose Trust Fund
Michigan Education Savings Program
Fiscal Year Ended September 30, 2010 (amounts in thousands)

Additions		
Contributions from participants		$ 819,987
Investment income:		
Net appreciation in fair value of investments	141,564	
Interest, dividends, and other	47,200	
Net investment income		188,764
Total additions		1,008,751

(continued)

TABLE 8-19	*(continued)*	
Deductions		
Benefits paid to participants or beneficiaries	643,593	
Administrative expense	4,084	
Total deductions		647,677
Net increase		361,074
Net Position Held in Trust for Others—Beginning of Fiscal Year		2,012,062
Net Position Held in Trust for Others—End of Fiscal Year		$2,373,136

Source: Adapted from the Comprehensive Annual Financial Report, State of Michigan, September 30, 2010.

TABLE 8-20	Statement of Fiduciary Net Position—Private Purpose Trust Fund—State of Michigan

State of Michigan
Statement of Fiduciary Net Position
Private Purpose Trust Fund
Michigan Education Savings Program
September 30, 2010 (amounts in thousands)

Assets		
Cash		$ 179
Dividend and interest receivables		1,466
Investments at fair value:		
Mutual funds	$2,125,970	
Pooled investment funds	247,159	
Total investments		2,373,129
Other current assets		2,714
Total assets		2,377,488
Liabilities		
Accounts payable and other liabilities		4,352
Net Position		
Held in trust for others		$2,373,136

Source: Adapted from the Comprehensive Annual Financial Report, State of Michigan, September 30, 2010.

FIDUCIARY-TYPE FUNDS: AGENCY FUNDS

Fund Overview

An Agency Fund is a fiduciary-type fund used when a governmental unit is the custodian for resources that belong to others. Agency Funds typically involve only the receipt, temporary investment, and remittance of fiduciary resources to individuals, private organizations, or other governments.[9] Because an Agency Fund is used for purely custodial purposes, there is no net position reported for this type of fund. Instead, all the assets held are offset by liabilities. Therefore, the Agency Fund accounting equation is assets = liabilities. No operating statements are prepared for Agency Funds because no inflows or outflows of resources are recorded.

One of the most common uses of an Agency Fund is as a clearing mechanism for recording the collection of property taxes by one government on behalf of other governments. For example, a county may collect the property taxes due to the county, one or more cities within the county, and a school district. A county Agency Fund would be used to account for the receipt of the tax proceeds and their subsequent disbursement to other governments. Of course, the county will retain the property taxes that are due to the county. Although some governments report these property tax receipts in an Agency Fund as a matter of convenience (as is done in the illustrative journal entries in this chapter), they should not be reported in an Agency Fund when a government prepares its financial statements because Agency Funds, by definition, are used only to account for assets held for those outside the government.

Agency Funds sometimes are used to record Social Security and other payroll deductions before these amounts are sent to the appropriate recipients, as well as to account for assets held in escrow and deposits from contractors doing business with the government. A key factor in determining whether an Agency Fund should be used is whether the governmental unit disburses the assets according to a previously agreed-upon formula, legal requirement, or instruction by the "owner." In short, Agency Funds should be used when the government has no discretionary use of the assets over which it has temporary custody and no trust agreement is established.

Accounting for Fund Activities

OPERATING ENTRIES   For illustrative purposes, assume that the City of Rubyville uses a Property Tax Collection Fund and that the city collects all property taxes and distributes two-thirds of the collections to other governments (the local school board and a levee district) and one-third to the General Fund of the city. Also, assume that the school board and the levee district are not part of the Rubyville government. The levy of the tax is recorded by each governmental unit. To keep the example manageable, however, we will illustrate only the General Fund and the Agency Fund for Rubyville. Entries similar to those for the General Fund are also made by the other governments. Assuming the amounts given, the appropriate entry for the General Fund books is this:

Property taxes receivable—current	5,000,000	
Estimated uncollectible property taxes—current		1,000
Revenues—property taxes		4,999,000
To record levy of property taxes for 2012.		

The entry for the City of Rubyville's Agency Fund is as follows:

Property taxes receivable for the city and other governmental units—current	15,000,000	
Due to the city and other governmental units		15,000,000
To record levy of 2012 property tax.		

---

[9]GASB Cod. Sec. 1300.114.

Because of the services provided, the city charges the school board and the levee district a 2 percent fee. This amount is deducted from the amount owed to them when the taxes are collected and recorded as revenues of the General Fund. If $9,000,000 is collected during 2012, the school board and the levee district will each receive $2,940,000 ($3,000,000 × .98), and the General Fund will receive $3,120,000 ($3,000,000 + $60,000 + $60,000). The entries in the Agency Fund necessary to record the collection and the distribution of cash are as follows:

Cash	9,000,000	
Property taxes receivable for the city and other governmental units—current		9,000,000
To record the collection of part of the 2012 property tax.		
Due to the city and other governmental units	9,000,000	
Due to General Fund		3,120,000
Due to School Board		2,940,000
Due to Levee District		2,940,000
To record allocation of taxes collected.		
Due to General Fund	3,120,000	
Due to School Board	2,940,000	
Due to Levee District	2,940,000	
Cash		9,000,000
To record distribution of 2012 property taxes collected.		

The journal entry in the General Fund to record the receipt of its share of the property taxes and the collection fee is this:

Cash	3,120,000	
Property taxes receivable—current		3,000,000
Revenues—miscellaneous		120,000
To record receipt of part of the 2012 property tax plus a collection fee.		

The other governmental units will recognize the difference between the debit to Cash and the credit to Property taxes receivable—current as a debit to an expenditure or an expense account, as appropriate. To illustrate, the entry that would be recorded on the books of the levee district follows:

Cash	2,940,000	
Expenditure—fee for collection of property taxes	60,000	
Property taxes receivable—current		3,000,000
To record receipt of part of the 2012 property tax.		

When uncollectible tax accounts are written off by the governments, an adjustment needs to be made in the Agency Fund. If the governments determine that $300 of the assessed taxes will not be collectible, the entry in the Agency Fund is this:

Due to the city and other governmental units	300	
Property taxes receivable for the city and other governmental units—current (delinquent or lien)		300
To record the write-off of uncollectible property taxes.		

TABLE 8-21 Trial Balance—Agency Fiduciary Fund

City of Rubyville
Agency Fund
Tax Collection Fund
Trial Balance
December 31, 2012

	Debits	Credits
Property taxes receivable for the city and other governmental units—current	$5,999,700	
Due to the city and other governmental units		$5,999,700
	$5,999,700	$5,999,700

In addition, the appropriate property tax–related entry or entries, as discussed in Chapter 5, are made on the books of the City of Rubyville's General Fund and in the funds of the other governments. Notice that the activities described do not result in either a revenue or an expenditure in the Agency Fund. Accordingly, no closing entry is needed for an Agency Fund. A trial balance for the fund at the end of the year is presented in Table 8-21.

Financial Statement Illustration

The financial statement of Agency Funds is a statement of net position. The statement for the City of Rubyville is illustrated in Table 8-22. In this statement of fiduciary net position, assets must equal liabilities. Therefore, there is no net position. Notice that the statement of net position includes only amounts held for other governments. The amounts within the Agency Fund accounts that pertain to other funds of the sponsoring government are not reported by the Agency Fund. Rather, these amounts are reported as assets and liabilities in the appropriate funds.[10] In this instance they are reported in the General Fund for the City of Rubyville.

TABLE 8-22 Statement of Fiduciary Net Position—Agency Fund

City of Rubyville
Agency Fund
Tax Collection Fund
Statement of Fiduciary Net Position
December 31, 2012

Assets	
Property taxes receivable for other governmental units—current	$3,999,800
	$3,999,800
Liabilities	
Due to other governmental units	$3,999,800
	$3,999,800

---

[10]GASB Cod. Sec. 2200.179.

Governmental Accounting in Practice

The City of Wichita Falls, Texas, Agency Fund

The City of Wichita Falls, Texas, has one Agency Fund. It is used to account for unclaimed vendor or payroll checks that will ultimately be sent to the State of Texas if not claimed. The city reports a statement of fiduciary net position (see Table 8-23). The statement is quite simple and demonstrates the assets = liabilities nature of the fund.

TABLE 8-23   Statement of Fiduciary Net Position—City of Wichita Falls, Texas

City of Wichita Falls, Texas
Statement of Fiduciary Net Position
Agency Fund
September 30, 2010

Assets	
Cash and cash equivalents	$300,715
Liabilities	
Due to others	$300,715

Source: Adapted from the Comprehensive Annual Financial Report, City of Wichita Falls, TX, September 30, 2010.

Review Questions

Q8-1   Does a government that offers pension benefits to its employees necessarily maintain a Pension Trust Fund? Explain.

Q8-2   Distinguish between a defined benefit pension plan and a defined contribution pension plan.

Q8-3   What is an actuary? What is the actuary's role in pension administration?

Q8-4   Distinguish between a pension contribution and pension cost.

Q8-5   What changes are expected to be made to pension accounting for employers?

Q8-6   What financial statements are prepared for Pension Trust Funds?

Q8-7   Identify and explain the schedules that are prepared for Pension Trust Funds.

Q8-8   What are other postemployment benefits?

Q8-9   Can the governmental unit sponsoring an external investment pool participate in it?

Q8-10 What financial statements are prepared for an Investment Trust Fund?

Q8-11 How are investments in an Investment Trust Fund valued? How are changes in value treated?

Q8-12 When are Private Purpose Trust Funds used?

Q8-13 How are Private Purpose Trust Funds controlled?

Q8-14 What financial statements are used for Private Purpose Trust Funds?

Q8-15 Define an agency relationship.

Q8-16 Is an operating statement prepared for an Agency Fund? Why or why not?

Q8-17 Does an Agency Fund have a fund balance? Why or why not?

Q8-18 Conduct a search on the Internet to find current news about the funded status of pension and OPEB plans for state and local governments. What do you find? State your source.

Discussion Scenarios and Issues

D8-1   J. S. Moneybaggs wants to include a provision in her will that will assure that her life's work of caring for small children will continue after her death. She is concerned that any resources given to the city might be used for some other purpose. Moneybaggs hires you as her financial consultant. How will you advise her?

D8-2   A new employee of the City of Kashime was working with the accounting records of several of its funds. This employee, John Fergie, found that a gift had been given to the city for the library. The gift mandated that only the earnings from the gift could be used for library operations. John wanted to set up a Permanent Fund for the principal of the donation to the library and use a Special Revenue Fund to account for the earnings of the investment and their use. Another employee argued that a Private Purpose Trust Fund should be used for both principal and income. Do you agree with either of these individuals, or do you have a better suggestion?

D8-3   The City of Macroville hires you as a consultant to help establish a procedure to simplify its property tax collection processing and to make the process more efficient. Currently the city and six special districts receive money from a property tax. Each district and the city have their own billing, recording, and collection functions. In addition, the taxpayers are upset about paying seven tax bills. At a recent town hall–type meeting, several citizens demanded that the city do something to simplify the process. As a consultant, how would you advise the city?

D8-4   Aaronsborough's city manager, Thomas Smith, is facing a financial dilemma. The General Fund will not have enough revenues to cover the current year's expenditures. After an all-night session, he reduced the expenditures by only 5 percent, which is not enough to balance the budget. His wife mentions to him that whenever they did not have enough money to meet their bills for a particular month, she merely borrowed money from the bank. Smith decides to borrow from the Pension Trust Fund. His intention is to repay the loan as soon as possible. Will the loan solve his problem? Explain. Is an ethical problem raised here? Explain.

D8-5   Assume the same facts as stated in D8-4 except that the Pension Trust Fund is operated by a five-member board of directors. Before the end of the current fiscal year, three of the board members' terms expire. If Smith appoints three new board members who are sympathetic to his plan, do you see a potential ethical problem?

Exercises

E8-1   (Fiduciary funds in practice)

Obtain a recent Comprehensive Annual Financial Report for a county or a municipality. Identify any fiduciary funds included in the report. Does the government have any Pension Trust Funds? If not, does the government contribute to an external pension plan?

E8-2   (Journal entries for a Pension Trust Fund)

The Pension Trust Fund maintained by the City of Linden had the following transactions during 2012. Record each transaction in the Pension Trust Fund. Ignore any other funds that may be involved in a transaction.

1. Contributions of $600,000 were received from General Fund employees, and the General Fund contributed its share of $100,000.
2. The fund paid $500 for investment management fees.
3. Investments held by the fund increased in value by $3,500.
4. Depreciation on fund capital assets totaled $800.
5. Retirement benefits of $7,700 were paid to retirees.
6. Interest of $2,500 and dividends of $1,400 were received from investments.

E8-3   (Terminology)

Define the following terms as they apply to pension plans and other postemployment benefit plans:

1. Defined benefit plan
2. Defined contribution plan
3. Other postemployment benefits
4. Annual required contribution
5. Unfunded actuarial accrued liability
6. Net pension obligation

E8-4   (Journal entries for an Investment Trust Fund)

Prepare the journal entries to record the following transactions in an Investment Trust Fund for Seggen County during the calendar year 2013.

1. Turtle Creek and Pineview contributed $60,000 and $40,000, respectively, to an Investment Trust Fund operated by Seggen County during 2013.
2. Investments totaling $75,000 were purchased.
3. Income from the investments during the year totaled $8,000.
4. The fund paid $1,500 to the county for investment management fees.
5. The investments increased in value by $3,000.
6. Income of $10,000 was paid to the two cities, based on the relative amount of their initial investment.

E8-5   (Financial statements for an Investment Trust Fund)

Based on the information in E8-4, prepare a statement of changes in fiduciary fund net position and a statement of fiduciary fund net position for Seggen County for its fiscal year ending December 31, 2013. (Assume that Seggen County's net position at the beginning of the year was zero.)

E8-6   (Discussion)

Why would one entity permit another entity to invest its resources?

E8-7   (Journal entries for a Private Purpose Trust Fund)

Record the following journal entries in the Children's Book Fund, a city's Private Purpose Trust Fund that supplies books for children in privately owned battered women's shelters.

1. A citizen donated $500,000 to a Private Purpose Trust Fund. The trust specified that this money was to be used to acquire children's books for battered women's shelters.
2. The fund invested $420,000 in CDs.
3. Books costing $45,000 were acquired.
4. Interest income of $20,000 was received in cash from the CDs.
5. The accounts were closed for the year.

E8-8   (Multiple choice)

1. Which of the following funds can be used to account for the spendable income from a Private Purpose Trust Fund?
   a. Agency Fund
   b. General Fund
   c. Capital Projects Fund
   d. Pension Trust Fund
   e. None of the above

2. To what provisions must the use of assets accumulated in a trust fund conform?
   a. State and local laws
   b. The trust agreement
   c. Both a and b
   d. The modified accrual basis of accounting
   e. None of the above

3. A citizen donated $1 million to a city upon her death. Her will provided that these resources be maintained in a trust and spent to provide schoolchildren with free tickets to local baseball games. In which fund is accounting for these activities done?

    a. General Fund

    b. Special Revenue Fund

    c. Investment Trust Fund

    d. Private Purpose Trust Fund

    e. Both c and d

E8-9   (Fill in the blanks)

    1. Private Purpose Trust Funds follow the _____ measurement focus and the _____ basis of accounting.

    2. Amounts originally contributed to a Private Purpose Trust Fund are recorded as _____.

    3. The following financial statements are prepared for a Private Purpose Trust Fund: _____ and _____.

    4. The operations of a Private Purpose Trust Fund are usually _____ (more or less) complex than those of the General Fund.

    5. The most important document, with respect to a Private Purpose Trust Fund, is the _____.

E8-10 (Compare and contrast an Investment Trust Fund with a Private Purpose Trust Fund)

Identify the major similarities and differences between an Investment Trust Fund and a Private Purpose Trust Fund. Be sure to specify when each is used.

E8-11 (Discussion of alternatives for use of trusts)

An individual wants to set up a long-lasting trust for the education of children of deceased schoolteachers. In a written statement explain the best method of achieving this goal.

E8-12 (Multiple choice)

    1. The principal and earnings of a gift held in a trust that can be spent for the college education of the children of deceased policemen should be accounted for in which of the following funds?

       a. Permanent Fund

       b. Special Revenue Fund

       c. Investment Trust Fund

       d. Private Purpose Trust Fund

    2. In what way can the amounts in an Investment Trust Fund be invested?

       a. Any way the government that operates the fund wishes

       b. Only in corporate stocks and bonds

       c. Only as provided in the trust agreement

       d. Only in governmental bonds

    3. To what type of account are contributions to a Pension Trust Fund usually credited?

       a. A revenue account

       b. An expenditure account

       c. An additions account

       d. A net position account

    4. Which account in a Private Purpose Trust Fund should be credited for the proceeds on the sale of an investment that *exceeds* its book value?

       a. Cash

       b. Accounts payable

       c. Investments

       d. Additions

    5. Financial statements for a Pension Trust Fund

       a. are included in a government's annual financial report.

       b. are categorized as governmental fund financial statements.

       c. are included with the General Fund for financial reporting purposes.

       d. are included with a Special Revenue Fund for financial reporting purposes.

E8-13 (Fill in the blanks)

    1. Agency Funds are classified as _____-type funds.

    2. An Agency Fund is used when the governmental unit is the _____ of resources that belong to some other organization.

3. Agency Funds _____ (do or do not) have title to the resources in the fund.
4. The financial statement for an Agency Fund is _____.
5. Revenues generated for a government by the activities recorded in its Tax Agency Fund are usually recorded in the _____ Fund.
6. Agency Funds _____ (are or are not) used only as tax collection funds.

E8-14 (Multiple choice)

1. The fee for the collection of property taxes by an Agency Fund will result in revenue in which of the following funds?
   a. General Fund and Agency Fund
   b. Agency Fund
   c. Capital Projects Fund
   d. Special Revenue Fund and Agency Fund
   e. None of the above
2. Blaken Township established an Agency Fund to account for the collection and distribution of a general sales tax. The tax is collected for the General Fund, an independent school district, and several independent drainage districts. The school district and the drainage districts are entities that are separate from the city. During the year, $500,000 was collected in sales taxes. Entries to record the collection and distribution of the resources for the city are recorded in which of the following funds?
   a. General Fund
   b. Agency Fund
   c. General Fund and Agency Fund
   d. Special Revenue Fund and Agency Fund
   e. None of the above
3. Collection of resources that must be distributed to other funds should be recorded in an Agency Fund as a debit to Cash and a credit to which account?
   a. Liability   DUe TO
   b. Expenditures
   c. Revenues
   d. Other financing sources
   e. Other financing uses
4. Which of the following funds does not have a fund balance account or net position account?
   a. General Fund
   b. Special Revenue Fund
   c. Capital Projects Fund
   d. Permanent Fund
   e. Agency Fund
5. For which of the following activities might an Agency Fund be used?
   a. Revenue generated from a property tax levy
   b. Expenditures of the General Fund
   c. Debt service for Enterprise Fund debt
   d. Debt service of general obligation bonds used to finance an addition to city hall
   e. None of the above
6. According to GAAP for Pension Trust Funds, which of the following is true?
   a. Revenues must be transferred to a Permanent Fund.
   b. Payments of resources are recorded as deductions.
   c. There is no concept of fund balance or net position.
   d. All disbursements must be made to the General Fund.
   e. None of the above

E8-15 (Journal entries for an Agency Fund)

Prepare the following journal entries in the Bid Deposits Fund, an Agency Fund. This fund is used to record all deposits made by contractors doing work for the city. Any earnings on these resources are required to be paid to the depositing companies.

1. Deposits totaling $750,000 were received.
2. The amount in the previous entry was invested in CDs.
3. Income from the investments totaling $70,000 was received.
4. Deposits of $93,750 were returned to contractors upon successful completion of the projects on which they had been working. In addition, these contractors received $8,750 of earnings on their deposits. (Hint: Do not forget to liquidate some of the investments.)
5. The books were closed for the year.

Problems

P8-1   (Journal entries and statements for a Pension Trust Fund)

The City of Green Meadows has had an employee pension fund for several years. The following is a trial balance for the fund at December 31, 2011, as well as several transactions that occurred during 2012. Prepare (a) the journal entries necessary to record the transactions, (b) a statement of changes in fiduciary net position for the fund for 2012, and (c) a statement of fiduciary net position as of December 31, 2012.

City of Green Meadows
Pension Trust Fund
Employees' Retirement Fund
Trial Balance
December 31, 2011

	Debits	Credits
Cash	$ 52,500	
Investment income receivable	210,000	
Investments—corporate stocks	20,000,000	
Investments—U.S. government securities	30,575,000	
Accrued expenses		$ 12,000
Net position held in trust for pension benefits		50,825,500
	$50,837,500	$50,837,500

1. Contributions from the General Fund totaled $750,000; included in this amount was $258,750 from the employees and $491,250 from the city.
2. Corporate stocks costing $500,000 were purchased.
3. The fund collected interest accrued as of December 31, 2011. Investment income for 2012 totaled $4,800,000, of which $4,290,000 was collected in cash. Investment income earned in 2012 included dividends of $850,000, and the remainder was interest.
4. Employee retirement benefits of $3,500,000 were paid.
5. Additional U.S. government securities totaling $1,100,000 were acquired.
6. Costs of operating the plan were $175,000; of this amount $150,000 was paid in cash, and the remainder was accrued. The accrued expenses at the beginning of the year were also paid. These expenses were administrative in nature.
7. U.S. government securities that had a book value of $500,000 were redeemed for $600,000.
8. The market value of the corporate stocks at the end of the year increased by $1,000,000.

P8-2   (Preparation of a statement of fiduciary net position for a Pension Trust Fund)

The following information is available for Russellville at June 30, 2012. Prepare a statement of fiduciary net position for Russellville's Pension Trust Fund as of June 30, 2012, by reporting the assets and liabilities from the information provided.

Additions—interest	$ 250,000
Member contributions	340,000
Loss on sale of investments	30,000
Cash	180,000
Accrued expenses	56,000
Interest receivable	20,000
Accounts payable	33,000
Due to other funds	54,000
Investments	10,000,000
Deductions—operating costs	42,000
Retirement annuities paid	987,000

P8-3 (Journal entries and financial statements for an Investment Trust Fund)

Pinnacle County operates an Investment Trust Fund for cities located in the county. The following entries are associated with the fund during 2012. Prepare (a) journal entries to record these transactions, (b) a statement of changes in fiduciary net position for the fund for the year ending December 31, 2012 (assume that the Investment Trust Fund began this year) and (c) a statement of fiduciary net position for the fund as of that date.

1. The cities of Clarksville and Kingsville contributed assets of $75,000 and $50,000, respectively.
2. The entire amount received in the previous transaction was invested: $65,000 in CDs and $60,000 in Treasury notes.
3. Interest income of $37,500 was received.
4. CDs totaling $40,000 and Treasury notes totaling $30,000 matured. Interest income of $1,000 was also received.
5. The money received in the previous transaction was reinvested in CDs.
6. Additional interest income was received: $17,500.
7. The General Fund charged the Investment Trust Fund $500 for administrative expenses. This amount was paid in cash.
8. Income of $50,000 was distributed to the participating cities according to the trust agreement (Clarksville 60 percent, Kingsville 40 percent).

P8-4 (Journal entries and financial statements for an Investment Trust Fund)

The City of Titanville established an Investment Trust Fund for Bay Town and Valley City. The cities contributed $200,000 and $100,000, respectively, to the fund. During 2012 the following transactions took place. Prepare journal entries to record the transactions in the Investment Trust Fund.

1. Bay Town contributed CDs valued at $200,000, and Valley City contributed $100,000 to the fund.
2. The cash contributed by Valley City was invested in U.S. government securities.
3. The CDs matured. The principal was $70,000, interest on the CDs was $3,000.
4. The principal amount received in the previous transaction was reinvested in municipal bonds.
5. The fund incurred internal administrative expenses totaling $700, of which $500 was paid in cash.
6. The General Fund charged the Investment Trust Fund $500 for managing the investments. This amount was paid in cash.
7. The trust fund income of $1,800 ($3,000 − $700 − $500) was distributed as provided in the trust agreement: two-thirds to Bay Town and one-third to Valley City.

P8-5 (Journal entries and financial statements for a Private Purpose Trust Fund)

Seaview Township received a $1,000,000 gift from J. R. Chancellor to sponsor an annual community picnic. All reasonable costs associated with sponsoring the picnic are to be paid from the gift. To guarantee proper use of the money, Chancellor made the donation in the form of a trust, which is accounted for as a Private Purpose Trust. The following events and transactions took place during 2012. Record these entries in the Chancellor Community Picnic Fund. Then prepare a statement of changes in fiduciary net position for 2012 and a statement of fiduciary net position as of December 31, 2012, for the fund.

1. The township received the gift.
2. The city paid $10,000 to an advertising agency to publicize the picnic.

3. The cost of permits for the picnic totaled $500.

4. The Seaview Cafe agreed to cater the entire picnic for $75,000, payable in advance.

5. Various performers were engaged to provide entertainment during the picnic at a total cost of $12,500. Cash was paid in advance.

6. The picnic was held and was a great success. The weather cooperated, and picnic attendance met all expectations.

7. The Police Department spent $15,000 for extra police to control the traffic and crowds at the picnic. The trust reimbursed the department in cash for these costs.

8. The Sanitation Department incurred $35,000 of costs in cleaning up after the picnic. The trust agreed to reimburse the department (in the General Fund) for these costs. No cash has yet been paid.

9. The remaining cash, except for $10,000, was invested in CDs. According to the trust agreement, this money could be invested and used to provide for the 2013 picnic.

P8-6   (Journal entries and financial statements for a Private Purpose Trust Fund)

Prepare (a) the journal entries for 2012 necessary to record the following events and transactions for the College Scholarship Fund; (b) a statement of changes in fiduciary fund net position for the fiscal year ending December 31, 2012, for the fund; (c) a statement of fiduciary fund net position as of that date; and (d) the 2012 closing entry (entries) for the fund.

1. The City of Rocky Basin received a $2,000,000 gift from a prominent citizen. The terms of the gift require the city to maintain the principal intact; investment income is to be used to provide college scholarships for deserving graduates of Rocky Basin High School.

2. The city invested the entire gift in CDs.

3. Interest income of $100,000 was received in cash.

4. That $100,000 was reinvested in short-term CDs.

5. The short-term CDs matured, yielding interest income of $1,000.

6. Interest income of $112,000 was received in cash.

7. Scholarships totaling $65,000 were paid to eligible students.

8. Interest income of $2,300 was accrued at the end of 2012.

9. The General Fund charged the Scholarship Fund $3,000: $2,000 for managing the investments and $1,000 for administering the fund. The amounts were unpaid at fiscal year-end.

P8-7   (Journal entries for three Agency Funds and a trial balance for each fund)

Assume that the Town of Boonsville maintains an Agency Fund for its employees' insurance withholdings, another for its employees' income tax withholdings, and a third for its employees' pension contributions. The following are selected transactions incurred during calendar year 2012 that are related to these funds. Prepare the journal entries necessary to record these transactions on the books of the Employees' Insurance Agency Fund, the Employees' Income Tax Agency Fund, and the Employees' Pension Agency Fund. Also, prepare a trial balance for each fund as of December 31, 2012.

1. The town recorded its monthly payroll; salaries totaled $350,000. The withholdings were as follows: $70,000 for employees' income taxes, $30,000 for employees' insurance, and $15,000 for employees' pension contributions. The General Fund paid the appropriate amount to each Agency Fund.

2. The Employees' Insurance Agency Fund made a payment of $25,000 to the various insurance companies providing insurance coverage to the employees.

3. The town recorded its monthly payroll; salaries totaled $375,000. The withholdings were as follows: $75,000 for employees' income taxes, $20,000 for employees' insurance, and $18,000 for employees' pension contributions. The General Fund paid the appropriate amount to each Agency Fund.

4. The town recorded its monthly payroll; salaries totaled $350,000. The withholdings were as follows: $70,000 for employees' income taxes, $30,000 for employees' insurance, and $15,000 for employees' pension contributions. The General Fund paid the appropriate amounts to each Agency Fund.

5. The appropriate Agency Funds made a payment of $215,000 to the U.S. government and $48,000 to the Pension Trust Fund.

6. The town recorded its monthly payroll; salaries totaled $375,000. The withholdings were as follows: $75,000 for employees' income taxes, $20,000 for employees' insurance, and $18,000 for employees' pension contributions. The General Fund paid the appropriate amounts to each Agency Fund.

P8-8   (Pension fund schedule of funding progress)

The following data come from the report prepared by the actuary for York City's retirement system as of December 31, 2012:

Investments (at actuarial value)	$2,921,000
Actuarial accrued liability	$5,586,000
Annual covered payroll	$1,128,000

The actuary's report also notes that the investment earnings assumption used in calculating the actuarial accrued liability was 8 percent, compared with 7.5 percent used in the preceding year.

Use the information to do the following:

1. Compute these ratios: (a) funded ratio and (b) unfunded actuarial accrued liability as a percentage of covered payroll.

2. Discuss the significance of the change in the investment earnings assumption in the calculation of the actuarial accrued liability.

3. Based solely on the information in this problem, discuss whether the system is reasonably funded. What additional data do you need to help reach a conclusion?

Summary Problems

Pension Trust Fund

Leisure City maintains a Pension Trust Fund for its employees. Following is a trial balance for the fund at December 31, 2011:

Leisure City
Pension Trust Fund
Employees' Retirement Fund
Trial Balance
December 31, 2011

	Debits	Credits
Cash	$ 178,750	
Investment income receivable	315,000	
Investments—U.S. government securities	25,287,500	
Investments—corporate stocks	50,575,000	
Accrued expenses		$ 18,000
Net position held in trust for pension benefits		76,338,250
	$76,356,250	$76,356,250

The following transactions took place during 2012:

1. Both Leisure City and its employees are required to contribute to the Employees' Retirement Fund. The fund contributions from the General Fund totaled $1,000,000; included in this amount was $500,000 from the employees and $500,000 from the city.

2. The Employees' Retirement Fund purchased CDs costing $600,000 and U.S. government securities costing $400,000.

3. The Employees' Retirement Fund collected interest accrued as of December 31, 2011. Interest income for 2012 totaled $7,000,000, of which $6,000,000 was collected in cash.
4. The Employees' Retirement Fund paid retirement benefits of $6,100,000.
5. The Employees' Retirement Fund purchased additional U.S. government securities costing $200,000.
6. Costs of operating the plan were $180,000; of this amount $100,000 was paid in cash, and the remainder was accrued. The accrued expenses at the beginning of the year were also paid. These expenses were administrative in nature.
7. The Employees' Retirement Fund redeemed for $510,000 CDs with a book value of $500,000.
8. The fair value of the corporate stocks increased by $50,000 by the end of 2012.

Prepare (a) the journal entries necessary to record these transactions, (b) a statement of changes in fiduciary net position for the fund for 2012, and (c) a statement of fiduciary net position as of December 31, 2012.

Investment Trust Fund

Leisure City established a new Investment Trust Fund to manage the investments of the cities of Odell and Whitt. The cities contributed $500,000 each to the fund. During 2012 the following transactions took place:

1. Leisure City received the contributions from Odell and Whitt.
2. The cash was immediately invested in U.S. government securities.
3. Some of the investments matured. The principal was $300,000. Interest on the securities was $5,000.
4. The principal amount received in the previous transaction was reinvested in municipal bonds.
5. The fund incurred internal administrative expenses totaling $1,000, of which $700 was paid in cash.
6. The Investment Trust Fund paid $900 to an investment adviser for managing the investments. This amount was paid in cash.
7. Accrued interest income at the end of the year totaled $30,000.
8. Cash in the amount of $1,800 was distributed as provided in the trust agreement: one-half to the City of Odell and one-half to Whitt.

Prepare (a) the journal entries to record these events and transactions in the Investment Trust Fund, (b) a statement of changes in fiduciary net position for 2012, and (c) a statement of fiduciary net position as of December 31, 2012.

Agency Fund

Leisure City annually hosts a state fair. The city collects a special 1 percent sales tax levied by the county on all sales made at the fair. The proceeds of the tax and all investment income are used to provide resources to the county to build new roads. The tax is collected by Leisure City and disbursed to the county as provided in the agreement between the two. The dates of the fair spanned two fiscal periods. The following trial balance was available at the end of 2011:

Leisure City
Agency Fund
State Fair Sales Tax Fund
Trial Balance
December 31, 2011

	Debits	Credits
Cash	$ 3,500	
Investments—certificates of deposit	46,600	
Due to other governments		$50,100
	$50,100	$50,100

The following transactions took place during 2012:

1. Investments costing $15,000 were redeemed for a total of $18,000; the difference was investment revenue.
2. The Agency Fund collected $150,000 of sales taxes.
3. The Agency Fund distributed $1,000 to the county.
4. The Agency Fund collected $800 in interest on investments.
5. An additional $13,500 was paid to the county.
6. The Agency Fund paid $35,000 to the county.
7. The remaining investments were redeemed by the Agency Fund for $36,000.
8. The remaining assets in the Agency Fund were transferred to the county.
9. The Agency Fund collected $48,000 of sales taxes in December 2012.

Prepare (a) the entries necessary for the Agency Fund during 2012 and (b) the statement of fiduciary net position for the Agency Fund at the end of 2012.

Chapter 9

Reporting Principles and Preparation of Fund Financial Statements

Statement of Revenues, Expenses, and Changes in Fund Net Position
Statement of Cash Flows

Preparing Fund Financial Statements for Fiduciary Funds

Preparing Notes to the Financial Statements

>   Governmental Financial Reporting in Practice: Disclosing Risks Associated with Bank Deposits and Investments

Preparing Required Supplementary Information
Budgetary Comparison Schedules
Pension and Other Employee Benefit Information

Preparing the Statistical Section

Review Questions

Discussion Scenarios and Issues

Exercises

Problems

Continuing Problems

After completing this chapter, you should be able to do the following:

- Describe the objectives of governmental financial reporting
- Explain how governmental standards define the "financial reporting entity"
- Describe how financial data for component units are incorporated in the financial statements of a reporting entity
- Identify the major sections of a comprehensive annual financial report (CAFR)
- Identify and describe the seven fund financial statements
- Describe the content of management's discussion and analysis
- Discuss the measurement focus and basis of accounting used in the fund financial statements
- Explain the relationship between fund financial statements and combining statements
- Describe the content of budgetary comparison schedules
- Discuss the significance of the notes to financial statements
- Describe the content of the statistical section of the CAFR

G ASB Statement No. 34, "Basic Financial Statements—and Management's Discussion and Analysis—for State and Local Governments," became effective in 2002. Before then, state and local government financial reporting had focused entirely on the fund types discussed in Chapters 4 through 8. Financial statements had separate columns for the General Fund, aggregated Special Revenue Funds, aggregated Capital Projects Funds, and so forth. Because the measurement focus and basis of accounting used for governmental-type funds differed from that used for proprietary-type funds, separate operating statements were prepared for each fund category.

Although this approach had many supporters, it also had many critics. Some critics believed that operating statements for governmental-type funds, based on the current financial resources measurement focus and modified accrual basis of accounting, could mislead the reader because they failed to report the financial effects of current operating transactions and events that did not result in current payment. Others believed there was a need for more highly aggregated financial statements that provided an overview of the operating results and financial position of the government as a whole.

After extensive due process and deliberation, the GASB issued Statement No. 34, a compromise that retained the existing fund-oriented reporting requirement (albeit in somewhat different form), but also added a highly aggregated top layer of "government-wide" financial statements. To prepare the top-layer statements, the fund financial statements for the governmental-type funds must be converted to the economic resources measurement focus and accrual basis of accounting.

To provide a framework for discussing the contents of governmental financial reports, this chapter starts with a brief summary of the GASB's stated objectives for governmental financial reporting and how GASB Statement No. 34 helps meet them. Because governments often conduct some activities through legally separate entities, we then discuss the financial reporting entity, a key aspect of financial reporting mentioned earlier in the text. Most of this chapter deals with the general principles underlying (a) the comprehensive annual financial report (CAFR) issued by many state and local governments and (b) preparation of the *fund* set of financial statements. Chapter 10 covers the *government-wide* set of financial statements, the adjustments to the fund statements needed to produce the government-wide statements, and certain other provisions of GASB Statement No. 34.

To illustrate the financial reporting principles, we continue using extracts from the actual financial statements prepared by Mt. Lebanon, Pennsylvania. You can access Mt. Lebanon's financial report at its web site at www.mtlebanon.org, then clicking on Departments, then Finance Department, then 2009 Comprehensive Annual Financial Report (CAFR).

FINANCIAL REPORTING OBJECTIVES AND GASB STATEMENT NO. 34

GASB Concepts Statement No. 1, "Objectives of Financial Reporting" (May 1987), suggests that state and local governmental financial reporting should meet the needs of three major groups of external users:

- The citizenry—those to whom the government is primarily accountable
- Legislative and oversight bodies—those who directly represent the citizens
- Lenders and creditors—those who provide resources to the government through the capital markets

The GASB considered the financial reporting needs of intergovernmental resource providers and other users of external financial reporting to be encompassed by the needs of the three primary external user groups.

The GASB issued Concepts Statement No. 1 after undertaking a user needs study. Based on the study, the GASB concluded that governmental financial reporting should provide information to assist users in assessing the accountability of public officials and in making economic, social, and political decisions. Accountability was considered to be the paramount objective from which all other objectives must flow. Specifically,

1. Financial reporting should assist in fulfilling government's duty to be publicly accountable and should enable users to assess that accountability by
   a. providing information to determine whether current-year revenues were sufficient to pay for current-year services

    b. demonstrating whether resources were obtained and used in accordance with the government's legally adopted budget, and demonstrating compliance with other finance-related legal or contractual requirements

    c. providing information to assist users in assessing the service efforts and accomplishments of the government

2. Financial reporting should assist users in evaluating the operating results of the government for the year by

    a. providing information about sources and uses of financial resources

    b. providing information about how it financed its activities and met its cash requirements

    c. providing information necessary to determine whether its financial position improved or deteriorated as a result of the year's operations

3. Financial reporting should assist users in assessing the level of services that can be provided by the government and its ability to meet its obligations as they become due by

    a. providing information about its financial position and condition

    b. providing information about its physical and other nonfinancial resources having useful lives that extend beyond the current year, including information that can be used to assess the service potential of those resources

    c. disclosing legal or contractual restrictions on resources and the risk of potential loss of resources[1]

In the Basis for Conclusions to GASB Statement No. 34, the board stated that, taken as a whole, the basic financial statements (including the notes) are designed to meet (or partially meet) all the foregoing objectives of governmental financial reporting. Objectives not met in the fund statements are met in the government-wide statements, to the extent possible, within the constraints of financial statements.

Similar to that of earlier financial reporting standards, the focus of governmental fund financial statements is on inflows, outflows, and balances of current financial resources; amounts available for appropriation; and fiscal compliance. Therefore, as stated by the board, the information provided by those statements should be useful in assessing (a) the sources, uses, and balances of current financial resources; (b) the extent of compliance with legally adopted budgets; (c) actual current financial results compared with legally adopted budgets; and (d) the amounts available for appropriation.

The focus of the government-wide statements is on reporting the operating results and financial position of the government as an economic entity. The GASB states that the government-wide statements will help users assess the finances of the government in its entirety, determine whether its overall financial position improved or deteriorated, evaluate whether the government's current-year revenues were sufficient to pay for current-year services, see the cost of providing services to the citizenry, see how the government financed its programs (through user fees and other program revenues versus general tax revenues), and understand the extent to which the government has invested in capital assets.[2]

In addition to the change in measurement focus and basis of accounting for governmental funds, the government-wide financial statements have several other distinguishing features:

- To avoid potential confusion caused by reporting resources for which the government has a fiduciary responsibility but which it cannot legally use to finance its own activities, fiduciary-type funds are omitted from the government-wide statements.

---

[1]GASB Cod. App. B, pars. 77–79.

[2]GASB Statement No. 34, Preface and Basis for Conclusions, pars. 230–238.

- To provide a broader overview of the government as a whole, certain legally separate entities for which the government has financial accountability are included in the government-wide statements. We will discuss these entities in the next section.
- To provide another perspective on governmental costs and revenues, the government-wide operating statement is formatted in a different manner from that of the fund operating statement. The focus of the government-wide operating statement is on the net expense of the government's activities, not on the change in fund net assets.

Does the financial reporting model introduced by GASB Statement No. 34 effectively achieve all the objectives set forth in GASB Concepts Statement No. 1? Perhaps the most important thing to remember about the data provided by the requirements of GASB Statement No. 34 is that the *fund* financial statements cannot be read in isolation; to overcome the limitations of governmental fund financial data, discussed in Chapter 5, fund financial statements must be read in conjunction with the accrual-basis government-wide statements and the notes.

Further, the objectives of Concepts Statement No. 1 are broad, and there are limits to the kinds of data that financial statements can provide. For example, as discussed later in this chapter, significant information regarding the government's financial condition—objective 3a—is provided outside the basic financial statements, in required information supplementary to the statements and in the statistical section of the CAFR. Also, although the requirement to report on the accrual basis of accounting for governmental-type funds is helpful in achieving objective 1c—"providing information to assist users in assessing the service efforts and accomplishments of the governmental entity"—more data are needed. To accomplish this objective, governments need to measure and report on the outputs (physical quantities of services provided) and outcomes (results achieved because of the services provided) of their programs. GASB Concepts Statement No. 2—"Service Efforts and Accomplishments Reporting," as amended by GASB Concepts Statement No. 5—provides general guidance on this subject.

THE FINANCIAL REPORTING ENTITY

We stated earlier that there are two dimensions to the entity concept in government. In Chapters 3 through 8, we focused on one aspect of the entity concept—funds, the accounting subdivisions *within* a governmental unit. However, there is another aspect to the entity concept in government— one that is similar to the entity concept in private-sector business enterprise.

When the term *reporting entity* is used in the private sector, it refers to the boundaries of a particular financial reporting unit; that is, it identifies *whose* assets, liabilities, revenues, expenses, and equities are embraced within the financial statements of that economic unit. A private-sector business enterprise may exercise control over legally separate organizations by owning a controlling share of their voting stock. Excluding the financial activities of those entities from the financial statements of the parent enterprise would cause the parent's statements to be incomplete and even misleading.

The same type of reporting entity issue also occurs in the public sector, because governments often create and control (or are otherwise financially accountable for) a number of legally separate entities. To illustrate, a government may provide sanitation and hospital services or may supply water to its residents through the legally constituted government, using the General Fund or an Enterprise Fund to account for the services. As an alternative, it may decide to provide these services by creating legally separate corporations. In fact, governments provide many business-type services—such as electricity and water, mass transit, hospitals, parking lots, and toll roads and bridges—through specially created, legally separate corporations. Often, these entities are authorized to sell debt to construct facilities, operate the facilities after they are built, and charge fees for services to pay off the debt and cover their operating costs. Governments even create legally separate entities to perform financing activities for the government itself, sometimes to circumvent constitutional limits on the government's ability to borrow. These entities (referred to as public authorities or public benefit corporations) generally are created by statute, but may be created through a state's not-for-profit corporation laws. Depending on the circumstances, not reporting the financial activities of these legally separate organizations within the financial statements of the parent government could cause the parent's statements to be incomplete and possibly misleading.

Defining the Financial Reporting Entity

Reporting-entity standards for state and local governments are set forth in GASB Statement No. 14, "The Financial Reporting Entity," as amended by GASB Statement No. 61. The reporting entity consists of a *primary government* and its *component units*.

- Primary government: All state governments and general-purpose local governments—such as counties, cities, towns, and villages—are primary governments. A special-purpose government (such as a local school district or hospital district) is also considered a primary government, provided it has a separately elected governing body, is legally separate (e.g., it is created as a body corporate and politic), *and* is *fiscally independent* of other state and local governments. To be fiscally independent, as defined by the GASB, the organization must be authorized to take all three of these specific actions without the approval of another government: (1) determine its budget, (2) levy taxes or set user charges, and (3) issue bonded debt.[3]
- Component units: Component units are legally separate organizations for which the elected officials of the primary government are *financially accountable*. In addition, component units can be other organizations for which, because of the nature and significance of their relationship with the primary government, exclusion would cause the entity's financial statements to be misleading.[4]

Under what circumstances is a primary government financially accountable for a legally separate organization so as to warrant including the legally separate organization in the primary government's financial statements? The issues surrounding those circumstances are sometimes complex because relationships among governmental organizations can be complex. The GASB identifies these two broad sets of circumstances—related to *governance* of the potential component unit—that create *financial accountability*:

1. *Primary government appoints a voting majority of the board.* A primary government is financially accountable for a legally separate organization if
   a. It appoints a voting majority of the organization's governing body, *and*
   b. (1) It is able to impose its will on that organization, *or*
      (2) There is a potential for the organization to provide specific financial benefits to, or impose specific financial burdens on, the primary government.

---

[3]GASB Cod. Sec. 2100.112 and 2100.115.
[4]GASB Statement No. 61, par. 4.b.

2. *Primary government does not appoint a voting majority of the board.* Even if the potential component unit has a separately elected governing board, a governing board appointed by a higher-level government, or a jointly appointed board, a primary government is financially accountable for a legally separate organization if

a. The organization is *fiscally dependent* on the primary government (i.e., the primary government has one or more of these powers over the organization—to approve and modify its budget, to approve its tax levy or user charge rates, or to approve its bonded debt issues), *and*

b. There is a potential for the organization to provide specific financial benefits to, or impose specific financial burdens on, the primary government.[5]

A primary government is able to *impose its will* on an organization if it can significantly influence the programs, activities, or level of services it provides. For example, a mayor can impose his or her will on an organization if he or she has the ability to remove members of the organization's governing board at will, modify or approve its budgets, modify or approve the rates or fees it charges for services, or veto or modify decisions of the governing body.

A primary government has a *financial benefit or burden* relationship with an organization if, for example, any of these conditions exist: (1) the primary government is legally entitled to or can otherwise access the organization's resources; (2) the primary government is legally obligated or has otherwise assumed the obligation to finance the deficits of, or provide financial support to, the organization; or (3) the primary government is obligated in some manner for the organization's debt.[6]

Here are some illustrations of circumstances wherein the "imposition of will" or "benefit/burden" requirements are met:

- A state lottery or off-track betting corporation meets the "benefit/burden" criterion because the law provides that the corporation's net revenues must be remitted to the state.
- A city toll bridge authority meets the "imposition of will" criterion because the law provides that the city council must approve toll rates or that the mayor can remove any board member at will.
- A county building construction authority meets the "benefit/burden" criterion because the law provides that the county will guarantee payment of principal and interest on the debt issued by the authority.

The following scenario describes a financial accountability situation in which the primary government appoints a voting majority of the board: A state creates a public authority to construct and operate a toll road. The authority has the power to issue revenue bonds payable from the tolls and other revenues. Four members of the six-member authority board are appointed by the governor, one is appointed by the senate majority leader, and another by the speaker of the assembly, all for fixed 5-year terms. The law creating the authority states that changes in toll rates may not take effect until approved by a majority of both houses of the legislature and the governor. *Conclusion:* The authority is a component unit of the state because the state (a) appoints a voting majority of the authority's board and (b) can impose its will on the authority through its ability to approve toll rate increases.

---

[5]GASB Statement No. 61, par. 6.a.

[6]GASB standards take a broad view of when a primary government is "obligated in some manner" for the debt of a legally separate entity. The standards provide that the obligation may be either expressed or implied by certain indications that make assumption of the debt probable (GASB Cod. Sec. 2100.132).

The following scenario describes a financial accountability situation even though the primary government does not appoint a voting majority of an organization's governing board: A board of education (BOE) administers the city's public school system. The BOE is separately elected by the citizenry and is organized as a separate legal entity. The BOE has no power to levy taxes or to issue bonds. Instead, the city is legally obligated to finance the BOE's operating and capital activities. The BOE's budget request takes the form of a lump-sum dollar amount, but it contains line items showing how it intends to spend the money. The city council can reject the BOE's request and appropriate a lesser amount, but cannot modify the individual line items. *Conclusion:* The BOE is a component unit of the city because (a) it is fiscally dependent on the city (the city can approve its operating and capital budgets) and (b) the city is legally obligated to financially support the BOE.

Even in the absence of financial accountability, the nature and significance of the relationship between a primary government and an organization may be such that the latter should be reported as a component unit of the primary government. That is, there may be financial or other factors that would cause the primary government's financial statements to be misleading if the organization were to be omitted from the primary government's statements. Professional judgment must be exercised in such situations. For example, for many years New York City's financial statements included the financial activities of a state-created agency whose governing board consisted primarily of state officials or state-appointed officials. The agency was created in the 1970s (during the city's fiscal crisis) for the sole purpose of refinancing a portion of the city's debt. The agency assumed the city's debt, and city sales taxes were diverted by law to that agency so the agency could pay the principal and interest on the debt. In the judgment of the city's officials, the agency's financial activities had to be reported as a Debt Service Fund in the city's financial statements because the city's statements otherwise would have been misleading.

Governmental Financial Reporting in Practice

When Is an Entity a Component Unit?

Here is an example of the thought process behind the decision as to whether an entity is a component unit of a primary government. The Oneida-Herkimer Solid Waste Management Authority was created in 1988 as a public benefit corporation under New York State law to provide solid waste management services for two counties, Oneida and Herkimer. The reporting entity footnote in Oneida County's 2009 financial statements explains that the authority is part of the Oneida County reporting entity because

a. *Oneida County appoints a voting majority of the authority's governing body.* The authority has a 10-member governing board, appointed as follows: four by the Oneida County executive and confirmed by the county legislature, three by the Oneida County legislature, and three by Herkimer County. (Appointing seven of the ten members gives Oneida a voting majority of the authority's governing body.)

b. *There is a potential for the authority to impose specific financial burdens on the county.* According to the note, "[Oneida] County officials do not exercise oversight responsibility for the Authority's operations." But "the County is obligated to finance deficits, if necessary, and the County is a joint guarantor with Herkimer County on the revenue bonds [sold by the Authority]." (The obligation to finance deficits and the guaranty of payment of the authority's debt imposes a potential financial burden on Oneida.)

The authority is not a component unit of Herkimer County because Herkimer does not appoint a majority of the authority's governing board; further, a component unit can be the component unit of only one government. Herkimer County would, however, disclose in a note to its financial statements its financial exposure resulting from the arrangement with Oneida and the authority.

Reporting Component Units in the Reporting Entity's Financial Statements

After all the organizations to be included in the reporting entity are identified, a decision needs to be made as to *how* these organizations should be included in the financial statements. The two methods for inclusion are blending and discrete presentation. *Blending* is the process of treating the funds used by the component unit as if they were the funds of the primary government. This is done by including them with the primary government's other funds in the fund financial statements. *Discrete presentation* of a component unit involves reporting the component unit's funds in a *separate column* in the reporting entity's government-wide financial statements.

Blending is used when the component unit, although legally separate from the primary government, is so intertwined with the primary government that it is, in substance, a part of the primary government. This occurs in any of the following circumstances:

- The component unit's governing body is substantively the same as that of the primary government and (a) there is a potential for the component unit to provide specific financial benefits to, or impose specific financial burdens on, the primary government, or (b) the primary government's management is responsible for the component unit's operations.
- The component unit provides services entirely (or almost entirely) to the primary government or otherwise exclusively (or almost exclusively) benefits the primary government—like an Internal Service Fund.

Governmental Financial Reporting in Practice

When Are Component Units Blended?

Although most component units are reported discretely, the financial statements of financing-type agencies are often blended with the Capital Projects Funds and Debt Service Funds of the primary government. The notes to New York City's financial statements for the year ended June 30, 2010, for example, refer to several blended component units that "despite being legally separate from the primary government, are so integrated with the primary government that they are in substance part of the primary government." Here are some excerpts from the notes regarding the New York City Transitional Finance Authority (TFA):

> TFA, a corporate governmental agency constituting a public benefit corporation and instrumentality of the State of New York, was created in 1997 to assist the City in funding its capital program, the purpose of which is to maintain, rebuild, and expand the infrastructure of the City. . . .
>
>   In addition to State legislative authorization to issue Future Tax Secured bonds for capital purposes . . ., TFA is also authorized to have outstanding Recovery Bonds of $2.5 billion to fund the City's costs related to and arising from events on September 11, 2001, at the World Trade Center . . . .
>
>   TFA does not have any employees; its affairs are administered by employees of the City and of another component unit of the City, for which TFA pays a management fee and overhead . . .

The notes make it clear that the TFA, though legally separate from New York City, is in essence a capital construction financing arm of the city. When it borrows to finance capital construction projects, it functions as a Capital Projects Fund of the city. When it receives personal income taxes (that would otherwise go to the city) so it can repay the debt, the TFA functions as a Debt Service Fund of the city. New York City's fund financial statements report TFA's financial activities as two governmental-type funds—as if the activities were undertaken by the city itself. When reporting its long-term liabilities on June 30, 2010, the city reported total bonds and notes payable of $67.6 billion, of which $20.1 billion represented TFA bonds.

- The component unit's outstanding debt is expected to be repaid entirely (or almost entirely) with resources of the primary government.[7]

Blending should be used, for example, when a specially created, legally separate financing agency issues debt solely to finance construction for the primary government and pays off the debt with rental payments received from the primary government. The financing agency, a component unit, is, in substance, a Debt Service Fund of the primary government and should be treated that way for financial reporting purposes. (See the box "When Are Component Units Blended?")

Discrete presentation is more common than blending. The typical discretely presented organization is one that provides services to the general public, much like an Enterprise Fund. For example, it may operate a toll road, a toll bridge, a lottery, an electric utility, or a public hospital.

In accordance with the reporting requirements of GASB Statement No. 34, the financial information of blended component units is reported in both the fund financial statements and the government-wide financial statements. Financial information of discretely presented component units is reported only in the government-wide statements, as illustrated in Chapter 10. Notes to the reporting entity's financial statements should contain a brief description of the component units and their relationship to the primary government, the rationale for including them in the financial reporting entity, and whether they are blended or discretely presented.

OVERVIEW OF THE COMPREHENSIVE ANNUAL FINANCIAL REPORT

In previous chapters we discussed the process of accumulating financial information for governments. This information is communicated to users of financial information through a *comprehensive annual financial report (CAFR)*. A CAFR should be prepared and published by all governmental entities as a matter of public record. Based on the GASB Statement No. 34 requirements, the major components of a CAFR are as follows:

I. Introductory section
II. Financial section
    A. Auditor's report
    B. Management's discussion and analysis (MD&A)
    C. Basic financial statements
        1. Government-wide financial statements
        2. Fund financial statements
        3. Notes to the financial statements
    D. Required supplementary information other than MD&A
    E. Combining statements, individual fund statements, and schedules
III. Statistical section

Preparing the CAFR is basically an aggregation process. Using the individual fund and component unit financial statements as building blocks, you first prepare the combining statements (see level II.E in the outline). Combining statements aggregate the elements of individual fund statements into totals that are carried forward to higher-level statements. Then the fund financial statements (level II.C.2) are prepared. The fund financial statements are then adjusted to prepare the government-wide financial statements (level II.C.1). The notes in level II.C.3 are often prepared as the financial statements are developed. The MD&A can be prepared after the

---

[7]GASB Cod. Sec. 2600.113 and GASB Statement No. 61, par. 8.a.

financial statements are completed; it is based on the statements and other relevant financial, economic, and demographic data.

The components of the CAFR are discussed briefly in the next few pages. They are covered in greater detail and illustrated in the rest of this chapter and in Chapter 10.

Introductory Section

The CAFR begins with an introductory section that includes a table of contents and a transmittal letter containing comments that the management of the government unit considers important to the reader. Care should be taken to avoid duplication of content in the introductory section and the MD&A.

Financial Section

AUDITOR'S REPORT   The financial section of the CAFR starts with the auditor's report, which contains the auditor's opinion on the government's financial statements. After describing the scope of their audit, the auditors state whether, in their opinion, the basic financial statements present fairly, in all material respects, the financial position and results of operations of the government, in conformity with generally accepted accounting principles. The auditors also indicate the extent to which they examined the other data contained in the CAFR and the nature of their opinion on the other data.

MANAGEMENT'S DISCUSSION AND ANALYSIS (MD&A)   MD&A introduces the basic financial statements and provides an objective analysis of the government's financial operations and financial position, based on facts known to management as of the date of the auditor's report. MD&A should be easily readable and should help the reader understand the fiscal policies, the economic factors, and other matters that affect the data reported in the financial statements.

BASIC FINANCIAL STATEMENTS   The basic financial statements consist of the following:

1. Government-wide financial statements
   a. Statement of net position
   b. Statement of activities
2. Fund financial statements
   a. Governmental funds
      (1) Balance sheet
      (2) Statement of revenues, expenditures, and changes in fund balances
   b. Proprietary funds
      (1) Statement of net position
      (2) Statement of revenues, expenses, and changes in fund net position
      (3) Statement of cash flows
   c. Fiduciary funds
      (1) Statement of fiduciary net position
      (2) Statement of changes in fiduciary net position

Notes to the financial statements provide information that is essential for fair presentation of the financial statements but is not shown on the face of the statements. Notes are, therefore, an integral part of the statements themselves.

REQUIRED SUPPLEMENTARY INFORMATION OTHER THAN MD&A   Required supplementary information includes schedules, statistical data, and other information that is identified by the GASB as essential for financial reporting and that should be presented with, but not as part of, the basic financial statements. For example, in addition to MD&A, the GASB requires that governmental units prepare budgetary comparison schedules for certain funds, as well as certain data on pensions and OPEB.

COMBINING STATEMENTS, INDIVIDUAL FUND STATEMENTS, AND SCHEDULES   Combining financial statements are needed if the primary government has more than one nonmajor fund or the reporting entity has more than one nonmajor component unit. Because the focus of the fund financial statements is on *major* funds (defined later in this chapter), financial information for the total nonmajor funds is presented in a single column of the fund financial statements. Combining financial statements for nonmajor funds and component units provide details on each of those funds or units. Although they are presented in the CAFR, combining statements are not classified as basic financial statements.

Schedules included in the CAFR provide useful details not otherwise included in the basic financial statements. Schedules might, for example, be prepared to present additional details regarding sources of revenues and object-of-expenditure data for each department. Schedules could also be used to pull together into a more useful format data that might be spread throughout the various financial statements.

Statistical Section

The *statistical section* of the CAFR provides financial report users with trend data helpful in assessing the government's financial and economic condition. The statistical section covers such matters as the government's capacity to raise revenues and the extent of the government's long-term debt burden. The GASB does not require a statistical section to be prepared as part of the basic financial statements or as required supplementary information; rather, the statistical section is prepared by governments that choose to issue a CAFR.

MINIMUM EXTERNAL FINANCIAL REPORTING REQUIREMENTS

CAFRs are often lengthy documents—Mt. Lebanon's CAFR, for example, is more than 130 pages long. For external financial reporting purposes, a government may wish to issue *general purpose financial reports* separately from the CAFR. For example, when official statements are prepared for bond offerings, financial statements are needed, but not in the detail provided in a CAFR. Also, some governments, especially smaller ones, question whether the benefits of issuing a CAFR justify the expense of preparing it.

To accommodate the need for financial reporting without the detail that goes into a CAFR, the GASB has established *minimum requirements* for general purpose external financial statements. The minimum requirements consist of the MD&A, the basic financial statements, and required supplementary financial information other than MD&A (levels II.B, II.C, and II.D of the CAFR). Exhibit 9-1 illustrates these minimum requirements and how they relate to each other.[8]

---

[8]GASB Cod. Sec. 2200.103.

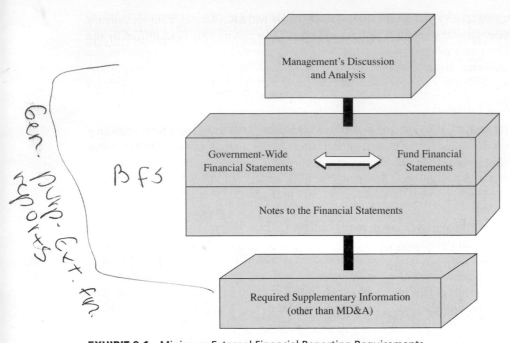

Gen. Purp. Ext. Fin?

BFS

EXHIBIT 9-1 Minimum External Financial Reporting Requirements

PREPARING MANAGEMENT'S DISCUSSION AND ANALYSIS

GASB Statement No. 34 requires that the basic financial statements be preceded by an objective analytical commentary called management's discussion and analysis (MD&A). MD&A provides an analysis of the government's financial activities and financial position; it is based on facts, decisions, and conditions known to management as of the date of the auditor's report. It should focus on the primary government, compare the current year with the previous one, and discuss both positive and negative aspects of that comparison. MD&A should cover the following:

- *Brief discussion of basic financial statements.* Discussion of how the government-wide and fund financial statements relate to each other, and why the results reported in the two sets of statements either reinforce each other or provide additional information.
- *Condensed financial information from the government-wide statements comparing the current and prior years.* Condensed year-to-year comparison of financial data (such as current assets and long-term assets, current liabilities and long-term liabilities, total revenues, total expenses, and excess of revenues over expenses before special items, extraordinary items, and transfers) supports narrative analysis of financial position and results of operations.
- *Analysis of the government's overall financial position and results of operations.* The objective of this analysis is to help users assess whether the government's financial position improved or deteriorated as a result of the year's operations. Covering both governmental and business-type activities, the analysis explains the causes of significant changes from the previous year, such as changes in tax rates and numbers of government employees. Major economic factors affecting operating results (such as changes in tax bases and employment rates) should also be discussed.

Governmental Financial Reporting in Practice

Explaining the Causes of Tax Revenue Increases or Decreases

Like many other governments with economy-sensitive tax bases, New York City's fiscal year 2009 tax revenues declined sharply from the previous year. Here are some of the reasons for the decrease, as explained in the MD&A section of the City's 2009 CAFR:

- The overall decrease in sales and use taxes was driven primarily by a large drop in mortgage tax collections due to a slowdown in mortgage originations and tighter lending standards that required higher down payments.
- The large decrease in personal income tax revenue was caused by employment losses, a steep decline in bonus payouts [in the financial services industry] in the first quarter of the calendar year, and a drop in nonwage income stemming from a decline in capital gains realizations.
- Record losses were posted by financial services entities in calendar years 2007 and 2008, affecting the general corporation taxes.
- A decrease in other taxes is primarily due to a large decrease in real property transaction taxes, caused by a steep decline in the volume and average sales price in both the residential and commercial markets.

By contrast, New York City reported in its 2010 MD&A that the overall increase in sales and use taxes was driven primarily by "a sales tax increase and strong tourism consumption."

Source: MD&A parts of CAFR, the City of New York, NY, June 30, 2009 (p. 11) and 2010 (p. 11).

- *Analysis of balances and transactions of individual funds.* This analysis covers reasons for significant changes in fund balances or fund net position. It also addresses restrictions and other limitations on the availability of fund resources for future use.
- *Analysis of budgetary variations.* A discussion is required of significant variances between the original budget, the final budget, and actual results on a budgetary basis for the General Fund. Currently known reasons for variations that might significantly affect future services or liquidity should also be discussed.
- *Capital asset and long-term debt activity.* This analysis covers significant transactions and events affecting capital assets and long-term debt (such as capital expenditure commitments, credit rating changes, and debt limitations) that might affect the financing of planned facilities or services.
- *Infrastructure assets.* For governments using the modified approach to report infrastructure assets (covered in Chapter 10), this discussion includes significant changes in the condition assessment of assets from previous assessments, how the current condition assessment compares with the desired condition level, and significant differences between estimated and actual amounts spent during the year to maintain the assets.
- *Future effects.* A description needs to be included of facts, decisions, or conditions currently known to management that are expected to significantly affect the financial position or results of operations of the government.

Exhibit 9-2 contains excerpts from the MD&A prepared by Mt. Lebanon, Pennsylvania, for its calendar year 2009 annual financial report. These excerpts cover the analysis of the government-wide and the fund financial statements. Notice the comparisons with data for both the previous year's actual results and the current year's budget.

> **Mt. Lebanon, Pennsylvania**
> **Management's Discussion and Analysis (Excerpts)**
> **December 31, 2009**
>
> **Financial Analysis of the Municipality as a Whole**
> Total government-wide revenues of $37.6 million were derived largely from charges for services, property taxes, and earned income taxes. Total revenues were virtually flat for the year, with a slight decrease in 2009 of $72,049 compared to 2008. . . .
>   Total program expenses in 2009 were $33.7 million, which is $1.3 million less than the previous year. Departments did an excellent job of controlling costs and only spending funds on necessary items. . . . Increases in fringe benefit costs affected results of police and fire [departments].
>
> **Financial Analysis of the Municipality's Funds—Revenues**
> Total operating revenues exceeded budget by $994,032. In 2009, a delinquent real estate tax account was settled, three commercial properties were sold (resulting in higher [than budgeted] transfer taxes), and earned income tax budgeted revenues proved to be low ([the budget] had anticipated a [greater] impact from the economic downturn). In addition, revenues were realized from an unbudgeted grant, from the recognition of previously escrowed alarm fines, and from assessment billings that were sent out in early 2009. Recreation and magazine revenues both were below budget in 2009, but expenditure controls offset the revenues shortfall.
>
> **Bond Ratings**
> The Municipality maintained a strong investment grade bond rating of As2 from Moody's Investor Service. This rating was upgraded in 2001 from As3 and was reaffirmed in 2009. More detailed information about the Municipality's general long-term debt activity can be found in Note 7 of the notes to financial statements.

EXHIBIT 9-2   Management's Discussion and Analysis

Source: Comprehensive Annual Financial Report, Mt. Lebanon, Pennsylvania, 2009, pp. 21, 25, and 29

PREPARING FUND FINANCIAL STATEMENTS: GENERAL

Focus on Major Funds

The fund financial statements are prepared from the individual fund statements illustrated in Chapters 4 through 8. Because the focus of fund financial statements is on the primary government's *major* funds, preparing them requires a determination as to which funds are major. GASB Statement No. 34, amended by Statement No. 37, defines a *major fund* as

a. The government's main operating fund (the General Fund or its equivalent), and

b. A governmental or Enterprise Fund (including a blended component unit) whose total assets, liabilities, revenues, or expenditures/expenses are at least 10 percent of the corresponding element total (assets, liabilities, and so forth) for all funds of that category or type (i.e., total governmental or total Enterprise Funds) and the same element that met the 10 percent criterion is also at least 5 percent of the corresponding element total for all governmental and Enterprise Funds combined, and

c. Any other governmental or Enterprise Fund that the government's officials believe is particularly important to financial statement users (e.g., because of public interest or consistency in reporting).[9]

---

[9]GASB Cod. Sec. 2200.152 and 153.

Financial information for each major fund is presented in a separate column of the fund financial statements. Funds that do not meet the definition of major are "nonmajor" funds, which are aggregated and displayed in a single column in the fund statements. Combining statements for nonmajor funds are not required, but may be presented as supplementary information. As a practical matter, many governments report the nonmajor funds in the combining statements section (level II.E) of the CAFR.

To illustrate the application of the 10 percent criterion, see Tables 9-1 through 9-4 on pages 325 through 328. Notice that Mt. Lebanon's Sewage Fund is major partly because its total assets ($4,370 thousand) are more than 10 percent of the total governmental fund assets ($18,306 thousand). Mt. Lebanon's Capital Projects Fund is major partly because its total expenditures ($4,496 thousand) are more than 10 percent of the total governmental fund expenditures ($37,936 thousand). If Capital Projects Fund expenditures were to dip below the 10 percent threshold in the next year, Mt. Lebanon's officials could nevertheless continue reporting that fund as major because of continuing public interest in it. Notice that Mt. Lebanon did not report its Debt Service Fund as major because it did not meet the 10 percent threshold in any element; if they believed it was useful to do so, however, Mt. Lebanon's officials could have reported that fund as major.

Major fund reporting requirements do not apply to Internal Service Funds. Instead, the combined totals for all Internal Service Funds should be presented in a single column to the right of the total Enterprise Funds column. A combining statement may be prepared to report the details of the individual Internal Service Funds.

Measurement Focus and Basis of Accounting

Financial statements for governmental funds should be presented using the *current financial resources measurement focus* and *modified accrual basis of accounting*, as described in Chapters 2, 4, 5, and 6. This means that capital assets acquired with governmental fund resources and general long-term debt (such as the unmatured principal of bonds and other forms of long-term indebtedness) are not reported as assets and liabilities in the governmental fund financial statements. These assets and liabilities are, however, reported in the government-wide financial statements, as described in Chapter 10. Financial statements for proprietary funds and fiduciary funds should be reported using the *economic resources measurement focus* and *accrual basis of accounting*, as described in Chapters 7 and 8, respectively.

Special and Extraordinary Items

GASB Statement No. 34, as amended by GASB Statement No. 62, paragraphs 45–49, requires that the effects of events or transactions that are special or extraordinary be displayed separately in operating statements prepared for governmental and proprietary funds. *Special items* are significant transactions or events *within the control of management* that are *either* unusual in nature *or* infrequent in occurrence; *extraordinary items* are transactions or events that are *both* unusual in nature *and* infrequent in occurrence. An item is unusual in nature if the underlying event possesses a high degree of abnormality, taking into account the environment in which the government operates. The GASB has stated specifically that Chapter 9 municipal bankruptcy meets the criteria for classification as extraordinary.[10]

---

[10]GASB Statement No. 58, Basis for Conclusions, par. 48.

The accounting effects of special or extraordinary transactions or events could be gains or losses (resulting, for example, from selling operating assets or remeasuring assets and liabilities), revenues or expenses (resulting, for example, from cleanup costs, professional fees, or grants from other governments), or a combination of those items. In its basis for conclusions to GASB Statement No. 34, the board noted that a reason for requiring separate reporting of special items is to highlight significant one-shot financing measures, such as certain sales of capital assets.[11] If the effects of special and extraordinary transactions and events were not highlighted, an analyst using past data to help assess future resource inflows and inflows could be misled.

PREPARING FUND FINANCIAL STATEMENTS FOR GOVERNMENTAL FUNDS

Balance Sheet

In the fund set of financial statements, the balance sheet prepared for governmental type funds provides, in columnar form, information about the current financial resources of each major fund, the total of the nonmajor funds, and the total of all funds. As discussed in Chapters 2 and 5, resources and claims against the resources are presented in balance sheet format: assets + deferred outflows of resources = liabilities + deferred inflows of resources + fund balance. The fund balance is reported in up to five classifications.

Table 9-1 shows the governmental funds balance sheet for Mt. Lebanon, Pennsylvania, as of December 31, 2009, and Table 9-2 shows the combining balance sheet for Mt. Lebanon's nonmajor governmental funds. The combining statement is not a basic statement, but is presented here to illustrate its relationship to the basic statement.

Notice that, because all the interfund transactions were among governmental-type funds, the totals of the "due from other funds" and "due to other funds" accounts equal each other in Table 9-1. The "due from" and "due to" totals are eliminated against each other when the government-wide financial statements are prepared.

The notes to Mt. Lebanon's financial statements (see Exhibit 9-3) later in the chapter indicate that Mt. Lebanon considers earned income tax revenues and certain other revenues to be "available" if collected within 30 days of the end of the accounting period. Many governments use periods greater than 30 days when defining *available* for income taxes and sales taxes, as noted in the footnote on page 136 in Chapter 5. GASB standards provide that when an asset is recorded in governmental fund financial statements but the revenue is not available, the government should report a deferred inflow of resources until the revenues become available. The deferred inflows reported in Table 9-1 relate to the tax and other receivables reported as assets.

Finally, notice how the fund balance section displays the constraints on the use of the governmental fund resources. The loans receivable in Mt. Lebanon's General Fund are long term and are, therefore, *currently* "nonspendable." The use of Sewage Fund, Capital Projects Fund, and Library Fund resources is "restricted" by requirements of a federal agency, bond covenants, and donor requirements, respectively.

Statement of Revenues, Expenditures, and Changes in Fund Balances

The governmental funds statement of revenues, expenditures, and changes in fund balances reports financial information about inflows, outflows, and balances of resources, based on the

---

[11]GASB Statement No. 34, Basis for Conclusions, par. 378.

TABLE 9-1	Governmental Funds—Balance Sheet

Mt. Lebanon, Pennsylvania
Balance Sheet
Governmental Funds
December 31, 2009
(in thousands of dollars)

non-major fund

major funds

	General	Sewage	Capital Projects	Other	Total
Assets	$ 5,641	$3,698	$447	$634	$10,420
Cash and cash equivalents					
Receivables:					
Taxes	3,751	—	—	—	3,751
Assessments	16	672	—	—	688
Accounts	565	—	17	—	582
Due from other funds	630	—	520	—	1,150
Due from other governments	472	—	—	—	472
Loans receivable	760	—	—	—	760
Other	468	—	—	15	483
Total assets	$12,303	$4,370	$984	$649	$18,306
Liabilities					
Accounts payable	$ 595	$ 941	$590	$ 9	$ 2,135
Advance deposits	480	—	—	95	575
Due to other funds	—	875	114	161	1,150
Accrued payroll	848	—	—	—	848
Total liabilities	1,923	1,816	704	265	4,708
Deferred Inflows of Resources					
Deferred revenue	2,613	302	17	—	2,932
Fund Balances					
Nonspendable	700	—	—	—	700
Restricted	—	2,252	263	165	2,680
Assigned for subsequent year's budget	1,896	—	—	—	1,896
Assigned for other purposes	1,426	—	—	219	1,645
Unassigned	3,685	—	—	—	3,685
Total fund balances	7,767	2,252	263	384	10,666
Total liabilities, deferred inflows of resources, and fund balances	$12,303	$4,370	$984	$649	$18,306

See accompanying notes to financial statements.

Source: Adapted from the Comprehensive Annual Financial Report, Mt. Lebanon, Pennsylvania, December 31, 2009. We updated the format of these statements to show the effects of changes in accounting standards after the statements were prepared.

| **TABLE 9-2** | Nonmajor Governmental Funds—Combining Balance Sheet |

Mt. Lebanon, Pennsylvania
Combining Balance Sheet
Other (Nonmajor) Governmental Funds
December 31, 2009
(in thousands of dollars)

	Highway Aid	Library	Capital Assessments	Debt Service	Total
Assets					
Cash and cash equivalents	$ —	$539	$ 95	$ —	$634
Other	—	15	—	—	15
Total assets	$ —	$554	$ 95	$ —	$649
Liabilities					
Accounts payable	$ —	$ 9	$ —	$ —	$ 9
Advance deposits	—	—	95	—	95
Due to other funds	—	161	—	—	161
Total liabilities	—	170	95	—	265
Fund Balances					
Restricted	—	165	—	—	165
Assigned for other purposes	—	219	—	—	219
Unassigned	—	—	—	—	—
Total fund balances	—	384	—	—	384
Total liabilities and fund balances	$ —	$554	$ 95	$ —	$649

Source: Adapted from the Comprehensive Annual Financial Report, Mt. Lebanon, Pennsylvania, December 31, 2009. The format was updated to show the effects of changes in accounting standards after these statements were prepared.

current financial resources measurement focus and modified accrual basis of accounting. Similar to the balance sheet, this statement contains separate columns for each major fund, the total of the nonmajor funds, and the total of all funds

Table 9-3 shows the governmental funds statement of revenues, expenditures, and changes in fund balances for Mt. Lebanon, Pennsylvania, for the year ended December 31, 2009. Table 9-4 shows Mt. Lebanon's combining statement for its nonmajor governmental funds. Notice, in particular, the relatively significant amount of activity reported under the caption "Other Financing Sources (Uses)" in both statements:

- Library Fund operations were financed not only with revenues, such as intergovernmental grants, but also with a transfer of resources from the General Fund. Mt. Lebanon's Debt Service Fund pays debt service with transfers from the General Fund and the Sewage Fund. Details of interfund transfers are required to be explained in the notes in order to aid in analyzing the financial statements.[12]

---

[12]GASB Cod. Sec. 2300.121.

Mt. Lebanon, Pennsylvania
Statement of Revenues, Expenditures, and Changes in Fund Balances
Governmental Funds
For the Year Ended December 31, 2009
(in thousands of dollars)

	General	Sewage	Capital Projects	Other	Total
Revenues					
Real estate taxes	$10,718	$ —	$ —	$ —	$10,718
Earned income taxes	9,539	—	—	—	9,539
Other taxes	2,504	—	—	—	2,504
Licenses, permits, fees, fines	832	7,043	—	72	7,947
Intergovernmental grants	1,241	—	—	1,224	2,465
Recreation	2,365	—	—	—	2,365
Other	2,048	41	6	192	2,287
Total revenues	29,247	7,084	6	1,488	37,825
Expenditures					
Current:					
General government	4,216	—	71	—	4,287
Community development	1,388	—	—	—	1,388
Public works	6,216	3,734	—	631	10,581
Human services	293	—	—	1,722	2,015
Culture and recreation	2,594	—	—	—	2,594
Public safety	9,846	—	—	—	9,846
Debt service:					
Principal	—	—	—	1,640	1,640
Interest	—	—	—	870	870
Capital outlay	280	—	4,425	10	4,715
Total expenditures	24,833	3,734	4,496	4,873	37,936
Excess (deficiency) of revenues over expenditures	4,414	3,350	(4,490)	(3,385)	(111)
Other Financing Sources (Uses)					
Transfers in	369	—	2,555	3,432	6,356
Transfers out	(3,364)	(2,992)	—	—	(6,356)
Proceeds—bond issuance	—	—	2,115	—	2,115
Bond issuance premium	—	—	3	—	3
Total other financing sources (uses)	(2,995)	(2,992)	4,673	3,432	2,118
Net change in fund balance	1,419	358	183	47	2,007
Fund balance, beginning of year	6,348	1,894	80	337	8,659
Fund balance, end of year	$ 7,767	$ 2,252	$ 263	$ 384	$10,666

See accompanying notes to financial statements.

Source: Adapted from the Comprehensive Annual Financial Report, Mt. Lebanon, Pennsylvania, December 31, 2009.

TABLE 9-4   Governmental Funds—Combining Statement of Revenues, Expenditures, and Changes in Fund Balances

Mt. Lebanon, Pennsylvania
Combining Statement of Revenues, Expenditures, and Changes in Fund Balances
Other (Nonmajor) Governmental Funds
For the Year Ended December 31, 2009
(in thousands of dollars)

	Highway Aid	Library	Capital Assessments	Debt Service	Total
Revenues					
Licenses, permits, fees, fines	$ —	$ 72	$—	$ —	$ 72
Intergovernmental grants	622	602	—	—	1,224
Other	9	173	10	—	192
Total revenues	631	847	10	—	1,488
Expenditures					
Current:					
Public works	631	—	—	—	631
Human services	—	1,722	—	—	1,722
Debt service:					
Principal	—	—	—	1,640	1,640
Interest	—	—	—	870	870
Capital outlay	—	—	10	—	10
Total expenditures	631	1,722	10	2,510	4,873
Excess (deficiency) of revenues over expenditures	—	(875)	—	(2,510)	(3,385)
Other Financing Sources (Uses)					
Transfer in from General Fund	—	922	—	2,443	3,365
Transfer in from Sewage Fund	—	—	—	67	67
Total other financing sources (uses)	—	922	—	2,510	3,432
Net change in fund balance	—	47	—	—	47
Fund balance, beginning or year	—	337	—	—	337
Fund balance, end of year	$ —	$ 384	$—	$ —	$ 384

Source: Adapted from the Comprehensive Annual Financial Report, Mt. Lebanon, Pennsylvania, December 31, 2009.

• Mt. Lebanon's capital projects were financed with the proceeds of a new bond issue and a transfer from the Sewage Fund.

The financial information in the governmental fund financial statements is reconciled with the financial information in the corresponding government-wide financial statements. The reconciliation, needed because different measurement focuses and bases of accounting are used in the two sets of statements, is illustrated in Chapter 10.

PREPARING FUND FINANCIAL STATEMENTS FOR PROPRIETARY FUNDS

As discussed in Chapters 2 and 7, there are two types of proprietary funds—Enterprise Funds and Internal Service Funds. Fund financial statements for Enterprise Funds are presented in the same manner as they are presented for governmental funds; that is, with separate columns for each major fund, a column for the aggregate of all nonmajor Enterprise Funds, and a total column. As is the case with governmental funds, combining statements for nonmajor Enterprise Funds are not required but may be presented as supplementary information. Major fund reporting requirements, however, do not apply to Internal Service Funds; instead, the combined totals of all Internal Service Funds are reported in a separate column to the right of the total Enterprise Funds column.

Also, as previously discussed, three financial statements are prepared for proprietary funds: a statement of net position; a statement of revenues, expenses, and changes in fund net position; and a cash flows statement. The financial statements are prepared using the economic resources measurement focus and the accrual basis of accounting.

Statement of Net Position

GASB Statement No. 63, "Financial Reporting of Deferred Outflows of Resources, Deferred Inflows of Resources, and Net Position" (June 2011), requires any deferred outflows of resources to be separated from assets and any deferred inflows of resources to be separated from liabilities when reporting on the net position of proprietary funds. The GASB encourages presentation of the statement of net position in this format: (assets + deferred outflows of resources) − (liabilities + deferred inflows of resources) = net position. However, the balance sheet format: assets + deferred outflows of resources = liabilities + deferred inflows of resources + net position, may also be used. Regardless of the format, assets and liabilities should be presented in *classified* form in order to distinguish between those that are current and those that are noncurrent. Current assets are assets that are expected to be converted to cash or consumed in operations within 1 year, and current liabilities are liabilities that are due to be paid within 1 year.

Net position should be classified in three components: (1) invested in capital assets, net of related debt, (2) restricted, and (3) unrestricted. The first component represents the capital assets of the proprietary funds minus accumulated depreciation and outstanding balances of bonds, notes, or other borrowings attributable to acquiring, constructing, or improving those assets.

A portion of the net position is reported as *restricted* when constraints are imposed on the use of resources either externally (by creditors, grantors, or laws or regulations of other governments) or by the entity's constitution or enabling legislation. For example, restrictions may be imposed by a debt covenant or by a higher-level government's requirement that resources be spent only for a particular capital project.

See Chapter 7 for illustrations of the statement of net position for proprietary funds. Although Mt. Lebanon has no proprietary funds, Table 2-9 in Chapter 2 (page 39) shows the statement of net position of the Mt. Lebanon Parking Authority, a component unit of Mt. Lebanon that uses proprietary fund accounting and financial reporting. Notice that Mt. Lebanon's statement of net position is presented in classified format, with current assets and liabilities separated from noncurrent assets and liabilities. Therefore, the portions of the long-term bonded debt and the note payable to Mt. Lebanon that are due to be paid in 1 year are classified as current.

Notice also the net position caption "Invested in capital assets, net of related debt" in the amount of $4,317 thousand. The amount invested in capital assets is the total of capital assets not being depreciated ($2,727 thousand), capital assets net of accumulated depreciation ($5,990 thousand), and deferred financing costs ($56 thousand—included in Prepaid expenses), for a total of $8,773 thousand. Related debt is the total of the current and noncurrent debt to bondholders and to Mt. Lebanon ($545 thousand, $34 thousand, $3,285 thousand, and $592 thousand), for a total of $4,456 thousand. Capital assets ($8,773 thousand) minus related debt ($4,456 thousand) equals $4,317 thousand.

Statement of Revenues, Expenses, and Changes in Fund Net Position

The proprietary funds operating statement is called the statement of revenues, expenses, and changes in fund net position. As discussed in Chapters 2 and 7, this statement should be prepared in a format that distinguishes between operating and nonoperating revenues and expenses, and that provides separate subtotals for *operating revenues, operating expenses, and operating income*. Nonoperating revenues (expenses) are then detailed, leading to a total that is generally captioned "Increase (decrease) in net position." If there are other resource inflows or outflows (such as capital contributions, special and extraordinary items, or interfund transfers), another subtotal captioned "Income before other revenues, etc." would be placed after adjusting for nonoperating revenues (expenses), as shown in Chapter 2 on page 41.

For illustrations of the format of the statement of revenues, expenses, and changes in fund net position, see Chapter 7 as well as the Mt. Lebanon Parking Authority statement in Table 2-8 on page 38. Notice, in particular, the nature of the items comprising operating expenses, the separate caption for operating income, and the nature of the items comprising nonoperating revenues (expenses).

Statement of Cash Flows

GASB Statement No. 34 also requires preparation of a statement of cash flows for proprietary activities, using the direct method of presenting cash flows from operating activities. For illustrations, see Chapter 7 as well as the Mt. Lebanon Parking Authority statement of cash flows in Table 2-10 on page 40. Notice that the statement of cash flows contains a reconciliation of the operating income to the net cash provided by operating activities.

The statement of cash flows supplements the accrual-basis statement of revenues, expenses, and changes in fund net position by giving the reader a more complete understanding of the nature of the fund's financing activities. For example, the statement of cash flows shows how much was spent to acquire capital assets and how much was spent to pay debt principal, neither of which is evident from the accrual-basis financial statements. With regard to the Mt. Lebanon Parking Authority, the statement of cash flows also shows that, because depreciation ($452 thousand) did not require a cash outlay, the net cash flows from operating activities ($761 thousand) helped provide cash to pay the principal ($564 thousand) and interest ($169 thousand) on long-term debt and to acquire capital assets ($217 thousand).

PREPARING FUND FINANCIAL STATEMENTS FOR FIDUCIARY FUNDS

As discussed in Chapters 2 and 8, GASB Statement No. 34 requires two fiduciary fund financial statements, a statement of fiduciary net position and a statement of changes in fiduciary net position. These statements should provide information about all fiduciary funds of the primary government, as well as component units that are fiduciary in nature. The statements should have separate columns for each *fund type*; that is, Pension and Other Employee Benefit Trust Funds, Investment Trust Funds, Private Purpose Trust Funds, and Agency Funds.

The requirement for showing individual major funds does not extend to fiduciary fund basic financial statements. Financial statements for *individual* pension and postemployment health care plans, however, must be presented in the notes to the financial statements if separate GAAP financial statements have not been issued. Generally, such statements are issued by the plan administrators; if so, the notes need only contain information about how to obtain the statements.

The statement of fiduciary net position should have information about the assets, liabilities, and net position for each fund type. The statement of changes in fiduciary net position reports additions to, deductions from, and net increase (or decrease) for the year in net position. For illustrations of the format of these statements, see Chapter 8 and Mt. Lebanon's Pension Trust Fund financial statements in Tables 2-12 and 2-13 on pages 44 and 45. For Pension Trust Funds, the financial statements do not sufficiently describe the financial position of the pension plan; to help the reader ascertain the financial position of the pension plan, additional data must be provided in the notes to financial statements and required supplementary information, as discussed in Chapters 8 and 14.

PREPARING NOTES TO THE FINANCIAL STATEMENTS

Notes to the financial statements contain information essential to a user's understanding of the reporting government's financial position and resource inflows and outflows. The notes provide (a) descriptions of the accounting and finance-related policies underlying amounts recognized in the financial statements; (b) more detail about or explanations of the amounts recognized in the financial statements; and (c) additional information about financial position or inflows and outflows of resources that does not meet the criteria for recognition in the statements. The notes are an integral part of the financial statements, as indicated by the notation "See accompanying notes" at the bottom of each statement.[13]

The focus of the notes should be on the primary government—specifically, its governmental activities, business-type activities, major funds, and nonmajor funds in the aggregate—but certain information should also be included on the major component units. Notes tend to be lengthy and may run 30 to 40 pages. The discussion that follows covers some, but by no means all, of the disclosure requirements.

The notes start with a summary of the primary government's significant accounting policies. Among the matters covered are these:

- Description of the government-wide financial statements
- Description of the component units of the financial reporting entity, the criteria for including them in the reporting entity, and their relationships with the primary government
- Description of the activities accounted for in certain columns (major funds, Internal Service Funds, and fiduciary-type funds) in the basic financial statements. For example, New York City's notes say: "General Fund. This is the general operating fund of the City.

---

[13]GASB Concepts Statement No. 3, "Communication Methods in General Purpose External Financial Reports That Contain Basic Financial Statements," par. 35.

Governmental Financial Reporting in Practice

Disclosing Risks Associated with Bank Deposits and Investments

During the 1980s, several governments suffered losses when they invested in a type of financial instrument called repurchase agreements. These instruments have characteristics similar to those of bank deposits, because they involve giving cash to another party who promises to return the cash (with interest) and who pledges collateral for the promise. When the governments didn't hold the collateral and the securities dealers handling the investments collapsed, the governments were left holding empty promises. This caused the GASB to require certain note disclosures on deposits and investments.

    One of the required disclosures concerns *custodial credit risk*—the risk that "in the event of failure of a depository financial institution, a government will not be able to recover deposits or will not be able to recover collateral securities that are in the possession of an outside party." GASB standards say that bank deposits are exposed to custodial risk if they are not covered by depository insurance and the deposits are uncollateralized, collateralized with securities held by the pledging financial institution, or collateralized with securities held by the pledging financial institution's trust department or agent but not in the name of the depositor government.

    If a government's bank deposits are exposed to custodial risk at the end of the accounting period, the government must disclose the amount of exposed balances and the nature of the exposure. For example, the notes to New York City's June 30, 2009, financial statements said that the carrying amount of the unrestricted cash and cash equivalents was $10.054 billion and the bank balances were $5.373 billion. Of the unrestricted bank balances, $29.2 million was exposed to custodial credit risk because the bank balances were uninsured or uncollateralized. The notes also said that the city uses independent bank rating agencies to determine the financial soundness of each bank and that it makes periodic operational and credit reviews of its banking relationships.

Substantially all tax revenues, Federal and State aid (except aid for capital projects), and other operating revenues are accounted for in the General Fund. This fund also accounts for expenditures and transfers as appropriated in the Expense Budget, which provides for the City's day-to-day operations. . . ."

- The measurement focus and basis of accounting used in the government-wide statements, and the revenue recognition policies (such as length of time used to define *available*) in the fund financial statements
- The policy for capitalizing assets and estimating their useful lives
- The policy for defining operating and nonoperating revenues of proprietary funds

    Governments are also required to make note disclosure of significant violations of finance-related legal and contractual provisions, as well as the actions taken to address the violations. A government might, for example, violate a statute that prohibits incurring a deficit in a particular fund, or it might violate the debt service coverage requirements of a bond covenant. In these cases, the government would need to disclose not only the violation, but also the nature of the action taken to overcome the violation (such as an increase in user charges).

    A note requirement of particular concern to analysts of a government's financial condition concerns short-term and long-term debt. A schedule of short-term debt shows beginning balances, increases, decreases, and ending balances, as well as the purposes for which the debt was issued. For long-term debt (including leases) governments need to disclose beginning- and end-of-year balances, increases and decreases during the year, and details of debt service requirements to maturity, including principal and interest requirements, stated separately, for each of the 5 subsequent fiscal years, and in 5-year increments thereafter. (The significance of this requirement is discussed in Chapter 14.)

Some governments have significant dollar amounts of interfund transfers and year-end interfund balances. The nature of interfund transactions and balances is generally not apparent from data shown on the face of the financial statements. Many transfers are routine in nature; for example, to move revenues from a collecting fund to another fund required by statute to expend them (such as a Debt Service Fund). Other transfers, however, are not routine and may be indicators of fiscal stress. Required disclosures, therefore, include such matters as (1) interfund balances that are not expected to be repaid within 1 year from the date of the financial statements and (2) significant interfund transfers that either do not occur routinely or are not consistent with the activities of the fund making the transfer.[14]

The notes to the financial statements prepared by Mt. Lebanon, Pennsylvania, for the year ended December 31, 2009, run almost 40 pages. In addition to a description of significant accounting policies, the notes cover such matters as the property tax calendar, deposits and investments, amounts due from component units and other governments, details regarding long-term debt and capital assets, interfund receivables and payables, pension plans, other postemployment benefits, risk financing, and contingent liabilities and commitments. Exhibit 9-3 shows excerpts from Note 1 on accounting policies, Note 2 on property taxes, and Note 7 on long-term debt obligations. We will discuss the note on long-term debt obligations in Chapter 14.

PREPARING REQUIRED SUPPLEMENTARY INFORMATION

Certain additional information—referred to as *required supplementary information* (RSI)—has been determined by the GASB to be an essential part of financial reporting. This information should be presented with, but not as part of, the basic financial statements of a governmental entity. Except for the MD&A, discussed previously, RSI should be presented immediately after the notes to the financial statements. Where applicable, this RSI may include budgetary comparison schedules, pension and other postemployment benefit information, and certain information about infrastructure assets. Budgetary comparison schedules and pension and other postemployment benefit information are discussed here; information about infrastructure assets is discussed in Chapter 10.

Budgetary Comparison Schedules

In addition to the basic fund financial statements, state and local governments are required to present budgetary comparison schedules for the General Fund and for each major Special Revenue Fund that has a legally adopted budget. (Rather than reporting budgetary comparisons as RSI, governments may choose to present them as basic financial statements.)

As discussed in Chapter 4, budgetary comparison schedules compare the original appropriated budget, the final appropriated budget, and the actual inflows, outflows, and balances for the year. A separate column showing the variance between the final budget and actual amounts may be shown but is not required. GASB Statement No. 34 defines the *original* budget as the first appropriated budget; this budget includes any modifications, such as transfers, allocations,

---

[14]GASB Cod. Sec. 2300.120 and 121.

Mt. Lebanon, Pennsylvania
Notes to Financial Statements (Excerpts)
December 31, 2009

NOTE 1. SUMMARY OF SIGNIFICANT ACCOUNTING POLICIES

C. Measurement Focus, Basis of Accounting, and Financial Statement Presentation

Revenues are considered to be available when they are collectible within the current period or soon enough thereafter to pay liabilities of the current period. For this purpose, the Municipality considers revenues to be available if they are collected within 30 days of the end of the current fiscal period. Governmental fund revenues accrued on this basis include earned income taxes, local services tax, sales tax, deed transfer tax. . . .

NOTE 2. PROPERTY TAXES

Based upon assessed valuations established by Allegheny County as of January 1 (approximately $2.2 billion in 2009), the Municipality bills and collects its own property taxes. The schedule for property taxes levied for 2009 is as follows:

June 1	Levy date
June 1—July 31	2% discount period
August 1—September 30	Face payment period
October 1—April 30	10% penalty period
May 1	Lien date

NOTE 7. LONG-TERM DEBT

The future annual payments required to amortize all debt outstanding as of December 31, 2009, are as follows:

	General Obligation Bonds		
	Prinipal	**Interest**	**Total**
2011	$ 1,675,000	$ 912,692	$ 2,587,692
2011	1,715,000	863,814	2,578,814
2012	1,755,000	817,781	2,572,781
2013	1,575,000	770,492	2,345,492
2014	1,130,000	740,617	1,870,617
2015–2019	6,260,000	3,065,368	9,325,368
2020–2024	7,580,000	1,728,490	9,308,490
2025–2028	3,425,000	374,115	3,799,115
	$25,115,000	$ 9,273,369	$34,388,369

The future annual payments listed here are to be funded entirely by the General Fund.

EXHIBIT 9-3 Notes to the Financial Statements

Source: Comprehensive Annual Financial Report, Mt. Lebanon, Pennsylvania, 2009, pp. 43, 50, and 60.

supplemental appropriations, and other legally authorized legislative and executive changes made before the start of the fiscal year. The *final* budget includes all subsequent legally authorized legislative and executive changes applicable to the fiscal year. The actual inflows, outflows, and balances for the year should be shown using the government's *budgetary* basis of accounting, which may be the cash basis, the modified accrual basis (similar to that used in governmental fund accounting), or some other hybrid basis.

Showing the original budget in the budgetary comparison schedule is useful not only for reporting on how much of the original budget was actually spent on each program or activity, but also in showing how management adapted to change. For example, if economic factors caused a reduction in tax collections, the budgetary comparison schedule provides a clue about the actions taken to keep expenditures in line with the reduced revenues.

In presenting the budgetary comparison schedules, governments may choose to use (a) the format, terminology, and classifications used in the budget document or (b) the same format used in the statement of revenues, expenditures, and changes in fund balances. In either event, the entity should reconcile the actual data from the budgetary basis of accounting, as shown in the budgetary comparison schedules, with the data presented in the fund financial statements of revenues, expenditures, and changes in fund balances.

Mt. Lebanon, Pennsylvania, presented its General Fund and Sewage Fund budgetary comparison information for the year ended December 31, 2009, as a basic financial statement, rather than as RSI. It supplemented the statement with detailed expenditure schedules in two formats, one on a program or activity basis and another on an object-of-expenditure basis. Mt. Lebanon's General Fund budgetary comparison statement is shown in Table 9-5. Notice that the original and final budget columns are the same—because there were no changes from the original budget. Notice also that the total amounts shown in the "actual" columns are the same in Tables 9-3 and 9-5—because Mt. Lebanon's budgetary basis of accounting (modified accrual) is the same as that used in the fund financial statement for the General Fund. Some line items differ because of the level of detail shown in the budgetary comparison statement and rounding differences. If the amounts shown in the "actual" columns differed, Mt. Lebanon would be required to show a reconciliation of the amounts.

In Table 9-5 notice that Mt. Lebanon's original budget projected a negative net change in fund balance, but that Mt. Lebanon actually ended the year with a $1,419 thousand surplus. Notice also the variance amounts for the revenue and expenditure items; then turn back to the excerpts from Mt. Lebanon's MD&A (Exhibit 9-2), and notice the discussion of the reasons for some of those variances.

Pension and Other Employee Benefit Information

Note disclosures regarding pension and other postemployment benefits are discussed in Chapter 8. In addition to those disclosures, the GASB requires, as RSI, presentation of 3-year trend information for all sole and agent employers, as follows:

- Information about the funding progress of the plan, including the actuarial value of assets, the actuarial accrued liability, and the funded ratio (i.e., the actuarial value of assets as a percentage of the actuarial accrued liability); also, the unfunded actuarial accrued liability, the annual covered payroll, and the ratio of the former to the latter
- Factors that significantly affect the identification of trends in the amounts and ratios, such as changes in benefit provisions, actuarial methods and assumptions, and the composition of the population covered by the plan

| **TABLE 9-5** | Budgetary Comparison Statement (or Schedule) |

Mt. Lebanon, Pennsylvania
Budgetary Comparison Statement—General Fund
Year Ended December 31, 2009
(in thousands of dollars)

| | Budget | | | |
	Original	Final	Actual	Variance
Revenues				
Taxes	$21,845	$21,845	$22,761	$ 916
Licenses, permits, fees	839	839	832	(7)
Fines, forfeitures	144	144	134	(10)
Investment, rental	71	71	32	(39)
Intergovernmental	1,106	1,106	1,241	135
Recreation	2,528	2,528	2,365	(163)
Other	1,720	1,720	1,882	162
Total revenues	28,253	28,253	29,247	994
Expenditures				
Current:				
General government	4,460	4,460	4,215	245
Community development	1,832	1,832	1,387	445
Public works	6,385	6,385	6,217	168
Human services	305	305	293	12
Culture and recreation	2,761	2,761	2,594	167
Public safety				
Police	6,399	6,399	6,156	243
Fire	2,892	2,892	2,885	7
Other	819	819	806	13
Capital outlay	429	429	280	149
Total expenditures	26,282	26,282	24,833	1,449
Other Financing Sources (Uses)				
Transfers in	402	402	369	(33)
Transfers out	(3,401)	(3,401)	(3,364)	37
Total other financing sources (uses)	(2,999)	(2,999)	(2,995)	4
Net change in fund balance	$(1,028)	$ (1,028)	1,419	$2,447
Fund balance, beginning of year			6,348	
Fund balance, end of year			$ 7,767	

Source: Adapted from the Comprehensive Annual Financial Report, Mt. Lebanon, Pennsylvania, December 31, 2009.

PREPARING THE STATISTICAL SECTION

Preparation of the *statistical section* of the CAFR is guided by GASB Statement No. 44, "Economic Condition Reporting: The Statistical Section" (May 2004). The trend data (generally for 10 years) contained in the statistical section provide users with financial, economic, and demographic data helpful in placing the financial statements, notes, and required supplementary information in a broader context. They thus give the analyst a starting point for assessing the government's financial condition.

The statistical section of the CAFR has the following five categories of data, generally presented in the form of tables:

- *Financial trends*—to help assess how the government's financial position has changed over time
- *Revenue capacity*—to help assess the factors affecting a government's ability to generate revenues from the most significant of its own source of revenues, generally property taxes
- *Debt capacity*—to help assess debt burden and the government's legal and financial capacity to borrow long term
- *Demographic and economic information*—to help understand the socioeconomic environment within which the government operates
- *Operating data*—to help understand how the reported financial information relates to the services the government performs

The information content of the various tables provided by general governments in the statistical section of the CAFR is shown next. Except as indicated, each table should present data for the year covered by the financial statements and the preceding 9 years.

Financial Trends

- Net assets by component (invested in capital assets, net of related debt; restricted; and unrestricted)
- Changes in net position, showing expenses by function and revenues by source
- Fund balances for the General Fund and other governmental funds
- Changes in fund balances, showing revenues by source and expenditures by function, for governmental funds

Revenue Capacity

- Taxable assessed value and estimated actual value of taxable property
- Direct and overlapping property tax rates
- Principal property tax payers (for current year and 9 years prior)
- Property tax levies and collections

Debt Capacity

- Total outstanding debt, showing amount of each type of debt, ratio of total debt to personal income, and per capita debt
- Total general obligation bond outstanding debt, showing ratio of debt to estimated actual value of taxable property and per capita debt
- Direct and overlapping outstanding governmental activities debt (for current year only)
- Legal debt margin
- Debt service coverage for long-term debt backed by pledged revenues

Demographic and Economic Information

- Demographic and economic statistics, such as population, personal income, per capita personal income, median age, education level (years of schooling), and unemployment rate
- Principal employers, showing number of employees and percentage of total employment (for current year and 9 years prior)

Operating Data

- Full-time equivalent number of government employees, by function/program
- Operating statistics by function/program—primarily workload-type data, such as number of arrests (for police) and tons of refuse collected (for sanitation)
- Capital asset and infrastructure statistics by function/program—such as number of police stations and number of refuse collection trucks

Illustrations of statistical tables are presented in Tables 9-6 and 9-7. Table 9-6 shows Mt. Lebanon's sources of tax revenues, presented on the modified accrual basis of accounting. Table 9-7 shows the 10-year trend in Mt. Lebanon's debt burden, expressed as debt per capita and debt as a percentage of full property value. Translating debt data into these ratios enables the reader to assess how Mt. Lebanon's debt burden compares with the debt burden of other municipalities. We explore how these tables may be used in financial analysis in Chapter 14.

TABLE 9-6	Statistical Tables—Tax Revenues by Source

Mt. Lebanon, Pennsylvania
Tax Revenues by Source, Governmental Funds
Last 10 Fiscal Years
(in thousands of dollars)

Year	Real Estate	Earned Income	Local Services	Real Estate Transfer	Utility	County Sales	Total
2009	$10,718	$9,539	$362	$1,443	$31	$668	$22,761
2008	10,927	9,523	354	1,191	28	673	22,696
2007	10,311	9,045	473	1,427	32	664	21,952
2006	10,125	8,554	502	1,606	34	634	21,455
2005*	9,599	8,530	484	1,569	31	603	20,816
2004	8,948	7,875	98	1,374	24	594	18,913
2003**	8,224	7,506	95	1,562	30	576	17,993
2002	8,406	6,708	93	1,447	27	567	17,247
2001	7,700	6,765	94	1,231	32	571	16,393
2000	7,054	7,093	95	1,033	59	566	15,900

*Beginning in 2005, the occupational privilege tax was eliminated and replaced with the emergency and municipal services tax (EMST). Beginning in 2008, the EMST was eliminated and replaced with the local services tax.

**The earned income tax rate was increased from 0.7% to 0.8% in 2003.

Source: Comprehensive Annual Financial Report, Mt. Lebanon, Pennsylvania, year ended December 31, 2009, p. 118.

TABLE 9-7	Statistical Tables—Long-Term Debt Trends

Mt. Lebanon, Pennsylvania
Ratios of Outstanding Debt
Last 10 Fiscal Years (columns 2–4 in millions of dollars)

As of December 31	Net Direct Outstanding Debt	Lease Rental Debt	Total Debt	Debt as a Percentage of Assessed Value	Total Debt per Capita
2009	$25.115	$ 4.362	$29.477	1.36%	$ 893
2008	24.640	4.879	29.519	1.36%	894
2007	26.045	5.386	31.431	1.46%	952
2006	23.615	5.882	29.497	1.36%	893
2005	23.175	6.400	29.575	1.36%	896
2004	24.485	6.885	31.370	1.48%	950
2003	21.965	7.765	29.730	1.39%	900
2002	15.895	4.965	20.860	0.98%	632
2001	13.250	5.385	18.635	1.00%	564
2000	7.285	5.790	13.075	0.93%	396

Source: Comprehensive Annual Financial Report, Mt. Lebanon, Pennsylvania, year ended December 31, 2009, p. 126.

Notes: Table has been modified slightly to enhance readability. Lease rental debt represents debt guaranteed by the Municipality of Mt. Lebanon for the Mt. Lebanon Parking Authority.

Review Questions

Q9-1 Which groups are the major external users of governmental financial reports?

Q9-2 List three ways in which financial reporting can assist in fulfilling government's duty to be publicly accountable and can also assist users in assessing that accountability.

Q9-3 Define the term *reporting entity.*

Q9-4 Assume a primary government appoints a voting majority of the governing board of a legally separate organization. When determining the financial reporting entity, what other requirements must be met for the primary government to be considered financially accountable for that organization?

Q9-5 When reporting component units in a governmental organization's financial statements, how does the process of blending differ from the process of discrete presentation?

Q9-6 List the major components of the financial section of a comprehensive annual financial report.

Q9-7 What are the minimum requirements established by the GASB for general purpose external financial reports?

Q9-8 List the two government-wide financial statements and seven fund financial statements that comprise the basic financial statements.

Q9-9 What is the purpose of management's discussion and analysis?

Q9-10 Discuss the difference between fund financial statements and government-wide financial statements, covering (a) the scope of the statements and (b) the measurement focus and basis of accounting used in each set of statements.

Q9-11 What are the requirements for a fund to be classified as a *major fund* in the fund financial statements?

Q9-12 What measurement focus and basis of accounting should be used in reporting each of the three fund categories in fund financial statements?

Q9-13 What is a *special item* in financial reporting?

Q9-14 What kind of information is compared in a budgetary comparison schedule?

Q9-15 Describe and illustrate the kind of information that should be reported in notes to the financial statements.

Q9-16 Briefly describe the kinds of information that should be reported in the statistical section of the CAFR.

Discussion Scenarios and Issues

D9-1 The Building Authority was created by the city and organized as a separate legal entity. The authority is governed by a five-person board appointed for 6-year terms by the mayor, subject to city council approval. The authority uses the proceeds of its tax-exempt bonds only to finance the construction or acquisition of general capital assets and only for the city. The bonds are secured by the lease agreement with the city and will be retired through lease payments from the city. Is the Building Authority a component unit of the city? If so, how should the city report the financial activities of the Building Authority? (GASB Statement 14, par. 134)

D9-2 The Municipal Electric Utility (MEU) was created as a separate legal entity in accordance with state law to own, manage, and operate an electric utilities system in the city. The MEU's governing body consists of five members. It is a self-perpetuating board composed of four citizens (customers) with the mayor of the city serving ex officio. The four citizen board members provide representation from each of the MEU's main service areas. When a board vacancy occurs, the remaining board members must nominate the successor. The MEU board chooses the nominee from a list of candidates proposed by an independent citizens' committee. The MEU's board may reject these candidates for any reason and request additional candidates. The MEU's nominee is then subject to confirmation by the city council. The council's confirmation procedure is essentially a formality. After confirmation, the council cannot remove a member for any reason.

The MEU uses various services provided by departments of the city, including insurance, legal, motor pool, and computer services. The MEU is billed for these services on a proportionate cost basis with other user departments and agencies. The MEU provides customer service and related functions to the city's water department. The cost of providing these services is paid by the water department. The MEU also provides electric service to the city and its agencies and bills the city for those services, using established rate schedules. The MEU selects and employs its executives, controls the hiring of its employees, and is responsible for rate setting and its overall fiscal management. The city is not legally or morally obligated by the MEU's debt. The MEU receives no appropriations from the city. In compliance with its charter, the MEU is required to make a payment in lieu of taxes annually to the General Fund, calculated according to a formula based on kilowatt-hour sales for the preceding 12-month period. Is the MEU a component unit of the city? If so, how should the city report the financial activities of the MEU? (GASB Statement 14, par. 141)

D9-3 The State Turnpike Commission (STC) was established by the state to construct, operate, and maintain the state turnpike system. The STC was created as an instrumentality of the state as a separate legal entity with powers to issue revenue bonds payable from tolls and other revenues. The governing body of the STC consists of eight members appointed by the governor for fixed 10-year terms and three state officials serving ex officio—the elected state treasurer, the elected state comptroller, and the appointed superintendent of highways.

The STC is financially self-sufficient, and the state cannot access its assets or surpluses, nor is it obligated to subsidize deficits of the STC. The STC sets its own rates and approves its own budget. The bond agreement states that the debt of the STC is not an obligation of the state. However, state statutes authorize the state's budget director to include in the budget submitted to the legislature an amount sufficient to make the principal and interest payments on the STC bonds in the event STC revenues are insufficient to meet debt service requirements. Is the STC a component unit of the state? If so, how should the state report the financial activities of the STC? (GASB Statement 14, par. 142)

D9-4   On page 315 in this chapter we referred to the thought process of the Oneida County, New York, officials regarding a potential component unit. Oneida County also sponsors the Mohawk Valley Community College. This is an excerpt from the county's financial statements for the year ended December 31, 2009:

> The Community College is administered by a Board of Trustees consisting of ten voting members. Five are appointed by the County Executive and confirmed by the Legislature, four by the Governor, and one student is elected by the student body. The Community College's budget is subject to the approval of the County Executive and the County Legislature, with the County providing substantial funding for the operation of the College.

Is the community college a component unit of the county? Explain.

D9-5   Several years ago the citizens of Jefferson Heights approved a 1/4 percent increase in the sales tax dedicated to law enforcement. The legislation provided that a Law Enforcement Special Revenue Fund (SRF) be established to account for the collection and disbursement of the tax resources. In addition, the legislation specifically included a provision that prohibited any other use of these funds. The chief financial officer (CFO) of Jefferson Heights discovered that the General Fund does not have enough resources to meet the final payroll of the fiscal year. At a staff meeting, the CFO suggested that the SRF loan resources to the General Fund until the General Fund could repay the loan. The county attorney said that, based on the wording of the law, such a loan probably would be illegal. After the meeting broke up, the mayor told the CFO to ignore the county attorney because "all the Special Revenue Funds are nonmajor and, when combined for financial reporting purposes, the loan would not show up in the basic financial statements as having come from the Law Enforcement SRF." How would you advise the CFO? Explain.

Exercises

E9-1   (Multiple choice—theory)
1. From the following, select the two conditions that together will cause an entity to be reported as a component unit of a primary government:
    a. The primary government's director of finance serves as a member of the entity's governing body.
    b. The primary government can appoint a voting majority of the entity's governing body.
    c. The primary government is required by law to finance the entity's deficits.
    d. The primary government is required by law to purchase its electricity from the entity, which also supplies electricity to the residents of the community.
    e. The primary government is authorized by law to bill the entity for the cost of police and fire protection.
2. What items are compared in a budgetary comparison schedule for the General Fund?
    a. Last year's final budget; current year's original budget; current year's final budget
    b. Last year's final budget; current year's final budget; current year's actual inflows and outflows on the budgetary basis of accounting
    c. Current year's original budget; current year's final budget; current year's actual inflows and outflows on the modified accrual basis of accounting
    d. Current year's original budget; current year's final budget; current year's actual inflows and outflows on the budgetary basis of accounting
3. Which of these items should be reported as "other financing uses" in a governmental funds statement of revenues, expenditures, and changes in fund balances?
    a. Transfers out
    b. Repayment of long-term debt principal

    c. Capital outlays

    d. Interest on long-term debt

4. Which of these items is normally reported as an "operating expense" in a proprietary fund statement of revenues, expenses, and changes in fund net position?

    a. Interest expense on long-term debt

    b. Transfers out

    c. Repayment of long-term debt principal

    d. Depreciation expense

5. In addition to the financial statements and notes, which two of the following items must be prepared to meet the *minimum requirements* for external financial reporting?

    a. Statistical data

    b. Management's discussion and analysis

    c. Combining statements for nonmajor funds

    d. Required supplementary information

    e. Schedules showing object-of-expenditure data for major departments or programs

6. In fund financial statements, for which category/categories of funds is depreciation reported?

	Governmental	Proprietary
a.	No	Yes
b.	Yes	No
c.	Yes	Yes
d.	No	No

7. For which of the following sets of funds is the modified accrual basis of accounting used for reporting in the fund financial statements?

    a. Special Revenue Funds and Pension Trust Funds

    b. Enterprise Funds and Internal Service Funds

    c. General Fund and Debt Service Funds

    d. All funds that meet the definition of *major*

8. How should the proceeds of debt be reported in a governmental fund's statement of revenues, expenditures, and changes in fund balances?

    a. As a revenue

    b. As an "other financing source"

    c. As an extraordinary item

    d. As an addition to the fund balance at the beginning of the period

E9-2   (True or False)

State whether these statements are true or false. For any false statement, explain why it is false.

1. In the fund financial statements, the General Fund should always be reported as a major fund.

2. In the fund financial statements, a government may elect to report any governmental or Enterprise Fund as major if the government considers financial information on that fund particularly important to statement users.

3. Notes to the financial statements are a form of required supplementary information.

4. When the financial data of a component unit are "blended" with the financial data of a primary government, the blended data are presented in both the fund financial statements and the government-wide statements.

5. In the fund financial statements, Enterprise Funds must be presented using the current financial resources measurement focus and the modified accrual basis of accounting.

6. Fiduciary funds are not reported in the fund financial statements, but instead are aggregated and reported in a single column in the government-wide financial statements.

7. A state government that receives a grant from the federal government to construct a firehouse should report the resource inflow as revenues in the Capital Projects Fund.

8. Net assets are reported as restricted in proprietary funds only if the restrictions are imposed by the entity's constitution or statute.

E9-3   State in which part of an entity's CAFR (MD&A, fund financial statements, notes to the financial statements, required supplementary information, and so forth) you are most likely to find the following information:

1. Description of the government's accounting policies
2. Ten-year trend in General Fund revenues and expenditures
3. Discussion of why the current year's tax revenues were greater than (or less than) the previous year's tax revenues
4. Comparison of the budgeted revenues and expenditures for the General Fund with the actual revenues and expenditures on the budgetary basis of accounting
5. Details of the year's expenditures for each nonmajor fund
6. Rationale for including component units as part of the reporting entity
7. Current year's revenues, expenditures, and changes in fund balance for the General Fund

E9-4   (Organization of the CAFR)
Explain the organization of the comprehensive annual financial report, as specified in GASB Statement No. 34. Outline your explanation.

E9-5   (Analysis of the MD&A section of a CAFR)
Obtain the CAFR of a governmental unit, and read the MD&A. Describe three significant comments made by management.

E9-6   (Analysis of the notes to the financial statements in a CAFR)
Obtain the CAFR of a governmental unit, and read the statement of significant accounting policies in the notes to the financial statements. Write a brief report summarizing those policies.

E9-7   (Analysis of the notes to the financial statements in a CAFR)
Obtain the CAFR of a governmental unit, and read the notes other than the statement of significant accounting policies. Write a brief report summarizing three of the notes.

E9-8   (Analysis of a budgetary comparison schedule or statement in a CAFR)
Obtain a CAFR of a governmental unit, and read the budgetary comparison schedule or statement. Also, read what, if anything, management says in its MD&A about the results of its budgetary activities for the year. What conclusions can you reach from reading the budgetary comparison schedule or statement? How do management's comments in the MD&A improve your understanding of the budgetary comparison schedule or statement?

Problems

P9-1   (Multiple choice—theory)

1. Which of the following types of governments is *always* considered to be a primary government for financial reporting purposes?
   a. A school district with a separately elected governing body
   b. A state university whose board members are appointed by the governor without the approval of the state legislature
   c. A town
   d. A legally separate public authority or public benefit corporation
2. Which of the following is an example of a "benefit or burden" relationship for purposes of determining whether a primary government is financially accountable for another organization?
   a. Primary government is authorized to audit the other organization.
   b. Primary government is obligated in some manner for the other organization's debt.
   c. Primary government is required to approve the other organization's debt issuances.
   d. Primary government is authorized to remove members of the other organization's governing board.
3. Which basis of accounting is used in preparing the budgetary comparison statement?
   a. The budgetary basis
   b. The accrual basis

    c. The modified accrual basis

    d. The cash receipts and disbursements basis

4. In fund financial statements, where are the revenues and expenditures (expenses) of governmental-type and proprietary-type funds reported?

    a. On different financial statements

    b. On the same financial statement

    c. On the same financial statement, provided all the funds are major funds

    d. On the same financial statement where fiduciary funds are reported

5. Fund financial statements have columns for which of the following?

    a. Major funds only, with separate columns for each fund

    b. All funds combined in a single column

    c. Each major fund plus a column for nonmajor funds combined

    d. All funds, with separate columns for each fund

6. Which of the following is an example of required supplementary information?

    a. Listing of revenues and expenditures for the current year and 9 previous years

    b. Statement of changes in fiduciary net assets for each nonmajor fiduciary fund

    c. Combining financial statement of Internal Service Funds

    d. Budgetary comparison schedule

7. Which of the following is part of the *minimum requirements* established by the GASB for general purpose external financial reports?

    a. An introductory section

    b. Management's discussion and analysis

    c. A statistical section

    d. A schedule of cash receipts and disbursements for all funds

8. The process of *blending* is accomplished by reporting a component unit's funds in which manner?

    a. In the notes to the primary government's financial statements

    b. In a separate column to the left of the primary government's funds

    c. As if they were fiduciary funds of the primary government

    d. As if they were the funds of the primary government

9. Which of the following situations would be defined as a *special item*?

    a. The amount of a revenue item or an expenditure item increased by at least 10 percent over the previous year.

    b. A significant transaction within the control of management is either unusual in nature or infrequent in occurrence.

    c. A significant event outside the control of management causes the expenses or expenditures of a fund to exceed its revenues.

    d. A vibrant economy causes an entity's tax revenues to rise by an extraordinary amount over the budgetary estimate.

10. Which of the following must be included when an entity issues general purpose financial reports separately from a CAFR?

    a. Notes to the financial statements

    b. Combining financial statements of nonmajor funds

    c. Statistical section

    d. Combining statement of blended component units

11. In fund financial statements, where are the categories capital assets, less accumulated depreciation and long-term bonds payable likely to appear?

    a. The General Fund, but not an Enterprise Fund

    b. An Enterprise Fund, but not a Capital Projects Fund

    c. Both an Enterprise Fund and a Capital Projects Fund

    d. An Enterprise Fund and a Capital Projects Fund or a Debt Service Fund

P9-2 (Preparation of a governmental funds balance sheet)
The following information is available for the governmental funds of Tom's Village. Prepare the governmental funds balance sheet for Tom's Village. The village officials do not consider either Special Revenue Fund as particularly important to financial statement users.

	General	Debt Service	Special Revenue Fund A	Special Revenue Fund B
Cash	$10,000	$5,000	$600	$1,000
Taxes receivable	5,000			
Due from other funds		2,000		
Accounts payable	9,000		200	400
Due to other funds	2,000			
Assigned fund balance	1,000		400	600
Restricted fund balance		7,000		
Unassigned fund balance	3,000			

P9-3 (Multiple choice—miniproblems)
The following information relates to the first three questions in the list that follows. A village levied property taxes in the amount of $800,000 for calendar year 2013. By year-end, the village had collected $775,000. It expected to collect $15,000 more in January and February of 2014 and the remaining $10,000 after February but before September 2014. Answer the following questions regarding the fund financial statements for the General Fund as of December 31, 2013, and for the calendar year 2013.

1. What amount of property tax revenues should be recognized for calendar year 2013?
    a. $775,000
    b. $785,000
    c. $790,000
    d. $800,000

2. What amount of property taxes receivable should be reported at December 31, 2013?
    a. $0
    b. $10,000
    c. $15,000
    d. $25,000

3. What amount of deferred property tax revenues should be reported at December 31, 2013?
    a. $0
    b. $10,000
    c. $15,000
    d. $25,000

4. A city operates on a calendar year basis. On April 1, 2012, the city issues general obligation bonds in the amount of $1,000,000 to build a new city hall. The debt is to be paid off at the rate of $100,000 a year, with interest of 5 percent per annum on the outstanding debt, starting April 1, 2013. Although it maintains a Debt Service Fund, the city has not transferred any resources to that fund to pay any interest or principal on the debt. When it prepares its governmental fund financial statements as of December 31, 2012, how much should the city report as Debt Service Fund expenditures?
    a. $0
    b. $37,500
    c. $50,000
    d. $100,000

5. Assume the same set of facts as in the previous problem, except that the debt has been issued by the Water Enterprise Fund to extend water mains. When it prepares its proprietary fund financial statements, how much should the city report as interest expense?
   a. $0
   b. $37,500
   c. $50,000
   d. $100,000

$1,000,000 \times .05 \times 9/12 = 37,500$

6. Nuevo York County maintains the Metro Bus Enterprise Fund to account for the activities of its municipal bus service. The following information is reported in the fund's statement of net position at year-end: Buses and bus garage—$2,500,000; Accumulated depreciation, buses and garage—$1,100,000; Current portion of bonds payable—$250,000; Noncurrent portion of bonds payable—$1,000,000. The bonds were issued to finance acquisition of the buses and the garage. How much should the fund report as Invested in capital assets, net of related debt in the statement of net position?
   a. $1,400,000
   b. $1,250,000
   c. $1,150,000
   d. $150,000

2,500,000
−1,100,000
1,400,000
−250,000
−1,000,000
150,000

7. Thomas Village operates on a calendar year basis. On January 1, 2012, it had outstanding property taxes receivable of $40,000 and deferred property tax revenue of $10,000. On that same date, it levied property taxes of $1,000,000 to cover its 2012 activities. During 2012, it collected the entire $40,000 of receivables that had been outstanding as of January 1, as well as $975,000 against the 2012 levy. With regard to the uncollected 2012 taxes, the village expected to collect $20,000 during the first 60 days of 2013 and the remaining $5,000 during the rest of 2013. How much should Thomas Village recognize as property tax revenues in its General Fund for calendar year 2012?
   a. $995,000
   b. $1,000,000
   c. $1,005,000
   d. $1,035,000

P9-4 (Preparation of governmental funds statement of revenues, expenditures, and changes in fund balance) The following information comes from the General Fund trial balance of West Chester County as of December 31, 2012. Prepare the county's General Fund statement of revenues, expenditures, and changes in fund balance for the year ended December 31, 2012. Consider the proceeds from the sale and leaseback of an office building as a special item.

Sales tax revenues	$ 2,200,000
Property tax revenues	2,000,000
Expenditures—county sheriff	1,500,000
Expenditures—all other departments	2,600,000
Fund balance, January 1, 2012	300,000
Transfer out to Debt Service Fund	1,000,000
Proceeds, sale and leaseback of office building	1,500,000

P9-5 (Preparation of proprietary funds statement of revenues, expenses, and changes in fund net position) The City of Breukelen maintains a rapid transit system, which is accounted for in a proprietary fund called Breukelen RTS. The following excerpt from the trial balance shows all the information needed to prepare an operating statement. Therefore, prepare a statement of revenues, expenses, and changes in fund net position for the Breukelen RTS for the year ended December 31, 2012, using the appropriate format.

Revenues from fares	$3,150,000
Train operating expenses	2,430,000

Track and train maintenance expenses	565,000
Depreciation	325,000
Investment income	50,000
Interest expense on long-term debt	320,000
Cash subsidy from the City of Breukelen	500,000
Net assets, January 1, 2012	7,430,000

P9-6   (Review problem—correction of errors and adjusting entries)

As the recently appointed chief accountant of the City of York, you asked the bookkeeper for a trial balance of the General Fund as of December 31, 2012. (York uses only a General Fund to record all its transactions.) This is what you received:

City of York
General Fund
Trial Balance
December 31, 2012

	Debits	Credits
Cash	$ 20,800	
Short-term investments	180,000	
Accounts receivable	11,500	
Taxes receivable—current	30,000	
Tax anticipation notes payable		$ 58,000
Appropriations		927,000
Expenditures	795,200	
Estimated revenues	927,000	
Revenues		750,000
General city property	98,500	
General obligation bonds payable	52,000	
Unassigned fund balance		380,000
	$2,115,000	$2,115,000

After glancing at the trial balance, you realize that the inexperienced bookkeeper made errors on some transactions and merely guessed at the correct accounting treatment of other transactions. This is what you found when you reviewed the journal entries and analyzed other transactions and events that had occurred during the year:

1. On December 1, 2012, the city received notice from the state that it would receive a grant to help train its police officers. The grant terms stipulated that, to be eligible for the grant, the city would need to incur certain allowable costs. The city received a check for $20,000 on December 10 as an advance on the grant. The bookkeeper recorded the advance in the Revenues account. As of December 31, however, the city had not yet started the training program.

2. On December 31, 2012, the state department of tax and finance advised the city that the state had collected $58,500 of sales tax revenues on behalf of the city and that a check would be sent to the city by January 20, 2013. No journal entry was made for this information.

3. York collects property taxes on behalf of the county in which it is located. The entire amount received in November 2012 ($15,000) was recorded as York's revenues and was not sent to the county.

4. Analysis of the Taxes receivable—current account shows the following:
   a. The entire $30,000 of receivables is delinquent.
   b. Based on the history of delinquent tax collections, you estimate that $15,000 of the receivables will be collected by the end of February 2013, that $12,000 of the receivable amount will not be received until later in 2013, and that $3,000 will ultimately need to be written off as uncollectible.

5. Analysis of the account General obligation bonds payable shows that the debit balance of $52,000 arose from a journal entry made on December 30, 2012, to record a payment of debt service ($40,000 bond principal and $12,000 interest).

6. Analysis of the account General city property shows that the $98,500 debit balance resulted from two journal entries:

    a. Sale of used truck for $6,400

    b. Purchase of new firefighting equipment for $104,900

7. Although the city's actuary estimated that the city would need to contribute $45,000 to its pension fund for the year, the York City Council decided not to make an appropriation for it because the city needed to conserve its cash. The bookkeeper decided that there was no need to make an accrual.

8. Two lawsuits were brought against the city as a result of damages caused by its trucks during trash collection. One case was settled in late December, for which York will pay $2,000 damages in January 2013. The city attorney believes the city will probably lose the other case as well and may need to pay out $6,000 to settle it. However, the case is complex and is not likely to be resolved for another 15 months. The bookkeeper didn't think any entry was needed because no cash was paid.

Prepare journal entries, as necessary, to correct the City of York's records. Record all adjustments to the revenue and expenditure accounts as simply "revenues" or "expenditures" without showing details. Make the adjusting journal entries in the General Fund only. If some other fund would normally be used to record the transaction, however, state which one would be used.

P9-7   (Review problem—journal entries for several funds and statement of revenues, expenditures, and changes in fund balance for a Capital Projects Fund)

The City of Lexington had the following transactions during the calendar year 2013. The transactions relate to financing and constructing a new firehouse. Lexington uses budgetary accounting in its Capital Projects Fund. Prepare journal entries to record all the transactions, and identify the fund(s) used. Also, prepare a statement of revenues, expenditures, and changes in fund balance for Lexington's Capital Projects Fund for the year ended December 31, 2013.

1. Lexington adopted a budget for the Capital Projects Fund on January 1, based on the following assumptions:

    Bonds would be issued for $2,000,000.
    Lexington would transfer $300,000 from its General Fund, and the state would contribute $200,000. Contracts would be awarded for $2,500,000 million.

2. On February 1, Lexington issued $2,000,000 of 5 percent general obligation bonds to build a new firehouse. Principal and interest payments are to be made each February 1 and August 1 for 20 years, starting August 1, 2013. Principal is amortized in equal semiannual payments of $50,000. The bonds were sold for $2,030,000.

3. On February 1, Lexington contracted with Howard Consultants for $100,000 to supervise construction.

4. On February 1, the Capital Projects Fund invested $1,000,000 in a CD.

5. On February 1, Lexington entered into a contract with Eddie Construction to build the firehouse for $2,400,000.

6. The CD matured on June 1. Lexington recorded the check for $1,010,000, which included $10,000 of interest, in the Capital Projects Fund.

7. Lexington transferred $300,000 from its General Fund to the Capital Projects Fund to help pay for construction of the firehouse.

8. Eddie Construction completed work on June 30. It billed Lexington $2,400,000. Lexington paid the bill less 10 percent retainage, pending final inspection of Eddie's work by Howard Consultants.

9. On July 10, Howard Consultants advised Lexington that Eddie had completed all work to its satisfaction. Lexington advised the state that work on the firehouse was completed. The state promptly wired its contribution of $200,000 to Lexington.

10. On July 15, Lexington paid the retainage to Eddie and also paid Howard the full $100,000 due on its contract.

11. On July 20, all cash remaining in the Capital Projects Fund was transferred to the Debt Service Fund to help defray the principal and interest payment due in August.

12. On July 31, the General Fund transferred to the Debt Service Fund the balance needed to pay the August installment of debt service.

13. On August 1, the Debt Service Fund paid the first installment of debt service on the bonds issued to build the firehouse.

P9-8 (Review problem—miscellaneous journal entries)

Prepare journal entries to record the following transactions, and identify all the affected funds. Many transactions require more than one journal entry.

1. The General Fund operating budget was approved as follows:

Appropriations	$5,200,000
Estimated revenues	5,000,000
Estimated other financing sources	300,000

2. Plans for a new criminal courts building were approved. General obligation bonds with a face value of $7,000,000 were issued for $7,200,000. Local laws stipulate that any premium must be transferred to the appropriate Debt Service Fund. In addition, a federal grant of $8,000,000 was received.

3. The city was notified by the state that the state had approved a grant of $200,000 for training civil defense personnel. The notification letter stated that the city would be reimbursed quarterly for 50 percent of all allowable costs incurred by the city. During the first quarter of the year, the city incurred total costs of $90,000 on the training program. It then billed the state for the state's share of the costs.

4. The city received $400,000 from the state. This amount was the city's share of the state gasoline tax. This money can be spent only to repair streets, and a separate accounting is required by the state.

5. $200,000 installment of general obligation bonds matured. The city paid the installment together with $120,000 of interest.

6. The city needed $3,200,000 to balance the budget. To provide that amount and an allowance for uncollectible taxes, the city levied property taxes in the amount of $3,230,000.

7. Salaries of governmental employees were paid, totaling $800,000. Of this amount, $65,000 was withheld and included in an account called Due to federal government as income tax payments. In addition, the city made a contribution of $100,000 to the city-operated pension system. Assume that all employees were paid through the General Fund.

8. The Central Supplies Fund, an Internal Service Fund, billed the General Fund $15,000 and the Gas Service Fund (an Enterprise Fund) $8,000 for supplies.

9. The Gas Service Fund billed the General Fund $2,500, the Central Supplies Fund for $1,000, and the remainder of its customers $2,500,000.

10. The city sent violation notices to restaurant owners for repeated failure to comply with local sanitary codes, along with notices of fines totaling $25,000. The city anticipates collecting the entire amount of the fines.

11. The city allows its employees to accumulate up to 30 days of annual leave and to receive pay for unused leave on termination or retirement. When it closed its General Fund books at year-end, the city owed two retired employees a total of $15,000 for unused leave, to be paid during the following month. The city also estimated that the year-to-year increase in the year-end annual leave liability for all working employees was $250,000.

12. Equity securities, carried in the city's pension fund at $3,200,000, had a fair value of $3,050,000 at year-end.

Continuing Problems

Continuing Problem 1. (Fund accounting and preparation of financial statements)
The scenario: At the start of the year beginning January 1, 2013, Coco City's General Fund had a cash balance of $40,000, vouchers payable of $35,000, and unassigned fund balance of $5,000. There were no balances in either the Capital Projects Fund or the Debt Service Fund. Coco City has adopted the following budgetary and accounting policies:
- Encumbrance accounting is used only for the acquisition of supplies. Open encumbrances lapse at the end of the year, but are considered in developing the next year's budget.
- For consistency with property taxes, "available" is defined for sales taxes as taxes expected to be collected within the first 60 days of the next year.

Part A (Chapter 2—Identification of funds)
Coco City uses separate funds for the following activities. State the names of the funds that Coco City will use for each of these activities.
  1. To account for its day-to-day operating activities
  2. To acquire or construct major capital assets
  3. To accumulate resources to service long-term debt
  4. To operate a municipal swimming pool

Part B (Chapter 3—Budgetary accounting for the General Fund)
Use the following information to (a) record the opening account balances; (b) prepare journal entries to record all four transactions; (c) post the journal entries to T-accounts; and (d) prepare an appropriations ledger for police supplies and post the budgetary transactions.
  1. The Coco City Council adopted the following budget for the General Fund at the beginning of the year:

Revenues—property taxes	$400,000
Revenues—sales taxes	70,000
Revenues—parks admission fees	10,000
Appropriations:	
Police salaries	300,000
Police supplies	40,000
Parks salaries	80,000
Transfer to Debt Service Fund	45,000

  2. Two purchase orders, one for $35,000 and one for $4,000, were placed against the appropriation for police supplies.
  3. Because the unit price was lower than anticipated, an invoice for $33,000 was received and approved for the supplies that had been ordered for $35,000.
  4. The invoice for $33,000 was paid.

Part C (Chapter 5—Other General Fund transactions)
Prepare journal entries, as appropriate, to record these transactions, and post the journal entries to T-accounts.
  1. Property taxes were levied in the amount of $404,000 in order to provide revenues of $400,000. Tax bills were sent to the property owners.
  2. The account of a taxpayer who owed $3,000 was written off as uncollectible.
  3. Property taxes of $370,000 were collected in cash.
  4. At year-end, all uncollected taxes were declared delinquent. The Coco City finance director concluded that all the property taxes would be collected, so there was no need for any allowance for uncollectible taxes. She estimated that $21,000 of the delinquent

taxes would be collected in January and February 2014 and that the rest of the taxes would be collected later in 2014.

5. The state collects sales taxes on behalf of all cities in the state. During the year, Coco City received $68,000 in sales taxes from the state. The state also advised Coco that it would remit an additional $6,000 in sales taxes (from sales made in 2013) by January 20, 2014.

6. Coco City collected parks admission fees of $18,000 during the year.

7. The unpaid vouchers of $35,000 at the beginning of the year were paid.

8. Salaries in the amount of $360,000 were paid ($290,000 for the Police Department and $70,000 for the Parks Department).

9. The payroll for the period ended December 31, 2013, which was included in the year 2013 budget, will be paid on January 5, 2014 ($8,000 for the Police Department and $5,000 for the Parks Department).

10. A Police Department sedan accidentally sideswiped a citizen's vehicle in November 2013. Coco City's corporation counsel estimated that the city would ultimately settle the citizen's claim for about $4,000. It usually takes about 18 months to settle cases of this kind.

Part D (Chapter 6—Capital Projects Fund and Debt Service Fund transactions)
Prepare journal entries for all funds, as appropriate, to record these transactions, and post the journal entries to T-accounts for each fund.

1. To provide financing for a new police station, Coco City sold bonds on April 1, 2013, in the amount of $500,000. Bond principal is payable over a 10-year period in 20 equal semiannual installments of $25,000, with interest of 6 percent per annum on the unpaid balance. The first payment is due on October 1, 2013.

2. Coco City purchased a prefabricated police station and paid $500,000 for it on delivery. The building, ready for occupancy on July 1, 2013, was expected to have a useful life of 25 years.

3. The General Fund transferred $45,000 to the Debt Service Fund in anticipation of the first installment of debt service.

4. The first installment of debt service became due and payable on October 1, 2013.

5. The first installment of debt service was paid.

Part E (Chapter 7—Enterprise Fund transactions)
Record the opening balances in T-accounts, prepare journal entries to record the transactions, and post the journal entries to T-accounts.

1. Coco City operates a municipal swimming pool. It started the year with cash of $5,000; net capital assets of $510,000 (the swimming pool cost $600,000, and the accumulated depreciation was $90,000); and outstanding bonds of $480,000 (the original debt of $600,000 was being paid off over 15 years in equal annual installments of $40,000 on December 31 of each year, with interest of 5 percent per annum on the outstanding balance).

2. Coco received swimming pool admissions fees of $70,000.

3. Salaries totaling $8,000 were paid to a lifeguard and a clerk.

4. Coco paid the annual debt service requirement on the swimming pool bonds.

5. Coco recorded depreciation on the swimming pool. The cost of the pool is amortized over 20 years.

Part F (Chapter 9—Preparation of fund financial statements)
Prepare preclosing trial balances for all funds. Also, prepare the following fund financial statements and schedules:

1. Governmental funds balance sheet (Note: Classify the fund balance of the Debt Service Fund as Assigned fund balance)

2. Governmental funds statement of revenues, expenditures, and changes in fund balances

3. General Fund budgetary comparison schedule
4. Proprietary funds statement of net position
5. Proprietary funds statement of revenues, expenses, and changes in fund net position

Part G (Chapter 10—Preparation of journal entries for government-wide financial statements and preparation of government-wide financial statements)
See Continuing Problems at the end of Chapter 10 for the remainder of this problem, to be completed after reading Chapter 10.

Continuing Problem 2. (Fund accounting and preparation of fund financial statements)
The scenario: Croton City started its calendar year 2013 with the following General Fund balances (all numbers are in thousands of dollars).

	Debits	Credits
Cash	$1,800	
Property taxes receivable	800	
Salaries payable		$ 700
Deferred property tax revenues		300
Unassigned fund balance		1,600
Totals	$2,600	$2,600

Croton has adopted the following budgetary and accounting policies:

- Encumbrance accounting is used only for the acquisition of supplies and for the award of contracts for construction and construction-related activities. Open encumbrances lapse at the end of the year, but are considered in developing the next year's budget.
- Because final income tax returns are not required to be filed until April 15 of the year following the end of a calendar year, "available" for income taxes is defined as taxes expected to be collected within 120 days after the end of the calendar year.
- Croton allows its employees to accumulate unused vacation days and to receive cash for up to 30 days of unused vacation leave at retirement. Such payments are charged to the department's appropriation for salaries.
- All revenues received by the library from fines, donations, and fundraising events are credited to Revenues—miscellaneous.

Part A (Chapter 2—Identification of funds)
Croton City maintains separate funds to account for the following activities. State the names of the funds that Croton City uses for each activity.
1. To account for its day-to-day operating activities
2. To account for its library activities
3. To acquire or construct capital assets
4. To accumulate resources to service long-term debt

Part B (Chapter 3—General Fund budgetary journal entries)
Use the following information to (a) record the opening account balances in T-accounts; (b) prepare journal entries to record all five transactions; (c) post the journal entries to general ledger T-accounts; and (d) prepare an appropriations ledger for the Public safety supplies appropriation.
1. The Croton council adopted the following General Fund budget for 2013:

Revenues—property taxes	$9,000
Revenues—personal income taxes	5,000
Revenues—intergovernmental	1,000
Revenues—recreation fees	600

Appropriations:

Public safety salaries	7,000
Public safety supplies	500
Public works salaries	5,000
Parks salaries	2,300
Transfer to Library Fund	100
Transfer to Debt Service Fund	1,200

2. Croton's Public Safety Department placed two purchase orders against its supplies appropriation, one for $300 for firearms and one for $150 for uniforms.
3. The firearms were received, with an invoice for $330. The purchase order allowed shipment of 10 percent over the amount ordered, so the invoice was approved.
4. The invoice for firearms was paid.
5. The Croton Cats won the World Series. To provide more funds for crowd control at the parade, the council increased the Public safety salaries appropriation by $100.

Part C (1) (Chapter 5—Journal entries for General Fund financial transactions)
Prepare journal entries, as appropriate, to record these transactions, and post the journal entries to T-accounts.

1. Of the $800 in property taxes receivable at January 1, $780 was collected in cash. The remaining $20 was written off as uncollectible. Deferred property taxes at the beginning of the year were recognized as revenue.
2. Accrued salaries from the previous year ($700) were paid.
3. Property taxes in the amount of $9,030 were levied in order to provide revenues of $9,000. Tax bills were sent to the property owners. An allowance for uncollectible taxes was established.
4. During the year, property taxes of $8,100 were collected in cash.
5. The state collects personal income taxes on behalf of the city. During the year, Croton received personal income taxes of $4,600 from the state.
6. The Parks Department collected $700 in recreation fees during the year.
7. Croton paid salaries of $13,600, charging the salary appropriations as follows:

Public safety	$6,700
Public works	4,700
Parks	2,200

8. The state sent the city a check for $1,000 to finance a special public safety program, stipulating that the resources could be used at any time during 2013 or 2014. The $6,700 in public safety salaries paid in the previous transaction includes $800 of salaries for this program, so $200 remains available for spending on the program in 2014.
9. Unpaid salaries at year-end (to be paid during the first week of 2014) were as follows:

Public safety	$350
Public works	250
Parks	100

10. At year-end, the uncollected property taxes were declared delinquent. Croton's director of finance estimated that $500 of the uncollected taxes would be collected in January and February 2014 and $400 would be collected during the rest of 2014. He decided to leave the allowance for uncollectible taxes on the books.
11. In January 2014, the state advised Croton that the state held $500 in personal income taxes on the city's behalf and that it would send the taxes to Croton by February 10. It also told Croton that it was likely that, by April 30, Croton would receive an additional $200 of taxes with final returns, but that tax refunds would probably be $300.

12. Police officers who retired at the end of 2013 will be paid $10 for unused vacation pay on January 6, 2014.

Part C (2) (Chapter 5—Journal entries for Special Revenue Fund transactions)
The Library Special Revenue Fund commenced calendar year 2013 with a cash balance of $5 and zero liabilities. Record the opening account balances in T-accounts. Also, prepare appropriate journal entries to record these transactions, and post the journal entries to T-accounts.

1. The General Fund transferred $100 cash to the Library Special Revenue Fund to help the library finance its activities for the year.
2. The library received a grant of $300 from the county. The grant must be used only for library purposes, but there is no requirement as to when it must be spent.
3. The library received $20 from fines, donations, and various fundraising events.
4. The library paid $350 for salaries and $40 to acquire books and periodicals. Charge the expenditures to Culture—salaries and Culture—supplies, respectively.

Part D (Chapter 6—Journal entries for Capital Projects Fund transactions)
At the start of 2013, Croton's Capital Projects Fund had no assets or liabilities. Prepare appropriate journal entries to record these transactions, and post the journal entries to T-accounts.

1. Croton undertook construction of a new police station, designed to house both the Croton police and the county sheriff and to serve as a detention center. To finance construction, Croton received a cash grant of $1,000 from the county and sold $2,000 of 20-year general obligation bonds. The bonds, sold April 1, 2013, were to be redeemed in equal semiannual installments of principal, with interest payable at the same time at the rate of 5 percent per annum, starting October 1, 2013.
2. Croton awarded two contracts, one for architectural and construction supervision services ($200) and one for construction ($2,800).
3. The construction contract was completed in a timely manner, and the contractor submitted an invoice for $2,800. The invoice was paid, except that 5 percent was withheld, pending completion of inspection.
4. All construction and construction supervision work was completed. The construction architect/supervisor was paid in full, and the contractor was paid the balance due.

Part E (Chapter 6—Journal entries for Debt Service Fund transactions)
At the start of 2013, Croton's Debt Service Fund had no assets or liabilities. Prepare appropriate journal entries to record these transactions, and post the journal entries to T-accounts.

1. The General Fund transferred $1,200 cash to the Debt Service Fund.
2. The first installment of principal and interest on the bonds sold in Part D came due for payment.
3. That principal and interest due for payment were paid.
4. Debt service on bonds sold by Croton in previous years came due and was paid. Principal and interest payments on those bonds were $600 and $470, respectively.

Part F (Chapter 9—Preparation of fund financial statements and schedules)
Prepare preclosing trial balances for all funds. Prepare a governmental funds balance sheet; a governmental funds statement of revenues, expenditures, and changes in fund balances; and a General Fund budgetary comparison schedule. Consider all funds as major funds for this exercise, and classify the fund balance for the Debt Service Fund as Assigned fund balance.

Part G (Chapter 10—Preparation of journal entries for government-wide financial statements and preparation of government-wide financial statements)
See Continuing Problems at the end of Chapter 10 for the remainder of this problem, to be completed after reading Chapter 10.

Chapter 10

Government-Wide Financial Statements

Chapter Outline

After completing this chapter, you should be able to do the following:

- Discuss the basic principles for preparing government-wide financial statements

- Describe the major differences in information content between the fund financial statements and the government-wide financial statements

- Describe the format of the government-wide statement of net position and statement of activities

- Discuss how interfund balances and transfers and Internal Service Fund activities are handled in government-wide statements

- Describe and prepare the major adjustments needed to convert fund financial statements to government-wide financial statements

- Prepare government-wide financial statements

- Describe and explain the content of the reconciliations between fund financial statements and government-wide statements

- Discuss the "modified approach" for reporting infrastructure assets

In addition to the fund financial statements described in Chapter 9, GASB Statement No. 34 (as amended) requires preparation of two government-wide financial statements: a statement of net position and a statement of activities. Government-wide financial statements are prepared using the following basic principles:

a. Assets, liabilities, revenues, and expenses are reported using the economic resources measurement focus and the accrual basis of accounting for *all* activities, regardless of the types of funds used to account for them.

b. Information is reported about the overall government, without showing individual funds or fund types.

   c. Financial statements are formatted to distinguish between the primary government and its discretely presented component units; also, for the primary government, the formatting distinguishes between governmental and business-type activities.

   d. Information about fiduciary activities is excluded from the statements.[1]

The fund financial statements provide the starting point for preparing the government-wide statements. Because of the way the fund financial statements are prepared, complying with the last three principles presents no major difficulties. Some effort is required, however, to convert the governmental-type fund financial data to the economic resources measurement focus and accrual basis of accounting, as required by the first principle. The major purpose of this chapter is to show how to make this conversion. We also discuss the standards for reporting on capital assets, including infrastructure assets, as well as methods for maintaining control over capital assets and long-term liabilities. First, however, we discuss the focus and format of the government-wide financial statements, using Mt. Lebanon's 2009 financial statements for illustration.

FOCUS AND FORMAT OF GOVERNMENT-WIDE STATEMENTS

The government-wide financial statements differ both in focus and in format from the fund financial statements. The most significant difference between the two sets of statements concerns the accounting measurements for activities reported in governmental-type funds. In the fund financial statements, the current financial resources measurement focus and modified accrual basis of accounting are used to measure resource inflows, outflows, and account balances for governmental-type funds. In the government-wide financial statements, however, the measurements for those funds are converted to the economic resources measurement focus and accrual basis of accounting. Because all activities—whether accounted for in governmental-type or proprietary-type funds—use the same measurement focus and basis of accounting, just one operating statement is needed for government-wide financial reporting.

A second difference concerns the reporting focus. The fund financial statements concentrate on individual major governmental and enterprise funds. The government-wide statements, however, focus on the government as a whole. The funds in each category are aggregated into two broad sets of activities: *governmental* (those whose resources come primarily from taxes and intergovernmental grants) and *business type* (those whose resources come primarily from user charges to third parties).

A third difference concerns accountability relationships. The fund statements include the fiduciary funds (for which the primary government has a fiduciary relationship) but exclude the discretely presented component units (for which the primary government has a financial accountability relationship). The government-wide statements, however, exclude the fiduciary funds but include the discretely presented component units.

Summarizing the foregoing distinctions from the perspective of funds and component units, preparation of the government-wide financial statements requires the financial data for the funds and the component units to be adjusted, aggregated, and/or excluded, as follows:

- *Governmental-type funds:* The financial data for governmental-type funds are converted to the economic resources measurement focus and accrual basis of accounting and are then consolidated to produce the governmental activities portion of the statements.

---

[1]GASB Cod. Sec. 2200.110.

- *Proprietary-type funds:* The financial data for Enterprise Funds are consolidated to produce the business-type activities portion of the statements. The revenues of Internal Service Funds are offset against expenditures of the funds that purchased services from them; net assets of the Internal Service Funds are then allocated as appropriate to either governmental or business-type activities.
- *Fiduciary-type funds:* Fiduciary funds are excluded from the government-wide financial statements because they cannot be used to support the government's programs.
- *Discretely presented component units:* Financial data for discretely presented component units are aggregated and presented in a separate column in the government-wide statements.

The Statement of Net Position

The *statement of net position* may have four columns of financial data: one for governmental activities, one for business type activities, one for the total of those two columns, and one for discretely presented component units. The column for discretely presented component units is shown to the right of the total column. The statement would, of course, have fewer columns if the entity had no business-type activities or component units.

Table 10-1 presents the government-wide statement of net position for Mt. Lebanon, Pennsylvania, as of December 31, 2009. Mt. Lebanon has no proprietary funds, so its statement of net position has just two columns, one for its governmental activities and one for its component units. If Mt. Lebanon had proprietary funds, this statement would also have had a column labeled business-type activities and a column for the total primary government—that is, for the governmental and business-type activities combined.

CHANGING THE ACCOUNTING MEASUREMENTS   When you compare the numbers in the governmental activities column in Table 10-1 with the total funds column in Table 9-1 on page 325, several differences are apparent: (a) capital assets and long-term liabilities appear in Table 10-1 but not in Table 9-1; (b) Table 10-1 shows evidence of more accruals than Table 9-1; and (c) the "due to" and "due from" amounts among the governmental funds in Table 9-1 do not appear in Table 10-1. The first two differences result from converting the accounting measurements made in the governmental funds to the economic resources measurement focus and accrual basis of accounting; the third difference results from consolidating the individual funds to a total for "governmental activities."

To help financial statement users assess the relationship between the fund statements and the government-wide statements, GASB Statement No. 34 requires that the statements be reconciled in summary form. The reconciliations explain the specific differences resulting from using different measurement focuses and bases of accounting in the two sets of statements. Two reconciliations are needed, one for the two financial position statements and one for the two operating statements. The reconciliations may be presented either at the bottom of the fund financial statements or in accompanying schedules.

Mt. Lebanon's reconciliation of the two financial position statements is shown in Table 10-2. Trace the numbers in the reconciliation schedule to the numbers in Tables 9-1 and 10-1. Notice that the most significant reconciling items relate to reporting capital assets and long-term debt in the government-wide statement but not in the funds statement. Significant reconciling items are also likely when governments routinely underfund pension and other postemployment benefits.

TABLE 10-1   Government-Wide Statement of Net Position

Mt. Lebanon, Pennsylvania
Statement of Net Position
As of December 31, 2009
(in thousands of dollars)

	Governmental Activities	Component Units
Assets		
Cash and cash equivalents	$10,420	$ 1,012
Receivables:		
Taxes	3,751	—
Assessments	688	—
Accounts	582	3
Due from other governments	472	2
Loans receivable from component unit and others	760	—
Other assets	483	340
Net pension and OPEB asset	491	—
Assets limited as to use, held by trustee	—	337
Capital assets not being depreciated	7,027	2,727
Capital assets, net of accumulated depreciation	22,554	6,210
Infrastructure assets, net of accumulated depreciation	35,726	—
Total assets	82,954	10,631
Liabilities		
Accounts payable	2,134	15
Accrued payroll and deductions payable	848	41
Accrued interest payable	268	81
Bonds payable, current portion	1,675	535
Loan payable to primary government, current portion	—	32
Unearned revenue	—	35
Advance deposits	575	—
Compensated absences, long-term	984	—
Loan payable to primary government, long-term portion	—	626
Bonds payable, long-term portion	23,440	3,827
Total liabilities	29,924	5,192
Net Position		
Invested in capital assets, net of related debt	40,192	4,334
Restricted	2,680	—
Unrestricted	10,158	1,105
Total net position	$53,030	$ 5,439

See accompanying notes.

Notes: We made some format changes to incorporate into the statements the effects of changes in accounting standards made after the statements were issued, as well as to serve pedagogical purposes.

Source: Adapted from the Comprehensive Annual Financial Report, Mt. Lebanon, Pennsylvania, December 31, 2009.

| **TABLE 10-2** | Reconciliation of Fund and Government-Wide Position Statements |

Mt. Lebanon, Pennsylvania
Reconciliation of the Governmental Funds Balance Sheet to the Statement of Net Position
December 31, 2009
(in thousands of dollars)

Total fund balance—governmental funds		$ 10,666
Amounts reported for governmental activities in the statement of net position are different because		
Capital assets used in governmental activities are not financial resources and, therefore, are not reported in the funds.		65,307
Other long-term assets are not available to pay for current-period expenditures and, therefore, are not reported in the funds.		2,932
Interest expense on long-term debt is not recognized in the fund statements until due.		(267)
The net pension and other postemployment benefit assets are not reported in the fund statements.		491
Long-term liabilities are not due and payable in the current period and, therefore, are not reported in the funds:		
Compensated absences	(984)	
Bonds payable	(25,115)	(26,099)
Net position—governmental activities		$ 53,030

See accompanying notes.

Source: Adapted from the Comprehensive Annual Financial Report, Mt. Lebanon, Pennsylvania, Decebmer 31, 2009.

FORMATTING THE STATEMENT   Similar to the reporting on proprietary funds, GASB Statement No. 63 (June 2011) requires deferred outflows of resources to be displayed separately from assets and deferred inflows of resources to be displayed separately from liabilities in the government-wide statement of net position. Mt. Lebanon, however, had no items specifically identified by the GASB as deferred outflows or inflows of resources. Therefore, Table 10-1 is presented in the format: assets − liabilities = net position, rather than (assets + deferred outflows of resources) − (liabilities + deferred inflows of resources) = net position. Notice, in particular, that the difference between assets and liabilities is reported as *net position*, not net assets or fund balances.

It is appropriate to comment on a few items in Table 10-1 that the GASB considers to be assets and liabilities, rather than deferred outflows and deferred inflows of resources. The caption Other assets ($483 thousand) includes various prepayments. *Prepayments* meet the GASB's definition of *assets*—resources with *present service capacity* (the existing capability to enable the government to provide services) that the government presently *controls*. The Net pension and OPEB asset ($491 thousand) is similar to a prepayment asset in the sense that it is a resource that can be used to pay future benefits to employees for services they will provide in the future. The *Unearned revenue* ($35 thousand) shown in the table meets the GASB's definition of *liabilities*—present obligations to sacrifice resources that a government has little or no discretion to avoid. The Unearned revenue occurred because the component unit received resources in advance of an exchange transaction, as a result of which it incurred a performance obligation—a promise to provide services to customers.

REPORTING ON LIQUIDITY GASB standards encourage reporting assets and liabilities in order of relative liquidity. For assets, relative liquidity means nearness in time to conversion to cash; an asset's liquidity is also affected by restrictions that limit the government's ability to use the resources. For liabilities, liquidity means nearness in time to payment. The statement of net position may be formatted by simply listing all assets and liabilities in order of liquidity or by using a classified format, wherein current items are separated from noncurrent items. For this purpose, *current* is distinguished from *noncurrent* using the business-type activity definition, wherein current assets are those expected to be converted to cash or consumed in operations within 1 year and current liabilities are those due to be paid within 1 year.

Some types of liabilities (such as bonds payable and compensated absences) often have both current and noncurrent elements. The GASB suggests that those liabilities be reported in two components—the amount due in 1 year and the amount due in more than 1 year. As a result, the liabilities sections of financial statements are often presented by first listing items that are entirely current and then reporting noncurrent liabilities in two components, those due within 1 year and those due in more than 1 year.

Notice that the assets and liabilities in Mt. Lebanon's statement of net position (Table 10-1) are presented in order of relative liquidity. Cash is shown as the first asset, and capital assets as the last; the portions of long-term liabilities that are due within 1 year (bonds payable and loans payable) are separated from the longer maturities and shown with the liabilities more currently due for payment.

CLASSIFYING COMPONENTS OF NET POSITION The difference between assets and liabilities—the net position—should be separated into three components: (1) invested in capital assets, net of related debt, (2) restricted, and (3) unrestricted. The net position component *invested in capital assets, net of related debt* represents the government's capital assets minus accumulated depreciation and outstanding balances of bonds, notes, or other borrowings attributable to acquiring, constructing, or improving those assets. In Table 10-1, the amount invested in capital assets, net of related debt in the governmental activities column ($40,192 thousand) is the total of the three capital asset lines ($65,307 thousand) minus the total of the two bonds payable lines ($25,115 thousand).

Net position is reported as *restricted* when constraints are imposed on the use of assets, either externally (by creditors, grantors, or laws or regulations of other governments) or by the government's charter or enabling legislation. For example, restrictions may be imposed by debt covenants or by higher-level governments when they provide resources with the explicit requirement that the resources be used only for a specific purpose, such as a particular capital project or a particular operating function. Amounts classified as restricted resources should be reduced by the specific liabilities that will be liquidated with those assets or by the specific liabilities from which the assets resulted. For example, amounts restricted for debt service should be reduced by related accrued bond interest payable. However, negative amounts are not reported for items classified as restricted net position; if related liabilities exceed an item of restricted net position, the resulting "shortfall" is, by default, covered by the unrestricted net position.[2]

The amount reported as *unrestricted net position* is the "residual" component of net position; it is simply the net position does not meet the definition of *restricted* or *invested in capital assets, net of related debt*. The amount of *unrestricted net position* in the governmental activities

---

[2]GASB 2010–2011 Comprehensive Implementation Guide, Q & A 7.24.13, p. 7–48.

column of the government-wide statement of net position may differ significantly from the total *unassigned fund balances* reported in the governmental funds balance sheet. One reason for the disparity is that commitments and assignments are not reported in the government-wide statement of net position. Another cause of the difference is the use of different bases of accounting in the two statements.

The Statement of Activities

The government-wide operations are reported in a *statement of activities,* presented in a format that shows the extent to which each function is self-financing (through fees and intergovernmental grants) and the extent to which it draws on the government's taxes and other general revenues. To accomplish that purpose, the statement of activities is presented in two sections: The upper portion shows the net expenses of each function or program (after deducting applicable revenues), and the lower portion shows the general revenues and the resulting change in net position for the year.

To prepare the statement, all gross expenses are listed in the first column in the upper left part of the financial statement. Revenues directly related to each function or program (called *program revenues*) are listed in the next three columns based on type of revenue—*charges for services, operating grants*, and *capital grants*—to the immediate right of gross expenses. The differences between gross expenses and program revenues are the net expenses or revenues for each function or program; these differences are presented in a column to the right of the program revenues columns. Then, in this same column, taxes, other general revenues (such as investment earnings and grants not restricted to specific purposes), and special and extraordinary items are displayed in the lower part of the statement to arrive at the change in net position.

Table 10-3 presents the government-wide statement of activities for Mt. Lebanon, Pennsylvania, for the year ended December 31, 2009. Notice that expenses and related program revenues are displayed in the upper half of the financial statement, with governmental activities separated from the component units. Taxes, other general revenues, and special and extraordinary items are shown in the lower part of the statement. A primary government may, of course, have both governmental activities and business-type activities. If Mt. Lebanon had business-type activities, captions for each function/program would be shown on the left side of the page just below the governmental activities, and the caption "total primary government" would include the data for the business-type activities. Also, instead of the two columns shown here, the right side of the statement would have four columns—three for the primary government (labeled for governmental activities, business-type activities, and a total of those two columns) and another column for the component units.

REPORTING EXPENSES   Governmental units report expenses by function or program (such as public safety and culture and recreation), except for expenses that meet the definition of special or extraordinary, which need to be shown separately, as discussed in Chapter 9. At a minimum, the statement of activities should show the direct functional expenses—those that are clearly identifiable to a particular function. Although not required to do so, governmental units may allocate certain indirect expenses (such as general government and support services) among the functions.

Depreciation expense for capital assets that can be specifically identified with a function (e.g., a police station or a firehouse) should be included with the direct expenses of the function. Depreciation expense for general infrastructure assets (such as water mains) may be reported either as a direct expense of the function that acquires and maintains the assets (such as public works) or as a separate line item in the statement of activities. Interest on general long-term debt generally should be shown separately.

TABLE 10-3 Government-Wide Statement of Activities

Mt. Lebanon, Pennsylvania
Statement of Activities
Year Ended December 31, 2009
(in thousands of dollars)

		Program Revenues			Net (Expenses) Revenues and Changes in Net Position	
	Expenses	Charges for Services	Operating Grants	Capital Grants	Governmental Activities	Component Units
Primary Government						
Governmental activities:						
General government	$ 4,346	$ 1,588	$ 606	$ —	$ (2,152)	$ —
Community development	1,386	190	18	—	(1,178)	—
Public works	12,177	7,507	716	190	(3,764)	—
Human services	1,549	88	753	—	(708)	—
Culture and recreation	3,126	2,364	7	—	(755)	—
Public safety:						
Police	6,247	217	137	—	(5,893)	—
Fire	3,160	126	212	—	(2,822)	—
Other	304	449	1	—	(354)	—
Interest on long-term debt	884	—	—	—	(884)	—
Total governmental activities	33,679	12,529	2,450	190	(18,510)	—
Total primary government	$33,679	$12,529	2,450	$190	(18,510)	—
Component Units						
Mt. Lebanon Parking Authority	$ 1,427	$ 1,540	—	—	—	113
Mt. Lebanon Ind. Develop. Auth.	13	4	—	—	—	(9)
Total component units	$ 1,440	$ 1,544	—	—	—	104
General revenues:						
Taxes: Real estate					10,589	—
Earned income					9,289	—
Other					2,503	—
Interest income					67	10
Gain on sale of capital assets					—	308
Total general revenues					22,448	318
Change in net position					3,938	422
Net position, beginning of year					49,092	5,017
Net position, end of year					$53,030	$5,439

See accompanying notes.
Source: Adapted from the Comprehensive Annual Financial Report, Mt. Lebanon, Pennsylvania, December 31, 2009.

Notice that Mt. Lebanon's statement of activities in Table 10-3 shows the same six functions in its governmental activities that it reports in its governmental funds statement of revenues, expenditures, and changes in fund balances (see Table 9-3 on page 327). Mt. Lebanon also reports expenses and revenues separately for each of its component units.

REPORTING NET FUNCTIONAL EXPENSES The statement of activities must be displayed in a manner that shows the net expense or revenue for each function or program. For this reason, the statement of activities uses columns for three types of program revenues associated directly with each function: charges for services, program-specific operating grants and contributions, and program-specific capital grants and contributions.

Charges for services are revenues based on exchange or exchange-like transactions. They include fees for specific services (such as garbage collection, water use, or parks admissions fees), licenses and permits (such as liquor licenses and building permits), and other amounts charged to service recipients. Charges for services also include fines and forfeitures (such as parking fines and fines arising out of inspections) because they are revenues generated by specific programs. Although charges for services tend to defray only a small part of the expenses of governmental activities, they generally exceed the expenses of business-type activities.

Program-specific operating grants and contributions arise out of revenues received from other governments, organizations, or individuals that are restricted for use in a particular program. Grants and contributions reported in this column are those received for operating purposes or for either operating or capital purposes at the receiving government's discretion. Program-specific operating grants and contributions include the typical program-oriented state aid programs such as aid for education and health care purposes.

Program-specific capital grants and contributions are reported in a separate column. In analyzing financial statements, amounts in this column need to be considered carefully because significant revenues from capital grants and contributions can distort amounts reported as net expenses or revenues. For example, the full amount of the revenue from a capital grant may be recognized in a single year, but program expenses may show only the year's depreciation on the asset acquired with the grant.

Examine the upper part of Mt. Lebanon's statement of activities (Table 10-3). Notice the amounts in the three columns headed "Program Revenues," as well as the amounts shown in the "Net (Expenses) Revenues and Changes in Net Position" columns. The amounts in the governmental activities column are all net expenses because gross expenses exceed program revenues. The aggregate of the net expenses in the governmental activities column ($18,510 thousand) is the amount that is financed by taxes, other general revenues, and net assets available at the beginning of the year, all of which are shown in the lower part of the statement.

CHANGING THE ACCOUNTING MEASUREMENTS Because of the conversion to the economic resources measurement focus and the accrual basis of accounting, the governmental activities column of the government-wide statement of activities will, of course, differ from the total governmental funds column in the funds statement of revenues, expenditures, and changes in fund balances. Mt. Lebanon's reconciliation of the two statements is shown in Table 10-4. Notice that the most significant items in the reconciliation relate to the treatment of capital asset outlays and long-term debt issuance and repayment. The need for these reconciling items is caused by the difference in measurement focus. The other differences are relatively small here, but they could be

TABLE 10-4 Reconciliation of Fund and Government-Wide Operating Statements

Mt. Lebanon, Pennsylvania
Reconciliation of the Statement of Revenues, Expenditures, and Changes in Fund
Balances of Governmental Funds to the Statement of Activities
For the Year Ended December 31, 2009
(in thousands of dollars)

Net change in fund balances—total governmental funds	$2,007
Amounts reported for governmental activities in the statement of activities are different because	
Governmental funds report capital outlays as expenditures. However, in the statement of activities, the cost of these assets is allocated over their estimated useful lives and reported as depreciation expense. This is the amount by which capital outlays ($5,174) exceeded depreciation ($3,024) in the current period.	2,150
The issuance of long-term debt provides current financial resources to governmental funds, while the repayment of principal of long-term debt consumes the current financial resources of governmental funds. The Municipality issued no debt during the current period but repaid debt principal.	(475)
Governmental funds do not report revenues that are not available to pay current obligations. In contrast, such revenues are reported in the statement of activities when earned.	(205)
The net effect of various transactions involving capital assets (i.e., sales, dispositions, and trade-ins) is to increase net assets.	188
Some expenses reported in the statement of activities do not require the use of current financial resources and, therefore, are not reported as expenditures in the governmental funds.	54
The accrued liability for compensated absences decreased by $20 thousand; other long-term liabilities decreased by $173 thousand; and the net pension and other postemployment benefit asset increased by $26 thousand. These changes did not affect the net change in fund balance in the fund statement but increased the change in net position in the government-wide statement.	219
Change in net position of governmental activities— statement of activities	$3,938

See accompanying notes.

Source: Adapted from the Comprehensive Annual Financial Report, Mt. Lebanon, Pennsylvania, December 31, 2009.

larger in some circumstances; for example, if a government does not finance pension and other postemployment benefits as the benefits are earned.

Interfund and Internal Service Fund Balances and Activity

As discussed in previous chapters, fund accounting often results in transfers among, charges to, and balances due to and from the various funds. As a general rule, these types of internal activities and balances—reported in the fund financial statements—are eliminated when preparing the government-wide statement of net position and statement of activities. Unless the eliminations are made, totals for the entity as a whole will be inflated. How are these eliminations made?

INTERFUND RECEIVABLES AND PAYABLES   Amounts due between individual governmental funds, as reported in the governmental funds balance sheet, are eliminated against each other and are not carried forward to the governmental activities column of the government-wide statement of net assets. The same should be done for amounts due between individual proprietary funds. However, amounts due between these two fund categories (e.g., governmental and proprietary) are carried forward to the respective columns for governmental- and business-type activities in the statement of net position and are reported as *internal balances*. Internal balances are eliminated against each other within the statement of net position.

To illustrate, turn to Mt. Lebanon's governmental funds balance sheet (Table 9-1 on page 325) and the statement of net position (Table 10-1). In Table 9-1, Due from other funds shows $1,150 thousand in the total column, and Due to other funds shows the same amount. These amounts do not appear, however, in the governmental activities column of the government-wide statement of net position, because they have been offset against each other to report the consolidated net financial position.

INTERFUND TRANSFERS   In the statement of activities, the treatment just described for interfund receivables and payables applies as well to interfund transfers and charges. Trace the elimination of the interfund activity by referring to Tables 9-3 and 10-3 of the Mt. Lebanon illustration. Notice that both transfers in and transfers out among the governmental-type funds were $6,356 thousand in Table 9-3. For government-wide reporting, these transfers cancel each other out and, therefore, do not appear in Table 10-3. If Mt. Lebanon had any proprietary funds and transfers had occurred between governmental-type and proprietary-type funds, they would have been eliminated against each other in Table 10-3.

The fact that interfund transfers are eliminated in the statement of activities does not mean that they should be ignored when analyzing governmental financial statements. Some transfers may be considered as routine transfers from a resource-collecting fund to a fund authorized by law to incur expenditures or expenses. Other interfund transfers, however, may indicate that a particular activity is experiencing financial difficulties and requires continuing subsidies.

INTERNAL SERVICE FUND BALANCES AND ACTIVITY   For government-wide financial reporting, the assets and liabilities of Internal Service Funds (ISFs) are aggregated with those of the activities that are the primary consumers of ISF services. (ISFs generally provide services primarily to departments accounted for in the General Fund, so ISF assets and liabilities are aggregated most often with those of governmental activities.) Also, to avoid artificially inflating the activity reported in the government-wide statements, an elimination is needed for ISF activity because (a) ISF operating statements show both revenues (from sales to other funds) and expenses and (b) funds that buy services from ISFs report expenditures or expenses as a result of the billings. Further, ISFs often generate "artificial" profits or losses as a result of their billing practices.

To understand the nature of the adjustments, assume the following set of facts: An ISF buys, stores, and sells supplies to two departments accounted for in the General Fund and reported in the public safety and recreation functions. During the year, the ISF billed Public Safety Departments for $60,000 and Recreation Departments for $40,000. The ISF had expenses of $95,000, so it had "net profit" of $5,000, equivalent to 5 percent of its revenues. As a result of

Governmental Financial Reporting in Practice

Turning Surpluses to Deficits

Changing the measurement focus and basis of accounting for governmental funds can significantly affect reported financial position. Positive fund balances resulting from using the current financial resources measurement focus and modified accrual basis of accounting can easily become net position deficiencies when using the economic resources focus and accrual basis. The State of New Jersey and Nassau County, New York, provide good illustrations—but they are not alone.

New Jersey's fund balance sheet at June 30, 2010, shows total fund balances for all governmental funds of $7.4 billion, but the governmental activities column in its government-wide statement of net assets (now called statement of net position) shows a net asset *deficiency* of $28.2 billion. The reconciliation of the two statements provides a starting point for determining the causes of the difference and their implications. New Jersey's reconciliation shows accrued liabilities of $18.4 billion resulting from significant underfunding of its pension and OPEB obligations. There is also evidence that New Jersey borrowed long-term to finance current operating expenditures—the reconciliation shows various forms of long-term borrowing (bonds and notes payable, installment obligations, loans payable, and tobacco settlement bonds) totaling more than $45 billion, but net capital assets of only $21.8 billion.

Nassau County's governmental funds balance sheet at December 31, 2009, shows total fund balances of $502 million in its governmental funds, but its statement of net assets shows a net asset *deficiency* of $5.0 billion. (The unrestricted *deficit* portion of its net asset deficiency is $6.6 billion, because the restricted net assets and the amount invested in capital assets, net of related debt are positive amounts.) The reconciliation shows that Nassau County also has a large underfunded OPEB obligation ($3.6 billion) and other long-term liabilities ($1.2 billion). Like New Jersey, its bonds payable exceed net capital assets, indicating that long-term debt may have been sold in the past to provide resources to finance current operating expenditures.

---

the year's activities, the ISF's net assets increased by $5,000, and its year-end net assets included cash of $3,000 and supplies inventory of $12,000.

When posted to the eliminations column of a work sheet containing columns for the General Fund and the ISF, the following journal entry would eliminate the interfund activity and the interfund profit:

Revenues (ISF)	100,000	
Expenses (ISF)		95,000
Public safety expenditures		3,000
Recreation expenditures		2,000

Notice that the credits to public safety and recreation expenditures represent 5 percent of the amounts purchased from the ISF—the interfund profit. Also, note that the assets of the ISF would be picked up automatically by extension of asset balances in the ISF column to a governmental activities column.[3]

---

[3]The same result could be accomplished with journal entries affecting only the governmental activities. The ISF balances could be assumed by governmental activities by debiting cash for $3,000 and supplies inventory for $12,000 and crediting net assets for $15,000. The interfund profit could be eliminated from governmental activities expenses by debiting net assets for $5,000 and crediting public safety and recreation expenditures for $3,000 and $2,000, respectively.

PREPARING GOVERNMENT-WIDE FINANCIAL STATEMENTS

Overview

GASB Statement No. 34 requires using the economic resources measurement focus and accrual basis of accounting for *all* activities, including the governmental activities, in the government-wide financial statements. Because the fund financial statements for governmental-type funds are based on the current financial resources measurement focus and modified accrual basis of accounting, those statements must be adjusted to produce the government-wide statements. The following types of adjustments are generally needed:

- Capital assets (including infrastructure assets) and related depreciation need to be recorded.
- Proceeds from issuing long-term debt need to be recorded as liabilities, and payments of debt principal need to be recorded as reductions of liabilities.
- Revenues need to be recognized on the accrual basis of accounting, so the "measurable and available" rule for recognizing tax revenues in the governmental-type funds is discarded.
- Expenses need to be recognized when incurred, so noncurrent liabilities resulting from current transactions and events must be reported.

In addition, adjustments are generally needed if a government sells capital assets, issues debt at a premium or discount, or maintains Internal Service Funds.

Proprietary fund financial statements are prepared using the economic resources measurement focus and accrual basis of accounting, so no measurement focus and basis of accounting adjustments are needed when Enterprise Funds are incorporated in the government-wide financial statements.

Process for Preparing Government-Wide Statements

The simplest way to prepare the government-wide financial statements—the method we use to illustrate the process later in the chapter—is to use a six-column work sheet to record the adjustments. (Later in the chapter we will show how keeping a separate set of accounts for capital assets can facilitate making some of the adjustments.) Using a work sheet requires three sets of debit and credit columns:

- Starting balances (an aggregation of the preclosing trial balances of the governmental-type funds)
- Adjustments to convert the measurement focus and basis of accounting of governmental-type funds from current financial and modified accrual to economic resources and accrual
- Adjusted preclosing trial balances

The adjustments made in the work sheet take the following forms:

- Entering beginning-of-year balances of accounts that affect the government-wide statements, such as capital assets and bonds payable
- Making adjustments for transactions and events that occurred during the year and that affect the accounts differently when the measurement focus and basis of accounting are changed
- Eliminating transfers and interfund balances among governmental-type funds

There is no need for concern with terminology in the work sheet because terms like *expenditures* can be converted to *expenses* and *fund balances* can be converted to *net position* when you prepare the government-wide statements.

Discussion of Adjustments for Government-Wide Statements

This section describes and illustrates some of the adjustments needed in preparing the government-wide financial statements, using the fund preclosing trial balances as a starting point. We also cover revenue and expense recognition standards under the accrual basis of accounting. The comprehensive illustration later in the chapter provides additional adjustments needed for preparing the government-wide financial statements.

ACQUIRING AND DEPRECIATING CAPITAL ASSETS   As you know, when capital assets are acquired with governmental fund resources, they are recorded in the funds as capital outlay expenditures, rather than as assets. Further, capital assets are not depreciated in the funds. Therefore, to report using the economic resources measurement focus and accrual basis of accounting, adjustments are needed to reverse capital outlay expenditures, record capital acquisitions as assets, and record depreciation expense. In all likelihood, the government will have reported capital assets at the beginning of the year. Therefore, beginning-of-year balances of capital assets and related accumulated depreciation also need to be entered in the work sheet.

To illustrate, assume a city had $1,000,000 of capital assets (equipment) at the start of its calendar year 2013 and that accumulated depreciation on those assets was $400,000. During 2013, the city had $200,000 of capital outlay expenditures. Depreciation on old and new assets during 2013 was $110,000. The only data reported in the fund financial statements for these transactions and events were the expenditures for acquiring the new equipment. Preparing the government-wide statements requires recording the opening balances, adjusting the accounting for equipment acquired during the year, and recording depreciation expense for the year. This is accomplished by making the following adjusting journal entries:

Capital assets—equipment	1,000,000	
Accumulated depreciation—equipment		400,000
Net position		600,000
To record account balances as of January 1, 2013.		
Capital assets—equipment	200,000	
Expenditures—capital outlay		200,000
To reverse 2013 expenditures and record capital assets.		
Depreciation expense—equipment	110,000	
Accumulated depreciation—equipment		110,000
To record depreciation expense for 2013.		

Notice that recording net capital assets at the start of the year requires a credit to net position. This is because reporting capital acquisitions as assets rather than as expenditures causes governmental "equity" (net position) to be greater than that reported under the current financial resources measurement focus. Similarly, as the next section shows, reporting proceeds from the sale of bonds as liabilities reduces governmental "equity."

SELLING AND REDEEMING LONG-TERM DEBT   Fund-level reporting on governmental-type funds requires that you report proceeds of long-term debt as financing sources, not as liabilities, and that you report the repayment of long-term debt as expenditures, not as reductions of liabilities. The economic resources measurement focus used in government-wide financial reporting requires adjustments to report long-term debt as liabilities. The adjustments needed to record beginning-of-year outstanding long-term debt, sale of new long-term debt, and redemption of outstanding long-term debt are similar to the adjustments described regarding capital assets—except that the effect on net position is just the opposite.

Assume, for example, that the city in the previous illustration had outstanding long-term debt of $500,000 at the start of the year. During the year, it sold $200,000 of debt to acquire capital assets and repaid $100,000 of debt that was outstanding at the beginning of the year. The following adjustments are needed to prepare the government-wide financial statements from the fund preclosing trial balances:

Net position	500,000	
Bonds payable		500,000
To record account balances as of January 1, 2013.		
Other financing sources—proceeds from bond issue	200,000	
Bonds payable		200,000
To reduce financing source and record liability.		
Bonds payable	100,000	
Expenditures—bond principal		100,000
To reduce expenditures and record repayment of liability.		

ACCRUING REVENUES   In reporting on governmental-type funds, taxes are recognized as revenues in the accounting period that they become measurable and available. For government-wide financial reporting, the GASB adopted specific accrual-basis standards for taxes and other nonexchange revenues in GASB Statement No. 33. The standards and resulting adjustments needed to prepare government-wide financial statements are summarized as follows:

Derived Tax Revenues (Sales Taxes, Income Taxes).   As discussed in Chapter 5, tax revenues from general sales, sales of specific commodities, and personal incomes are derived from assessments imposed by a government on external exchange transactions. Tax revenues from corporate incomes are obtained in the same manner.

For government-wide financial reporting, these "derived" tax revenues are recognized (net of estimated refunds and estimated uncollectible amounts) when the assets are recognized—generally, on occurrence of the exchange transaction on which the tax is imposed. With regard to sales taxes, for example, the practical effect of the standard is to require revenue recognition at the time of the taxable sale, regardless of when the cash is received.[4]

To illustrate, suppose a state collects sales taxes on behalf of a city whose fiscal year ends December 31, 2013. The state's practice is to remit the taxes to the city between 90 and 120 days after the end of the quarter for which it has collected the taxes. When preparing its 2013 fund financial statements, the city—based on its accounting policy regarding the definition of *available*—reports sales taxes receivable for the quarter ended December 31, 2013, but defers recognition of the revenues because they are not "available." For its 2013 government-wide financial statements, however, the city would recognize sales tax revenues for the quarter ended December 31, 2013, even though it will not receive the taxes until April 2014.

Imposed Nonexchange Revenues (Real Property Taxes, Fines).   Imposed nonexchange revenues are taxes and other assessments levied without an underlying external exchange,

---

[4]GASB Cod. Sec. N50.113.

such as real property taxes and fines. For government-wide financial reporting, real property tax revenues are recognized (net of estimated refunds and estimated uncollectible amounts) in the period for which the taxes are levied, even if the enforceable legal claim arises or the due date for payment occurs in a different period.[5] The accrual-basis standard makes no reference to the term *measurable and available*. Therefore, for government-wide reporting, if a city levies real property taxes on January 1, 2013, for calendar year 2013, property tax revenues are recognized in 2013 for the amount levied (net of estimated refunds and uncollectible amounts), even though some of the taxes may be collected after the 60-day availability criterion discussed in Chapter 5.

Adjustments for Preparing Government-Wide Statements.   Modified accrual accounting for tax revenues makes it likely that deferred inflows of resources will be reported at year-end for tax revenues applicable to a particular year that have not yet met the "measurable and available" criteria for revenue recognition. Therefore, two adjustments are needed when the government-wide statements are prepared: (1) to take account of the beginning-of-year deferral and (2) to remove the current year's deferral. You need to be careful when making the first adjustment because the deferral was reversed in the funds when the receivable was collected during the year.

To illustrate, assume a city started calendar year 2013 with deferred property taxes of $10,000. The entire $10,000 was collected in 2013. Property taxes of $800,000 were levied for 2013. Although the city expected to collect the entire $800,000, it actually collected only $760,000 in 2013; it expected to collect $25,000 more by February 28, 2014, and the remaining $15,000 in the latter part of 2014.

Based on the foregoing data, the city reported $15,000 of deferred property tax revenues in its fund financial statements for 2013. The city also reported $795,000 of property tax revenues in 2013—$10,000 from reversing the prior year's deferral, plus $785,000 that met the measurable and available criteria for the 2013 tax levy. Based on the accrual accounting criteria, however, $800,000 of property tax revenues—the entire 2013 property tax levy—should be recognized in the government-wide statements. Therefore, the net effect of the adjustments must be to increase property tax revenues by $5,000 and to remove the $15,000 of deferred property tax revenues. The following adjustments to the data reported in the fund financial statements accomplish this result:

Revenues—property taxes	10,000	
Net position		10,000
To reverse revenues applicable to 2012 but recognized in the fund statements during 2013.		
Deferred property tax revenues	15,000	
Revenues—property taxes		15,000
To recognize additional revenues from 2013 property tax levy by removing the deferral.		

Intergovernmental Aid.   Higher-level governments often provide resources to lower-level governments to be used for specific purposes set forth in the higher-level government's enabling legislation. In addition to purpose restrictions, the provider government may establish other eligibility requirements, such as time and expenditure-incurrence requirements. The GASB standard requires that the receiving government recognize receivables and revenues (net of uncollectible amounts) when all eligibility requirements, including time requirements, are met.[6] For

---

[5]GASB Cod. Sec. N50.115.
[6]GASB Cod. Sec. N50.118.

example, a state law may provide that the state reimburse counties 50 percent of all allowable costs incurred on a specific health program, subject to maximum amounts specified in annual contracts between the state health department and the counties. In these so-called expenditure-driven grants, counties recognize receivables and revenues as they incur allowable costs—the point when they meet the eligibility requirements—up to the maximum amount specified in the contract.

In these situations, financial reporting in the fund and the government-wide financial statements are likely to be the same. If, for some reason, revenue recognition is deferred in the fund financial statements because it isn't considered "available," an adjustment similar to that made for deferred taxes would be needed for the government-wide statements.

ACCRUING EXPENSES As discussed in Chapters 5 and 6, the modified accrual basis of accounting provides for several significant departures from accrual accounting when recognizing expenditures. You need to adjust for these accrual accounting departures to report expenses for governmental activities in the government-wide financial statements. Here are some examples.

"Stub Period" Interest on General Obligation Long-Term Debt. As discussed in Chapter 6, under modified accrual accounting, interest on general obligation long-term debt and capital leases is, as a general rule, recognized only to the extent that the interest matures and is payable. Interest for the "stub period"—the period between the last interest payment in one fiscal year and the fiscal year-end—is generally not accrued. Therefore, accruing the stub period interest is a common adjustment in preparing the accrual-basis government-wide financial statements.

To illustrate, assume a city that operates on a calendar year basis sold long-term debt of $200,000 on October 1, 2012. The debt matures at the rate of $50,000 a year, starting September 30, 2013. Interest is payable each September 30 at the rate of 4 percent per annum on the outstanding balance. What adjustment to the fund financial statements is needed for interest when the city prepares its government-wide statements at December 31, 2013?

Answer: The city had no matured interest during 2012, so it recorded no interest in its 2012 fund financial statements. But for its 2012 government-wide statements, the city reported an expense and a liability of $2,000 for the stub period October 1–December 31, 2012 ($200,000 × 4% × 1/4 year). For its 2013 governmental fund statements, the city reported interest expenditures of $8,000 ($200,000 × 4% × 1 year) because that was the amount of matured interest during the year. For its 2013 government-wide statements, the interest expense should be $7,500, consisting of these two components:

- Interest for 9 months (previously paid) on $200,000 at 4 percent, or $6,000
- Unpaid accrued interest for 3 months on $150,000 at 4 percent, or $1,500

Therefore, the $8,000 interest expenditure reported in the 2013 fund statements must be reduced by $500. You also want to report an accrued interest liability of $1,500—the accrual for the stub period October 1–December 31, 2013. You can accomplish both tasks by first recording the beginning-of-year interest liability and then adjusting it to the end-of-year liability, as follows:

Net position	2,000	
Accrued interest payable		2,000
To record interest liability on January 1, 2013.		
Accrued interest payable	500	
Expenditures—interest on bonds		500
To adjust expenditure and liability to the accrual basis of accounting.		

When reporting interest in the government-wide financial statements, you should describe it as *expense* rather than *expenditure,* because the journal entries adjusted the amount from the modified accrual expenditure to the full accrual expense.

Expenses Incurred but Not Currently Due and Payable.   As discussed in Chapter 5, when the modified accrual basis of accounting is used, certain specific expenditures are recognized as fund liabilities only to the extent the liabilities are "normally expected to be liquidated with expendable available resources." In effect, these items—which include compensated absences, judgments and claims, and landfill closure and postclosure costs—are not recognized as expenditures until they come due for payment. Under accrual accounting, however, expenses are recognized when the liabilities are incurred, regardless of when the cash outflows occur. For example, compensated absences are recognized as employees earn the right to the benefits. In preparing government-wide financial statements, it is likely that additional expenses will need to be accrued and additional liabilities (mostly noncurrent) will need to be recognized. The adjustment is similar to that just described for interest; that is, you should first record the beginning-of-year liability and then adjust it to the appropriate end-of-year liability.

Pensions and Other Postemployment Benefits.   In reporting on governmental-type funds, expenditures for pension, retiree health care, and other postempoyment benefits are "equal to the amount contributed to the plan or expected to be liquidated with expendable available financial resources" (see Chapter 5). For government-wide reporting on governmental activities, however, an adjustment may be needed to recognize expenses and liabilities using the GASB's accrual-basis standards, briefly discussed in Chapter 8. Because most governments finance retiree health care and other postemployment benefits (collectively called OPEB) only when payments are made on behalf of retirees, virtually all governments that provide such benefits need to make an adjustment.

As discussed in the box entitled "New York City Takes a Big Accounting Bang!" GASB standards permit the OPEB obligation to be accreted gradually onto the government-wide statements. The amount accreted annually is the difference between the annual accrual basis OPEB expense and the contribution made during the year. (The annual accrual basis OPEB expense covers the year's normal cost plus amortization of the unfunded actuarial accrued liability over a period not to exceed 30 years; the contribution made generally is the amount of benefit expenditures made during the year on behalf of retired employees.) To illustrate, in a note to its financial statements for the year ended June 30, 2010, the State of California presented a schedule of changes in long-term obligations, including its OPEB obligation. The schedule shows an obligation of $4.6 billion as of July 1, 2009; an addition of $3.8 billion (the annual OPEB expense); a deduction of $1.3 billion (the benefit expenditures during the year on behalf of the retirees); and a balance of $7.1 billion as of June 30, 2010. The year-to-year increase in the obligation is $2.5 billion, the difference between the annual OPEB expense and the benefit expenditures.

To prepare the governmental activities column of its government-wide statements, using the procedure just discussed, California would have made these journal entries:

Net position	$4.6 billion	
Net OPEB obligation		$4.6 billion
To record OPEB liability at start of year.		
OPEB expense	$2.5 billion	
Net OPEB obligation		$2.5 billion
To record net increase in OPEB obligation.		

> **Governmental Financial Reporting in Practice**
>
> **New York City Takes a Big Accounting Bang!**
>
> As discussed in Chapter 8, GASB Statement No. 45 (June 2004) requires employers to report the expense of postemployment health care and other benefits in the period the employees work, rather than when the benefits are paid. For many governmental employers, transition to the new accounting standard resulted in the need to take account of a large actuarial accrued liability for postemployment health care benefits attributable to retired employees and to the past service of active employees.
>
> The standard allows employers to record this liability gradually (over 30 years) or all at once. Unlike the State of California (previously discussed), New York City opted to record the entire actuarial accrued liability at once. The result: a huge accounting bang—$53.5 billion! That number appears in the city's reconciliation of its fund and government-wide operating statements for the fiscal year ended June 30, 2006. The fund balances of its governmental-type funds (shown in the fund statement) declined by $736 million, but the decision to record the $53.5 billion transition liability for postemployment health care benefits all at once caused the net position of its governmental activities (which appears in the government-wide statement) to decline by a total of $53.7 billion. According to New York City's financial statements for the fiscal year ended June 30, 2010, that liability has increased to $75.0 billion.

CREATING GOVERNMENT-WIDE FINANCIAL STATEMENTS FROM FUND FINANCIAL DATA: COMPREHENSIVE ILLUSTRATION

This section illustrates the preparation of government-wide financial statements by making adjustments to the fund financial statements on a work sheet. Our objective is to illustrate the adjustments within the context of opening balances and a full series of transactions and events that had been recorded in the funds. The illustration contains basic transactions in three governmental-type funds: a General Fund, a Debt Service Fund, and a Capital Projects Fund.

Opening Balances, Transactions, and Events

Assume, for simplicity, that Eunee City's General Fund has just two programs, Public Safety and Parks. To further simplify the illustration, all numbers are expressed in thousands of dollars, and budgetary accounting is not shown.

On January 1, 2013, there were zero account balances in both the Debt Service Fund and the Capital Projects Fund. The General Fund had the following balances:

Cash	$25	
Property taxes receivable—delinquent	35	
Deferred property tax revenues		$10
Unassigned fund balance		50
Totals	$60	$60

Eunee City's government-wide financial statements for the year ended December 31, 2012, reported that the city had (a) capital assets of $400 and accumulated depreciation on the assets of $280; (b) outstanding long-term general obligation bonds of $60; (c) accrued interest of $2 on the long-term bonds; and (d) an accrual of $4 for long-term compensated absences.

The following transactions and events occurred during the calendar year 2013:

1. On January 1, the city levied property taxes of $710, all of which were expected to be collected.
2. During the year, the city collected $35 of delinquent property taxes outstanding on January 1, 2013. (This amount included $10 for which revenue had been deferred because the city did not expect to collect it until July 2013.)
3. During the year, the city collected $660 of the $710 levied for property taxes. At year-end, the remaining $50 was declared delinquent. The city expected to collect $32 of it in the first 60 days of 2014 and the other $18 during the rest of 2014.
4. The city paid $610 cash for salaries and supplies, charging $470 to Public Safety and $140 to Parks.
5. The Parks Department collected fees of $20 for parking in the city's parks.
6. At the beginning of the year, the city sold the police chief's old sedan for $1. The sedan had originally cost $20 and had accumulated depreciation of $16.
7. The General Fund transferred $65 to the Debt Service Fund to provide resources for paying debt service. Assume the bond agreement results in classifying Debt Service Fund resources as Restricted.
8. On April 1, 2013, the city paid off its outstanding general obligation debt of $60, together with interest of $4 for the period of October 1, 2012, to April 1, 2013.
9. On April 1, 2013, the city sold $400 of general obligation debt, to be used to acquire capital assets. It will repay the debt in 10 equal annual installments of principal, starting April 1, 2014, together with interest at the rate of 5 percent per annum on the unpaid principal.
10. On July 1, 2013, the city used $300 of bond proceeds to acquire capital assets. The capital assets have a useful life of 20 years and no salvage value.
11. At year-end, the city estimated that the long-term liability for compensated absences had increased to $5. All compensated absences apply to Public Safety.
12. Depreciation for the year on the city's capital assets was $30. The entire depreciation amount applies to Public Safety.

Journal Entries to Record Transactions in Funds

Journal entries to record the foregoing transactions in the three governmental-type funds are as follows:

Entry in General Fund	1. Property taxes receivable	710	
	Revenues—property taxes		710
	To record property tax levy for 2013.		
Entries in General Fund	2. Cash	35	
	Property taxes receivable—delinquent		35
	To record collection of property taxes.		
	Deferred property tax revenues	10	
	Revenues—property taxes		10
	To recognize revenues previously deferred.		
Entries in General Fund	3. Cash	660	
	Property taxes receivable		660
	To record collection of 2013 property taxes.		

	Property taxes receivable—delinquent	50	
	Property taxes receivable		50
	To record delinquent tax receivables.		
	Revenues—property taxes	18	
	Deferred tax revenues		18
	To record property taxes not available.		

Entry in General Fund	4. Expenditures—public safety	470	
	Expenditures—parks	140	
	Cash		610
	To record expenditures paid in cash.		

Entry in General Fund	5. Cash	20	
	Revenues—parking fees		20
	To record parking fee revenues.		

Entry in General Fund	6. Cash	1	
	Other financing sources—sale of assets		1
	To record sale of used sedan.		

Entry in General Fund	7. Transfer out to Debt Service Fund	65	
	Cash		65
	To record transfer out.		

Entry in Debt Service Fund	Cash	65	
	Transfer in from General Fund		65
	To record transfer in.		

Entries in Debt Service Fund	8. Expenditures—bond principal	60	
	Expenditures—bond interest	4	
	Matured bond principal payable		60
	Matured bond interest payable		4
	To record liability for matured debt service.		
	Matured bond principal payable	60	
	Matured bond interest payable	4	
	Cash		64
	To record payment of debt service.		

Entry in Capital Projects Fund	9. Cash	400	
	Other financing sources—proceeds of bonds		400
	To record proceeds of bonds.		

Entry in Capital Projects Fund	10. Expenditures—capital outlay	300	
	Cash		300
	To record acquisition of capital assets.		

11. No entry required in funds.

12. No entry required in funds.

Preclosing Trial Balances and Fund Financial Statements

Preclosing trial balances, based on the foregoing journal entries, are shown in Table 10-5. Eunee City's governmental funds balance sheet at December 31, 2013, is shown in Table 10-6, and its governmental funds statement of revenues, expenditures, and changes in fund balances for the year ended December 31, 2013, is shown in Table 10-7. Trace the items shown in the trial balances to the two financial statements.

TABLE 10-5   Preclosing Trial Balances

Eunee City
Preclosing Trial Balances
General Fund
December 31, 2013

	Debits	Credits
Cash	$ 66	
Property taxes receivable—delinquent	50	
Deferred tax revenue		$ 18
Unassigned fund balance		50
Revenues—property taxes		702
Revenues—parking fees		20
Other financing sources—sales of assets		1
Expenditures—public safety	470	
Expenditures—parks	140	
Transfer out to Debt Service Fund	65	
Totals	$791	$791

Debt Service Fund

	Debits	Credits
Cash	$ 1	
Expenditures—bond principal	60	
Expenditures—bond interest	4	
Transfer in from General Fund		$ 65
Totals	$ 65	$ 65

Capital Projects Fund

	Debits	Credits
Cash	$100	
Expenditures—capital outlay	300	
Other financing sources—proceeds of bonds		$400
Totals	$400	$400

TABLE 10-6   Fund Financial Statement—Balance Sheet

Eunee City
Balance Sheet
Governmental Funds
December 31, 2013

	General	Debt Service	Capital Projects	Total
Assets				
Cash	$ 66	$1	$100	$167
Property taxes receivable—delinquent	50	—	—	50
Total assets	$116	$1	$100	$217
Liabilities				
Deferred Inflows of Resources				
Deferred tax revenue	$ 18	$	$	$ 18
Fund Balances				
Restricted		1	100	101
Unassigned	98	—	—	98
Total fund balances	98	1	100	199
Total liabilities, deferred inflows of resources, and fund balances	$116	$1	$100	$217

Adjustments for Preparing Government-Wide Statements

To prepare the government-wide financial statements, we start by making adjusting entries and posting them to our six-column work sheet. The adjusting entries take account of (a) the opening balances in the accounts needed to produce the government-wide statements, (b) the transactions and events during the year that affected those accounts, and (c) the elimination of interfund transfers. For illustrative purposes, we present the adjustments in five groups: capital asset adjustments, long-term debt adjustments, revenue adjustments, expense adjustments, and interfund transfer eliminations. Each adjustment is keyed to the data provided in the previous section titled "Opening Balances, Transactions, and Events." Trace the journal entries to the data provided in that section.

Capital Asset Adjustments

a. Capital assets 400
       Accumulated depreciation—capital assets 280
         Net position 120
       To record beginning-of-year account balances. (*Opening Balances data*)

b. Accumulated depreciation—capital assets 16
     Other financing sources—sale of assets 1
     Loss on sale of assets 3
       Capital assets 20
     To adjust for loss on sale of assets under economic resources
       measurement focus. (*Transaction 6*)

TABLE 10-7 Fund Financial Statement—Statement of Revenues, Expenditures, and Changes in Fund Balances

Eunee City
Statement of Revenues, Expenditures, and Changes in Fund Balances
Governmental Funds
December 31, 2013

	General	Debt Service	Capital Projects	Total
Revenues				
Property taxes	$702			$702
Parking fees	20			20
Total revenues	722			722
Expenditures				
Current:				
Public safety	470			470
Parks	140			140
Debt service:				
Principal		$60		60
Interest		4		4
Capital outlay			$300	300
Total expenditures	610	64	300	974
Excess (deficiency) of revenues over expenditures	112	(64)	(300)	(252)
Other Financing Sources (Uses)				
Proceeds of bonds			400	400
Sales of assets	1			1
Transfers in		65		65
Transfers out	(65)			(65)
Total other financing sources (uses)	(64)	65	400	401
Net change in fund balances	48	1	100	149
Fund balances—beginning	50	0	0	50
Fund balances—ending	$ 98	$ 1	$100	$199

Comment on adjustment b: Governments dispose of capital assets relatively often, sometimes realizing significant amounts of financial resources. Under the current financial resources measurement focus, the sale of capital assets results either in a financing source or a special item. When capital assets are reported under the economic resources measurement focus, the assets need to be reduced when sold or otherwise disposed of. Eunee City sold an asset during the year, so an adjusting entry is needed to account for the sale under the economic resources measurement focus. Although the sale resulted in a financing source of $1 under the current financial resources measurement focus, there was a $3 loss under the economic resources measurement focus.

c. Capital assets	300	
Expenditures—capital outlay		300

To reverse 2013 expenditures and record capital assets. (*Transaction 10*)

d. Depreciation expense—public safety	30	
Accumulated depreciation		30

To record depreciation for 2013. (*Transaction 12*)

Long-Term Debt Adjustments

e. Net position	60	
Bonds payable		60

To record beginning-of-year account balances. (*Opening Balances data*)

f. Bonds payable	60	
Expenditures—bond principal		60

To reduce expenditures and record repayment of liability. (*Transaction 8*)

g. Proceeds of bonds	400	
Bonds payable		400

To reverse financing source and record liability. (*Transaction 9*)

Revenue Adjustments

h. Revenues—property taxes	10	
Net position		10

To reverse revenues applicable to 2012 but recognized in fund statements
in 2013. (*Transaction 2*)

i. Deferred tax revenues	18	
Revenues—property taxes		18

To recognize 2013 property tax revenues on accrual basis of accounting.
(*Transaction 3*)

Comment on adjustments h and i: As shown in Table 10-7, Eunee recognized $702 of prop-
erty tax revenues in the 2013 fund financial statements. (The entire 2013 property tax levy
of $710 was expected to be collected, but $18 of that amount was deferred; on the other
hand, an additional $10 from the 2012 tax levy was recognized in 2013.) On the accrual-
basis government-wide statements, however, property tax revenues of $710 are recognized
(eliminating the deferral) because the "availability" criterion does not apply. Adjustments h
and i increase revenues by a net of $8 and remove the deferral.

Expense Adjustments

j. Net position	2	
Accrued interest payable		2

To record beginning-of-year liability. (*Opening Balances data*)

k. Interest expense	13	
Accrued interest payable		13

To record increase in interest liability on accrual basis of accounting.
(*Transaction 9*)

Comment on adjustments j and k: As a result of Transaction 8, Eunee City recognized interest
expenditures of $4 in the fund statements. Under the accrual basis of accounting, Eunee
would have recognized only $2 in 2013 because there was an accrued liability of $2 as of

December 31, 2012. Therefore, the expenditures shown in the work sheet are overstated by $2 for government-wide reporting purposes. But Eunee sold new debt in 2013 (Transaction 9) and, under the modified accrual basis of accounting, made no accrual for the unpaid interest of $15 on that debt ($400 × 5% × 9 months). The government-wide financial statements at December 31, 2013, need to show the full liability of $15. However, because we recorded the opening liability of $2 in adjustment j, we need to record only the $13 *increase* in adjustment k. The effect of adjustment k on the government-wide statements is that total interest expense will be $17 ($4 previously reported as expenditures plus the $13 adjustment).

l.	Net assets	4	
	Accrued compensated absences		4
	To record beginning-of-year balance. (*Opening Balances data*)		
m.	Compensated absences expense	1	
	Accrued compensated absences		1
	To record increase in long-term compensated absences liability. (*Transaction 11*)		

Interfund Transfer Eliminations

n.	Transfer in from General Fund	65	
	Transfer out to Debt Service Fund		65
	To eliminate transfers among governmental funds. (*Transaction 7*)		

Preparing Government-Wide Financial Statements and Reconciliations

The work sheet in Table 10-8 has two columns for the combined balances of the preclosing governmental fund trial balances (based on Table 10-5), two for the adjusting entries, and two for the adjusted trial balance. Trace the adjusting entries to the work sheet, using the letter symbols shown for each adjusting entry. The work sheet can now be used to prepare the government-wide financial statements (see Tables 10-9 and 10-10). The reconciliations between the fund financial statements and the government-wide statements can be prepared by referring to the two sets of financial statements and the adjusting entries. The reconciliations are presented in Table 10-11. Trace the government-wide financial statements back to the "adjusted balances" columns of the work sheet. Also, trace the amounts appearing in the reconciliations back to the two sets of financial statements and the adjusting entries.

Notice the following items in the government-wide financial statements:

- Long-term bonds payable are presented in two amounts in the government-wide statement of net position, due within 1 year and due in more than 1 year. The amount due in 1 year ($40) is based on the data in Transaction 9.
- The amount reported in the statement of net position as *invested in capital assets, net of related debt* is $86 (capital assets net of accumulated depreciation [$386] less *related* debt [$300]). The total amount of bonds payable is $400, but only $300 is *related* to the capital assets because the remaining $100 of bonds payable has not yet been invested in capital assets. Also, because the $100 is reported as bonds payable, it cannot be shown as an amount restricted for capital projects. To avoid misleading inferences from the face of the statement of net position, this restriction on the use of assets should be disclosed in a note to the statements.
- Although the $1 fund balance for the Debt Service Fund (in the governmental funds balance sheet) is reported as restricted, no restriction regarding debt service resources is reported in the government-wide statement of net position because the $15 accrued liability

TABLE 10-8 Work Sheet for Preparing Government-Wide Financial Statements

	Aggregated Balances of Fund Statements		Adjustments		Adjusted Balances	
	Debit	**Credit**	**Debit**	**Credit**	**Debit**	**Credit**
Cash	167				167	
Property taxes receivable	50				50	
Deferred tax revenues		18	18 (i)			
Unassigned fund balance		50				50
Revenues:						
Property taxes		702	10 (h)	18 (i)		710
Parking fees		20				20
Expenditures:						
Public safety	470				470	
Parks	140				140	
Bond principal	60			60 (f)		
Bond interest	4		13 (k)		17	
Capital outlay	300			300 (c)		
Other financing items:						
Sales of assets		1	1 (b)			
Proceeds of bonds		400	400 (g)			
Transfers in		65	65 (n)			
Transfers out	65			65 (n)		
	1,256	1,256				
Capital assets			400 (a)	20 (b)		
			300 (c)		680	
Accumulated depreciation			16 (b)	280 (a)		
				30 (d)		294
Accrued interest payable				2 (j)		
				13 (k)		15
Bonds payable			60 (f)	60 (e)		
				400 (g)		400
Accrued comp. absences				4 (l)		
				1 (m)		5
Net position			60 (e)	120 (a)		
			2 (j)	10 (h)		
			4 (l)			64
Loss on sale of assets			3 (b)		3	
Depreciation expense			30 (d)		30	
Comp. absences expense			1 (m)		1	
			1,383	1,383	1,558	1,558

TABLE 10-9 | Government-Wide Statement of Net Position

Eunee City
Statement of Net Position
December 31, 2013
(amounts in thousands)

	Governmental Activities
Assets	
Cash	$167
Property taxes receivable—delinquent	50
Capital assets, net of $294 accumulated depreciation	386
Total assets	603
Liabilities	
Accrued interest payable	15
Bonds payable:	
Due within 1 year	40
Due in more than 1 year	360
Other long-term liabilities	5
Total liabilities	420
Net Position	
Invested in capital assets, net of related debt	86
Restricted for	
Capital projects (see note)	
Unrestricted	97
Net position	$183

Note to financial statements: Cash and bonds payable include $100 of proceeds from bonds that are restricted for spending on capital projects.

TABLE 10-10 | Government-Wide Statement of Activities

Eunee City
Statement of Activities
For the Year Ended December 31, 2013
(amounts in thousands)

	Expenses	Charges for Services	Net (Expense) Revenue
Programs			
Public safety	$504		$(504)
Parks	140	$ 20	(120)
Interest on long-term debt	17		(17)
Total governmental activities	$661	$ 20	(641)
General revenues—property taxes			710
Change in net position			69
Net position, beginning			114
Net position, ending			$ 183

TABLE 10-11   Financial Statement Reconciliations

A. Reconciliation of Funds Balance Sheet to Government-Wide Statement of Net Position (amounts in thousands)

Total fund balances (Table 10-6)	$199
Amounts reported in the statement of net position are different because	
Capital assets used in governmental activities are not financial resources and, therefore, are not reported in the funds.	386
A portion of the revenues is not available to pay for current-period expenditures and, therefore, is deferred in the funds.	18
Bonds payable are not due and payable in the current period and, therefore, are not reported in the funds.	(400)
Interest on long-term debt and other liabilities are not due and payable in the current period and, therefore, are not reported in the funds.	(20)
Net assets of governmental activities (Table 10-9)	$183

B. Reconciliation of Funds Statement of Revenues, Expenditures, and Changes in Fund Balances to Government-Wide Statement of Activities (amounts in thousands)

Net change in fund balances (Table 10-7)	$149
Governmental funds report capital assets as expenditures. In the statement of activities, the costs of capital assets are allocated over their useful lives as depreciation. The amount by which capital outlays in the current period ($300) exceeded depreciation ($30) is	270
Bond proceeds provide current financial resources (and debt repayments are expenditures) in governmental funds. Issuing debt increases liabilities (and repaying debt decreases them) in the statement of net assets. The amount by which bond proceeds ($400) exceeded repayments ($60) is	(340)
Revenues in the statement of activities that do not provide current resources are not reported as revenues in the funds. The increase in deferred inflows of resources is	8
Expenses reported in the statement of activities that did not require use of current financial resources and, therefore, are not reported as expenditures in the funds were	(14)
The disposal of assets resulted in reporting a $3 loss in the statement of activities. The sale resulted in reporting $1 of other financing source in the funds, causing a difference of	(4)
Change in net position (Table 10-10)	$ 69

for interest (made for government-wide reporting purposes) exceeds the restricted resources. As discussed earlier, negative amounts are not reported for restricted resources. Having calculated the portion of net position represented by "invested in capital assets, net of related debt" and having determined that there are no restricted resources, the amount reported as *unrestricted* is the "residual" amount needed to report the total net position.

• The amount shown in the statement of activities as net position at the beginning of the year ($114) consists of the Unassigned fund balance at the beginning of the year ($50) plus the net amount of the adjustments to net assets ($64).

- The amount shown in the statement of activities for public safety expenses ($504) consists of the public safety expenditures reported in the fund statements ($470) plus other items applicable to the public safety function (depreciation expense—$30; compensated absences expense—$1; loss on sale of assets—$3).

CAPITAL ASSETS, INCLUDING INFRASTRUCTURE ASSETS

GASB Statement No. 34 prescribes standards for reporting on capital assets and provides for special treatment of certain infrastructure assets. The basic rules regarding capital assets are these:

- Capital assets of proprietary funds are reported in both the government-wide and fund financial statements.
- Capital assets of fiduciary funds are reported only in the statement of fiduciary net position.
- All other capital assets are general capital assets; general capital assets are not reported as assets in governmental funds, but are reported in the governmental activities column of the government-wide statement of net position.[7]

Capital assets are reported at historical cost, which includes ancillary charges needed to place the asset into its intended location and condition for use, such as freight and transportation costs and site preparation costs. The assets are depreciated over their estimated useful lives, unless they are inexhaustible (such as land) or are infrastructure assets that are reported using the *modified approach*, as described in the next section.

Reporting on Infrastructure Assets

Infrastructure assets are defined as

> long-lived capital assets that normally are stationary in nature and normally can be preserved for a significantly greater number of years than most capital assets. Examples of infrastructure assets include roads, bridges, tunnels, drainage systems, water and sewer systems, dams, and lighting systems. Buildings, except those that are an ancillary part of a network of infrastructure assets, should not be considered infrastructure assets.[8]

All governments, regardless of their size, are required to capitalize their infrastructure assets. (Governments with total annual revenues of less than $10 million were not required to capitalize infrastructure assets in existence before implementation of GASB Statement No. 34.) Further, once they are capitalized, infrastructure assets must be depreciated over their estimated useful lives, unless the government adopts the *modified approach.*

The modified approach was developed in response to concerns about the usefulness of depreciation based on historical costs for assets likely to have long lives if appropriately preserved, such as roads and bridges. Under the modified approach, infrastructure assets need not be depreciated, provided the government has an asset management system and documents that the assets are being preserved at or above a condition level that it establishes and discloses.

---

[7]GASB Cod. Sec. 1400 Statement of Principle.
[8]GASB Cod. Sec. 1400.103.

To meet the requirement for having an asset management system, a government would need to do the following:

- Have an up-to-date inventory of its infrastructure assets.
- Make periodic assessments of the physical condition of the assets and summarize the results using a measurement scale.
- Estimate each year the annual amount needed to maintain and preserve the assets at the condition level that it establishes and discloses.[9]

Governments would also need to document that

- Complete condition assessments are made at least every 3 years.
- The results of the three most recent condition assessments give reasonable assurance that the assets are indeed being preserved approximately at or above the established condition levels.[10]

If these sets of requirements are met and the infrastructure assets are not depreciated, all preservation expenditures are treated as expenses in the year they are incurred. Additions or improvements increase the capacity or efficiency of the assets (rather than preserve their useful lives) and should be capitalized.

It should be recognized that the requirements for adopting the modified approach are relatively rigorous. Governments may begin using the modified approach after at least one complete condition assessment is available and the government documents that the assets are being preserved approximately at or above the established condition level. Assume, for example, that a government's established condition level for a network of roads is 4 out of a maximum of 5, but the roads are actually being preserved at a level of 2. In that event, the government may begin using the modified approach only after it has made sufficient preservation expenditures so that a complete condition assessment shows the actual condition level to be 4.

Documentation regarding the management and preservation of infrastructure assets needs to be provided in the financial report as required supplementary information (RSI). To illustrate the data reported in support of the *modified approach*, Table 10-12 contains excerpts from the RSI reported by the State of Ohio in its CAFR for the year ended June 30, 2010.

Capital Asset Accounting

Governments need to maintain financial control over their capital asset inventories to ensure accountability for the assets and to provide data for the government-wide financial statements. At a minimum, the accounting system needs to be structured so that postings to the capital outlay expenditure account are accompanied with postings to the detailed capital asset inventory records. Two factors, however, can create some complications because (a) government-wide accounting for the sale of capital assets is different from such accounting within governmental-type funds and (b) government-wide accounting calls for reporting the amount invested in capital assets, net of *related* debt.

One way to accomplish financial control and to deal with the complications is to maintain a capital investment account group (CIAG). Maintaining a CIAG requires journal entries for transactions that affect the amount reported as invested in capital assets, net of related debt. This

---

[9]GASB Cod. Sec. 1400.105.
[10]GASB Cod. Sec. 1400.106.

| **TABLE 10-12** | Infrastructure Asset Accounting Using the Modified Approach |

State of Ohio
Required Supplementary Information
Infrastructure Assets Accounted for Using the Modified Approach (Excerpts)

Pavement Network

The Ohio Department of Transportation conducts annual condition assessments of its Pavement Network. The State manages its pavement system by means of annual, visual inspections by trained pavement technicians. Technicians rate the pavement using a scale of 1 (minimum) to 100 (maximum) based on a Pavement Condition Rating (PCR). This rating examines items such as cracking, potholes, deterioration of the pavement, and other factors. It does not include a detailed analysis of the pavement's subsurface conditions.

For the Priority Subsystem [interstate highways, freeways, and multilane portions of the National Highway System], it is the State's intention to maintain at least 75 percent of the pavement at a level of at least 65, and to allow no more than 25 percent of the pavement to fall below a 65 PCR level. . . .

Condition Assessment Data—Priority Subsystem

Pavement Condition Ratings (PCR)

Year	Total Lane Miles	**Percent of Lane-Miles Excellent** PCR 85–100	**Percent of Lane-Miles Good** PCR 75–84	**Percent of Lane-Miles Fair** PCR 65–74	**Percent of Lane-Miles Poor** PCR below 65
2009	12,932	66.98%	22.80%	8.24%	1.98%
2008	12,826	67.70	21.04	9.00	2.26
2007	12,718	66.50	21.63	8.81	3.06
2006	12,655	70.47	15.33	11.07	3.13
2005	12,500	68.65	15.69	12.04	3.62

Comparison of Estimated and Actual Maintenance and Preservation Costs
(in thousands of dollars)

Year	Estimated	Actual
2010	$357,393	$394,017
2009	352,644	407,564
2008	357,396	405,258
2007	403,067	418,936
2006	376,588	410,049

Source: Adapted from the Comprehensive Annual Financial Report, State of Ohio, June 30, 2010, pp. 148–149.

net asset subdivision is affected when the government acquires, depreciates, or disposes of capital assets and when it issues debt to acquire capital assets or repays that debt.

The CIAG has these balance sheet accounts: Capital assets, Accumulated depreciation, Available for investment in capital assets, Bonds payable, and Invested in capital assets, net of related debt. It also has accounts for increasing and decreasing amounts invested in capital assets, net of related debt.

To illustrate the journal entries used to maintain a CIAG, go back to the transactions provided in the comprehensive Eunee City illustration. Based on the opening balances provided in that illustration, Eunee's CIAG accounts would be as follows: Capital assets—$400; Accumulated depreciation—$280; Bonds payable—$60; and Invested in capital assets, net of related debt—$60. The entries to record the applicable 2013 transactions in the CIAG are listed here by transaction number. They are generally similar to the adjusting entries needed to prepare the government-wide financial statements from the balances in the fund accounts, except that they are designed also to keep track of the amount invested in capital assets, net of related debt.

6.	Accumulated depreciation—capital assets	16	
	Decreases—realized on sale of capital asset	1	
	Decreases—loss on sale of asset	3	
	Capital assets		20
	To record disposal of capital asset.		
8.	Bonds payable	60	
	Increases—repayment of debt		60
	To record increase in net assets invested in capital assets.		
9.	Available for investment in capital assets	400	
	Bonds payable		400
	To record issuance of long-term debt.		
10.	Capital assets	300	
	Increases—capital outlay expenditures		300
	To record increase in net assets invested in capital assets.		
	Decreases—debt used to acquire capital assets	300	
	Available for investment in capital assets		300
	To record decrease in net assets invested in capital assets.		
12.	Decreases—depreciation expense	30	
	Accumulated depreciation—capital assets		30
	To record decrease in net assets invested in capital assets.		

The increase and decrease accounts, which net to an increase of $26, are closed to Invested in capital assets, net of related debt. That amount, together with the opening balance of $60, leaves a net balance of $86, the amount shown in the statement of net position in Table 10-9.

The CIAG, though not essential for accounting purposes, improves internal control over the government's capital assets and facilitates preparation of the government-wide financial statements. It is possible to construct other forms of memorandum accounts to aid in preparing the government-wide statements.

Review Questions

Q10-1   List four basic differences between the information content of the fund financial statements and the government-wide financial statements.

Q10-2   Describe the column headings generally used in the government-wide statement of net position.

Q10-3   Describe the three components of net assets in the government-wide statement of net position.

Q10-4   What is the purpose of a *classified* statement of net position?

Q10-5   What three categories of revenues are deducted from expenses to compute the net expenses or revenues for each function or program shown in the government-wide statement of activities?

Q10-6   How are interfund activities and balances reported in government-wide financial statements?

Q10-7   How is Internal Service Fund activity reported in government-wide statements?

Q10-8   When should sales tax revenues and property tax revenues be recognized for governmental activities in the government-wide statement of activities?

Q10-9   Describe the difference between expenditure recognition and measurement in the governmental funds financial statements and expense recognition for governmental activities in government-wide financial statements.

Q10-10   Describe the difference in reporting capital assets and long-term debt in the governmental funds financial statements and reporting those elements for governmental activities in government-wide financial statements.

Q10-11   Describe three items that require reconciliation between fund financial statements and government-wide financial statements.

Q10-12   Define and give illustrations of infrastructure assets.

Q10-13   Discuss under what circumstances a government may choose not to depreciate infrastructure assets.

Discussion Scenarios and Issues

D10-1   Mayor Meier served for many years as the chief executive officer of a city. During that time he used his red pencil liberally when reviewing the draft of the introductory section of the CAFR, prepared by finance director Ted Gee. For example, when Ted made reference to large amounts of accumulating leave and unsettled claims that might affect future General Fund expenditures, Meier struck it out. When Ted discussed the implications of the city's recent issuance of large amounts of general obligation debt, with debt service payments scheduled to begin 10 years after the bonds were issued, Meier crossed it out. When Ted mentioned in the introductory section that the city had been neglecting to maintain its capital assets, Meier struck that out also. Ted never even bothered to mention that the city's credit rating had been gradually reduced during Meier's tenure, knowing that the mayor would surely delete it.

Last year, the city implemented the requirements of GASB Statement No. 34. Ted Gee read its requirements carefully. He made the necessary accruals when he prepared the government-wide financial statements. He also concluded that many of the deleted comments he had made in previous years' drafts of the introductory section and other comments that he hadn't made should now be made in the MD&A. Ted made all the comments he felt were needed to comply with the MD&A requirements of GASB Statement No. 34 and gave his draft of the MD&A to the mayor. The mayor applied his red pencil in the usual manner and dumped the draft on Ted's desk. What should Ted do?

D10-2   The section "Preparing Government-Wide Financial Statements" points out that the State of California is accreting gradually its obligation for postemployment benefits other than pensions, while New York City recorded the entire obligation immediately. Do you believe one method is preferable to the other? Why? Would you change the accounting standard to require one or the other method? (Consider the perspectives of both the user and the preparer of the financial statements.)

Exercises

E10-1   (Analysis of financial statements)
Use the Internet to review a government's CAFR. Examine the governmental fund financial statements, the governmental activities sections of the government-wide financial statements, and the reconciliations between the two sets of statements. Trace the items that make up the reconciliations back to the financial statements as best you can. Write a brief report explaining the nature of each item of the reconciliation.

E10-2   (Analysis of the MD&A)
Use the Internet to review a government's CAFR. Review all financial statements carefully. Read the MD&A. Consider the comments made in the MD&A in light of the financial statements. Write a brief report assessing the quality of the MD&A, based on the data in the financial statements.

E10-3   (Multiple choice)
1. In government-wide financial statements, for which activities is depreciation reported?
   a. Only for governmental activities
   b. Only for business-type activities
   c. For both governmental and business-type activities
   d. For neither governmental nor business-type activities
2. In government-wide financial statements, for which activities is the economic resources measurement focus and accrual basis of accounting used?
   a. Only for governmental activities
   b. Only for business-type activities
   c. For both governmental and business-type activities
   d. For neither governmental nor business-type activities
3. In which set of financial statements are fiduciary-type funds reported?
   a. Only in the fund financial statements
   b. Only in the government-wide financial statements
   c. In both fund and government-wide financial statements
   d. In neither fund nor government-wide financial statements
4. If the General Fund makes a transfer to the Debt Service Fund, how should the transfer be reported in the financial statements?
   a. The transfers in and out should be reported in both the fund operating statement and the government-wide operating statement.
   b. The transfers in and out should be reported in neither the fund operating statement nor the government-wide operating statement.
   c. The transfers in and out should be reported in the fund operating statement but not in the government-wide operating statement.
   d. The transfers in and out should be reported in the government-wide operating statement but not in the fund operating statement.
5. A primary government has two component units, called CA and CB. CA meets the criteria for blending with other governmental funds; CB meets the criteria for discrete reporting. How should CA and CB be reported in the primary government's government-wide financial statements?
   a. Report neither CA nor CB in those statements.
   b. Report both CA and CB in a separate column headed "Component Units."
   c. Report CA in the column headed "Governmental Activities," and report CB in a separate column headed "Component Units."
   d. Do not report CA in those statements, but report CB in a separate column headed "Component Units."
6. A city issues $500,000 of 10-year general obligation bonds on April 1, 2013. It is required to redeem debt principal of $50,000 on April 1 of each year, starting April 1, 2014, with interest of 4 percent per annum paid on the unpaid principal. How much interest expenditure or expense should the city recognize in its operating statements for the calendar year 2013?

	Fund Statement	Government-Wide Statement
a.	$15,000	$15,000
b.	0	0
c.	15,000	0
d.	0	15,000

7. A village issues $3,000,000 of general obligation bonds to build a new firehouse. How should the debt be reported?
   a. As a liability in the government-wide statement of net position
   b. As a liability in the fund balance sheet
   c. As proceeds of debt in the government-wide statement of activities
   d. As a liability in both the fund balance sheet and the government-wide statement of net position

8. A village levies property taxes in the amount of $4,290,000 for the fiscal year ended June 30, 2013. It collects $4,200,000 during the year. Regarding the $90,000 of delinquent receivables, it expects to collect $60,000 in July and August of 2013 and another $20,000 after August 2013 but before March 2014. It expects to write off $10,000 as uncollectible. How much should the village recognize as property tax revenue in its government-wide statement of activities for the fiscal year ended June 30, 2013?
   a. $4,290,000
   b. $4,280,000
   c. $4,270,000
   d. $4,260,000
   e. $4,200,000

4,200,000
60,000

E10-4 (True or false) For any false statement, indicate why it is false.
   1. In government-wide financial statements, information about fiduciary funds should be presented in a discrete column to the right of the business-type activities.
   2. In government-wide financial statements, expenses for each program should be presented in such a way that charges for services directly related to the programs are shown to reduce the gross expenses of the programs.
   3. In government-wide financial statements, interest on long-term general obligation debt should be recognized in the period that the interest is due and payable.
   4. In government-wide financial statements, real property tax revenues are recognized (net of estimated refunds and estimated uncollectible amounts) in the period for which the taxes are levied.
   5. The economic resources measurement focus and accrual basis of accounting are used in reporting on Enterprise Funds in both the fund statements and the government-wide statements.
   6. The existence of Internal Service Funds does not affect amounts reported as expenses in the governmental activities column of government-wide financial statements, as compared with the expenditures reported in the fund statements.
   7. Fiduciary funds are reported in fund financial statements but are not reported in government-wide financial statements.
   8. Only the major proprietary funds are reported in government-wide financial statements.

E10-5 (Capital asset adjustments for government-wide financial statements)
Oliver City reported capital assets of $4,300,000 and accumulated depreciation of $2,000,000 in the governmental activities column of its government-wide statement of net position for the year ended December 31, 2012. The total governmental funds column in Oliver's calendar year 2013 statement of revenues, expenditures, and changes in fund balances showed that Oliver's capital outlay expenditures were $340,000. Oliver City's director of finance estimated that total depreciation for 2013 was $200,000. Based on this information, prepare journal entries to adjust Oliver's 2013 fund financial statements so government-wide statements can be prepared.

E10-6 (Sale of assets adjustments for government-wide financial statements)
Simon County realized $2,500 in cash when it auctioned off three automobiles previously used by its inspectors. It deposited the proceeds in its General Fund. According to its capital asset records, Simon had originally purchased these automobiles for $70,000. Accumulated depreciation on the automobiles as of the date of the auction was $66,000. Prepare the journal entry needed to adjust Simon's 2013 fund financial statements so government-wide statements can be prepared.

E10-7   (Long-term debt adjustments for government-wide financial statements)
Sai-Tu Village reported outstanding long-term bonds payable of $6,000,000 in the governmental activities column of its government-wide statement of net position for the year ended December 31, 2013. During 2014, Sai-Tu Village sold $500,000 of new general obligation bonds and redeemed $300,000 of bonds outstanding at the beginning of the year. Prepare journal entries needed to adjust Sai-Tu's fund financial statements so government-wide statements can be prepared for the year ended December 31, 2014.

E10-8   (Adjusting for claims in government-wide financial statements)
Punkeytown carries no insurance for possible claims and, as of January 1, 2013 (the start of its fiscal year), Punkeytown had no outstanding claims. During 2013 a town water main burst, flooding the basements of two property owners. The property owners sued the town for damages. The town settled one claim in December 2013 for $4,000 and expected to pay it in early January 2014. The town's counsel thought he could settle the second claim for about $11,000, but he expected negotiations to drag on for 18 months before reaching agreement. Based on this information, prepare the journal entry (if needed) to adjust Punkeytown's 2013 fund financial statements so government-wide statements can be prepared.

E10-9   (Adjusting for accrued vacation leave in government-wide financial statements)
Sophie County allows its employees to earn 10 days of vacation leave every year. It also allows employees to accumulate vacation leave and to receive cash for up to 20 days of leave on termination or retirement. Sophie's annual appropriations for salaries include salaries plus a provision for cashed-out vacation leave payments to be made to those who are likely to retire during the year. However, Sophie does not make an appropriation for the accumulating vacation leave liability. In its government-wide financial statements for the year ended December 31, 2012, Sophie reported a liability of $215,000 for the accumulating vacation leave liability. Sophie's finance officer estimated this liability to be $285,000 as of December 31, 2013. Prepare journal entries needed to adjust Sophie's 2013 fund financial statements so government-wide statements can be prepared.

E10-10   (Interest expense adjustments for government-wide financial statements)
Thomas County pays all the debt service on its long-term general obligation bonds on April 1 and October 1 of each year. Accrued interest on these bonds for the stub period October 1–December 31, 2012, was $75,000. During its fiscal year ended December 31, 2013, Thomas paid $350,000 interest on its long-term general obligation bonds. Accrued interest for the stub period October 1–December 31, 2013, was $88,000. Prepare journal entries needed to adjust Thomas County's 2013 fund financial statements so government-wide statements can be prepared.

E10-11   (Interest expense adjustments for government-wide financial statements)
Mike Village sold $1,000,000 of general obligation bonds on October 1, 2012, maturing at the rate of $100,000 every 6 months starting April 1, 2013, and paying interest at the rate of 4 percent per annum on the unpaid balance. Compute (a) the interest expenditure Mike will report in its fund statement of revenues, expenditures, and changes in fund balances for the calendar years ended December 31, 2012, and 2013 and (b) the interest expense Mike will report in its government-wide statement of activities for the same calendar years. Also, prepare journal entries needed to adjust Mike's 2013 fund financial statements so government-wide statements can be prepared.

E10-12   (Property tax adjustments for government-wide financial statements)
When Oscar City prepared its fund balance sheet for the year ended December 31, 2012, the General Fund column contained the following items: Property taxes receivable—delinquent: $18,000; Allowance for uncollectible taxes: $2,000; Deferred property taxes: $5,000. During 2013, Oscar collected $16,000 of the delinquent taxes and wrote off the balance of the allowance account.

Oscar levied real property taxes in the amount of $1,350,000 to finance its General Fund budget for the calendar year 2013. During the year, Oscar collected $1,280,000 against this levy. With regard to the remaining $70,000, Oscar expected to collect $47,000 during the first 2 months of calendar year 2014 and $20,000 later in the year between March and August 2014. Oscar wrote off $3,000 as uncollectible.

Using this information, (a) calculate how much property tax revenue Oscar will recognize in its governmental fund statements for 2013; (b) calculate how much property tax revenue Oscar will recognize in its government-wide statements; and (c) prepare the journal entries needed to adjust the fund statements so government-wide statements can be prepared.

E10-13 (Reporting Internal Service Fund financial information)

The Village of Delmar is preparing its government-wide statement of activities for the year ended December 31, 2013. Analysis of the data accumulated thus far shows the following expenses for each of its programs:

Program	Salaries	Supplies	ISF Billings	Total Expenses
General	$ 250,000	$ 45,000	$ 20,000	$ 315,000
Police	675,000	75,000	35,000	785,000
Fire	380,000	40,000	30,000	450,000
Parks	200,000	35,000	15,000	250,000
Totals	$1,505,000	$195,000	$100,000	$1,800,000

The Internal Service Fund (ISF) billings are from the village's Motor Pool ISF. The ISF column of the proprietary funds statement of revenues, expenses, and changes in fund net position, prepared by the Village of Delmar, shows the following:

Charges for services	$100,000
Operating expenses:	
Personal services	70,000
Repairs and maintenance	5,000
Depreciation	15,000
Total operating expenses	90,000
Operating income	10,000
Total net assets—beginning of year	45,000
Total net assets—ending of year	$ 55,000

Calculate the amounts that the Village of Delmar should report as expenses for each of its programs in its government-wide statement of activities for the year ended December 31, 2013.

Problems

P10-1 (Accounting for and reporting on capital assets acquired using governmental funds)

Marilyn County operates on a calendar year basis. It uses a Capital Projects Fund to account for major capital projects and a Debt Service Fund to accumulate resources to pay principal and interest on general obligation debt. It does not use encumbrance accounting in the Capital Projects Fund. The following transactions occur:

1. On January 1, 2013, Marilyn County issues general obligation bonds in the amount of $1,000,000 to build a community center. The debt will be paid off in 20 equal semiannual installments of $50,000 over a 10-year period commencing October 1, 2013, with interest of 4 percent per annum paid on the outstanding debt.
2. The county realizes that the community center will cost more than it originally anticipated. On May 1, the county transfers $20,000 from its General Fund to its Capital Projects Fund to help meet project costs.
3. Construction is completed on July 1, 2013, and the community center is ready for occupancy. The county pays the contractor a total of $1,020,000 on July 1. The county anticipates that the community center will have a useful life of 20 years.

4. On September 30, 2013, the General Fund transfers an amount to the Debt Service Fund that is sufficient to pay the first debt service installment, which is due October 1.

5. The county pays the debt service due on October 1.

Use the preceding information to do the following:

a. Prepare journal entries to record these transactions in the Capital Projects Fund, the General Fund, and the Debt Service Fund.

b. Prepare the adjustments needed to develop the governmental activities column of the government-wide financial statements.

c. Calculate the amount that Marilyn County will report in its December 31, 2013, government-wide statement of net position as Invested in capital assets, net of related debt. Also, assuming all debt service installments are paid when due in 2014, calculate the amount invested in capital assets, net of related debt as of December 31, 2014.

P10-2   (Preparation of statement of activities)

The following information is taken from Hamilton Township's December 31, 2013, trial balance after all adjustments were made for preparation of the government-wide financial statements. Hamilton Township has governmental activities but no business-type activities. Using the appropriate format, prepare a statement of activities for the Town of Hamilton for the year ended December 31, 2013.

Revenues—property taxes	$3,250,000
Revenues—sales taxes	2,175,000
State operating aid—police program	410,000
State operating aid—town road maintenance	250,000
State capital aid—town road maintenance	50,000
Fees—sanitation	75,000
Fees—programs for youth and seniors	65,000
Fees—parks admissions	85,000
Revenue from disposal of donated property	425,000
General government expenses	625,000
Police program expenses	2,615,000
Road maintenance program expenses	975,000
Sanitation program expenses	1,410,000
Parks and recreation program expenses	525,000
Youth and senior program expenses	325,000
Net position—beginning of year	3,125,000

P10-3   (Property tax revenue transactions and measurement in financial statements)

Honesdale levies property taxes in March of each year to help finance the General Fund expenditures for the calendar year. Property owners are required to pay the taxes in equal installments in April and October. Taxes remaining uncollected are declared delinquent at the end of the year. The facts regarding property taxes levied and collected for calendar years 2012 and 2013 are as follows:

2012: Honesdale levied property taxes of $700,000, anticipating the entire amount to be collected. It actually collected $650,000 during the year. When the village prepared its financial statements, it assumed all the delinquent taxes would be collected during 2013: $37,000 in the first 60 days and the remaining $13,000 later in 2013.

2013: Regarding the $50,000 of delinquent 2012 taxes, Honesdale collected $40,000 in the first 60 days of 2013 and $8,000 during the rest of 2013, and the village wrote off the remaining $2,000 as uncollectible.

For calendar year 2013, Honesdale levied property taxes of $730,000, again expecting the entire amount to be collected. It actually collected $690,000 in the year of the levy. When it prepared its 2013 financial statements, the village assumed $37,000 of the delinquent 2013 taxes would be collected during 2014: $30,000 in the first 60 days and $7,000 later in the year. It established an allowance of $3,000 for uncollectible taxes.

Prepare journal entries as follows:

a. Record the year 2012 transactions in the General Fund, including the year-end adjustment needed to prepare the fund financial statements.

b. Make the adjustment needed to prepare the governmental activities column of the 2012 government-wide statements.

c. Record the year 2013 transactions in the General Fund, including the year-end adjustment needed to prepare the fund financial statements.

d. Make the adjustment needed to prepare the governmental activities column of the 2013 government-wide statements.

e. Also, calculate the amount of property tax revenues Honesdale should recognize in its fund financial statements and in its government-wide statements for 2012 and 2013.

P10-4 (Conversion to government-wide financial statements)

Harlan City, a small city with revenues less than $10,000,000 a year, is planning to issue its first set of GAAP financial statements for the year ended December 31, 2013. To prepare for the transition, the city comptroller wants to have a government-wide statement of net position as of January 1, 2013, the beginning of the year. The available information includes extracts from the governmental funds portion of the balance sheet prepared as of December 31, 2012, together with other data necessary to prepare a government-wide statement of net position for governmental activities, using the economic resources measurement focus and accrual basis of accounting.

The balance sheet for the combined governmental funds as of December 31, 2012, is as follows:

Assets	
Cash	$175,000
Property taxes receivable	85,000
Total assets	$260,000
Liabilities	
Accounts payable	$ 43,000
Accrued salaries and other expenses	14,000
Total liabilities	57,000
Deferred Inflows of Resources	
Deferred property tax revenues	18,000
Fund Balances	
Unassigned	185,000
Total liabilities, deferred inflows of resources, and fund balances	$260,000

The following additional information is available as of December 31, 2012:

Capital assets: Harlan's capital asset records show that the total cost of the assets in use as of December 31, 2012, is $8,400,000. Estimated accumulated depreciation on the assets is $4,600,000.

Bonds payable: Harlan has outstanding bonds payable of $2,600,000 as of December 31, 2012. Of this amount, principal due to be paid during the calendar year 2013 is $150,000. Analysis of the outstanding bonds shows that all of the debt was used to finance the acquisition of capital assets.

Interest on long-term debt: In its fund statements, Harlan recognizes interest on bonds payable when it is due and payable. It does not accrue interest for year-end stub periods that will be paid early in the following year. Stub period interest as of December 31, 2012, was $20,000.

Property taxes: Harlan expects that all of its property taxes receivable will be collected in 2013. Property tax revenues of $18,000 were deferred because Harlan did not expect to collect them during the first 60 days of 2013.

Other expenses: Employees may accumulate vacation pay, subject to certain limits, that they may receive in cash on retirement. Accrued expenses of $14,000 include $2,000 of accrued vacation pay that the city will pay early in 2013 to retired employees. Other employees have accumulated vacation pay of $42,000 that Harlan expects to pay when they retire in future years. No accrual has been made for this amount.

Use the preceding information to do the following:

a. Prepare a six-column work sheet similar to that shown in Table 10-8, providing the balances in the fund accounts, the adjusting entries needed to prepare a government-wide statement of net position as of January 1, 2013, and the adjusted balances. Make the adjustments needed to prepare a government-wide statement of net position, and support the adjustments with journal entries. (Hint: Reclassify the fund balance to net position. Because no statement of activities is required, the adjustments to report the additional assets and liabilities will directly affect net position.)

b. Prepare a statement of net position as of January 1, 2013, in classified format. Show the net position either as invested in capital assets, net of related debt or as unrestricted.

c. Prepare a reconciliation of the funds balance sheet to the government-wide statement of net position.

P10-5   (Expenditure/expense accruals)

A city was incorporated as of January 1, 2013. It is preparing its first set of financial statements as of December 31, 2013, and is examining transactions and events affecting its General Fund to see if any accruals need to be made. Based on the following data, prepare journal entries to record (a) accruals needed to prepare the city's fund financial statements and (b) the additional accruals needed to prepare the city's government-wide financial statements.

1. Salaries for the period ended December 31, 2013, and totaling $25,000 will be paid on January 6, 2014.

2. The city permits its employees to receive cash for unused accumulated vacation pay when they retire or are terminated. Employees who were terminated as of December 31, 2013, will receive $3,000 in cash on January 6, 2014, for accumulated vacation pay. The active employees accumulated vacation pay totaling $14,000.

3. Newly hired sanitation employees accidentally sideswiped several vehicles. The vehicle owners filed claims. The city settled one claim for $2,000 in December and will pay it on January 10, 2014. The city attorney thinks the other claim will cost the city at least $10,000, but there is no indication when it will be resolved.

4. The city adopted a pension plan for its employees. Based on GASB accounting standards, the city actuary calculated the annual required contribution (ARC) for 2013 to be $18,000. However, the city made no appropriation for that purpose.

Continuing Problems

Continuing Problem 1. (Preparation of government-wide financial statements)

This problem is a continuation of Continuing Problem 1 at the end of Chapter 9. It is Part G of the problem.

Prepare journal entries needed to convert the governmental funds financial statements to the governmental activities column of the government-wide financial statements. Post the journal entries to a six-column work sheet similar to that shown in Table 10-8. Also, prepare Coco City's financial statements: the government-wide statement of net position and the government-wide statement of activities.

Continuing Problem 2. (Preparation of government-wide financial statements)

This problem is a continuation of Continuing Problem 2 at the end of Chapter 9. The following additional information is furnished to complete this part of the problem.

1. Croton has no activities other than governmental activities. The city's government-wide statement of net position for the year ended December 31, 2012, showed general capital assets of $14,000 and related accumulated depreciation of $6,400.

2. Depreciation expense on Croton's general capital assets for 2013 (including assets acquired in 2013) was $700, all of which was applicable to public safety.

3. The city's government-wide statement of net position for the year ended December 31, 2012, showed bonds payable of $5,500. All the debt had been issued to finance capital assets. Analysis

of Croton's debt service requirements showed that $700 of the total bonds payable as of December 31, 2013, should be reported as current because it is due to be paid during 2014.

4. The city's government-wide statement of net position for the year ended December 31, 2012, showed accrued interest payable of $120 on its outstanding long-term debt. Analysis of the city's debt service requirements showed accrued interest payable of $135 on all outstanding long-term debt as of December 31, 2013, including the debt sold by the city during 2013.

5. Croton's government-wide statement of net position for the year ended December 31, 2012, showed accrued vacation pay of $75. Vacation leave records showed that, as of December 31, 2013, accumulated vacation leave had increased to $87, exclusive of the $10 due to be paid to retired police officers early in 2014. (Assume vacation leave applies only to the public safety function.)

Use the preceding information to do the following:

a. Prepare journal entries needed to convert the governmental funds financial statements to the governmental activities columns of the government-wide financial statements. Post the journal entries to a six-column work sheet similar to that shown in Table 10-8.

b. Prepare Croton City's government-wide financial statements—a statement of net position and a statement of activities.

c. Prepare Croton's financial statement reconciliations—the funds balance sheet to the government-wide statement of net position and the funds statement of revenues, expenditures, and changes in fund balances to the government-wide statement of activities.

Chapter 11

Federal Government Accounting and Reporting

Chapter Outline

Learning Objectives

Background
- The Accounting and Financial Reporting Structure
- The Budget Process
- Types of Funds Used
- Consolidated U.S. Government Financial Statements
  - Federal Financial Reporting in Practice: A Perspective on the Federal Deficit

The Federal Accounting and Financial Reporting Model
- The Budgetary Accounting Track
- The Proprietary Accounting Track
- Accounting Standards

Recording Transactions and Events
1. Recording the Authority to Spend
2. Accounting for Acquisition and Use of Materials
3. Accounting for Salaries Paid and Accrued
4. Accounting for Other Types of Expenses
5. Year-End Adjusting Entries
6. Trial Balance and Closing Entries

Federal Agency Financial Reporting
- Federal Financial Reporting in Practice: The Status of Social Security

Review Questions

Discussion Scenarios and Issues

Exercises

Problems

After completing this chapter, you should be able to do the following:

- Discuss the federal budget process and the roles of the major agencies involved in federal accounting and financial reporting

- Describe the major elements of the federal accounting model, including the two-track accounting system (budgetary and proprietary)

- Explain the function of the Federal Accounting Standards Advisory Board and discuss several of its accounting standards

- Prepare budgetary and proprietary accounting journal entries to record basic transactions of a federal agency

- Describe and prepare simple financial statements of a federal agency

The Chief Financial Officers Act of 1990, as amended by the Government Management Reform Act of 1994, mandated issuance of annual audited financial statements for the 24 largest federal agencies and for the U.S. government as a whole. By 1996, the Federal Accounting Standards Advisory Board (FASAB) completed a basic body of accrual-basis accounting standards, providing the accounting underpinning for the U.S. government to issue its first set of consolidated financial statements for the fiscal year ended September 30, 1997.

Consolidated financial statements for the government as a whole have been issued every year since 1997, although the auditor—the U.S. Government Accountability Office (GAO)—has yet to express an opinion on them. The main obstacles to an opinion on the statements for the fiscal year ended September 30, 2010, were serious financial management problems at the Department of Defense, an inability to adequately account for and reconcile intragovernmental activity and balances, and an ineffective process for preparing the consolidated statements.[1] Nevertheless, 19 of the 24 major federal agencies received "clean" audit opinions on all their individual statements. In our opinion, the fiscal year 2010 Financial Report of the U.S. Government, along with the related GAO audit report, is an extremely informative document. It is available at the GAO web site at http://www.gao.gov/financial.html.

This chapter provides an overview of federal government accounting and financial reporting. It discusses the responsibilities of the various federal agencies involved in the process, outlines the relevant budgetary processes, discusses the major components of the federal government's accounting model, describes the basic journal entries made by federal agencies to record budgetary and financial transactions and events, and describes several financial statements prepared by federal agencies.

BACKGROUND

The Accounting and Financial Reporting Structure

Accounting within the federal government is decentralized to the individual departments and agencies, each of which is responsible for maintaining the ledger accounts and preparing agency

---

[1]U.S. Government Accountability Office, press release December 21, 2010, accompanying U.S. Government 2010 consolidated financial statements, www.gao.gov.

financial statements. Historically, three agencies have had oversight responsibilities for financial management, including accounting and financial reporting, within the federal government: the Office of Management and Budget (OMB) and the Department of the Treasury (Treasury) in the executive branch, and the GAO in the legislative branch. Treasury also has significant responsibilities for day-to-day accounting activities.

- *OMB.* In addition to assisting the president in preparing the U.S. budget and overseeing its execution, the OMB, through its Office of Federal Financial Management, provides direction for improving financial management and systems throughout the federal government. Annually, the OMB issues Circular A-136, "Financial Reporting Requirements," which sets forth the form and content of the "Performance and Accountability Report" prepared by federal agencies. The financial section of this report contains the required agency financial statements. Circular A-136 is accessible at the OMB web site at http://www.whitehouse.gov/omb/circulars.

- *Treasury.* Treasury's Financial Management Services Bureau provides central payment services for the federal government's program agencies, operates the collection and deposit systems, and provides government-wide accounting and reporting services. Treasury maintains the government's central cash accounting system and, through its Treasury Financial Manual, advises agencies regarding the processing of their receipts and disbursements. Treasury also prepares the government's annual consolidated financial statements based on the data provided by its central cash accounting system and the accounting reports prepared by the individual agencies. To that end, Treasury publishes the U.S. Standard General Ledger (USSGL), the government's chart of accounts that defines the accounts and describes the journal entries needed by all governmental agencies to record their budgetary and financial transactions. The USSGL can be accessed at http://www.fms.treas.gov/ussgl/index.html.

- *GAO.* As the federal government's legislative auditor, the GAO also plays a major role in the accounting and financial reporting process. Among other things, the GAO has the authority to evaluate agency accounting systems for conformance with prescribed principles. The GAO has overall responsibility for auditing and expressing an opinion on the consolidated financial statements prepared by Treasury. Much of the detailed auditing of the individual federal agencies, however, is performed by the various agency inspectors general.

In October 1990, the director of the OMB, the secretary of the Treasury, and the comptroller general established the FASAB to "consider and recommend accounting standards and principles for the Federal Government." After undergoing some structural changes, the FASAB was designated by the American Institute of Certified Public Accountants as the body that promulgates GAAP for federal entities in the United States. The FASAB currently has nine members, including six public (nonfederal) members and one each representing the OMB, the Treasury, and the GAO.

After considering the information needs of the public, the Congress, agency managers, and other users of federal financial information, the FASAB publishes Statements of Federal Financial Accounting Concepts (SFFAC) and Statements of Federal Financial Accounting Standards (SFFAS). It also publishes interpretations and technical bulletins. It follows due process, soliciting public comment on "exposure drafts" of all proposed statements. After completing deliberations, the FASAB submits proposed statements to its sponsors, who have 90 days to respond. If neither the director of OMB nor the comptroller general objects to a proposed statement, it becomes GAAP for federal entities. As of this writing, the FASAB has issued 6 SFFAC and 39 SFFAS. The FASAB documents are available at http://www.fasab.gov.

The Budget Process

Budgetary accounting is incorporated into federal accounting and financial reporting to a much greater extent than in state and local governments. The following summary of the federal budget process will help you understand the terminology and the journal entries used to record budgetary transactions and events.[2]

The federal government operates on a fiscal year that begins October 1, but the budget process starts some 18 months before that date. Based on general budget and fiscal policy guidelines, agencies submit budget requests to OMB in the fall of the preceding year. OMB analysts identify issues, most of which are resolved with agency officials; some, however, may require resolution by the president and White House policy staff. The president transmits budget proposals to Congress about 8 months before the fiscal year begins. Congress considers the proposals and may change funding levels of individual programs, add or eliminate programs, and add or eliminate revenue sources.

Congress first considers budget totals before taking action on specific appropriations. This is done by means of a concurrent resolution by the budget committees of the House of Representatives and the Senate that sets levels for total receipts and total budget authority and outlays. *Appropriations* bills are then initiated in the House. After approval by the House, bills are forwarded to the Senate for review and approval. They are then sent to the president for approval or veto. When an appropriations bill is signed by the president, *appropriations warrants* are sent to the various agencies by the Treasury. Each agency then revises its proposed budget in accordance with the enacted appropriation and submits a request for *apportionment* of the appropriation to the OMB.

Congressional appropriations are one form of *budget authority*, which gives federal agencies authority to obligate the government to make disbursements for expenditures, repayment of loans, and the like.[3] Most appropriations are for 1 year only. If they are not spent or obligated by the end of the fiscal year, they expire. Congress may also make multiyear or indefinite appropriations, as it does in funding Social Security and servicing the public debt. The illustration provided in this chapter deals with 1-year appropriations.

A congressional appropriation, however, does not give agencies the immediate authority to spend; several additional budgetary processes occur before that can happen. Upon an agency's request, the OMB makes an *apportionment* of part of the appropriation (generally, based on a quarterly time period) to the department that administers the agency. The purposes of the apportionment system are to help prevent agencies from obligating or spending more than their appropriations, to help Treasury manage cash, and to help the OMB monitor expenditure levels in relation to revenues. The administering department then makes an *allotment* of all or part of the apportionment to the agency. When it receives the allotment, the agency may obligate or spend up to the amount of the allotment, within budgetary guidelines.

Depending on the nature of its system, an agency may commit resources before it obligates them. A *commitment* is based on an internal request to purchase, say, supplies, equipment, or services. Commitment accounting helps maintain control over availability of resources, particularly if there is a relatively long "lead time" between the request to purchase and the placement of a purchase order or contract.

---

[2]For more details on the federal budget process, see *Budget Concepts and Budget Process* in the Analytical Perspectives volume of the U.S. Budget at www.whitehouse.gov/omb/budget/Analytical_Perspectives.

[3]Budget authority may take several forms, the most common of which is appropriations. Budget authority may also take the form of borrowing authority, contract authority (which generally requires a subsequent appropriation), and authority to spend from offsetting collections.

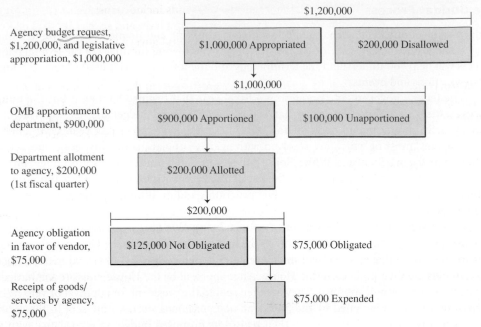

EXHIBIT 11-1 The Federal Budgetary Accounting Cycle

The key point of budget control is the obligation—a legally binding agreement that will result in outlays, immediately or in the future. An obligation is incurred when an agency places an order, signs a contract, awards a grant, purchases a service, or takes other actions that require the government to make payments to the public.[4] It is a violation of the Antideficiency Act (31 U.S.C. of the Revised Statutes) to incur an obligation without sufficient budget authority to do so. Resources are *obligated*—and identified in the accounting system as an *undelivered order*—when, for example, a purchase order is placed or a contract is signed.

When the goods or services are received (and, in the financial accounting sense, the liability to pay is established), the undelivered orders become *delivered orders—unpaid*. Instead of making direct payment, however, the agency requests the Treasury to make payment by sending it a *disbursement schedule*. When the Treasury notifies the agency that payment has been made, the order becomes a *delivered order—paid*. Payments by the Treasury are called outlays. *Outlays*, defined as payments to liquidate obligations, are the *budgetary measure of federal government spending*. Outlays generally are recorded on a cash basis, but they also include some other items like interest accrued on the public debt.

The budget process is illustrated in Exhibit 11-1. We return to it, with illustrative journal entries, later in the text.

Types of Funds Used

The federal government uses several types of funds to account for its activities, distinguishing between funds that are earmarked for specific purposes and funds that are nonearmarked. Earmarked funds are financed by specifically identified revenues, which may be supplemented by

---

[4]OMB Circular No. A-11, Section 20.5(a) (2010).

other financing sources. The more than 600 earmarked funds include trust funds (the most significant of the earmarked funds), public enterprise revolving funds, and special funds. Following is a brief description of the types of funds used by the federal government. The journal entries covered later in this chapter relate to General Fund activities.

GENERAL FUND   The General Fund comprises the greater part of the federal budget. It accounts for receipts (primarily individual and corporation income taxes, other taxes, and the proceeds of general borrowing) that are not earmarked for a specific purpose. It also accounts for most of the expenditures of the federal departments, such as the Departments of Defense and Health and Human Services. General fund expenditures are recorded in appropriation accounts maintained by the individual departments and agencies.

TRUST FUNDS   Trust funds account for receipts and expenditures of resources used to carry out specific purposes and programs in accordance with the terms of a statute that designates the fund as a trust fund. Many significant governmental activities, such as Social Security and Medicare, are financed through trust funds. The federal budget meaning of *trust fund* differs from the private-sector fiduciary notion; use of the term *trust fund* in the federal government means only that the fund is accounted for separately, is used only for a specified purpose, and is designated as a trust fund.

PUBLIC ENTERPRISE REVOLVING FUNDS   These funds are used for programs authorized by law to conduct business-type activities, primarily with the public. They are "revolving" funds because outlays from the funds generate *offsetting collections* that are credited directly to the funds and are available for expenditure without further congressional action. They are similar to state and local government Enterprise Funds.

SPECIAL FUNDS   These funds are used to account for resources from specific sources earmarked by law for special purposes and for spending in accordance with specific legal provisions. They are similar to state and local government Special Revenue Funds.

Cash receipts collected from the public for an earmarked fund are deposited in the US Treasury, which uses the cash for general government purposes. In exchange, the federal agencies that administer the earmarked funds (such as the Social Security Administration and the Office of Personnel Management) receive Treasury securities. As of September 30, 2010, earmarked funds held about $4.5 trillion of Treasury securities. The largest amount (almost $2.6 trillion) was held by the two Social Security funds—the Federal Old Age and Survivors Insurance and the Federal Disability Insurance Trust Funds. If an earmarked fund's disbursements exceed its receipts, Treasury securities will need to be redeemed. Such redemption will increase the government's financing needs and require more borrowing from the public, higher taxes, less spending on other programs, or a combination of the three.[5]

Consolidated U.S. Government Financial Statements

To provide a framework for discussing accounting within the government's agencies, we reproduced several of the government-wide financial statements for the fiscal year ended September 30, 2010. (We deleted some details to simplify the presentation.) These are the statement of net cost, the statement of operations and changes in net position, the reconciliation of net operating cost and unified budget deficit, and the balance sheet. Another statement, the statement of social

---

[5]*2010 Financial Report of the United States Government*, Note 24, Earmarked Funds.

insurance, is discussed at the end of this chapter. As previously noted, the complete report, including notes and supplemental information, is available at the GAO web site. When reading the financial statements, keep the following in mind:

- They are prepared in accordance with GAAP promulgated by the FASAB. Expenses are generally recognized when incurred, except for the costs of social insurance programs, which are recognized only for amounts currently due and payable. Tax revenues are recognized on a "modified cash" basis; that is, when collected, adjusted by the change in net measurable and legally collectible amounts receivable. Actual financial statements show financial data for the current and previous years.
- The statement of net cost (see Table 11-1) shows the full costs (including payroll fringe benefits costs) of all departments, net of revenues from providing goods and services to the public at a price.

TABLE 11-1 U.S. Government Statement of Net Cost

United States Government
Statement of Net Cost
For the Year Ended September 30, 2010
(in billions of dollars)

	Gross Cost	Earned Revenue	Net Cost
Department of Defense	$ 929.0	$ 39.8	$ 889.2
Department of Health and Human Services	920.4	62.7	857.7
Social Security Administration	754.2	0.3	753.9
Department of the Treasury	402.3	29.4	372.9
Department of Veterans Affairs	240.2	4.7	235.5
Interest on Treasury securities held by the public	214.8	—	214.8
Department of Labor	179.0	—	179.0
Department of Agriculture	136.6	6.0	130.6
Department of Education	100.8	11.3	89.5
Department of Transportation	80.4	0.6	79.8
Department of Homeland Security	58.9	8.9	50.0
U.S. Postal Service	57.3	65.7	(8.4)
Department of Housing and Urban Development	56.7	1.3	55.4
Office of Personnel Management	43.5	18.0	25.5
Department of Justice	32.7	1.2	31.5
Other agencies (see note)	265.5	59.3	206.2
Subtotal	4,472.3	309.2	4,163.1
Loss from changes in assumptions in 2010	132.9	—	132.9
Total	$4,605.2	$309.2	$4,296.0

Note: We combined entities whose gross costs were less than $30 billion. The notes accompanying these financial statements are an integral part of the statements.

TABLE 11-2 U.S. Government Statement of Operations and Changes in Net Position

United States Government
Statement of Operations and Changes in Net Position
For the Year Ended September 30, 2010
(in billions of dollars)

	Nonearmarked Funds	Earmarked Funds	Consolidated
Revenue			
Individual income tax, tax withholdings	$ 902.6	$ 830.3	$ 1,732.9
Corporation income taxes	179.6	—	179.6
Unemployment taxes	—	45.2	45.2
Excise taxes	22.6	49.0	71.6
Estate and gift taxes	18.8	—	18.8
Customs duties	25.1	—	25.1
Other taxes and receipts	96.9	30.6	127.5
Miscellaneous earned revenues	11.3	4.5	15.8
Intragovernmental interest	—	195.0	(Note)
Consolidated revenue	1,256.9	1,154.6	2,216.5
Net cost			
Net cost	2,553.5	1,742.5	4,296.0
Intragovernmental interest	195.0	—	(Note)
Consolidated net cost	2,748.5	1,742.5	4,296.0
Intragovernmental transfers	(482.1)	482.1	—
Other—unmatched transactions, balances	(0.8)	—	(0.8)
Net operating (cost) revenue	$ (1,974.5)	$ (105.8)	$ (2,080.3)
Net position, beginning of period	$(12,208.6)	$ 752.7	$(11,455.9)
Prior period adjustments—changes in accounting principles	63.4	—	63.4
Net operating (cost) revenue	(1,974.5)	(105.8)	(2,080.3)
Net position, end of period	$(14,119.7)	$ 646.9	$(13,472.8)

Note: Intragovernmental interest of $195.0 billion was eliminated in consolidation. We changed the format of this statement slightly to simplify it. The notes accompanying these financial statements are an integral part of the statements.

- The statement of operations and changes in net position (see Table 11-2) shows all revenues and expenses. The consolidated net cost shown here is the net cost reported in Table 11-1. Activities financed by nonearmarked funds are separated from those financed by earmarked funds, which include the Social Security and Medicare trust funds. The net operating cost—more than $2 trillion—is the year's deficit on the accrual basis of accounting.

TABLE 11-3 U.S. Government Reconciliation of Net Operating Cost and Unified Budget

United States Government
Reconciliation of Net Operating Cost and Unified Budget
For the Year Ended September 30, 2010
(in billions of dollars)

Net operating cost	$(2,080.3)
Components of net operating cost not part of budget deficit:	
Increase in liability for military employee benefits	164.2
Increase in liability for veterans compensation	223.8
Increase in liability for civilian employee benefits	115.1
Decrease in environmental and disposal liabilities	(20.5)
Depreciation expense	57.5
Increase in other liabilities	62.4
TARP year-end downward reestimate	(23.6)
Increase in liabilities of government-sponsored enterprises	268.0
Other (see note)	6.1
Components of the budget deficit not part of net operating cost:	
Acquisition of capital assets	(92.5)
Other (see note)	25.7
Unified budget deficit	$(1,294.1)

Note: Actual statement is more detailed than that shown here; we showed the major reconciling items and summarized the other items in the "other" categories. The notes accompanying these statements are an integral part of the statements.

- The basis of accounting in federal budgeting is primarily a "cash and obligation" basis. Hence, the reconciliation (see Table 11-3) of the net operating deficit of $2.080 trillion with the unified budget deficit of $1.294 trillion helps you understand the cash-basis nature of the budget, about which you hear so much in the media. It also helps you understand the nature of the major accruals.
- An unusually significant amount of detailed data is provided in the notes and in supplemental information to the financial statements. Indeed, the significance of the data reported *(and not reported)* on the face of the statements cannot be grasped without reading the notes and the supplementary information. This includes extensive data on social insurance and financial sustainability.
- The net deficit reported in the balance sheet (see Table 11-4) is almost $13.5 trillion as of September 30, 2010. Four years earlier, the reported deficit stood at about $9 trillion. Notice the accrued liability for federal employee and veteran benefits, which are not provided for in the cash-basis budget. Depending on how you view Social Security and Medicare, discussed at length in notes and supplemental information to the financial statements, you may conclude the deficit is much greater than that reported in this statement.

TABLE 11-4	U.S. Government Balance Sheet

United States Government
Balance Sheet
As of September 30, 2010
(in billions of dollars)

Assets

Cash and other monetary assets	$ 428.6
Accounts and taxes receivable	94.6
Loans receivable and mortgage-backed securities, net	688.6
TARP direct loans and equity investments, net	144.7
Beneficial interest in trust	20.8
Inventories and related property, net	286.2
Property, plant, and equipment, net	828.9
Debt and equity securities	98.9
Investments in government-sponsored enterprises	109.2
Other assets	183.3
Total assets	$ 2,883.8

Stewardship land and heritage assets

Liabilities

Accounts payable	$ 72.9
Federal debt securities held by the public and accrued interest	9,060.0
Federal employee and veteran benefits payable	5,720.3
Environmental and disposal liabilities	321.3
Benefits due and payable	164.3
Insurance and guarantee program liabilities	175.6
Loan guarantee liabilities	65.8
Liabilities to government-sponsored enterprises	359.9
Other liabilities	416.5
Total liabilities	16,356.6

Contingencies and commitments

Net Position

Earmarked funds	646.9
Nonearmarked funds	(14,119.7)
Total net position	(13,472.8)
Total liabilities and net position	$ 2,883.8

Note: Captions shown without amounts are described in notes to the financial statements. The notes accompanying these financial statements are an integral part of the statements.

Federal Financial Reporting in Practice

A Perspective on the Federal Deficit

As students of accounting or public administration, you are aware that you cannot look at financial statements in a vacuum. So we look at trends to put into perspective some of the details regarding the annual deficit and the outstanding debt (shown in Tables 11-2 and 11-4). To do that, we extracted data from financial statements for fiscal years 1997 (the first set of audited consolidated financial statements), 2000, 2005, and 2010. Here are the trends (all amounts in billions of dollars):

	Change in Net Position		
Year	Revenues	Net Cost	Change*
1997	$1,588	$1,603	$ (3)
2000	2,045	1,998	53
2005	2,186	2,950	(760)
2010	2,217	4,296	(2,080)

	Major Liabilities and Net Position		
Year	Public Debt	Employee, Veteran Benefits	Net Position
1997	$3,768	$2,244	$ (5,003)
2000	3,409	2,758	(5,937)
2005	4,624	4,492	(8,459)
2010	9,060	5,720	(13,473)

*The change in net position—the surplus or deficit for the year—differs slightly from the amount obtained by subtracting the net cost from the revenues. The difference—see Table 11-2—results from "unmatched transactions" in preparing the consolidation.

Analysis of the foregoing data shows that the federal government's revenues were about equal to the net costs—on a GAAP basis—in 1997 and 2000. In fact, there was a small "surplus" in 2000, and the debt held by the public actually *declined* between 1997 and 2000. Since 2000, however, annual revenues have been relatively flat while net costs have more than doubled. As a result, there has been a sharp rise in the two major liabilities reported in the balance sheet (federal debt held by the public and federal employee and veteran benefits payable). And the negative net position (the excess of liabilities over assets) increased from $5,003 billion to $13,473 billion.

In addition to the public debt of $9,060 billion as of September 30, 2010, the Treasury also owes $4,477 billion to the Social Security and other trust funds. (The amount owed to the various trust funds has also increased significantly since 1997, when it was $1,620 billion.) The total of the public debt and the debt owed to the trust funds represents the amount of debt subject to the "federal debt ceiling."

THE FEDERAL ACCOUNTING AND FINANCIAL REPORTING MODEL

Accounting and financial reporting in the federal government is designed to achieve objectives related to (a) budgetary integrity, (b) operating performance, (c) stewardship, and (d) and systems and control. FASAB SFFAC No. 1, "Objectives of Federal Financial Reporting," states that federal financial reporting should provide information to help readers determine the things listed here, among others. Notice the concerns with budgeting, management, program costs, and financial sustainability.

- How budgetary resources were obtained and used and whether their acquisition and use were in accordance with legal authorization
- The status of budgetary resources
- How information on the use of budgetary resources relates to information on the costs of program operations
- The costs of providing specific programs and activities and the composition of, and changes in, these costs
- The efforts and accomplishments associated with federal programs and the changes over time and in relation to costs
- The efficiency and effectiveness of the government's management of its assets and liabilities
- Whether the government's financial position improved or deteriorated over the period
- Whether future budgetary resources will likely be sufficient to sustain public services and to meet obligations as they come due
- Whether financial management systems and controls are adequate to ensure that transactions are executed in accordance with budgetary and financial laws and that assets are properly safeguarded to deter fraud, waste, and abuse

Accounting and financial reporting procedures for budgetary control purposes differ from the procedures needed to help meet program management objectives. Therefore, to achieve the objectives just enumerated, federal agencies use a two-track accounting system. One track is a self-balancing set of budgetary accounts, to help ensure budgetary control and compliance and to facilitate budgetary reporting. (Budgetary accounting is much more extensive in the federal government than in state and local governments.) The other is a self-balancing set of proprietary accounts, to help in financial and program management and to facilitate financial reporting.

Federal agencies are required to prepare annual reports, called "Performance and Accountability Reports," that have a management discussion and analysis, a performance section (showing goals and accomplishments), a financial section (containing audited financial statements), and a section with other information. (Agencies may issue separate performance and financial reports.) All agency annual reports are posted on the FASAB web site at www.fasab.gov. We suggest you examine the report, particularly the financial statements and the related notes, prepared by one of the departments, such as the Department of Commerce or the Department of Veterans Administration.

The Budgetary Accounting Track

The federal budgetary equation is net resources = status of resources. In this equation, the net resources accounts normally have debit balances, and the status of resources accounts normally have credit balances. The titles of the status of resources accounts describe the budgetary actions taken during the year, and the budgetary journal entries track the budgetary actions from congressional appropriation to payment for services or property. As a result, the account balances show the status of the appropriations.

In this text, we illustrate the use of eight basic budgetary accounts. The account numbers and definitions of those accounts follow, taken from the USSGL. All the accounts except "Other appropriations realized" are status of resources accounts:

4119—*Other appropriations realized:* A net resources account for all appropriations not specifically classified

4450—*Unapportioned authority:* Amounts of unobligated budgetary resources not yet apportioned by OMB and, hence, not available for obligation

4510—*Apportionments:* Amounts apportioned by OMB and, hence, available for allotment

4610—*Allotments—realized resources:* Current-period amounts available for obligation or commitment

4700—*Commitments:* Amounts of allotment or lower-level authority committed in anticipation of obligation

4801—*Undelivered orders—obligations, unpaid:* Amounts of goods and/or services ordered but not received for which there have been no prepayments (equivalent to encumbrances in state and local government accounting)

4901—*Delivered orders—obligations, unpaid:* Amounts accrued or due for services performed by employees, contractors, grantees, etc., and goods and property received

4902—*Delivered orders—obligations, paid:* Amounts paid for services performed by employees, contractors, grantees, etc., and goods and property received

The summary of basic journal entries in Table 11-5 illustrates how these accounts are used to record budgetary and proprietary transactions and events. Notice that some transactions and events require only a budgetary or a proprietary entry, while others require both. Use of all these accounts and several others will be illustrated in more detail in the next section.

Notice also the debit to the account Allotments—realized resources made as a result of a commitment action. This entry assumes use of commitment accounting. If an agency does not use commitment accounting, the debit to Allotments—realized resources is made at the time of obligation. If an action that consumes budgetary resources is taken without recording an obligation (for routine, regularly recurring items such as salary payments), the debit to Allotments—realized resources is made when the liability for payment is established. Thus, the credit balance in Allotments—realized resources at any time shows the amount of resources available to the agency for spending.

At year-end, amounts that have been obligated but unpaid (budgetary accounts 4801 and 4901) remain open and are carried forward for payment in the subsequent year. Unless the resources have been obligated, however, most appropriations expire, and unused resources cannot be used to finance operations of subsequent years. Expired resources may be used to pay for adjustments to outstanding obligations that have been carried forward. After 5 years, expired resources are returned to the Treasury.

The Proprietary Accounting Track

The accounting equation within the proprietary set of federal government accounts is assets = liabilities + net position. Although federal government budgeting is essentially cash-based, the economic resources measurement focus and accrual basis of accounting are used in the proprietary accounting and financial reporting system. Therefore, the proprietary balance sheet includes capital assets, and the operating statement (called a statement of net costs) shows expenses such as depreciation.

Most of the proprietary accounts used by federal agencies are similar to those found in state and local governments and commercial accounting. There are five major object classes—personnel compensation and benefits, contractual services and supplies, acquisition of assets, grants and fixed charges, and other—each of which is subdivided into more detailed accounts. For example, the major object class contractual services and supplies includes such accounts as travel, rent, communication, and utilities.

TABLE 11-5	Summary of Basic Journal Entries		
Who Acts?	**What Action?**	**Budgetary Entry**	**Proprietary Entry**
Congress	Appropriates	Other appropriations realized Unapportioned authority	Fund balance with Treasury Unexpended appropriations— appropriations received
OMB	Apportions	Unapportioned authority Apportionments	None
Department	Allots	Apportionments Allotments—realized resources	None
Agency	Commits	Allotments—realized resources Commitments	None
Agency	Obligates	Commitments Undelivered orders— obligations, unpaid	None
Agency	Receives goods or equipment	Undelivered orders— obligations, unpaid Delivered orders— obligations, unpaid	Assets such as operating materials and supplies held for use Accounts payable Unexpended appropriations— used Expended appropriations
Agency	Asks Treasury to pay	None	Accounts payable Disbursements in transit
Agency	Receives notice of payment	Delivered orders—obligations, unpaid Delivered orders— obligations, paid	Disbursements in transit Fund balance with Treasury
Agency	Uses goods or equipment	None	Operating expenses/ program costs Assets, or Accumulated depreciation
Agency	Accrues year-end payroll (for budgeted resources)	Allotments—realized resources Delivered orders— obligations, unpaid	Program costs—salaries Accrued funded payroll Unexpended appropriations—used Expended appropriations

Note: The budgetary transactions assume use of commitment accounting. If an obligation is made without a commitment, there is no need for a debit and credit to Commitments; the obligation entry becomes Debit, Allotments—realized resources and Credit, Undelivered orders—obligations, unpaid. Similarly, as may occur in acquiring services, an agency may incur an expense without either a commitment or an obligation. In that event, there is also no need for a debit and credit to Undelivered orders—obligations, unpaid; the budgetary entry is Debit, Allotments—realized resources and credit, Delivered orders—obligations, unpaid.

A few unfamiliar accounts serve the same purpose as counterpart accounts in state and local governments. Those accounts, which are used in the illustrative journal entries discussed in this text, are described here. Account 1010 is an asset account (used like a cash account); accounts 3310, 3101, and 3107 are agency net position accounts; and account 5700 is a financing source account (somewhat like a transfer in).

> 1010—*Fund balance with Treasury:* Funds on deposit with the Treasury; the aggregate amount for which the entity is authorized to make expenditures and pay liabilities. The account is increased (debited) when appropriations are received and decreased by disbursements made to purchase assets, goods, and services and by cancellations of expired appropriations.

> 3310—*Cumulative results of operations:* Net difference, since inception, of activity between (a) expenses and (b) financing sources, including appropriations and revenues.

> 3101—*Unexpended appropriations—appropriations received* and 3107—*Unexpended appropriations—used:* These accounts are the two sides of *Unexpended appropriations.* Credit 3101 to record the amount of new appropriations received during a fiscal year, and debit 3107 to record reductions to Unexpended appropriations during a fiscal year when goods or services are received.

> 5700—*Expended appropriations:* Credit to record appropriations used during a fiscal year when goods or services are received.

Accounting Standards

The accrual basis of accounting is used within the proprietary track. Following are brief descriptions of some of the standards, developed by the FASAB, applicable to the proprietary financial statements prepared by federal agencies and to the consolidated U.S. government statements prepared by Treasury.

INVENTORY AND RELATED PROPERTY   This caption includes primarily inventory (items held for sale, mostly within the same department), operating materials and supplies (items to be consumed in normal operations), and stockpile materials (strategic and critical materials held for use in national defense or national emergencies). FASAB SFFAS No. 3, "Accounting for Inventory and Related Property," requires that inventory held for sale and operating materials and supplies be valued at historical cost (first-in-first-out, weighted average, or moving average) or any other valuation method that approximates historical cost. The Department of Defense (DOD) holds more than 80 percent of the inventories shown in Table 11-4.

PROPERTY, PLANT, AND EQUIPMENT (PP&E)   FASAB SFFAS No. 6, "Accounting for Property, Plant, and Equipment," as amended, establishes three categories of PP&E: general PP&E, heritage assets, and stewardship land. General PP&E includes tangible assets that have estimated lives of 2 years or more, are not intended for sale in the ordinary course of operations, and are intended to be used by the entity. It includes equipment, buildings, assets acquired through capital leases, and DOD military equipment (ships, aircraft, combat vehicles, and weapons). The DOD holds more than 70 percent of the gross ($1,641 billion) and net ($829 billion) PP&E shown in Table 11-4.

General PP&E is capitalized if the acquisition cost (estimated acquisition cost in the case of DOD) exceeds capitalization thresholds, which vary considerably among federal agencies. Depreciation is recognized on a straight-line basis over the estimated useful lives of the assets.

SFFAS No. 6 also requires *disclosure* of deferred maintenance costs—the estimated cost of bringing property to an acceptable condition, resulting from not performing maintenance on a timely basis. According to the 2010 consolidated financial statements, based on condition assessment surveys of government property, deferred maintenance totals approximately $250 billion, $100 billion of which is deemed "critical."

The existence of heritage assets and stewardship land is disclosed in the notes, without values. Heritage assets are government assets that have historical or natural significance—or cultural, educational, or artistic importance—such as the Washington Monument and the Declaration of Independence. The cost of these assets is either not determinable or not relevant to their significance. Stewardship land is land the government does not expect to use to meet its obligations. Most of it is part of the 1.8 billion acres of public domain land acquired between 1781 and 1867. It constitutes about 28 percent of the U.S. landmass.

FEDERAL LIABILITIES—GENERAL   FASAB SFFAS No. 5, "Accounting for Liabilities of the Federal Government," provides that liabilities arising from exchange transactions (in which each party sacrifices value and receives value in return) should be recognized on the accrual basis of accounting; that is, when the exchange occurs. Therefore, salaries and salary-related benefits (such as pensions and annual leave) are recognized at the time employee services are rendered, and accruals are made to record liabilities for the other exchange transactions engaged in by federal agencies.

Federal agencies also engage in many nonexchange transactions, wherein agencies promise to provide benefits pursuant to law or grant without directly receiving value in return, such as payments to health care providers under Medicaid. In that program, the agency recognizes a liability for any unpaid amounts as of the reporting date, including an estimate for services rendered by providers but not yet reported to the agency.

Federal liabilities may also arise from government-related events—events involving interaction between federal entities and their environment. SFFAS No. 5 requires that a liability be recognized for a future outflow of resources resulting from a government-related event *when the event occurs* if a future outflow of resources is probable and measurable. SFFAS No. 6 expands on this standard in regard to *cleanup costs*—the costs of removing, containing, and/or disposing of hazardous waste. The environmental and disposal liability of $321 billion in Table 11-4 is the estimated current cost (assuming use of current technology) of removing, containing, treating, and/or disposing of radioactive waste, hazardous waste, chemical and nuclear weapons, and other contaminations.

FEDERAL EMPLOYEE AND VETERAN BENEFITS PAYABLE   Federal agencies generally participate in defined benefit pension plans administered by other federal agencies. In accordance with SFFAS No. 5, employer agencies should recognize an expense equal to the *service cost* for their employees for the accounting period less the amount contributed to the plan by the employees. (The service cost, synonymous with *normal cost*, is the actuarial present value [APV] of benefits attributed by the benefit formula to services rendered by employees during the current period.)

Except for the federal debt held by the public and the related accrued interest, the most significant liability reported in Table 11-4 is the accrued liability of $5,720 billion for federal employee and veteran benefits. The benefits include pensions, postemployment health care, and veterans' compensation. The liability, calculated by subtracting the APV of future normal cost contributions from the APV of future benefits, represents the APV of benefits earned as of the balance sheet date. Actuarial gains and losses, including gains and losses from changes in assumptions, are recognized immediately in the year they occur. Funding of these benefits is somewhat complex and is beyond the scope of this text.

SOCIAL INSURANCE PROGRAMS   Perhaps the most controversial issue dealt with by the FASAB concerns the recognition of liabilities for Social Security and other social insurance programs. Throughout the FASAB's existence, some of its members have believed that liabilities for these programs should be reported only for amounts due but unpaid as of the financial reporting date. They have argued that Social Security is a compulsory intergenerational transfer program and that the government can cancel or significantly reduce program benefits. Other FASAB members have believed that liabilities should be reported, similarly to pension plans, for the unfunded present value of amounts due in the future to current Social Security beneficiaries and for benefits earned to date by active participants. They have argued that Social Security has elements of exchange programs and that the commitments, citizen expectations, and political climate affecting the program make future payment so highly probable as to meet the liability definition.[6]

The issue regarding recognition was resolved with the publication of FASAB SFFAS No. 17, "Accounting for Social Insurance," which requires that liabilities for social insurance programs be recognized only for benefits that are *due and payable at the end of the reporting period*—basically, the amount due for the month of September. However, the standard as amended through FASAB SFFAS No. 37, "Social Insurance: Additional Requirements for Management's Discussion and Analysis and Basic Financial Statements," also requires a statement of social insurance, together with extensive information on assumptions and other data to help financial statement users assess long-term program sustainability. Indeed, the 2010 consolidated U.S. government financial report has 3 pages of financial statements and more than 40 pages of data in the MD&A, notes, and supplemental information regarding Social Security, Medicare, and other social insurance programs. We discuss the financial status of Social Security later in the chapter.

RECORDING TRANSACTIONS AND EVENTS

This section illustrates the journal entries needed to record some basic budgetary and proprietary transactions and events of a federal agency. Financial statements based on these journal entries are presented in the next section.

Assume the agency is called the Bureau of Food Inspection, which is a unit of the Federal Inspection Department. Also, assume the agency was created in September 2012 and that it had received a start-up appropriation to purchase inspection equipment. As a result, the agency's balance sheet at the start of the fiscal year beginning October 1, 2012, showed an asset captioned General property, plant and equipment and a net position item captioned Cumulative results of operations, each for $40,000. (To better understand the relationship among the budgetary accounts, we suggest you post the budgetary entries to ledger accounts.)

1. Recording the Authority to Spend

    a. The accounting cycle begins at the start of the fiscal year when the Congress makes and the president approves an appropriation. If the appropriation is for $150,000, the agency makes the following entries:

Budgetary	Other appropriations realized	150,000	
	Unapportioned authority		150,000
	To record receipt of appropriation authority.		

---

[6]Controversy regarding this issue commenced during discussions leading to the issuance of SFFAS No. 5 in September 1995. The summary section of SFFAS No. 37, issued 15 years later, notes that the compromise regarding enhanced disclosures about social insurance programs still "does not resolve the two strongly held views" regarding recognition in the financial statements!

Proprietary	Fund balance with Treasury	150,000	
	Unexpended appropriations—appropriations received		150,000
	To record receipt of appropriation warrant.		

The budgetary entry establishes initial accountability for the appropriation. The account, Other appropriations realized, distinguishes the agency's basic operating appropriation from other special purpose appropriations it might have received. The proprietary entry records the establishment of a "line of credit" with the Treasury. The credit to Unexpended appropriations—appropriations received increases the agency's net position.

b. After Congress makes the appropriation, the OMB apportions it to the department that administers the agency. The OMB generally makes quarterly apportionments, so receipt of the appropriation does not mean the agency may spend all of it. For simplicity, however, assume the entire appropriation is apportioned. The agency makes this entry:

Budgetary	Unapportioned authority	150,000	
	Apportionments		150,000
	To record apportionment of resources by OMB.		

| Proprietary | None | | |

c. For budgetary control purposes, the administering department may decide to make quarterly allotments to the agency. For simplicity, assume the department allots the entire $150,000 to the agency. The following entry records the allotment:

Budgetary	Apportionments	150,000	
	Allotments—realized resources		150,000
	To record allotment of resources to finance operations.		

| Proprietary | None | | |

Having received notice of the allotment, the agency has the authority to start spending.

2. Accounting for Acquisition and Use of Materials

Accounting for acquisition and use of materials results in a relatively large number of journal entries. The budgetary entries help the agency keep track of the status of resources available for spending. The proprietary entries provide the financial accounting for the transactions and also help keep track of the status of payment, which is needed to ensure integration of the agency's records with Treasury records.

a. To enhance budgetary control, an agency may use *commitment* accounting, which reserves budgetary authority before purchase orders are actually placed; that is, based on internal requests to acquire materials and supplies. If the food inspectors require materials and the purchasing department estimates that the cost will be $40,000, the following entry records the commitment and reduces the amount available for spending:

Budgetary	Allotments—realized resources	40,000	
	Commitments		40,000
	To record request for materials.		

| Proprietary | None | | |

b. Supplies and services purchased by contract are recorded as obligations when there is a binding agreement, usually when the contract is signed. The resulting journal entry replaces the commitment with an obligation. If the contract (or purchase order) is for an amount more or less than the committed amount, the account Allotments—realized resources must be adjusted. If the contract is for $42,000, the following entry is made:

Budgetary	Commitments	40,000	
	Allotments—realized resources	2,000	
	Undelivered orders—obligations, unpaid		42,000
	To obligate funds for materials ordered.		

Proprietary	None		

c. When the materials arrive and are accepted, the budgetary account Undelivered orders—obligations, unpaid is replaced with the account Delivered orders—obligations, unpaid. (A further adjustment to Allotments—realized resources is needed if the invoice amount differs from the contract amount.) Acceptance of delivery also results in a financial accounting (proprietary) event—the need to record the asset and the liability. If the invoice is for $42,000, the following entries are made:

Budgetary	Undelivered orders—obligations, unpaid	42,000	
	Delivered orders—obligations, unpaid		42,000
	To record acceptance of delivery.		
Proprietary	Operating materials and supplies held for use	42,000	
	Accounts payable		42,000
	To record acceptance of materials.		
	Unexpended appropriations—used	42,000	
	Expended appropriations		42,000
	To record financing of materials purchased.		

Regarding the second proprietary entry, the credit to the account Expended appropriations records the financing source—the appropriation used by the agency to acquire the asset.

d. To improve internal accounting controls, payment requires two sets of entries, one when a *disbursement schedule* is sent to Treasury requesting payment and another when the agency receives notification from Treasury that payment has been made. This entry records the request for payment:

Budgetary	None		
Proprietary	Accounts payable	42,000	
	Disbursements in transit		42,000
	To record request to Treasury for check.		

e. Both budgetary and proprietary journal entries are needed to record receipt of notification from Treasury that payment was made; the budgetary entry is needed because payment changes the budgetary status of the event from an unpaid obligation to a paid obligation.

Budgetary	Delivered orders—obligations, unpaid	42,000	
	Delivered orders—obligations, paid		42,000
	To record confirmed payment by Treasury.		

Proprietary	Disbursements in transit	42,000	
	Fund balance with Treasury		42,000
	To record confirmed payment by Treasury.		

f. As noted previously, the federal government uses the accrual basis of accounting in its proprietary accounts. Therefore, when materials are used, a proprietary entry is needed to record the program cost and reduction of the asset. No budgetary entry is needed because use of the budgetary resource was recorded previously. If the agency uses $35,000 of supplies, the following entry is made:

Budgetary	None		
Proprietary	Program costs—materials	35,000	
	Operating materials and supplies held for use		35,000
	To record materials used in operations.		

g. The foregoing transactions illustrate the full budgetary accounting cycle. To more fully illustrate required budgetary resource reporting, we need a transaction that creates an obligation that has not been paid at year-end. So, assume the agency recorded a commitment for $4,000 for materials and placed a purchase order for the same amount but did not receive delivery of the materials by year-end. The journal entries would be as follows:

Budgetary	Allotments—realized resources	4,000	
	Commitments		4,000
	To record request for materials.		
Budgetary	Commitments	4,000	
	Undelivered orders—obligations, unpaid		4,000
	To obligate funds for materials ordered.		
Proprietary	None		

If you have posted the budgetary journal entries to ledger accounts, you will notice that the net effect of the budgetary entries is that Allotments—realized resources was reduced by $46,000 (i.e., budgetary resources of $46,000 were used up), based on paid delivered orders of $42,000 and undelivered orders of $4,000. In the proprietary accounts, $42,000 of resources was used (and Fund balance with Treasury was reduced) to finance program costs of $35,000 and an inventory asset of $7,000, Operating materials and supplies held for use.

3. Accounting for Salaries Paid and Accrued

Close controls are maintained over salaries in both the budget formulation and the execution processes. OMB, for example, requires reporting on the number of full-time equivalent personnel within the personnel compensation and benefits object class. As a general rule, salaries are recorded as obligations "as the amounts are earned during the reporting pay period."[7] As a practical matter, because of the close control over salary line items and the short time lapse between the earning and payment of salaries, the first journal entries to record salaries are made when a

---

[7]OMB Circular No. A-11, Section 20.5(b).

disbursement request is sent to Treasury. Nevertheless, when those journal entries are made, they produce the same net accounting effect as the series of entries made to record the acquisition of materials, including a charge to the budgetary status account Allotments—realized resources and a credit to the proprietary financing source account Expended appropriations.

a. The following entries are made when a disbursement request is sent to Treasury for salary checks totaling $85,000:

Budgetary	Allotments—realized resources	85,000	
	Delivered orders—obligations, unpaid		85,000
	To record use of resources for salaries.		
Proprietary	Program costs—salaries	85,000	
	Disbursements in transit		85,000
	To record request to Treasury for checks.		
	Unexpended appropriations—used	85,000	
	Expended appropriations		85,000
	To record financing of salary costs.		

b. These entries are made when the agency is told that Treasury has made payment:

Budgetary	Delivered orders—obligations, unpaid	85,000	
	Delivered orders—obligations, paid		85,000
	To record confirmed payment by Treasury.		
Proprietary	Disbursements in transit	85,000	
	Fund balance with Treasury		85,000
	To record confirmed payment by Treasury.		

c. Assume a year-end accrual is needed for $6,000 of unpaid salaries and that resources have been budgeted for that purpose. The following entries record the use of budgetary resources, the proprietary expense and liability, and the financing source. Notice that, because the payroll has been accrued but not yet paid, the budgetary status is Delivered orders—obligations, *unpaid*, rather than paid.

Budgetary	Allotments—realized resources	6,000	
	Delivered orders—obligations, unpaid		6,000
	To record use of resources for salary accrual.		
Proprietary	Program costs—salaries	6,000	
	Accrued funded payroll		6,000
	To record accrual of year-end payroll.		
	Unexpended appropriations—used	6,000	
	Expended appropriations		6,000
	To record financing of salary accrual.		

4. Accounting for Other Types of Expenses

a. The agency is likely to obligate resources when travel orders are issued, without making a previous commitment entry. If the agency issues travel orders for $8,000, an entry is made that has the same budgetary effect as transactions 2a and 2b, combined:

Budgetary	Allotments—realized resources	8,000	
	Undelivered orders—obligations, unpaid		8,000
	To record issuance of travel orders.		

Proprietary   None

b. When the travel is completed and a travel voucher for, say, $9,000 is submitted and approved, entries are made that are similar to 2c. Notice the adjustment to Allotments—realized resources because an additional $1,000 of resources has been used up.

Budgetary	Undelivered orders—obligations, unpaid	8,000	
	Allotments—realized resources	1,000	
	Delivered orders—obligations, unpaid		9,000
	To record approved travel voucher.		

Proprietary	Program costs—travel expenses	9,000	
	Accounts payable		9,000
	To record approved travel expense.		
	Unexpended appropriations—used	9,000	
	Expended appropriations		9,000
	To record financing of travel expense.		

c. If a disbursement schedule is sent to the Treasury and the agency is notified that the voucher is paid, journal entries would be made that are similar to those in 2d and 2e. To better illustrate the data appearing in the financial statements, however, we will assume the travel occurred late in the year before a disbursement schedule could be sent to the Treasury.

d. The federal government's central supporting services agency, the General Services Administration (GSA), provides supplies and services (such as occupancy and utilities) to many agencies. Obligations for intragovernmental services are incurred when the services are rendered; also, obligations for rental payments to the GSA are incurred in the year the premises are occupied, whether or not a bill has been rendered.[8] Because the OMB makes quarterly apportionments, effective control is enhanced by recording obligations for service arrangements with the GSA at the beginning of each quarter, crediting Undelivered orders—obligations, unpaid. If this is not done, the agency should record the obligation (and the accounting liability) when it has received the services, as follows:

Budgetary	Allotments—realized resources	
	Delivered orders—obligations, unpaid	
	To record use of resources for services.	

Proprietary	Operating expenses/program costs	
	Accounts payable	
	To record liability for services.	
	Unexpended appropriations—used	
	Expended appropriations	
	To record financing for services.	

---

[8]OMB Circular No. A-11, Section 20.5(d).

5. Year-End Adjusting Entries

a. The adjustment for year-end salary accrual, for which budgetary funds are available, was illustrated in 3c. But the appropriation normally does not include a provision for accrued vacation leave. For proprietary accounting purposes, an accrual must be made to record the expense and the liability as shown here—assume the amount is $4,000. However, in the absence of budgetary resources, a budgetary entry is not made; for the same reason, a proprietary entry is not made to record a financing source.

Budgetary	None		
Proprietary	Future funded expenses	4,000	
	Unfunded leave		4,000
	To record accrual for unfunded leave.		

b. Recall that the agency started the fiscal year with $40,000 in General plant, property, and equipment. For proprietary accounting purposes, it needs to record depreciation of the asset. No budgetary entry is made because the equipment was acquired with the previous year's budgetary resources and depreciation is not a budgetary event. Further, no proprietary entry is needed to record a financing event because the asset was financed with the previous year's appropriation. If the assets are depreciated over a period of 5 years, the entry to record the $8,000 depreciation is as follows:

Budgetary	None		
Proprietary	Program costs—depreciation	8,000	
	Accumulated depreciation		8,000
	To record depreciation of equipment.		

6. Trial Balance and Closing Entries

A preclosing trial balance based on the foregoing journal entries (including account balances at the start of the year) is presented in Table 11-6. The trial balance will be used to prepare the financial statements shown in the next section. The closing journal entries are shown here; trace them to the accounts in the preclosing trial balance.

> **Budgetary accounts:** The accounts Undelivered orders—obligations, unpaid ($4,000) and Delivered orders—obligations, unpaid ($15,000) remain open until they are paid in the next year. The first closing entry records the unused budgetary authority ($4,000 balance remaining in Allotments—realized resources) as Allotments—expired authority. (Any remaining balances in the budgetary accounts Apportionments and Commitments would also be closed into Allotments—expired authority.) The second budgetary entry has the effect of gathering the unexpended authority into a separate account called Total actual resources—collected. The total in this account ($23,000) equals the total of the Allotments—expired authority ($4,000) and the unpaid obligation accounts ($19,000).

Allotments—realized resources	4,000	
Allotments—expired authority		4,000
To close expired appropriation authority.		

TABLE 11-6	Preclosing Trial Balance

Federal Inspection Department
Bureau of Food Inspection
Preclosing Trial Balance
September 30, 2013

Budgetary Accounts

Other appropriations realized	$150,000	
Unapportioned authority		$ —
Apportionments		—
Allotments—realized resources		4,000
Commitments		—
Undelivered orders—obligations, unpaid		4,000
Delivered orders—obligations, unpaid		15,000
Delivered orders—obligations, paid		127,000
Totals	$150,000	$150,000

Proprietary Accounts

Fund balance with Treasury	$ 23,000	
Operating materials and supplies held for use	7,000	
General property, plant, and equipment	40,000	
Accumulated depreciation		$ 8,000
Accounts payable		9,000
Accrued funded payroll		6,000
Unfunded leave		4,000
Unexpended appropriations—appropriations received		150,000
Unexpended appropriations—used	142,000	
Cumulative results of operations		40,000
Expended appropriations		142,000
Program costs—materials	35,000	
Program costs—salaries	91,000	
Program costs—travel expenses	9,000	
Program costs—depreciation	8,000	
Future funded expenses	4,000	
Totals	$359,000	$359,000

Delivered orders—obligations, paid	127,000	
Total actual resources—collected	23,000	
Other appropriations realized		150,000

To close expended appropriations and establish collected
resources account.

Proprietary accounts: The financing source and program cost accounts are closed to the
net position account Cumulative results of operations. The two unexpended appropriations

accounts (received and used) are closed to a single net position account captioned Unexpended appropriations.

Expended appropriations	142,000	
Cumulative results of operations	5,000	
Program costs—materials		35,000
Program costs—salaries		91,000
Program costs—travel expenses		9,000
Program costs—depreciation		8,000
Future funded expenses		4,000
To close accounts to Cumulative results of operations.		
Unexpended appropriations—appropriations received	150,000	
Unexpended appropriations—used		142,000
Unexpended appropriations		8,000
To close accounts to Unexpended appropriations.		

FEDERAL AGENCY FINANCIAL REPORTING

Federal agencies report in accordance with standards established by the FASAB, as implemented by the Treasury and the OMB. As previously stated, the OMB requires all federal agencies to prepare an annual Performance and Accountability Report. The financial section of the report contains (for both the current and the previous year) a balance sheet, a statement of net costs, a statement of changes in net position, and a statement of budgetary resources. Where applicable, agencies must also prepare a statement of custodial activity, a statement of social insurance, and a statement of changes in social insurance.

The financial statements illustrated in this section are presented in the format prescribed by the OMB. Because the statements cover only the transactions shown in the preceding section, however, they are much less detailed than the financial statements of a typical federal agency. To prepare these statements, we start with the preclosing trial balance shown in Table 11-6. The financial statements are shown in Tables 11-7 through 11-10.

In the *balance sheet* (Table 11-7), intragovernmental assets and liabilities are reported separately from other assets and liabilities. Notice that the net position ($43,000) consists of two components: Unexpended appropriations and Cumulative results of operations. The amount shown as Unexpended appropriations ($8,000) is the difference between the appropriations received ($150,000) and the appropriations used ($142,000). Notice these amounts in the trial balance. Cumulative results of operations represents amounts accumulated over the years by the entity from its financing sources, less net costs, plus the cumulative amount of prior period adjustments. These elements of net position are discussed in greater detail in connection with the statement of changes in net position.

The *statement of net costs* (Table 11-8) shows objects of account because those accounts were used in the simplified set of illustrative journal entries. This statement supports congressional and managerial needs for cost data useful in evaluating program performance and in making decisions about allocating federal resources to programs. Therefore, in accordance with FASAB SSFAS No. 4, "Managerial Cost Accounting Concepts and Standards for the Federal Government," the net costs reported in this statement are the *full* costs of each program operated by the agency,

| **TABLE 11-7** | Balance Sheet of Federal Agency |

Federal Inspection Department
Bureau of Food Inspection
Balance Sheet
September 30, 2013

Assets

Intragovernmental:

Fund balance with Treasury	$ 23,000	
Operating materials and supplies held for use	7,000	
General property, plant, and equipment, net of $8,000 accumulated depreciation	32,000	
Total assets		$62,000

Liabilities and Net Position

Liabilities:

Accounts payable	$ 9,000	
Accrued funded payroll	6,000	
Unfunded leave	4,000	
Total liabilities		$19,000

Net position:

Unexpended appropriations	8,000	
Cumulative results of operations	35,000	
Total net position		43,000
Total liabilities and net position		$62,000

including not only the direct and indirect agency costs, but also the costs of identifiable supporting services provided by other segments within the reporting entity and by other reporting entities. Also, revenues earned by the agency (e.g., from fees charged for services or products) are deducted from gross program costs to report the net costs.

| **TABLE 11-8** | Statement of Net Costs of Federal Agency |

Federal Inspection Department
Bureau of Food Inspection
Statement of Net Costs
For Fiscal Year Ended September 30, 2013

Net Program Costs

Materials	$ 35,000
Salaries	91,000
Travel expenses	9,000
Depreciation	8,000
Future funded expenses	4,000
Net cost of operations	$147,000

TABLE 11-9	Statement of Changes in Net Position of Federal Agency

Federal Inspection Department
Bureau of Food Inspection
Statement of Changes in Net Position
For the Year Ended September 30, 2013

Cumulative Results of Operations		
Beginning balance		$40,000
Budgetary financing sources:		
Appropriations used	$142,000	
Other financing sources	—	
Net cost of operations	147,000	
Net change		(5,000)
Cumulative results of operations		35,000
Unexpended Appropriations		
Beginning balance		—
Appropriations received	$150,000	
Appropriations used	142,000	
Total unexpended appropriations		8,000
Net position, end of period		$43,000

The *statement of changes in net position* (Table 11-9) summarizes the factors that caused increases or decreases in the components of net position. In this illustration, the agency's net position increased from $40,000 to $43,000 because of the following factors:

- The component Unexpended appropriations increased from zero at the start of the year to $8,000 at the end of the year. As described in OMB's Circular A-136, appropriations are considered used as a financing source *when goods or services are received or benefits are provided*. The agency received appropriations of $150,000 but used only $142,000. (See the Unexpended appropriations accounts in the proprietary portion of the trial balance in Table 11-6.) The $142,000 of Appropriations used does not include unobligated appropriations of $4,000 and undelivered orders of $4,000. (See the Allotments—realized resources and Undelivered orders accounts in the budgetary portion of the trial balance.)
- The component Cumulative results of operations decreased by $5,000 from $40,000 at the start of the year to $35,000 at the end of the year, because the net cost of operations for the year ($147,000) exceeded the financing source—the appropriations used ($142,000). The $5,000 decrease is the net result of three items: a decrease of $12,000 because the net cost of operations includes two items that were not financed with current-year appropriations (depreciation of $8,000 and accrued leave of $4,000) and an increase of $7,000 because $42,000 of financing was provided to purchase inventory, but only $35,000 was used in operations.

TABLE 11-10	Statement of Budgetary Resources of Federal Agency

Federal Inspection Department
Bureau of Food Inspection
Statement of Budgetary Resources
For the Year Ended September 30, 2013

Budgetary Resources	
Appropriation	$150,000
Other (not illustrated)	—
Total budgetary resources	$150,000
Status of Budgetary Resources	
Obligations incurred	$146,000
Unobligated balance	—
Unobligated balance not available	4,000
Total status of budgetary resources	$150,000
Change in Obligated Balance	
Unpaid obligations, beginning of period	—
Obligations incurred	$146,000
Less, gross outlays	127,000
Unpaid obligated balance, end of period	$ 19,000
Net (and Gross) Outlays	$127,000

The *statement of budgetary resources* (Table 11-10) has four parts: budgetary resources, status of budgetary resources, change in obligated balance, and outlays.

- The budgetary resources part of the statement, derived from the left column of the budgetary part of the trial balance in Table 11-6, shows the appropriations and other forms of budget authority made available to the agency.
- The status part of the statement comes from the right column of the budgetary part of the trial balance. Obligations incurred ($146,000) in Table 11-10 includes the three items in Table 11-6 containing the word *obligations* in the caption—Undelivered orders, unpaid and Delivered orders, both unpaid and paid. The $4,000 balance in the account Allotments—realized resources in Table 11-6 is not available for future obligation by the agency because the appropriation expires at year-end.
- The change in obligated balance is determined by deducting gross outlays from the total of unpaid obligations at the beginning of the period and the obligations incurred during the period. In this illustration, the $19,000 of Unpaid obligations in Table 11-10 consists of the two items in Table 11-6 with "obligations, unpaid" in the caption.
- Outlays are defined as payments by the U.S. Treasury to liquidate obligations. The outlay of $127,000 in this illustration is the balance in the budgetary account Delivered orders—obligations, paid in Table 11-6. It is also the difference between the opening proprietary entry of $150,000 in Fund balance with Treasury (see journal entry 1a on page 415) and the $23,000 closing balance of that account.

Federal Financial Reporting in Practice

The Status of Social Security

To understand the status of Social Security, you need to look not only at the financial statements previously discussed, but also at the statement of social insurance, which reports the present value of the 75-year actuarial projection of Social Security revenues and expenditures. Because of the way Social Security is financed, you also need to review economic and demographic factors affecting Social Security inflows and outflows. This information can be found in the notes and supplementary data to the financial statements. (See the consolidated U.S. government financial report and the financial report issued by the Social Security Administration [SSA] at www.gao.gov and www.ssa.gov/finance/.)

SSA administers Social Security through two trust funds: the Federal Old Age and Survivors Insurance (OASI) Trust Fund and the Federal Disability Insurance Trust (DI) Fund. Social Security is financed largely pay-as-you-go; that is, payroll taxes paid by the working population and employers are used to provide benefits to those who are already retired. However, amendments to the law in 1977 and 1983 caused tax revenues to exceed benefit payments. These excesses, which we will call a reserve, are recorded in the two Trust Funds and are invested in U.S. Treasury securities. The investments pay interest, which is also invested in Treasury securities.

The government has used these investments to help finance the annual deficits in the nonearmarked portion of the budget. So from the perspective of the *consolidated financial position of the U.S. government*, the Social Security reserve has been spent. As of September 30, 2010, the reserve stood at $2.586 trillion—a significant amount compared to the total liquid assets shown in the consolidated U.S. financial statements (see Table 11-4), but much less than the aggregate benefits payable under current law to those already retired and those working.

The notion behind creation of the reserve was that SSA would call upon it (first the interest on the investment, then the investment) when Social Security benefit payments started to exceed its revenues. But, to pay the interest or redeem the securities, the federal government needs to raise taxes, cut other expenditures, or borrow from the public. Let us look at the status of Social Security.

Near-Term Perspective: Trust fund investments in Treasury securities have grown from $1.007 trillion as of September 30, 2000, to $2.586 trillion on September 30, 2010. But trust fund tax revenues leveled off in FY 2009 and *declined* in FY 2010, while benefit payments *increased*, as shown in the following schedule (amounts in billions of dollars):

Fiscal Year	Tax Revenues	Program Costs
2000	$502	$408
2005	588	528
2008	671	610
2009	668	666
2010	647	697

Notice that Social Security program costs (almost entirely benefit payments) exceeded tax revenues in FY 2010. The leveling off and decline of tax revenues in 2009 and 2010 apparently were caused by the severe economic recession. (The 2009 spike in program costs is attributable to the eligibility of the "baby boomers" for benefits.) In its 2010 financial report, the SSA projects that program costs will exceed tax revenues in 2011 as well, that revenues will exceed costs for the next 3 years, and that costs will exceed revenues permanently starting in 2015 unless the revenue/benefit structure is changed. In any event, the SSA calculates that, even with no tax inflows, the trust fund investments of $2.586 trillion are sufficient to cover benefit payments for 42.2 months; considering projected tax inflows, interest on the investments, and benefit outflows, the trust funds will not be exhausted until 2037. (The 2012 report of the Social Security trustees lowered the estimated exhaustion date to 2033.)

In short, despite the revenue drop-off in 2009 and 2010, the accumulation of resources in the trust funds makes Social Security fully solvent in the near term. The near term problem lies not with Social Security, but rather with the actions the government as a whole may take to meet its $2.586 trillion obligation to the trust funds.

Long-Term Perspective: The SSA projects that current Social Security tax rates cannot sustain current benefit levels over the long term. According to the supplemental data in the 2010 consolidated U.S. financial report, current tax rates will be sufficient to pay 78 percent of scheduled benefits when the trust funds are exhausted in 2037 and 75 percent of benefits in 2084. Here are some of the factors underlying the SSA projection.

First, consider some demographics—specifically, the number of Social Security beneficiaries relative to the number of workers who pay the taxes that provide the benefits. In 1960, there were about 20 Social Security beneficiaries for every 100 workers; by 2006, that number had increased to about 30. When the baby boom generation became eligible for Social Security benefits in 2009, the number of beneficiaries started to increase much more rapidly than the number of workers. In 2010, there were about 34 Social Security beneficiaries for every 100 workers. The SSA projects that, by 2030, there will be 46 beneficiaries for every 100 workers—and the ratio will gradually worsen after that.

Now, consider some projected long-term numbers. The trust fund investments of $2.586 trillion may seem large but are very small compared with Social Security obligations. Here are the calculations of the SSA actuaries comparing the estimated present values of Social Security tax revenues and estimated benefit payments over the next 75 years (in trillions of dollars):

Population Group	Revenues	Benefits
Currently eligible for benefits	$ .672	$ 8.096
Working, not yet eligible	19.914	32.225
Total	20.586	40.321
Future participants	19.532	7.744
Total	$40.118	$48.065

Thus, because Social Security benefits basically are financed pay-as-you-go, the trust fund reserve of $2.586 trillion clearly is not large enough to pay the lifetime benefits due to those who are either already obtaining benefits or who are otherwise eligible for benefits ($8.096 trillion minus $0.672 trillion, or $7.424 trillion). The addition of those who are currently working but not yet eligible for benefits increases the disparity between revenues and benefit payments. It is not until the net resources of future participants are added to the mix that long-term revenue inflows start to approach the benefit outflows. But even then, over the 75-year period used by the SSA to assess sustainability, the negative difference between the present values of the revenues and the benefits is almost $8 trillion ($5.4 trillion if the trust fund assets are deducted).

The Social Security trustees equate this "negative actuarial balance" to 1.92 percent of taxable payroll. That percentage, according to the SSA 2010 Performance and Accountability Report, "represents the magnitude of an increase in the combined payroll tax rate for the entire 75-year period that would allow the trust funds to remain solvent throughout the period with a small amount of assets remaining in the trust funds at the end of the period" (pp. 138–139).

Long-term projections regarding Social Security inflows and outflows are best estimates. They depend on many economic and demographic factors, such as the vibrancy of the economy, long-term birth and mortality rates, immigration rates, and inflation rates—all of which can vary greatly from the best estimates. Only a few years ago, the SSA estimated that benefit payments would exceed Social Security tax revenues in about 2017; now it is down to 2015. But current best estimates indicate that there is indeed a long-term Social Security problem . . . unless you are content with the thought that, even after 2037, the cup will still be three-quarters full, based on Social Security's pay-as-you-go financing system.

Review Questions

Q11-1   The terms *appropriation, apportionment,* and *allotment* are used in the federal budget process. Describe what each is and which unit of the government makes it.

Q11-2   The Congress appropriates $5 million to fund the fiscal year 2013 activities of a bureau within a department. Can the bureau director immediately place a purchase order to buy needed supplies? If not, why not?

Q11-3   The term *obligation* is commonly used in federal government accounting. What is an obligation, and what is its equivalent in state and local government accounting?

Q11-4   What are *earmarked funds*? Which funds are characterized as earmarked?

Q11-5   Briefly describe the federal accounting standards regarding inventory and related property; property, plant, and equipment; and liabilities.

Q11-6   What is the budgetary equation? Briefly describe the components of each side of the equation.

Q11-7   What is the nature of the account Fund balance with Treasury? When is that account debited, and when is it credited?

Q11-8   Compare the use of accrual accounting in federal government financial reporting with the use of accrual accounting in state and local government financial reporting.

Q11-9   How is depreciation handled in the federal government's General Fund? How does it differ from depreciation in state and local government General Funds?

Q11-10   Describe four financial statements prepared by federal agencies.

Q11-11   What are the two components of an agency's net position? Describe the major causes of the year-to-year changes in each component.

Q11-12   How does the financing of Social Security differ from the financing of most state and local government pension plans?

Discussion Scenarios and Issues

D11-1   Financial reporting of Social Security has been a controversial subject in the federal government. Current federal accounting standards require that liabilities be reported only for Social Security payments that are currently due and payable, but that no liability be reported for the unfunded actuarial present value of amounts due to retirees or their beneficiaries or for the unfunded actuarial present value of benefits earned by other participants in the Social Security system. However, the standard does require various disclosures regarding the financial status of Social Security. Give arguments for and against the current financial reporting standard, and state your opinion about the soundness of the standard.

D11-2   A federal agency receives a separate appropriation for supplies. A large number of purchase orders marked "Rush" are processed in August. Because several clerks are on vacation, they are not recorded as obligations. The supplies are received in early September, before the end of the fiscal year. After matching the invoices with the receiving reports, the accountant finds the agency has insufficient funds to process many of the payments. On further inquiry, the accountant locates the batch of unrecorded purchase orders. He also finds that the supplies were used immediately upon receipt. He explains the problem to his immediate supervisor, who says, "Forget it. Just charge the bills to next year's appropriation." Explain the nature of the accountant's dilemma, and discuss what you think he should do.

Exercises

E11-1   (Multiple choice)
1. Which funds are used by federal agencies to account for receipts of resources from specific sources, earmarked by law for special purposes?
   a. Special Revenue Funds
   b. Trust Funds

  c. Revolving Funds
  d. Deposit Funds

2. Who sets federal accounting standards?
   a. Congress
   b. Financial Accounting Standards Board (FASB)
   c. Federal Accounting Standards Advisory Board (FASAB)
   d. Governmental Accounting Standards Board (GASB)

3. What does an unliquidated obligation represent?
   a. Resources that cannot be spent for any purpose
   b. Resources that have already been disbursed
   c. Resources that must be returned to the Treasury
   d. Resources earmarked for a specific purpose

4. Who makes apportionments of appropriations?
   a. Congress
   b. Office of Management and Budget (OMB)
   c. The agency
   d. The department of which the agency is a part

5. What is the function of commitments?
   a. To legally encumber an allotment
   b. To formally disclose purchase requests before actual orders are placed
   c. To represent the authority to spend money for a particular project
   d. To represent legally enforceable promises to specific vendors

6. What account is used to show that an agency has requested payment by the Treasury to vendors?
   a. Fund balance with Treasury
   b. Accounts payable
   c. Disbursements in transit
   d. Processed invoices

7. To prepare the "Status of Budgetary Resources" section of the Statement of Budgetary Resources, you would use the balances in which of the following accounts?
   a. Expended authority, undelivered orders, and commitments
   b. Cumulative results of operations, undelivered orders, and disbursements in transit
   c. Fund balance with Treasury, expended authority, and undelivered orders
   d. Fund balance with Treasury, undelivered orders, and commitments

E11 2 (Matching)

Match the items in the following right column with those in the left column:

_____ 1. An act of Congress that gives a department and/or agency authority to obligate the federal government to make disbursements for goods and services

_____ 2. Document sent to the Treasury ordering it to pay vendors and employees

_____ 3. Sets standards for federal government accounting

_____ 4. Type of fund used to account for commercial-type operations of federal agencies

_____ 5. Action by which the OMB distributes amounts appropriated by Congress

_____ 6. Payments of obligations

_____ 7. Reserves budgetary authority from an allotment in anticipation of an obligation

_____ 8. Federal equivalent of encumbrances used by state and local governmental units

_____ 9. Type of fund that finances Social Security payments

a. Outlays
b. Obligation
c. Disbursement schedule
d. GASB
e. Appropriation
f. Revolving Fund
g. Apportionment
h. FASAB
i. Allotment
j. Trust Fund
k. Deferral
l. Commitment

E11-3   (Use of the budgetary accounts)
Following are some basic budgetary accounts used in federal accounting:
Other appropriations realized
Unapportioned authority
Apportionment
Allotments—realized resources
Commitments
Undelivered orders—obligations, unpaid
Delivered orders—obligations, unpaid
Delivered orders—obligations, paid
>   Determine which account title best describes each of the following situations:

____ 1. Spending authority allotted but not yet committed
____ 2. Resources obligated, but goods or services not yet received
____ 3. Spending authority apportioned but not yet allotted to an agency
____ 4. Amounts paid for services and goods received
____ 5. Spending authority appropriated but not yet apportioned by the OMB
____ 6. Amounts due or accrued for services and goods received

E11-4   (True or False)
State whether the following assertions are true or false. If false, explain why.

1. Depreciation of general property, plant, and equipment is reported as an expense in the consolidated U.S. government statement of net cost, but not in the statement of net cost prepared by individual agencies.
2. Abraham Lincoln's face appears on Mount Rushmore, but Mount Rushmore's cost does not appear on the face of the consolidated U.S. balance sheet.
3. A year-to-year increase in an agency's liability for vacation leave may not be accrued in the agency's proprietary accounts unless sufficient budgetary resources are available to finance the accrual.
4. The ending balance in the account Expended appropriations is used to report a financing source in an agency's statement of changes in net position.
5. The ending balance in the account *Delivered* orders—obligations, unpaid remains open at year-end because it is available for payment in the following year; however, the ending balance in the account *Undelivered* orders—obligations, unpaid is closed out because it is not available for payment in the following year.
6. In the federal government, trust funds are accounted for separately from other funds, but they are not "fiduciary" in nature, so the federal government may borrow from them.

E11-5   (Accounting for the acquisition and use of equipment)
Prepare budgetary and proprietary journal entries to record the following transactions of the Bureau of Shipping Security (BOSS), a unit of the Department of National Security.

1. BOSS received an appropriation of $3,000,000 for fiscal year 2013.
2. OMB apportioned the entire amount of the appropriation.
3. The secretary of the department allotted $750,000 to provide for BOSS operations during the first quarter of the year.
4. The BOSS planning unit asked the purchasing department to buy a new piece of equipment (estimated cost—$190,000) capable of scanning shipping containers.
5. The BOSS purchasing department awarded a contract for $210,000 for the scanning equipment. The purchasing department said the additional cost over the estimate was caused by the need for research to meet the specifications.
6. BOSS received the equipment ordered in the previous transaction, with an invoice for $200,000. The supplier said it was passing along the savings resulting from a breakthrough on the research.
7. BOSS sent a disbursement schedule to the Treasury, requesting payment of the $200,000 invoice.

8. The Treasury notified BOSS that the invoice for $200,000 had been paid.

9. BOSS recorded 6 months' depreciation ($10,000) on the equipment.

E11-6 (Accounting for acquisition and use of materials and supplies)

On November 1, 2013, a federal agency had the following balances in two of its accounts: The budgetary account Allotments—realized resources had a credit balance of $250,000, and the proprietary account Fund balance with Treasury had a debit balance of $800,000. Prepare journal entries to record the following transactions, which occurred in November and December, regarding a single purchase of materials:

1. The agency's inventory control department sent a purchase request to the purchasing department to order materials at an estimated cost of $140,000.

2. After soliciting competitive bids, the purchasing department ordered the materials at a cost of $150,000.

3. The materials arrived, together with an invoice for $150,000. After inspection, the materials were accepted.

4. A disbursement schedule was sent to Treasury requesting payment of the invoice.

5. Treasury notified the agency that the invoice was paid.

6. To prepare its quarterly financial statements, the agency took an inventory and found that $35,000 of the materials were still on hand.

E11-7 (Year-end adjusting journal entries)

Prepare budgetary and proprietary journal entries to record the following year-end adjustments:

1. An accrual of $60,000 was made for salaries earned the last week of September, to be paid in October. Budgetary funds were available for this purpose.

2. The agency's liability for unused vacation leave increased by $40,000 as a result of the year's activities. The budget makes no provision for this expense until vacation leave is actually taken.

3. The agency discovered that a purchase order for $15,000 was inadvertently issued twice for the same thing. Therefore, one of the orders was cancelled.

4. The agency recorded depreciation of $25,000 on its equipment.

E11-8 (Accounting for salaries)

A federal agency receives a separate allotment to finance the salary costs of its program. The allotment is sufficient to cover salaries earned in the last month of the fiscal year but paid early in the next fiscal year. The account Allotments—realized resources has a credit balance of $300,000. The agency maintains budgetary control by means of a vacancy control system. Make journal entries to record the following transactions and events:

1. A disbursement schedule is sent to Treasury requesting salary checks $275,000.

2. Treasury notifies the agency that payment was made.

3. The agency accrues salaries of $18,000 at the end of the fiscal year.

4. The agency accrues $20,000 for unused vacation leave. Budgetary resources for vacation leave are provided when leave is actually taken.

E11-9 (Journal entries—emphasis on budgetary entries and statements)

The Central Think Tank (CTT) receives a separate appropriation from Congress for the acquisition of advanced intelligence-gathering materials. The following is a summary of transactions affecting the CTT's intelligence-gathering material appropriation for the year ended September 30, 2013. Prepare journal entries to record these transactions; state which entries are budgetary and which are proprietary. Also, prepare a statement of budgetary resources. Assume that all resources not obligated by year-end are not available for future obligation.

1. The CTT received an appropriation of $400,000.

2. The OMB apportioned to the agency the entire amount that Congress appropriated.

3. To keep control over its rate of expenditures, the agency used an allotment system. During the year, the entire apportionment was allotted.

4. Commitments placed during the year for intelligence-gathering materials totaled $390,000.

5. Purchase orders issued against the commitments totaled $375,000.

6. Of the intelligence-gathering materials ordered, $360,000 worth was delivered this year; the remaining $15,000 worth will be delivered next year. The delivered materials were accepted and placed in inventory.
7. During the year, intelligence-gathering materials worth $140,000 were consumed in operations.
8. The CTT sent a disbursement schedule to the Treasury requesting payment of the invoice for $360,000 received from the vendor.
9. The Treasury later notified the CTT that the invoice had been paid.

Problems

P11-1   (Accounting cycle and financial reporting)
Following is a trial balance of the accounts of the Bureau of Bridge Inspection (BOBI), a relatively new unit of the Department of Transportation (DOT), as of October 1, 2013.

Budgetary accounts:		
Total actual resources—collected	$20,000	
Delivered orders—obligations, unpaid		$20,000
Totals	$20,000	$20,000
Proprietary accounts:		
Fund balance with Treasury	$20,000	
Inventory, materials, and supplies	6,000	
General property, plant, and equipment	30,000	
Disbursements in transit		20,000
Cumulative results of operations		36,000
Totals	$56,000	$56,000

BOBI is responsible for overseeing state inspections of bridges constructed with federal funds. It reports program expenses by object of account. BOBI does not use commitment accounting, but does obligate budgetary resources when it enters into contracts or sends purchase orders to buy capital assets and supplies and materials. It also obligates resources for operating leases. The following transactions occurred during the month of October 2013:

1. Congress appropriated $2,000,000 for BOBI's bridge inspection program activities in fiscal year 2014.
2. OMB notified DOT that it had apportioned the entire amount of BOBI's appropriation.
3. DOT notified BOBI that it had allotted $500,000 of its appropriation for the first quarter of fiscal year 2014.
4. During the month of October, BOBI entered into the following contracts:

For testing equipment	$ 100,000
For materials and supplies	50,000

    BOBI also obligated the full amount of its operating lease payments ($90,000) for the first quarter of 2014.
5. Treasury advised BOBI that it paid the $20,000 invoice that BOBI had forwarded for payment before October 1, 2013.
6. BOBI received the materials and supplies ordered in transaction 4. However, the invoice was for $52,000 because the supplier sent additional supplies, as permitted by the contract. BOBI accepted the entire shipment. BOBI also recorded as a liability the $30,000 rent due October 1.
7. BOBI sent a disbursement schedule to Treasury requesting the following payments:

For materials and supplies	$ 52,000
For rent	30,000

8. BOBI sent a disbursement schedule to Treasury requesting salary checks totaling $90,000.
9. Treasury advised BOBI that it had made payments totaling $172,000, pursuant to the schedules forwarded by BOBI in transactions 7 and 8.
10. To prepare accrual-basis financial statements for the month of October, BOBI made adjusting journal entries for the following items:
    a. To accrue salaries earned in October but not paid—$10,000
    b. To record materials and supplies used—$12,000
    c. To record 1 month's depreciation on equipment—$1,000

Use the preceding information to do the following:
a. Prepare journal entries to record the foregoing transactions and events.
b. Prepare a preclosing trial balance based on transaction 1.
c. Prepare a balance sheet, a statement of net costs, and a statement of changes in net position.

P11-2 (Accounting cycle for 1 month)

The Star Exploration Agency, a unit of the Space Department, was established by Congress to begin operations at the beginning of fiscal year 2014. Following are the agency's transactions during October, its first month of operations:

October 1	Congress passed and the president approved a $1,000,000 appropriation for this agency.
October 1	Of the amount appropriated, $950,000 was apportioned by the OMB.
October 1	The Space Department allotted the agency $100,000 to carry out its October operations.
October 1	Purchase requests were made for materials and supplies, estimated to cost $88,000.
October 4	Purchase orders were placed for materials and supplies, estimated to cost $85,000. The other requests (for $3,000) were cancelled.
October 10	Materials and supplies previously ordered were received, together with invoices for $80,000. All items received were placed in inventory. The remaining items (for $5,000) will be received at a later date.
October 14	A disbursement schedule was sent to the Treasury, requesting that it pay invoices amounting to $80,000.
October 24	The Treasury informed the agency that it had paid invoices amounting to $76,000.
October 31	An inventory count showed that $15,000 of materials and supplies was on hand. The rest was used in operations.

Use the preceding information to do the following:
a. Prepare journal entries to record the events of October.
b. Prepare a preclosing trial balance.
c. Prepare the following month-end statements: balance sheet, statement of net costs, statement of changes in net position, and statement of budgetary resources

P11-3 (Financial statements after initial month of operations)

The Black Hole, a unit of the Space Department, was established October 1, 2013. Its purpose is to probe deep space. It is financed by an appropriation from Congress. Following are the transactions of the agency during October 2013:

October 1	The agency received a certified copy of an appropriation warrant from the Department of the Treasury for $900,000.
October 1	The entire appropriation of $900,000 was apportioned by the OMB.
October 1	Of the amount apportioned, $400,000 was allotted to the agency by the Space Department to finance its October operations.
October 4	The agency ordered special training equipment at an estimated cost of $275,000.
October 14	The equipment arrived, together with an invoice for $300,000. The equipment was accepted at the price charged, because the contract permitted a 10 percent cost overrun.

October 24   The agency sent a disbursement schedule to Treasury requesting payment of the following items. (The agency does not obligate salaries or utility bills but maintains off-line controls to ensure allotments are not exceeded.)

Equipment	$300,000
Salaries	75,000
Utilities	20,000

October 27   Treasury notified the agency that all items on the disbursement schedule had been paid.

October 31   The agency recorded depreciation of $5,000 on the equipment.

Use the preceding information to do the following:

a. Prepare journal entries to record these transactions and events.

b. Prepare a preclosing trial balance.

c. Prepare a balance sheet, a statement of net costs, and a statement of changes in net position.

Chapter 12

Accounting for Not-for-Profit Organizations

Chapter Outline

After completing this chapter, you should be able to do the following:

- Describe the characteristics that distinguish not-for-profit organizations (NFPOs) from for-profit organizations and from governmental entities
- Describe the financial statements prepared by NFPOs
- Discuss the characteristics of the three classifications of net assets reported in the financial statements
- State the basic rule for reporting on contributions, including contributed services
- Discuss the accounting for various types of donor-imposed restrictions
- Discuss the accounting entries needed when resources are released from restrictions
- Discuss the difference in accounting between unconditional and conditional promises to give
- Discuss the accounting for various types of contributed services
- Discuss the accounting for collections of works of art, rare books, and similar assets
- Discuss how investments are measured for financial reporting purposes
- Prepare journal entries to record the activities of NFPOs
- Describe the major types of funds used internally by NFPOs

CHARACTERISTICS OF NOT-FOR-PROFIT ORGANIZATIONS

Not-for-profit organizations (NFPOs) perform a wide range of activities. Many of these activities (particularly in such fields as health care, social services, and education) are also performed by for-profit enterprises and governmental agencies. Knowing whether an activity is being performed by an NFPO, a for-profit enterprise, or a governmental agency is important because the accounting and financial reporting standards applicable to these entities are somewhat different. This chapter discusses the accounting and reporting standards promulgated by the Financial Accounting Standards Board (FASB) for entities it defines as NFPOs.

The FASB defines NFPOs by listing the characteristics that distinguish them from for-profit business enterprises; that is, NFPOs (1) receive contributions of significant amounts of resources from resource providers who do not expect to receive proportionate monetary benefits in return; (2) operate for purposes other than to provide goods or services at a profit; and (3) lack defined ownership interests that can be sold, transferred, or redeemed.[1] NFPOs possess these characteristics in varying degrees; for example, there are significant variations in the extent to which NFPOs receive revenues from exchange transactions versus contributions. Clearly, however, investor-owned enterprises and dividend-paying entities fall outside the realm of NFPOs. As we shall see, the need for demonstrating accountability to donors and the lack of ownership interests have influenced the development of accounting and financial reporting standards for NFPOs.

The distinction between an NFPO and a governmental entity is sometimes fuzzy, because governments have increasingly provided social services and other functions by contracting with NFPOs. Indeed, many NFPOs receive all or most of their resources from governments. Entities such as states, cities, counties, and towns (including public corporations and "bodies corporate and politic") are clearly governmental. However, an entity created by charter under state corporation or not-for-profit corporation laws may perform activities so closely related to what governments do that it may not be clear what kind of entity it is. As distinguished from NFPOs, governmental entities have one or more of these characteristics: (1) their officers are either popularly elected, or a controlling majority of their governing boards are appointed or approved by entities that are clearly governmental; (2) they may have the power to tax; (3) they may have the power to issue tax-exempt debt; or (4) they can be dissolved unilaterally by a government, and their net assets assumed by it without compensation.[2]

Examples of Not-for-Profit Organizations

The four broad NFPO categories are voluntary health and welfare organizations (VHWOs), health care organizations, colleges and universities, and other not-for-profit organizations (ONPOs). The accounting and financial reporting principles covered in this chapter apply to all four NFPO categories, but the illustrations relate primarily to VHWOs and ONPOs. Not-for-profit colleges and universities are discussed in an appendix to this chapter. The unique aspects of accounting and financial reporting for health care entities are discussed in Chapter 13.

VHWOs are entities formed for the purpose of providing voluntary services for various segments of society, in the fields of health, welfare, and other social services. These entities obtain resources primarily from donations from the general public. They may also receive grants and

---

[1]FASB Concepts Statement No. 4, "Objectives of Financial Reporting by Nonbusiness Organizations," (Norwalk, CT: FASB, 1980), par. 6. Also, FASB Accounting Standards Codification (ASC), Section 958-10-20 (formerly Statement No. 116, "Accounting for Contributions Received and Contributions Made," Glossary).

[2]*AICPA Audit and Accounting Guide—Health Care Organizations* (New York: AICPA, 2006), par.1.02.c.

contracts from governmental agencies to provide specific social services. Because they are organized for the benefit of the public, they are exempt from many taxes. Well-known examples of VHWOs are the American Cancer Society, the Boy Scouts of America, the National Urban League, and the Young Women's Christian Association of the USA. VHWOs may provide such services as family counseling, recreation and work for youth, and meals for the needy and the elderly, often at no charge or low charge to the service recipients.

The category ONPOs includes other types of NFPOs that are not VHWOs, colleges and universities, or health care entities. Some of them provide services similar to those provided by VHWOs and charge user fees. Many of them, however, are organized to provide benefits to their members and hence derive their revenues primarily from membership dues and fees. Examples of ONPOs include the following:

- Cemetery organizations
- Civic and community organizations
- Labor unions
- Nongovernmental libraries and museums
- Performing arts organizations
- Political parties
- Private foundations
- Private not-for-profit elementary and secondary schools
- Professional associations and trade associations
- Religious organizations
- Research and scientific organizations
- Social and country clubs

Major Sources of Accounting and Financial Reporting Guidance

The FASB *Accounting Standards Codification* (ASC; formerly issued in the form of FASB Statements and Interpretations) is the primary source of accounting and financial reporting guidance for NFPOs. Although most FASB standards apply equally to for-profit entities and NFPOs, some are unique to NFPOs. The most significant were originally issued as FASB Statement No. 116, "Accounting for Contributions Received and Contributions Made," and FASB Statement No. 117, "Financial Statements of Not-for-Profit Organizations" (both are incorporated into FASB ASC Topic 958). This chapter concentrates on these unique standards. In addition, FASB ASC Topic 958 incorporates NFPO accounting standards originally established by AICPA Audit and Accounting Guide, *Not-for-Profit Entities*.

FINANCIAL REPORTING

Overview

NFPOs account for revenues, expenses, assets, and liabilities on the full accrual basis of accounting. Before the FASB issued Statement No. 117 in 1993, NFPOs used fund accounting to maintain accountability for restrictions placed by donors and others on the use of resources; they also prepared financial statements by fund type. Although some continue to use funds for internal accounting purposes, the FASB changed the focus of NFPO financial reporting and requires their financial reporting to focus on the organization as a whole, rather than on fund type.

The FASB states that the primary purpose of NFPO financial statements is to provide information that meets the common interests of donors, members, creditors, and other resource providers. To meet these needs, all NFPOs must prepare (1) a statement of financial position, (2) a statement of activities, and (3) a statement of cash flows. In addition, VHWOs are required to provide information in a separate financial statement about expenses by natural classification. Reporting by natural classification further classifies the broad functional categories shown in the statement of activities into components such as salaries, supplies, and depreciation.

Reporting by Net Asset Classification

Donor-imposed restrictions significantly influence NFPO accounting and financial reporting. Donor-imposed restrictions affect the *purposes* for which NFPOs may spend the donated resources, *when* they may spend them, and even *whether* they may spend them. The FASB requires that the net assets shown in NFPO statements of financial position and the inflows and outflows of resources shown in NFPO statements of activities be reported as unrestricted, temporarily restricted, or permanently restricted, depending on the existence and nature of donor-imposed restrictions.

Sometimes, restrictions on the use of resources arise out of circumstances other than those imposed by donors, such as from other contracts and bond agreements. However, only donor-imposed restrictions are classified as temporarily or permanently restricted net assets. Information about the amounts and nature of different types of such donor-imposed restrictions must be reported on the face of the statement of financial position or in notes to the financial statements.

Permanently restricted net assets are resources resulting from the following:

a. Contributions and other asset inflows whose use by the organization is limited by donor-imposed stipulations that neither expire by passage of time nor can be fulfilled or otherwise removed by actions of the organization

b. Other enhancements and diminishments subject to the same kinds of stipulations

c. Reclassifications from (or to) other classes of net assets as a consequence of donor-imposed stipulations[3]

Temporarily restricted net assets are resources resulting from the following:

a. Contributions and other asset inflows whose use by the organization is limited by donor-imposed stipulations that either expire by passage of time or can be removed by actions of the organization pursuant to donor stipulations

b. Other asset enhancements and diminishments subject to the same kinds of stipulations

c. Reclassifications to (or from) other net asset classes as a consequence of donor-imposed stipulations, their expiration by passage of time, or their fulfillment and removal by actions of the organization pursuant to donor stipulations[4]

Unrestricted net assets are resources that are neither permanently nor temporarily restricted. The only limits on their use are those resulting from the nature of the organization and the environment in which it operates, including contractual agreements with creditors, suppliers, and others that are entered into in the ordinary course of business. Information about the limits should be disclosed only in notes to the financial statements. Because they are *not donor-imposed*, however, those limits do not meet the FASB's definition of restrictions and are not reported as restricted.

---

[3]FASB ASC Section 958-205-20.
[4]Ibid.

To illustrate, assume an individual donates $1 million to a not-for-profit university, stipulating that the corpus of the donation must be held intact in perpetuity. The donor also stipulates that the corpus must be invested in high-grade corporate bonds, the income from which must be used to perform research on the causes of autism. Assume further that the investments produce income of $40,000 in a particular year. The donation of $1 million would be classified as *permanently restricted* because the donor-imposed restriction does not expire with the passage of time, nor can it be removed by university action. The investment revenue is also donor-restricted because it can be used only for a particular purpose. However, the investment revenue is classified as *temporarily restricted* because the restriction can be removed by university action based on the donor's stipulation, namely, performing research on the causes of autism. More on this later.

Statement of Financial Position

A statement of financial position provides financial information about the assets, liabilities, and net assets of the organization and their relationship to each other. This information, when used with information in other financial statements and related disclosures, helps donors, members, and other interested parties assess the organization's ability to continue its operations, as well as its liquidity, financial flexibility, ability to meet obligations, and future financing needs.[5] To help accomplish some of these purposes, assets are presented in order of liquidity, and liabilities are presented in order of anticipated liquidation. Showing the amount and nature of donor-imposed restrictions in the statement of net assets helps the reader assess the NFPO's financial flexibility.

FASB standards do not specify or preclude any one format of financial statement, so long as it shows the amounts and flows of unrestricted, temporarily restricted, and permanently restricted resources. Following is a skeletal outline of the broad elements of an NFPO statement of financial position:

Assets (presented generally in order of nearness to cash)	XXX
Total assets	XXX
Liabilities and net assets:	
Liabilities (presented generally in order of nearness to liquidation)	XXX
Total liabilities	XXX
Net assets:	
Unrestricted	XXX
Temporarily restricted	XXX
Permanently restricted	XXX
Total net assets	XXX
Total liabilities and net assets	XXX

Statement of Activities

A statement of activities provides information about "the effects of transactions and other events and circumstances that change the amount and nature of net assets" and "how the organization's resources are used in providing various programs or services."[6] The changes in the three asset

---

[5]FASB ASC par. 958-210-05-2.
[6]FASB ASC par. 958-225-05-2.

classifications can be presented in multicolumn format or in single-column "pancake" style. Some prefer the multicolumn format because it lets the reader observe, at a glance, the effects of revenues, gains, other support, expenses, and losses on each category of net assets. Others prefer a single-column format that permits emphasis on operating performance, as shown by changes in unrestricted net assets. (We discuss this matter in Chapter 13 regarding not-for-profit hospital financial statements.) Following is a skeletal outline of the elements of an NFPO statement of activities, prepared in a multicolumn format:

	Unrestricted	Temporarily Restricted	Permanently Restricted	Total
Revenues, Gains, and Other Support (details by source):	XXX	XXX	XXX	XXX
Net assets released from restrictions	XXX	(XXX)		
Total	XXX	XXX	XXX	XXX
Expenses and Losses:				
Program (details by program)	XXX			XXX
Management and general	XXX			XXX
Fund-raising	XXX			XXX
Total expenses	XXX			XXX
Losses	XXX	XXX	XXX	XXX
Total expenses and losses	XXX	XXX	XXX	XXX
Change in net assets	XXX	XXX	XXX	XXX
Net assets at beginning of year	XXX	XXX	XXX	XXX
Net assets at end of year	XXX	XXX	XXX	XXX

Notice that Revenues, Gains, and Other Support in the statement of activities are reported as increases in either Unrestricted or Restricted assets, depending on whether the use of assets is limited by donor-imposed restrictions. However, the FASB requires that all expenses be reported as decreases in *unrestricted* net assets, even if they were financed with restricted resources. This is accomplished by means of journal entries that reduce restricted assets and increase unrestricted assets, as donor restrictions are satisfied by incurring program expenses or by the passage of time. In the foregoing skeletal outline, next to the caption "Net assets released from restrictions," notice the reduction reported for temporarily restricted net assets and the corresponding increase in unrestricted net assets. (Regarding the illustration on page 440, when the university receives investment revenues, the resources would be classified as temporarily restricted; when it performs research on autism, a journal entry would be made reclassifying the resources from temporarily restricted to unrestricted.)

Notice also that the first caption in the outline is Revenues, Gains, and Other Support. What is the difference between revenues and gains? Revenues are inflows from selling goods and providing services that constitute the organization's ongoing major or central operations, such as fees for providing child care services, college and university tuition, and charges for services to hospital patients. Gains are inflows from peripheral or incidental transactions, such as profits from selling securities or operating a parking lot in conjunction with an NFPO's major activities. It is possible that an activity considered by one organization to produce revenues will be considered by another organization to produce gains. In fact, donor contributions received by NFPOs may be called revenues or gains, depending on whether they are actively sought and frequently received. The term *support* describes broadly the nature of the resources received by many NFPOs and is used throughout the FASB's literature on NFPOs.

Expenses incurred by NFPOs must be reported in the statement of activities or in the notes to the financial statements "by their functional classification such as major classes of program services and supporting activities."[7] When functional classifications are used, individual expenses (such as salaries and supplies) within a function or program are aggregated and reported by function or program. Functional classifications are required because they enable the reader to determine the cost of various programs offered by the organization. The organization's programs should also be described in the notes to the financial statements.

For financial reporting purposes, a *program* is considered to be an activity that is directly related to the purpose(s) for which the organization was established. Although most organizations are involved in several programs, it is possible that an organization may have only one such activity.

Expenses identified as *management and general* or *administrative* are those associated with the overall direction and management of the organization, in addition to those associated with record keeping, the annual report, and so forth. *Fund-raising* and other supporting services are associated with the solicitation of money, materials, and the like, for which the individual or organization making the contribution receives no direct economic benefit. These expenses include such items as printing, personnel, the cost of maintaining a mailing list, and the cost of any gifts that are sent to prospective contributors.

The distinction between program, management and general, and fund-raising expenses is useful to those interested in knowing the percentage of total expenses that an NFPO devotes to program activities. IRS Form 990, "Return of Organization Exempt from Income Tax," used both by the Internal Revenue Service and by state agencies responsible for oversight of charitable organizations, also requires program service, management and general, and fund-raising expenses to be reported on separate lines.

Statement of Functional Expenses

All VHWOs are required to prepare both a statement of activities and a statement of functional expenses. The statement of functional expenses, which provides another perspective on the way resources are spent, is presented in matrix format. For each program or function, this statement identifies the expenses by natural or object classification (e.g., salaries, supplies, travel, depreciation expense, and occupancy expense). Although they are not required to prepare a statement of functional expenses, many ONPOs choose to do so because the statement is useful to managers and others.

Statement of Cash Flows

A statement of cash flows provides the financial statement user with information on the cash receipts and cash payments of the organization during the same period as the statement of activities. The statement is organized to show the effect of operating, investing, and financing activities on cash flows.

---

[7]FASB ASC par. 958-720-45-2.

> ## Not-for-Profit Financial Reporting in Practice
>
> ### How Much "Program Activity" Will a Donation Buy?
>
> Charity Navigator (CN) seeks to "advance a more efficient and responsive philanthropic marketplace" by evaluating and rating individual charitable entities. One of the key factors used by CN in its rating process is "organizational efficiency." Using data derived from IRS Form 990, CN ascertains and assesses (a) the percentage of total expenses spent on program activities; (b) the percentage spent on administration; (c) the percentage spent on fund-raising; and (d) fund-raising efficiency, that is, how much the NFPO spends to raise each $1 of contributions. Here are some of CN's rating criteria and findings:
>
> - **Program activities.** CN finds that 7 of every 10 charities it evaluates spend at least 75 percent of their budgets on program activities, and 9 of every 10 spend at least 65 percent on program activities. CN determines the program expense percentage and multiplies it by 10, so if an NFPO spends 90 percent of its total expenses on program activities, it gets a score of 9 out of a maximum 10.
> - **Administrative expenses.** CN finds that the median administrative expense rate for all charities is 9.5 percent. In general, CN gives an NFPO a score of 10 (the maximum) if its administrative expense rate is 0–15 percent, a score of 7.5 if it is 15–20 percent, and so on. Administrative expense rates often vary by type of NFPO (e.g., CN finds the median for food banks to be 2 percent), so CN takes that into account when rating individual NFPOs.
> - **Fund-raising expenses.** CN finds the median fund-raising expense rate for all charities to be 7.3 percent. It assigns a score of 10 if the fund-raising expense rate is 0–10 percent, 7.5 if the rate is 10–15 percent, and so on.
> - **Fund-raising efficiency.** CN finds that the median cost for a charity to raise $1 in charitable contributions is 10 cents. CN gives a score of 10 to the NFPO if it costs 0–10 cents to raise each dollar of contributions, 7.5 if it costs 10–20 cents, and so on.
>
> *Source:* Available online at www.charitynavigator.org.

Illustration of NFPO Financial Statements

The following illustration of NFPO financial reporting is based on the statements of several food distribution entities. Assume that County Food Harvest, an NFPO, rescues and distributes surplus and donated food to social service agencies, soup kitchens, homeless shelters, and other agencies that provide free meals to the hungry and homeless throughout the county. Food donors include retailers, wholesalers, bakeries, and other entities. Included here are County Food Harvest's financial statements for the year ended June 30, 2013 (amounts in thousands of dollars): a statement of financial position (Table 12-1), a statement of activities (Table 12-2), a statement of functional expenses (Table 12-3), and a cash flows statement (Table 12-4).

In Table 12-1, notice the classification of net assets among unrestricted ($3,035), temporarily restricted ($2,992), and permanently restricted ($835). Details of the nature and amounts of the restrictions could be presented either on the face of the statement of financial position or in the notes. In this instance, the notes show the following:

Temporarily restricted net assets are available for the following purposes:	
Acquisition of warehouse and office facility	$2,140
Food distribution program, on expiration of time restrictions	300
Food distribution program, on expiration of purpose restrictions	552
Total	$2,992

TABLE 12-1 Statement of Financial Position—NFPO	

County Food Harvest
Statement of Financial Position
June 30, 2013
(amounts in thousands)

Assets	
Cash and cash equivalents	$2,094
Contributions receivable	654
Grants receivable	310
Food inventory	452
Other current assets	215
Equipment, net of $215 depreciation	640
Assets restricted to acquiring land, buildings, and equipment	2,140
Long-term investments	835
Total assets	$7,340
Liabilities and Net Assets	
Liabilities:	
Accounts payable and accrued expenses	$ 478
Total liabilities	478
Net assets:	
Unrestricted	3,035
Temporarily restricted	2,992
Permanently restricted	835
Total net assets	6,862
Total liabilities and net assets	$7,340

Permanently restricted net assets are restricted to investments perpetuity, with the investment return available to support the food distribution program.

In Table 12-2, notice the form of the contributions, which include food and services, and consider how those contributions might have been valued for financial reporting purposes. Notice also the side-by-side reporting of the reclassification of net assets upon their release from restrictions. Finally, notice how the statement of functional expenses in Table 12-3 provides detail on each of the programs reported in Table 12-2.

CONTRIBUTIONS OTHER THAN SERVICES AND COLLECTIONS

General Rule

A contribution is an unconditional transfer of cash or other assets from one entity to another; the entity making the contribution does not directly receive value in exchange.[8] NFPOs may receive contributions in the form of cash, investments, supplies and materials, rights to use facilities,

---

[8] FASB ASC Section 958-605-20.

TABLE 12-2 Statement of Activities

County Food Harvest
Statement of Activities
Year Ended June 30, 2013
(amounts in thousands)

	Unrestricted	Temporarily Restricted	Permanently Restricted	Total
Revenues, Gains, and Other Support				
Contributions—food	$ 9,752			$ 9,752
Contributions—support	5,854	$2,084		7,938
Contributions—services	420			420
Revenues—government grants	612			612
Special events	820			820
Investment income	75	90		165
Net unrealized and realized gains on long-term investments		28	$ 35	63
Net assets released from restriction due to satisfaction of:				
Program restrictions	312	(312)		
Time restrictions	156	(156)		
Total revenues, gains, and other support	18,001	1,734	$ 35	19,770
Expenses				
Food distribution program	14,804			14,804
Management and general	956			956
Fund-raising	1,714			1,714
Total expenses	17,474			17,474
Change in net assets	527	1,734	35	2,296
Net assets at beginning of year	2,508	1,258	800	4,566
Net assets at end of year	$ 3,035	$2,992	$835	$ 6,862

pledges of cash, personal services, works of art, and so on. NFPOs may also receive contributions with "strings attached;" that is, with restrictions on the purposes for which the donations may be used or when they may be used. The general rule for reporting the receipt of contributions other than services and collections is that they must be reported or measured as follows:

a. Reported as revenues or gains in the period received
b. Reported as assets, decreases of liabilities, or expenses, depending on the form the benefits take
c. Measured at the fair value of the contribution received
d. Reported as either restricted support or unrestricted support[9]

---

[9]FASB ASC par. 958-605-25-2.

TABLE 12-3   Statement of Functional Expenses

County Food Harvest
Statement of Functional Expenses
Year Ended June 30, 2013
(amounts in thousands)

	Food Distribution	Management and General	Fund Raising	Total
Salaries	$ 3,420	$380	$ 473	$ 4,273
Employee benefits	861	95	118	1,074
Food rescued	9,700			9,700
Food packing supplies	178			178
Rent and utilities	315	40	38	393
Communication	52	21	53	126
Professional fees	110	180	250	540
Advertising			678	678
Office expenses	73	210	74	357
Depreciation	95	30	30	155
Total expenses	$14,804	$956	$1,714	$17,474

TABLE 12-4   Cash Flows Statement

County Food Harvest
Cash Flows Statement
Year Ended June 30, 2013
(amounts in thousands)

Cash Flows from Operating Activities

Change in net assets	$2,296
Adjustments to reconcile change in net cash (used in) provided by operating activities:	
Depreciation and amortization	155
Increase in contributions receivable	(85)
Increase in grants receivable	(15)
Decrease in other current assets	10
Increase in accrued expenses and accounts payable	30
Net unrealized and realized gains on long-term investments	(63)
Net cash provided by operating activities	2,328

Cash Flows from Investing Activities

Purchase of securities	(2,000)
Net cash (used in) investing activities	(2,000)
Net increase in cash and cash equivalents	328
Cash and cash equivalents at beginning of year	1,766
Cash and cash equivalents at end of year	$2,094

Unrestricted Contributions

When an NFPO receives a contribution without a donor-imposed restriction, it should report the contribution in the statement of activities as unrestricted revenues or gains (unrestricted support). It should report expenses incurred from unrestricted net assets as decreases in those assets. To illustrate, assume an NFPO operates a clinic that provides services to substance abusers. During calendar year 2012, it receives the following donations that may be used for any purpose and at any time: (a) $25,000 of cash, (b) 100 shares of stock having a fair value of $40 a share at the time of the donation, and (c) medical supplies (from a pharmaceutical company) having a fair value of $10,000. The NFPO's accounting policies provide that medical supplies be recorded in inventory until they are used. The NFPO would make the following journal entry in the period the resources are received:

Cash	25,000	
Investments	4,000	
Inventory—medical supplies	10,000	
Unrestricted support—contributions		29,000
Unrestricted support—supplies		10,000
To record unrestricted contributions.		

In the foregoing illustration, all the contributions resulted in increases in assets. But a contribution could also result in a simultaneous increase in expenses. For example, if a utility provides free electricity to an NFPO, the NFPO would recognize as revenues and expenses simultaneously the fair value of the electricity used.

Contributions with Donor-Imposed Restrictions

A donor-imposed restriction limits the use of the contributed resources beyond the broad limits resulting from the nature of the organization and the purposes for which it was organized. Contributions received with donor-imposed restrictions must be reported as *restricted* support. These contributions will increase either temporarily restricted or permanently restricted net assets. As an option, if the NFPO receives donor-restricted contributions whose restrictions are met in the *same reporting period the contributions are received*, the contribution may be reported as unrestricted support, provided the entity reports similar types of contributions that way consistently from one period to another.

For example, a contributor may stipulate that a cash donation be used only to perform a specific research project or to construct a building. These *purpose-type* restrictions are classified as temporary restrictions, because they may be satisfied by the NFPO's performance of the research or construction of the building. (Notice that even though the building may have a long life, the restriction itself is *temporary* because it is satisfied once the resources are spent to construct the building.) Another donor may stipulate that his or her cash contribution be maintained permanently, with the income from investing the cash to be used to perform a specific research project. The permanent restriction can never be removed by action of the entity, so the donation itself is classified as permanently restricted. However, the income from investing the permanently restricted resources is classified as temporarily restricted because only a purpose restriction—the performance of specific research—applies to the investment income.

Rather than purpose-type restrictions, a donor may impose a *time* restriction on the use of resources. For example, a donor may make a $30,000 cash contribution to an NFPO, stipulating that the contribution may be used for any purpose the trustees choose, but only at the rate of

Not-for-Profit Financial Reporting in Practice

Placing a Value on Donated Food

The requirement to record donated noncash assets, such as supplies and materials, at fair value some-times can be a daunting task. Food banks, for example, receive millions of pounds of donated perishable and packaged food (and even prepared food) from restaurants, bakeries, retailers, and manufacturers to help feed the needy and the homeless. Using estimates to place a value on donated food makes the task much easier. Here's how two food banks valued donated food:

- In a note to its 2010 financial statements, Feeding America writes:

  Feeding America reports the fair value of gifts of donated food and grocery products . . . as unre-stricted public support and, shortly thereafter, as expense when granted to member food banks. During the years ended June 30, 2010, and 2009, Feeding America distributed approximately 364 million pounds and 340 million pounds, respectively, of donated product received from approxi-mately 320 national donors. The approximate average wholesale value of one pound of donated product at the national level, which was determined to be approximately $1.60 during 2010 and $1.58 during 2009, was based on a study by Feeding America. . . .

- In its Form 990 for the fiscal year ended June 30, 2010, City Harvest writes:

  In addition to donations of food products, City Harvest also accepts donations of prepared food and meals. All food has been valued based on the wholesale value of donated product at the national level, as determined by an independent study, which has been calculated by City Harvest at $1.28 and $1.25 per pound for fiscal years 2010 and 2009, respectively.

Source: Feeding America financial statements available online at www.feedingamerica.org and City Harvest Form 990 available online at www.cityharvest.org.

$10,000 a year, starting at the beginning of the next year. This type of restriction also causes the contribution to be classified as temporarily restricted.

To illustrate the accounting effect of donor-imposed restrictions, assume the NFPO in the preceding section received three additional cash donations: (1) $5,000 from a donor who said it must be used only for research into a new method for treating substance abusers; (2) $7,000 from a donor who said it may be used for any purpose the trustees choose, but not until the following year; and (3) $25,000 from a donor who said the gift must be maintained in perpetuity, with the income from it to be used for any purpose the trustees choose. Donation 1 has a temporary (pur-pose) restriction; donation 2 has a temporary (time) restriction; and donation 3 has a permanent restriction. The NFPO would make this journal entry:

Cash	37,000	
Temporarily restricted support—contributions		5,000
Temporarily restricted support—contributions		7,000
Permanently restricted support—contributions		25,000
To record temporarily and permanently restricted gifts.		

Accounting for Reclassifications

An NFPO must recognize the expiration of a donor-restricted contribution in the period the restriction expires. A restriction expires when the stipulated purpose for which the contribution was made has been fulfilled, when the stipulated time period has elapsed, or both. FASB standards require, however, that *all expenses* must be reported in the statement of activities as decreases in *unrestricted* net assets, even though the original contribution that financed the expense was reported as an increase in temporarily restricted net assets. To accomplish this result, an additional journal entry is needed to reclassify restricted net assets to unrestricted net assets when the restriction expires.

Reclassifications have an effect similar to interfund transfers in governmental accounting. They decrease the net assets of the temporarily restricted assets class and correspondingly increase the net assets of the unrestricted net assets class. As shown in the skeletal statement of activities, reclassification transactions are reported as Revenues, Gains, and Other Support under the caption Net assets released from restrictions. The journal entry to record these transactions should be prepared in sufficient detail to enable reporting the cause of the reclassification, such as satisfaction of program restrictions or expiration of time restrictions.

To illustrate, let's return to the illustration in the preceding section, Contributions with Donor-Imposed Restrictions. As the NFPO spends the $5,000 to do research on the substance abuse project, the gift is being used as intended, and the purpose restriction is being satisfied. As the spending occurs, the resources are released from the temporary restriction and become unrestricted; at the same time, the expense is reported as a reduction of unrestricted net assets. The NFPO would make the following journal entries to record the program expense and the expiration of the restriction:

Expenses—special research programs	5,000	
Cash		5,000
To record payment for research expenses.		
Temporarily restricted asset reclassifications out—satisfaction of purpose restrictions	5,000	
Unrestricted asset reclassifications in—satisfaction of purpose restrictions		5,000
To record satisfaction of purpose restriction on donation 1.		

The time restriction regarding donation 2 for $7,000 is satisfied as soon as the new year arrives, because the gift becomes available for spending at the start of the new year. The NFPO would make the following journal entry to record expiration of that restriction:

Temporarily restricted asset reclassifications out—satisfaction of time restrictions	7,000	
Unrestricted asset reclassifications in—satisfaction of time restrictions		7,000
To record satisfaction of time restriction on donation 2.		

Donation 3 will remain in permanently restricted status in perpetuity. Because the donor stipulated that income from the investment could be used for any purpose, the investment income would be recorded as Unrestricted revenue—investment income. If, however, the donor had stipulated that the investment income had to be used for a specific purpose, the investment income would be recorded as Temporarily restricted revenue—investment income; when used for the specified purpose, a reclassification entry would be made, similar to that for donation 1.

Financial reporting of reclassification transactions is shown in the statement of activities illustrated in Table 12-2 on page 445. Notice that the debit to Reclassifications out is reported as a negative amount under Net assets released from restriction, in the Temporarily restricted column. The credit to Reclassifications in is reported as a positive amount—alongside the negative amount—under Net assets released from restriction in the Unrestricted column. Thus, the reclassifications cancel each other out.

From an organization-wide perspective, the contribution revenue is recognized at the time of the donation, and the expense is recognized when incurred, even if the transactions occur in different accounting periods. However, when viewed from the perspective of changes in unrestricted net assets, the inflow (reported by means of the reclassification) and the outflow (the expense) occur in the same accounting period.

Unconditional Promises to Give (Pledges)

A *promise to give,* sometimes called a pledge or a charitable subscription, is a written or oral agreement to contribute cash or other assets to another entity. The FASB concluded that *unconditional promises to give*—those that depend only on the passage of time or demand by the receiver of the promise—meet the definition of assets because promise makers generally feel bound to honor them. Therefore, unconditional promises to give should be recognized in the financial statements as receivables and as revenues or gains when the promises are received.

To report receivables at net realizable value, an allowance for uncollectible promises should be established, based on the NFPO's experience with collecting pledges and current economic circumstances. Instead of recording "bad debts expense" for estimated uncollectible pledges, NFPOs generally record contribution revenues net of the allowance for uncollectible promises, like the way governments record property tax revenues.

Notice that a promise to give cash contains an *inherent time restriction*, because the NFPO cannot spend the cash until it has the cash in hand. Thus, as a practical matter, whether promises to give are recorded initially as unrestricted or temporarily restricted depends on the accounting period in which the cash is likely to be received. FASB standards say that "receipts of unconditional promises to give with payments due in future periods shall be reported as restricted support [generally, temporarily restricted] unless explicit donor stipulations or circumstances surrounding the receipt of a promise make clear that the donor intended it to be used to support activities of the current period."[10]

Consistent with the requirement for measuring donations at fair value, the FASB requires that promises to give cash in the future (i.e., more than 1 year after the balance sheet date) be discounted to present value. The discount rate is generally the NFPO's average earning rate on investments or average borrowing rate. Contributions receivable are reported net of the discount in the statement of financial position. As time passes, the discount is accreted and recorded as contribution revenue.

When reporting promises to give, the following must be disclosed:

a. Amounts of promises receivable within 1 year, in 1 to 5 years, and in more than 5 years
b. The allowance for uncollectible pledges[11]

For an illustration of the reporting of contributions receivable, see the discussion of the Contributions receivable note in Appendix 12A, page 485. To illustrate the journal entries used to record pledges, assume the NFPO in our earlier illustration received unconditional promises to give totaling $50,000 and expected to receive the gifts in the current period. Based on experience, the NFPO

---

[10]FASB ASC par. 958-605-45-5.
[11]FASB ASC par. 958-310-50-1.

expects to collect 90 percent of the promised cash. It also received a promise from an individual to give $10,000 in cash in two payments: $5,000 in the next year and $5,000 in the year following. It expects that person to fulfill the promise. The NFPO would make the following journal entries:

Contributions receivable	50,000	
Allowance for uncollectible contributions		5,000
Unrestricted support—contributions		45,000
To record receipt of promises to give cash this year, less provision for estimated uncollectible promises.		
Contributions receivable	10,000	
Temporarily restricted support—contributions		9,700
Discount on contributions receivable		300
To record receipt of promises to give cash next year and the year following, discounted to present value.		

Conditional Promises to Give

Conditional promises to give are promises that bind the donor on the occurrence of a specified "future and uncertain" event. Examples of conditional promises to give are (a) a donor promises to give $15,000 in cash to an NFPO, but only if the NFPO raises an equal amount from other contributors by a specific date; and (b) a donor promises to contribute $20,000 as soon as the NFPO establishes a day care center and starts admitting children. A bequest is also a conditional promise—based on a future and uncertain event—because the person making the will may change his or her mind prior to death.

Conditional promises to give are not recognized as receivables and as revenues (or gains) until the conditions on which they depend are *substantially met*. At that point, the conditional promise becomes unconditional and should be recognized as a receivable and as revenue. When an NFPO receives conditional promises to give, it must disclose the total amount promised and describe each group of promises having similar characteristics, such as amounts of promises conditioned on completing a building and raising matching gifts by a specified date.

If a donor actually transfers assets to an NFPO simultaneously with a conditional promise, the NFPO should not recognize revenues. Instead, the receipt of the assets should be accounted for as a refundable advance (deferred revenue) until the conditions are substantially met.

Notice how the accounting treatment of *conditions* differs from that regarding *restrictions*. Conditions may involve significant uncertainty, including events outside the organization's control. Recognizing assets before the uncertainty is sufficiently resolved may cause the information to be unreliable. Therefore, judgment must be exercised in determining when a condition is "substantially met." For example, suppose a donor promises on April 1, 2012, to give an NFPO $50,000, payable March 31, 2013, provided the entity raises a total of $50,000 from other donors by March 15, 2013. By December 31, 2012, when it closes its books, the NFPO has raised only $20,000 from other donors, and the contribution rate has been declining. Has the condition been "substantially met" as of December 31, 2012? Probably not.

If a promise is received with ambiguous donor stipulations, the promise should be presumed to be conditional until the ambiguities are resolved. On the other hand, if a donor attaches a condition to a promise and the possibility that the condition will not be met is remote, the promise should be considered to be unconditional. (An example of the latter is an administrative requirement to file a routine annual report.)

Now, let's continue with the NFPO in our earlier illustration. Suppose it received a matching grant from Ted Elias on January 15, 2012. He promised to contribute up to $25,000, dollar for dollar, for each dollar obtained from other donors through December 31, 2012. The NFPO received no gifts from other donors during January and February but did receive $8,000 in cash on March 15. Ted's matching grant is a conditional promise to give, and the condition is met each time a dollar is collected from other donors. Therefore, the NFPO would make no entry on January 15, when it received Ted's conditional promise. It would, however, make the following journal entry on March 15:

Cash	8,000	
Contributions receivable (Ted Elias)	8,000	
Unrestricted support—contributions		16,000
To record receipt of $8,000 cash from various donors and related promise by Ted Elias to match those donations.		

CONTRIBUTED SERVICES

Contributions of services must be recognized in the financial statements of an NFPO if the services received (1) create or enhance nonfinancial assets or (2) require specialized skills, are provided by individuals who possess those skills, *and* would typically need to be purchased if the services were not donated. Services requiring "specialized skills" are those provided by "accountants, architects, carpenters, doctors, electricians, lawyers, nurses, plumbers, teachers, and other professionals and craftsmen."[12] When these criteria are met, contribution revenue and an asset or an offsetting expense should be recorded for the fair value of the donated services.

The rule regarding contributed services is intended to be restrictive, so that contributed services that do not meet the enumerated criteria may not be recognized. For example, assume a lawyer donates 5 hours to a performing arts center. She spends 3 hours preparing contracts with artists and 2 hours selling tickets at the box office. The fair value of the time she spends drawing up contracts should be recognized as contribution revenue and as an expense. The 2 hours she spends selling tickets should not be recognized, however, because the work—even though needed by the center—does not require specialized skills.

An NFPO that receives contributed services must describe, in notes to its financial statements, the nature and extent of services received, programs or activities for which they were used, and the amount recognized as revenues. If practicable, the fair value of contributed services received but not recognized should also be disclosed. For example, a note to the financial statements of a performing arts center might say: "Donated service revenues and program expenses include the fair value of professional services contributed by performing artists. During the year, performing artists contributed services valued at $60,000 for the free summer concert series. Local residents donated about 200 hours serving as ushers, but those services do not meet the requirement for recognition in the financial statements."

To illustrate accounting for contributed services, assume a psychiatrist donates 25 hours to the NFPO in our continuing example. She spends 20 hours counseling drug abuse patients and 5 hours serving food to them at lunchtime. The NFPO would have paid for both types of

---

[12]FASB ASC par. 958-605-25-16.

services had the psychiatrist not donated her time. She earns $150 an hour when counseling her patients (or the NFPO normally pays $150 an hour when purchasing those services); and the NFPO pays $10 an hour when hiring food servers. The NFPO would make the following journal entry:

Expenses—counseling services	3,000	
Unrestricted support—services		3,000
To record donation of professional services—20 hours @ $150 per hour.		

No entry is made for the 5 hours she spent serving meals, because that service requires no specialized skills.

CONTRIBUTIONS TO COLLECTIONS

A museum in dire financial straits receives a gift of a painting with a fair value of $1 million that it plans to display. The museum's trustees think it would be misleading to report the contribution as revenue and as an asset. They fear that potential donors, noting the revenue, might conclude that the museum does not need financial support for day-to-day operating expenses. Must the museum recognize the contribution as revenue and an asset?

The FASB resolved this controversial issue by giving NFPOs the option of not recognizing donated works of art, historical artifacts, rare books, and similar assets as revenues or gains and assets, provided the donated items are added to collections and the collections meet *all* of the following conditions:

a. Held for public exhibition, education, or research in furtherance of public service rather than financial gain
b. Protected, kept unencumbered, cared for, and preserved
c. Subject to an organizational policy that requires the proceeds from sales of collection items to be used to acquire other items for collections[13]

Thus, NFPOs—such as museums, art galleries, and similar entities that have collections meeting all three of these conditions—have a choice when new items are added: to either capitalize them or not. If they choose to capitalize their collections, they must recognize new items as revenues or gains. If they choose not to capitalize their collections, revenues or gains cannot be recognized. Furthermore, NFPOs must follow a consistent policy. They cannot capitalize selected collections or items within a collection.

On the other hand, NFPOs must recognize contributions of works of art, historical treasures, and similar items that are not part of a collection as revenues or gains and assets when received. For example, suppose an NFPO holds a collection of art that meets all three criteria for triggering the choice either to capitalize or not to capitalize the collection. The NFPO chooses not to capitalize the collection. But what if it receives a donation of a work of art that it intends to sell rather than add to its collection? In that situation, the NFPO must recognize the fair value of the donation as assets (using an account such as Donated art held for sale) and revenues or gains when the work of art is received.

---

[13]FASB ASC Section 958-360-20.

If an NFPO chooses not to capitalize its collections, it must report the following information on the face of its statement of activities, *separately* from revenues, expenses, gains, and losses:

a. Costs of collection items purchased
b. Proceeds from the sale of collection items
c. Proceeds from insurance recoveries of lost or destroyed collection items[14]

In addition, an NFPO that does not capitalize its collections must make various disclosures in the notes to the statements. It must describe its collections, "including their relative significance, and its accounting and stewardship policies for collections."[15] If items in the collection are deaccessed (removed from the collection) during the period, the NFPO must describe the items deaccessed during the period or disclose their fair value. In addition, these disclosures must be referred to in a line item shown on the face of the statement of financial position.

Not-for-Profit Financial Reporting in Practice

Art . . . and Bones, Rocks, Frozen Tissues

Before issuing its accounting standard on contributions, the FASB had proposed that collection items be capitalized, both retroactively and in the future. The proposal was met with a storm of protest from many museums, which argued that the cost of doing so would outweigh the benefits. After further deliberation, the FASB provided the option discussed in the text. Here are some excerpts from the notes to financial statements issued by large museums that have chosen not to capitalize their collections.

American Museum of National History (**Collections note, 2010**)

The Museum has extensive collections of specimens and artifacts that constitute a record of life on Earth. These valuable, and sometimes irreplaceable, collections have been acquired through field expeditions, contributions, and purchases since the Museum's inception and represent one of the largest natural history collections in the world. New collection areas include the Museum's frozen tissue collection of DNA and tissue samples and access to large scientific databases and genomic and astrophysical data. The collections provide a resource for scientists around the world.

The collections are the property of the Museum and are not recognized as assets in the accompanying statements of financial position.

The Art Institute of Chicago (**Art Objects and Library Collections note, 2009**)

The value of the art objects in the permanent collection, as well as the holdings of the libraries, is excluded from the consolidated statements of financial position. . . . All works of art and certain library collections are held for public exhibition, education, or research; are protected, kept unencumbered, cared for, and preserved; and are subject to strict organizational policies governing their use. The value of the Institute's permanent collection is not subject to reasonable estimation.

The Museum of Modern Art (**Collections note, 2009**)

The Museum's collections, acquired through purchase and contributions, are not recognized as assets. . . . Purchases of collection items are recorded in the year in which the items were acquired as decreases in unrestricted net assets.

The 2009 statement of unrestricted revenues, expenses, and changes in unrestricted net assets shows—as a separate item after the caption "Excess of operating revenues and support over operating expenses"—a $33.6 million expense for acquisitions of works of art.

---

[14]FASB ASC par. 958-360-45-5.
[15]FASB ASC par. 958-360-50-6.

INVESTMENTS AND SPLIT-INTEREST AGREEMENTS

Fair Value Reporting and Investment Gains and Losses

Some NFPOs carry large amounts of investments, primarily as a result of donor contributions. Indeed, for many museums and universities, investments rank with property, plant, and equipment as the largest assets reported in the financial statements. Income from investments plays an important role in financing the activities of these NFPOs.

Investments are recorded initially at their acquisition cost if purchased by the NFPO and at fair value if received as a contribution. For financial reporting purposes, FASB standards require that investments held by NFPOs in equity securities that have readily determinable fair values, and all investments in debt securities, be reported at fair value. The FASB defines *fair value* as the "price that would be received to sell an asset or paid to transfer a liability in an orderly transaction between market participants on the measurement date."[16] Thus, when preparing financial statements, an NFPO holding actively traded equity securities would value them at the closing sales price reported on a registered securities exchange.

Reporting investments at fair value means that the carrying amount of investments in the financial statements will usually need to be adjusted every year to the new fair value. It also requires simultaneous recognition, in the statement of activities, of any *unrealized* gains and losses caused by changes in fair value. What if an investment acquired in early 2012 is sold, say, in 2014? In that case, the amount of gain or loss reported in 2014 on that investment should exclude the amount previously recognized in 2012 and 2013.

The simplest way to account for investment gains and losses is to use a single account (called Net unrealized and realized investment gains and losses) to report *all* investment gains and losses, whether realized or not. To illustrate, assume an NFPO received 100 shares of a stock as a contribution in October 2012. Because it had a fair value of $40 a share when received, it was recorded at $4,000. Assume the investment was worth $43 a share when the NFPO prepared its financial statements on December 31, 2012, and was subsequently sold for $44 a share on March 15, 2013. The NFPO would make the following journal entries:

Entry at December 31, 2012:

Investments	300	
Net unrealized and realized investment gains and losses		300
To record unrealized gain on investments.		

Entry at March 15, 2013 (time of sale):

Cash	4,400	
Net unrealized and realized investment gains and losses		100
Investments		4,300
To record sale of investment and gain in investment value.		

The effect of these entries is to report a net gain of $400, resulting from a gain of $300 in 2012 and a gain of $100 in 2013. In an economic (opportunity cost) sense, there was indeed a gain of $300 in 2012, followed by a gain of $100 in 2013. But some NFPOs prefer to separate realized gains and losses from unrealized gains and losses. They do this by maintaining the Investment account at the original carrying value and using an Investment valuation account to record changes in unrealized gains and losses. Although the net effect of the accounting is the same each

---

[16]FASB ASC Section 820-10-20.

year, it allows the financial reporting to be structured so as to separate realized gains and losses from changes in the fair value (unrealized gains and losses) in the investments it still owns. (This matter is discussed further in Chapter 13.) Using the same illustration, the journal entries to accomplish this result are as follows:

Entry at December 31, 2012:		
Investment valuation account	300	
Change in net unrealized investment gains and losses		300
To record change in unrealized investment gains and losses.		
Entries at March 15, 2013 (time of sale):		
Change in unrealized investment gains and losses	300	
Investment valuation account		300
To reverse unrealized investment gain.		
Cash	4,400	
Realized gains and losses on investments		400
Investments		4,000
To record realized gain on sale of investment.		

Investment Disclosures

It is not uncommon to see a significant quantity of notes to the financial statements regarding an NFPO's investments. In its Statement No. 157, the FASB established a three-level fair value hierarchy that prioritizes the types of data used (inputs) to measure fair value. Level 1 inputs are quoted prices in *active markets* for identical assets at the reporting date. (An active market is one in which transactions occur with sufficient frequency and volume to provide pricing data on an ongoing basis.) Level 2 inputs are inputs other than quoted prices that are *observable* for the asset, either directly or indirectly. (Observable inputs may be obtained, for example, from noncurrent prices in inactive markets or from other inputs such as yield curves.) Level 3 inputs are unobservable inputs, based on the reporting entity's pricing assumptions. Regarding its investments, an NFPO must disclose the following:

- The aggregate carrying amount of investments by major types, such as equity securities, U.S. Treasury securities, corporate debt securities, and so on
- The fair value measurements for each major type of investment as of the reporting date
- The various levels within the fair value hierarchy (i.e., levels 1, 2, and 3) in which the fair value measurements fall
- For those investments whose measurements are based on unobservable inputs (level 3), a reconciliation of the beginning and ending balances, separately showing the changes due to realized and unrealized gains and losses, purchases, and sales

Investment Income

Investment income, such as interest and dividends, should be recognized as the income is earned. Such income should be reported in the statement of activities as increases in unrestricted net assets, unless use of the income is limited by donor-imposed restrictions. For example, if a donor stipulates that investment income from a permanently restricted contribution be used to support a particular program, the investment income should be reported as an increase in temporarily restricted net assets. As the income is used in support of the program, a reclassification from temporarily restricted to unrestricted net assets would be necessary. See Appendix 12A, page 486, for an illustration of the reporting of investment income by a university.

Split-Interest Agreements

A donation may take the form of a split-interest agreement, whereby a donor enters into a trust or other arrangement with an NFPO, giving the NFPO a beneficial interest in the agreement, but not the sole interest. The NFPO may have a *lead interest* (receiving distributions during the term of the agreement) or a *remainder interest* (receiving all or a part of the assets when the term of the agreement ends). Accounting for a split-interest agreement depends generally on whether the donor may revoke it, what form it takes, and who holds the assets. Accounting for one form of these agreements (an irrevocable charitable remainder trust) is discussed here. See Appendix 12A, page 485, for discussion of another form of agreement and an illustration of how a university reports on it.[17]

When a *revocable* split-interest agreement is executed—that is, one that the donor may cancel—contribution revenue and related assets should not be recognized. A revocable split-interest agreement is simply an intention to give. But when an *irrevocable* split-interest agreement is executed, an NFPO should recognize contribution revenue and related assets at the fair value of the beneficial interest. Classification of the net assets of an irrevocable split-interest agreement depends on the donor's stipulations and when the resources are available for use by the NFPO.

To illustrate, assume a donor establishes an irrevocable *charitable remainder trust*, wherein the donor's spouse receives a specified percentage of the fair value of the trust's assets during the spouse's lifetime, and the NFPO receives the remaining assets of the trust at the spouse's death. The donor also specifies that the NFPO is to treat the assets as a permanent endowment. To administer the trust during the lifetime of the spouse, the donor names a trustee other than the NFPO. When the NFPO is made aware of the existence of the trust, it recognizes receivables and contribution revenues, measured at the fair value of its beneficial interest in the trust. The fair value is the present value of the estimated future benefits to be received when the trust assets are distributed. If the fair value is $200,000, the NFPO makes the following journal entry:

Contributions receivable—charitable remainder trust	200,000	
Permanently restricted support—contributions		200,000
To record beneficial interest in remainder trust.		

Notice that this gift is classified as permanently restricted because the donor stipulated that the assets were to be treated as a permanent endowment. If the donor had stipulated that the gift could be used at the trustees' discretion, the net assets would be classified as temporarily restricted because they could not be used until some time in the future.

The fair value of the asset will change with the passage of time and the changing fair value of the underlying trust assets. This change should be recognized when financial statements are prepared. If the fair value of the trust increases by $5,000, the following journal entry is made:

Contributions receivable—charitable remainder trust	5,000	
Change in value of remainder trust—permanently restricted		5,000
To record change in fair value of remainder trust.		

---

[17]For a more complete discussion of this subject, see FASB ASC subtopic 958-30.

OTHER ACCOUNTING MATTERS

Exchange Transaction Revenues

Many NFPOs obtain revenues from exchange transactions. As distinguished from contributions, an exchange is a transaction wherein each participant both receives and sacrifices value, as in the case of a purchase of services. NFPOs provide many types of social and health-related services by contracting with state and local governments. NFPOs may also provide day care for children, the elderly, or others with special needs, charging fees for their services.

NFPOs account for exchange revenues and receivables in a manner similar to that of for-profit enterprises. Revenues from exchange transactions should be recognized using accrual accounting principles. Related estimated bad debts should be recognized as an expense, and accounts receivable should be reported net of an allowance for uncollectible amounts.

When an NFPO provides services to a government agency under a cost-reimbursement-type contract, revenues should be recognized as costs are incurred. If the NFPO receives advance payments under the contract, it would report the advance as deferred revenue. Assume, for example, that the NFPO in our continuing illustration provides treatment planning, counseling, urine testing, and other services to parolees who have been substance abusers. The contract provides that the government agency will make monthly advance payments to the NFPO and that the NFPO will bill the agency at the end of the month for costs incurred, offsetting the advance against the costs. If the government agency provides an advance payment of $10,000 and the NFPO subsequently incurs costs of $12,000, it should record the advance and the subsequent revenue as follows:

Cash	10,000	
Deferred contract revenue		10,000
To record advance payment on contract.		
Deferred contract revenue	10,000	
Accounts receivable	2,000	
Revenues from services		12,000
To record service revenues on government contract and billing		
for costs incurred in excess of advance.		

Subscription and Membership Income

Subscription and membership dues are the primary means of support for the operating activities of many ONPOs. Membership dues are recognized as revenue in the period(s) during which they are used to provide services to the organization's members. Membership dues collected in advance of the service period are initially recorded as deferred revenue and then recognized as revenue during the period in which members receive services.

Nonrefundable initiation fees are generally reported as revenues in the period(s) in which the organization is entitled to receive them. Initiation fees are generally reported as unrestricted revenue. If, however, there is a clear understanding with the membership that the fees will be used to acquire or improve capital assets, they are reported as temporarily restricted.

Board Designations

The trustees of an NFPO may act to designate a portion of its unrestricted funds for a particular purpose, such as the acquisition of capital assets or a research program. Such actions do not create restrictions; instead, board designations should continue to be reported as unrestricted net assets, with the designated purpose shown either on the face of the financial statements or in the notes. If, for example, the trustees designate $100,000 of an NFPO's unrestriced net assets for future plant expansion, the following entry is made:

Unrestricted net assets	100,000	
Unrestricted net assets—designated for plant expansion		100,000
To record board designation of unrestricted net assets.		

Sometimes, particularly if several years are required to fulfill the purpose of the designation, the board may also wish to set aside specific assets (such as investments) for the purpose. If that had occurred in this illustration, an additional entry would be made reducing Investments and debiting an account such as Investments internally designated for plant expansion.

Depreciation Expense

As a general rule, NFPOs must allocate the cost of their long-lived tangible assets, whether acquired in exchange transactions or through donation, over the estimated lives of the assets. Like other expenses, depreciation expense is reported as a decrease in unrestricted net assets. (If the capital asset is temporarily restricted, because of donor-imposed restrictions on its use, a reclassification from temporarily restricted to unrestricted is needed.) Disclosures regarding long-lived assets and depreciation methods are also required.

Separate rules, however, apply to works of art, historical treasures, and collections. The circumstances under which NFPOs are permitted not to capitalize these assets were discussed previously. But suppose NFPOs elect to capitalize works of art, historical treasures, and collections. If they capitalize them, must they depreciate them? The answer is "not necessarily." Consistent with practice regarding land used as a building site, depreciation need not be recognized on individual works of art or historical treasures "whose economic benefit or service potential is used up so slowly that their estimated useful lives are extraordinarily long."[18] A work of art or historical treasure is deemed to have this characteristic only if verifiable evidence indicates that the NFPO has the technological and financial capacity to preserve the asset.

Fund-Raising Expenses

NFPOs may undertake significant fund-raising activities to induce potential donors to contribute resources. Costs that relate solely to fund-raising are reported separately as fund-raising expenses. Sometimes, however, an NFPO may incur costs relating both to fund-raising and to one of its programs. Joint costs may be incurred, for example, when an NFPO distributes a brochure containing information about the entity's programs as well as an appeal for funds.

When an NFPO incurs costs on a brochure (or similar activity) that has elements of both fund-raising and program, the appropriate accounting for the costs depends on three factors or criteria—the brochure's *purpose,* the *audience* it is intended to reach, and its *contents.* As a general rule, if the purpose, audience, and content criteria are met, the joint costs should be allocated between the fund-raising and program functions. If *any* of the three criteria is not met, however, all costs of the joint activity should be reported as fund-raising.

The purpose and content criteria of the rule are met if the solicitation for support also calls on the audience to take specific action that will help accomplish the organization's mission. For example, if an organization's mission is to improve individuals' physical health, sending a brochure that urges the audience to stop smoking and that suggests specific methods that may be used to stop smoking is an activity that helps accomplish that mission.

---

[18]FASB ASC par. 958-360-35-3.

The presumption is that the audience criterion is not met if the audience includes prior donors or was selected based on the likelihood of their contributing to the organization. This presumption can be overcome, however, if the audience was also selected for other reasons, such as a need to take the specific action called for in the brochure.

To illustrate, assume that one mission of the NFPO in our continuing illustration is to prevent teenage drug abuse. The NFPO mails a brochure to the parents of all high school students, describing methods for counseling children against drug abuse and showing how parents can detect signs of drug abuse. The mailing also appeals for contributions. In this illustration, the nature of the action requested and the audience contacted are such that the three criteria are met. The audience was not limited to persons likely to contribute. The audience was called on to take actions related to the purposes of the NFPO, and the brochure described specific actions to be taken. Therefore, the cost of preparing and mailing the brochure should be allocated between fund-raising and program expenses, using appropriate cost accounting techniques.[19] If the cost of preparing and mailing the brochure was $8,000 and the NFPO estimates that 75 percent of the costs should be allocated to program and 25 percent to fund-raising, it would make the following journal entry:

Program expenses—drug abuse prevention	6,000	
Fund-raising expenses	2,000	
Cash		8,000
To record payment of expenses related to drug abuse prevention brochure.		

Not-for-Profit Financial Reporting in Practice

Telemarketing as a Source of Donations

New York State attorneys general have been issuing annual reports titled *Pennies for Charity* for many years. The reports show what share of the total funds raised by telemarketers actually goes to the charitable organizations. The 2009 report shows that, on average, for every dollar raised by the fund-raisers, only 39½ cents goes to the charity. *Pennies for Charity 2009* is based on financial reports filed by professional fund-raisers for 584 telemarketing campaigns conducted on behalf of 444 charitable organizations during 2008. (Reports prepared for earlier years show that the situation is improving; the 2000 report shows that, on average, the charities received only 28½ cents for each dollar raised by telemarketers.)

During 2008, telemarketers raised a total of $204.8 million; of this amount, $123.9 million was paid to the fund-raisers for fees and costs of conducting the campaigns, and $80.9 million went to the charities. There were wide differences, however, among individual campaigns in the ratio of funds received by the charity to the gross amount raised by the telemarketer. In 7 campaigns, the charity received from 90 percent to 100 percent of the amount raised; in another 21 campaigns the charity received from 70 percent to 89 percent of the amount raised. But in 285—almost half—of the campaigns, the charity received less than 30 percent of the amount raised, and in 42 of those campaigns, the charities actually lost money. The report noted that losses can occur if the fund-raising contract does not guarantee the charity a specific dollar amount or percentage of the gross receipts or does not hold the charity harmless when expenses or fees exceed the gross amount contributed by donors.

Source: Pennies for Charity, New York State Department of Law, Charities Bureau, October 2009, available online at www.charitiesnys.com.

---

[19]For extensive discussion of this subject, see FASB ASC Section 958-720-45.

FUND ACCOUNTING IN NFPOs

Although not permitted for GAAP financial reporting purposes, some NFPOs use fund accounting for internal record-keeping purposes. The way funds are used differs to some extent among the various types of NFPOs. Fund accounting can cause additional record-keeping complexities:

- Using funds may cause the need to record resource transfers from one fund to another. At the same time, to comply with financial reporting requirements, there is also a need to record net asset classifications and reclassifications within the funds.
- The notion of "restricted" has traditionally been broader in the funds than it is in the current requirement for financial reporting. Therefore, when funds are used in the accounting process, the NFPO may need to separate fund balances into more than one net asset classification when preparing financial statements.

When they use funds, NFPOs generally use the following types:

1. *Unrestricted Current Fund*—**UCF** (also called Unrestricted Operating Fund, General Fund, or Current Unrestricted Fund). UCFs are used to account for resources over which governing boards have discretionary control. Therefore, the resources of the UCF are available not only for general operating purposes, but also for transfer to other funds. UCF resources come primarily from unrestricted donor contributions; exchange-type transactions with members, clients, students, customers, and others; and unrestricted investment income.

   As previously noted, board trustees may designate portions of the UCF resources for specific purposes, such as capital asset acquisition or research activities. When this happens, the resources either remain in the UCF or are transferred to some other fund, such as a Plant Fund. For financial reporting purposes, however, designations of resources made by the governing board are classified as unrestricted because they are not donor-restricted. Depending on fund accounting policies adopted by the NFPO, capital assets may be accounted for in the UCF or in a separate Plant Fund.
2. *Restricted Current Funds*—**RCFs** (also called Restricted Operating, Specific-Purpose, or Current Restricted Funds). For financial reporting purposes, temporarily restricted net assets are those whose restrictions are donor imposed. When funds are used, however, RCFs may include not only donor contributions that are restricted for specific operating purposes, but also resources received on contracts whose use is limited by external parties other than donors. Therefore, for financial reporting purposes, if the NFPO uses fund accounting, the fund balances need to be separated between net assets restricted by donors (classified as temporarily restricted) and net assets restricted as to use by contract or other limitation (classified as unrestricted).
3. *Endowment Funds*—**EFs.** Several types of endowments may be included in EFs. For financial reporting purposes, however, how they are classified depends on the nature of the endowment:

   - Permanent or pure endowments are those wherein the donor specifies that the principal be invested and maintained in perpetuity and only the income earned may be used for operations. These endowments are classified as permanently restricted for financial reporting purposes.

- Term endowments are those wherein the resources originally contributed become available for use in operations after a specific time period or the occurrence of a specified event. They are classified as temporarily restricted net assets until the term expires or the specified event occurs.
- Quasi-endowment funds, often used by colleges and universities, are funds set aside by the governing board for lengthy but unspecified periods of time. Because they are not donor restricted, they are classified as unrestricted for financial reporting purposes.

4. *Plant Funds—PFs* (or Land, Building, and Equipment Funds or Plant Replacement and Expansion Funds). These funds take a variety of forms. Some contain only financial resources to be used for plant (capital asset) acquisition. Some account not only for financial resources, but also for land, buildings, and equipment currently used in operations, together with associated depreciation and long-term debt. Colleges and universities sometimes divide their plant funds into four subfund account groups: Unexpended Plant Funds, Funds for Renewal and Replacement, Funds for Retirement of Indebtedness, and Net Investment in Plant. Depending on the nature of restrictions imposed by donors on the use of Plant Fund resources, the net assets may need to be separated among unrestricted, temporarily restricted, or permanently restricted for financial reporting purposes.

Some NFPOs also use other types of funds, such as Loan Funds, Annuity Funds, and Agency Funds. Colleges and universities, for example, commonly use Loan Funds to account for loans made to students. Loan Fund resources are classified as unrestricted if unrestricted resources were designated by the governing board for use as a Loan Fund. Or they may be classified as temporarily or permanently restricted, depending on the nature of donor-imposed restrictions.

Interfund Transfers

Using fund accounting may result not only in reclassification transactions, but also interfund transfers. For example, an interfund transfer occurs when a governing board transfers resources from the UCF to a Plant Fund for capital acquisition purposes. To record the transfer, the fund that transfers resources debits a "Transfer to . . ." account, and the fund that receives the resources credits a "Transfer from . . ." account.

Colleges and universities classify interfund transactions as either nonmandatory or mandatory. *Nonmandatory transfers* are those made at the discretion of the governing board for such purposes as additions to Loan Funds, Plant Funds, or Quasi-Endowment Funds. *Mandatory transfers* are those arising out of binding legal agreements, such as requirements to set aside amounts for debt service or to match gifts or grants.

ILLUSTRATION USING FUNDS

This section illustrates NFPO accounting and financial reporting when fund accounting is used. It also serves as a review of some of the NFPO accounting principles previously discussed. Note that revenues and gains within the funds are classified as unrestricted, temporarily restricted, or permanently restricted to facilitate reporting by net asset classification.

Assume that Kezar Cares, a VHWO that offers counseling services to abused persons of all ages, is formed at the beginning of 2013. It receives contributions from various sources and performs counseling services under a government contract. Kezar classifies expenses by object of account (salaries and other) within four major functions—counseling program, education program, administration, and fund-raising.

Kezar uses fund accounting because it believes fund accounting is useful for internal accounting purposes. It prepares financial statements, however, in accordance with generally accepted accounting principles. Kezar uses a UCF, an RCF, an EF, and a PF. Donor gifts with time or purpose restrictions are recorded in the RCF. Resources received and expenses incurred under the government contract are also recorded in the RCF, even though the net assets are not donor restricted, because Kezar believes it will improve controls over contract costs. To simplify its accounting, Kezar accounts for its capital assets in the UCF and uses the PF to account only for financial resources that will be used to acquire capital assets.

Kezar has the following transactions in 2013. For each transaction, the fund in which the transaction is recorded is shown in **bold type** to the left of the journal entry, and the net asset classification, where applicable, is shown in **bold type** within the journal entry.

1. At the beginning of the year, Kezar receives unrestricted promises of cash donations in the amount of $130,000. Kezar expects to collect $115,000 of that amount in 2013 and estimates that $15,000 will not be collected.

UCF	Contributions receivable	130,000	
	Allowance for uncollectible contributions		15,000
	Unrestricted support—contributions		115,000
	To record unrestricted promises to give cash.		

2. Kezar collects $118,000 of the unrestricted promises to donate cash and writes off $12,000 as uncollectible. It reverses the remaining $3,000 allowance for uncollectible receivables. (Notice that the effect of the reversal is to increase unrestricted support.)

UCF	Cash	118,000	
	Allowance for uncollectible contributions	15,000	
	Contributions receivable		130,000
	Unrestricted support—contributions		3,000
	To record collection of pledges and write-off of uncollectible contributions.		

3. Kezar receives two donations that contain restrictions imposed by the donors: (a) cash in the amount of $20,000 that can be used only for research into counseling methodology and (b) investments that have a fair value of $100,000. The donor making the second contribution stipulates that the investment corpus should be maintained in perpetuity, but the investment income may be used for any purpose the Kezar trustees designate.

RCF	Cash	20,000	
	Temporarily restricted support—contributions		20,000
	To record temporarily restricted contribution.		
EF	Investments	100,000	
	Permanently restricted support—contributions		100,000
	To record permanently restricted contribution.		

4. Kezar receives the following donated services:

- A psychologist donates 20 hours of her time to Kezar's counseling program. Kezar would have paid $4,000 for these services if they had not been donated.
- A lawyer donates 10 hours of his time to review a contract Kezar is negotiating with a government. He would normally charge Kezar $2,000 for the services.

UCF	Expenses—counseling services (other)	4,000	
	Expenses—administration (other)	2,000	
	Unrestricted support—donated services		6,000
	To record receipt of donated services.		

5. Kezar holds a book sale as part of its fund-raising program. It raises $12,000 in cash but pays $2,000 of that amount for various expenses. Several high school students donate 16 hours of their time, selling refreshments and books at the event. Kezar would have paid them $5 an hour for these services had they not been donated.

UCF	Cash	10,000	
	Expenses—fund-raising (other)	2,000	
	Unrestricted gains—special events		12,000
	To record net gain from fund-raising event.		

Note: The revenue from this event was recorded as a gain because it was considered as a peripheral or incidental transaction. The refreshment and bookselling services were not recognized as expenses and revenues because they did not require specialized skills.

6. Kezar pays salaries of $14,000 and other expenses of $2,000 in performing research into counseling methodology, using the restricted gift in transaction 3.

RCF	**Temporarily restricted** net asset reclassifications out— satisfaction of program restrictions	16,000	
	Cash		16,000
	To record payment of research expenses and reclassification of temporarily restricted net assets due to satisfaction of restrictions.		

UCF	Expenses—counseling (salaries)	14,000	
	Expenses—counseling (other)	2,000	
	Unrestricted net asset reclassifications in— satisfaction of program restrictions		16,000
	To record reclassification to unrestricted net assets due to satisfaction of restrictions and payment of expenses.		

Note: Expenses are recorded in the UCF because temporarily restricted net assets have been reclassified as unrestricted. The journal entries are organized differently from those shown on page 449 because of the use of fund accounting, but the net result of the entries is the same.

7. Income of $4,000 is earned and received on the investments in the endowment fund.

UCF	Cash	4,000	
	Unrestricted revenue—investment income		4,000
	To record income, usable for any purpose, on endowment investments.		

8. Kezar's contract with a government agency for counseling services provides for quarterly advance payments. At the end of each quarter, Kezar is required to submit a statement of actual costs incurred. Based on the statement, Kezar is entitled to receive the difference between the advance and its actual costs. In accordance with these arrangements, Kezar receives an advance payment of $27,000 on October 1 and incurs actual costs of $30,000 ($26,000 salaries and $4,000 other costs) between October 1 and December 31, 2013.

RCF	Cash	27,000	
	Deferred revenues		27,000
	To record advance payment received on contract.		

RCF	Expenses—counseling (salaries)	26,000	
	Expenses—counseling (other)	4,000	
	Cash		30,000
	To record expenses incurred on contract.		

RCF	Deferred revenues	27,000	
	Accounts receivable	3,000	
	Unrestricted revenue—contract		30,000
	To record revenues earned on contract.		

9. Kezar incurs the following expenses in undertaking its unrestricted programs. All the expenses are paid in cash, except for $4,000, which is accrued.

Function	Salaries	Other
Counseling	$30,000	$ 5,000
Education	20,000	
Administration	9,000	
Fund-raising	5,000	2,000
Total	$64,000	$ 7,000

UCF	Expenses—counseling (salaries)	30,000	
	Expenses—counseling (other)	5,000	
	Expenses—education (salaries)	20,000	
	Expenses—administration (salaries)	9,000	
	Expenses—fund-raising (salaries)	5,000	
	Expenses—fund-raising (other)	2,000	
	Cash		67,000
	Accrued expenses		4,000
	To record payment of expenses and accrual of unpaid expenses.		

10. Before preparing financial statements, Kezar ascertains that the investments held in its endowment fund have a fair value of $102,000.

EF	Investments	2,000	
	Permanently restricted net unrealized and realized investment gains/losses		2,000
	To record increase in fair value of investments.		

11. Kezar's trustees decide that Kezar Cares should construct a building rather than continue to rent space. Kezar approaches several philanthropists to raise funds. Sara Dawn says she will contribute up to $50,000 to match other contributions as received, dollar for dollar. Oscar Catt says he will contribute $25,000, provided Kezar raises a total of $100,000 from all other donors. As a result of its fund-raising program, Kezar raises $12,000 from other donors. Kezar then sends a letter to Ms. Dawn, advising her of the receipt of the $12,000.

PF	Cash	12,000	
	Temporarily restricted support—contributions		12,000
	To record receipt of contributions for building.		
PF	Contributions receivable	12,000	
	Temporarily restricted support—contributions		12,000
	To record promise to give from Sara Dawn.		

Note: Sara Dawn's promise of $50,000 and Oscar Catt's promise of $25,000 are conditional promises to give, which cannot be recognized as revenue until the conditions regarding the promises have been substantially met. In this situation, Ms. Dawn's condition is met each time other donors make cash contributions. Therefore, $12,000 should be recognized as contributions receivable and revenue based on her promise. Mr. Catt's promise, however, cannot be recognized because his condition has not been substantially met.

12. Kezar receives a gift of $5,000 in cash. The donor stipulates that the gift may be used for any activities the trustees direct, except that it must be used to finance 2014 activities.

RCF	Cash	5,000	
	Temporarily restricted support—contributions		5,000
	To record receipt of gift for 2014 activities.		

Note: At the beginning of 2014, the time restriction on this gift will expire, and journal entries will be made to reclassify the net assets from temporarily restricted to unrestricted, because of satisfaction of time restrictions. The cash will also be transferred to the UCF. For fund accounting purposes, Kezar could record the receipt of cash initially in the UCF but would still need to classify the net assets as temporarily restricted and reclassify the net assets as unrestricted at the beginning of 2014.

Fund Trial Balances

Based on the foregoing journal entries, preclosing trial balances for each fund are shown in Tables 12-5, 12-6, 12-7, and 12-8, respectively.

Preparing Financial Statements from Fund Trial Balances

The required financial statements can be prepared directly from the fund trial balances with the help of a multicolumn spreadsheet. Kezar's statement of activities, statement of financial position, and statement of functional expenses are shown in Tables 12-9, 12-10, and 12-11, respectively. Trace the information from the fund trial balances to the financial statements, noticing the following matters in particular:

1. All expenses are reported in the unrestricted column of the statement of activities, even though some expenses are recorded in the RCF.

TABLE 12-5 Trial Balance—UCF

Kezar Cares
Unrestricted Current Fund
Preclosing Trial Balance
December 31, 2013

Cash	$ 65,000	
Accrued expenses		$ 4,000
Unrestricted support—contributions		118,000
Unrestricted support—donated services		6,000
Unrestricted revenue—investment income		4,000
Unrestricted gains—special events		12,000
Unrestricted net asset reclassifications in—satisfaction of program restrictions		16,000
Expenses—counseling (salaries)	44,000	
Expenses—counseling (other)	11,000	
Expenses—education (salaries)	20,000	
Expenses—administration (salaries)	9,000	
Expenses—administration (other)	2,000	
Expenses—fund-raising (salaries)	5,000	
Expenses—fund-raising (other)	4,000	
Totals	$160,000	$160,000

TABLE 12-6 Trial Balance—RCF

Kezar Cares
Restricted Current Fund
Preclosing Trial Balance
December 31, 2013

Cash	$ 6,000	
Accounts receivable	3,000	
Temporarily restricted support—contributions		$25,000
Unrestricted revenue—contract		30,000
Temporarily restricted net asset reclassifications out—satisfaction of program restrictions	16,000	
Expenses—counseling (salaries)	26,000	
Expenses—counseling (other)	4,000	
Totals	$55,000	$55,000

2. Required reporting by net asset classification is facilitated by (a) designating the appropriate net asset classification for revenues as the transactions are recorded and (b) recording net asset reclassifications within each fund as they occur.

3. Restrictions on the use of resources are reported on the face of the statement of financial position. (Financial reporting standards provide that such restrictions may be reported either on the face of the statements or in the notes to the statements.)

TABLE 12-7 Trial Balance—EF

Kezar Cares
Endowment Fund
Preclosing Trial Balance
December 31, 2013

Investments	$102,000	
Permanently restricted support—contributions		$100,000
Permanently restricted net unrealized and realized investment gains and losses		2,000
Totals	$102,000	$102,000

TABLE 12-8 Trial Balance—Plant Fund

Kezar Cares
Plant Fund
Preclosing Trial Balance
December 31, 2013

Cash	$12,000	
Contributions receivable	12,000	
Temporarily restricted support—contributions		$24,000
Totals	$24,000	$24,000

TABLE 12-9 Statement of Financial Position

Kezar Cares
Statement of Financial Position
December 31, 2013

Assets

Cash	$ 83,000
Accounts receivable	3,000
Contributions receivable, restricted for building acquisition	12,000
Investments, restricted for endowment	102,000
Total assets	$200,000

Liabilities and Net Assets

Liabilities:	
Accrued expenses	$ 4,000
Net assets:	
Unrestricted	61,000
Temporarily restricted:	
For next year's general activities	5,000
For counseling research	4,000
For building acquisition	24,000
Permanently restricted	102,000
Total net assets	196,000
Total liabilities and net assets	$200,000

TABLE 12-10   Statement of Activities

Kezar Cares
Statement of Activities
Year Ended December 31, 2013

	Unrestricted	Temp. Restricted	Perm. Restricted	Total
Revenues, Gains, Other Support				
Contributions	$118,000	$49,000	$100,000	$267,000
Donated services	6,000			6,000
Contract revenue	30,000			30,000
Special events	12,000			12,000
Investment income	4,000			4,000
Unrealized and realized investment gains			2,000	2,000
Net assets released from restrictions— satisfaction of program restrictions	16,000	(16,000)		
Total revenues, gains, other support	186,000	33,000	102,000	321,000
Expenses				
Counseling	85,000			85,000
Education	20,000			20,000
Administration	11,000			11,000
Fund-raising	9,000			9,000
Total expenses	125,000			125,000
Change in net assets	61,000	33,000	102,000	196,000
Net assets, beginning of year	—	—	—	—
Net assets, end of year	$ 61,000	$33,000	$102,000	$196,000

TABLE 12-11   Statement of Functional Expenses

Kezar Cares
Statement of Functional Expenses
Year Ended December 31, 2013

Function	Total	Salaries	Other
Counseling	$ 85,000	$ 70,000	$15,000
Education	20,000	20,000	
Administration	11,000	9,000	2,000
Fund-raising	9,000	5,000	4,000
Total	$125,000	$104,000	$21,000

Review Questions

Q12-1   What characteristics distinguish NFPOs from for-profit organizations? What characteristics distinguish government organizations from NFPOs?

Q12-2   What financial statements must be prepared by all VHWOs and ONPOs? What additional financial statements must be prepared by VHWOs?

Q12-3   Identify and briefly describe the three classifications of net assets on the financial statements of NFPOs.

Q12-4   State the four elements of the general rule for reporting the receipt of contributions other than services and collections.

Q12-5   Illustrate the kinds of restrictions that donors may impose on the use of resources they contribute to NFPOs.

Q12-6   How are pledges that are expected to be uncollectible reported in the financial statements of NFPOs?

Q12-7   Discuss the differences between a donor-imposed restriction and a conditional promise to give. How is each reported in the financial statements?

Q12-8   Describe the circumstances under which contributed services must be recognized as revenues and expenses in the financial statements.

Q12-9   When should an NFPO make a reclassification of its net assets?

Q12-10   Under what circumstances must an NFPO recognize a contributed work of art as revenue? Under what circumstances does the organization have an option not to recognize it as revenue?

Q12-11   Discuss the meaning of *fair value* when applied to an NFPO's investments, and give examples of how fair value may be determined.

Q12-12   Identify and briefly describe the major funds used internally by NFPOs.

Discussion Scenarios and Issues

D12-1   The text states that NFPOs have the option of not recognizing donated works of art, historical artifacts, and similar items as assets and revenues, provided they are added to collections and the NFPOs meet certain other conditions. The practices of several major museums are illustrated in the practice example "Art . . . and Bones, Rocks, Frozen Tissues." Discuss the arguments for and against this option.

Exercises

E12-1   (Identifying the appropriate net asset classification)

For each of the following transactions, identify the net asset classification (unrestricted, temporarily restricted, permanently restricted) that is affected in the NFPO's financial statements for the year ended December 31, 2012. More than one net asset class may be affected in some transactions.

1. Donor A gave an NFPO a $50,000 cash gift in June 2012, stipulating that the NFPO could not use the gift until 2013.

2. Donor B gave an NFPO a $25,000 cash gift in July 2012, telling the NFPO the gift could be used only for research on a specific project.

3. In response to an NFPO's fund-raising campaign for a new building, a large number of individuals promised to make cash contributions totaling $2 million in 2012. The NFPO believes it will actually collect 80 percent of the promised cash.

4. Donor C gave an NFPO several investments having a fair value of $3 million in March 2012. Donor C stipulated that the NFPO must hold the gift in perpetuity, but it could use the income from the gift for any purpose the trustees considered appropriate. Between March and December, the investments produced income of $100,000.

5. Using the funds raised in transaction 3, an NFPO paid an architect $50,000 in 2012 to make preliminary designs for a new building.

E12-2 (Recording journal entries for NFPOs)
Prepare journal entries to record the transactions in E12-1.

E12-3 (Identifying the appropriate net asset classification)
For each of the following transactions, identify the net asset classification (unrestricted, temporarily restricted, permanently restricted) that is affected in the NFPO's financial statements for the year ended December 31, 2013. More than one net asset class may be affected in some transactions.

1. Donor A gave the NFPO a cash gift of $50,000 in June 2012, telling the NFPO the gift could not be used until 2013. Identify the net asset classification(s) in the journal entry made at the start of 2013.

2. Attorney Howard Gorman volunteered his services to Taconic Singers, an NFPO. He spent 12 hours preparing contracts for the services of professional singers and 8 hours serving as an usher before performances. Gorman normally gets $200 an hour for legal services, and Taconic normally pays $8 an hour when it hires ushers.

3. Donor B sent a letter to an NFPO, saying she would donate $20,000 in cash to the NFPO, to be used for any purpose the NFPO's trustees desired, provided the NFPO raised an equal amount of cash from other donors.

4. Regarding the previous transaction, the NFPO raised $23,000 in cash from other donors and then notified Donor B of its success in meeting her condition for the gift.

5. Donor C donates to a local museum a work of art having a fair value of $5,000, with the understanding that the museum will sell it at auction and use the funds for its general activities.

6. Donor D advises a university that he has established an irrevocable charitable remainder trust, administered by his attorney, whereby his wife will receive income from the trust as long as she lives. At her death, the remaining trust assets will be distributed to the university as a permanent endowment. The university's actuary estimates the fair value of the university's beneficial interest to be $400,000.

7. By December 31, 2013, the fair value of investments held in perpetuity by an NFPO increased by $30,000.

E12-4 (Recording journal entries for NFPOs)
Prepare journal entries to record the transactions in E12-3.

E12-5 (Investment transactions and events)
An NFPO had the following transactions and events. Prepare journal entries to record these transactions and events, based on the assumption that the NFPO uses a single account to record all unrealized and realized investment gains and losses. Then, prepare journal entries for events 2 and 3, based on the assumption that the NFPO separates unrealized from realized investment gains and losses.

1. On July 15, 2012, an NFPO received a donation of Google stock that had a fair value of $75,000 at the time of the donation. The donor told the NFPO that the stock could be sold and used only to finance a particular research project.

2. On December 31, 2012, when the NFPO closed its books, the stock had a fair value of $76,500.

3. On February 15, 2013, the NFPO sold the stock for $76,000.

4. On March 15, 2013, the NFPO spent the entire $76,000 on the research project for which the donor made the gift.

E12-6 (True or False)
State whether each of these sentences is true or false. If false, state why.

1. FASB standards require that NFPO financial statements report on activities by major fund.

2. If an NFPO reports temporarily restricted resources, it is likely the restrictions could have been placed either by donors or by the NFPO's board of directors.

3. When an NFPO spends temporarily restricted resources on the project for which a donor made the contribution, the expenses are reported in the temporarily restricted column of the statement of activities.

4. Members of an NFPO donated their time to construct a garage for the NFPO's automobile. The NFPO would have paid $8,000 for the labor, had it not been donated. The garage will last 20 years. The NFPO should report the contributed labor as an asset and as contribution revenue.

5. Cash donated specifically for constructing a building that will have an estimated life of 40 years should be reported as temporarily restricted.

6. Depending on the circumstances, a not-for-profit museum has the option to either record or not record an asset when it receives a donation of a valuable art work.

7. From the perspective of NFPO accounting, there is no difference between a donor-imposed restriction and a donor-imposed condition.

8. An NFPO held a fund-raising campaign at year-end. It received pledges of $45,000, but it did not receive any cash until the following year. The NFPO should not report any revenue in the year it conducted its fund-raising campaign, but it should report the amount of the pledges in a note to the financial statements.

9. Gains and losses on investments must be reported in the unrestricted column of the statement of activities.

10. If a donor makes an unconditional promise to give cash to an NFPO 2 years after the NFPO's balance sheet date, the gift should be classified as temporarily restricted.

E12-7 (Multiple choice)

1. How should expenses be reported in an NFPO's statement of activities?
   a. As decreases in the net asset classification in which the revenues were reported
   b. As decreases of permanently restricted net assets
   c. As decreases of temporarily restricted net assets _revenue_
   d. As decreases of unrestricted net assets

2. Which of the following is a general rule established by the FASB regarding contributions received by an NFPO in the form of investments?
   a. They must be recorded either in a restricted fund or in an unrestricted fund.
   b. They must be reported either as restricted support or unrestricted support.
   c. They must be recorded at the amount paid by the donor for the investment.
   d. They must be reported in an endowment fund.

3. Which of the following financial statements is required for VHWOs but not for ONPOs?
   a. Statement of financial position
   b. Statement of activities
   c. Statement of functional expenses
   d. Statement of cash flows

4. If a donor provides that interest earned on an endowment be used to finance a particular program, how should the interest revenue be classified?
   a. As unrestricted
   b. As temporarily restricted
   c. As permanently restricted
   d. As quasi-endowment income

5. How should land and buildings owned by an NFPO be classified in its financial statements?
   a. As unrestricted
   b. As temporarily restricted
   c. As permanently restricted
   d. They need not be reported

6. At the balance sheet date, the fair value of an investment is greater than the amount at which the investment was initially recorded. What adjustment, if any, is needed?
   a. No adjustment is needed.
   b. The increase should be recorded as an unrestricted gain.
   c. The increase should be recorded as a temporarily restricted gain.
   d. The increase should be recorded as a gain in the same net asset class in which the investment is reported.

7. The Prevent Cancer Organization incurred several expenses during 2013. Which of the following would not be classified as program support?
   a. Postage for announcements of the 2013 Kickoff Dinner
   b. Pamphlets mailed to the general public regarding the "danger signals of cancer"
   c. Pamphlets on the relationship of smoking to cancer
   d. Salaries of personnel who perform cancer research

8. As a result of its annual fund-raising program, an NFPO receives pledges in the amount of $300,000 during December 2012, the last month of its reporting period. Based on its previous history regarding pledges, the NFPO believes that about $250,000 will be collected in the first 60 days of 2013; $35,000 will trickle in during the rest of 2013; and $15,000 will not be collected at all. How much should the NFPO report as net contributions receivable on its 2012 financial statements?
   a. $0
   b. $250,000
   c. $285,000
   d. $300,000

9. Computer expert J. Leveille donated 60 hours of time to the Boston Museum, an NFPO. He spent 40 hours designing a web site for the museum and 20 hours selling merchandise at the museum store. Mr. Leveille normally earns $150 an hour when he designs web sites, and the museum normally pays $10 to its salespeople. How much should the museum report as contribution revenue for Mr. Leveille's services?
   a. $0
   b. $200
   c. $6,000
   d. $6,200

10. The trustees of an NFPO decide to designate a portion of the NFPO's resources for use in a specific research program. How should the designation be reported in the NFPO's financial statements?
   a. Board designations should never be reported in NFPO financial statements.
   b. As temporarily restricted net assets, either on the face of the statements or in a note
   c. As temporarily restricted net assets designated for research, in a note
   d. As unrestricted net assets designated for research, either on the face of the statements or in a note

E12-8   (Statement of activities for a country club)
The following information was excerpted from the records of the East End Golf and Tennis Club, an NFPO. All account balances are as of the fiscal year ended June 30, 2013, except for the net asset balances at the beginning of the year. Prepare a statement of activities for the East End Golf and Tennis Club.

Revenues—dues	600,000
Revenues—golf lessons	80,000
Revenues—tennis lessons	55,000
Expenses—golf and tennis pros	105,000
Other expenses associated with golf courses and tennis courts	475,000
Administration expenses	65,000
Assessments against members, restricted for capital improvements	200,000
Net assets released from restriction due to satisfaction of program restrictions	70,000
Net unrealized and realized gains on temporarily restricted investments	20,000
Net assets at beginning of year—unrestricted	60,000
Net assets at beginning of year—temporarily restricted	80,000

E12-9   (Journal entries for an NFPO)
Good Health, an NFPO, conducts two types of programs: education and research. It does not use fund accounting. During 2013, the following transactions and events took place. Prepare journal

entries for these transactions, identifying increases and decreases by net asset classification as appropriate.

1. Pledges amounting to $100,000 were received, to be used for any purpose designated by the trustees. Good Health normally collects 80 percent of the amount pledged.
2. Good Health collected $75,000 in cash on the amount pledged in the previous transaction. It wrote off the balance as uncollectible.
3. Ed Victor donated $5,000, stipulating that it could be used for any purpose, but only during 2014.
4. Howard Gore donated $875,000, stipulating that the donation must be used solely to purchase a building that Good Health could use for research.
5. Good Health invested $20,000 of unrestricted resources in equity securities. Earnings on these resources amounted to $1,000 in 2013.
6. Late in the year, Good Health used Howard Gore's donation (see transaction 4) and unrestricted resources of $140,000 to purchase a building for research purposes.
7. The following services were donated to Good Health:
    a. Audit of the financial statements by an accounting firm—$5,000
    b. Professional services by an advertising agency in connection with a fund-raising campaign—$3,000
    c. Ushering services at educational meetings, provided by high school students. If paid for, these services would cost $1,000.
8. At year-end, the investments referred to in transaction 5 had a fair value of $22,000.
9. Good Health conducted a fund-raising campaign; the donations were to be used solely for research into the causes of a particular disease. Donations totaled $45,000 in cash.
10. Good Health paid $35,000 for expenses on the research project in the previous transaction.

E12-10 (Journal entries using classifications of net assets)

The Mon Elisa Museum of Fine Arts is an NFPO that derives most of its resources from wealthy patrons. Mon Elisa has recently changed its accounting system to eliminate the use of separate funds. All journal entries are made so as to indicate which of the three net asset classifications are affected. The following transactions and events occurred during 2013. Prepare journal entries for these transactions and events, and identify the affected classification(s) of net assets.

1. Cash of $40,000 was received from donors, who stated that it could be used for any purpose desired by the museum.
2. A donor gave the museum $10,000, stipulating that the money be used only to acquire fine examples of Weller Dickensware pottery.
3. Elias Gotbucks sent Mon Elisa a letter, stating that he would donate $15,000 to the museum to purchase examples of Sara Dawn's quilt work, provided the museum conducted a special campaign that raised at least $25,000 to buy additional examples.
4. The museum spent $4,000 to acquire a fine Weller Dickensware vase. Assume that Mon Elisa capitalizes its pottery collection.
5. Mon Elisa contacted wealthy patrons to raise funds to buy Sara Dawn's quilt work. It obtained $30,000 in pledges, all likely to be collected. Mon Elisa then wrote to Elias Gotbucks, advising him it had raised $30,000.
6. Attorney Ted Floot donated his services to the museum. He spent 4 hours on museum legal matters and 3 hours as a salesperson in the museum shop. Mr. Floot bills $250 an hour when he works as an attorney.
7. During the year, Mon Elisa received several art works having a total fair value of $45,000. Mon Elisa does not capitalize its art collection, but it holds the art for public exhibition, protects and preserves the works, and uses the proceeds of any sales to acquire other works for its collection.
8. A wealthy patron donated *The Portrait of Samantha*, which had a fair value of $6,000, to the museum. The museum accepted the gift with the understanding that it would be sold at auction and the proceeds used for any purpose the museum wished.

9. Another wealthy patron entered into an irrevocable charitable remainder trust with Mon Elisa, whereby the patron's wife would receive annual distributions until her death. At that time, Mon Elisa would receive the remaining assets, to be used to augment Mon Elisa's art collection. The patron's bank will administer the trust. Mon Elisa's actuary estimated the fair value of the gift at $95,000.

Problems

P12-1 (Journal entries for contributions to a VHWO)

Feed the Needy (FTN), a VHWO, has three programs: (a) providing meals for the needy in its own facility (Service to Needy program); (b) providing meals for senior citizens through a contract with the County Department for the Aging (Service to Seniors program); and distributing food to other facilities in the area that serve the needy (Food Distribution program). FTN maintains a warehouse to store donated food and has cooking and serving facilities. It does not use fund accounting. Prepare journal entries to record the following transactions and events, which occurred during calendar year 2013:

1. On January 10, 2013, in response to its annual fund-raising drive to finance day-to-day operations, FTN received $150,000 of cash donations and $400,000 of promises to donate cash. Based on experience, FTN expected to collect 80 percent of the promises to donate cash, all of which was to be used to finance its activities during 2013.
2. During the year, FTN received cash of $310,000 from the promises to give (see transaction 1) and wrote off the remaining receivables as uncollectible.
3. To meet its expanding operations, FTN determined that it needed to add storage facilities at an estimated cost of $400,000. Dr. Ted Golfit, noted research engineer, advised FTN that he would contribute $200,000, provided FTN raised an equal amount from other sources.
4. Attorneys A. and E. Gorman provided free legal services to FTN during the year. FTN would have purchased the services for $10,000 if they had not been donated.
5. FTN raised $220,000 in cash as a result of its fund-raising campaign to add to its storage facilities (see transaction 3). FTN contacted Dr. Golfit, who gave FTN a check for $200,000.
6. FTN constructed additional storage facilities at a cost of $425,000. It paid for the facilities by using $420,000 it had raised for that purpose (see transaction 5) and by using $5,000 of its unrestricted available cash.
7. FTN's contract with the County Department for the Aging called for the county to make quarterly advance payments to FTN. The contract required FTN to report to the county after the end of each quarter, showing actual costs to provide food during the quarter and billing for any difference between actual costs and the advance. On January 5, 2013, FTN received a $20,000 advance payment from the county.
8. Between January and March 2013, FTN spent $23,000 in cash providing services through its contract with the county (see transaction 7). On April 4, 2013, FTN sent an invoice to the county, showing it had spent $23,000 on the program, deducting the $20,000 advance, and requesting an additional $3,000.
9. During 2013, FTN received donations of 600,000 pounds of food from supermarkets, bakeries, and food wholesalers. FTN valued the food at $1.50 per pound, based on a national study. All donated food is initially recorded in inventory.
10. FTN distributed 540,000 pounds of food to other facilities under its Food Distribution program and used 30,000 pounds of food in its Service to Needy program (see transaction 9).
11. Local residents donated 1,000 hours of their time serving food at FTN's facility. If the residents had not donated their time, FTN would have paid $7 an hour for the services.
12. FTN paid $200,000 to store food in its warehouse, to package and deliver food to other facilities, and to cook at its own facility. The $200,000 was charged to the following programs: Food Distribution—$175,000; Service to Needy—$25,000.

P12-2   (Journal entries, statement of activities, statement of functional expenses for an NFPO)
Sing Sing Singers (SSS) is a local opera company. It finances its activities through contributions and admissions fees. It accounts for its expenses though four major functions: regular events, special events, administration, and fund-raising. For each function, it maintains three object accounts: salaries, supplies and other, and occupancy. On July 1, 2012, the start of its fiscal year, SSS had cash on hand amounting to $12,000, of which $7,000 represented unrestricted net assets and $5,000 represented temporarily restricted net assets. The following transactions and events occurred during the year. Prepare journal entries to record these transactions; also, prepare a statement of activities and a statement of functional expenses for the year ended June 30, 2013.

1. The $5,000 of temporarily restricted net assets resulted from a donation made during the previous year that could be used only during the year beginning July 1, 2012.

2. SSS held its annual fund-raising dinner at a cost of $3,000 (use object account supplies and other). As a result of the dinner, SSS received cash contributions of $10,000 and pledges totaling $40,000. Based on prior experience, SSS estimated it would collect 90 percent of the pledges in cash.

3. SSS collected $37,000 in cash on the pledges received in transaction 2 and wrote off the other pledges as uncollectible.

4. SSS trustees received the following cash donations:
    a. $15,000 from T. Robbins, to be used solely for the purpose of a special presentation of *The Marriage of Figaro* at the Shawshank Correctional Center in Ossining.
    b. $25,000 from the Chester County Council on the Arts, to be used for any purpose deemed appropriate by the trustees.

5. SSS performed *The Marriage of Figaro* at Shawshank, spending the entire $15,000 donation on salaries for the performers. Expenses were charged to Special events.

6. SSS collected $162,000 in admissions fees from its opera performances during the year. It also had the following expenses, which it paid in cash:

	Regular Events	Special Events	Administration
Salaries	$150,000	$15,000	$12,000
Supplies and other	30,000	3,000	1,000
Occupancy	20,000	2,000	
Total	$200,000	$20,000	$ 13,000

7. SSS received the benefit of the following donated services during the year:
    a. M. Freeman, a lawyer, prepared contracts with the performers. Had Freeman charged for this work, the cost to SSS would have been $4,000.
    b. W. A. Mozart, a carpenter, constructed sets for the regular events. Had Mozart charged for this work, the cost to SSS would have been $8,000.
    c. Local bankers G. Donizetti and G. Puccini served as ushers for all performances. Had SSS paid for this work, the cost would have been $1,000.

P12-3   (Journal entries for an NFPO)
Oliver's Place is a not-for-profit entity that cares for dogs until they are adopted. It uses a UCF, an RCF, and an EF. It charges its expenses to the care of animals program, special programs, and administrative expenses. Following are some of its transactions for 2013. Prepare the journal entries needed to record these transactions; also, indicate the fund used for each entry. (You can check the accuracy of your work by preparing trial balances and comparing them with the trial balances in P12-4.)

1. During the year, Oliver's Place received unrestricted pledges of $100,000. It estimated that 95 percent of the pledges would be collected in cash.

2. It received the following gifts from various donors:
   a. Donor A made a gift of common stock that had a fair value of $20,000. Donor A stated that the gift could be used for any purpose.
   b. Donor B made a cash gift of $5,000, stipulating that it could be used only for a new program to take calm dogs to visit elderly people.
   c. Donor C made a gift of common stock that had a fair value of $50,000. Donor C stipulated that the gift, and any gains on the sale of the stock, should be maintained in perpetuity and that the dividends received on the investment could be used for any purpose.
3. Volunteers contributed their time to Oliver's Place as follows:
   a. Dr. D, a veterinarian, spent 10 days caring for the medical needs of the dogs. Those services would normally cost Oliver's Place $10,000.
   b. Dr. E, a kidney surgeon, spent 12 days feeding the dogs, keeping them occupied, and placing them for adoption. He earns $2,000 a day as a surgeon.
4. Oliver's Place received dividends of $400 on the common stock donated by Donor A and $600 on the common stock donated by Donor C.
5. At year-end, the stock donated by Donor A had a fair value of $22,000, and the stock donated by Donor C had a fair value of $47,000.
6. During the year, Oliver's Place collected $80,000 in cash on the pledges made in transaction 1.
7. Oliver's Place spent $3,000 on the special program designed to take calm dogs to visit elderly people.
8. Oliver's Place paid the following expenses:

Care of animals	$40,000
Administrative expenses	30,000

9. Cash gifts of $12,000 were received from various donors who stipulated that the resources must be used in 2014.

P12-4 (Preparation of financial statements for an NFPO)
Following are the preclosing fund trial balances as of December 31, 2013, for Oliver's Place, an NFPO. (The trial balances are based on the transactions contained in P12-3.) Prepare a statement of activities for the year ended December 31, 2013; also prepare a statement of financial position as of December 31, 2013.

Oliver's Place
Preclosing Trial Balances
December 31, 2013
Unrestricted Current Fund

	Debit	Credit
Cash	$ 11,000	
Contributions receivable	20,000	
Investments	22,000	
Allowance for uncollectible contributions		$ 5,000
Unrestricted support—contributions		115,000
Unrestricted support—donated services		10,000
Unrestricted revenue—investment income		1,000
Unrestricted gains—unrealized investment gains		2,000
Unrestricted asset reclassifications in—satisfaction of program restrictions		3,000
Care of animals expenses	50,000	
Special programs expenses	3,000	
Administrative expenses	30,000	
	$136,000	$136,000

Restricted Current Fund

	Debit	Credit
Cash	$14,000	
Temporarily restricted support—contributions		$17,000
Temporarily restricted asset reclassifications out—satisfaction of program restrictions	3,000	
	$17,000	$17,000

Endowment Fund

	Debit	Credit
Investments	$47,000	
Permanently restricted support—contributions		$50,000
Permanently restricted losses—unrealized investment losses	3,000	
	$50,000	$50,000

P12-5 (Journal entries for a VHWO)

Youth Services Agency (YSA) is a VHWO that provides counseling and recreation programs for youthful offenders. YSA's programs are financed through a contract with the county in which the agency is located and through contributions from local citizens. Its contract with the county provides for reimbursement of allowable costs based on monthly billings to the county. YSA does not use fund accounting, but it does identify all revenues by net asset class. Following are some transactions and events that occurred during 2013. Prepare journal entries to record these transactions. Identify all revenues within the journal entries as unrestricted, temporarily restricted, or permanently restricted.

1. YSA received pledges of gifts in the amount of $30,000, to be used as the YSA trustees consider appropriate. Based on experience, YSA's CEO believed that 90 percent of the pledges would be collected.
2. YSA collected $25,000 in cash on the pledges received in transaction 1. It also wrote off $1,500 of the pledges as uncollectible.
3. YSA received a gift of 100 shares of equity securities that had a fair value of $3,000 at the time of the gift. The donor sent the CEO a letter with the gift, saying that proceeds of the securities should be used only to purchase athletic equipment and uniforms for the basketball team.
4. YSA realized $2,800 in cash from the sale of the securities received in transaction 3.
5. YSA paid $800 in cash for athletic equipment, using the proceeds received in transaction 4. The expense was charged to Recreation programs.
6. YSA spent $12,000 in cash on the following:

Counseling programs	$ 8,000
Recreation programs	3,000
Administration expenses	1,000
Total	$12,000

7. YSA billed the county $6,500 for costs incurred under its contract.
8. The YSA trustees sent a letter to potential donors, soliciting contributions toward a building improvement program that would include a new gymnasium. The board designated $5,000 of its unrestricted resources for that purpose but did not establish a separate cash account.
9. YSA received a letter from a donor, saying he would contribute $20,000 in cash to the building improvement program as soon as YSA received an equal amount of cash from other donors.

P12-6   (Preparation of financial statements for a VHWO)

Following are the preclosing trial balances of Marilyn Township Senior Citizens Center as of December 31, 2013. Prepare a statement of financial position and a statement of activities at and for the year ended December 31, 2013.

	Unrestricted		Temporarily Restricted	
	Debit	Credit	Debit	Credit
Cash	$ 3,000		$1,600	
Pledges receivable	1,000		500	
Allowance for uncollectible pledges		$ 300		
Investments	3,200			
Accrued interest receivable	100			
Net assets, January 1, 2013		6,700		$2,000
Contributions		1,000		500
Membership dues		1,500		
Program service fees		3,000		
Grant from county		2,500		
Grant from state		2,500		
Unrealized and realized gains on investments		200		
Investment income		100		
Luncheon program expenses	7,200			
Recreation program expenses	3,400			
Administration expenses	300			
Temporarily restricted asset reclassifications out— satisfaction of program restrictions			400	
Unrestricted asset reclassifications in—satisfaction of program restrictions		400		
	$18,200	$18,200	$2,500	$2,500

P12-7   (Discussion problems for specific not-for-profit transactions)

For each of the following transactions, discuss the issues, and state the appropriate accounting solution:

1. The Society to Eliminate Hunger spent $8,000 to prepare and mail a two-page brochure to potential contributors. The brochure contained general information about the society, described its accomplishments, pointed out that a contribution of $25 would provide 25 dinners, and urged recipients to contribute. The trustees want the accountant to charge the cost of preparing and mailing the brochures to the Distribution of Food Program. The executive director thinks the expenses should be charged to fund-raising expenses.

2. The Good Folk Society commenced operations on January 1, 2012. On December 26, 2012, the society conducted a telethon and received pledges of $2,500,000. By December 31, 2012, when it closed its books, it had received $40,000 in cash. The trustees told the society's accountant to report the $40,000 in cash as contributions for 2012 and to ignore the other pledges because (a) "we didn't get the cash in 2012 and can't use in 2012 what we didn't get in 2012" and (b) "we are a new organization and cannot estimate how much additional cash we are going to receive." What should the accountant do?

3. Professional lawyers and accountants volunteered to perform all the legal and audit services required by Youth Services, an NFPO. The trustees of the NFPO take great pride in their low overhead rate. They tell the accountant: "We didn't pay for these services, so there's really no point in recording any expenses for them."

4. Sam Rich made annual contributions of $100,000 for the past 3 years to Cardinal House, a not-for-profit drug treatment center. On December 20, 2012, Cardinal House received a letter from

Sam, promising to contribute $500,000 if the organization would change the name of the entity to Rich House. The trustees debated the name change until it was time to issue the annual financial report but could not decide whether to make the change. They told the accountant: "We'd really like to report Sam's pledge as a receivable, because it will cause other donors to contribute. Besides, Sam has been a major supporter in the past and will probably contribute even if we don't change the name. We think we ought to recognize Sam's offer of $500,000 as revenue and as a receivable."

5. A wealthy individual donated a valuable work of art to a museum. The museum intends to keep the work, protect it from harm and deterioration, and hang it in a location so all can see it. The accountant sees no need either to recognize the asset or to depreciate it. However, one of the newer trustees, the chief executive of a large business entity, said, "In our company, we depreciate everything. And we know that, ultimately, everything turns to dust. So why don't we recognize the work of art as an asset and depreciate it?"

6. On March 1, 2012, Dr. Rebecca offered to contribute $15,000, which was 50 percent of the estimated cost of a special program to be undertaken by the Shelley Center, an NFPO. Dr. Rebecca stated, however, that she would make the contribution only if the center would raise the rest of the needed funds from other donors during the next 12 months. By December 31, 2012, the center had raised $6,000 of the additional amount needed. The center expected to mount a special campaign to obtain the other $9,000 and thought it would be successful. Should the center recognize Dr. Rebecca's promise as revenue for the year ended December 31, 2012?

P12-8   (Journal entries for a not-for-profit museum)
Londonderry Fine Arts Center (LFAC) is a museum dedicated to collecting and displaying works of Vermont artists. It acquires works of art primarily from direct donations and from income provided by permanent endowments. It does not, however, capitalize its art collection and does not recognize revenue when art works are contributed to the collection. LFAC protects and cares for its art works and has a policy of using the proceeds from the sale of collection items solely to acquire new works of art. LFAC charges all expenses to four programs: curatorial and exhibition, art acquisition, education and public service, and administration. Make journal entries to record the following transactions and events.

1. Donor A contributed several works by N. Rockwell, which had an estimated fair value of $30,000 and were accepted by LFAC for its permanent collection.

2. Donor B contributed a painting not done by a Vermont artist. The donor agreed that LFAC would hold it for sale (it had an estimated fair value of $2,000) and use the proceeds to enhance its art collection.

3. LFAC sold the non-Vermont artist painting, referred to in the previous transaction, for $2,100. It used the proceeds, together with $1,900 of its unrestricted resources, to acquire several serigraphs by H. Shokler.

4. One of LFAC's permanent endowments provided investment income of $6,000. When she made the gift to LFAC, the donor had stipulated that all investment income be used solely for a special program to train local residents in the art of print making.

5. LFAC spent $6,000 on the training program described in transaction 4.

6. Local residents donated 1,000 hours of time collecting museum admissions fees; LFAC estimated these services had a value of $10,000. Also, a retired skilled craftsman donated 80 hours cleaning and preserving works of art recently acquired by the museum; LFAC estimated these services had a value of $4,000.

7. Admissions fees to the museum totaled $30,000.

8. As a result of a weakened stock market, the fair value of the permanent endowments held by the museum declined by $60,000.

9. LFAC paid curatorial and exhibition expenses of $80,000.

P12-9   (Journal entries for a not-for-profit college)
Manny Saxe College is a small, not-for-profit college known for its excellence in teaching accounting. The college uses fund accounting and has an Unrestricted Current Fund, a Restricted Current

Fund, a Plant Fund, and an Endowment Fund. It charges its expenses to Instruction and research, Student services, Plant operations, and Auxiliary enterprises. It had the following transactions and events during 2013. Prepare the journal entries necessary to record these transactions, identifying the net asset classification as appropriate. Show which fund is used to record each transaction.

1. Revenues from student tuition and fees were $2,500,000, all of which was collected.
2. Revenues from auxiliary enterprises were $400,000 in cash.
3. Salaries and wages, all of which were paid, were $1,800,000 million, chargeable as follows:

Instruction and research	$1,200,000
Student services	200,000
Plant operations	250,000
Auxiliary enterprises	150,000

4. Materials and supplies costing $800,000 were purchased on account and placed in inventory during the year.
5. Materials and supplies used during the year were $700,000, chargeable as follows:

Instruction and research	$300,000
Student services	50,000
Plant operations	150,000
Auxiliary enterprises	200,000

6. A cash transfer of $100,000 was made from the Unrestricted Current Fund to the Plant Fund to start the design work on a new student services building.
7. The college received a cash gift of $20,000 from K. Schermann to finance a 3-year research project on the usefulness of fund accounting.
8. The college paid R. Attmore $7,000 to do research on the project in transaction 7.
9. P. Defliese donated $1,000,000 in equity securities to the college, stipulating that the corpus and all gains and losses on the sale of the securities remain intact in perpetuity. He also stipulated that income on the investments be used solely to finance a chair in governmental accounting.
10. At year-end, the securities donated by Mr. Defliese in transaction 9 had a fair value of $1,030,000. Income earned on the investments during the year was $45,000.
11. Antonio Harmer sent a letter to the college at the end of the year, promising to contribute $25,000 to equip the new student services building if the college raised an equal amount from other contributors. The college planned to write to the alumni to seek additional funds.

Appendix 12A

Not-for-ProfIt Colleges
and Universities

Not-for-profit colleges and universities are required to follow the same accounting standards used by other not-for-profit organizations, as discussed in this chapter. These colleges and universities also prepare financial statements using the unrestricted, temporarily restricted, and permanently restricted net asset classifications. Those that use fund accounting also use the fund types previously discussed.

The major functional expense categories used by colleges and universities in financial reporting are instruction, research, public service, academic support, student services, auxiliary enterprises, and institutional support. Instruction, research, and public service are considered to be the primary programs, while academic support, student services, and auxiliary enterprises support the primary programs. Auxiliary enterprises include the operation of bookstores, residence halls, dining services, and intercollegiate athletics. Institutional support includes management and general expenses and fund-raising expenses. Costs of operating and maintaining the physical plant, including depreciation, are generally allocated to the other functions.

FINANCIAL STATEMENTS OF NOT-FOR-PROFIT COLLEGES AND UNIVERSITIES

Not-for-profit colleges and universities, like other not-for-profit organizations, are required to prepare a statement of financial position, a statement of activities, and a cash flow statement. Tables 12A-1 and 12A-2 illustrate not-for-profit college and university statements of financial position and statements of activities, using the fiscal year 2010 financial statements of Fordham University. Located in the city of New York, Fordham University serves about 8,000 undergraduate students and 6,700 graduate and professional students.

Notice that Fordham University prepares its statement of activities in "pancake" format, separating the changes in unrestricted net assets from the changes in temporarily restricted and permanently restricted net assets. The FASB permits this type of display as an alternative to a columnar format. In Table 12A-2, the $8,858,835 of Net assets released from restrictions, reported among the operating revenues for fiscal year 2010, is the same amount as the decrease shown for that caption under changes in temporarily restricted net assets.

Notice also that Fordham University's statement of activities for unrestricted net assets distinguishes between "net operating revenue" and "nonoperating activities." Generally, captions such as "net operating revenue" and "excess of operating revenues over expenses" are used to provide the reader with a measure of operating results from basic operations. In deliberations leading to FASB Statement No. 117 (FASB ASC Topic 958), the FASB explored the use of such intermediate captions but decided not to prescribe specific operating measures, choosing instead to let them evolve for the various types of NFPOs.

TABLE 12A-1	Statements of Financial Position—Not-for-Profit University

Fordham University
Statements of Financial Position
As of June 30, 2010 and 2009

	2010	2009
Assets		
Cash and cash equivalents	$ 2,138,875	$ 1,659,672
Accounts and grants receivable:		
Students, net	12,641,134	7,042,386
Government	6,957,235	5,246,196
Other	6,955,283	8,001,882
Contributions receivable [see text]	59,226,790	70,564,525
Prepaid expenses and other assets	4,291,234	4,167,871
Investments [see text]	396,281,058	372,365,640
Student loans receivable, net	15,656,153	15,524,777
Deposits with bond trustees	6,756,577	53,382,423
Bond issuance costs	6,678,727	6,966,904
Investment in plant assets, net	629,865,069	560,195,542
Total assets	$1,147,448,135	$1,105,117,818
Liabilities and Net Assets		
Liabilities		
Accounts payable and accrued expenses	$ 72,912,606	$ 77,605,407
Borrowings under line of credit	10,000,000	10,000,000
Deferred revenues and deposits	20,629,407	24,107,077
Amounts held for others	2,958,062	2,046,772
U.S. government refundable advances	4,711,423	4,861,235
Postretirement benefit obligation	38,869,000	32,023,000
Long-term debt	292,117,372	301,710,742
Total liabilities	442,197,870	452,354,233
Commitments and contingencies		
Net Assets		
Unrestricted	337,364,070	299,086,184
Temporarily restricted	179,095,197	179,576,219
Permanently restricted	188,790,998	174,101,182
Total net assets	705,250,265	652,763,585
Total liabilities and net assets	$1,147,448,135	$1,105,117,818

Note: The notes accompanying these statements and the related note references made in the captions are not reproduced in this text. However, captions labeled "see text" are discussed in this appendix.

Source: Fordham University 2010 Financial Statements.

Fordham University
Statements of Activities
For the Years Ended June 30, 2010 and 2009

	2010	2009
Operating Revenues		
Tuition and fees, net	$327,611,596	$307,186,756
Government grants	26,641,458	18,502,329
Investment return [see text]	13,257,380	17,242,911
Contributions and private grants	17,204,783	16,048,430
Auxiliary enterprises, net	52,596,112	50,238,341
Other revenues	13,380,001	15,023,964
Net assets released from restrictions	8,858,835	8,239,440
Total operating revenues	459,550,165	432,482,171
Operating Expenses		
Program services:		
Instruction	167,216,513	164,986,784
Research	13,415,253	10,806,112
Public service	17,576,022	17,665,837
Academic support	59,665,504	60,031,615
Student services	52,870,677	50,145,227
Auxiliary enterprises	62,262,140	57,627,321
Total program services	373,006,109	361,262,896
Supporting services—institutional support	60,040,903	60,275,236
Total operating expenses	433,047,012	421,538,132
Net operating revenue	26,503,153	10,944,039
Nonoperating Activities		
Investment return [see text]	20,282,201	(83,570,860)
Change in value of interest rate swap	(4,624,468)	(6,268,240)
Adjustment to student accounts receivable	—	(9,553,224)
(Loss) gain not yet recognized as a component of net periodic benefit cost	(3,883,000)	362,000
Increase (decrease) in unrestricted net assets	38,277,886	(88,086,285)
Changes in temporarily restricted net assets:		
Contributions and private grants, net	6,221,443	27,080,208
Investment return [see text]	2,156,370	(36,441,073)
Net assets released from restrictions	(8,858,835)	(8,239,440)
Decrease in temporarily restricted net assets	(481,022)	(17,600,305)
Changes in permanently restricted net assets:		
Contributions	12,974,836	4,803,276
Investment return [see text]	1,331,980	(682,845)
Appreciation (depreciation) in fair value of perpetual trust	383,000	(1,921,000)
Increase in permanently restricted net assets	14,689,816	2,199,431
Increase (decrease) in net assets	52,486,680	(103,487,159)
Net assets at beginning of year	652,763,585	756,250,744
Net assets at end of year	$705,250,265	$652,763,585

Note: The notes accompanying these statements and the related note references made in the captions are not reproduced in this text. However, captions labeled "see text" are discussed in this appendix.

Source: Fordham University 2010 Financial Statements.

NOTES TO THE FINANCIAL STATEMENTS

Notes are an integral part of financial statements, and you need to read them carefully to understand the information content of the statements. Space limitations preclude presentation of all the notes to Fordham University's statements. Several of them are discussed here, however, to further illustrate matters covered in this chapter.

Contributions Receivable

Contributions receivable, reported in the statement of financial position as of June 30, 2010, consist of the following:

Amounts expected to be collected in	
Less than 1 year	$24,427,426
1 to 5 years	27,744,817
More than 5 years	19,820,000
Less, allowance for uncollectible amounts	(15,683,406)
Less, discount to present value (ranging from 1.79% to 5.00%)	(5,698,038)
Subtotal	50,610,799
Funds held in perpetual trust	5,637,000
Charitable remainder trusts	2,978,991
Total	$59,226,790

Notice that the allowance for estimated uncollectible contributions is significant in relation to the total contributions receivable. Also, notice that the receivables have been discounted to present value. This adjustment is in accordance with FASB standards, which provide that unconditional promises to contribute cash that are expected to be collected more than 1 year after the balance sheet date should be discounted to their present value. Subsequent accretion of the interest element is reported as contribution revenue.

As discussed on page 457, colleges, universities, and other NFPOs may be beneficiaries of various types of trusts or other arrangements, generally called split-interest agreements.

- A perpetual trust is one in which the NFPO has an irrevocable right to receive the *income* from the trust assets in perpetuity, but not the assets held in trust. When the trust is established, the fair value of the asset—the present value of estimated future cash receipts from the trust—is reported as contributions receivable, and the related contribution revenue is classified as permanently restricted support. Subsequent distributions from the trust are recorded as unrestricted or restricted investment income (based on trust stipulations) in the year received. Changes in the underlying fair value of the trust assets are recorded each year with a journal entry similar to that shown on page 457 for charitable remainder trusts.

- Charitable remainder trusts are discussed on page 457. The notes to Fordham's statements say: "At the dates these charitable remainder trusts are established or the University becomes aware of their existence, contribution revenue and receivables are recognized at the present value of the estimated future benefits to be received when the trust assets are distributed. The receivable is adjusted during the term of the trust for changes in the value of the assets, accretion of the discount, and other changes in the estimates of future benefits."

Investments and Investment Income

Fordham's statement of financial position reports investments having a fair value of more than $396 million as of June 30, 2010. The extensive disclosures include a description of the types of investments held and the fair value levels (see page 456) in which each type of investment is categorized. Fordham categorizes its $396 million of investments as $185 million in level 1, $139 million in level 2, and $72 million in level 3.

Fordham's statement of activities (Table 12A-2) reports Investment return in four places: under Operating Revenues and Nonoperating Activities in the section on unrestricted net assets and among the Changes in both temporarily and permanently restricted net assets.

As Fordham explains in a note to the financial statements, dividends, interest, and gains and losses on investments are reported as increases or decreases in unrestricted net assets unless their use is limited by explicit donor-imposed restrictions or by law. But why is some investment income reported as operating revenue and some as nonoperating? Some colleges and universities include all *realized* gains and losses as part of operating revenues and all *unrealized* gains and losses as nonoperating. Others manage their investments on a total return basis, focusing on the long-term overall return on investment, which includes both investment income and net appreciation. The latter use a trustee-authorized spending rate formula to determine how much of the income will be used for current operations. The trustees may also authorize additional spending from investment return. The balance is reported as nonoperating income.

A note to Fordham's financial statements indicates that the university manages its investment pool to achieve the maximum prudent long-term total return. Its policy is "to preserve the value of these investments in real terms (after inflation) and provide a predictable flow of funds to support operations. This policy permits the use of total return at a rate (spending rate) of 4.0% of the average quarterly fair value during the three preceding calendar years for the permanently restricted and other board-designated portions of the pool." The investment return for the unrestricted net assets in fiscal year 2010 consisted of the following components:

Dividends and interest (net of expenses of $1,761,254)	$ 1,488,250
Net appreciation on investments	32,051,331
Total return on investments	33,539,581
Investment return recognized in operating activities	13,257,380
Investment return greater than amounts recognized in operating activities [included in nonoperating activities]	$20,282,201

Chapter 13

Accounting for Health Care Organizations

Chapter Outline

Learning Objectives

Health Care Service Providers

Introduction to Hospital Accounting and Financial Reporting
  Sources of Generally Accepted Accounting Principles
  Financial Reporting Framework

Patient Service Revenues
  Nature of Hospital Payment Systems
  Accounting for Net Patient Service Revenues
    Gross Patient Service Revenues and Contractual Adjustments
    Provision for Uncollectible Receivables
    Estimated Third-Party Settlements
  Accounting for Capitation Premiums
  Notes to Financial Statements Regarding Patient Revenue Recognition
    Reporting on Charity Care

Investment Income, Other Revenues, and Gains
  Investment Returns
  Other Revenues, Gains, and Operating Support
    Parking and Other Revenues or Gains
    Contributions of Cash and Supplies
    Contributed Services

Expenses
  Operating Expenses
  Medical Malpractice Claims
    Reporting on Medical Malpractice Claims

Other Transactions
  Contributions Received by a Not-for-Profit Hospital's Foundation
  Governmental Hospital Foundations
  Transactions Creating Assets Limited as to Use

After completing this chapter, you should be able to do the following:

- Identify the sources of generally accepted accounting principles for health care organizations
- Prepare journal entries related to hospital patient service revenue and patient receivables
- Prepare journal entries used to record investment income and other revenues and gains
- Describe the accounting principles regarding hospital medical malpractice claims
- Prepare journal entries to account for transactions with restrictions
- Describe how not-for-profit hospitals calculate an indicator of financial performance
- Identify and prepare financial statements for not-for-profit and governmental hospitals

Health care is one of the most rapidly growing industries in the United States. The U.S. health care system is also one of the most controversial political topics. In March 2010, the president signed into law a sweeping overhaul of the U.S. health care system. If upheld in the courts, the new law will affect nearly everyone—individuals, insurance companies, health care providers, and employers.

As an industry, health care continues to outpace nearly every other in its growth. In 2008, the U.S. Bureau of Labor Statistics reported that as one of the country's largest industries, health care provided 14.3 million jobs. In addition, the bureau projects that health care will generate 3.2 million new wage and salary jobs between 2008 and 2018, largely in response to the rapid growth in the country's elderly population.

Health care in the United States is characterized not only by rapidly rising employment among service providers, but also by increasing costs and the involvement of third parties (such as government, private insurance companies, and health maintenance organizations) in financing health care services. We read almost daily about threats to the financial health of Medicare, increased taxes related to increasing Medicaid costs, disputes between health maintenance organizations and service providers, and reductions in employer-provided health care benefits.

Public programs that receive the most attention are Medicare and Medicaid. The Medicare program is financed primarily by the federal government. Medicaid is a public assistance–type program financed by the federal, state, and sometimes local governments.

Accounting and financial reporting are important tools in health care administration, not only in keeping track of costs, but also because third parties often base their payments to health care providers on allowable costs, some form of fixed-rate reimbursement, or a combination of both. Measurement and control of costs are critical, both to health care providers and to third-party payers.

HEALTH CARE SERVICE PROVIDERS

Health care services are provided in many types of settings and by entities having different ownership structures and operating orientations. Health care services may be provided, for example, in hospitals, surgery centers, clinics, laboratories, group medical practices, nursing homes (that differ in the intensity of the medical care they provide), home health agencies, and continuing care retirement communities. Health care organizations may be organized as not-for-profit, governmental, or private for-profit (investor-owned) entities. Not-for-profit health care entities may be classified as having either a business orientation or a nonbusiness orientation. Governmental health care entities may also recover their costs with patient fees and charges (generally reported in Enterprise Funds or as component units) or may charge no fees at all (reported in governmental funds). This chapter focuses on accounting and financial reporting by a major health care provider—hospitals—organized either as governmental entities that use Enterprise Fund accounting or as not-for-profit entities with a business orientation.

The characteristics of governmental entities, as distinguished from not-for-profit entities, are discussed in Chapter 12. Some governmental hospitals are organized within departments of state or local governments. Others are organized as legally separate corporations, governed by boards appointed by government officials. Legally separate governmental corporations may have the power to tax and to issue tax-exempt debt directly, rather than through a state or local government agency.

Not-for-profit hospitals, like other not-for-profit entities, have no ownership interests and, thus, do not operate to maximize profits for owners. Not-for-profit health care entities with a business orientation are basically self-supporting as a result of fees they charge for their services, but they may also receive relatively small amounts of contributions. Non-business-oriented not-for-profit health care entities are considered so because they obtain most of their revenues from contributions, grants, and other support. Non-business-oriented not-for-profit health care entities are included within voluntary health and welfare organizations (VHWOs) discussed in Chapter 12.

INTRODUCTION TO HOSPITAL ACCOUNTING AND FINANCIAL REPORTING

Sources of Generally Accepted Accounting Principles

The Financial Accounting Standards Board (FASB) establishes accounting standards for for-profit (investor-owned) and not-for-profit hospitals and other health care entities. The Governmental Accounting Standards Board (GASB) establishes them for governmental hospitals and other health care entities. Governmental health care entities also apply the industry-specific guidance provided in the AICPA's Audit and Accounting Guide, *Health Care Entities*. Although some differences exist in the standards established for investor-owned, not-for-profit, and governmental health care entities, the move for comparability among entities that perform similar functions has resulted in far more similarities than differences among the three types of entities.

Governmental hospitals—those that meet the definition of *government* discussed in Chapter 1—apply only GASB pronouncements, not FASB pronouncements. In addition, governmental hospitals that meet the definition of Enterprise Funds as discussed in Chapter 7 (or that are organized as public benefit corporations and use Enterprise Fund accounting) apply the full accrual basis of accounting. As noted in that chapter, the GASB recently adopted all pre-1989 FASB and AICPA pronouncements that it considered applicable to Enterprise Funds.[1] However, that guidance *excludes* all FASB and AICPA pronouncements developed primarily for not-for-profit entities, including not-for-profit hospitals.

Investor-owned and not-for-profit business-oriented hospitals are required to follow the industry-specific incremental requirements of FASB Accounting Standards Codification (ASC) Topic 954, Health Care Entities. In addition, all not-for-profit hospitals are required to follow the requirements of FASB ASC Topic 958, Not-for-Profit Entities, because they are not-for-profit entities, regardless of whether they are business-oriented or funded in large part by contributions, grants, and other support.

In this chapter we discuss transactions simultaneously for not-for-profit and governmental entities, pointing out differences where they exist. Most of the differences occur in accounting for certain contributions and in financial reporting. Keep the following factors in mind as you read this chapter:

- Governmental hospitals are subject to the accounting and reporting requirements for governmental *proprietary funds,* discussed in Chapter 7. Not-for-profit hospitals are subject to the accounting and reporting requirements for *not-for-profit organizations,* discussed in Chapter 12.
- Governmental hospitals use the economic resources measurement focus and the full accrual basis of accounting, as discussed in Chapter 7.
- Not-for-profit business-oriented health care entities also use full accrual accounting. But even though most of their revenues are obtained from fees and charges for services, they are subject to the accounting and financial reporting standards of FASB ASC Topic 958, Not-for-Profit Entities, because they are not-for-profit entities. Incremental accounting and reporting requirements related to the health care industry also apply as provided by FASB ASC 954, Health Care Entities.

Financial Reporting Framework

Like all not-for-profit entities, not-for-profit hospitals are required to report net assets and changes in net assets by net asset classification—unrestricted, temporarily restricted, and permanently restricted. To more clearly present operating results, FASB ASC 954-205-45-1 states that the basic financial statements of health care entities consist of a balance sheet, a statement of operations, a statement of changes in equity (or net assets), a statement of cash flows, and notes to

---

[1]GASB Statement No. 62, "Codification of Accounting and Financial Reporting Guidance Contained in Pre-November 30, 1989 FASB and AICPA Pronouncements."

the financial statements. In effect, not-for-profit hospitals present two operating statements. One, the statement of operations, reports on the basic day-to-day revenues and all expenses by covering only changes in *unrestricted* net assets. (Recall from Chapter 12 that expenses affect only *unrestricted* net assets.) The statement of operations must include a performance indicator (such as "revenues over expenses" (analogous to income from continuing operations of a for-profit enterprise). The other statement, called the statement of changes in net assets, reports on changes in all three net asset classifications as well as changes in net assets for the hospital as a whole. This statement deals primarily with transactions and events other than day-to-day operating activities involving permanently and temporarily restricted net assets. Information presented in this statement for unrestricted net assets is highly aggregated. Not-for-profit hospitals have the option to combine these two statements.

Later in the chapter, we present a more detailed discussion and illustrations of hospital financial reporting. The following skeletal outline of a not-for-profit hospital statement of operations provides a framework for the ensuing discussion of hospital accounting.

Unrestricted revenues, gains, and other support:	
Net patient service revenues	XXX
Premium revenue	XXX
Other revenue	XXX
Net assets released from restrictions, used for operations	XXX
Total revenues, gains, and other support	XXX
Expenses:	
Details by function or natural classification	XXX
Provision for bad debts	XXX
Total expenses	XXX
Operating income	XXX
Other income (or expenses)	
Details, such as investment income	XXX
Excess of revenues over expenses	XXX
Change in net unrealized gains and losses on securities other than trading securities	XXX
Change in interest in net assets of NFP Hospital Foundation	XXX
Net assets released from restrictions, used to purchase capital assets	XXX
Increase in unrestricted net assets	XXX

Net assets of governmental hospitals are classified as either unrestricted or restricted. Permanent endowments are included in restricted net assets and, when present, must be further broken down between expendable and nonexpendable. Recall that the GASB does not distinguish between temporarily restricted and permanently restricted assets, and it does not limit restricted net assets to those subject to donor-imposed restrictions. The operating statement of governmental hospitals is all-inclusive, showing all revenue sources, including operating and capital grants and contributions of capital assets. The operating statement—called a statement of revenues, expenses, and changes in net position—is presented in the same format as that of other governmental Enterprise Funds/activities (see Chapter 7). In this statement, operating expenses are deducted from operating revenues to show operating income. Nonoperating revenues (such as investment income) and expenses (such as interest expense) are then added or subtracted to show income before capital contributions and transfers. The latter are then added or subtracted to report total change in net position. Net position is reported in three categories—net investment in capital assets, restricted, and unrestricted.

PATIENT SERVICE REVENUES

Nature of Hospital Payment Systems

Hospitals obtain operating revenues primarily from patient services (based on charges for nursing and other professional services) and health care insurance premiums (based on agreements to provide care). Most of these revenues come from third-party payers, including both public sources such as Medicare and Medicaid and private insurers such as health maintenance organizations (HMOs) and Blue Cross.

Third-party payers have developed various payment systems, generally paying hospitals at amounts less than the hospitals' established rates. Differences between a hospital's established rates and the amounts set by or negotiated with third-party payers are referred to as *contractual adjustments*. Hospitals also provide services to uninsured patients, some of whom may receive discounts from established rates or who may not pay at all (called "charity care"). The different payment arrangements affect the way hospitals account for patient service revenues and receivables.

Hospital payment systems include prospectively determined rates per discharge; reimbursed costs; negotiated fee schedules; per diem payments; discounts from established charges; and capitation premiums paid per member, per month (PMPM). Some payment rates are established prospectively (i.e., in advance of service delivery) at fixed amounts. Others are based on interim billing amounts, subject to retrospective adjustment (i.e., after the accounting period ends).

Medicare generally pays hospitals at prospectively determined rates, which vary according to a patient classification system based on clinical, diagnostic, and other factors. Under the diagnosis-related group (DRG) system, all potential diagnoses are classified into a number of medically meaningful groups, each of which has a different value. Each hospital in a specific geographic region receives the same amount for each DRG, depending on whether the hospital is classified as urban or rural. Thus, an uncomplicated appendectomy results in the same basic reimbursement to all hospitals in a given urban or rural area. Other factors, such as whether the hospital is a teaching hospital and the intensity of service rendered, are also considered in the payments a hospital will receive.

Third-party payers that pay hospitals retrospectively reimburse hospitals initially on the basis of interim payment rates. The interim payment rates are then adjusted retrospectively based on stipulated allowable costs after the hospitals submit required cost reports to the third-party payers. The rates reached on final settlement may differ significantly from the interim payment rates. Therefore, to ensure that revenues and net assets are reported on the accrual basis of accounting, reasonable estimates of the amounts receivable from or payable to the third-party payers need to be made in the period that the services are rendered.

Under *capitation agreements* with HMOs, hospitals generally receive agreed-upon premiums per member, per month, based on the number of participants in the HMO. In exchange, the hospitals agree to provide all medical services to the HMO's subscribers. The hospitals thus earn these revenues from *agreeing to provide* care and will receive the capitation payments regardless of the actual services they perform. The hospitals may also receive fees from the HMO for certain services.

Accounting for Net Patient Service Revenues

Revenues based on fees for services *actually provided* by hospitals are classified as *patient service revenues.* These revenues include those derived from Medicare and Medicaid beneficiaries. Revenues based on *agreements to provide* care (regardless of whether care is actually provided) are classified as premium revenues and include revenues from capitation arrangements with HMOs. If the amount is significant, patient service revenues must be reported separately from premium revenues in the financial statements.

Hospitals record patient service revenues and receivables initially at their gross (established) rates, even if they do not expect to collect those amounts. As previously noted, several factors are likely to cause the amount realized from these services to be significantly less than the established rates. These factors include contractual rate adjustments with third-party payers, provision of charity care, discounts granted to various persons, bad debts, and retrospective adjustments.

For financial reporting purposes, patient service revenue is reported on the operating statement *net* of contractual rate adjustments, charity care, and similar items that the hospital does not expect to collect. For governmental hospitals, patient service revenues are also reported net of estimated uncollectible amounts. For not-for-profit hospitals, however, patient service revenue is not reduced by a provision for uncollectible accounts. Instead, not-for-profit hospitals report bad debts expense in the expenses section of the operating statement (see the skeletal outline on page 491 for financial reporting by not-for-profit hospitals of net patient service revenues and provision for bad debts). Both governmental and not-for-profit hospitals must exercise their judgment to distinguish uncollectible amounts from charity care. Receivables resulting from health care services are reported on the balance sheet at the amount likely to be realized in cash. Therefore, gross receivables must be reduced by allowances needed to present the receivables at their *net realizable value.*

GROSS PATIENT SERVICE REVENUES AND CONTRACTUAL ADJUSTMENTS To illustrate, assume that a hospital's regular charges (at established rates) for nursing and other professional services (including services provided to patients covered by Medicare and other third-party payers, self-pay patients, and charity patients) are $1,700,000. To record this information, the following entry is made:

Patient accounts receivable	1,700,000	
Patient service revenue		1,700,000
To record gross patient service revenue at established rates.		

Although we use one account for each type of revenue, remember that this *control account* is used in the same manner as a control account in general accounting. Subsidiary records are used to accumulate the revenues for the unit to which the patient was admitted or whose services were used—for example, general nursing services, surgery, pediatrics, and radiology.

As previously stated, payment rates may be established either prospectively or retrospectively. When established prospectively, the full contractual adjustment is known at billing time. When established retrospectively, the full adjustment may not be known until a later date, such as when the person is discharged, when the third party is billed, or when payment or partial payment is received. For this reason, interim rates reflecting a tentative contractual adjustment may be used for billing purposes. Provision for further contractual adjustment (upward or downward), however, may be needed at year-end to report revenues and receivables from third-party payers at net realizable amounts.

For example, assume that under a prospective billing arrangement with third-party payer X, the hospital has contractual adjustments of $80,000. Under a retrospective rate arrangement with third-party payer Y, it has tentative contractual adjustments of $40,000 based on interim rates, pending later negotiation of final rates. The hospital would make the following entry at the time of the billings:

Provision for contractual adjustments	120,000	
Patient accounts receivable		120,000
To record adjustments to revenue and receivables, based on prospective billing contract with payer X and interim rates negotiated with payer Y.		

After reducing the patient accounts receivable by the provision for contractual adjustments, the outstanding receivables from third-party payers would include only the amount the hospital expects to collect from them.

Other types of adjustments to gross patient revenues are made for charity care and "discounts" granted to clergy, volunteers, and employees. These adjustments also represent the amount of the established rates that the hospital will not collect. The only difference between these and the contractual adjustments lies in the reason they will not be collected. Assume, for example, that the previously recorded revenues include services of $50,000 to patients who may be unable to pay. As soon as the hospital determines that the patients meet its established criteria for charity care, the following entry is made:

Provision for charity services	50,000	
Patient accounts receivable		50,000
To record adjustment to revenues and receivables because of charity care.		

If collections of receivables during the year total $1,400,000, they would be recorded as follows:

Cash	1,400,000	
Patient accounts receivable		1,400,000
To record collection of receivables.		

PROVISION FOR UNCOLLECTIBLE RECEIVABLES Accounts receivable must be stated in the financial statements at their net realizable value. Therefore, patient accounts receivable need to be reviewed for likelihood of collection. As previously noted, an estimate for uncollectible accounts receivable is reported as a *bad debts expense* by not-for-profit hospitals and as an *adjustment of patient service revenue* by governmental hospitals. Both not-for-profit and governmental hospitals report the credit part of the journal entry—the allowance for uncollectible accounts—as a contra to accounts receivable. If a hospital's management estimates uncollectible amounts from self-pay patients to be $30,000, the following entry would be made:

Bad debts expense (or Provision for bad debts)	30,000	
Allowance for uncollectible accounts		30,000
To record allowance for uncollectible accounts.		

If $20,000 of individual patient accounts becomes uncollectible, both types of hospitals would reduce patient accounts receivable and the allowance for uncollectible accounts as follows:

Allowance for uncollectible accounts	20,000	
Patient accounts receivable		20,000

To record write-off of accounts determined to be uncollectible.

ESTIMATED THIRD-PARTY SETTLEMENTS   As previously stated, arrangements with some third-party payers may call for billing at interim rates, subject to retrospective adjustment based on a review of cost reports submitted by the hospital. To ensure that amounts reported as net patient service revenues, receivables, or payables in the financial statements are valid, estimates must be made of the settlement amounts for all billing arrangements that have not been settled as of the date of the financial statements. The adjustment, which takes the form of an additional contractual adjustment, must be made even if the final settlement amount has not been negotiated.

Regarding its retrospective rate arrangement with third-party payer Y, assume the hospital estimates at year-end that it will need to refund $15,000 because its analysis of reimbursable costs shows that the interim rates negotiated with Y were too high. If Y had paid all amounts previously billed by the hospital, the following entry would be needed at year-end:

Provision for contractual adjustments	15,000	
Estimated third-party payer settlements		15,000

To record provision for estimated refund to payer Y, pending
negotiation of retrospective rate.

Based on these journal entries, the amount reported in the not-for-profit hospital's operating statement as net patient service revenue would be $1,515,000—gross billings of $1,700,000, less the $135,000 provision for contractual adjustments and the $50,000 provision for charity services. Net patient accounts receivable reported on the hospital's balance sheet would be $100,000—gross outstanding receivables of $110,000, less $10,000 remaining in the contra account allowance for uncollectible accounts. The $15,000 estimated third-party payer settlements account would be reported as a liability. (Note that, in the previous journal entry, we assumed that third-party payer Y had paid all amounts previously billed by the hospital. If Y had not paid all amounts previously billed, the $15,000 estimated settlement would be reported as a reduction of the outstanding receivables in order to state the receivables at net realizable value.)

Accounting for Capitation Premiums

In addition to billing fees for services, hospitals also have capitation agreements with various HMOs, wherein they receive agreed-upon premiums per member, per month. If a hospital receives $400,000 of capitation fees at the beginning of the month, it would make the following entry:

Cash	400,000	
Premium revenue		400,000

To record capitation premium revenues.

Assume that, at the end of the month, hospital records show that it provided services to participants in these HMOs amounting to $375,000 at its established billing rates. Although this information is valuable for internal management purposes, no entry is made in the financial accounting records.

For an example of the effect of these entries on financial reporting, see Patient accounts receivable and Estimated third-party payer settlements in Table 13-1 (page 511) and Net patient service revenue in Table 13-2 (page 512).

Notes to Financial Statements Regarding Patient Revenue Recognition

The nature of the third-party arrangements, revenue recognition practices, and charity care policies should be described in notes to the financial statements. The following is an illustration of a note regarding these arrangements that might be made in the summary of significant accounting policies.

- *Net Patient Service Revenue.* The hospital has agreements with third-party payers, providing for payments at amounts different from its established rates. The agreements provide for both prospectively and retrospectively determined rates. Net patient service revenue is reported at estimated net realizable amounts from patients, third-party payers, and others for services rendered, including estimated retroactive adjustments under agreements with third-party payers. Estimated retroactive adjustments are accrued in the period services are provided and adjusted in future periods as final settlements are made.
- *Premium Revenue.* The hospital has agreements with various health maintenance organizations to provide services to subscribing participants. In accordance with the agreements, the hospital receives monthly capitation payments based on the number of participants, regardless of the services the hospital actually performs.
- *Charity Care.* The hospital provides care to patients either without charge or at less than its established rates. These patients must meet the criteria under the hospital's charity care policy. The value of these services is not reported as revenue because the hospital does not seek to collect amounts that qualify as charity care. (see "Reporting on Charity Care")

Reporting on Charity Care

All U.S. not-for-profit hospitals are required to give charity care equal to at least 5 percent of their net patient revenue in order to maintain their tax-exempt status. Not-for-profit hospitals are required by FASB ASC 954-605-50 to disclose in their notes to their financial statements their policy for providing charity care. Disclosures must include the level of charity care provided, based on the provider's direct and indirect costs of providing that care. This cost-based measure of charity care is a recent development in GAAP. Previously, measures varied, and many not-for-profit hospitals reported the level of charity care provided, based on their established or contract revenue rates. For example, this is how the Geneva Valley Hospital Center might have reported on charity care before the change in required disclosures:

> The Hospital provides a significant amount of partially or totally uncompensated patient care to patients who are unable to compensate the Hospital for their treatment either through third-party coverage or their own resources. Patients who meet certain criteria under the Hospital's charity care policy are provided care without charge or at amounts less than established rates. Because charity care amounts are not expected to be paid, they are not reported as revenue. The amount of charges forgone for total uncompensated care (including uncompensated care reported as bad debt expense), based on established rates under the Hospital's policy for the years ended December 31, 2012 and 2011, was approximately $7,258,000 and $8,538,000, respectively.

Similar disclosures are required for governmental hospitals by the AICPA's Audit and Accounting Guide.[2] However, governmental hospitals often bear more of the burden and finance it with taxpayer dollars. A case in point is the Parkland Health & Hospital System—a component unit of Dallas County,

---

[2]AICPA Audit and Accounting Guide, Health Care Entities, par. 15.112.

Texas. The system provides health care to Dallas County residents, along with three not-for-profit health care systems also located in Dallas County. Parkland disclosed the following information:

> **Uncompensated Care**—Parkland provides services to uninsured patients who qualify for tax-supported care. The program is called Parkland Health*Plus* and is designed for Dallas County indigent patients with family incomes up to 200% of the federal poverty level and no third-party coverage such as Medicaid, Medicare, or commercial insurance. Parkland recognized ad valorem tax revenues of approximately $446 million to fund services for qualified patients. . . . Management estimates the cost of uncompensated health care, including charity care, as the excess direct and indirect costs of providing services over the estimated collection amounts. The cost of uncompensated care, including charity care, was approximately $599 million during the year ended September 30, 2011.
>
> *Source:* Adapted from a recent annual report of the Dallas County Hospital District, Texas.

Parkland's cost of uncompensated care was more than 100 percent of its net patient service revenue. In comparison, the *Dallas Morning News* reported in 2011 that the three not-for-profit systems operating in the Dallas County area provided 12.4 percent, 6.2 percent, and 5.4 percent of their net patient revenue as free and unreimbursed medical care.

INVESTMENT INCOME, OTHER REVENUES, AND GAINS

Investment Returns

Investment activities often provide a major source of revenue for hospitals. Not-for-profit hospitals account for investments in accordance with FASB ASC Subtopic 958-320, discussed in Chapter 12. Governmental hospitals account for investments in accordance with GASB Statement No. 31, "Accounting and Financial Reporting for Certain Investments and for External Investment Pools," discussed in Chapter 8. Both standards require that, in general, hospitals report investments in equity and debt securities at fair value on the balance sheet. Reporting investments at fair value on the balance sheet means that investment returns in the operating statement include dividends and interest, realized gains and losses, and unrealized gains and losses.

As noted earlier, FASB ASC 954-225-45-4 requires not-for-profit hospitals to include a performance indicator in their statement of operations. Realized gains and losses must be included in the performance indicator, but unrealized gains and losses on securities other than trading securities must be excluded from that measure. (A security is classified as *other than trading* if it is acquired without the intent to sell it in the near term.) GASB accounting standards on investments, which are applicable to governmental hospitals, generally do not permit realized gains and losses to be displayed in the financial statements separately from the net increase or decrease in the fair value of investments.[3]

Accomplishing the different methods of financial reporting requires differences in financial accounting. Combining realized and unrealized gains and losses in a single account is the simpler of the two methods. To illustrate, assume a governmental and a not-for-profit hospital each purchase a security for $100,000 on March 15, 2012. (The not-for-profit hospital considers it to be other than trading.) Both would make the following entry:

Investments	100,000	
Cash		100,000
To record purchase of investment.		

---

[3]GASB Statement No. 31, par. 13. The GASB does, however, permit note *disclosure* of realized gains and losses.

Both securities increase in value to $115,000 as of December 31, 2012, the balance sheet date, and both are sold in the year 2013 for $120,000. Both hospitals have an unrealized gain of $15,000 in 2012, and both have an additional gain of $5,000 in 2013. The $5,000 gain in 2013 can be separated into two components—a realized gain of $20,000 and a decrease in the unrealized gain of $15,000. The governmental hospital would carry the investment at fair value and report both the unrealized and the realized gain in a single account called Net realized and unrealized gains and losses on investments. It would make the following entries to record the transactions:

Investments	15,000	
Revenues—net realized and unrealized gains and losses on investments		15,000
To record unrealized gain on investments in 2012.		
Cash	120,000	
Investments		115,000
Revenues—net realized and unrealized gains and losses on investments		5,000
To record gain on sale of investments in 2013.		

The governmental hospital would report the investment revenue as nonoperating revenue in its operating statement.

The not-for-profit hospital would carry the investment at original cost and use an Investment valuation account to record the adjustment to fair value. It would also use separate accounts for the unrealized gain and the realized gain. It would make the following journal entries:

Investment valuation account	15,000	
Unrestricted revenue—change in net unrealized gains and losses on investments		15,000
To record unrealized gain on investments in 2012.		
Cash	120,000	
Unrestricted revenue—realized gain on investments		20,000
Investments		100,000
Unrestricted revenue—change in net unrealized gains and losses on investments	15,000	
Investment valuation account		15,000
To record realized gain on investments and reverse unrealized gain in 2013.		

For financial reporting purposes, the not-for-profit hospital would add the $15,000 balance in the Investment valuation account to the Investments account in order to report investments at fair value at the end of 2012. It would report the $15,000 unrealized gain below Excess of revenues over expenses. In 2013, the realized gain of $20,000 would be included with other investment income and reported above Excess of revenues over expenses. The negative $15,000 net change in unrealized gains and losses would be reported below that caption. Despite the different presentation methods, the net effect for both hospitals is to increase net assets by $15,000 in 2012 and by $5,000 in 2013.

Other Revenues, Gains, and Operating Support

Hospitals may also derive revenues and gains from services and activities other than services to patients and investing. Other sources of revenue and gains include educational program fees (including tuition for schools), sales of medical and pharmaceutical supplies to doctors and others, parking fees, cafeteria sales, and gift shop sales. Contributions also provide a source of operating support for hospital activities. For analytical purposes, other forms of revenue, gains, and support are reported in captions separate from net patient service revenue and premium revenue.

Accountants sometimes make a fine distinction between revenues and gains. Revenues are inflows from delivering goods, providing services, or performing other activities that constitute the hospital's ongoing major or central operations. Gains are increases in net assets from a hospital's peripheral or incidental transactions. An activity peripheral to one hospital might be a normal, ongoing activity of another. Depending on materiality of individual items, revenues and gains may be aggregated as Other revenues for reporting purposes.

PARKING AND OTHER REVENUES OR GAINS Revenues received from parking fees, the cafeteria, educational programs (such as nursing school tuition), and so forth are recorded as follows (amounts assumed):

Cash	245,000	
Other receivables	5,000	
Other revenues (or gains)		250,000
To record other revenues.		

CONTRIBUTIONS OF CASH AND SUPPLIES Contributions to hospitals may take the form of unrestricted or restricted cash donations, supplies and commodities (such as medicines or materials) to cover the cost of charity services, and professional or nonprofessional services. Unrestricted contributions are recorded as other revenues or gains, measured at fair value. Restricted contributions are discussed later in this chapter.

Contributions received by not-for-profit hospitals are accounted for and reported in accordance with FASB ASC Topic 958, as discussed in Chapter 12. Contributions received by governmental hospitals are accounted for and reported in accordance with GASB standards for voluntary nonexchange transactions, as described in GASB Statement No. 33. For example, a governmental hospital should recognize the fair value of donated commodities as revenue in the period when all eligibility requirements are met, which is usually in the period when the commodities are received.

To illustrate, assume a private organization makes an unrestricted cash donation of $100,000 and medicines having a fair value of $75,000 to both a not-for-profit hospital and a governmental hospital. Both hospitals would report both donations as revenues on receipt of the contributions. The not-for-profit hospital would report the contributions as increases in unrestricted net assets (other revenue), and the governmental hospital would report them as nonoperating revenue:

Cash	100,000	
Other revenue (or gains)—unrestricted support		100,000
To record receipt of unrestricted cash donation.		
Inventory—medicines and drugs	75,000	
Other revenue (or gains)—donated commodities		75,000
To record receipt of medicines at fair value.		

CONTRIBUTED SERVICES   Services donated to not-for-profit hospitals are accounted for based on the criteria set forth in FASB ASC Topic 958, discussed in Chapter 12. For example, if doctors and nurses donated professional services having a fair value of $10,000 to a not-for-profit hospital and the services would typically need to be purchased, the following entry would be made:

Patient care expense	10,000	
Other revenue (or gains)—donated services		10,000
To record receipt of donated services.		

If donated services do not meet the criteria discussed in Chapter 12 (i.e., if they do not require specialized skills, are not provided by individuals who possess those skills, and would not need to be purchased), the hospital should not recognize the expenses and revenues. Thus, a not-for-profit hospital should not recognize the value of many donated services that do not require specialized skills, such as moving wheelchairs and selling at gift shops.

GASB Statement No. 33 does not apply to donated services. In the absence of standards regarding donated services, governmental hospitals often do not record them. Others record them if the hospital controls the employment and duties of the donors and the services are of significant value.

EXPENSES

Operating Expenses

Expenses related to the general operation of a hospital consist of nursing and other professional services, general services, fiscal services, and administrative services. FASB ASC Subtopic 958-225 states that expenses may be reported on the face of the financial statements either by natural classification (e.g., salaries and benefits, medical supplies and drugs, insurance) or by function (e.g., patient care expense, dietary services).[4] Not-for-profit entities that report by natural classification on the face of the financial statements are required also to show expenses by functional classification in the notes. In this chapter, we illustrate expenses by functional classification. The entry used to record some of these expenses follows (amounts assumed):

Patient care expense	750,000	
Dietary services expense	50,000	
General services expense	200,000	
Administrative services expense	145,000	
Interest expense	155,000	
Cash		1,100,000
Accounts payable, salaries payable, and so on		200,000
To record certain operating expenses.		

For simplicity, we combined the recording and payment of expenses in the preceding entry, and we combined several liability items. Because we are dealing with summary journal entries that cover an entire year, this aggregation will have no effect on the results of our illustrations.

---

[4]FASB ASC 954-225-45-4.

During the year, the acquisition and use of inventory items is recorded as follows (amounts assumed):

Inventories	150,000	
Accounts payable		150,000
To record purchase of inventory.		

Patient care expense	70,000	
Dietary services expense	50,000	
Administrative services expense	20,000	
Inventories		140,000
To record use of inventory.		

Because full accrual accounting is used for hospitals, items of property, plant, and equipment are recorded as assets when acquired and are depreciated over their useful lives. The entry to record this expense is as follows (amounts assumed):

Depreciation expense	200,000	
Accumulated depreciation—plant and equipment		200,000
To record depreciation for the year.		

Medical Malpractice Claims

Settlements and judgments on medical malpractice claims constitute a potential major expense for hospitals. Whether expenses and liabilities need to be recognized on malpractice claims depends on whether risk has been transferred by the hospital to third-party insurance companies or to public entity risk pools.

FASB ASC Subtopic 450-20 and GASB Statement No. 10, "Accounting and Financial Reporting for Risk Financing and Related Insurance Issues," provide similar guidance regarding medical malpractice claims. The basic rule is this: If risk of loss has not been transferred to an external third party, expenses must be recognized and liabilities reported if it is probable that a loss has been incurred and the amount of the loss can be reasonably estimated.

The basic rule applies whether or not claims are known for incidents occurring before the balance sheet date. These claims are called incurred but not reported (IBNR) claims. An estimate must be made for losses on IBNR claims if it is probable that claims will be asserted and losses can be reasonably estimated. Historical experience of both the hospital and the industry may be used in estimating the probability of IBNR claims.

Estimates of losses from malpractice claims may be based on a case-by-case review of all claims or by applying historical experience regarding losses to outstanding claims (e.g., the ratio of settlement amounts to claimed amounts) or both. For example, if an uninsured hospital has 10 medical malpractice claims aggregating $1,000,000 and historical experience shows that claims have been settled for an average of 30 percent of the amount claimed, the hospital should accrue an expense and a liability for $300,000.

What if one patient has filed a claim for $500,000 and negotiations between the attorneys, though not complete, indicate that the claim probably can be settled for an amount within the range of $150,000 to $300,000? For that situation, the basic rule is this: If it is probable that a loss has occurred but analysis shows that the amount of loss is within a range of amounts, the most likely amount within the range should be accrued as an expense. If no amount in the range is more likely than any other, the minimum amount in the range should

Reporting on Medical Malpractice Claims

Risks regarding medical malpractice claims are generally transferred to third-party insurers by means of claims-made policies. A claims-made policy covers losses from claims that have been asserted or filed against the policyholder during the policy period, regardless of whether the events occurred during the current or any previous period in which the policyholder was insured. Such a policy, however, does not insure the policyholder for incidents not reported to the insurer. Therefore, the hospital needs to make an accrual in its financial statements for incurred but not reported (IBNR) claims. To illustrate, the Geneva Valley Hospital Center might make the following disclosure on medical malpractice claims:

> The Hospital maintains a commercial claims-made policy for its medical malpractice insurance. The policy does not represent a transfer of risk for claims and incidents incurred but not reported (IBNR) to the insurance carrier. Therefore, the Hospital has recorded an estimated malpractice liability related to IBNR of approximately $2.9 million and $2.6 million as of December 31, 2012, and December 31, 2011, respectively.

be accrued, and the potential additional loss should be disclosed in the notes if a reasonable possibility exists for loss greater than the amount accrued. As a practical matter, care should be taken in presenting this disclosure in order to preserve the hospital's ability to negotiate an appropriate settlement.

For financial reporting purposes, amounts accrued that are expected to be paid within 1 year after the date of the financial statements should be reported as current liabilities, and the rest of the accrual should be reported as noncurrent. Hospitals should also disclose their programs of malpractice insurance coverage and their basis for recording accruals.

OTHER TRANSACTIONS

Contributions Received by a Not-for-Profit Hospital's Foundation

As a means of obtaining contributions, a not-for-profit hospital may establish a separate but financially interrelated fund-raising foundation. A financial interrelationship exists if the hospital is able to influence the foundation's operating and financial decisions and has an ongoing economic interest in the foundation's net assets. A hospital has the ability to influence the foundation's operating and financial decisions if, for example, the foundation's charter limits its activities to those that are beneficial to the hospital or the hospital has considerable representation on the foundation's governing board.

Under those circumstances, the not-for-profit hospital would report in its financial statements its interest in the foundation's net assets and adjust that interest for the hospital's share of the change in the foundation's net assets. (This is known as the "equity method" of accounting.) Assume, for example, that a hospital established a foundation on January 2 for the sole purpose of raising funds on behalf of the hospital. During the year, the foundation obtained contributions of $900,000. Of this amount, $100,000 was unrestricted, and $800,000 was restricted by the donors to acquisition of new equipment. At the hospital's request, the foundation transferred cash of $280,000 to the hospital, consisting of $30,000 that was unrestricted and $250,000 that was restricted for equipment acquisition. The hospital used the restricted cash immediately to acquire equipment. The hospital would make the following journal entries:

Interest in Hospital Foundation	900,000	
Unrestricted gains—change in interest in net assets of Hospital Foundation		100,000
Temporarily restricted gains—change in interest in net assets of Hospital Foundation		800,000
To record change in interest in net assets of Hospital Foundation.		
Cash, restricted for capital acquisition	250,000	
Cash	30,000	
Interest in Hospital Foundation		280,000
To record receipt of cash from Hospital Foundation.		
Equipment	250,000	
Cash, restricted for capital acquisition		250,000
To record acquisition of equipment.		
Temporarily restricted net asset reclassifications out—satisfaction of equipment acquisition restrictions	250,000	
Unrestricted net asset reclassifications in—satisfaction of equipment acquisition restrictions		250,000
To record reclassification of net assets.		

For financial reporting purposes, Interest in Hospital Foundation is an asset account. Temporarily restricted gains—change in interest in net assets is reported as increases in temporarily restricted net assets in the statement of changes in net assets. And Unrestricted gains—change in interest in net assets is reported as increases both in the statement of operations and in the unrestricted net assets section of the statement of changes in net assets.

Governmental Hospital Foundations

Governmental hospitals also may establish separate but financially interrelated fund-raising foundations, particularly when the hospital is part of a state college or university. GASB standards, as applied to a governmental hospital's financial statements, provide that a legally separate, tax-exempt organization should be reported (in a separate column) as a component unit of the hospital if *all* of these criteria are met: (a) the economic resources received or held by the separate organization are entirely or almost entirely for the direct benefit of the hospital; (b) the hospital is entitled to, or has the ability to otherwise access, a majority of the economic resources received or held by the organization; and (c) the economic resources received or held by the organization are significant to the hospital.[5] The presentation of a legally separate foundation as a component unit of a governmental hospital is illustrated in Tables 13-5 through 13-7 later in this chapter.

---

[5]GASB Statement No. 39, "Determining Whether Certain Organizations Are Component Units," par. 5.

Transactions Creating Assets Limited as to Use

Not-for-profit hospital balance sheets often show resources as "assets limited as to use" or "assets whose use is limited." These are designations of unrestricted resources that have been set aside either as a result of a contractual agreement with an external party other than a donor or as a result of an internal decision by a hospital's governing board. For example,

- To secure payment of debt service, a hospital that sells revenue bonds may be required by the bond agreement to maintain a deposit with a trustee equal to, say, 1 year's debt service. Or a hospital may be required by a third-party payer to fund depreciation on certain capital assets.
- A hospital's governing board may decide to set aside funds for a specific project or function, such as a special training program or a capital acquisition. Although these resources have been set aside, the segregation has no legal consequence because the board can readily reverse its decision.

To illustrate how the resources are set aside, assume a not-for-profit hospital sells revenue bonds for $10,000,000. From the proceeds of the sale, $800,000 is forwarded to a trustee to hold in escrow until the hospital makes final payment of debt service on the bonds. The hospital would make the following journal entry:

Cash	9,200,000	
Cash with trustee	800,000	
Bonds payable		10,000,000
To record proceeds from sale of bonds and cash held in escrow by trustee.		

If the hospital's governing board formally sets aside $750,000 of existing investments to create a fund to modernize equipment, it would make the following entry:

Investments—board-designated for equipment	750,000	
Investments		750,000
To record board designation of resources for equipment modernization.		

ACCOUNTING FOR TRANSACTIONS WITH RESTRICTIONS WHEN USING FUNDS

Many not-for-profit and governmental hospitals use fund accounting for internal accounting and managerial control purposes. These funds are not included in the external financial reports of governmental hospitals. The FASB requires not-for-profit hospitals to report externally on the entity as a whole, with net assets and changes in net assets classified as unrestricted, temporarily restricted, and permanently restricted; however, not-for-profit hospitals may provide disaggregated information by fund groups in external financial reports.[6]

When hospitals use funds for internal purposes, the funds are categorized in two groups: the General Fund and restricted funds. Resources and liabilities included within a hospital's General Fund fall into four broad categories:

---

[6]FASB ASC 958-205-45-3.

- *Operating resources* are assets and liabilities associated with the day-to-day hospital activities.
- *Assets limited as to use* are resources set aside internally by the hospital's governing board or in accordance with an agreement with an external party other than a donor or grantor.
- *Agency resources* are resources held by a hospital that belong to other persons, such as doctors and patients.
- *Plant resources* are the property, plant, and equipment used by a hospital in its general operations, and any related liabilities.

Restricted funds are used to account for resources that must be used in compliance with the terms of agreements, like those related to donor gifts or grants. Restricted funds are used only when an external limitation is placed on the use of resources and the resources are not related to a bond agreement or third-party reimbursement. The most common types of restricted funds used by hospitals are these:

- *Specific Purpose Funds* are resources that are restricted by donors or grantors for specific operating purposes, such as a gift that must be used for cancer research.
- *Plant Replacement and Expansion Funds* are resources contributed by outsiders that can be used only to replace or expand the existing plant. The assets acquired from those resources are recorded in the General Fund.
- *Endowment Funds* may be either permanent or term. A permanent endowment is one in which the donor requires that the principal be maintained in perpetuity. A term endowment is one in which the donor requires that the principal be maintained for a specific period or the donor imposes other restrictions. After the term restrictions have been satisfied, the principal can be unrestricted or restricted. Income from Endowment Funds may be unrestricted (and recorded in the General Fund) or restricted (and recorded in one of the other restricted funds).

Except for the part of the illustration concerning hospital foundations, the transactions discussed in the earlier part of this chapter dealt with a hospital's basic operating activities. Therefore, if fund accounting is used, those transactions are accounted for primarily in the General Fund and are not subject to restrictions. But hospitals may receive restricted resources; for example, a donor may stipulate that a gift be used only for a particular purpose. These restrictions need to be recorded in the internal accounting records to ensure management compliance. They also need to be reported in the financial statements so users are not misled regarding the availability of these resources for the hospital's general purposes.

The discussion of transactions with restrictions is complicated by two factors:

- The notion of *restricted,* as used in not-for-profit *fund accounting,* is broader than the FASB definition of the term for financial reporting. Specific Purpose Funds, for example, can include both unrestricted and temporarily restricted resources because they can include both gifts contributed by donors and grants made by resource providers other than donors.
- The GASB defines the term *restricted* differently then the FASB. The GASB does not distinguish between temporarily restricted and permanently restricted, and it does not limit restricted net assets to those subject to donor-imposed restrictions.

Because of these complications, we discuss accounting for transactions with restrictions by not-for-profit hospitals separately from governmental hospitals.

Not-for-Profit Hospital Accounting for Restrictions

GENERAL RULES The general rules for not-for-profit hospital accounting within each of the funds are similar to those discussed in Chapter 12 for other not-for-profit organizations. The rules are as follows:

- All donor-restricted contributions are recorded as either temporarily or permanently restricted revenues or gains when received.
- When temporarily restricted resources are released from restriction, not-for-profit hospitals record a reclassification out of temporarily restricted resources and a reclassification in to unrestricted net assets.
- Expenses resulting from use of the reclassified resources are reported as decreases in unrestricted net assets.

SPECIFIC PURPOSE FUNDS Specific Purpose Funds are used to account for resources that are restricted for specific operating purposes. Restrictions on their use are temporary, expiring either with the passage of time or by fulfillment of the purpose stipulated by the donor. Assume a not-for-profit hospital receives a $500,000 gift, to be used specifically for research into methods of counseling individuals who have become addicted to drugs. Later, the hospital incurs $25,000 in research program expenses. The entries to record those transactions and the funds used to record them are as follows:

Entries to accounts for Specific Purpose Funds	Cash	500,000	
	Temporarily restricted support—contributions		500,000
	To record contribution for research.		
	Temporarily restricted asset reclassifications out— net assets released from restriction, used for operations	25,000	
	Cash		25,000
	To record payment of research program expenses and net assets released from restriction.		
Entry to accounts for General Fund	Research program expenses	25,000	
	Unrestricted asset reclassifications in—net assets released from restriction, used for operations		25,000
	To record research program expenses and net assets released from restriction.		

PLANT REPLACEMENT AND EXPANSION FUNDS Plant Replacement and Expansion Funds accumulate resources from donors or grantors that can be used only to replace or expand existing plant assets. Because the hospital plant is reported in the General Fund, Plant Replacement and Expansion Funds contain only *financial resources* that will be used to acquire capital resources. To illustrate, assume that Colonel Corwin donates $100,000 in cash to a not-for-profit hospital and that the gift must be used to replace existing assets. Then, $80,000 of the contribution is used to acquire equipment, causing expiration of the temporary restriction. The entries to record these transactions are as follows:

Entries to accounts for Plant Replacement and Expansion Fund	Cash	100,000	
	Temporarily restricted support—contributions		100,000
	To record Corwin gift for capital assets replacement.		
	Temporarily restricted asset reclassifications out—net assets released from restriction for purchase of equipment	80,000	
	Cash		80,000
	To record release of net assets from restriction and payment for equipment.		
Entry to accounts for General Fund	Equipment	80,000	
	Unrestricted asset reclassifications in—net assets released from restriction for purchase of equipment		80,000
	To record purchase of equipment and release of net assets from restriction.		

If fund resources are invested in marketable securities until the plant is acquired, the recording of income from the securities is determined by the restrictions, if any, placed on that income. If no restrictions are placed on the use of the investment income, it is recorded in the General Fund as unrestricted. Assume income from the securities in this illustration must be used for the same purpose as the gift itself, which is what usually occurs. If $2,000 of income accrues from investment of the Colonel Corwin gift, the investment income is recorded in the Plant Replacement and Expansion Fund as follows:

Interest receivable	2,000	
Temporarily restricted revenue—investment income		2,000
To record investment income from Colonel Corwin's gift.		

ENDOWMENT FUNDS   Endowment funds are used when a donor gives a hospital assets whose principal must be maintained intact. Income from the investment of the assets can be either restricted or unrestricted in use. Assume that Mrs. Corwin gives a hospital marketable securities with a fair market value of $500,000. The principal of the fund must be maintained in perpetuity and is, therefore, considered a permanent or pure Endowment Fund. The income from the endowment is restricted to finance the cost of cancer research. Income of $30,000 is received during the year. The entries to record those transactions are as follows:

Entry to accounts for Endowment Fund	Marketable securities	500,000	
	Permanently restricted support—contributions		500,000
	To record receipt of Mrs. Corwin's gift.		
Entry to accounts for Specific Purpose Fund	Cash	30,000	
	Temporarily restricted revenue—investment income		30,000
	To record investment income from Mrs. Corwin's gift to be used for cancer research.		

Note: In the preceding entry, investment income was recorded directly in the Specific Purpose Fund. To provide control over the investment income, some prefer to record the revenue initially in the Endowment Fund and establish a "due to" the Specific Purpose Fund. When the resources of the Specific Purpose Fund are used to conduct research, the expenses are reported in the General Fund, and the temporarily restricted net assets are released from restriction. This journal record is made with reclassification entries, as shown in the journal entries on page 506.

If the contribution specified that the income from the endowment could be used for any purpose desired by the hospital's management, the investment income would be reported in the General Fund with a credit to Unrestricted revenue—investment income.

FINANCIAL REPORTING EFFECT   The foregoing illustrations assume the use of fund accounting for internal control purposes. For external financial reporting, however, not-for-profit hospitals must report on the entity as a whole (distinguishing among unrestricted, temporarily restricted, and permanently restricted resources), just like any other not-for-profit entity.

Donor-restricted contributions are reported in a not-for-profit hospital's second operating statement, the statement of changes in net assets, as increases in temporarily or permanently restricted net assets. Net assets released from restrictions are reported in that statement as decreases in temporarily restricted net assets. Net assets released from restrictions and used for operations and related program expenses are reported on the statement of operations (see again the skeletal outline on page 491) and in the statement of changes in net assets. Net assets released from restrictions (reclassification in) and used for purchase of property and equipment are also reported on both operating statements, but below the line showing Excess of revenues over expenses (see skeletal outline).

Governmental Hospital Accounting for Restrictions

GENERAL RULES   For financial reporting purposes, the GASB defines the term *restricted* differently than the FASB. The GASB requires that net assets be reported as restricted when constraints are imposed in either of these ways:

- Externally, by creditors (such as through debt covenants), grantors, contributors, or laws or regulations of other governments
- By law, through constitutional provisions or enabling legislation.[7] (*Enabling legislation*, as the term is used by the GASB, includes a legally enforceable requirement that resources be used only for the purposes stipulated in the legislation.)

Governmental hospitals engaged in business-type activities follow GASB standards for proprietary funds. Pursuant to GASB Statement No. 34, all proprietary fund revenues, including capital contributions and additions to permanent and term endowments, should be reported in the all-inclusive statement of revenues, expenses, and changes in net position.[8]

Hospital transactions accounted for in restricted funds are often what the GASB defines as *voluntary nonexchange transactions.* They include certain governmental grants and entitlements, as well as donations by nongovernmental entities, including individuals. Governmental hospitals, receiving such grants and donations should recognize revenues when all applicable eligibility requirements, including time requirements, are met.[9]

---

[7]GASB Statement No. 34, par. 34, as amended.
[8]GASB Statement No. 34, par. 101.
[9]GASB Statement No. 33, par. 21.

GASB Statement No. 33 distinguishes between time requirements and purpose restrictions. *Time requirements* specify the period when resources must be used or when use may begin. Time requirements affect revenue recognition. For example, if a hospital receives resources before it is eligible to use them, the grant or gift should be reported as an advance. *Purpose restrictions* specify the purpose for which the resources are required to be used. They do not affect revenue recognition but instead affect whether the net assets should be classified as restricted or unrestricted.

In addition to time requirements, other types of eligibility requirements affect the timing of revenue recognition. For example, a higher-level government may specify that the recipient of a hospital construction grant does not qualify for resources until allowable costs are incurred (as in the case of expenditure-driven grants). In those instances, revenues are recognized as allowable costs are incurred. Gifts received as endowments should be recognized as revenues upon receipt, provided all eligibility requirements are met.

When restricted fund resources are used for the intended purposes, expenses or assets should be recorded in the General Fund. The credit part of the entry to record these transactions in the General Fund should be labeled "Amounts released from restriction," which is narrower and, hence, more descriptive than the term *transfers.*

ILLUSTRATION OF PRIVATE DONATION WITH PURPOSE RESTRICTION   A corporation makes a donation to a governmental hospital, stipulating that the donation must be used solely for the purpose of training nurses. For this voluntary nonexchange transaction, the hospital should recognize the entire amount as revenue (reported as nonoperating revenues) when the gift is received. The resulting net assets should be reported as restricted until the purpose restriction (training nurses) is fulfilled. If $50,000 is donated and $20,000 of that amount is used, the following entries would be made to record the transaction:

Entries to accounts for Specific Purpose Funds	Cash	50,000	
	Restricted revenue (nonoperating)— contributions		50,000
	To record contribution for nurse training.		
	Amounts released from restriction to General Fund	20,000	
	Cash		20,000
	To record fulfillment of purpose restriction for nurse training.		
Entry to accounts for General Fund	Training expenses	20,000	
	Amounts released from restriction from Specific Purpose Funds		20,000
	To record research expenses financial by restricted contribution.		

ILLUSTRATION OF CONSTRUCTION GRANT WITH ELIGIBILITY REQUIREMENT   A federal agency makes a cash grant of $500,000 to finance a governmental hospital's acquisition of special equipment. The grant agreement contains an eligibility requirement; namely, the hospital does not qualify for the grant without first incurring allowable costs. In this situation, the hospital should report the grant as an advance until it incurs expenditures under the grant. If the hospital spends $200,000 to acquire equipment and sends an invoice to the federal agency for that amount, it would make the following entries:

Entries to accounts for Plant Replacement and Expansion Fund	Cash	500,000	
	Advance received for equipment		500,000
	To record receipt of grant for equipment acquisition.		
	Amounts released from restriction to General Fund	200,000	
	Cash		200,000
	To record capital expenditure.		
	Advance received for equipment	200,000	
	Revenue—capital contributions		200,000
	To record revenue recognition.		
Entry to accounts for General Fund	Equipment	200,000	
	Amounts released from restriction from Plant Replacement and Expansion Fund		200,000
	To record purchase of equipment under federal grant.		

If the hospital does not receive an advance payment from the federal agency, it makes no entry until it incurs expenditures under the grant. When it incurs expenditures, it should record both receivables and revenues.

FINANCIAL REPORTING EFFECT   Although the preceding illustrations assume the use of fund accounting for internal purposes, governmental hospitals prepare external financial reports on the entity as a whole, as illustrated in Tables 13-5 and 13-6 (pages 515 and 516). Therefore, when the hospital prepares its operating statement, amounts recorded in the funds as "released from restriction" are eliminated against each other. In the first illustration, the entire $50,000 contribution would be reported as nonoperating revenue, as shown in Table 13-6. At year-end, the unspent portion of the contribution ($30,000) would be reported as restricted net assets. In the second illustration, the $200,000 of recognized revenue should be reported as capital contributions after Income before other revenues and expenses, as shown in the skeletal outline in Chapter 7, page 231.

FINANCIAL STATEMENTS

There are many similarities in the financial statements prepared by not-for-profit and governmental hospitals, but there are also some differences. The differences result from the differing standards of the FASB and the GASB. The financial statements of both not-for-profit and governmental hospitals focus on the hospital as a whole, rather than on individual funds. Not-for-profit hospitals report changes in net assets separately for unrestricted, temporarily restricted, and permanently restricted funds and emphasize a performance indicator within the changes in unrestricted net assets. Governmental hospitals prepare an all-inclusive statement of revenues, expenses, and changes in net position.

    Not-for-profit hospital financial statements are illustrated in Tables 13-1 through 13-4. These statements are derived from the actual financial statements of a hospital in New York State.

TABLE 13-1 Balance Sheets—Not-for-Profit Hospital

Geneva Valley Hospital Center
Balance Sheets
December 31, 2012 and 2011

	2012	2011
Assets		
Current assets:		
Cash and cash equivalents	$ 9,544,764	$10,524,715
Investments	17,665,267	9,570,503
Patient accounts receivable, less allowance for uncollectible accounts of approximately $4,240,000 in 2012 and $4,880,000 in 2011	12,317,650	10,657,163
Other receivables	1,516,119	576,110
Supplies and prepaid expenses	1,744,525	1,669,344
Total current assets	42,788,325	32,997,835
Interest in Foundation of Geneva Valley Hospital Center	5,947,723	5,313,105
Assets whose use is limited—externally restricted	6,692,714	7,064,422
Long-term investments	1,674,619	669,163
Property, plant, and equipment, net	32,436,683	30,516,903
Other assets	1,785,804	1,231,723
Total assets	$91,325,868	$77,793,151
Liabilities and Net Assets		
Current liabilities:		
Current portion of long-term debt	$ 645,349	$ 639,238
Current portion of capital lease obligations	904,412	1,421,699
Accounts payable and accrued expenses	6,419,826	6,852,313
Accrued salaries and benefits	6,089,351	5,222,043
Estimated payable to third-party payers	1,761,172	694,000
Total current liabilities	15,820,110	14,829,293
Long-term debt	17,321,911	18,120,671
Capital lease obligations	1,839,810	1,722,328
Estimated payable to third-party payers, malpractice and other liabilities	14,883,123	12,857,742
Total liabilities	49,864,954	47,530,034
Net assets:		
Unrestricted	34,245,544	24,280,849
Temporarily restricted	5,540,751	5,313,105
Permanently restricted	1,674,619	669,163
Total net assets	41,460,914	30,263,117
Total liabilities and net assets	$91,325,868	$77,793,151

TABLE 13-2   Statements of Operations—Not-for-Profit Hospital

Geneva Valley Hospital Center
Statements of Operations
Years Ended December 31, 2012 and 2011

	2012	2011
Operating revenues:		
Net patient service revenue	$89,517,295	$84,542,802
Premium revenue	2,342,573	2,415,522
Total operating revenues	91,859,868	86,958,324
Operating expenses:		
Salaries	37,531,888	34,763,509
Physician fees	1,918,099	2,001,851
Fringe benefits	7,580,312	6,995,657
Supplies and other expenses	27,366,422	28,610,259
Provision for bad debts	1,775,068	3,238,525
Interest	1,341,181	1,518,418
Depreciation and amortization	4,488,172	4,962,198
Total operating expenses	82,001,142	82,090,417
Operating gain	9,858,726	4,867,907
Investment income	806,560	554,012
Loss on transfer	(477,840)	—
Excess of revenues over expenses	10,187,446	5,421,919
Change in net unrealized gains and losses on investments	(75,897)	230,272
Net assets released from restrictions for capital expenditures	—	3,126,250
Increase in unrestricted net assets before cumulative effect of change	10,111,549	8,778,441
Cumulative effect of change in accounting principle	(146,854)	—
Increase in unrestricted net assets	$ 9,964,695	$ 8,778,441

Governmental hospital financial statements are illustrated in Tables 13-5 through 13-7. They are the recent financial statements of the Dallas County Hospital District, Texas, prepared in accordance with GASB standards for business-type activities.

Balance Sheet

Notice the following items, in particular, about the balance sheets illustrated in Tables 13-1 and 13-5:

- Current assets and current liabilities are presented separately from other assets and liabilities.
- *Assets whose use is limited* are separated from other assets, and externally imposed limitations are shown separately from internal limitations (either on the face of the statements or in the notes).
- The resources and activities of fund-raising foundations are reported differently in not-for-profit and governmental hospitals. Not-for-profit hospitals report their interests in the

TABLE 13-3 Statements of Changes in Net Assets—Not-for-Profit Hospital

Geneva Valley Hospital Center
Statements of Changes in Net Assets
Years Ended December 31, 2012 and 2011

	Unrestricted Net Assets	Temporarily Restricted Net Assets	Permanently Restricted Net Assets	Total Net Assets
Balances, December 31, 2010	$15,502,408	$7,433,741	$ 669,163	$23,605,312
Changes in net assets				
Excess of revenues over expenses	5,421,919	—	—	5,421,919
Net assets released from restrictions for capital expenditures	3,126,250	(3,126,250)	—	—
Change in net unrealized gains and losses on investments	230,272	—	—	230,272
Change in interest in net assets of the Foundation of Geneva Valley Hospital Center	—	1,005,614	—	1,005,614
Total changes in net assets	8,778,441	(2,120,636)	—	6,657,805
Balances, December 31, 2011	24,280,849	5,313,105	669,163	30,263,117
Changes in net assets				
Excess of revenues over expenses	10,187,446	—	—	10,187,446
Cumulative effect of change in accounting principle	(146,854)	—	—	(146,854)
Change in net unrealized gains and losses on investments	(75,897)	—	—	(75,897)
Endowment transfer	—	—	1,005,456	1,005,456
Change in interest in net assets of the Foundation of Geneva Valley Hospital Center	—	227,646	—	227,646
Total changes in net assets	9,964,695	227,646	1,005,456	11,197,797
Balances, December 31, 2012	$34,245,544	$5,540,751	$1,674,619	$41,460,914

foundation's net assets and changes in net assets by recording them using the equity method of accounting described on page 502. Governmental hospitals report on the resources of their foundations by incorporating the foundations as component units in separate columns of the financial statements, consistent with the component unit methods described in Chapter 10.

• *Net assets* of Geneva Valley Hospital Center are separated among unrestricted, temporarily restricted, and permanently restricted, in accordance with FASB standards, discussed in Chapter 12. The Dallas County Hospital District's net position is separated among net investment in capital assets, restricted, or unrestricted, in accordance with GASB standards, as discussed in Chapter 7. Major categories of restricted net position should be shown on the face of the statements.

TABLE 13-4	Statements of Cash Flows—Not-for-Profit Hospital

Geneva Valley Hospital Center
Statements of Cash Flows
Years Ended December 31, 2012 and 2011

	2012	2011
Cash Flows from Operating Activities		
Change in net assets	$11,197,797	$ 6,657,805
Adjustments to reconcile change in net assets to cash provided by operating activities:		
Depreciation and amortization	4,488,172	4,962,198
Provision for bad debts	1,775,068	3,238,525
Realized losses and change in unrealized gains and losses on investments	(69,703)	(212,979)
Change in interest in net assets of the Foundation of Geneva Valley Hospital Center	(227,646)	(1,005,614)
Cumulative effect of a change in accounting principle	146,854	—
Endowment transfer	(1,005,456)	—
Changes in operating assets and liabilities:		
Patient accounts receivable	(3,435,555)	(5,775,078)
Other receivables, supplies and prepaid expenses, other assets	(1,569,271)	1,711,353
Accounts payable and accrued expenses	(432,487)	171,185
Accrued salaries and benefits	867,308	714,963
Estimated payable to third-party payers, malpractice, and other liabilities	2,979,235	3,975,848
Net change in due from Foundation of the Geneva Valley Hospital Center	(406,972)	85,339
Net cash provided by operating activities	14,307,344	14,523,545
Cash Flows Used in Investing Activities		
Acquisition of property, plant, and equipment	(4,302,565)	(2,085,717)
Net purchase of investments and assets whose use is limited	(9,610,279)	(3,403,170)
Net cash used in investing activities	(13,912,844)	(5,488,887)
Cash Flows Used in Financing Activities		
Principal payments on long-term debt and capital lease obligations	(2,379,907)	(2,421,721)
Proceeds from endowment transfer	1,005,456	—
Net cash used in financing activities	(1,374,451)	(2,421,721)
Net (decrease) increase in cash and cash equivalents	(979,951)	6,612,937
Cash and cash equivalents at beginning of year	10,524,715	3,911,778
Cash and cash equivalents at end of year	$ 9,544,764	$10,524,715

TABLE 13-5 Balance Sheet—Governmental Hospital

Dallas County Hospital District
Parkland Health and Hospital System
(A Component Unit of Dallas County, Texas)
Balance Sheet
As of September 30, 2011
(amounts in thousands)

	Hospital and Health Plan	Foundation
Assets		
Current assets:		
Cash and cash equivalents	$ 108,763	$ 6,990
Short-term investments	—	1,374
Assets limited as to use	20,182	—
Ad valorem taxes receivable, less allowance for uncollectible taxes of $17,290	6,277	—
Patient accounts receivable, less allowance for uncollectible accounts	85,971	—
Due from Parkland Foundation	567	—
Other receivables	59,261	1,119
Inventories and other assets	11,885	—
Total current assets	292,906	9,483
Capital assets—net	411,715	—
Long-term investments	201,432	30,579
Assets limited as to use	1,056,938	—
Other noncurrent assets	25,048	20,978
Total	$1,988,039	$61,040
Liabilities and Net Position		
Current liabilities:		
Accounts payable and accrued expenses	$ 163,611	$11,352
Due to Parkland Hospital	—	567
Due to third-party reimbursement programs	6,025	—
Interest payable	4,880	—
Other current liabilities	22,907	—
Total current liabilities	197,423	11,919
Other long-term liabilities	15,099	—
Long-term debt	707,159	—
Total liabilities	919,681	11,919
Commitments and contingencies		
Net position:		
Net investment in capital assets	387,403	—
Restricted	—	47,057
Unrestricted	680,955	2,064
Total net position	1,068,358	49,121
Total	$1,988,039	$61,040

Source: Adapted from a recent annual report of the Dallas County Hospital District, Texas.

TABLE 13-6	Operating Statement—Governmental Hospital

Dallas County Hospital District
Parkland Health and Hospital System
(A Component Unit of Dallas County, Texas)
Statement of Revenues, Expenses, and Changes in Net Position
For the Year Ended September 30, 2011
(amounts in thousands)

	Hospital and Health Plan	Foundation
Operating revenues:		
Net patient service revenue	$ 475,384	—
Premiums	437,862	—
Other, net	237,804	$11,472
Total operating revenues	1,151,050	11,472
Operating expenses:		
Salaries, wages, and benefits	655,339	—
Purchased medical services	112,922	—
Supplies and other	230,434	5,541
Pharmaceuticals	92,166	—
Claims	400,872	—
Depreciation and amortization	53,756	—
Total operating expenses	1,545,489	5,541
Operating (loss) income	(394,439)	5,931
Nonoperating revenues (expenses):		
Ad valorem tax support	445,902	—
Grants and contributions	19,119	—
Investment income	71,776	—
Interest expense	(36,094)	—
Total nonoperating revenues and expenses	500,703	—
Change in net position	106,264	5,931
Net position—beginning of year	962,094	43,190
Net position—end of year	$1,068,358	$49,121

Source: Adapted from the September 30, 2011, annual report of the Dallas County Hospital District, Texas.

Statements of Operations and Changes in Net Assets

NOT-FOR-PROFIT HOSPITALS FASB ASC Subtopic 958-205 permits differing formats for not-for-profit operating statements, allowing entities to report information in what they consider to be the most meaningful way to financial statement users. However, FASB ASC Topic 954 requires hospitals to present two operating statements: One, called the statement of operations, covers only changes in unrestricted net assets and includes the details of revenues and expenses that constitute a *performance indicator*. The other, called a statement of changes in net assets, covers the changes in net assets for all three net asset classifications. Hospitals are permitted to combine the two statements.

TABLE 13-7 Cash Flows Statement—Governmental Hospital

Dallas County Hospital District
Parkland Health and Hospital System
(A Component Unit of Dallas County, Texas)
Combined Statement of Cash Flows
For the Year Ended September 30, 2011
(amounts in thousands)

Cash flows from operating activities:	
Receipts from third-party payers and patients	$ 908,280
Payments to suppliers	(852,771)
Payments to employees	(651,748)
Other receipts	266,842
Net cash (used in) operating activities	(329,397)
Cash flows from capital and related financing activities:	
Purchases of capital assets	(121,329)
Bond reimbursement for new hospital expenditures	33,749
Interest paid	(35,573)
Build America Bonds subsidy	12,117
Net cash (used in) capital and related financing activities	(111,036)
Cash flows from noncapital financing activities:	
Ad valorem taxes	447,860
Grants and contributions	18,842
Net cash provided by noncapital financing activities	466,702
Cash flows from investing activities:	
Interest received	31,133
Investments purchased	(1,850,720)
Investment maturities	1,772,201
Designated assets	(17,635)
Net cash (used in) investing activities	(65,021)
Decrease in cash and cash equivalents	(38,752)
Cash and cash equivalents—beginning of year	147,515
Cash and cash equivalents—end of year	$ 108,763
Reconciliation of operating income to net cash provided by operating activities:	
Operating loss	$ (394,439)
Adjustments to reconcile operating loss to net cash used in operating activities:	
Depreciation and amortization	53,756
Loss on disposal of assets	530
Changes in operating assets and liabilities:	
Patient accounts receivable	(7,658)
Other receivables, inventories, and other assets	26,711
Accounts payable and accrued expenses	(3,827)
Due to third-party reimbursement programs	(247)
Other current liabilities	(5,271)
Net pension asset	(838)
Other long-term liabilities	1,886
Net cash used in operating activities	$ (329,397)

Source: Adapted from the September 30, 2011, annual report of the Dallas County Hospital District, Texas.

To emphasize the importance of the performance indicator within the statement of operations, FASB ASC 954-225-45-4 calls for it to be clearly labeled, using terms such as *revenues over expenses, revenues and gains over expenses and losses, earned income,* or *performance earnings.* The performance indicator should be presented in a statement that also presents the total changes in unrestricted net assets. To accomplish this purpose, changes in net assets other than those that affect the performance indicator are reported in the operating statement below the performance indicator line.

To illustrate, turn to Table 13-2 on page 512. First, notice that this operating statement relates only to unrestricted net assets. Transactions affecting temporarily restricted and permanently restricted net assets are not included in a hospital's statement of operations, except to the extent those net assets have been released from restrictions into unrestricted net assets.

Next, notice that patient service revenue is Geneva Valley Hospital Center's main source of revenue. As discussed previously, Net patient service revenue is the excess of gross billings for services less provisions for charity care, contractual adjustments with third-party payers, and other similar items the hospital does not expect to collect. These adjustments do not include a provision for bad debts.

Other revenue is generated by normal day-to-day activities, other than patient care, that are related to the organization's central operations. Notice that in Table 13-2, all resource inflows that enter into the performance indicator, which is the line captioned Excess of revenues over expenses, are reported under Operating revenues, except for investment income. Investment income, which is part of the performance indicator, could also be reported as part of Other revenue.

Notice also that the performance indicator, *Excess of revenues over expenses,* is separated from other factors causing the net increase in unrestricted net assets. Consider the difference in the transactions affecting the performance indicator from those presented below that line.

- **Change in net unrealized gains and losses on investments.** As described earlier in this chapter, with regard to their unrestricted net assets, not-for-profit hospitals report realized gains and losses on investments separately from unrealized gains and losses on securities other than trading securities. Realized gains and losses are included with investment income as part of the measure of operating performance, while unrealized gains and losses are shown below that measure. The notes show that interest income represents most of Geneva Valley Hospital Center's investment income.

- **Net assets released from restrictions for capital expenditures.** Part of the resources held by Geneva Valley Hospital Center's Foundation were used to acquire capital assets in 2011, resulting in reclassifying the net assets from temporarily restricted to unrestricted. Because the resources were used to acquire capital assets, the reclassification was reported *below* the measure of operating performance. If Geneva Valley Hospital Center had net assets released from restrictions and used for *operations,* the reclassification in would have been shown as operating revenues and, therefore, as part of the performance measure. Why the difference? The answer lies in the matching principle of accounting. Reclassified net assets used for operations can be matched with related expenses. But only the current year's depreciation is shown as an expense when reclassified net assets are used to acquire capital assets; showing the entire amount released from restrictions as part of the performance indicator would overstate the hospital's performance.

The statement of changes in net assets is a summary reconciliation of the beginning and ending net assets of each of the three net asset classifications. Table 13-3 illustrates the statement of changes in net assets. Notice that, for the unrestricted net assets, the details constituting the performance indicator Excess of revenues over expenses, which were in the operating statement, are not repeated in the statement of changes in net assets. Notice also the following:

- For 2011, the amount shown as Net assets released from restrictions for capital expenditures ($3,126,250) under Temporarily Restricted Net Assets is the same as the amount reported as a reclassification in to Unrestricted Net Assets.
- For 2012 and 2011, Temporarily Restricted Net Assets were increased by a change in the interest in the net assets of Geneva Valley Hospital Center's foundation.

GOVERNMENTAL HOSPITALS Governmental hospitals report in accordance with the GASB's standards for proprietary funds. GASB Statement No. 34 requires that the proprietary fund operating statement take the form of an all-inclusive statement of revenues, expenses, and changes in fund net position, as illustrated in Chapter 7 (page 231). No provision is made in GASB Statement No. 34 for separate "statements of operations" for unrestricted funds and "statements of changes in net assets" covering both unrestricted and restricted funds.

The statement of revenues, expenses, and changes in fund net position is required to distinguish between operating and nonoperating revenues and expenses and to provide a separate subtotal for operating income. The GASB does not define *operating* and *nonoperating*, but it allows each government to establish and disclose definitions appropriate to the activity being reported. However, revenues from capital contributions, additions to the principal of permanent and term endowments, special and extraordinary items, and transfers must be reported separately, after nonoperating revenues and expenses.

Table 13-6 illustrates a statement of revenues, expenses, and changes in fund net position for a governmental hospital. Notice the captions of the various subtotals and the items constituting nonoperating income and expenses, such as interest on long-term debt. If present, capital contributions and endowment contributions would be reported toward the end of the statement, just before Change in net position. Because governmental hospital operating statements are all-inclusive, covering both unrestricted and restricted resources, reporting of amounts released from restrictions is not necessary.

Statement of Cash Flows

Tables 13-4 and 13-7 illustrate the cash flow statements of not-for-profit and governmental hospitals, respectively. Cash flow statements describe the causes of increases and decreases in cash from the beginning of the year to the end of the year. Notice that the end-of-year amounts for cash and cash equivalents, shown in the last line of the cash flow statements, are the same as the amounts reported for cash and cash equivalents on the balance sheets.

Because of differences in the standards adopted by the FASB and the GASB, several major differences can be found in the details of these two statements.

1. The not-for-profit hospital cash flow statement is presented using the indirect method, whereas the governmental cash flow statement is presented using the direct method.
2. The not-for-profit hospital cash flow statement presents three classifications of cash flows: operating activities, investing activities, and financing activities. The governmental hospital cash flow statement provides four classifications: operating activities, capital and related financing activities, noncapital financing activities, and investing activities.
3. The starting point for the operating activity portion of the not-for-profit cash flow statement is the change in net assets. Notice that the first line of Geneva Valley Hospital Center's

2012 statement is $11,197,797, which is the increase in net assets for the year, as shown in the statement of changes in net assets. The reconciliation point for the governmental cash flow statement, however, is operating income (loss) for the year.

Review Questions

Q13-1   Which organizations establish GAAP for not-for-profit health care organizations? Do these organizations establish GAAP also for governmental health care organizations?

Q13-2   Many hospitals use funds for internal record keeping. Distinguish between the kinds of resources accounted for in the General Fund and the kinds accounted for in Restricted Funds.

Q13-3   What are the four basic financial statements required for not-for-profit hospitals, and what does each report?

Q13-4   What is a contractual adjustment?

Q13-5   A not-for-profit hospital has contractual adjustments, takes charity cases, grants discounts to employees and to clergy, and has bad debts. How does each affect net patient service revenue? Would your answers be the same for a governmental hospital?

Q13-6   How does charity care affect the patient service revenue reported by hospitals, and what measure of charity care are hospitals required to disclose in the notes to their financial statements?

Q13-7   How do prospective and retrospective payment agreements affect the amount reported as net patient service revenue?

Q13-8   A not-for-profit hospital invests a $10,000 restricted donation in equity securities. At the date of its financial statements, the securities have a fair value of $12,000. How would the hospital report the increased value in its financial statements? Would your answer be the same for a governmental hospital?

Q13-9   Under what circumstances, if any, would a not-for-profit hospital recognize donated services and donated drugs in its records?

Q13-10   Illustrate the difference between recording a hospital's expenses by natural classification and recording by function. Discuss which is more informative.

Q13-11   Describe the basic rule for recognizing expenses and liabilities for medical malpractice claims.

Q13-12   Describe the accounting process or journal entry to record the segregation of resources by the managing board of a hospital.

Q13-13   Describe how the resources raised by a not-for-profit hospital's fund-raising foundation are reported in the hospital's financial statements.

Q13-14   If a governmental hospital receives a cash grant that contains a time requirement, when should the hospital recognize revenues for the grant?

Q13-15   How is the information provided to a user of a not-for-profit hospital's financial statements different from that provided by a "generic" not-for-profit? Focus on the statement of operations and the statement of changes in net assets.

Discussion Scenarios and Issues

D13-1   Several young doctors started a small not-for-profit out-patient-type hospital in a poor neighborhood in their spare time. Because the doctors received their education free from the state in the form of scholarships, they plan to work at the hospital without pay. The chief administrative officer does not believe that the value of the donated services should appear in the financial statements of the hospital. The comptroller feels that the conditions under which the services were donated require that they be recorded. The CEO feels that if the revenue associated with the services is recorded, it will look like the hospital has a great deal more revenue than it actually has, which may cause it a problem when seeking donations and grants. The doctors do not want the value of their services recorded. How would you respond to this situation?

D13-2   The chief administrative officer of a not-for-profit hospital, Vera Thomas, is attempting to find resources to add a new wing to the hospital. For the past several years, many patients have been turned away because of a lack of space. The hospital has a large endowment, but all earnings from these funds are restricted to various operating purposes; for example, providing continuing education for nurses and maintaining the parking lot. Thomas approaches you and asks whether a recently received gift from T. W. Wealthy could be used to begin expansion. Wealthy donated $1 million to the hospital in his deceased wife's name. She recently died from cancer, and in her memory Wealthy established a cancer research fund. How would you respond to Ms. Thomas?

D13-3   Dr. Rebecca Friend, the chief administrative officer of a hospital, is having an argument with the hospital's comptroller. Dr. Friend recently received a gift of $100,000 from a benefactor. She wants to put the money into a board-designated fund to allow the board to do whatever it wants with the money. The comptroller, however, feels that the hospital should talk with the donor to determine whether he wishes any particular use for his donation. Dr. Friend is concerned that if the donor wishes to use the money in a manner that does not meet the hospital's immediate needs, the hospital may have to turn away some patients because of a lack of facilities. How would you handle this dilemma?

D13-4   A not-for-profit hospital is seeking a loan from a bank to finance a major acquisition of equipment. The hospital is preparing its financial statements for 2012, which the bank's loan officer wants to review before completing the loan agreement. Based on preliminary data, the hospital's treasurer thinks the loan officer will be troubled with the amount the hospital will report as "excess of revenues over expenses" in the hospital's statement of operations. The treasurer knows the hospital comptroller plans to report the allowance for bad debts at 20 percent of patient accounts receivable, the same rate used in preparing the 2010 and 2011 financial statements. The treasurer goes to the comptroller and says: "I'd really like to improve our bottom line a bit. Seems to me the economy is better than last year. I suggest you reduce the bad debts allowance to 12 percent." What should the comptroller do?

Exercises

E13-1   (Fill in the blanks—general terminology)
1. The FASB publishes its Accounting Standards Codification (ASC) as the source of accounting and reporting guidance for _____ hospitals.
2. FASB standards _____ (always, sometimes, never) apply to governmental hospitals.
3. Board-designated resources in a not-for-profit hospital are classified as _____ (unrestricted, temporarily restricted, permanently restricted) net assets.
4. Endowment Funds, Plant Replacement and Expansion Funds, and Specific Purpose Funds are internal accounting funds used for _____ (restricted, unrestricted) resources.
5. The daily operations of a hospital are internally accounted for in the _____ Fund.
6. Hospitals use the _____ basis of accounting.

E13-2   (Use of funds)
The Brite-Hope Hospital uses the following types of funds:

GF   General Fund
EF   Endowment Funds
PREF   Plant Replacement and Expansion Funds
SPF   Specific Purpose Funds

Gf
Ef
RRGf
SPf

Using these codes, identify which fund(s) would be used to account for the following events or activities:

_____ 1. The operations of the cafeteria.

_____ 2. A gift received from an individual for medical research (consider only the receipt of the gift).

_____ 3. Income is earned on investments of money donated by the Manybucks Corporation (the original gift and all income earned must be used to provide up-to-date equipment for the hospital).

_____ 4. The hospital received $1 million in securities from an individual; the principal of the gift must be maintained intact (consider only the receipt of the gift).

_____ 5. The managing board of the hospital decided to start a fund for cancer research. It transferred $30,000 into the fund. Which fund would be used to record the receipt of the money?

_____ 6. The payment of salaries to the nursing staff.

_____ 7. Depreciation is recorded on equipment in use.

_____ 8. The purchase of additional hospital equipment.

E13-3 (Identification of net asset classifications)

Assume that Brite-Hope Hospital in E13-2 is a not-for-profit hospital. Using the following letters, identify which net asset classification would be affected by the events or activities listed in E13-2:

    a. Unrestricted net assets

    b. Temporarily restricted net assets

    c. Permanently restricted net assets

E13-4 (Journal entries)

Prepare journal entries to record the following transactions of a not-for-profit hospital:

    1. The hospital billed its patients for $250,000.

    2. Nurses and doctors employed by the hospital were paid their salaries, $100,000.

    3. The chief administrative officer was paid her salary of $10,000.

    4. The hospital paid its utility bill, $5,000.

    5. Depreciation on the equipment was $34,000.

    6. Several adults donated their time (worth $5,000) selling merchandise in the hospital gift shop.

    7. The hospital billed Medicare $100,000 for services provided at its established rates. The prospective billing arrangement gives Medicare a 40 percent discount from these rates.

    8. An unrestricted donation of $4,000 was received.

E13-5 (Accounting for board-designated resources)

On January 1, 2013, the managing board of a not-for-profit hospital set aside $35,000 to upgrade the skills of its newly hired nurses. During January, the hospital spent $15,000 to train the nurses. Prepare journal entries to record the transactions.

E13-6 (Accounting for uncollectible patient accounts)

The Metro County Hospital could not collect the amount billed to a patient who declared bankruptcy and had no assets with which to pay his debts. Assuming the patient owed the hospital $3,000, prepare the entry or entries necessary to record the uncollectible account if the hospital uses the allowance method. After preparing the necessary entry or entries, state what effect the write-off will have on the balance sheet.

E13-7 (Discussion scenarios)

Discuss the accounting and financial reporting principles in the following scenarios:

    1. A governmental hospital does not carry insurance. Several patients have filed malpractice claims against the hospital, but the claims have not yet been adjudicated. Hospital attorneys think the hospital will probably lose one of the cases and have started settlement negotiations with the other patients. The hospital is preparing its financial statements at year-end.

    2. A billing arrangement with a third-party payer provides for a retrospective adjustment. The hospital estimates it will need to refund $45,000 to the third party, but it has not started settle-

ment negotiations on the amount of the adjustment. The hospital is preparing its year-end financial statements.

3. A not-for-profit hospital has just opened a gift shop. The merchandise for the gift shop is bought by a hospital employee, but all the selling is done by volunteers. The hospital comptroller estimates that, if she had to pay the volunteers for their services, it would cost the hospital $25,000 a year. She wants to know how to handle the donated services in the financial statements.

4. A not-for-profit hospital provides services to Medicare patients amounting to $40 million at its established billing rates. But the billing arrangement with Medicare provides for a contractual adjustment of 40 percent from the established rates. The hospital also provides charity care that has a value of $5 million at its established billing rates. A hospital board member wants to report the lost revenues as bad debt expenses.

5. A governmental hospital provides $20,000 of services at established rates to a patient. The patient does not meet the hospital's criteria for charity care. When the patient tells the hospital that he will not be able to pay the bill, how should the lost revenues be reported?

E13-8 (Accounting for contractual adjustments)

A hospital arranges with a third-party payer to charge the third party 75 percent of its established billing rates. During January 2012, the hospital provided services amounting to $1 million at the established billing rates. Prepare journal entries to record the January billings.

E13-9 (Accounting for premium revenues)

A hospital arranges with an HMO to provide hospital care to the HMO's members at a specific rate per member, per month. During June, the HMO paid the hospital $850,000, in accordance with the agreement. The hospital's cost accounting records showed that, if it had billed the HMO in accordance with its established billing rates, it would have billed the HMO $975,000. Prepare the appropriate journal entry (or entries) to record this transaction.

E13-10 (Accounting for net patient service revenue)

Ruby Ruth Hospital had the following transactions during the year ended December 31, 2012. Prepare journal entries to record these transactions, and state the amount that Ruby Ruth Hospital would report as net patient service revenue in its operating statement.

1. The hospital provided services to patients insured by third-party payer A amounting to $5 million at its established billing rates. The hospital's prospective billing arrangement with this third party stipulates payment to the hospital of 70 percent of its established rates for services performed. All billings were paid during the year.

2. The hospital provided services to patients insured by third-party payer B amounting to $3 million at its established billing rates. Its retrospective billing arrangement with this third party stipulates that the hospital should receive payment at an interim rate of 90 percent of its established rates, subject to retrospective adjustment based on agreed-upon allowable costs. By year-end, B had paid all the billings. Before issuing its financial statements, the hospital estimated that it would need to refund $250,000 to B, based on allowable costs.

3. The hospital provided services to charity patients amounting to $1 million at its established billing rates.

E13-11 (Journal entries to record investment transactions)

A hospital purchased 100 shares of stock on June 30, 2011, for $3,100, using its unrestricted resources. On December 31, 2011, the date of its financial statements, the stock's fair value was $3,200. On November 30, 2012, the hospital sold the stock for $2,800. Assuming it is a governmental hospital, prepare journal entries to record all the transactions and events related to this investment. Then, assuming it is a not-for-profit hospital, prepare journal entries to record all the transactions and events related to this investment.

E13-12 (Financial reporting of investment gains and losses)

Reread the material on reporting investment gains and losses in the section "Investment Returns," and consider the journal entries you made in E13-11. Which of the two reporting methods (if either) do you think is the more informative? Which of the two reporting methods (if either) do you think better expresses the hospital's financial performance? Give reasons for your answers.

E13-13 (Journal entries to record the receipt and use of contributions by a not-for-profit hospital)

Ellen Falk Hospital, a not-for-profit hospital, had the following transactions during the year ended December 31, 2012. Prepare journal entries necessary to record the transactions. The hospital does not use fund accounting.

1. Joe Joseph, a high school senior, donated his services to the hospital for an entire summer, serving food to patients and performing general tasks. If paid for, these services would have cost the hospital $8,000.
2. D. Bean donated $20,000 to the hospital, stipulating that the resources be used only to resurface its parking lot, a maintenance function that the hospital performs every 3 years.
3. The hospital used D. Bean's donation for the stipulated purpose.
4. J. Blythe's estate donated $500,000 to the hospital to help pay for new MRI equipment.
5. The hospital used J. Blythe's donation for new MRI equipment.

E13-14 (Use of funds)

The following transactions relate to the Rohan Hospital, a not-for-profit hospital that uses fund accounting for internal record keeping purposes. Indicate which fund(s) would be used to record the data.

1. Collected $2,345 from a patient.
2. Received a $100,000 grant from Christine Drug Company for a study of the effects of morphine on female patients.
3. Received unrestricted gifts of $50,000.
4. Purchased equipment for $125,000 by using resources previously accumulated in the Plant Replacement and Expansion Fund.
5. Research expenses totaling $12,000 were incurred in studying the effects of morphine on female patients, using the Christine grant.
6. The board decided to begin a fund for nursing education. Initially $10,000 of general hospital resources was transferred to the fund.
7. Marketable securities with a fair value of $15,000 were donated by CHR, Inc., to help the hospital acquire new equipment.
8. The hospital received a dividend check for $2,000 from the securities donated in transaction 7. Assume that the investment income is restricted in the same way as the original gift.

E13-15 (Transactions involving General Fund and restricted funds)

Using the same information given in E13-14, prepare the journal entries that would be used to record the data. Identify each type of fund used.

E13-16 (Financial statements)

Using the following codes, indicate which statement would be used to report each item for a not-for-profit hospital.

BS   Balance sheet
SO   Statement of operations
SCNA   Statement of changes in net assets only

_____ 1. Land, buildings, and equipment
_____ 2. Unrestricted contributions
_____ 3. General services expense
_____ 4. Contributions receivable
_____ 5. Realized gain on sale of permanently restricted investments
_____ 6. Assets limited as to use
_____ 7. Change in interest in hospital foundation's temporarily restricted assets
_____ 8. Estimated liability for malpractice costs

Problems

P13-1   (Matching)

Match items on the right with those on the left by placing the letter of the best match in the space provided.

a. Temporarily restricted net asset
b. Prepared for a not-for-profit hospital's changes in unrestricted net assets only
c. Permanently restricted net asset
d. *Audit and Accounting Guide—Health Care Entities*
e. Used to account for resources that are donor-restricted for a particular operating purpose
f. General Fund
g. Assets whose use is limited
h. Reported on a not-for-profit hospital's statement of changes in net assets

_____ 1. Used to account for day-to-day operations of a hospital
_____ 2. Gift that must be used for a specific purpose, such as capital asset acquisition
_____ 3. Resources set aside for a specific purpose by a hospital's governing board
_____ 4. Revenues from restricted resources
_____ 5. Resources donated to a hospital for which the principal must be maintained intact
_____ 6. Specific Purpose Funds
_____ 7. AICPA audit guide for hospitals
_____ 8. Statement of operations

P13-2   (Multiple choice)

1. In accordance with its established billing rates, Alpha Hospital provided services amounting to $14 million during the year ended December 31, 2012. Included in the $14 million were contractual adjustments of $3 million and charity patient care of $1 million. What amount should Alpha report as net patient service revenue in its year 2012 financial statements?
    a. $10 million
    b. $11 million
    c. $13 million
    d. $14 million

2. Beta Hospital provided services to patients who were covered by the Corwin Health Plan. Beta's arrangement with Corwin called for interim billing rates at 25 percent less than the established rates, as well as a retrospective rate adjustment. Based on its established billing rates, Beta provided services amounting to $4,000,000 to patients covered by Corwin during the year ended December 31, 2012. At year-end, Beta estimated that it would need to refund $150,000 to Corwin in accordance with the cost standards set forth in the retrospective rate arrangement. What amount should Beta report as net patient service revenue in its year 2012 financial statements?
    a. $2,850,000
    b. $3,000,000
    c. $3,850,000
    d. $4,000,000

3. Gamma Hospital provided services amounting to $10 million at its established billing rates in the year ended December 31, 2012. Included in the $10 million were services of $8 million to Medicare patients. Medicare paid Gamma at 60 percent of Gamma's established rates. Also included in the $10 million were $2 million of services to self-pay patients who did not meet Gamma's criteria for charity care when admitted. Gamma collected $1.5 million from the self-pay patients during the year and estimated that 40 percent of the uncollected amount would not be collected. What amount should Gamma report as net patient service revenue in its year 2012 financial statements?
    a. $6.3 million
    b. $6.6 million

    c. $6.8 million

    d. $10 million

4. On January 10, 2012, Delta Hospital received a bequest in the form of equity securities. Delta was required to hold the securities in perpetuity, but it could spend the income. The securities had cost the donor $2.7 million, but their fair value was $3.4 million when Delta received them. The fair value of the securities fluctuated during the year, and Delta's comptroller calculated that the average fair value during the year was $3.1 million. When Delta prepared its financial statements as of December 31, 2012, the fair value of the securities was $3.3 million. At what amount should Delta report the securities in its financial statements at December 31, 2012?

    a. $2.7 million

    b. $3.1 million

    c. $3.3 million

    d. $3.4 million

5. Abbott and Costello Labs donated drugs to Epsilon Hospital, a not-for-profit entity, in January 2012. If Epsilon had purchased the drugs, it would have paid $600,000. During the year, Epsilon used all the drugs in providing services to patients. How should Epsilon report the donation in its financial statements for the year ended December 31, 2012?

    a. Report nothing

    b. Report the donation in a note to its financial statements

    c. Report $600,000 as other revenues (or gains)

    d. Report $600,000 as a reduction of operating expenses

6. Omicron Hospital, a not-for-profit entity, received $6 million in premium revenue under an agreement with Zeta HMO to provide services to subscribing participants. Its internal records showed that Omicron spent $5.6 million in caring for Zeta's subscribers. How should Omicron report the transactions with Zeta in its financial statements?

    a. Report $400,000 as unrestricted premium revenue

    b. Report $400,000 as temporarily restricted premium revenue

    c. Report $6 million as unrestricted premium revenue

    d. Report $6 million as temporarily restricted premium revenue

7. Which of the following is the most likely description of the resources reported by Kappa Hospital on its balance sheet as assets limited as to use?

    a. A donation that can be used only for cancer research

    b. A donation that must be held in perpetuity in an Endowment Fund

    c. An investment of unrestricted resources that is not readily marketable

    d. An amount designated by Kappa's governing board for plant expansion

8. How should Phi Hospital, a not-for-profit hospital, report an increase in the fair value of its temporarily restricted investments?

    a. Only in the notes to its statements

    b. As part of nonoperating revenues (expenses) in its statement of revenues, expenses, and changes in net assets

    c. As a gain in its statement of changes in net assets

    d. As a direct addition to total net assets

P13-3   (Multiple choice)

1. A hospital has not transferred risk on malpractice claims to a third-party insurer. Which of the following statements best expresses the general rule regarding the reporting of liabilities for malpractice claims on the face of the balance sheet (or statement of net position)?

    a. They should be reported only to the extent that judgments and settlements are due and payable.

    b. Outstanding claims should be described in the notes to the statements; adjudicated and settled claims should be reported if they have not been paid.

c. They should be reported if it is highly likely that the disputes ultimately will be resolved in favor of the claimants.

d. They should be reported if it is probable that a loss has been incurred and the amount of the loss can be reasonably estimated.

2. Historical experience shows that a hospital sometimes receives malpractice claims in the year after the incidents occur. Which of the following statements best expresses the general rule for reporting liabilities for such claims, if risk of loss has not been transferred to a third-party insurer?

a. No mention is required to be made of these claims anywhere in the financial statements.

b. A note should be prepared discussing the likelihood that claims will be received after the balance sheet date, but no estimate needs to be made of the possibility of loss.

c. Liabilities should be recognized in the statements if it is probable that claims will be asserted for incidents occurring before the balance sheet date and the losses can be reasonably estimated.

d. Liabilities should be recognized in the statements if claims have been received before the statements are issued; a note should be prepared discussing the likelihood of receiving additional claims after the statements have been issued.

3. A not-for-profit hospital receives a gift from a donor who specifies that the gift must be used only to further its research into the treatment of Parkinson's disease. When the hospital incurs expenses in this program, in which classification of net assets should the expenses be reported?

a. Unrestricted net assets

b. Temporarily restricted net assets

c. Permanently restricted net assets

d. Assets limited as to use

4. A not-for-profit hospital sells long-term bonds in the amount of $25 million to finance the construction of a new wing. The bond agreement requires the hospital to pay $1 million of this amount to a trustee as security until the debt is fully repaid. How should the $1 million payment be reported in the financial statements?

a. As an expense, to be amortized over the life of the debt

b. As assets limited as to use

c. As noncurrent assets, with all other long-term investments

d. As temporarily restricted net assets

5. A not-for-profit hospital creates a foundation whose sole purpose is to raise funds on behalf of the hospital. The hospital appoints all members of the foundation's governing board and directs its activities. The foundation raises $200,000 in unrestricted cash gifts during the year. The hospital does not need the cash, so the foundation continues to hold the cash at year-end. How should the hospital report on the foundation's activities in its financial statements?

a. Report an asset in its balance sheet and a "change in interest in the foundation" in its statement of operations

b. Report an asset in its balance sheet and a "change in interest in the foundation" in the temporarily restricted net asset section of its statement of changes in net assets

c. Report nothing on the face of its financial statements but disclose the foundation's activities in a note to its financial statements

d. Report the foundation in a separate column to the right of the hospital balances on the face of the hospital's financial statements

6. During the year ended December 31, 2012, a not-for-profit hospital had both unrealized and realized gains on investments made with its unrestricted net assets. How should these gains be reported in the hospital's statement of operations for the year 2012?

a. Both the realized and the unrealized gains should be reported.

b. Neither the realized nor the unrealized gains should be reported.

      c. Realized gains should be reported, but unrealized gains should not.

      d. Unrealized gains should be reported, but realized gains should not.

   7. Under which of these circumstances would a not-for-profit hospital report restricted net assets?

      a. Whenever there are external limitations on using the resources

      b. When a donor places limitations on using the resources

      c. When the hospital's board of directors sets resources aside for plant expansion

      d. When a bond agreement requires the hospital to set resources aside

P13-4 (Multiple choice—governmental hospital)

   1. What are the components of the net position section of a governmental hospital's balance sheet?

      a. Unrestricted; temporarily restricted; permanently restricted

      b. Assets limited as to use; assets unlimited as to use

      c. Net investment in capital assets; restricted; unrestricted

      d. Restricted; unrestricted

   2. A county hospital receives grants from higher-level governments that must be used to construct and equip a special trauma unit. How should the hospital report the grants in its financial statements?

      a. As nonoperating revenues

      b. After nonoperating revenues (expenses) to arrive at total change in net position

      c. As a direct addition to "net investment in capital assets"

      d. As an item of extraordinary or special revenue

   3. A county hospital receives $1 million from the county's General Fund to help cover the hospital's annual operating deficit. How should the hospital report that receipt of cash?

      a. As operating revenues

      b. As nonoperating revenues

      c. After nonoperating revenues (expenses) to arrive at total change in net position

      d. As a direct addition to unrestricted net position

   4. A county hospital receives a grant of $250,000 from the State Health Department, which specifies that the grant may be used for any purpose the trustees wish, provided it is used at the rate of $50,000 a year for the next 5 years, starting the following year. How should the hospital report the gift in its financial statements in the year the cash is received?

      a. As an advance

      b. As revenue in the amount of $250,000

      c. As revenue in the amount of $250,000, discounted at the government's borrowing rate over the 5-year period

      d. As a direct addition to unrestricted net position

   5. How is interest on long-term bonds issued by a county hospital generally reported?

      a. As operating expenses

      b. As nonoperating expenses

      c. As a separate item after nonoperating revenues (expenses) to arrive at total change in net position

      d. As a direct reduction of beginning net position

P13-5 (Accounting for and reporting patient service revenues)

The Maggie King Hospital, a not-for-profit hospital, had the following transactions regarding its patient service billings.

   1. The total services provided by the hospital to all patients during the year amounted to $19 million at the hospital's established billing rates.

   2. Transaction 1 includes billings to Medicare (for services to program beneficiaries) at prospectively determined rates. Under this program contractual adjustments to the predetermined rates were $1.5 million.

3. Transaction 1 also includes billings to third-party payer X under an agreement that calls for retrospective final rates. Interim billing rates under this agreement resulted in contractual adjustments of $1 million.
4. The hospital provided charity care included in transaction 1 valued at $500,000 at the established rates.
5. The hospital made a provision for bad debts in the amount of $300,000.
6. The hospital collected $13.5 million from third-party payers and direct-pay patients. The hospital also wrote off bad debts of $200,000.
7. The hospital estimated it would need to refund $100,000 to payer X in transaction 3 when retrospective rates are determined. (The hospital's receivables include no amounts due from payer X.)

Prepare the journal entries needed to record these transactions. State (a) the amount of net patient service revenue the hospital will report on its operating statement and (b) the amount of net patient accounts receivable the hospital will report on its balance sheet. Also, state (c) how the estimated third-party payer settlements should be reported and (d) how charity care should be reported.

P13-6 (Accounting for medical malpractice claims)

Caire-Less Hospital carries no insurance for medical malpractice claims. Analysis of medical malpractice claims at year-end shows the following:

1. Claim A is for $500,000. The hospital's attorneys are 90 percent confident that the hospital will win the claim if it goes to trial. The hospital will not settle the claim for any amount and is awaiting trial.
2. Claim B is for $400,000. The hospital's attorneys are not confident of winning if the case goes to trial. They believe the claim can be settled out of court, within the range of $100,000 to $200,000.
3. The hospital also has 20 outstanding smaller claims. The average claim is for $10,000. Experience shows that the hospital loses 60 percent of the claims, and the average loss on them is 30 percent of the amount claimed.
4. Experience also shows that two patient claims, each for $10,000 and relating to incidents occurring before year-end, are likely to be made during the following year.

Compute the amount, if any, that the hospital ought to establish as a liability on its balance sheet for malpractice claims. Discuss the content of any note disclosures that the hospital should make. Also, describe the accounting principles leading to your conclusions.

P13-7 (Comprehensive set of journal entries and financial statements)

Cort Hospital was established as a not-for-profit organization on January 1, 2013, to take over the assets of an existing hospital. The hospital does not use fund accounting. It had the following transactions during 2013.

1. The hospital sold revenue bonds in the amount of $40 million. The hospital received $38 million in cash from sale of the bonds. To provide security for payment of the debt service, the other $2 million was deposited in an escrow account with a trustee. The trustee immediately invested the cash in U.S. Treasury bills.
2. The physical assets of the existing hospital were purchased for $35 million in cash. The appraised values of the assets were as follows: land—$3 million; buildings—$28 million; and equipment—$4 million.
3. The hospital provided services of $20 million at its established rates to Medicare patients. Its agreement with Medicare provided for contractual adjustments of 30 percent against the established rates. By year-end, the hospital had collected $12.5 million against the billings.
4. The hospital provided services of $10 million at its established rates to patients insured by a third-party payer. Its agreement with the third party provided for contractual adjustments of 20 percent from the established rates. It also provided for a retrospective adjustment, based on a cost submission by the hospital 30 days after the end of the year. By year-end, the hospital had collected the entire amount that it was owed by the third-party payer. When it prepared its

financial statements, the hospital estimated that it owed the third party $80,000, but the final settlement had not yet been negotiated.

5. The hospital provided services to members of an HMO at rates per member, per month, receiving cash premiums totaling $15 million for the year. The hospital's internal records showed that, if billings had been made at its established rates, it would have charged the HMO $18 million for these services.

6. The hospital provided care to charity patients amounting to $2 million at its established billing rates. It estimated the direct and indirect costs of that care to be $1.4 million.

7. The hospital provided care to self-pay patients in the amount of $5 million at its established rates. The hospital collected $2 million against these billings. At year-end, the hospital established an allowance for uncollectible receivables of 40 percent of the remaining amount due from the self-pay patients.

8. The hospital had the following functional expenses. Of the amounts shown, $29 million was paid in cash. Depreciation on building and equipment (included in each function) was $1.4 million and $600,000, respectively.

Health care services	$22 million
Dietary services	4 million
Maintenance expenses	2 million
Administrative expenses	3 million

9. The hospital paid debt service of $4 million on its bonds ($1.6 million in amortization of principal and $2.4 million in interest). It also made a year-end journal entry, reclassifying $1.6 million of long-term debt as current.

10. The hospital recorded accrued expenses at year-end as follows:

Health care services	$2 million
Administrative expenses	500,000

11. The hospital paid $1 million for a claims-made policy for medical malpractice insurance through December 31, 2013. Because the policy did not transfer risk to the insurance carrier for incurred but not reported claims (IBNR), the hospital accrued $300,000 as a liability. (Note: Charge the expenses to the health care services function.)

12. The hospital received a check from the trustee for $100,000, representing earnings on the investment made by the trustee with the escrow money. The investment income is available for the hospital's general operations.

13. The hospital received equity securities from a donor who specified that the securities, together with any earnings thereon, be used for the purpose of upgrading the hospital buildings. The securities had a fair value of $250,000 when the donor made the gift. During the year, the hospital received dividends of $10,000 on the securities. At year-end, when the hospital prepared its financial statements, the securities had a fair value of $270,000. (Assume the hospital's accounting policy provides for recording realized and unrealized gains and losses on *restricted* net assets in a single account.)

14. During 2013, the hospital created Cort Hospital Foundation, whose sole purpose is to obtain donations for the hospital. At year-end, the foundation advised the hospital that it had received cash donations of $300,000. Of this amount, $50,000 was unrestricted, and $250,000 was restricted for upgrading the hospital's equipment. At the hospital's request, the foundation sent to the hospital the entire $50,000 of cash received from unrestricted donations.

Use the preceding information to do the following:
a. Prepare the necessary journal entries to record these transactions.
b. Prepare a statement of operations for 2013.
c. Prepare a statement of changes in net assets for 2013.
d. Prepare a balance sheet as of December 31, 2013.

P13-8   (Journal entries and financial statements)
Following is a trial balance for the Jayce County General Hospital, a governmental hospital. The
hospital does not use fund accounting.

Jayce County General Hospital
Trial Balance
December 31, 2011

Cash	$ 6,000	
Patient accounts receivable	20,000	
Allowance for uncollectible receivables		$ 3,000
Inventories	5,000	
Land	300,000	
Building	2,000,000	
Accumulated depreciation—building		80,000
Equipment	500,000	
Accumulated depreciation—equipment		100,000
Accounts payable		8,000
Bonds payable		2,400,000
Net position		240,000
	$2,831,000	$2,831,000

During 2012, the following transactions took place:
1. Services provided to patients amounted to $3,300,000 at established billing rates. Following is
   an analysis of the billings:
   a. Medicare patients were billed for $2,000,000 at established rates. However, contractual
      allowances against these billings were $400,000.
   b. Billings under a retrospective arrangement with a third party were $600,000 at the estab-
      lished rates. However, the interim billing rates called for contractual adjustments of $100,000.
   c. Billings to self-pay patients were $500,000 at established rates. Based on experience, the
      hospital anticipated that $25,000 of the billings would not be collected.
   d. Services to charity patients were $200,000 at established rates.
2. Inventories of $56,000 were purchased on credit.
3. Operating expenses were incurred as follows:

Health care services	$2,140,000
General expenses	$200,000
Administrative expenses	$90,000

Assume that all the expenses were incurred on credit.
4. The board decided to set aside $30,000 in cash in a separate account to provide for the continu-
   ing education of nurses.
5. The hospital entered into a capitation agreement with the county in which it was located, agreeing to provide hospital services to certain groups of county employees and their dependents.
   The agreement provided for the county to make a monthly payment for each covered county
   employee. Cash payments received by the hospital under this agreement were $300,000.
6. Collections of patient receivables totaled $2,200,000. In addition, $13,000 of patient receivables
   were written off as uncollectible.
7. Payments of accounts payable totaled $1,900,000.
8. The use of inventories was recorded as follows:

Health care services	$30,000
General expenses	$20,000

9. Depreciation was recorded as follows: building, $40,000; equipment, $50,000.

10. During the year, the hospital paid debt service of $220,000 on the outstanding bonds, consisting of interest of $120,000 and principal of $100,000. At year-end, the hospital made an entry to report $100,000 of its outstanding long-term debt as current. (Assume the debt was used to finance the purchase of the hospital's capital assets.)

11. During the year, a self-pay patient instituted legal action in the amount of $200,000 against the hospital for medical malpractice. The hospital does not carry insurance. Hospital attorneys have started negotiations with the claimant and believe it is highly probable that the claim can be settled for $50,000. (Charge the expense to Health care services.)

12. At year-end, the hospital reviewed its cost accounting records in connection with the retrospective billing arrangement made with the third-party payer in transaction 1.b. The hospital believes it will need to refund $40,000 to that third party in accordance with that agreement. (The third party had paid all the billings made by the hospital in 1.b.)

Use the preceding information to do the following:

a. Prepare all the journal entries necessary to record these transactions.
b. Prepare a statement of revenues, expenses, and changes in net position for 2012.
c. Prepare a balance sheet as of December 31, 2012.

P13-9   (Journal entries using funds and net asset classifications; preparation of financial statements)
Christy General Hospital, a not-for-profit organization, accounts for its activities using a General Fund (GF), and three restricted fund groups—Specific Purpose Funds (SPF), Endowment Funds (EF), and Plant Replacement and Expansion Funds (PREF). The hospital had the following transactions during 2012. Prepare journal entries to record these transactions in the hospital's General Fund and restricted funds. Identify the fund and, where appropriate, the net asset classification. Also, prepare a statement of changes in net assets for the temporarily and permanently restricted net assets for 2012.

1. The hospital received a gift of $300,000 in equity securities from Brady Johnson. The terms of the gift specified that the principal amount of the gift and any investment gains must be maintained intact permanently. The gift terms also stipulated that the income from the investments could be spent only for cancer research.

2. Beynon Associates gave the hospital a cash gift of $50,000 and equity securities having a fair value of $150,000 at the date of the gift. The donor stipulated that the gift and all income derived from the gift (including proceeds from sale of the securities) could be used only for cancer research.

3. Diane Shaw promised to donate $50,000 to the hospital to provide equipment for the hospital's new gastroenterology unit, provided the hospital raised an equal amount of cash from other donors.

4. The hospital undertook a fund-raising campaign to purchase equipment for its new gastroenterology unit and raised cash of $80,000. Diane Shaw immediately sent the hospital a check for $50,000.

5. The hospital spent the entire $130,000 to buy equipment for its gastroenterology unit.

6. The hospital received interest and dividends totaling $20,000 on the gifts made by Brady Johnson and Beynon Associates.

7. The hospital sold some of the securities donated by Beynon so it could hire a well-known cancer researcher. It received $35,000 in cash from investments that had a fair value of $30,000 at the time of the gift. (The hospital's accounting polices call for recording in a single account both realized and unrealized gains and losses on securities held in *restricted* net assets.)

8. The hospital spent $70,000 on cancer research, using the resources provided by the Johnson and Beynon gifts.

9. At year-end, the fair values of the equity securities from the Johnson and Beynon gifts were as follows:

Johnson	$310,000
Beynon	$122,000

10. The hospital created the Christy General Hospital Foundation, over which it had full control. At year-end, the foundation notified the hospital that it had received $25,000 in cash donations, to be used only to purchase equipment for its gastroenterology unit.

P13-10 (Journal entries using funds and net asset classifications)

Following is a trial balance for Porschen Memorial, a not-for-profit hospital:

Porschen Memorial Hospital
General Fund
Trial Balance
July 1, 2012

Cash	$ 12,000	
Patient accounts receivable	40,000	
Allowance for uncollectible patient accounts		$ 4,000
Land	600,000	
Buildings	2,500,000	
Accumulated depreciation—buildings		650,000
Equipment	2,000,000	
Accumulated depreciation—equipment		400,000
Accounts payable		15,000
Notes payable		100,000
Bonds payable		2,000,000
Unrestricted net assets		1,983,000
	$5,152,000	$5,152,000

The hospital uses a General Fund (GF) and several restricted funds—Specific Purpose Funds (SPF), Endowment Funds (EF), and Plant Replacement and Expansion Funds (PREF). During the 2012–2013 fiscal year, the following selected transactions took place. Prepare all the journal entries necessary to record these transactions. Identify the fund and, where appropriate, the net asset classification.

1. Porschen had capitation agreements with several HMOs, wherein the HMOs agreed to pay monthly premiums per member at the beginning of every month in exchange for Porschen's agreement to provide hospital services to the HMO members. Porschen received premiums of $2,000,000 in cash during the year. In addition, Porschen billed its self-pay patients a total of $100,000.
2. Several self-pay patient accounts that were classified as uncollectible were written off. These accounts totaled $2,000.
3. The MP2 Corporation gave the hospital a grant for research into the use of a voice-activated microscope. The grant was for $500,000. The entire amount was immediately invested in marketable securities.
4. Operating expenses were incurred as follows:

Nursing and other professional services	$850,000
General expenses	$300,000
Administrative expenses	$175,000
Dietary services	$100,000

Assume that all expenses were incurred on credit.
5. Self-pay patient receivables of $110,000 were collected.
6. Accounts payable of $1,400,000 were paid.
7. Several individuals in the community contributed a total of $1,000,000 for the expansion of the burn unit of the hospital. This money was invested in marketable securities until the plans for the unit were completed. The fund was titled the Burn Unit Fund.
8. Debt service of $210,000 on the outstanding debt was paid in cash. Of this amount, $110,000 was for interest, and the rest was for debt principal.

9. The managing board decided to set aside $25,000 in cash from general hospital resources for the development of its professional nursing staff.

10. The construction and planning costs incurred on the new burn unit totaled $200,000. This amount was paid from the Burn Unit Fund cash account. To make these payments, investments that originally cost $190,000 were sold for $205,000. In addition, $10,000 in cash income was received on the investments. Assume that (a) the income from the investments has the same restrictions as the original donation and (b) the hospital's accounting policy calls for realized and unrealized gains and losses on *restricted* net assets to be recorded in a single account.

11. During the year, the hospital received $25,000 in cash income from the investment of the MP2 grant money. Assume that the investment income is restricted in the same way as the original grant.

12. Research costs associated with the MP2 grant were $20,000. These costs were paid with cash generated by the investment of the original grant.

13. Larry Porschen III gave the hospital $15,000, which must be maintained intact. The income from the gift can be used in any way the managing board feels is helpful to the hospital. The money was immediately invested in marketable securities.

14. Investments in the Larry Porschen III Fund earned $2,000 during the year. Of this amount, $1,900 was received in cash.

15. The fair value of the remaining investments in the Burn Unit Fund at the end of the year was $850,000.

Chapter 14

Analysis of Financial Statements and Financial Condition

Chapter Outline

After completing this chapter, you should be able to do the following:

- Explain how financial statement format and content assist in financial analysis

- Explain how using ratios facilitates analysis of financial data

- Explain how time-series analysis and comparative analysis facilitate financial analysis

- Describe and calculate indicators of liquidity

- Describe and calculate indicators of asset turnover or efficiency

- Describe and calculate indicators of budgetary solvency and operating results

- Describe and calculate indicators of debt burden and long-term financial flexibility

- Describe the factors, other than ratios derived from financial statements, needed to assess an entity's financial condition

Financial statements provide the primary source of data used by financial analysts and others in assessing an entity's operating results and short-term financial position, including liquidity. Financial statement analysis also plays a key role in assessing financial condition—the likelihood that the entity will meet its longer-term obligations. For example, analysts for credit-rating agencies examine the financial statements (as well as economic, demographic, and managerial matters) to help reach conclusions about creditworthiness when governmental and not-for-profit entities borrow in the capital markets. Analysts for state governments also use financial statements in connection with their oversight of local government finances.

    Converting various elements of financial statements to ratios (such as the ratio of current assets to current liabilities) or other useful formats (such as debt per capita) helps the analyst spot deviations from industry norms or from earlier-year entity patterns. When trends in the ratios are assessed in relation to relevant economic, demographic, and managerial information, insight may be gained into the causes of deviations and into the entity's likely future financial health.

    This chapter discusses and illustrates some commonly used indicators of operating results and financial position of state and local governments and not-for-profit entities. Some of the ratios used in analyzing the finances of for-profit business-type entities are readily adaptable to governmental and not-for-profit business-type activities, such as hospitals. Other indicators have been developed specifically for assessing the finances of general-purpose governments.

When reading this chapter, keep in mind that analyzing an organization's financial health is an art, not a science. An analyst may be interested in knowing a particular ratio for a particular purpose, but no single ratio or indicator will suffice to reach a conclusion about an entity's overall financial condition. Instead, many ratios and other indicators—financial, economic, demographic, administrative, and political—must be considered.

INFORMATION CONTENT OF FINANCIAL STATEMENTS: A FINANCIAL ANALYSIS PERSPECTIVE

Before discussing the techniques of financial statement and financial condition analysis, let's reexamine the information content of the financial statements and related data:

- Statement of net position, also called the statement of financial position or the balance sheet
- Statement of activities, also called the statement of operations or the statement of revenues, expenses (expenditures), and changes in net position (or fund balances)
- Notes to the financial statements and required supplementary information

Although there are formatting differences in the financial statements prepared by the various types of organizations covered in this text, there are sufficient similarities to allow some general observations about the purposes served by the statements and the related data.

Statement of Net Position

The statement of net position (or equivalent designation) provides information about an organization's assets, liabilities, and net position as of the statement date. The formatting and information content of this statement allows the analyst to reach some conclusions about the entity's liquidity and financial flexibility.

Assets are generally listed in order of *liquidity*—their nearness to becoming cash and nearness to being consumed in operations. Liabilities are listed in terms of nearness to being paid. To provide further emphasis on liquidity, assets and liabilities may be classified as *current* and *noncurrent*. Current assets include cash, those that are expected to be converted to cash in the following year, or those that are expected to be consumed in operations in the following year. Current liabilities are those that are expected to be paid in the following year. For example, the portion of long-term bonds that is due to be paid in the following year is shown as current while the rest is reported as noncurrent.[1]

Evidence of financial flexibility is provided by the captions attached to the various assets and liabilities, by the liquidity order in which they are listed, and by the classifications shown in the net position section of the statement of net position. For example, both governmental and not-for-profit organizations show the extent to which there are constraints on using the net assets. When net assets are classified as unrestricted or unassigned, they can be used for any purpose within the scope of the entity's charter that its management considers appropriate. When classified as restricted or otherwise constrained, the net assets are available only for the

---

[1]As discussed in previous chapters, the term *current* has a shorter time frame in fund statements for governmental-type funds than it does for government-wide financial statements and for not-for-profit entity and hospital financial statements.

specific activity, function, or time period designated by law or by the party that placed limits on use of the assets.

Obviously, management's financial flexibility is greater if its resources are relatively liquid and the level of its unrestricted net assets (or unassigned fund balance) is relatively high. For example, a relatively high level of unrestricted net assets (or unassigned fund balance) provides a cushion against future revenue shortfalls. How the analyst determines an entity's relative degree of liquidity will be discussed shortly.

Statement of Activities

The statement of activities (or equivalent designation) shows both the details and the totals of an organization's revenues, expenses, and other elements leading to the change in net position for the year. Depending on the measurement focus and basis of accounting used in preparing the statements, the analyst can ascertain the following,

- Whether the resources obtained during the year were sufficient to cover the costs of services provided that year
- The various sources of revenues obtained during the year
- The nature of the services provided during the year
- Whether unusual factors, such as significant one-time resource inflows, influenced operating results for the year

Separating revenues by source provides a clue as to the volatility and reliability of revenue streams available to finance future activities. For example,

- In financing governments, property tax revenues tend to be more stable from year to year than personal income tax and sales tax revenues, which are more sensitive to economic factors. Also, revenues from higher-level governments tend to be less reliable than taxes and other revenues raised directly by the entity being analyzed.
- Not-for-profit entities that rely heavily on contributions may experience revenue shortfalls during periods of recession. Those that are heavily endowed may experience volatile revenues because of stock market fluctuations, although unrealized gains and losses on securities in a particular year may not affect the entities' long-run financial health.

Subtotals and formats in the statement of activities also play a useful role in conveying information. For example, the not-for-profit hospital's statement of operations provides measures of financial performance by separating the "operating gain" and the "excess of revenues over expenses" from other factors affecting the increase in unrestricted net assets for the year. For another example, the government-wide statement of activities prepared by governments reports the relative burden each function places on the taxpaying public by showing gross expenses by function and revenues directly related to those functions. Also, by separating program expenses from administrative and fund-raising expenses, a not-for-profit organization's statement of activities shows readers how resources were used.

A financial analyst needs to recognize that the statement of activities has limitations as an indicator of future events. Its limitations are particularly evident in government, where the statement of activities measures the cost of services provided but not the cost of unmet service needs. The fact that a governmental entity's net position at year-end increased over the previous year does not necessarily mean that its financial condition improved. Unmet service needs that cannot be readily financed must be considered in examining a government's financial condition.

Notes to the Financial Statements and Required Supplementary Information

As previously stated, notes are an integral part of the financial statements, providing information not shown on the face of the statements but nevertheless essential to fair presentation of the statements. Required supplementary information also provides information considered essential to financial reporting. Here are some examples of how the notes and required supplementary information provide data useful in assessing financial position and condition:

- *Property Tax Calendar.* Some governments obtain large amounts of revenues from property taxes. Although property taxes generally are collected twice a year, 6 months apart, the first payment may be due before the fiscal year begins, at any time during the year, or even in the next year. The tax calendar can therefore affect an entity's cash flows and need for short-term borrowing. It may also help explain the size of amounts reported as cash, taxes receivable, deferred inflows of resources, notes payable, interest revenue, and interest expenditure/expense.
- *Debt Service Requirements to Maturity.* Debt service requirements affect an entity's financial flexibility. An entity that can balance its current budget and simultaneously redeem relatively large amounts of debt has greater financial flexibility than one that needs to push its debt redemption off to the long-term future. Governmental entities are required to disclose their debt service requirements to maturity, showing amounts due each year for the next 5 years and amounts due in 5-year increments thereafter.
- *Pension and Other Postemployment Benefit Obligations.* Defined benefit pension plans and other postemployment benefit plans create future debtlike commitments. As discussed in Chapter 8, governments with such plans must disclose funding progress and actual contributions to the plans compared to required contributions. All other factors being equal, an entity that has a high funded ratio and contributes the full annual funding requirement is likely to be in better fiscal health than one with a low ratio that does not contribute the full requirement.

AN APPROACH TO FINANCIAL STATEMENT AND FINANCIAL CONDITION ANALYSIS

The extent to which one might analyze financial statements depends on the purpose of the analysis. An analyst might be concerned only with a particular data element, such as the size of a not-for-profit organization's unrestricted fund balance and how it compares with that of the previous year. Another might be concerned with how a hospital's overall financial position and results of operations compare with those of the previous year. A third might want to review the overall financial condition of a governmental entity to assess its long-term ability to finance anticipated debt and expanded services.[2]

The first analyst is interested in a single element of an organization's financial position at two points in time, which can be obtained by reading that data element in the statement of financial position. The second needs to read the statements and related notes, select certain data elements

---

[2]Robert Berne defines financial condition as "the probability that a government will meet both (a) its financial obligations to creditors, consumers, employees, taxpayers, suppliers, constituents, and others as they become due and (b) the service obligations to constituents, both currently and in the future." Robert Berne, *The Relationships between Financial Reporting and the Measurement of Financial Condition,* Norwalk, CT: GASB, 1992, p. 17.

from the statements, convert them to financial ratios, do the same with the previous year's statements, and interpret the results. The third needs to use a longer time period, select additional data elements (including economic and demographic data obtained outside the financial statements), and develop a frame of reference based on other governments to aid in interpreting the results.

Converting Data to More Useful Formats

To aid in interpreting data for financial statement and financial condition analysis, the analyst needs to convert data elements to more useful formats. The numbers take on a different meaning when compared with another relevant statistic. For example, an analyst may conclude that the accounts receivable collection process got worse if the accounts receivable balance at December 31, 2013, was $420,000, up from $400,000 at December 31, 2012. Considering the increase in revenues during 2013 by converting the accounts receivable balance to the number of days' revenue represented by the balance might show, however, that the collection process actually improved during the year.

Data formats used in financial analysis include ratios, per capita information, and common size statements. In addition, analyzing data can be made easier by developing percentage change information.

- *Ratios* are developed by relating one data element to another to produce an indicator of a particular characteristic. We just saw how relating the receivables balance to revenues provides a good indicator of receivables collection efficiency. Using ratios also allows the analyst to assess trends for the entity itself and to compare the entity with other organizations—things that could not be done in a meaningful way using just the raw numbers.
- *Per capita information* is produced by dividing financial data elements by the entity's population. Converting financial data to per capita information also makes it easier to trace trends for the entity and to compare the entity with other organizations.
- *Common size statements* are obtained by converting financial statement elements to percentages of 100. Using common size statements allows the analyst to readily identify changes over time in the proportion that individual data elements bear to the total (e.g., the share of total expenses represented by a government's public safety expenses, or a not-for-profit entity's fund-raising expenses).
- *Percentage change information* is obtained by comparing data elements for a later year with data elements for an earlier year. For example, if the cash balance increased from $200,000 in 2012 to $250,000 in 2013, the percentage change was plus 25 percent [($250,000 − $200,000)/$200,000]. The calculations help in making comparisons over time within an entity or with other entities.

Time-Series Analysis

Financial analysts generally review financial statements over a period of time for the organization under study, called *time-series analysis*. At a minimum, data (such as raw numbers, ratios, per capita information, or other formats) for the current year need to be compared with data for the previous year so observations can be made about the nature and extent of improvement or deterioration. To assess financial condition, however, analysts generally study changes for 5 to 10 years. (Ratios for some indicators may be unusually high or low for a year or two because of changes in general economic conditions.) To ascertain the implications of trends in economic and demographic factors (such as population shifts), data for even longer periods are reviewed.

Comparative Analysis

Suppose the operating margin (discussed later in this chapter) for a not-for-profit hospital was 2.5 percent in a particular year. How can the analyst assess whether 2.5 percent is favorable or not? To answer that question, the analyst might ask: "What is the median operating margin of other not-for-profit hospitals of similar size and similar patient mix in the same state?" *Comparative analysis* is a valuable tool for the analyst because it provides an external reference point—a type of standard or norm—for assessing the data developed for the organization under study.

Analysts concerned with assessing operating results, financial position, and financial condition of individual organizations maintain extensive databases to facilitate comparative analysis among generally similar organizations. For example,

- Several state agencies, such as the New York State Comptroller's Office and the North Carolina Department of State Treasurer, publish annual reports containing comparative financial data on local governments within the state. Some state agencies publish annual reports showing financial indicators for all hospitals or school districts within the state.
- Municipal bond-rating agencies maintain extensive nationwide databases to help in their bond-rating processes. These agencies often publish documents containing ratios that can serve as "rules of thumb" (general guidelines) for governmental entities seeking to compare their ratios with others'.

Information obtained from sources such as these can help in assessing the implications of ratios developed for a particular entity. Also, professional organizations may publish "best practices," industry averages, or other generally recognized standards concerning a particular measure of financial position. If such information is not readily available, analysts should construct their own "reference groups" or "peer groups" for comparison purposes. However, rule of thumb and reference group data need to be developed and used with care because of the potential for distortion caused by environmental differences, such as the nature of functions performed, mix of population served, size of entity, revenue sources, and location.

Although nationwide data may serve as good frames of reference for some ratios, it is often better to compare the organization under study with a reference group of similar organizations. For example, if an analyst is studying the financial condition of a city, a reference group of about 10 other *city* governments *within the state* might be developed, because all the cities are likely to perform the same functions and be subject to the same laws. They should also be of generally similar population size. For some ratios, data on all local governments within the state and available nationwide rules of thumb will serve as a useful check on the ratios developed for the smaller reference group.

FINANCIAL STATEMENT AND FINANCIAL CONDITION ANALYSIS INDICATORS

Many indicators used in financial analysis are developed entirely from financial statement data elements (or the notes or required supplementary information), or from the relationship of a financial statement data element to a demographic or economic element. The indicators may be classified as (a) liquidity indicators, (b) asset turnover or efficiency indicators, (c) budgetary solvency and operating results indicators, and (d) debt burden and other long-term financial flexibility indicators. Other indicators (used in the more extensive financial condition analysis) are derived entirely from economic and demographic data.

The indicators covered in this text are illustrative of the many ratios suggested by writers on this subject. We focus on indicators we have observed in practice or consider particularly useful. Some indicators are used for analyzing all three types of entities covered in the text: governmental, general not-for-profit entities, and not-for-profit hospitals. Others have been adapted to or developed for the operating characteristics of a particular type of entity, such as a government. The indicators are discussed in this section and summarized in Table 14-1 at the end of the section; they are applied to specific situations later in the chapter.

In considering the indicators, remember that no indicator taken alone can be used to measure an entity's financial position or condition. Also, ratios based on balance sheet information are as of a single point in time and may not be representative of what occurs during the year. Appropriate judgments can be made, however, when the indicators are considered as a group, examined over a period of years, and assessed in relation to those of a representative group of similar organizations.

Liquidity Indicators

New York City's fiscal crisis of the late 1970s was preceded by a sharp increase in short-term debt. Increased short-term borrowings and a buildup of unpaid bills are often the first signs of fiscal stress. *Liquidity indicators* provide information on the ability of an organization to meet its short-term obligations.

Commonly used liquidity indicators are the *current ratio, quick ratio,* and *number of days' cash on hand.* The general formulae for calculating them are as follows:

$$\text{current ratio} = \frac{\text{current assets}}{\text{current liabilities}}$$

$$\text{quick ratio} = \frac{\text{cash} + \text{cash equivalents} + \text{short-term investments}}{\text{current liabilities}}$$

$$\frac{\text{number of days'}}{\text{cash on hand}} = \frac{\text{cash} + \text{cash equivalents} + \text{short-term investments}}{(\text{total expenses} - \text{bad debts} - \text{depreciation})/365}$$

These ratios are used in varying degrees to analyze the financial statements of governmental business-type activities and not-for-profit entities, including not-for-profit hospitals. In these financial statements, current assets are cash and other assets as of the balance sheet date that will be converted to cash or consumed in operations in the following year. Current liabilities in both the current and the quick ratios are obligations that are due to be paid in the following year.

Those who analyze general-purpose governments often concentrate on the quick ratio, using the governmental fund financial statements. As stated in Chapter 5, governmental fund liabilities are current liabilities with a short-time horizon—generally payable in no more than 60 days; further, fund liabilities generally do not include accrued interest on long-term debt.

When calculating the quick ratio, current assets that are less readily convertible to cash are excluded from the numerator. At a minimum, the assets in the quick ratio are cash, cash equivalents, and other short-term (temporary) investments. *Cash equivalents* are short-term liquid investments readily convertible to known amounts of cash and are so close to maturity (having had an original maturity of 3 months or less) that there is little risk of loss in value. *Short-term investments* other than cash equivalents have slightly longer maturities and include CDs, money market assets, and U.S. Treasury bills.

Analysts of business-type activities often include accounts receivable in calculating the quick ratio. Analysts of general-purpose governments exclude taxes receivable in calculating the quick ratio but consider them separately in assessing the ratio.

From the perspective of the financial condition analyst, higher current and quick ratios signify a greater ability to meet current obligations. Historically, many organizations (including business enterprises) have found that a current ratio of 2.0 and a quick ratio of 1.0 provide reasonable margins for safety in meeting current obligations. These historical rules of thumb, however, are not etched in stone. Many business enterprises have found more productive uses for their cash and have current ratios well below 2.0. Hospitals that carry large amounts of slow-paying accounts receivable may need a current ratio higher than 2.0 to meet current obligations.

A quick ratio of 1.0 says enough cash is on hand to pay currently due bills, but a lower ratio may suffice if some current liabilities are not due for immediate payment and if cash received early in the next year from the next year's activities will help pay them. A New York State comptroller publication observes that cash balances tend to be lowest at year-end and suggests that year-end cash and investments generally should be about 50 percent of current liabilities.[3] The International City/County Management Association considers a quick ratio of less than 1 to be a negative factor.[4]

Monthly cash forecasts help supplement the liquidity ratios. Increasingly large amounts of notes payable due early in the next year (tax anticipation notes and revenue anticipation notes, in the case of governments) can signal an onset of liquidity problems.

Number of days' cash on hand, widely used as a liquidity indicator by not-for-profit hospitals, provides another perspective on liquidity. This indicator is a quick ratio converted to another form, because it shows how many days the entity can continue to pay its regular operating expenses without new inflows of cash. In making this calculation, depreciation and bad debts expenses are removed from total expenses because they do not require cash outlays. Some analysts include debt principal repayments in the denominator.

Asset Turnover or Efficiency Indicators

Cash can be invested or used to pay bills, but accounts receivable cannot. Receivables can be sold or used as collateral to borrow cash, but both come at a price—the payment of interest. Generally, the more rapidly an entity converts its receivables to cash, the more liquid it is.

You can express receivables collection efficiency in several ways. Hospitals and governmental business-type activities generally express *accounts receivable collection efficiency* in terms of number of days' revenue in receivables or average collection period. General governments measure property tax collection efficiency in terms of percentage of taxes collected (or *not* collected) in the year of the tax levy, or the ratio of property taxes receivable to property tax revenues. The general formulae for calculating these indicators are as follows:

$$\frac{\text{days' revenue in}}{\text{receivables}} = \frac{\text{net patient accounts receivable}}{\text{net patient service revenue}/365}$$

$$\frac{\text{property tax}}{\text{collection rate}} = \frac{\text{current-year real property taxes collected}}{\text{current-year real property tax levy}}$$

$$\frac{\text{property tax}}{\text{receivable rate}} = \frac{\text{real property taxes receivable}}{\text{real property tax revenues}}$$

---

[3]"Local Government Management Guide—Financial Condition Analysis," Office of the New York State Comptroller, Albany, NY, 2003, p. 30.

[4]"Evaluating Financial Condition," Sanford M. Groves and Maureen Godsey Valente, International City/County Management Association, Washington, DC, 1994, p. 77.

The number of days' revenue in receivables also can be calculated using the *asset turnover* method. Accounts receivable turnover is calculated by dividing revenues by accounts receivable. Days' revenue in receivables (or average receivables collection period) is then determined by dividing 365 by the accounts receivable turnover.

These indicators may provide evidence of weak administration, such as poor follow-up on slow payers or insufficient penalties for nonpayment of real property taxes. Increasing rates of real property tax delinquency, however, could also be a sign of the onset of fiscal stress, caused by an inability of property taxpayers to make their payments because of economic hardship. For example, referring again to the New York City fiscal crisis, analysis of the city's real property tax collection experience showed a gradual increase in delinquencies as the crisis of the 1970s worsened and better collections as the city emerged from the crisis.[5]

Another common asset turnover or efficiency ratio is the *total asset turnover*, which is calculated as follows:

$$\frac{\text{total asset}}{\text{turnover}} = \frac{\text{unrestricted revenues, gains, and other support}}{\text{unrestricted net assets}}$$

Total asset turnover is sometimes used by hospitals as an efficiency indicator. Assets used in producing revenues can be thought of as inputs, and the revenues can be considered as outputs. The greater the quantity of output for a given quantity of input (i.e., the higher the asset turnover), the greater is the entity's efficiency in using its resources.

Budget Solvency and Operating Results Indicators

Budget solvency means being able to generate sufficient recurring revenues each year to meet recurring expenses (or expenditures) and having a sufficiently large "cushion" of readily available resources to weather unforeseen economic downturns and expenditure needs. Entities with relatively volatile revenue structures (such as governments that obtain large amounts of revenue from economy-sensitive taxes like personal income and sales taxes) should maintain a larger cushion than those with relatively stable revenue structures.

The general formulae for the ratios discussed in this section are as follows:

$$\frac{\text{operating margin or}}{\text{earnings margin}} = \frac{\text{excess of revenues over expenses (or expenditures)}}{\text{total revenues, gains, and other support (or total revenues or other corresponding item)}}$$

$$\text{or } \frac{\text{net change in fund balances (adjusted)}}{\text{total revenues + certain transfers in}}$$

$$\text{budgetary cushion} = \frac{\text{available fund balance}}{\text{total revenues + certain transfers in}}$$

$$\text{program service ratio} = \frac{\text{program expenses}}{\text{total expenses}}$$

One indicator of budgetary solvency is the operating or earnings margin, determined by comparing the excess of revenues over expenses (or expenditures) with a base such as total revenues. The *AICPA Audit and Accounting Guide—Health Care Organizations* emphasizes the need for statements of operations prepared by health care entities to have clearly labeled operating

---

performance indicators, using terms such as "revenues over expenses" and "performance earnings." This indicator should be presented in a statement that also presents the total changes in unrestricted net assets.[6] (As discussed later in the text, hospitals often distinguish between "operating" margin—which considers only *operating* revenues and *operating* expenses—and "total" margin—a broader measure of earnings.) Significant transactions or events reported below the performance indicator also warrant scrutiny, however, in assessing financial health. An analyst might question, for example, whether unrealized securities losses might ultimately be realized.

For general-purpose governments, analysts generally measure operating margin by using only the General Fund or a combination of the General Fund and the Debt Service Fund, but some analysts add selected Special Revenue Funds. In this measure of operating margin, the numerator is the net change in fund balances (adjusted), and the denominator is the revenues plus certain transfers in, or the expenditures plus certain transfers out. We use the term "net change in fund balances (*adjusted*)" for the numerator because the reported net change may require downward adjustment for items that affect the *quality* of the change. For example, the net change in fund balances might require adjustment for (a) nonrecurring financial inflows, such as proceeds of debt used to finance operating expenditures or transfers in from closed-out funds, and (b) significant nonaccruals caused by using the modified accrual basis of accounting. We discuss this issue later in the chapter.

Operating margins need to be examined for a period greater than 1 year. A 1-year decline in operating results or even a negative net change in fund balances is not necessarily a cause for concern. For example, a government may budget deliberately for an operating deficit in a particular year to use up a small portion of its unassigned fund balance or to avoid raising tax rates. The analyst, thus, needs to understand the reasons for the year-to-year change and to examine the longer-term trends in the operating results indicator.

A significant indicator for analysts of general-purpose government financial statements is the budgetary cushion—the ratio of available fund balance to total revenues (or revenues plus certain transfers in). We use the term *available* fund balance here because fund balance consists of five components and not all of them are available to cushion the entity against future revenue shortfalls or emergency expenditure needs. That part of fund balance classified as Unassigned is clearly available as a budgetary cushion, and all or most of Assigned fund balance is likely to be available because of management's ready ability to change the purposes for which it intends to spend its resources.

What is a reasonable level of available fund balance? In the past, credit-rating agencies have suggested rates in the 5–10 percent range. Several years ago, a credit-rating agency said a General Fund balance of 5–10 percent of revenues is typically sufficient to address *normal* contingencies; another referred to 5 percent as "sound," but added that local governments that consistently maintain a level of 10 percent or more are viewed more favorably. More recent credit agency publications do not cite specific percentages but note that the size of a government's budgetary cushion depends heavily on its operating environment and managerial practices. For example, a higher budgetary cushion is warranted by such factors as a relatively high level of revenues from economy-sensitive income and sales taxes, concentration of the tax base in a few large taxpayers, and continuous negative deviations of actual financial performance relative to budgets.

The Government Finance Officers Association (GFOA) suggests a higher budgetary cushion than the credit-rating agencies have used in the past. The GFOA recommends that general-purpose

---

[6]*AICPA Audit and Accounting Guide—Health Care Organizations* (2006), par. 10–20.

Financial Analysis in Practice

State Budgetary Cushions and the Economy

The Fiscal Survey of the States, prepared by the National Governors Association and the National Association of State Budget Officers in the fall of 2010, shows how economic contractions can wreak havoc with budgetary cushions. The survey computes the budgetary cushion (which includes both ending fund balances and rainy day funds) as a percentage of expenditures. The survey says: "Though budget experts' views vary, the informal rule-of-thumb has previously been to build up total budget reserve balances to a level that equals at least five percent of total expenditures. . . ."

According to the survey, aggregate fund balances of the 50 states were 10.4 percent of expenditures in fiscal 2000. A recession at the start of the decade caused the aggregate fund balance level to drop to 3.2 percent by 2003, but strong revenue growth caused it to swell to 11.5 percent by 2006. As a result of the severe economic deterioration in 2009 and 2010, the fund balance level declined to 6.4 percent in 2010 (preliminary data) and 5.6 percent in 2011 (estimate). However, the situation in 2010 was much worse than the aggregate numbers indicate, because two states (Texas and Alaska) accounted for almost two-thirds of the total fund balance. In fact, 13 of the 50 states had fund balances equivalent to less than 1 percent of expenditures.

As the survey notes, lower fund balance levels impede the ability to respond to negative events that may occur during the year, including unanticipated budget gaps that appear toward year-end.

---

governments have a financial policy that calls for the General Fund unrestricted fund balance to be "no less than *two months* of regular general fund operating revenues or regular general fund operating expenditures."[7] It defines unrestricted fund balance as the total of committed, assigned, and unassigned fund balance.

Some governments have adopted financial policies concerning fund balance size. For example, the North Carolina treasurer suggests that local governments maintain a fund balance in the General Fund of at least 8 percent of the prior year's expenditures to meet current obligations and prevent cash flow difficulties. Financial status reports issued by Minneapolis, Minnesota, indicate that the city's practice is to maintain a fund balance of at least 15 percent of the next year's revenue budget. Some governments hold budgetary cushions in the form of "tax stabilization funds" or "rainy day" funds, their laws requiring that all or part of the General Fund surplus be placed in a separate fund until it reaches a specified level, such as 5 percent of revenues.

Examination of the composition of expenses of not-for-profit organizations is useful to those concerned with how donations are being spent. The FASB requirement to show program expenses separately from administrative and fund-raising expenses enables the reader to calculate the percentage of total expenses devoted to program—the program services ratio. See Chapter 12, page 443, for discussion of median administrative and fund-raising expense rates in not-for-profit entities.

Debt Burden and Other Long-Term Financial Flexibility Indicators

Investors (through credit-rating agencies), the general citizenry, and other stakeholders are concerned with the ability of governments and not-for-profit entities to meet their long-term obligations. Long-term obligations include not only the interest and principal on long-term debt, but

---

[7]"Replenishing Fund Balance in the General Fund (Budget and CAAFR)," Best Practice, GFOA of the US and Canada, 2011.

also promises made to employees to provide pensions and health care benefits after retirement. To enable the legislature and others to assess the level of their outstanding debt, some state governments routinely prepare "debt affordability studies." Also, credit-rating agencies issue periodic guidelines concerning debt and debt service burdens.

DEBT ISSUED BY GENERAL-PURPOSE GOVERNMENTS   The general formulae for calculating a general-purpose government's debt and debt service burdens are as follows:

$$\text{debt burden} = \frac{\text{outstanding long-term debt}}{\substack{\text{population (or full value of taxable real} \\ \text{property or personal income)}}}$$

$$\text{debt service burden} = \frac{\text{total debt service}}{\text{total revenues (or total expenditures)}}$$

Governments generally sell long-term bonds to finance acquisition of long-lived capital assets, but long-term debt may also be issued to finance operating needs in periods of fiscal stress. Governments that have a policy of financing a portion of their capital asset needs from tax revenues tend to have greater financial flexibility than those that finance all their capital asset needs by long-term borrowing.

State constitutions or statutes generally limit the amount of debt a local government can issue. Debt limits are usually expressed as a percentage of the full value of taxable real property. The closer a government is to its maximum debt limit, the less flexibility it has to borrow for its capital needs. Further, even if it has the legal capacity to borrow, a government may still find it difficult to borrow at reasonable interest rates because of recurring imbalances between its revenues and expenditures.

Common measures of a government's *debt burden* are those that relate outstanding long-term debt to bases that measure its ability to pay the debt and that can be tracked over time and compared with other governments. These measures include debt per capita, debt as a percentage of full value of taxable real property, and debt as a percentage of personal income. Debt per capita is a simple measure but does not take account of the wealth (and, hence, ability to pay) of the government's citizens. Full value of taxable real property provides a general measure of wealth; such information is readily available for local governments, so debt as a percentage of full value of taxable real property is often used to measure a local government's debt burden. Debt as a percentage of personal income, a measure frequently used in assessing state debt levels, is also a good measure of debt burden because it takes account of the ability to pay the debt service.

Outstanding debt for purposes of calculating debt burden includes the *net direct debt* of the government itself and *overlapping debt,* which is the proportionate share of debt issued by other governmental units that provide services to that government's citizens. Net direct debt includes both general obligation debt and other forms of tax-supported debt, such as lease-purchase obligations. Depending on the circumstances, net direct debt may exclude "self-supporting" debt, such as debt supported by Enterprise Fund revenues. Overlapping debt includes debt issued by related entities (such as school districts, park districts, and counties) that tax the same real property base taxed by the government, thus, placing a burden on the government's citizens.

For local governments, Fitch considers overall debt (e.g., direct plus overlapping debt) of less than 2 percent of full value to be low and greater than 5 percent to be above average; it considers overall per capita debt to be low if it is less than $2,000 and above average if it is more

---

Financial Analysis in Practice

Debt Affordability Studies

Debt affordability studies are useful financial management tools. North Carolina's debt affordability study provides a basis of assessing the effect of future debt issuance on the state's fiscal position. It also provides some guidelines for students interested in the financial analysis of governments.

North Carolina has AAA bond ratings from the three major credit-rating agencies and wants to maintain them. To help do that, its debt affordability advisory committee adopted the following targets to serve as the basis for calculating the amount of General Fund-supported debt the state could prudently issue over the next 10 years:

- Net tax-supported debt service as a percentage of general tax revenues should be targeted at no more than 4 percent and should not exceed 4.75 percent.
- Net tax-supported debt as a percentage of personal income should be targeted at no more than 2.5 percent and should not exceed 3.0 percent.
- The amount of debt to be retired over the next 10 years should be targeted at no less than 55 percent and should not decline below 50 percent.

Source: State of North Carolina Debt Affordability Study, February 1, 2011, available at www.nctreasurer.com; select Debt Affordability Studies under State and Local Government online.

---

than $4,000.[8] For state governments, Fitch considers ratios of net tax-supported debt to personal income in the range of 2–7 percent as "moderate" and a ratio greater than 10 percent as "very high, a point at which servicing debt poses a significant ongoing constraint on resources."[9]

A government's *debt service burden* is the portion of its revenues (or expenditures) that is consumed by the annual payment of principal and interest on long-term debt and interest on short-term debt. Because refinancing outstanding debt may be costly, the annual debt service requirement is a relatively fixed expense. Therefore, the greater the portion of an entity's revenues that is consumed by its debt service requirements, the less flexibility it has to issue additional debt, to meet operating expenditure needs, and to weather the effects of an economic downturn.

Credit-rating agencies recognize that debt service burdens vary among governments; ratios are likely to be higher among single-purpose governments (such as school districts) than general-purpose governments. One credit-rating agency suggests that debt service greater than 10 percent of general and debt service spending is "above average"; another says the burden is "high" when debt service payments are "15–20 percent of the combined operating and debt service fund expenditures." Another reported the median debt service expenditure as a percentage of total expenditures to be in the 8–9 percent range for all cities in 2005.

A factor closely related to the annual debt service burden is the rate of payback of debt principal. State constitutions or statutes generally limit the length of debt issuances. For example, some require that debt be issued for a period no greater than the useful life of the capital asset to be financed with the debt. Others require that debt be issued for no more than a specific number of years. To keep interest costs down, some governments repay their debt faster than is legally required. On the other hand, a government may decide to stretch its debt repayment schedule further into the future by refinancing its outstanding debt, which is often a sign of fiscal stress.

---

[8]"U.S. Local Government Tax-Supported Rating Criteria," FitchRatings, October 8, 2010, p. 6.

[9]"U.S. State Government Tax-Supported Rating Criteria," FitchRatings, October 8, 2010, p. 4.

Municipal credit-rating agencies generally consider a debt repayment schedule "average" if 25 percent of the outstanding debt is paid off in 5 years and 50 percent is paid off in 10 years. As long as it is not placing a strain on the operating budget, a faster rate of payback not only reduces interest costs, but also gives an entity greater financial flexibility; the more rapidly the existing debt is paid off, the greater is the ability to issue new debt to meet new capital asset needs.

DEBT ISSUED BY GOVERNMENTAL ENTERPRISES AND NOT-FOR-PROFIT ORGANIZATIONS
Debt analysis for governmental enterprises and not-for-profit organizations generally focuses on capital structure and coverage. *Capital structure* concerns the extent to which the organization is leveraged; that is, the extent to which its assets are financed through use of debt. Capital structure ratios are calculated in a variety of ways. The numerator in these ratios is often some formulation of total long-term debt or total liabilities. The denominator is some formulation of either total assets or net assets (i.e., assets minus liabilities). The result is either a *debt to total capitalization* ratio or a *debt to equity* ratio. In either calculation, as the use of debt increases—and the ratio increases—the entity's financial flexibility tends to decrease.

Coverage analysis focuses on the entity's ability to repay the debt, as demonstrated by its level of net earnings. Coverage indicators measure the number of times debt service (or interest on debt) is covered by the earnings. Thus, the greater number of times debt service (or interest on debt) is covered by earnings, the greater is the cushion against possible nonpayment. The general formulae for these ratios are as follows:

$$\frac{\text{long-term debt to}}{\text{capitalization}} = \frac{\text{long-term debt}}{\text{long-term debt} + \text{unrestricted net assets}}$$

$$\frac{\text{long-term debt}}{\text{to equity}} = \frac{\text{long-term debt}}{\text{net assets or unrestricted net assets}}$$

$$\frac{\text{debt service}}{\text{coverage}} = \frac{(\text{excess of revenues over expenses}) + \text{depreciation} + \text{interest expense}}{\text{principal payment} + \text{interest expense}}$$

$$\text{times interest earned} = \frac{(\text{excess of revenues over expenses}) + \text{interest expense}}{\text{interest expense}}$$

PENSION AND OTHER OBLIGATIONS Pension, retiree health care, and other post-employment benefit arrangements create long-term debtlike commitments. To be adequately funded, these plans must receive annual employer contributions and employee contributions (if required) so that amounts contributed plus earnings on them will be sufficient to pay benefits earned by the employees as the benefits come due. Failure to fund the plans appropriately each year as benefits are earned could place a future strain on an entity's operating budgets.

The most common measure of the adequacy of pension and retiree health care funding is the *funded ratio*, discussed in Chapter 8. Another good measure, particularly when different measures of the actuarial accrued liability make comparisons difficult, is *payout coverage*. These indicators are calculated as follows:

$$\text{funded ratio} = \frac{\text{fund assets available for benefits}}{\text{benefit obligation (actuarial accrued liability)}}$$

$$\text{payout coverage} = \frac{\text{fund assets available for benefits}}{\text{benefits paid last year}}$$

The most frequently cited level for what constitutes a "reasonable" funded ratio is 80 percent. Keith Brainard writes that 80 percent is "a threshold often cited by actuaries as a benchmark

---

Financial Analysis in Practice

Survey of Public Pension Funds

The *Public Fund Survey Summary of Findings*, published annually by the National Association of State Retirement Administrators, provides useful reference information for analysts in and out of government. The survey analyzes data provided by about 125 large pension plans (primarily state administered) and comments on trends in the funded status of the plans, factors affecting the funded status, investment returns, asset allocation practices, employer and employee contribution rates, investment return assumptions, and other significant factors affecting the plans.

The 2010 survey traces the annual aggregate funded level of the pension plans from 1990 through 2009. The funded level stood at 79 percent in 1990, increased to more than 100 percent in 2001, and declined to 79.8 percent in 2009. Both the increase and the decrease during the two decades were attributed primarily to changes in the value of equity securities held by the plans. The decline from 2008 to 2009 was particularly steep—from 85.3 percent to 79.8 percent—and would have been steeper but for the practice of smoothing investment gains and losses into the actuarial value of assets over a median period of 5 years.

From the perspective of analyzing the financial condition of individual governments, it is important to recognize that not all governments have similar pension-funding practices. The funded status of a government's pension plan depends not only on the value of the assets held by the plan, but also on the commitment of the government to finance the plan. Some governments consistently underfinance their pension plans, shifting both costs and risks to the future. Thus, the survey for 2007, before the onset of the 2008–2009 stock market decline, shows that, while some pension plans were more than 100 percent funded, some were less than 60 percent funded. A government that consistently underfinances its pension plans may be currently in fiscal stress and is at risk of future fiscal stress. Indeed, routine underfunding of pension systems is a major reason that some governments currently are in bankruptcy or on the verge of declaring bankruptcy.

---

of a pension plan's actuarial health" and that a level below 80 percent "may create fiscal stress" because of the need for higher future contribution rates.[10] Fitch says a funded ratio of at least 70–80 percent "typically indicates that the system is adequately funded given the assumptions underlying the plan."[11] An excessively high earnings assumption on plan investments, used in computing the funded ratio, will overstate the ratio.

Table 14-1 presents a summary of the financial analysis indicators discussed in this text.

GOVERNMENTAL FINANCIAL CONDITION ASSESSMENT

Financial statement analysis provides information about one or more aspects of financial position. *Financial condition assessment* uses financial statement analysis as a starting point for drawing inferences about the likely future ability of a government to meet its financial obligations as they come due, to provide services to its individual and corporate citizens, and to maintain these activities in the face of periodic economic contractions. Financial condition analysis, therefore, has a longer time horizon and is broader in scope than financial statement analysis.

---

[10]"Public Fund Survey Summary of Findings for FY 2004," prepared by Keith Brainard, Research Director, National Association of State Retirement Administrators, September 2005.

[11]"U.S. Local Government Tax-Supported Rating Criteria," Fitch Ratings, October 8, 2010, p. 7.

TABLE 14-1   Summary of Financial Analysis Indicators

Liquidity Indicators

Purpose: To help assess an entity's ability to meet its short-term obligations

Common Indicators:

Current ratio (current assets *divided by* current liabilities)

Quick ratio (cash + cash equivalents + short-term investments *divided by* current liabilities)

Number of days' cash on hand (cash + cash equivalents + short-term investments *divided by* cash needs per day); cash needs per day (total expenses − bad debts − depreciation *divided by* 365)

Asset Turnover or Efficiency Indicators

Purpose: To help assess an entity's efficiency in using its resources

Common Indicators:

Number of days' revenue in accounts receivable (net patient accounts receivable *divided by* net patient service revenue per day)

Property tax collection rate (current-year real property taxes collected *divided by* current-year real property tax levy)

Property tax receivable rate (real property taxes receivable *divided by* real property tax revenues)

Total asset turnover (unrestricted revenues, gains, and other support *divided by* unrestricted net assets)

Budget Solvency and Operating Results Indicators

Purpose: To help assess an entity's ability to generate sufficient recurring revenues to meet expenses and to meet unforeseen operating budget needs

Common Indicators:

Operating or earnings margin (excess of revenues over expenses *divided by* total revenues, gains, and other support [or equivalent]) or (net change in fund balances [adjusted] *divided by* total revenues + certain transfers in)

Budgetary cushion (available fund balance *divided by* total revenues + certain transfers in)

Program services ratio (program expenses divided by total expenses)

Debt Burden and Other Long-Term Financial Flexibility Indicators

Purpose: To help assess an entity's likelihood of having sufficient resources to meet its long-term obligations and to finance long-term capital and other needs

Common Indicators:

Debt issued by *general-purpose governments:*

Debt burden (outstanding long-term debt *divided by* population or full value of taxable real property or personal income)

Debt service burden (total debt service *divided by* total revenues or expenditures)

Debt issued by *governmental enterprises and not-for-profit organizations:*

Long-term debt to capitalization (long-term debt *divided by* long-term debt + unrestricted net assets)

Long-term debt to equity (long-term debt *divided by* net assets or unrestricted net assets)

Debt service coverage ([excess of revenues over expenses] + depreciation + interest expense *divided by* principal payment + interest expense)

Times interest earned ([excess of revenues over expenses] + interest expense *divided by* interest expense)

Pension and retiree health care obligations:

Funded ratio (fund assets available for benefits *divided by* benefit obligation)

Payout coverage (fund assets available for benefits *divided by* benefits paid last year)

To assess financial condition, the analyst must consider not only the results of financial statement analysis, but also the numerous factors—economic, demographic, administrative, and political—influencing a government's previous, current, and likely future finances. Financial condition analysis is undertaken for many reasons. For example,

- Credit-rating agencies provide an independent, objective assessment of the relative credit-worthiness of state and local government debt obligations. These assessments, generally made before sale of a particular issue of long-term bonds or short-term notes, help the issuer raise capital and help the investor decide whether to invest in the obligation. Credit-rating agencies consider four major factors: economic strength, financial strength, debt and other long-term obligations, and management and administration.
- Credit enhancers also assess the creditworthiness of debt obligations to decide whether to insure the payment of future debt service. Insurance lowers the net interest cost to the borrower and provides a guarantee of payment to the lender.
- Some state oversight agencies gather financial and other information from local governments within the state as part of their fiscal oversight responsibilities. The process is designed primarily to help both the state and the local governments detect early signals of fiscal stress.

Here are some of the specific matters—beyond the ratios previously discussed—that one might consider in assessing municipal financial condition:[12]

- Behavior and composition of the entity's *tax revenue bases.* The tax revenue bases are the specific sources of wealth, income, or transactions tapped to produce tax revenues, such as real property values, personal incomes, and general sales. From a financial condition analysis perspective, tax revenue growth resulting from increasing tax bases is preferable to tax revenue growth from increases in tax rates. However, insufficient diversity of tax revenue bases poses a risk of future revenue loss. (Fitch considers a tax revenue base to be "concentrated"—and at greater risk of revenue loss—if the largest taxpayer constitutes 5 percent of it or the 10 largest constitute 15 percent or more.)
- Nature of and trends in the economic and demographic base. Economics and demographics play a major role in tax revenue growth and expenditure needs. The financial condition analyst examines such factors as trends in resident personal income; risk of tax revenue loss because of insufficient employer, industry sector, and taxpayer diversity; trends in poverty, labor skills, and population growth; and trends in the nature of employment within the jurisdiction. Economic and demographic trends for the government under study are compared with peer group trends within the state and nationwide.
- Relative *tax bite* or *burden.* Tax bite is computed as the ratio of tax revenues to the tax revenue base. The greater the entity's current tax bite relative to similar entities, the less flexibility it has to raise tax rates in the future.
- Managerial skill and political will. History shows that some governments with a strong economic base have encountered fiscal stress because of a failure of political will, while some with a weaker economic base have avoided fiscal stress because of strong financial management and conservative fiscal practices. A financial condition analyst might raise

---

[12]For an extensive discussion of this subject, see Martin Ives, *Assessing Municipal Financial Condition,* Croton-on-Hudson, NY: Ives and Hancox, 2006.

questions such as these: Does the entity prepare longer-term financial plans? Are its annual budgets routinely balanced both in form and in substance? What are its practices regarding expenditure control? Has it adopted policies concerning debt affordability and size of its budget cushion? Does it routinely finance some of its capital needs from tax revenues? Does it adequately finance its pension systems?

ILLUSTRATION OF ANALYSIS OF GOVERNMENTAL FINANCIAL STATEMENTS

This section illustrates some of the ratios used in analyzing the financial statements of general-purpose governments. To make the calculations, we adapted the ratios shown earlier in this chapter to the government environment and used the data provided in the 2009 financial statements issued by Mt. Lebanon, Pennsylvania.

When analyzing the financial statements of general-purpose governments, analysts generally focus on the General Fund or on the total of the General and Debt Service Funds. Some analysts include the Special Revenue Funds that account for normal, day-to-day operating activities of government, such as libraries. In developing or assessing the ratios, analysts also need to consider the data provided in the government-wide financial statements as well as the statistical data provided in the comprehensive annual financial report (CAFR).

To simplify this illustration, most of our calculations are based on Mt. Lebanon's General Fund. For ease in tracing the numbers used in the calculations, the relevant elements of Mt. Lebanon's General Fund financial statements (presented earlier in the text) are shown in Tables 14-2 and 14-3. Remember that, except as otherwise indicated, the numbers shown in the ratio calculations are in thousands of dollars.

TABLE 14-2 Balance Sheet Elements for Ratio Calculations

Mt. Lebanon General Fund Balance Sheet (Condensed)
December 31, 2009 (amounts in thousands)

Assets	
Cash and cash equivalents	$ 5,641
Other assets	6,662
Total assets	$12,303
Liabilities	$ 1,923
Deferred Inflows of Resources	2,613
Fund Balances	
Nonspendable	760
Assigned for subsequent year's budget	1,876
Assigned for other purposes	1,446
Unassigned	3,685
Total fund balances	7,767
Total liabilities and fund balances	$12,303

TABLE 14-3 Operating Statement Elements for Ratio Calculations

Mt. Lebanon General Fund Statement of Revenues,
Expenditures, and Changes in Fund Balances (Condensed)
December 31, 2009 (amounts in thousands)

Total revenues	$29,247
Total expenditures	24,833
Excess of revenues over expenditures	4,414
Other financing sources (uses):	
Transfers in	369
Transfers out	(3,364)
Total other financing sources (uses)	(2,995)
Net change in fund balance	1,419
Fund balance, beginning of year	6,348
Fund balance, end of year	$ 7,767

Liquidity Indicator (Quick Ratio)

The quick ratio provides a conservative measure of liquidity for general-purpose governments. In calculating Mt. Lebanon's liquidity ratio, we did not include deferred inflows of resources as a liability because the deferral relates to taxes receivable under the modified accrual basis of accounting and not from receipt of cash. Mt. Lebanon's quick ratio, calculated from the data in Table 14-2, is as follows:

$$\frac{\text{cash and cash equivalents}}{\text{current liabilities}} = \frac{\$5,641}{\$1,923} = 2.9$$

The calculation shows that Mt. Lebanon has sufficient quick assets to cover its current liabilities almost three times. The quick assets of $5,641 thousand are also sufficient to cover about 2.4 months' expenditures. (Table 14-3 shows Mt. Lebanon's General Fund expenditures [$24,833 thousand] and transfers out [$3,364 thousand] totaled $28,197 thousand for the year, which is equivalent to $2,350 thousand a month; $5,641/$2,350 = 2.4.) Based on the previously cited rule of thumb guidelines regarding cash liquidity, Mt. Lebanon's liquidity as shown by its quick ratio is very favorable.

Efficiency Indicator (Tax Collection Rate)

One way to examine the efficiency of a municipality's property tax collections is to review the schedule of levies and collections, which many governments include with their statistical data. Mt. Lebanon's schedule shows that between 2005 and 2009, it collected (during the year of the levy) an average of 96 percent of the amount levied. The schedule also shows that Mt. Lebanon collects most of the tax delinquencies and eventually collects more than 99 percent of the adjusted levy. This is how Mt. Lebanon computed its 2009 property tax collection rate:

$$\frac{\text{face value of current collections}}{\text{total adjusted tax levy}} = \frac{\$10,244}{\$10,637} = 96.3\%$$

In an earlier publication, Moody's suggested that a current tax collection rate of less than 95 percent is a sign of potential credit distress. Mt. Lebanon's collection rate is better than that rule of thumb. Further, although Mt. Lebanon has experienced some delinquencies, it has been successful in collecting most of them.

Budgetary Solvency and Operating Results Indicators

A government's fund balance is basically the cumulative result of previous net changes in fund balance. Therefore, the size of the General Fund budgetary cushion depends on the size of the annual net changes in fund balance. But the net change in fund balance in any year is affected not only by the difference between revenues and expenditures, but also by factors of particular concern to the analyst, such as nonrecurring resource inflows. Therefore, for financial analysis purposes, the *quality* of the net change in fund balance needs to be analyzed, and the operating margin and the budgetary cushion should be considered together.

OPERATING MARGIN When calculating governmental activity operating margins, the analyst needs to use both the fund financial statements and the government-wide statements. Using only the fund statements may produce misleading ratios because they are prepared on the modified accrual basis of accounting and lack certain accruals. Using only the governmental activities column of the government-wide statements also may produce misleading results, primarily because the requirement to reduce program expenses by program-related *capital* grants and contributions can overstate the margin resulting from operating activities; although capital grants increase net assets, they are not operating revenues.

Many analysts assess operating results by starting with the fund statements and then considering the items in the reconciliation of the fund and government-wide operating statements. The analyst might adjust the operating results if the reconciliation shows large expense accruals in the government-wide statements that were not made in the fund statements. When using the fund financial statements, it is necessary to focus on the transactions reported between the captions "Excess (deficiency) of revenues over expenditures" and "Net change in fund balance." We started with Mt. Lebanon's General Fund statement of revenues, expenditures, and changes in fund balances (Table 14-3) and calculated the operating margin as follows:

$$\frac{\text{net change in fund balance}}{\text{total revenues} + \text{transfers in}} = \frac{\$1,419}{\$29,247 + \$369} = 4.8\%$$

To assess the *quality* of the net change in fund balance, we raised the following questions:

- What is the nature of the transactions after the caption "Excess (deficiency) of revenues over expenditures"—in this case, the transfers in and out? Were they for recurring activities or were they one-shot transactions (like asset sales or long-term borrowings) that should be removed from resource inflows? Analysis of the note disclosures shows that the entire amount of transfers out was for recurring operating items (to finance library activities and to pay debt service) and should be treated as recurring expenditures for financial analysis purposes. The transfer in was for recurring sanitary sewer maintenance activities provided to the Sewer Fund and should be treated as recurring revenue for this analysis. Therefore, in this illustration, there is no need to adjust the net change in fund balance.
- Does the data provided by the government-wide financial statements and the reconciliation between the fund and government-wide statements materially modify the operating results shown in the fund statements? The reconciliation of the operating statements (see

Table 10-4 on page 365) shows that the potential accrual adjustments are relatively small amounts, so the answer to that question is no.

- What conclusions can we draw from the budgetary comparison statement about Mt. Lebanon's budgetary practices? The budgetary comparison statement (see Table 9-5 on page 336) shows that Mt. Lebanon budgeted for a negative net change in fund balance of $1,028 thousand, but finished 2009 with a positive net change of $1,419 thousand. Actual tax revenues exceeded budgeted tax revenues by $916 thousand, and actual expenditures were $1,449 thousand less than budget. In short, Mt. Lebanon's General Fund financial position improved as a result of 2009 activities, even though it had originally budgeted a reducton of fund balance. Although data for more than 1 year are needed to assess the quality of Mt. Lebanon's budgeting and expenditure management practices, the 2009 data show that Mt. Lebanon budgets revenues conservatively and is able to "hold the line" on expenditures.

BUDGETARY CUSHION   The larger the budgetary cushion, the more likely it is that the entity can withstand revenue shortfalls caused by economic contraction and meet emergency expenditure needs. The total fund balance of Mt. Lebanon's General Fund is $7,767 thousand (see Table 14-2). Of this amount, Nonspendable fund balance of $760 is clearly not available; Unassigned fund balance of $3,685 thousand is clearly available; and fund balance Assigned for other purposes than meeting 2010 budget needs ($1,446 thousand) is also available, if needed, because management can readily remove the assignment. If Mt. Lebanon can accomplish in 2010 what it accomplished in 2009 regarding expenditure management, a portion of the $1,876 thousand assigned for subsequent year's budget may also be available to cushion future budget shortfalls. Thus, the available fund balance is at least $5,131 thousand ($3,685 thousand plus $1,446 thousand). Mt. Lebanon's General Fund budgetary cushion is calculated from Tables 14-2 and 14-3 as follows:

$$\frac{\text{available fund balance}}{\text{total revenues + transfers in}} = \frac{\$5,131}{\$29,247 + \$369} = 17.3\%$$

Historically, credit-rating agencies have considered a General Fund budgetary cushion of 5–10 percent as sufficient to address normal contingencies and have considered a cushion greater than 10 percent as very favorable. Although Mt. Lebanon derives about one-half of its tax revenues from real property taxes, it also obtains significant revenues from economy-sensitive income taxes. Therefore, a cushion toward the higher end of the 5–10 percent range is desirable. Mt. Lebanon's budgetary cushion of 17.3 percent is well above that range.

Mt. Lebanon's budgetary cushion is also well above the GFOA's suggested best practice for fund balance levels. Mt. Lebanon's unrestricted fund balance of $7,007 thousand (total fund balance minus nonspendable fund balance from Table 14-2) is equivalent to almost 3 months of revenue (one month's revenue is $29,247 thousand divided by 12, or $2,437 thousand). Further, the more conservative "available fund balance" of $5,131 thousand is equivalent to more than 2 months' revenues.

Conclusion: As a result of favorable operating margins, Mt. Lebanon's General Fund combined Unassigned and Assigned fund balance increased from $2,586 thousand to $7,007 thousand between 2005 and 2009. Thus, from the operating margin and budgetary cushion perspectives, Mt. Lebanon's financial condition is very favorable.

Debt Burden and Other Financial Flexibility Indicators

DEBT BURDEN   State laws generally limit the amount of long-term debt that municipalities can have outstanding at any time. As shown in its statistical section, under Pennsylvania laws, Mt. Lebanon had a legal debt limit of $108,757 thousand, against which it had outstanding debt of

$29,477 thousand as of December 31, 2009. Therefore, it had a legal debt margin (the amount of additional long-term debt that it could legally issue) of $79,280 thousand. Thus, Mt. Lebanon has ample *legal capacity* to borrow long term, if needed. Calculating debt burden ratios provides an indicator as to whether it also has the *financial capacity* to do so.

To assess the relative amount of a local government's debt burden, analysts generally consider only the *tax-supported debt.* "Self-supporting" debt (i.e., debt financed by user charges) and amounts set aside in debt service reserve funds are excluded. Even though Mt. Lebanon's parking activity debt of $4,362 thousand is guaranteed by the municipality, we excluded it from our calculations because it is self-supporting. This is our calculation of Mt. Lebanon's debt burden as of June 30, 2009 (all numbers shown here are the actual amounts):

Direct debt	$ 25,115,000
Overlapping debt:	
Mt. Lebanon School District	$ 71,140,396
Allegheny County	25,773,287
Total overlapping debt	$ 96,913,683
Overall net debt	$ 122,028,683
Measurement base:	
Market value of taxable real property	$2,175,275,286
Population	33,017
Direct debt as a percentage of property value	1.15%
Direct debt per capita	$ 761
Overall debt as a percentage of property value	5.61%
Overall debt per capita	$ 3,696

To put these indicators into perspective, we can use the Fitch rules of thumb discussed earlier in the chapter. Fitch considers overall debt (i.e., direct plus overlapping debt) of less than 2 percent of full property value to be low and greater than 5 percent to be above average; it considers overall per capita debt to be low if it is less than $2,000 and above average if it is more than $4,000. Analysis of debt medians developed by the rating agencies shows that direct debt ratios tend to run about 40–50 percent of the overall debt; therefore, assume that direct debt would be considered "above average" if it ranged from 2.0 to 2.5 percent, and per capita direct debt would be "above average" if it ranged from about $1,600 to $2,000. Using those criteria, Mt. Lebanon's direct debt burden is about at the median, but the overall debt burden on its citizens is on the high side as a result of the overlapping school district and county debt.

DEBT SERVICE BURDEN Debt service is a relatively fixed expenditure, which reduces the ability of a governmental entity to finance operating activities (and nondebt financed capital activities) from taxes and other resources. Debt service burden can be calculated from the information reported in the General Fund operating statement (see Table 14-3 on page 554) and the combining statement of revenues, expenditures, and changes in fund balances (see Table 9-4 on page 328). Mt. Lebanon's Debt Service Fund made debt service expenditures of $2,510 thousand in 2009, of which $2,443 thousand was transferred in from the General Fund and $67 thousand was transferred in from the Sewage Fund. The debt service burden on the General Fund was, therefore, as follows:

$$\frac{\text{debt service expenditures}}{\text{revenues + transfers in}} = \frac{\$2,443}{\$29,247 + \$369} = 8.2\%$$

We said previously that the debt service burden is related to rate of payback of debt principal; a more rapid debt principal payback will increase total debt service expenditures in the short run but reduce interest expenditures in the long run. A note to Mt. Lebanon's financial statements shows that Mt. Lebanon is scheduled to pay down $7,850 thousand (31.3 percent) of its $25,115 thousand debt principal in 5 years and $14,110 thousand (56.2 percent) in 10 years.

We believe credit-rating agencies would consider Mt. Lebanon's debt service burden to be manageable, probably better than the median. Even though it is paying down its debt principal somewhat more rapidly than the credit-rating agency norm of 25 percent in 5 years and 50 percent in 10 years, its debt service burden of 8.2 percent is about at the median. In summary, we think Mt. Lebanon's annual payment for capital assets through debt service is not at the level of creating undue competition with other programs for tax resources.

PENSION AND RETIREE HEALTH CARE BENEFIT BURDENS   Mt. Lebanon provides pension, retiree health care, and other postemployment benefits for its employees and maintains trust funds for that purpose. Notes to the financial statements and required supplementary information report the funded status of the pension funds on the January 1, 2009, valuation date as follows (numbers in thousands). To simplify the presentation, we added the values for the three pension funds together:

$$\frac{\text{actuarial value of assets}}{\text{actuarial accrued liability}} = \frac{\$54,375}{\$60,585} = 89.8\%$$

Based on the funded ratio "reasonableness" norm of 80 percent and the sharp stock market declines during 2008, the 89.8 percent funded ratio of Mt. Lebanon's pension systems is particularly good. Further, as reported in the required supplementary information, Mt. Lebanon's aggregate pension systems were more than 100 percent funded at the January 1, 2004, through January 1, 2008, valuation dates. Further yet, Mt. Lebanon used a 7.5 percent investment return rate for its 2009 actuarial valuation, which is more conservative than the median 8 percent reported in the Public Fund Survey of pension systems. In short, we consider Mt. Lebanon's pension systems to be well funded.

Using the same formula, Mt. Lebanon's retiree health care and other benefits plans were 14.8 percent funded at the January 1, 2009, valuation date. Because most governments finance these benefits pay-as-you-go, the fact that Mt. Lebanon's plans were funded even at this low level is a positive factor in assessing its financial position.

Overall Assessment

We designed this illustration to provide an overview of some of the factors considered in analyzing state and local government financial statements. Based on the ratios we calculated, Mt. Lebanon's financial position is very favorable. But analysis of financial condition for credit-rating purposes requires consideration of several factors not covered here. Mt. Lebanon's outstanding general obligation bonds were rated Aa1 by Moody's in late 2010. An Aa rating by Moody's means that the bonds are of high quality by all standards and, together with Aaa bonds, are referred to as high-grade bonds. The symbol Aa1 puts Mt. Lebanon at the upper end of all governments with Aa ratings. See the Financial Analysis in Practice box for excerpts from Moody's credit report on Mt. Lebanon.

Financial Analysis in Practice

Credit Report on Mt. Lebanon

The following excerpts from Moody's October 2010 credit report on Mt. Lebanon illustrate the matters considered in assessing the ability of a government to repay long-term debt obligations. The analysis requires a review not only of financial statements (as discussed in the text), but also of economic and demographic influences on the community and the actions of its managers.

The Aa1 rating reflects the municipality's stable and wealthy residential tax base, solid and well-managed financial position, and manageable debt burden.

Moody's anticipates that the healthy financial position will remain stable given conservative budgeting practices, timely tax rate increases, and effective expenditure management. After recording operating deficits in fiscal years 2003 and 2004, management implemented several revenue enhancing and expenditure saving initiatives to return operations to structural balance. . . . By fiscal year-end 2009, General Fund balance increased to $7.77 million, or a healthy 26.2 percent of General Fund revenues, with [unassigned fund balance] increasing to $3.69 million, or a satisfactory 12.4 percent of General Fund revenues. . . . Property tax collection rates have averaged a satisfactory 96 percent over the past five years.

Moody's believes the municipality's $2.5 billion [property] tax base will remain stable, given its almost fully built out residential nature and favorable location outside of Pittsburgh . . . Mt. Lebanon's income levels well exceed state and national medians and are amongst the highest in this region of the state.

Moody's expects the municipality's average 1.0 percent direct debt burden will remain manageable given limited additional borrowing plans in the medium term. . . . After accounting for the municipality's prorata share of overlapping county and school debt obligations, the municipality's overall debt burden increases to a well above-average 7.5 percent of full value, two times the national median. . . . Debt service comprised a manageable 9.0 percent of fiscal 2009 operating expenditures. . . .

ILLUSTRATION OF ANALYSIS OF NOT-FOR-PROFIT HOSPITAL FINANCIAL STATEMENTS

The more commonly used measures of hospital financial performance include the current ratio and number of days' cash on hand (liquidity indicators); number of days' revenues in patient accounts receivable (efficiency indicator); operating margin and total margin (operating results indicators); and capitalization and coverage ratios (debt burden and financial flexibility indicators). Data elements from the financial statements of Model Hospital, a short-term acute care hospital, will be used to illustrate the calculations of these ratios. As you read the text, trace the numbers used in the calculations to the financial statements found in Tables 14-4 and 14-5 (financial data are in thousands of dollars).

Some of the factors that affect hospital financial ratios in general are hospital type (acute care versus long-term or specialized care), size (number of beds), and whether the hospital is not-for-profit or for-profit, rural or urban, and teaching or nonteaching. To provide a frame of reference for assessing this particular hospital's ratios, we used financial ratios published annually by the Florida Agency for Health Care Administration (Florida AHCA).[13] This agency and similar

---

[13]For Florida AHCA ratios, see www.fdhc.state.fl.us; select Publications, then Certificate of Need/Financial Analysis Publications, then Florida Hospital Financial Data—Fiscal Year 2009.

| **TABLE 14-4** | Balance Sheets—Not-for-Profit Hospital |

Model Hospital
Balance Sheets
December 31, 2009 and 2008
(amounts in thousands)

	2009	2008
Assets		
Current assets:		
Cash and cash equivalents	$ 9,700	$ 9,500
Short-term investments	3,600	3,600
Patient accounts receivable, net of allowance for uncollectible accounts of approximately $4,200 in 2009 and $4,800 in 2008	13,300	12,600
Other receivables	1,500	500
Supplies and prepaid expenses	1,700	1,700
Total current assets	29,800	27,900
Interest in Model Hospital Foundation	5,900	5,300
Assets whose use is limited—externally restricted	4,700	5,000
Long-term investments	1,600	700
Property, plant, and equipment, net	32,500	30,500
Other assets	1,700	1,200
Total assets	$76,200	$70,600
Liabilities and Net Assets		
Current liabilities:		
Current portion of long-term debt	$ 600	$ 600
Current portion of capital lease obligations	900	1,400
Accounts payable and accrued expenses	3,400	3,300
Accrued salaries and benefits	4,200	3,700
Estimated payable to third-party payers	4,500	4,100
Total current liabilities	13,600	13,100
Long-term debt	17,400	18,100
Capital lease obligations	1,800	1,700
Estimated payable to third-party payers, malpractice and other liabilities	6,000	5,000
Total liabilities	38,800	37,900
Net assets:		
Unrestricted	30,200	26,700
Temporarily restricted	5,500	5,300
Permanently restricted	1,700	700
Total net assets	37,400	32,700
Total liabilities and net assets	$76,200	$70,600

TABLE 14-5	Statements of Operations—Not-for-Profit Hospital

Model Hospital
Statements of Operations
Years Ended December 31, 2009 and 2008
(amounts in thousands)

	2009	**2008**
Operating revenues:		
Net patient service revenue	$89,500	$84,500
Other operating revenue	2,300	2,400
Total operating revenues	91,800	86,900
Operating expenses:		
Salaries	39,000	36,800
Physician fees	2,000	2,000
Fringe benefits	7,600	7,000
Supplies and other expenses	32,300	30,000
Provision for bad debts	1,800	3,200
Interest	1,300	1,500
Depreciation and amortization	4,500	4,900
Total operating expenses	88,500	85,400
Operating gain	3,300	1,500
Investment income	800	500
Excess of revenues over expenses	4,100	2,000
Change in net unrealized gains and losses on investments	(100)	(200)
Net assets released from restrictions for capital expenditures	—	3,000
Increase in unrestricted net assets	$ 4,000	$ 4,800

ones in other states publish statewide averages based on reports prepared by hospitals within the respective states. We also used some medians developed from nationwide data derived from annual Medicare cost reports, which appeared in an article by T. M. Schuhmann, published by the Healthcare Financial Management Association.[14]

Liquidity Indicators

CURRENT RATIO Model Hospital's current ratio as of December 31, 2009, was 2.19, calculated as follows from the balance sheet in Table 14-4:

$$\frac{\text{current assets}}{\text{current liabilities}} = \frac{\$29,800}{\$13,600} = 2.19$$

The hospital's 2009 current ratio of 2.19 was slightly higher than the previous year, when it was 2.13 ($27,900/$13,100). We did not compute a quick ratio for this hospital, but if we did, we

---

[14]Thomas M. Schuhmann, "Hospital Financial Performance Trends to Watch," in *hfm*, published by Healthcare Financial Management Association, July 2008.

would be inclined to limit the quick assets to cash and cash equivalents plus short-term investments, because inclusion of accounts receivable would cause the current ratio and the quick ratio to be virtually the same.

NUMBER OF DAYS' CASH ON HAND   Calculating the number of days' cash on hand requires reference to both financial statements. First, estimate the average amount of cash needed each day to pay operating expenses. To do this, start with the total expenses (see Table 14-5), subtract depreciation and the provision for bad debts (because they do not require cash outlays), and divide the result by 365. Then, to get the number of days' cash on hand, divide cash and cash equivalents plus the short-term investments (see Table 14-4) by the average cash needs per day. The 2009 calculations for Model Hospital are as follows:

$$\frac{\text{total expenses} - (\text{depreciation and amortization} + \text{provision for bad debts})}{365}$$

$$= \frac{\$88,500 - (\$4,500 + \$1,800)}{365} = \$225.21$$

$$\frac{\text{cash and cash equivalents} + \text{short-term investments}}{\text{average cash needs per day}}$$

$$= \frac{\$9,700 + \$3,600}{\$225.21} = 59.1 \text{ days}$$

Thus, the hospital had sufficient cash and short-term investments as of December 31, 2009, to pay operating expenses for about 59.1 days. This is slightly worse than the previous year, when cash and short-term investments on hand covered operating expenses for 61.9 days. (First, $85,400 − [$4,900 + $3,200] / 365 = $211.78; then, [$9,500 + $3,600] / $211.78 = 61.9).

As a general frame of reference for these liquidity ratios, the Florida AHCA reported that the weighted average current ratio for all acute care hospitals in the state of Florida was 2.1 in both 2008 and 2009. Also, Schuhmann reported that current ratios for not-for-profit short-term acute care hospitals averaged approximately 1.9 between 2003 and 2007 and that the number of days' cash on hand ranged between 32.5 and 36.4 during that period. Based on these frames of reference, Model Hospital is liquid; its current ratio is in line with the averages, and its number of days' cash on hand to pay operating expenses compares favorably with the Schuhmann data.

How much cash should a hospital have on hand? W. O. Cleverley suggests that most hospitals lack sufficient cash to cover all their short-term working capital needs, capital investment needs, and contingencies. He says that, in 2005, the average not-for-profit U.S. hospital held about 15 to 20 days' cash and short-term investments to cover working capital needs. But much more than that might be needed to finance capital investment needs, depending on projected levels of capital expenditures and the extent to which capital needs would be financed from debt.[15] In this illustration, Model Hospital may be accumulating cash to acquire capital assets.

Efficiency Indicator (Number of Days' Revenue in Receivables)

Calculating the number of days' revenue in year-end receivables also requires using both the balance sheet and the statement of operations. First, use the caption Net patient service revenue in

---

[15]William O. Cleverley, "How Much Cash Should Your Hospital Hold?" *Strategic Financial Planning,* Spring 2007, pp. 14–15.

Table 14-5 to determine the net patient service revenue per day. Then, to get the number of days' revenues in year-end receivables, divide the net patient accounts receivable (see Table 14-4) by that net patient service revenue per day. As of December 31, 2009, Model Hospital had 54.2 days' revenues in its net patient receivables, calculated as follows:

$$\frac{\text{net patient service revenue}}{365} = \frac{\$89,500}{365} = \$245.21$$

$$\frac{\text{net patient accounts receivable}}{\text{net patient service revenue per day}} = \frac{\$13,300}{\$245.21} = 54.2 \text{ days}$$

Model Hospital's 54.2 days' revenue in accounts receivable at December 31, 2009, is similar to the previous year's figure of 54.4 days' revenues in receivables ($84,500 / 365 = $231.51; then $12,600 / $231.51 = 54.4 days). As a frame of reference, the Florida AHCA reported that the weighted average days' revenue in accounts receivable for all acute care hospitals in the state declined from 56.1 days in 2008 to 51.3 days in 2009. Further, according to the Schuhmann paper, the collection medians of nationwide receivables for not-for-profit acute care hospitals improved year-by-year from 56.4 in 2003 to 48.9 in 2007. Hence, there may be room for improvement in this aspect of Model Hospital's financial operations.

Operating Results Indicators (Operating Margin and Total Margin)

Hospitals often use two measures of operating results, the operating margin and the total margin. The operating margin represents the excess of operating revenues over operating expenses (or the operating gain) divided by operating revenues; the total margin includes nonoperating items, such as investment income, in the numerator and the denominator. The statement of operations (Table 14-5) provides the data for calculating these indicators. Model Hospital's operating margin for 2009 was 3.6 percent, calculated as follows:

$$\frac{\text{operating gain}}{\text{total operating revenues}} = \frac{\$3,300}{\$91,800} = 3.6\%$$

Model's 2009 operating margin of 3.6 percent was significantly higher than its 2008 operating margin of 1.7 percent ($1,500 / $86,900)—a favorable indicator. To determine the reasons for the improvement over the prior year (or the decline, if that had occurred), the analyst would need to compare the details of the revenue and expense components and determine the reasons for the major changes. In this situation, one of the major causes for the improved operating margin lies in the significantly reduced provision for bad debts.

Model Hospital's operating margins for both years lag behind the average operating margins reported by the Florida AHCA—4.0 percent in 2009 and 2.5 percent in 2008. On the other hand, the Schuhmann paper reports that nationwide median operating margins for not-for-profit acute care hospitals were consistently negative from 2003 through 2007 (negative 1.86 percent to negative 0.54 percent.). If we consider both sets of data, Model Hospital's operating performance appears to be satisfactory.

Model Hospital's total margin for 2009 (which, in this illustration, takes account of investment income) was 4.4 percent, calculated as follows and based on the data in Table 14-5. Model's total margin was slightly below the 5.0 percent average reported by the Florida AHCA for that year.

$$\frac{\text{excess of revenues over expenses}}{\text{operating plus nonoperating revenues}} = \frac{\$4,100}{\$91,800 + \$800} = 4.4\%$$

Debt Burden and Other Financial Flexibility Indicators

LONG-TERM DEBT TO CAPITALIZATION RATIO Model Hospital's ratio of long-term debt to capitalization as of December 31, 2009, can be computed from the balance sheet in Table 14-4. The current portion of the debt is sometimes included in this calculation, but we excluded it because it was covered in the current ratio.

$$\frac{\text{long-term debt (including capital lease obligations)}}{\text{long-term debt} + \text{unrestricted net assets}}$$

$$= \frac{\$17,400 + \$1,800}{\$17,400 + \$1,800 + \$30,200} = \frac{\$19,200}{\$49,400} = 38.9\%$$

DEBT SERVICE COVERAGE AND TIMES INTEREST EARNED Most of the data needed to calculate an entity's debt service coverage and number of times it earned its interest expense come from the statement of operations (Table 14-5). The cash outflow for the principal portion of debt service can be found in the cash flows statement. (Assume Model Hospital's cash flows statement shows the principal payment was $2,400 in 2009.)

The denominator of these ratios shows what was covered: either the total debt service requirement or just the interest. The numerator is based on the hospital's earnings; to get the numerator, start with the excess of revenues over expenses and add back either the depreciation plus the interest or just the interest. Depreciation is added back because it does not require a cash outflow and because it is, in a sense, a surrogate for part of what is covered—the principal payment. Interest is added back because it is part of what is covered and because it had been deducted as an expense in determining the excess of revenues over expenses.

In 2009, Model Hospital covered its debt service 2.7 times and its interest expense 4.2 times, calculated as follows:

$$\frac{\text{excess of revenues over expenses} + \text{depreciation} + \text{interest expense}}{\text{principal payment} + \text{interest expense}}$$

$$= \frac{\$4,100 + \$4,500 + \$1,300}{\$2,400 + \$1,300} = \frac{\$9,900}{\$3,700} = 2.7 \text{ times}$$

$$\frac{\text{excess of revenues over expenses} + \text{interest expense}}{\text{interest expense}}$$

$$\frac{\$4,100 + \$1,300}{\$1,300} = \frac{\$5,400}{\$1,300} = 4.2 \text{ times}$$

The hospital improved its times interest earned performance in 2009 over 2008, when it was 2.3 times ([$2,000 + $1,500] / $1,500).

As a frame of reference for assessing these ratios, we used data reported in a 2008 study prepared for the New Jersey Commission on Rationalizing Health Care Resources, which was based on 2005 financial data derived from Medicare cost reports.[16] The study covered acute care hospitals in the state of New Jersey, most of which are not-for-profit facilities. Model Hospital's long-term debt to capitalization ratio of 38.9 percent is at the nationwide median of 38.6 percent; it is also much better than the average long-term debt to captalization ratio for

---

[16]Available online at www.nj.gov/health/rhc/finalreport/documents/chapter_5.pdf

New Jersey hospitals (52.5 percent). However, Model Hospital's debt service coverage of 2.7 times, while better than the New Jersey average of 2.43 in 2005, was well below the nationwide median of 3.98.

Review Questions

Q14-1   How does the organization of the statement of net position help the reader assess an entity's financial position?

Q14-2   How does the organization of the statement of activities help the reader assess an entity's operating results?

Q14-3   How do the calculations of ratios and per capita amounts assist in assessing an entity's financial position and financial condition?

Q14-4   How do time-series analysis and comparative analysis help in assessing an entity's operating results, financial position, and financial condition?

Q14-5   What is the purpose of preparing common size financial statements?

Q14-6   What is the purpose of calculating the current ratio and the quick ratio?

Q14-7   What is the purpose of calculating the number of days' revenue in accounts receivable?

Q14-8   How is the budgetary cushion calculated, and why should a governmental entity maintain such a cushion?

Q14-9   What can a potential donor to a not-for-profit organization learn by calculating the organization's program services ratio?

Q14-10 Discuss why an analyst might prefer to calculate a governmental entity's debt burden as a percentage of full value of property rather than on a per capita basis.

Q14-11 Describe the relationship, if any, between a governmental entity's debt service burden and the rate at which it pays off debt principal.

Q14-12 What is the purpose of calculating debt service coverage?

Q14-13 What is the purpose of calculating a pension plan's funded ratio?

Q14-14 Why is it necessary to consider the economic and demographic environment in assessing a governmental entity's financial condition?

Discussion Scenarios and Issues

D14-1   Ken Mead, newly elected mayor of Bronson City, promised the citizens during his campaign that he would not raise taxes during his tenure as mayor. He asks his new commissioner of finance to analyze the city's financial statements to see whether the city has "any extra money lying around" to help keep taxes down. The commissioner of finance notices the caption "Unassigned fund balance" on the city's General Fund balance sheet. The commissioner shows the financial statements to the mayor and says: "See that Unassigned fund balance? Looks like a slush fund to me. Why don't we just use it to help keep taxes down?" How would you advise the mayor about this matter?

D14-2   Good Faith Hospital needs to sell bonds to finance major renovations and purchases of modern equipment. The hospital recently experienced difficulties, however, and its operating margin for the past 3 years fell below the median operating margin for hospitals of similar size. The hospital is preparing its financial statements, and preliminary indications are that its operating margin will continue its downward slide. The CFO is concerned that the bond-rating agency will lower the hospital's bond rating, resulting in an increase in the interest rate on the new bonds.

The CFO wants to report a higher operating margin than that of the previous year. He tells the chief accountant: "I don't want you to do anything you shouldn't do, but we both know that higher interest rates on the new bonds will reduce our operating margin even further. Just sharpen your pencil to see if you can reduce this year's provision for uncollectible patient receivables and estimated third-party settlements." If you were the chief accountant, how would you react to the CFO's request?

Exercises

E14-1   (Multiple choice)
   1. To prepare common size statements, what do you do to the financial statement data elements?
      a. Convert them to amounts per capita
      b. Present them on a single page
      c. Show them as percentages of 100
      d. Convert them to percentage change data
   2. Which of the following is considered an asset in computing the quick ratio?
      a. Supplies inventory
      b. Prepaid insurance
      c. Investments in long-term bonds
      d. Certificates of deposit purchased with an original maturity of 30 days
   3. Which of the following belongs in the numerator when computing the budgetary cushion of a municipal government?
      a. Infrastructure assets
      b. Unassigned fund balance
      c. Proceeds of bonds issued for capital construction purposes
      d. Restricted fund balance
   4. In computing the program services ratio, which of these expenses would *not* be considered part of the program service expenses?
      a. Donated services of an administrative nature, such as legal fees
      b. Depreciation of equipment used by a program
      c. Expenses of a program financed from temporarily restricted funds
      d. Donated services applicable to a program
   5. What does the number of days' revenue in a hospital's receivables reveal?
      a. Its bad debts expense for the year
      b. The amount of its charity services
      c. Its accounts receivable collection efficiency
      d. The amount of its net patient service revenue
   6. *Overlapping debt* is which of the following?
      a. General obligation debt sold to finance the capital assets of Enterprise Funds
      b. Debt sold by a public authority on behalf of a primary government
      c. The proportionate share of debt issued by other governmental units that provide services to the citizens of the government
      d. The portion of total debt issued by a government that is due in future years
   7. What does the *funded ratio* show?
      a. The portion of bonds payable that has been set aside in a debt service reserve fund
      b. The portion of the pension benefit obligation that is covered by assets available for pension benefits
      c. The portion of the future cost of fixed assets that is financed by a new bond issue
      d. The portion of the current year's tax levy collected during the year

E14-2   (Computation of a government's operating margin)
Following is an excerpt from a city's General Fund statement of revenues, expenditures, and changes in fund balance. Calculate the numerator of the city's operating margin. State the factors you considered in making your calculation.

Revenues	$670,000
Expenditures	640,000
Excess of revenues over expenditures	30,000
Other financing sources (uses):	
Transfer in from closed Special Revenue Fund	50,000
Proceeds from sale of capital assets	40,000
Net change in fund balance	$120,000

E14-3   (Computation of a government's budgetary cushion)
The fund balance components of a city's General Fund are as follows. Calculate the numerator of the city's budgetary cushion. State the factors you considered in making your calculation.

Nonspendable (supplies inventory)	$ 30,000
Restricted (intergovernmental grant)	20,000
Assigned (for future pension obligations)	15,000
Unassigned	50,000
Total fund balance	$115,000

E14-4   (Computation and assessment of a city's budgetary cushion)
The following information is extracted from the General Fund column of a city's fund financial statements. Compute the city's budgetary cushion. Based on your computation and the textbook discussion of the budgetary cushion rule of thumb, assess the city's ability to withstand a potential near-term economic contraction.

Fund balance:		
Nonspendable	$	85,392
Unassigned		423,185
Total fund balance	$	508,577
Revenues:		
Property taxes		$12,480,500
Sales taxes		14,325,700
Other revenues		1,683,800
Total revenues		$28,490,000

E14-5   (Computation of a city's debt burden)
The following information is extracted from a city government's CAFR. Compute the city's debt burden based on population and on property value. Make separate computations for (a) net direct debt and (b) combined net direct and overlapping debt.

Net direct debt	$ 15,841,000
Overlapping debt	$ 12,142,000
Population	13,243
Full value of taxable real property	$484,481,000

E14-6   (Computation of a village's operating margin)
The following information is extracted from a village's governmental funds statement of revenues, expenditures, and changes in fund balances (amounts in thousands). Compute the village's operating margin (a) for the General Fund and (b) for the General, Debt Service, and Library Funds aggregated. (Hint: The transfers out are routine transfers to the other two funds and should be considered as expenditures in calculating the General Fund's operating margin. Because the transfers in

are from the aggregated funds, they should be ignored in calculating the denominator for the aggregated funds operating margin.)

	General	Debt Service	Library
Total revenues	$8,640	$ 26	$ 15
Total expenditures	7,412	842	234
Excess (deficiency) of revenues over expenditures	1,228	(816)	(219)
Transfers in		850	225
Transfers out	(1,075)		
Net change in fund balances	$ 153	$ 34	$ 6

E14-7   (Computation of current ratio and quick ratio)
The following information is extracted from Alpha Hospital's balance sheet. Compute (a) Alpha's current ratio and (b) the number of days' revenue in patient accounts receivable. (Alpha reported net patient service revenue of $76,245,000.)

Cash and cash equivalents	$ 5,432,000
Short-term investments	2,317,000
Long-term investments	15,641,000
Patient accounts receivable, net	10,903,000
Supplies inventory	1,815,000
Current portion of long-term debt	2,900,000
Long-term debt, net of current portion	22,600,000
Accounts payable and accrued expenses	5,615,000

E14-8   (Computation of a hospital's operating margin, total margin, debt service coverage, and times interest earned)
The following information is extracted from Beta Hospital's financial statements. Compute Beta's operating margin, total margin, debt service coverage, and times interest earned.

Net patient service revenue		$75,458,000
Operating expenses	$62,490,000	
Depreciation and amortization	3,765,000	
Interest on long-term borrowings	2,200,000	
Provision for bad debts	3,000,000	71,455,000
Operating income		4,003,000
Investment income		500,000
Excess of revenues over expenses		$ 4,503,000
Principal payment on debt		$ 3,000,000

E14-9   (Computation of days' revenue in patient accounts receivable)
The following information is extracted from Gamma Hospital's financial records. Compute the number of days' revenue in patient accounts receivable.

Patient accounts receivable, net	$14,710,000
Patient service revenue, gross	97,478,000
Provision for contractual adjustments	12,609,000

E14-10 (Computation of a not-for-profit organization's program services ratio)
A voluntary health and welfare organization obtains contributions to perform various social services. The following information is extracted from its statement of activities. Compute the organization's program services ratio.

Expenses:

Youth services program	$ 89,000
Senior citizens health services program	312,000
Adult counseling services program	248,000
Management and general	156,000
Fund-raising	98,000
Total expenses	$903,000

Problems

P14-1   (Computation of financial analysis ratios for a hospital from a trial balance)
Following is a condensed trial balance of the accounts of Leveille Hospital as of December 31, 2013 (amounts in thousands).

	Debits	Credits
Cash and cash equivalents	$ 4,700	
Short-term investments	5,400	
Patient accounts receivable	14,700	
Allowance for uncollectible receivables		$ 2,600
Drugs and supplies inventories	2,100	
Buildings and equipment	72,000	
Accumulated depreciation, buildings, and equipment		22,000
Accounts payable and accrued expenses		5,400
Estimated third-party payer settlements (currently due)		2,300
Long-term debt		35,000
Unrestricted net assets, beginning of year		27,600
Patient service revenue (gross)		66,300
Provision for contractual adjustments	7,100	
Provision for charity care	1,500	
Operating expenses	45,300	
Depreciation expense	3,200	
Interest expense	2,400	
Provision for bad debts	1,300	
Other expenses	1,700	
Investment income		200
Totals	$161,400	$161,400

Additional information (amounts in thousands):

1. The amount of long-term debt principal paid during the year ended December 31, 2013, was $1,800.
2. The current portion of the long-term debt payable on December 31, 2013, was $2,000.

Use the preceding information to do the following:

a. In preparation for calculating ratios, compute the net patient accounts receivable, the net patient service revenue, the operating gain, the excess of revenues over expenses, and the unrestricted net assets at end of year.
b. Compute the current ratio and the number of days' cash on hand.
c. Compute the number of days' revenue in receivables.
d. Compute the operating margin and the total margin.
e. Compute the long-term debt to capitalization ratio, the debt service coverage, and the times interest earned.

P14-2   (Computation of financial analysis ratios for a hospital, using financial statements)
Following are condensed balance sheets and statements of operations for Elias Hospital for the years ended December 31, 2013 and 2012 (amounts in thousands of dollars).

Balance Sheets

	2013	2012
Assets		
Current assets:		
Cash and cash equivalents	$ 9,758	$ 10,877
Short-term investments	10,836	5,740
Assets limited as to use	970	1,300
Patient accounts receivable, net	15,100	14,194
Supplies inventory	2,670	2,856
Total current assets	39,334	34,967
Assets limited as to use, net of current portion	17,979	18,541
Long-term investments	6,695	6,570
Property and equipment, net	51,038	50,492
Total assets	$115,046	$110,570
Liabilities and Net Assets		
Current liabilities:		
Current portion of long-term debt	$ 1,470	$ 1,750
Accounts payable and accrued expenses	7,787	7,496
Estimated third-party payer settlements	2,143	1,942
Total current liabilities	11,400	11,188
Long-term debt, net of current portion	23,144	24,014
Total liabilities	34,544	35,202
Net assets:		
Unrestricted	70,846	66,199
Temporarily restricted	2,115	2,470
Permanently restricted	7,541	6,699
Total net assets	80,502	75,368
Total liabilities and net assets	$115,046	$110,570

Statements of Operations

	2013	2012
Unrestricted revenues, gains, and other support:		
Net patient service revenue	$ 97,156	$ 92,942
Other revenue	2,051	2,162
Total revenues, gains, and other support	99,207	95,104
Expenses:		
Operating expenses	87,521	80,585
Depreciation and amortization	4,782	4,280
Interest	1,752	1,825
Provision for bad debts	2,000	2,600
Total expenses	96,055	89,290
Operating gain	3,152	5,814
Other income—investment income	1,900	1,025
Excess of revenues over expenses	5,052	6,839
Other items (not detailed)	(405)	(1,140)
Increase in unrestricted net assets	$ 4,647	$ 5,699

Use the preceding information to do the following:
a. Compute the following ratios for both 2013 and 2012:
   1. Current ratio
   2. Number of days' cash on hand
   3. Number of days' patient service revenue in receivables
   4. Operating margin
   5. Total margin

6. Long-term debt to capitalization ratio
7. Debt service coverage (Note: Assume that $1,750 of long-term debt was redeemed in 2013, and $1,850 was redeemed in 2012.)
8. Times interest earned

b. Using these ratios and any other observations you make from reviewing the financial statements, discuss whether the hospital's financial position and results of operations improved or worsened in 2013 compared with 2012.

P14-3 (Computation of financial analysis ratios for a county government)
Following are extracts from the financial statements of Elisa County for the year ended December 31, 2013. The funds shown are the governmental operating funds; Capital Projects Funds are omitted. (All amounts are in thousands of dollars.)

Balance Sheet

	General	Special Revenue	Debt Service
Assets:			
Cash and cash equivalents	$ 6,700	$2,100	$100
Property taxes receivable (net)	19,500		
Other receivables	500	3,100	
Due from state government	3,500		
Total assets	$30,200	$5,200	$100
Liabilities:			
Accounts payable	$16,700	$1,100	
Accrued liabilities	1,800	300	
Matured bonds payable			$100
Total liabilities	18,500	1,400	100
Fund balances:			
Assigned	800	3,800	
Unassigned	10,900		
Total fund balances	11,700	3,800	
Total liabilities and fund balances	$30,200	$5,200	$100

Statement of Revenues, Expenditures, and Changes in Fund Balances

	General	Special Revenue	Debt Service
Revenues:			
Real property taxes	$ 46,000		
Sales taxes	45,000		
State and federal aid	36,500	$ 5,400	
Other revenues	27,200	9,400	$ 1,200
Total revenues	154,700	14,800	1,200
Expenditures:			
General government	15,100		
Public safety	26,600		
Public health	17,100		
Economic assistance	68,300		
Other expenditures	15,200	16,800	
Debt service:			
Principal			6,200
Interest	500		4,100
Total expenditures	142,800	16,800	10,300

(continued)

Statement of Revenues, Expenditures, and Changes in Fund Balances			
	General	Special Revenue	Debt Service
Excess of revenues over expenditures	11,900	(2,000)	(9,100)
Other financing sources (uses):			
Transfers in		1,900	9,100
Transfers out	(11,000)		
Net change in fund balances	900	(100)	0
Fund balances—beginning of year	10,800	3,900	0
Fund balances—end of year	$ 11,700	$ 3,800	$ 0

Use the preceding information to compute the following ratios for Elisa County:

a. Quick ratio (aggregated governmental operating funds)

b. Property tax receivable rate (Note: All taxes receivable are delinquent.)

c. Operating margin, computed separately for General Fund and for aggregated operating funds (Note: Consider the transfers out as if they were routine expenditures when computing the General Fund operating margin.)

d. Budgetary cushion, for General Fund only (Note: Assume the Assigned fund balance in the General Fund is not available for budgetary cushion purposes.)

e. Debt service burden (aggregated General and Debt Service Funds)

P14-4   (Assessment of governmental financial analysis ratios)
The state in which Elisa County (P14-3) is located publishes certain financial analysis ratios for all counties within the state. To provide a reference group for assessing Elisa County's financial analysis ratios, the median county ratios are listed here. Based on the reference group ratios, prepare a brief report assessing the implications of the financial analysis ratios computed for Elisa County in P14-3.

Quick ratio	110%
Property tax receivable rate	47%
Operating margin	
General Fund	2.4%
Aggregated funds	2.3%
Budgetary cushion—General Fund	12.0%
Debt service burden	4.9%

P14-5   (Assessment of a government's results of operations and budgetary cushion)
You are assessing the financial condition of Teddy County. As part of your assessment, you obtain the following summary of the General Fund column of the statement of revenues, expenditures, and changes in fund balance for Teddy County for the year ended June 30, 2012.

Total revenues	$14,350,000
Total expenditures	14,755,000
Excess (deficiency) of revenues over expenditures	(405,000)
Other financing sources (uses):	
Transfer out to Library Special Revenue Fund	(235,000)
Proceeds of debt	650,000
Total other financing sources (uses)	415,000
Net change in fund balance	10,000
Fund balance—beginning of year	165,000
Fund balance—end of year	$ 175,000

Analysis of county revenues shows that approximately 50 percent are from the sales tax. The year-end fund balance is entirely classified as Unassigned. On inquiry, you learn that the county makes transfers every year to the Library Special Revenue Fund to finance the library's operations and that the county sold $650,000 of bonds during 2012 to finance a looming deficit for the year.

Make a preliminary assessment of Teddy County's financial condition, based on the financial information provided here. Consider the following factors in making your assessment: (a) the county's operating margin, (b) the quality of the operating margin, (c) the budgetary cushion, and (d) relevant credit-rating agency rules of thumb.

Chapter 15

Fundamentals of Accounting

Chapter Outline

Closing the Books

Other Transactions and Other Matters
>   Withdrawals by the Owner
>   Control and Subsidiary Accounts
>   Credit Sales and Bad Debts
>   Buying and Selling Merchandise

Review Questions

Exercises

Problems

After completing this chapter, you should be able to do the following:

- Define and distinguish among assets, liabilities, and equity

- Explain the logic of the accounting equation

- Analyze transactions to distinguish between those that affect only assets and liabilities and those that affect equity

- Define and illustrate the accrual basis of accounting

- State the rules of debit and credit for assets, liabilities, equity, revenues, and expenses

- Record transactions in a general journal

- Post transactions from a general journal to a general ledger

- Prepare a trial balance from the general ledger

- Prepare adjusting journal entries

- Prepare an income statement, a statement of changes in owner's equity, and a balance sheet

- Prepare closing journal entries

THE ACCOUNTING EQUATION: TRANSACTION ANALYSIS

The basic processes of accounting—whether they are done for governments, not-for-profit entities, or business enterprises—are similar.[1] They all must keep records of their resources, their use of the resources, and claims against the resources. These resources, commonly called *assets*, represent items of value that are either owned or controlled by the entity as a result of past transactions and events. Assets might be financial in nature (like cash and accounts receivable) or nonfinancial (like buildings and equipment). An entity's operations are centered on using its resources for the purpose for which the entity was established.

A business-type entity obtains assets primarily from three sources: (1) investing by its owners, (2) incurring economic obligations (commonly called *liabilities*), and (3) earning profits from its operations. These activities can be illustrated as follows: An owner might provide additional assets (such as cash) by investing to expand operations. An asset (cash) is also created when a business incurs a liability (called a note payable) by borrowing from a bank. And, an asset (merchandise

---

[1]We have used simple business enterprises in this chapter to introduce you to the basic accounting processes because the transactions and terminology are likely to be familiar to you.

inventory) is created when a business incurs another liability (an account payable) by buying merchandise on credit from a supplier. Finally, a net increase in assets (perhaps in the form of cash or accounts receivable) occurs when merchandise inventory is sold or services are provided to a customer at a profit—a price that is greater than the cost of providing the goods or services.

The Accounting Equation

The difference between assets and liabilities is called *equity* or *capital*. Equity comes from investments in the business by its owners and from profits earned by the business. The relationship among these three elements can be expressed in the form of the following equation, known as the *accounting equation:*

$$\text{assets} = \text{liabilities} + \text{equity}^2$$

This equation states that the assets (resources) of an entity are equal to the sources of those assets: liabilities and equity.

At any point in time—for example, at the beginning or at the end of the year—the assets, liabilities, and equity of a business can be presented in a financial statement. This statement is based on the accounting equation and is commonly called a *balance sheet.* The dollar value of the assets will always equal the dollar value of the liabilities plus the dollar value of the equity. The balance sheet is a status statement—a statement of financial position—at a particular point in time. In fact, most not-for-profit entities now refer to this statement as the statement of financial position.

Effect of Transactions and Events on the Accounting Equation

In the course of the year, an entity will engage in numerous transactions and be affected by many events that change one or more of the elements of the accounting equation: assets, liabilities, or equity. Changes that affect the equity of the entity are expressed in another financial statement, generally called an *income statement* or an *operating statement.* The income statement thus serves as a link between the balance sheet at one point in time (the beginning of the accounting period) and the balance sheet at a later point in time (the end of the period).

Some transactions or events affect only assets, only liabilities, or a combination of assets and liabilities. In those situations, no increase or decrease in the entity's equity occurs. Here are two examples of these types of situations: (1) If an entity buys equipment on credit, an asset (equipment) is increased, and a liability (accounts payable) is increased. (2) If an entity buys merchandise inventory for cash, an asset (merchandise inventory) is increased, and another asset (cash) is decreased. Notice that, in both of these transactions, the accounting equation assets = liabilities + equity is always in balance. In the first situation, an asset increase is offset by a liability increase; in the second, an asset increase is offset by an asset decrease. Equity is not affected in either case.

Other transactions may affect an asset or a liability and, at the same time, increase or decrease the entity's equity. For example, if an entity bills a customer for a service, an asset (accounts receivable) is increased, and equity is increased because there is an increase in the entity's net assets. As a second example, if an entity pays an employee to provide the service just referred to, an asset (cash) is decreased, and equity is decreased because of the decrease in the

---

[2]In business enterprise accounting, equity stands for *owners' equity.* Because there are no ownership interests in not-for-profit entities, the difference between assets and liabilities is simply *net assets.* In governmental accounting, the difference is referred to as *net position, net assets,* or *fund balance.*

entity's net assets. If the price charged by the entity for the service is greater than the salary and other costs incurred by the entity, a net increase in the entity's equity will result.

Changes in Equity

Increases in assets generated through profit-oriented activities of a business (e.g., by providing services to a customer) increase the owner's equity. These increases in equity are called *revenues*. On the other hand, assets used in or liabilities incurred through the profit-oriented activities of a business (e.g., by paying an employee to provide the services) reduce the owner's equity. These decreases in equity are called *expenses*. When an owner adds capital to (or withdraws capital from) the business, however, it is neither a revenue nor an expense. It is a direct change in equity.

We can look upon revenues and expenses as temporary subsets of equity and, thus, broaden our equation to express both the point-in-time and the operating concepts:

$$\text{assets} = \text{liabilities} + \text{equity [opening equity} + (\text{revenues} - \text{expenses})$$
$$+ (\text{owner additions to} - \text{withdrawals from equity})]$$

Recording Business Transactions

The process of accounting involves the following: first, analyzing economic transactions and events to see how they have affected assets, liabilities, and equity; and, second, recording the effects as changes (increases or decreases) to one or more of those elements. To understand this process, consider the following transactions of a computer service started on January 2, 2013, by Kyle Thomas. Thomas intends to provide computer education to individuals who purchase personal computers.

1. On January 2, Kyle deposited $10,000 of his personal cash into a bank account, to be used exclusively by the business.
2. On January 2, Kyle also purchased 10 computers. The computers cost $30,000. He made a down payment of $3,000 in cash and financed the remainder through the French Quarter Bank. The agreement with the bank requires that Kyle pay back $9,000 on each succeeding January 2 for 3 years, together with interest of 10 percent a year on the unpaid balance of the loan.
3. In order to have an office for the operation of the business, Kyle rented office space on January 2 from the Mardi Gras Realty Company for $2,000 a month. Because the rental contract required payments at the beginning of each month, he immediately wrote a check for $2,000.
4. At the end of January, Kyle sent bills to his students. The amount due him for services performed in January was $5,000.
5. During the month, Kyle paid a salary of $1,500 to an employee who helped train his students.
6. Kyle received a utility bill for $300 for the month of January. Because the due date on the bill is February 10, the bill will not be paid until then.

Now, let us analyze each transaction and show how the accounting equation applies to it.

1. *The $10,000 Investment*   The entity concept (which relates to the scope of the activities covered in financial reporting) requires that the operations of an organization be kept separate from the owner's personal financial records. Therefore, we will consider only those transactions that affect the assets, liabilities, and equity of the business. The $10,000 deposit causes an increase

TABLE 15-1	Effect of Owner Investment					
		Assets	=	Liabilities	+	Equity
		Cash				K. Thomas, Capital
Owner invests cash in the business	+	$10,000 $10,000	= =	-0-	+ +	$10,000 $10,000

in the asset Cash. It also causes a corresponding increase in equity. To show the increase in equity, we will use the caption K. Thomas, Capital. This transaction is reflected in the accounting equation as shown in Table 15-1.

Two important observations about the transaction in Table 15-1 should be made:

- The dollar amount of the items included in the transaction must balance in terms of the equation; that is, the net change in the assets must equal the net change in the liabilities plus (minus) the net change in equity.
- The equation itself must balance after the transaction has been recorded.

2. *The $30,000 Purchase of Computers*   Recording this transaction causes the accounting equation to expand, as shown in Table 15-2.

Several observations should be made regarding this purchase:

- The assets of the business increased by $27,000: Cash decreased by $3,000, and computers increased by $30,000.
- The business now owes the bank $27,000. Thus, a liability exists that must be reflected in the system.
- The computers are recorded at their full cost, $30,000, even though Kyle borrowed $27,000 to purchase them.

In summary, the business now has assets totaling $37,000—that is, $27,000 contributed by creditors (the bank) and $10,000 contributed by the owner. Notice that the acquisition of the computers did not affect the owner's equity because he did not contribute any additional assets to the business as a result of this transaction.

TABLE 15-2	Effect of Computer Purchase						
		Assets		=	Liabilities	+	Equity
					Notes Payable to Bank		
		Cash	Computers	=			K. Thomas, Capital
Previous balances		$10,000		=			$10,000
The firm purchased computers	−	3,000 $ 7,000	+ $30,000 + $30,000	= =	+$27,000 $27,000	+	$10,000

A simple method of analyzing a transaction in terms of its effect on the accounting equation is to ask four questions:

- **a.** Did any asset increase or decrease?
- **b.** Did any liability increase or decrease?
- **c.** Did the equity increase or decrease?
- **d.** Does the transaction have a balanced effect on the equation?

For example, consider the acquisition of the computers:

- **a.** The asset Cash decreased by $3,000, and the asset Computers increased by $30,000.
- **b.** The liability Notes payable to bank increased by $27,000.
- **c.** No change in equity occurred.
- **d.** The transaction increased assets by $27,000 and had a similar effect on total liabilities and equity. Therefore, the accounting equation is still in balance.

Although this type of analysis may seem cumbersome, it will be a great help when more complex transactions are encountered.

3. The $2,000 Office Rental Applying the four-step analysis, the transaction has the following effects on the accounting equation:

- **a.** The asset Cash decreased by $2,000. Because the business now has "control" over the use of office space for the month of January, another asset has been acquired. This type of asset is usually called Prepaid rent, and it increased by $2,000. No other assets changed as a result of this transaction.
- **b.** Because the business does not owe any more or any less as a result of this transaction, no liabilities changed.
- **c.** Because the net effect of this transaction resulted in a decrease in one asset and an increase in another, the owner's share of the total assets did not change. Therefore, no change in equity took place.
- **d.** The transaction had a balanced effect on the accounting equation. The decrease in one asset was offset by an increase in another asset. Liabilities and equity were not affected by this transaction.

The result of this analysis on the accounting equation is shown in Table 15-3. Notice that the total of the assets ($37,000) is equal to the total of the liabilities plus equity ($37,000).

4. The $5,000 Billings By applying the four-step analysis, we can determine the following:

- **a.** Sending out the bills is a formal recognition that Kyle's customers owe $5,000 for services he rendered. As a result, he has a claim against each of them. These claims are assets because they give him the right to collect the amounts due. The title usually given to these assets is *Accounts receivable*. No other assets changed as a result of this transaction.
- **b.** Because the business does not owe any more or any less as a result of this transaction, no liabilities changed.
- **c.** Because the $5,000 net increase in assets was generated by Kyle's profit-oriented activities—services provided to customers—his equity increases by $5,000. (We can also "back into" this conclusion by noting that steps a and b produce an increase in assets without any change in liabilities. Because each transaction must have a balancing effect on the equation, an increase in equity must occur.)
- **d.** The transaction has a balanced effect on the accounting equation: Assets increased by $5,000, and liabilities + equity increased by $5,000.

TABLE 15-3 Effect of Office Rental

	Assets				=	Liabilities	+	Equity
				Prepaid		Notes Payable		K. Thomas,
	Cash		Computers	Rent		to Bank		Capital
Previous balances	$7,000	+	$30,000		=	$27,000	+	$10,000
The firm paid the rent for the month	− 2,000			+ $2,000	=			
	$5,000	+	$30,000	+ $2,000	=	$27,000	+	$10,000

The results of this analysis on the accounting equation are shown in Table 15-4. Notice that the total of the assets ($42,000) is equal to the total of the liabilities plus equity ($42,000).

5. ***The $1,500 Salary Payment*** Applying the four-step analysis, we find the following:

a. The asset Cash decreases by $1,500 as a result of the payment to the employee.
b. Technically, Kyle has a liability to his employee from the moment the employee starts to work. However, it is impractical to record that liability continuously. If he has not paid the employee, an increase in a liability rather than a decrease in an asset has occurred. But because he has made the payment, there is no liability to record.
c. The salary is an expense of doing business and, therefore, a decrease in equity. (We can also "back into" this conclusion by noting that, because each transaction must have a balancing effect on the equation, and because steps a and b showed only a decrease in an asset, there must be a decrease in equity.)
d. The transaction has a balanced effect on the equation: Assets decrease by $1,500, and liabilities + equity decrease by the same amount.

The result of this analysis is shown in Table 15-5. Notice that the total of the assets ($40,500) equals the total liabilities + equity ($40,500).

TABLE 15-4 Effect of Billing Customers

	Assets						=	Liabilities	+	Equity
				Prepaid		Accounts		Notes Payable		K. Thomas,
	Cash		Computers	Rent		Receivable		to Bank		Capital
Previous balances	$5,000	+	$30,000	+ $2,000			=	$27,000	+	$10,000
The firm billed customers					+	$5,000	=		+	5,000
	$5,000	+	$30,000	+ $2,000	+	$5,000	=	$27,000	+	$15,000

TABLE 15-5	Effect of Salary Payment						

			Assets			= Liabilities +	Equity
	Cash	Computers	Prepaid Rent	Accounts Receivable		Notes Payable to Bank	K. Thomas, Capital
Previous balances	$5,000 +	$30,000	+ $2,000 +	$5,000	=	$27,000 +	$15,000
The firm paid salaries	−1,500				=	−	1,500
	$3,500 +	$30,000	+ $2,000 +	$5,000	=	$27,000 +	$13,500

6. The $300 Utility Bill   The four-step analysis results in the following effects on the accounting equation:

a. Because the business does not have title to or control over any items of value that it did not have before this transaction, no changes in assets occur.
b. The business now owes money to an additional creditor. The receipt of the bill is a formal recognition of this fact. It necessitates recording a liability of $300. The title normally given to this account is *Accounts payable.*
c. The result of this analysis (steps a and b) is an increase in liabilities with no corresponding increase in assets. Because each transaction must contribute to a balanced effect on the equation, a decrease in equity of $300 must occur.
d. The transaction had a balanced effect on the accounting equation: Assets did not change, and the net effect on liabilities + equity was zero (+$300 − $300).

The result of this analysis on the accounting equation is shown in Table 15-6. Notice that the total of the assets ($40,500) is equal to the total of the liabilities plus equity ($40,500).

Although numerous other types of transactions could be illustrated for the operations of a business, those selected here should be sufficient to enable you to understand the process used for determining the effect of each transaction on the accounting equation.

TABLE 15-6	Effect of Receiving Utility Bill						

		Assets			=	Liabilities	+ Equity
	Cash	Computers	Prepaid Rent	Accounts Receivable	Notes Payable to Bank	Accounts Payable	K. Thomas, Capital
Previous balances	$3,500 +	$30,000 +	$2,000 +	$5,000 =	$27,000		+ $13,500
The firm received a bill for utilities				=		+ $300	− 300
	$3,500 +	$30,000 +	$2,000 +	$5,000 =	$27,000 +	$300	+ $13,200

Review Exercise

The following exercise should be completed by using the approach previously described. After completing a work sheet, compare it with the solution that follows so that you can determine how well you understand the concepts involved.

In this exercise, assume that Paige Keith is an independent tour guide who works for several large tour companies. Her income is determined by the number of individuals on each tour she hosts. To start her business, Paige had the following transactions:

2013

June 1 Paige placed $5,000 in cash into a bank account to be used in the operations of her business, Kaki Tours.

2 Paige signed a contract with Tel-Ans, a telephone-answering service. The service cost $50 per month, payable at the beginning of each month. Paige paid Tel-Ans $50.

4 Paige paid Print Faster $55 for stationery and the various forms she needed.

5 Paige purchased office equipment for $250. She paid $25 down and will pay the remainder in 30 days.

7 Paige purchased additional office supplies costing $125. She paid cash for these supplies.

10 Paige billed several tour companies for tours she conducted during the month. The total billing was $300.

15 Paige received $250 from companies she billed earlier that month.

18 Paige hired an assistant and agreed to pay him 25 percent of her revenue from the tours that he helped to organize.

20 Paige deposited $130 in her bank account. This amount was collected from various walking tours she conducted.

25 Paige paid $75 for the June rent (including utilities).

30 Paige billed several tour companies for a total of $400 for tours she conducted during the month.

Solution

The solution is found in Table 15-7.

THE ACCRUAL BASIS OF ACCOUNTING

Before moving on, you need to get a better understanding of the nature of assets, liabilities, expenses, and revenues, and of the purpose of accounting and financial reporting. Assume, for example, that you own a department store. You ask: "Can I find out how much profit I made last month just by seeing how much cash I had in the bank at the beginning of the month and at the end of the month?" If you think about your question a bit, you might ask: "How about the unpaid bills for the merchandise I bought? What about the items I sold on credit for which customers have not yet paid? What about the new fixtures I bought that are likely to last 10 years?" Knowing your cash position is important, but it's not enough to let you know how

| **TABLE 15-7** | Solution to Paige Keith's Transactions | | | | | | |

	Assets					= Liabilities	+ Equity
	Cash	Accounts Receivable	Prepaid Services	Office Supplies	Office Equipment	Accounts Payable	P. Keith, Capital
2013							
June 1	+$5,000						+$5,000
2	−$ 50		+$50				
4	−$ 55			+$ 55			
5	−$ 25				+$250	+$225	
7	−$ 125			+$125			
10		+$300					+$ 300
15	+$ 250	−$250					
18	No transaction—no assets, liabilities, or equity have changed. Nothing is owed to the assistant until he completes some work.						
20	+$ 130						+$ 130
25	−$ 75						−$ 75
30		+$400					+$ 400
	$5,050	$450	$50	$180	$250	$225	$5,755

Total assets[a] = $5,980   Total liabilities + Equity[a] = $5,980

[a]Cumulative totals after each transaction were omitted in order to conserve space.

much profit you made because it doesn't consider the effect of transactions and events that did not involve cash.

A major purpose of accounting is measuring performance (such as profitability) and financial position. To measure performance, an entity first needs to know what it is trying to measure, which is called its *measurement focus*. To achieve a particular measurement focus, accountants adopt what is called a *basis of accounting*. If an entity wants to measure inflows and outflows of cash, it uses the cash basis of accounting. But, as we have just seen, the cash basis of accounting will not provide a good measure of net income, because it recognizes the effect of transactions and events only when cash is received or disbursed. To measure net income, accountants use the *accrual* basis of accounting. Under the accrual basis of accounting, revenues are recorded when earned. Expenses are recorded when incurred, not necessarily when cash changes hands.

Accruals, Deferrals, and Amortizations

Accrual accounting is accomplished by certain processes known as *accruals, deferrals,* and *amortizations*. An accrual recognizes assets, liabilities, revenues, and expenses attributable to one period but not expected to be received or paid in cash until a future period. A deferral has just the opposite effect. In a deferral, cash has been received or paid in the past, but the economic benefit lies in the future. Thus, the recognition of the revenue or expense is deferred to a future period.

Amortization includes recognizing an expense by periodically writing down an asset. In the examples that follow, observe that every accrual, deferral, or amortization affects equity (as either an expense or a revenue) and either an asset or a liability:

- If employees earn their salaries in year 1 but will be paid in year 2, a salary expense and a liability are *accrued* (added to) in year 1.
- If revenues are earned in year 1 but the cash will be received in year 2, a revenue and an asset are *accrued* (added to) in year 1.
- If cash is paid in year 1 for a 3-year insurance policy, the payment creates an asset called "prepaid insurance." Recognition of insurance expense is *deferred* to the years actually covered by the insurance, some of which might be in year 1, some in year 2, and so on.
- If cash is paid in year 1 for equipment that will last 10 years, the payment creates an asset called "equipment." The expense of using the equipment is *deferred* and recognized by means of *amortizing* the asset over its 10-year life.

The Matching Process

The discussion of accrual accounting allows us to broaden our concept of the nature of assets. As previously noted, some assets either are cash or will soon be converted to cash, like accounts receivable. But buildings and equipment, previously described as nonfinancial resources, can also be described as unexpired bundles of future services, awaiting recognition as expenses as they are used up with the passage of time. Prepaid insurance and rent are also unexpired bundles of future services. So are inventories, which become expenses in the period they are sold. The notion of relating expenses to the same period of time that revenues are recognized is called "matching." Accrual accounting also helps broaden the notion of liabilities; that is, liabilities may result not only from borrowing and from not paying expenses, but also from receiving cash to provide services or products in the future.

Now, let us return to Kyle Thomas to see whether any of the transactions referred to previously require further consideration when applying the concepts of accrual accounting. Our analysis shows that if Kyle requested financial statements to measure accurately his financial performance for January and his financial position at the end of January, these matters must be taken into account:

1. Interest of $225 would need to be accrued because, even though he did not pay it, Kyle incurred interest expense for January because of the loan from French Quarter Bank. The accrual decreases equity (Interest expense) and increases a liability (Interest payable). The calculation is $27,000 \times 10\% \times 1/12$.
2. The asset Computers (an unexpired bundle of future services) would need to be amortized to recognize an expense because 1 month of the computers' estimated useful lives has expired. Assuming the computers have estimated useful lives of 50 months, the expense for the month would be $600 ($30,000/50). This decrease in equity (an expense called *depreciation*) parallels the reduction in the asset Computers.
3. Rent expense of $2,000 would need to be recognized because the asset Prepaid rent (another unexpired bundle of future services) expired at the end of January. Recognizing rent expense decreases equity and also decreases the asset Prepaid rent.

The result of this analysis is shown in Table 15-8. Notice that the total assets ($37,900) equal the total of the liabilities ($27,525) plus equity ($10,375).

TABLE 15-8 Effect of Accrual Adjustments

	Assets				=	Liabilities			+	Equity
	Cash	Computers	Prepaid Rent	Accounts Receivable		Notes Payable to Bank	Accounts Payable	Interest Payable		K. Thomas, Capital
Previous balances (Table 15-6)	$3,500 +	$30,000 +	$2,000 +	$5,000	=	$27,000 +	$300 +	+	+	$13,200
Accrual of interest								$225		225 −
Using up of computers		600 −								600 −
Expiration of prepaid rent			2,000 −							2,000 −
	$3,500 +	$29,400 −	— +	$5,000	=	$27,000 +	$300 +	$225 +		$10,375

RECORDING TRANSACTIONS: DEBITS AND CREDITS

Journals, Ledgers, and Accounts

In the previous sections we discussed how analysis of business transactions and events leads to recording increases and decreases to various components of assets, liabilities, and equity. The use of a work sheet to accomplish that recording procedure, however, is too cumbersome. Consider, for example, the size of the work sheet that would be needed to record the huge number of transactions and the numerous kinds of assets, liabilities, revenues, and expenses of any large corporation.

Because of the awkwardness of the previously discussed systems of analysis and record keeping, a more efficient system has been developed. This system is based on the same concepts previously discussed: Transactions and events are analyzed and recorded by increasing and decreasing components of the accounting equation. The actual recording of transactions, however, is accomplished through the use of journals, ledgers, and accounts. Transactions are analyzed and recorded in journals, from which they are then posted to a ledger that contains accounts.

- *Journals* are books in which every transaction that affects the accounting equation is recorded in chronological order. Journals, often referred to as "books of original entry," are the permanent records of all the transactions of a business.
- *Posting* is the process of transferring information from the journals to the ledger.
- A *ledger* is a book with a separate page that accumulates transaction data (increases and decreases) for each account (component of assets, liabilities, or equity). For example, separate accounts are kept for cash, accounts receivable, and accounts payable. Each account is in the general form of a "T," with one side of the T representing increases to the account balance and the other representing decreases.

Double-Entry Accounting—Debits and Credits

Recall from the earlier sections of this chapter that every transaction resulted in changes to at least two components of assets, liabilities, and equity. For example, when Kyle Thomas sent bills to his students, an asset (accounts receivable) was increased, and equity was increased. The practice of increasing or decreasing two or more accounts as a result of each transaction is known as double-entry accounting. We will now discuss how the T-form of the account facilitates the recording of increases and decreases.

As noted, rather than use columns on a work sheet, an *account* is used to accumulate the increases and decreases in assets, liabilities, and equity. It is much easier to accumulate changes if like items are grouped, so the increases are accumulated on one side of the account, and the decreases on the other. Arbitrarily, the increases ($+$) in assets have been accumulated on the left, and the decreases ($-$) on the right. As a result, it is much easier and faster to calculate the balance in an account at any point in time. This convention produces the following situation:

$$\text{Assets}$$
$$+ \mid -$$

TABLE 15-9 Debits and Credits		
Type of Account	**Increases**	**Decreases**
Assets	Debits	Credits
Liabilities	Credits	Debits
Equity	Credits	Debits

Because the system is based on the accounting equation, the following relationship develops:

$$\underset{+\,|\,-}{\text{Assets}} = \underset{|}{\text{Liabilities}} + \underset{|}{\text{Equity}}$$

When the account form is transferred to the right side of the equation and is used to accumulate changes in liabilities and equity, the signs must change. The increases are accumulated on the right side, and the decreases on the left side. This maintains the mathematical integrity of the transaction analysis and of the system:

$$\underset{+\,|\,-}{\text{Assets}} = \underset{-\,|\,+}{\text{Liabilities}} + \underset{-\,|\,+}{\text{Equity}}$$

Debit and Credit Analysis

In accounting terminology the left side of an account is referred to as the *debit side,* and the right side is referred to as the *credit side.* Note that the terms *debit* and *credit* refer only to position. Without any association with a particular account, these terms do not mean plus or minus. When a particular type of account has been considered, however, the terms do refer to plus or minus. For example, when assets are considered (see the previous illustration), increases are accumulated on the left, or debit side, and decreases are accumulated on the right, or credit side. Liabilities and equity, however, are increased or decreased in the opposite manner: Debits represent decreases, and credits represent increases. These rules are summarized in Table 15-9.

To complete the system, revenues and expenses must be analyzed in terms of their debit/credit effect. At the end of each period, it is important that management study the relative size of the individual revenues and expenses incurred in operating an organization. In the previous illustrations, revenues and expenses were recorded as direct increases or decreases in equity. To make the analysis easier, however, we will begin to accumulate the changes in each of the revenues and expenses in separate accounts. This practice will avoid the rather cumbersome task of sorting out the revenues and expenses after they have been combined in the equity account.

The debit/credit analysis of revenues and expenses is based on the relationship of each to equity. Remember that revenues and expenses were defined as temporary subsets of the equity of a firm. Because revenues cause equity to increase, they are recorded as credits. Any reductions of revenues are recorded as debits, as shown in the following illustration:

$$\underset{-\,|\,+}{\text{Revenues}}$$

Note the *direct* relationship with equity. Equity is increased with credits. Because revenues increase equity, *revenues* are increased with *credits*. Equity is decreased with debits. Because decreases in revenue are decreases in equity, revenues are decreased with debits.

Expenses follow the same logic. The analysis, however, is a bit more complex. *Expenses* have been defined as those decreases in equity associated with the profit-oriented activities of the business. Therefore, as expenses increase, the amount of equity decreases. A decrease in equity is recorded as a debit. Continuing with this logic, then, an increase in an expense must be recorded with a debit. This procedure reflects the decrease in equity that is taking place.

This analysis can be extended to include a decrease in an expense, which results in a credit to the expense account and reflects the increase in equity that is taking place, as shown in the following illustration:

Expenses

Debits	Credits
+	−

To summarize, it is helpful to return to our earlier comment about considering revenues and expenses as temporary subsets of equity. In this context, revenues may be viewed as the increase side (credits) of equity and expenses as the decrease side (debits) of equity. Thus, an increase in expenses (a debit) is really a decrease in equity. This relationship is shown in the following illustration:

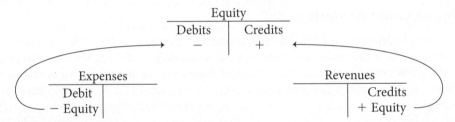

Notice that this system is based on the mathematical integrity of the accounting equation. As a result, the equality mentioned in the section "The Accounting Equation: Transaction Analysis" still exists—that is, the accounting equation must be balanced after the result of each transaction has been recorded. In terms of debits and credits, this equality can be stated as follows:

The total dollar amount of debits for any transaction must EQUAL the total dollar amount of credits.

This rule is critical because it affects the integrity of the entire accounting system.

Transaction Analysis Using Debits and Credits

The effects of a transaction can now be recorded in terms of debits and credits that increase or decrease the accounts. Following are several examples taken from the Review Exercise in the previous section:[3]

---

[3]The effects of the transactions on the individual accounts are summarized in Table 15-10.

Transaction		Analysis	
June 1	Paige invested $5,000 in cash in a bank account to be used in the operations of her business, Kaki Tours.	Debit:	Cash, $5,000—to record the increase in this asset.
		Credit:	P. Keith, Capital, $5,000—to record the increase in equity.
June 2	She signed a contract with Tel-Ans, a telephone-answering service. The service cost $50 per month, payable at the beginning of each month. She paid Tel-Ans $50.	Debit:	Prepaid services, $50—to record the increase in this asset.
		Credit:	Cash, $50—to record the decrease in this asset.
June 4	She paid Print Faster $55 for stationery and the various forms she needed.	Debit:	Office supplies, $55—to record the increase in this asset.
		Credit:	Cash, $55 to record the decrease in this asset.
June 5	She purchased office equipment for $250. She paid $25 down and will pay the remainder in 30 days.	Debit:	Office equipment, $250—to record the increase in this asset.
		Credit:	Cash, $25—to record the decrease in this asset.
		Credit:	Accounts payable, $225—to record the increase in this liability.

Review Exercise

Using the following information, prepare an analysis of the remaining transactions of Paige Keith's tour business that is similar to the previous analysis. Compare your results with the solution that follows.

Transaction	
June 7	Paige Keith purchased additional office supplies costing $125. She paid cash for these supplies.
June 10	She billed several tour companies for tours she conducted during the month. The total billing was $300.
June 15	She received $250 from companies she billed earlier that month.
June 18	She hired an assistant and agreed to pay him 25 percent of her revenue from the tours that he helped to organize.
June 20	Paige Keith deposited $130 in her bank account. This amount was collected from various walking tours she conducted.
June 25	She paid $75 for the June rent (including utilities).
June 30	She billed several tour companies for a total of $400 for tours she conducted during the month.

Solution

June 7   *Debit:*   Office supplies, $125—to record the increase in this asset.
          Credit: Cash, $125—to record the decrease in this asset.

June 10   *Debit:*   Accounts receivable, $300—to record the increase in this asset.
          Credit: Tour revenue, $300—to record the increase in equity from profit-oriented activities.

June 15   *Debit:*   Cash, $250—to record the increase in this asset.
          Credit: Accounts receivable, $250—to record the decrease in this asset.

June 18   No transaction: no assets, liabilities, or equity have changed.
          Nothing is owed to the assistant until he completes some work.

June 20   *Debit:*   Cash, $130—to record the increase in this asset.
          Credit: Tour revenue, $130—to record the increase in equity from profit-oriented activities.

June 25   *Debit:*   Office rent expense, $75—to record the decrease in equity from profit-oriented activities.
          Credit: Cash, $75—to record the decrease in this asset.

June 30   *Debit:*   Accounts receivable, $400—to record the increase in this asset.
          Credit: Tour revenue, $400—to record the increase in equity from profit-oriented activities.

The results of these transactions in the accounts are summarized in Table 15-10.

TABLE 15-10 Paige Keith Transactions—Ledger Accounts

Cash		Accounts Receivable		Prepaid Services		Office Supplies	
5,000	50	300	250	50		55	
250	55	400				125	
130	25	700	250			180	
	125	450					
	75						
5,380	330						
5,050							

Office Equipment		Accounts Receivable		P. Keith, Capital		Tour Revenue	
250			225		5,000		300
							130
							400
							830

Office Rent Expense	
75	

Completion of Review Exercise

Table 15-10 covers each transaction in the Review Exercise in the section "The Accounting Equation: Transaction Analysis." Several transactions were omitted in that section, however, because we had not yet discussed accrual accounting. The items that follow are similar to those covered in the section "The Accrual Basis of Accounting":

1. The assistant was not paid for the services he performed. Because this amount is owed at the end of the month, the amount earned must be recorded. This entry will record the liability owed and the effect on equity of the services performed by the assistant. Assuming this owed amount is $40, the following entry is necessary:

   Debit: Salary expense, $40—to record the decrease in equity from profit-oriented activities.

   Credit: Salary payable, $40—to record the increase in liabilities.

2. By the end of June, the services performed by Tel-Ans for the month were "used up" and no longer had any value. The following entry, therefore, is necessary:

   Debit: Telephone-answering expense, $50—to record the decrease in equity from profit-oriented activities.

   Credit: Prepaid services, $50—to record the decrease in this asset.

   Note: To save time, most companies record repetitive monthly payments for services such as answering services directly in an expense account. This practice eliminates the need for a second entry like the one described here. If this procedure had been followed here, the June 2 entry would have required a debit to Telephone answering expense and a credit to Cash for $50. Notice that the effect of these two procedures on the accounting equation is the same: Assets decrease and Equity decreases.

3. Office supplies totaling $180 were purchased in June. During the month some of these supplies were used. Assuming the cost of the supplies used was $30, the following entry is necessary:

   Debit: Office supplies expense, $30—to record the decrease in equity from profit-oriented activities.

   Credit: Office supplies, $30—to record the decrease in this asset.

4. The final item that must be considered is office equipment. Whenever a business purchases an asset, it is really buying a "bundle of future services." As these services are used up, an expense is recorded. Using the services of an asset such as Office equipment is generally referred to as *depreciation*. Because it is the using up of an asset in the profit-oriented activities of the business, it is recognized as an expense. The following entry is, therefore, necessary (assume the amount is $5):

   Debit: Depreciation expense—office equipment, $5—to record the decrease in equity from profit-oriented activities.

   Credit: Accumulated depreciation—office equipment, $5—to record the decrease in the asset. Accumulated depreciation is credited instead of the asset itself because it is important to maintain the original cost in a separate account. The Accumulated depreciation account is treated as a negative, or contra, asset—the effect is the same as crediting the Office equipment account directly (see Table 15-15 on page 601).

TABLE 15-11	Paige Keith Transactions—Ledger Accounts

Cash		Accounts Receivable		Prepaid Services		Office Supplies	
5,000	50	300	250	50	50	55	30
250	55	400		-0-		125	
130	25	700	250			180	30
	125	450				150	
	75						
5,380	330						
5,050							

Office Equipment		Accumulated Depreciation— Office Equipment		Accounts Payable	
250			5		225

Salary Payable		P. Keith, Capital		Tour Revenue		Office Rent Expense	
	40		5,000		300	75	
					130		
					400		
					830		

Salary Expense		Telephone- Answering Expense		Office Supplies Expense		Depreciation Expense— Office Equipment	
40		50		30		5	

After these transactions have been entered into the system, the accounts will appear as shown in Table 15-11.

A More Complete Look at the Transaction Recording Process

Now that we have discussed the principles of recording transactions through the use of debits and credits, let us return to the actual process of maintaining accounting records by using journals and ledgers. We said that a journal is a permanent record of all the transactions of a business. The process of recording transactions in a journal is referred to as making journal entries, or *journalizing*. Although there are various types of journals, the one we will illustrate is called a *general journal*. Exhibit 15-1 illustrates the form of a general journal. (To simplify the recording process, entities use separate journals—such as cash receipts, cash disbursements, sales, and purchase journals—to record similar types of transactions.)

GENERAL JOURNAL   Page 1

Date 2013		Description	P.R.	Debit	Credit
June	1	Cash	101	5000 –	
		P. Keith, Capital	301		5000 –
		Owner invested $5,000 in the business.			

EXHIBIT 15-1   General Journal

Continuing the example used in the previous two sections, let us reconsider the first transaction illustrated. The following steps are used when entering information in the journal (follow each step by referring to the journal entry in Exhibit 15-1):

1. The year is written at the top of each page in the Date column.
2. The month of the transaction is entered. As additional transactions are entered, the month is usually not rewritten unless the same journal page is used for more than 1 month.
3. The third item of information is the date of the transaction. Because this helps separate the transactions, the date for each transaction is usually entered—even if it is the same as that of the preceding transaction.
4. The debit account is entered next to the left-hand margin in the Description column. If more than one debit account is involved in a transaction, all the debit items must be entered before any credit items are entered.
5. Each debit amount is entered in the Debit money column.
6. The credit account or accounts are entered and are *slightly indented* to the right.
7. The respective credit amount or amounts are placed in the Credit money column.
8. The final part of the entry is the explanation. Here a brief description of the transaction is entered. It helps explain the event that was recorded. It can be useful when attempting to analyze the events that caused a particular account to change.
9. A line is usually skipped between journal entries to help separate the entries and to make the information included in the journal easier to read.

The Ledger and Posting

Changes in the accounting equation are accumulated in the journal by transaction. To provide information to decision makers, these data must be summarized in useful categories. This summarization is provided in the ledger. We said earlier that the ledger is a book with a separate page for each account. The traditional two-column ledger account is shown in Exhibit 15-2. We also said that posting is the process of transferring information from the journal to the ledger. The following steps are used when posting a debit entry to the ledger (follow each step by referring to the ledger in Exhibit 15-2):

1. The year is entered as the first item in the Date column on the debit side of the account. As in the journal, it is entered only once.

GENERAL LEDGER

Cash   Account No. 101

Date 2013		Item	P.R.	Debit	Date 2013		Item	P.R.	Credit
June	1		1	5000 –					

P. Keith, Capital   Account No. 301

Date 2013		Item	P.R.	Debit	Date 2013		Item	P.R.	Credit
					June	1		1	5000 –

EXHIBIT 15-2   General Ledger

2. The next item of information is the month. It is placed beneath the year and is entered only once unless the same ledger page is used for more than 1 month.
3. The date of the transaction is the next piece of information placed in the ledger.
4. The amount of the transaction is then entered in the Debit money column.
5. Finally, the P.R. (Posting Reference) column is used to enter the page number where the transaction is recorded in the journal.
6. The account number (for Cash it is 101) is entered in the journal in the P.R. column (see Exhibit 15-1). Thus, the cross-referencing system has been completed. The journal entry can be traced to the ledger, and the ledger entry can be traced back to the original transaction in the journal.

These steps follow the posting of a debit to the Cash account. The process is the same for each credit entry except that the recording is made on the credit side of the account. See Exhibit 15-2 for the P. Keith, Capital account, and follow the steps previously listed. The ledger referred to in Exhibit 15-2 is a *general ledger*.

Review Exercise

Following the format in Exhibit 15-1, record the entries for Kaki Tours that are found on pages 582 and 591. Then post the entries to the appropriate accounts, following the format in Exhibit 15-2. You should begin by recording the first transaction—the deposit by Paige Keith—in the journal. After performing these steps, compare your answers with the solution provided in the next section.

Solution

GENERAL JOURNAL

Page 1

Date 2013		Description	P.R.	Debit		Credit	
June	1	Cash	101	5000	–		
		P. Keith, Capital	301			5000	–
		Owner invested $5,000 in the business.					
	2	Prepaid services	102	50	–		
		Cash	101			50	–
		Paid Tel-Ans for telephone-answering services.					
	4	Office supplies	104	55	–		
		Cash	101			55	–
		Purchased stationery from Print Faster.					
	5	Office equipment	107	250	–		
		Cash	101			25	–
		Accounts payable	201			225	–
		Purchased office equipment.					
	7	Office supplies	104	125	–		
		Cash	101			125	–
		Purchased office supplies.					
	10	Accounts receivable	103	300	–		
		Tour revenue	401			300	–
		Billed tour companies for tours conducted.					
	15	Cash	101	250	–		
		Accounts receivable	103			250	–
		Collected accounts receivable.					
	20	Cash	101	130	–		
		Tour revenue	401			130	–
		Collected cash for tours conducted.					
	25	Office rent expense	501	75	–		
		Cash	101			75	–
		Paid rent on office.					
	30	Accounts receivable	103	400	–		
		Tour revenue	401			400	
		Billed tour companies for tours conducted.					

GENERAL JOURNAL

Page 2

Date 2013		Description	P.R.	Debit	Credit
June	30	Salary expense	502	40 –	
		Salary payable	202		40 –
		Recorded unpaid salary of assistant.			
	30	Telephone-answering expense	503	50 –	
		Prepaid services	102		50 –
		Recorded telephone-answering services used.			
	30	Office supplies expense	504	30 –	
		Office supplies	104		30 –
		Recorded office supplies used.			
	30	Depreciation expense—office equipment	505	5 –	
		Accumulated depreciation—office equipment	108		5 –
		Recorded depreciation for June.			

GENERAL LEDGER

Cash 101

Date 2013		Item	P.R.	Debit	Date 2013		Item	P.R.	Credit
June	1		1	5000 –	June	2		1	50 –
	15		1	250 –		4		1	55 –
	20		1	130 –		5		1	25 –
		(5,050)		5380 –		7		1	125 –
						25		1	75 –
									330 –

Prepaid Services 102

Date 2013		Item	P.R.	Debit	Date 2013		Item	P.R.	Credit
June	2	(Ø)	1	50 –	June	30		2	50 –

Accounts Receivable 103

Date 2013		Item	P.R.	Debit	Date 2013		Item	P.R.	Credit
June	10		1	300 –	June	15		1	250 –
	30		1	400 –					
		(450)		700 –					

Office Supplies 104

Date 2013		Item	P.R.	Debit	Date 2013		Item	P.R.	Credit
June	4		1	55 –	June	30		2	30 –
	7		1	125 –					
		(150)		180 –					

Office Equipment 107

Date 2013		Item	P.R.	Debit	Date 2013	Item	P.R.	Credit
June	5		1	250 –				

Accumulated Depreciation — Office Equipment 108

Date 2013	Item	P.R.	Debit	Date 2013		Item	P.R.	Credit
				June	30		2	5 –

Accounts Payable 201

Date 2013	Item	P.R.	Debit	Date 2013		Item	P.R.	Credit
				June	5		1	225 –

Salary Payable 202

Date 2013	Item	P.R.	Debit	Date 2013		Item	P.R.	Credit
				June	30		2	40 –

P. Keith, Capital 301

Date 2013	Item	P.R.	Debit	Date 2013		Item	P.R.	Credit
				June	1		1	5000 –

Tour Revenue   401

Date 2013		Item	P.R.	Debit	Date 2013		Item	P.R.	Credit
					June	10		1	300 –
						20		1	130 –
						30	(830)	1	400 –
									830 –

Office Rent Expense   501

Date 2013		Item	P.R.	Debit	Date 2013		Item	P.R.	Credit
June	25		1	75 –					

Salary Expense   502

Date 2013		Item	P.R.	Debit	Date 2013		Item	P.R.	Credit
June	30		2	40 –					

Telephone-Answering Expense   503

Date 2013		Item	P.R.	Debit	Date 2013		Item	P.R.	Credit
June	30		2	50 –					

Office Supplies Expense   504

Date 2013		Item	P.R.	Debit	Date 2013		Item	P.R.	Credit
June	30		2	30 –					

Depreciation Expense—Office Equipment   505

Date 2013		Item	P.R.	Debit	Date 2013		Item	P.R.	Credit
June	30		2	5 –					

FINANCIAL STATEMENTS

The Accounting Cycle

Thus far, we have discussed the recording aspects of the accounting cycle, which consist of (1) analyzing transactions and events to see how they affect assets, liabilities, and equity; (2) recording the transactions and events by making entries in a journal; and (3) posting the journal entries to ledger accounts.

The ultimate purpose of accounting is to provide information to decision makers. Information about the results of past operations and current financial position assists in making decisions about the future. Financial reporting organizes the mass of data that the accounting system has gathered into statements that can help users interpret the information. The financial reporting aspects of the accounting cycle are (1) preparing a trial balance, (2) adjusting the accounts as necessary, and (3) preparing financial statements. The final aspect of the accounting cycle is closing the temporary subsets of equity. This cycle is repeated every accounting period. In specific cases, the cycle may be expanded or contracted to fit the particular circumstances facing the organization.

The Trial Balance

To help prepare financial statements and locate errors that may have been made in the recording or posting processes, a *trial balance* is prepared. The trial balance is a columnar listing of each ledger account, together with its balance. If the debit and credit columns equal each other, the system is in balance. The trial balance in Table 15-12 was prepared from the ledger accounts on pages 596–598.

TABLE 15-12 Trial Balance

Kaki Tours
Trial Balance
June 30, 2013

	Debits	Credits
Cash	$5,050	
Accounts receivable	450	
Office supplies	150	
Office equipment	250	
Accumulated depreciation—office equipment		$ 5
Accounts payable		225
Salary payable		40
P. Keith, Capital		5,000
Tour revenue		830
Office rent expense	75	
Salary expense	40	
Telephone-answering expense	50	
Office supplies expense	30	
Depreciation expense—office equipment	5	
	$6,100	$6,100

Errors can occur within the system even if the debit and credit columns in the trial balance are equal. Examples of such errors include (1) entries that are not recorded, (2) amounts debited (credited) to incorrect accounts, and (3) complete entries recorded for incorrect amounts.

The financial statements are usually prepared directly from the trial balance. In some systems, a formal adjusting process must be completed before the statements can be prepared. Such a process is discussed next.

Adjusting Entries

After the trial balance has been prepared, *adjusting entries* may be needed to bring the financial records up-to-date before statements are prepared. Adjusting entries, as discussed previously, are needed if the books have not been adjusted continuously to the full accrual basis of accounting. A good example is depreciation. Recall that in the Kaki Tours illustration depreciation was recorded to recognize the fact that the services of the asset Office equipment were being used up.

Logic would indicate that the using-up process is gradual and does not occur suddenly at the end of an accounting period. If the books were to be maintained on a current basis, an entry for depreciation would need to be made daily. Because financial statements are prepared only periodically, however, it is not necessary to have the books fully up-to-date until the statements are prepared. Therefore, adjusting entries are made at the end of each period before the financial statements are prepared.

In addition to depreciation in the Kaki Tours illustration, Prepaid services must be adjusted. Although the services were used each day, it was not necessary to record the using up (or gradual expiration) of the asset until the end of the period. In the illustration, note that adjustments were also made for using up office supplies, as well as for salaries earned by an employee but not yet paid to him. The previous section "The Accrual Basis of Accounting" discusses other examples of accruals, deferrals, and amortizations for which adjusting entries might be needed if not otherwise recorded.

Financial Statements

After adjusting entries have been made, we are ready to prepare financial statements. Statements commonly prepared are (1) an income (or operating or activity) statement, (2) a statement of changes in owner's equity, (3) a balance sheet, and (4) a statement of cash flows.

An *income statement* compares the revenues earned with the expenses incurred in earning those revenues, and it reports the resulting net income or net loss. For a profit-oriented organization, this statement is called an income statement. An income statement for Paige Keith's business—Kaki Tours—is shown in Table 15-13.

The *statement of changes in owner's equity* provides a reconciliation of the beginning and ending owner's capital balance. Items that increase owner's capital include investments by the owner and net income for the period. Items that decrease the balance are owner's withdrawals and net losses. Owner's withdrawals are covered later in this chapter. A statement of changes in owner's equity is shown in Table 15-14.

The final statement that will be illustrated is the *balance sheet.* This statement reports the balances of the asset, liability, and capital accounts at the end of the period (see Table 15-15).

An understanding of the accounting system requires an understanding of the relationship between the financial statements. Notice that the net income for the period is taken from the income statement and is used to determine the ending balance in the owner's capital account. Notice also that the ending balance in the owner's capital account is used to balance the balance sheet.

TABLE 15-13 Income Statement

Kaki Tours
Income Statement
For the Month Ended June 30, 2013

Revenue		
Tour revenue		$830
Expenses		
Office rent expense	$75	
Salary expense	40	
Telephone-answering expense	50	
Office supplies expense	30	
Depreciation expense—office equipment	5	200
Net Income		$630

TABLE 15-14 Statement of Changes in Owner's Equity

Kaki Tours
Statement of Changes in Owner's Equity
For the Month Ended June 30, 2013

P. Keith, Capital, June 1, 2013	$ 0
Investment during June	5,000
Income for June	630
P. Keith, Capital, June 30, 2013	$5,630

TABLE 15-15 Balance Sheet

Kaki Tours
Balance Sheet
June 30, 2013

Assets		
Cash		$5,050
Accounts receivable		450
Office supplies		150
Office equipment	$250	
Less, accumulated depreciation	5	245
Total assets		$5,895
Liabilities and Equity		
Liabilities:		
Accounts payable		$ 225
Salary payable		40
Total liabilities		265
Equity:		
P. Keith, Capital		5,630
Total liabilities and equity		$5,895

Assets =
Liabilities +
Equity

A *statement of cash flows* should also be prepared for a business, but a discussion of its preparation is beyond the scope of this chapter.

Financial Statement Work Sheet

To facilitate preparation of the financial statements, accountants use a *work sheet* that starts with the trial balance and spreads this information across columns for the income statement, the statement of changes in owner's equity, and the balance sheet. Often, the work sheet will contain 12 columns: the first two for the unadjusted trial balance, the next two for adjusting entries, the next two for the adjusted trial balance, and the last six for the financial statements. For Kaki Tours, the trial balance shown in Table 15-12 already contains the effect of the adjusting journal entries, so we will prepare an eight-column work sheet—starting with the adjusted trial balance. Preparing the work sheet requires an ability to distinguish between accounts that belong in the income statement and accounts that belong in the balance sheet.

When you review the work sheet in Table 15-16, notice the following:

- When you extend the income statement accounts from the adjusted trial balance columns to the income statement columns, the total of the credit amounts exceeds the total of the debit amounts by $630. This means that net revenues exceed net expenses, resulting in net income—an increase in owner's equity. To keep the statements in balance, the $630 net credit in the income statement columns is extended to the credit column of the statement of changes in owner's equity by putting a $630 debit in the income statement columns and a corresponding credit in the statement of changes in owner's equity columns.
- It is also necessary to extend the owner's equity accounts from the trial balance to the columns for changes in owner's equity. As a result of this year's net income, the owner's equity now shows total credits of $5,630. Because there were no debits, the new owner's equity amount is $5,630. That net credit is extended to the balance sheet by putting a $5,630 debit into the columns for the statement of changes in owner's equity and a corresponding credit into the balance sheet columns.
- Finally, the balance sheet accounts are extended from the trial balance to the columns for the balance sheet. Notice that the original balance for P. Keith, Capital has been changed by the net effect of the "temporary" revenue and expense accounts. If there are no errors in extending the amounts from the adjusted trial balance to the appropriate columns, the amount of the total debits will equal the amount of the total credits in the balance sheet columns.

Now, trace the figures from each column of the work sheet to the corresponding financial statements illustrated in Tables 15-13 through 15-15.

CLOSING THE BOOKS

The final step in the accounting process is closing the books and getting them ready for the next year.

In this chapter the accounting equation was originally used to account for the acquisition and use of the resources of an organization. Table 15-1, which explained how transactions affect the equation, contained only three types of accounts: assets, liabilities, and equity. These accounts are generally referred to as the *permanent* or *real accounts*. They are labeled *permanent* because they are carried from one period to another. Thus, for example, the ending balance of Cash of one period will be the beginning balance of Cash for the next period.

TABLE 15-16 Work Sheet for Preparing Financial Statements

Kaki Tours
Work Sheet for Preparing Financial Statements
June 30, 2013

	Adjusted Trial Balance		Income Statement		Changes in Owner's Equity		Balance Sheet	
	Debits	Credits	Debits	Credits	Debits	Credits	Debits	Credits
Cash	$5,050						$5,050	
Accounts receivable	450						450	
Office supplies	150						150	
Office equipment	250						250	
Acc. dep.—off. equip.		$ 5						$ 5
Accounts payable		225						225
Salary payable		40						40
P. Keith, Capital		5,000				$5,000		
Tour revenue		830		$830				
Office rent expense	75		$ 75					
Salary expense	40		40					
Tel. ans. expense	50		50					
Office supplies exp.	30		30					
Dep. exp.—off. equip.	5		5					
	$6,100	$6,100	200	830				
Net income			630			630		
			$830	$830		5,630		
P. Keith, Cap. 6/30					$5,630			5,630
					$5,630	$5,630	$5,900	$5,900

As the illustrations in this chapter became more complex, the changes in equity resulting from operations of the business were accumulated in separate accounts called revenues and expenses. The purpose of these accounts is to identify the particular operating items causing equity to change. These accounts become the source of the data presented on the activity (income) statement. These data are used to help decision makers evaluate the effectiveness of the use of the resources available to management.

After such an evaluation has been made for the current period, however, the data lose their importance. The generation of revenue and the incurrence of expenses are relative to a certain period of time. It serves little purpose to know that a business that has been in operation for 100 years has generated $500 million in revenue. Information on revenues and expenses is useful only for evaluating the operations of an organization on a period-by-period basis. As a result, revenue and expense accounts are generally referred to as *temporary* or *nominal accounts*.

If temporary (revenue and expense) accounts are to be used to generate information relative to certain periods, they must be closed out (reduced to a zero balance) at the end of each period, and the balances in those accounts must be transferred to equity. The ledger in Table 15-11

GENERAL JOURNAL   3

Date 2013		Description	Ref.	Debit	Credit
June	30	Tour revenue	401	8 3 0 –	
		Office rent expense	501		7 5 –
		Salary expense	502		4 0 –
		Telephone·answering expense	503		5 0 –
		Office supplies expense	504		3 0 –
		Depreciation expense—office equipment	505		5 –
		P. Keith, Capital	301		6 3 0 –
		Record closing the revenue and expense accounts			
		and transfer the net income to capital.			

EXHIBIT 15-3   Closing Entry

shows a balance in the P. Keith, Capital account of $5,000, the initial contribution by Paige Keith. Analysis of the balance sheet in Table 15-15, however, indicates a capital balance of $5,630. The reason for the difference between these two figures is that the former, the one found in the ledger, does not include the income for the period. Because the effects of operations have already been recorded in the asset and liability accounts, they must also be reflected in the capital account so that the balance sheet will balance.

In summary, the trial balance figure for capital does not include the effect of operating the business. Therefore, it must be updated. In addition, the revenue and expense accounts must be reduced to zero to begin accumulating data for the next period. The process of achieving these goals is referred to as *closing the books*. The closing entry for Kaki Tours as of June 30, 2013, is shown in Exhibit 15-3.

The purpose of the closing process is to zero out the balances of the temporary accounts and transfer the net income for the period to the capital account. The steps involved in this process are as follows:

1. Debit each revenue account for the credit balance currently in the account.
2. Credit each expense account for the debit balance currently in the account.
3. Debit or credit the capital account for the amount needed to balance the journal entry—that is, make the debits equal the credits—thereby providing the amount of the net income or loss.

After posting these entries to the accounts, the revenue and expense accounts will no longer have any balances. A double line should be drawn under the date and amount columns for each of those accounts, and the accounts will then be ready for the next year's postings. The asset, liability, and equity accounts all have balances that will be carried into the next period as the beginning balances in those accounts.

OTHER TRANSACTIONS AND OTHER MATTERS

Withdrawals by the Owner

In the example just discussed, Kaki Tours had net income of $630 for the month of June. What if Paige Keith had decided—just before the end of the month—to withdraw $200 in cash as compensation for her work? Withdrawals by the owner of a business are not treated as expenses. Instead, they are recorded as reductions of equity. An account called P. Keith, Withdrawals would be debited for $200, and Cash would be credited. When closing the books, P. Keith, Capital would be debited for $200, and P. Keith, Withdrawals would be credited. For financial reporting purposes, the withdrawal is reported not in the income statement, but rather in the statement of changes in owner's equity—Table 15-14.

Control and Subsidiary Accounts

Until now, we have shown just single accounts for accounts receivable and for accounts payable. In practice, large entities will have thousands of individual accounts receivable and accounts payable, representing amounts owed by their customers and to their creditors. Maintaining separate accounts for each receivable and each payable in the general ledger would make the general ledger extremely unwieldy. To simplify record keeping, most entities maintain a separate accounts receivable ledger, with a page for each customer. They also keep a separate accounts payable ledger, with a page for each creditor. These ledgers are called *subsidiary ledgers,* and the individual accounts are called *subsidiary accounts.*

To record individual receivable and payable transactions, postings are made to each affected account in the subsidiary ledger. Summary postings for the total of the amounts affecting the accounts receivable and accounts payable accounts are made to those accounts in the general ledger. The accounts receivable and accounts payable accounts maintained in the general ledger are referred to as *control accounts.* The totals of the control accounts must be equal at all times to the total of the individual accounts kept in the subsidiary ledgers.

Credit Sales and Bad Debts

The U.S. economy is basically a credit economy. Instead of paying cash immediately, customers are allowed a certain period of time to pay. Although this practice may stimulate sales, selling on credit also has a cost. Some customers may not pay their bills, resulting in an expense called *bad debts expense.* When should you record this expense: in the year of the sale or in the year the bad debt is written off?

To determine the answer, think about the question in another way: Is this expense attributable to the year the sales were made or to the year the customer failed to pay the bill? Remember that, under accrual accounting, expenses need to be matched with the revenues to which the expenses relate. Therefore, the bad debts expense should be recorded in the year the sales revenue was recorded.

Recording this expense raises a few questions:

- If specific bad debts have not yet occurred, how do you know how much to record as an expense?

  Answer: Make an estimate, generally based on past experience and calculated as a percentage of the year's sales or as a percentage of the unpaid accounts receivable.

- If bad debts have not yet occurred, how do you reduce the balance of the Accounts receivable account? Which specific account in the accounts receivable subsidiary ledger should you reduce if you don't know which receivables will not be collected?

  Answer: Don't reduce any specific account receivable at the time you record the bad debts expense. Instead, create another account, called Allowance for uncollectible accounts. This account stands in place of the credit to Accounts receivable until an actual bad debt becomes known. When an actual bad debt becomes known, reduce Accounts receivable, as well as the Allowance account.

To illustrate this process, return to the Kaki Tours illustration. Notice from Table 15-13 that Kaki Tours had tour revenue of $830. Notice also (see Accounts receivable in Table 15-15) that some customers had not yet paid their bills. They owed Kaki a total of $450. These financial statements were based on the assumption that everyone would pay. Suppose, however, based on her experience, Paige Keith believes that not everyone will pay. She estimates that about 10 percent of the $450 owed to her on June 30, 2013, will not be paid. To record this estimate, the following entry is needed:

Bad debts expense	45	
Allowance for uncollectible accounts		45
To record estimated bad debts.		

The $45 bad debts expense would be reported as one of the expenses on the income statement, thereby reducing Kaki Tours' net income from $630 to $585. The Allowance for uncollectible accounts would be shown as a reduction of Accounts receivable on the balance sheet, so that the net Accounts receivable would be reported as $405.

Now, assume one of the individuals included in Accounts receivable at June 30 goes bankrupt in August, after the statements are issued. Because he cannot pay the $30 he owes, Accounts receivable must be reduced. Also, because the Allowance for uncollectible accounts had been set up for that purpose, that account is also reduced. The entry is as follows:

Allowance for uncollectible accounts	30	
Accounts receivable		30
To record write-off of bad debt.		

What is the financial reporting effect of these transactions? The account Allowance for uncollectible accounts is called a *contra-asset*. For financial reporting purposes, it serves to reduce the reported Accounts receivable balance, so that Accounts receivable is stated at its net realizable value; that is, the amount expected to be realized in cash. A balance sheet prepared as of June 30, 2013, would show Accounts receivable of $450, less Allowance for uncollectible accounts of $45, for a net asset of $405. A balance sheet prepared immediately after the write-off of the bad debt would show Accounts receivable of $420, less Allowance for uncollectible accounts of $15, leaving the *same net asset of $405*.

Buying and Selling Merchandise

For simplicity, the illustrations in this chapter deal with the sale of services. Much of what takes place in the U.S. economy, however, concerns the purchase (or manufacture) and sale of products. How would a retail store, for example, account for the purchase and sale of clothing? Assume Sammi's Dresses purchases 12 dresses on credit at a cost of $100 each. She sells five of them for cash at $160 each. You can tell from inspection that Sammi made a profit of $300 on the sale, because she sold five dresses and made a profit of $60 on each. You reached that conclusion because you "matched" the selling price of each dress ($160) with the cost of each dress ($100). The accounting process follows the same matching process, as the following entries show:

Merchandise inventory	1,200	
Accounts payable		1,200
To record merchandise purchases (12 dresses @ $100).		
Cash	800	
Sales revenue		800
To record sales of merchandise (5 dresses @ $160).		

Cost of goods sold	500	
Merchandise inventory		500
To record cost of sales (5 dresses @ $100).		

Consider the effect of these transactions. Merchandise inventory is an asset account. After the journal entries were made, that account has a balance of $700, representing seven dresses that cost Sammi $100 each. Sales revenue and Cost of goods sold are equity accounts (a revenue and an expense account). Matching the Sales revenue ($800) with the Cost of goods sold ($500) shows that Sammi's gross profit was $300.

Review Questions

Q15-1 Define the following terms:
    a. Assets
    b. Liabilities
    c. Equity
    d. Revenue
    e. Expense
Q15-2 Write the accounting equation.
Q15-3 Must the accounting equation always balance? Why?
Q15-4 Describe the difference between the cash basis of accounting and the accrual basis.
Q15-5 Describe and illustrate the difference between an accrual and a deferral.
Q15-6 Identify the rules of debit and credit with respect to assets, liabilities, equity, revenues, and expenses.
Q15-7 A student of basic accounting made the following statement: "For each account debited, there must be another account credited for the same amount." Do you agree? Why or why not?
Q15-8 What is a journal, and how is it used in the accounting process?
Q15-9 What is a ledger, and how is it used in the accounting process?
Q15-10 How are journals and ledgers interrelated in an accounting system?
Q15-11 If the columns of a trial balance total to the same amount, the information included in the accounts must be correct. Do you agree or disagree? Why?
Q15-12 What are the three basic financial statements illustrated in the text?
Q15-13 Describe the interrelationship among the three statements in Q15-12.
Q15-14 Why is it important to put the appropriate date or time period on a financial statement?
Q15-15 What is the purpose of adjusting entries?
Q15-16 Which accounts are closed at the end of an accounting period? Why are these accounts closed?

Exercises

E15-1 (Preparing transactions)
For each of the following categories, compose a transaction that will cause that category to increase and one that will cause it to decrease:
    1. Assets
    2. Liabilities
    3. Equity
    4. Revenues
    5. Expenses

E15-2   (Associating changes with specific accounts)
For each of the following transactions of Vicky's Day Care Center, identify the accounts that would be increased and those that would be decreased:
1. The center borrowed $10,000 from a bank.
2. Rent for the months of July and August was paid, a total of $4,000.
3. An assistant was hired at a monthly salary of $3,000.
4. Customers were billed for day care services: $17,000.
5. The utilities bill for the month was paid: $350.

E15-3   (Calculating the change in equity from balance sheet data)
The beginning and ending balances in certain account categories of the Release Company are as follows:

Account Categories	Beginning Balances	Ending Balances
Assets	$318,000	$331,000
Liabilities	$107,000	$110,000

Based on this information, what was the change in equity for the period?

E15-4   (Associating accrual-type changes with specific accounts)
For each of the following events affecting Vicky's Day Care Center in E15-2, identify the accounts that would be increased and those that would be decreased:
1. The first of the 2 months for which rent had been paid, expired.
2. The assistant in E15-2 worked for a full month and earned $3,000 but was not paid.

E15-5   (Associating accrual-type changes with specific accounts)
For each of the following events affecting Youth Services, identify the accounts that would be increased and those that would be decreased on April 30 in order to accurately measure the results of operations for the month of April:
1. Youth Services borrowed $10,000 on April 1 to provide working capital. It promised to repay the loan in 12 months with interest at 6 percent a year.
2. Youth Services did not plan to use the entire $10,000 immediately. On April 1, it invested $2,000 in a 90-day Treasury bill that would pay 4 percent interest.
3. Youth Services paid $1,800 on April 1 for a 3-year fire insurance policy.

E15-6   (Using debits and credits)
Bobby Hooks, licensed master plumber, had the following transactions and events during his first month of business. Prepare journal entries to record them. After you have prepared the journal entries, scan the accounts, and state which ones you would use to determine Bobby's net profit for the month.
1. Purchased a truck for $24,000. He paid $4,000 in cash and signed a note for the rest.
2. Purchased, on credit, copper pipes and a variety of other items for use in repair jobs at a cost of $3,500. He recorded these items as Supplies inventory.
3. Billed customers $6,000 for work done during the month.
4. Paid $1,500 in salary to a young apprentice plumber.
5. Estimated that $1,200 of supplies was used in performing repair jobs.
6. Paid the $3,500 invoice in transaction 2.
7. Received $5,300 from collections of accounts receivable.
8. At month-end, owed $200 salary to his apprentice plumber.

E15-7   (Associating debits and credits with account categories)
Each of the account categories listed in E15-1 is increased with either a debit or a credit. Indicate which is used to record an increase in each type of account, and state whether the normal account balance is a debit or a credit.

E15-8 (Associating transactions with their effects on the accounting equation)

Life Support, a not-for-profit nursing home, had the following transactions in 2013. For each transaction, state whether an asset increased or decreased, a liability increased or decreased, or equity (revenues or expenses) increased or decreased. (Each transaction has two answers.)

1. Borrowed $100,000 in cash from a bank.
2. Bought equipment on credit.
3. Sent bills to Medicaid for care of residents.
4. Paid rent on January 1 for the 3-month period January–March.
5. Recorded depreciation on equipment it owned.
6. Paid salaries to its employees.
7. Made a year-end accrual for interest owed the bank on money it had borrowed.

E15-9 (Recognizing asset, liability, revenue, and expense accounts)

Based on the following data, calculate the net income for the period and the balance in the account for Nuno Texeira, Capital after the closing entry has been posted.

Cash	$12,000
Accounts receivable	15,000
Prepaid rent	1,000
Ironworking equipment	30,000
Accumulated depreciation, equipment	9,000
Accounts payable	5,000
Notes payable to bank	10,000
Nuno Texeira, Capital	25,000
Service revenue	30,000
Depreciatión expense, equipment	3,000
Rent expense	6,000
Salary expense	14,000

E15-10 (Using debits and credits)

Ken Cascioli and Bill Ryder, master painters and paperhangers, formed a partnership. They had the following transactions during their first month of business. Record the debits and credits, without making explanations.

1. Ken and Bill each invested $3,000 in the business. (Note: Use separate capital accounts for each.)
2. Ken and Bill acquired the following items of equipment for use in the business:
   a. Ladders and other equipment, for which they paid $1,800 in cash. They estimated that the equipment would have an average useful life of 6 years.
   b. A pickup truck, which they bought for $10,000. They paid $2,000 in cash as a down payment and signed a note for the remainder, agreeing to pay $1,000 a month for the next 8 months, together with interest at the rate of 5 percent per annum on the unpaid balance of the loan. They estimated the truck would have a useful life of 4 years.
3. They took out a 3-year insurance policy related to their business activities, paying $1,200 cash.
4. They paid $380 for paint and other supplies, all of which was consumed on the various painting jobs they did during the month.
5. They paid $80 for gasoline for the pickup truck.
6. Ken and Bill expect payment from their customers every Friday for work done during the week. During the month they collected $9,380 in cash for their work.

E15-11 (Using debits and credits for adjusting journal entries)

Ken Cascioli and Bill Ryder (see E15-10) need to make adjusting journal entries to prepare financial statements based on their first month's activities. Make adjusting journal entries for the following events, referring to the transactions in E15-10 as necessary.

1. Record depreciation for 1 month on the ladders and other equipment.
2. Record depreciation for 1 month on the pickup truck.

3. Accrue interest for 1 month on the note referred to in transaction 2b.

4. Record the cost of insurance for 1 month (see transaction 3).

5. Ken and Bill worked on the last 2 days of the month and earned a total of $850, but they did not collect cash because the last day of the month fell on a Tuesday. Make an accrual for their earnings.

E15-12 (Preparing a trial balance and financial statements)

Ken Cascioli and Bill Ryder (see E15-10 and E15-11) want to know the net income for their first month's activities. Post the journal entries prepared for E15-10 and E15-11 to general ledger T-accounts, and prepare a trial balance. From the trial balance, prepare an income statement, a statement of changes in owners' equity, and a balance sheet.

E15-13 (Recording transactions in a general journal)

Mario and John, who run the best barber shop in Westchester, decided to expand their business. They sold their old equipment and moved to larger quarters in the Arcadian Mall, doing business as the Arcadian Barber Shop. Record the following transactions in general journal form; then, compute the net profit for the month by subtracting expenses from revenues (do not consider owner withdrawals as expenses).

2013

January	2	Mario and John each invested $10,000 in the business.
	2	They borrowed $24,000 from a local bank. The loan must be repaid over 6 years (in equal annual installments of $4,000 each by December 31), with interest at the rate of 6 percent per annum on the unpaid balance.
	2	They paid $36,000 for barber chairs and other equipment, including installation cost.
	2	They paid $5,000 in rent for January and February.
3–31		The barber shop collected cash amounting to $18,500 for services performed during the month.
	31	They paid $3,000 in salaries each to barbers Joe and Pat.
	31	Mario and John each withdrew $3,500 in cash as compensation for their own work.
	31	In preparation for month-end financial statements, they recorded the following expenses for 1 month: (a) depreciation of barber chairs and equipment (estimated life 20 years); (b) interest on the bank borrowing; and (c) expiration of 1 month's rent.
	31	Utility bills arrived in the mail; they totaled $800. The bills will be paid in February.

E15-14 (Preparing a trial balance)

Using the following information, prepare a trial balance for the Bilello Electric Repair Company as of June 30, 2013, grouping together the asset, liability, equity, revenue, and expense accounts.

Accumulated depreciation—truck and tools	$ 4,800
Accounts receivable	1,200
Truck and tools	24,000
Cash	4,000
Utilities expense	1,000
Depreciation expense—truck and tools	2,400
Electrical supplies inventory	3,000
Joe Bilello, Withdrawals	55,000
Joe Bilello, Capital	6,300
Electrical supplies expense	4,000
Service revenue	68,000
Rent expense	3,000
Notes payable	20,000
Truck expense	1,500

E15-15 (Preparing closing entries and determining the ending balance in capital)

Prepare the appropriate closing entry based on the information in E15-14. Compute Joe Bilello's net income for the period, and determine the ending balance in his Capital account.

E15-16 (Computation of balance sheet amounts)

Based upon the following information, compute total assets, total liabilities, and total capital; in addition, determine whether all of the accounts are listed. (Note: This is the first month of operations of the business.)

Cash	$22,000
Accounts receivable	12,000
Accounts payable	15,000
Equipment	50,000
Rent expense	11,000
Service revenue	74,000
Notes payable	17,000
Accumulated depreciation	25,000
Depreciation expense	12,500
Office supplies	3,000
Office supplies expense	8,000
Salaries payable	4,000

E15-17 (Relating accounts and financial statements)

Identify the financial statement on which each of the following items would appear:

a. Bonds payable
b. Rent revenue
c. Owner's capital, beginning balance
d. Cash
e. Equipment
f. Supplies expense
g. Depreciation expense
h. Service revenue
i. Accounts receivable
j. Accounts payable
k. Owner's capital, ending balance
l. Rent expense
m. Accumulated depreciation
n. Net income
o. Salaries payable
p. Land
q. Supplies on hand

E15-18 (Matching accounts and financial statements)

Following are several financial statement classifications and accounts. Identify the proper financial statement classification for each account by placing the appropriate letter key in the space provided. (Some items may appear in more than one statement classification.)

R	Revenue
E	Expense
A	Asset
L	Liability
C	Owner's capital (balance sheet)
SC	Statement of changes in owner's equity

Example: __A__ Cash
_____ 1. Notes payable
_____ 2. Additional investment by owner
_____ 3. Automobile
_____ 4. Depreciation expense—automobile
_____ 5. Prepaid rent
_____ 6. Utilities expense
_____ 7. Consulting revenue
_____ 8. Accounts payable

_____ 9. Ending balance in owner's capital

_____ 10. Office supplies

_____ 11. Accumulated depreciation—automobile

_____ 12. Salaries payable

_____ 13. Office supplies expense

_____ 14. Service revenue

_____ 15. Interest expense

_____ 16. Accounts receivable

_____ 17. Loans made to other companies

_____ 18. Deposit made with utility company (to be repaid in 5 years to the company for which we are keeping the records)

_____ 19. Cash held in a separate bank account from that mentioned previously (to be used to buy a building in a few years)

E15-19 (Fill in the blanks—definitions)

Match the items in the right column with those in the left column.

_____ 1. Statement of changes in owner's equity

_____ 2. Income statement

_____ 3. Net income

_____ 4. Additional investment by the owner

_____ 5. Ending balance in owner's capital

_____ 6. Balance sheet

a. A financial statement that presents the revenues and expenses of a business

b. A financial statement that presents a reconciliation of the owner's beginning and ending capital

c. An increase in owner's capital

d. A financial statement that presents a business's assets, liabilities, and owner's capital

e. Can be found on a balance sheet and a statement of changes in owner's equity

f. An excess of revenues over expenses

E15-20 (Accounting for uncollectible accounts receivable)

South Salem Day Care Center is a not-for-profit organization that provides day care services. Prepare journal entries for the center to record the following events. After making all the journal entries, calculate the net realizable value of the center's accounts receivable.

1. The center billed its clients $120,000 for day care services during the year.

2. The center received $105,000 from its clients in payment of the bills.

3. The center established an allowance for uncollectible accounts receivable in the amount of 10 percent of its outstanding receivables.

4. The center could not locate three clients who owed a total of $800, and it decided to write off their accounts as being uncollectible.

E15-21 (Accounting for the purchase and sale of merchandise)

Nomoto Cars is an automobile dealership. Prepare journal entries to record these transactions. Then, based on the journal entries, determine the total profit Nomoto made on the sales.

1. Nomoto receives 14 automobiles from a manufacturer and puts them into its inventory for resale. Nomoto bought the autos on credit for $22,000 each.

2. During the following week, Nomoto sells five of the automobiles for $26,000 each. The customers pay in cash. (Hint: Prepare two journal entries, one to record the sale proceeds and one to record the cost of the autos sold. For the second entry, debit the account Cost of goods sold.)

Problems

P15-1 (Analyzing transactions on a work sheet)

Sally Golfo, a registered nurse, opens a business called Sally's Elder Care. Golfo plans to care for the elderly herself in a facility that she will rent. The following transactions occurred during July 2013, her first month in business. Analyze these transactions on a work sheet similar to that illustrated in the text. You will need columns for Cash, Accounts receivable, Prepaid rent, Furniture, Notes payable, Accounts payable, and Sally Golfo, Capital.

1	Ms. Golfo invested $5,000 of her own money to start the business.
1	She borrowed $20,000 from the bank to provide her with additional cash. She agreed to repay the bank $1,000 on the last day of every month, starting July 31, with interest at the rate of 6 percent a year on the unpaid balance.
1	She rented the house next to hers for a 3-month period, paying a total of $6,000, to provide a facility to care for her patients.
1	She purchased furniture for the facility. She received an invoice for $4,800, payable in 10 days.
10	She paid the $4,800 invoice for the furniture.
18	She paid her assistant $800 for 2 weeks' work.
20	During the month, she billed her clients $12,000 for services rendered.
25	She received $9,000 in cash from the clients who were previously billed.
30	At month-end, she received a bill for electric service in the amount of $300. She will pay the bill in August.
30	During the month, she paid $500 for food to provide lunch to her clients. (Hint: For this problem, consider the food as an expense when it is purchased.)
31	She paid the bank $1,100 on the borrowing. Of that amount, $1,000 was for the principal payment on the loan, and $100 was for interest.

P15-2 (Analyzing accrual transactions on a work sheet)
Analyze the following accrual-type events, and add them to the work sheet you prepared for P15-1.
1. Adjust for the expiration of 1 month's rent.
2. Adjust for the "using up" of the furniture during the month. (Assume the furniture will have a useful life of 4 years.)
3. Accrue for $800 of salary earned by the assistant during the last 2 weeks of the month but not yet paid to her.

P15-3 (Recording transactions in journals and ledgers)
Using the information given in P15-1 and P15-2, record the transactions in general journal form. Then, post the journal entries to ledger T-accounts, like those shown in Table 15-11. (To help keep track of your postings, give each journal entry the same reference number or letter shown in the problems, and insert that number or letter to the left of the amount recorded in the T-accounts.)

P15-4 (Preparing a trial balance and financial statements)
From the ledger accounts prepared for P15-3, prepare a trial balance. Extend the trial balance to an eight-column work sheet like that shown in Table 15-16, and use the work sheet to prepare the following financial statements: (a) income statement, (b) statement of changes in owner's equity, and (c) balance sheet.

P15-5 (Preparing a closing entry)
Based on the answers you obtained in P15-4, prepare the closing entry.

P15-6 (Analyzing transactions on a work sheet)
Dr. Harlan Elliott opened a magnetic resonance imaging (MRI) facility, to be known as Harlan MRI. The following transactions took place during his first month of operation. Analyze these transactions on a work sheet similar to that illustrated in the text. You will need columns for Cash, Accounts receivable, Supplies inventory, Prepaid rent, Equipment, Notes payable, Accounts payable, Withholding taxes payable, and H. Elliott, Capital.
1. Dr. Elliott invested $80,000 in the business.
2. He purchased MRI equipment from the manufacturer for $1,800,000. To pay for the equipment, Harlan gave the manufacturer a note. He was required to repay the note in five annual payments of $360,000 each, together with interest of 6 percent a year on the unpaid balance.
3. He purchased supplies for $25,000 on credit. The supplies were received and put in inventory.

4. At the beginning of the month, he paid rent in the amount of $3,000.
5. He paid the bill for supplies in the amount of $25,000.
6. During the month, he incurred technician salaries of $12,000. Of this amount, he paid $11,000 in cash to employees. He withheld the other $1,000 from their salaries for taxes, which he will pay the government next month.
7. He billed his patients in the amount of $40,000 for MRI services.
8. On receiving the bills, the patients paid Dr. Elliott a total of $35,000.
9. During the month, he paid bills amounting to $4,000 for utility services.
10. He took inventory of the supplies and found that he had consumed $2,000 of those supplies in the course of the month's activities.

P15-7   (Analyzing accrual transactions on a work sheet)
Analyze the following accrual-type events, and add them to the work sheet you prepared for P15-6.
1. Adjust for the "using up" of the MRI equipment during the month. (Assume the equipment will have a useful life of 10 years.)
2. Accrue 1 month's interest owed on the note payable. (Add a column for Interest payable.)
3. Adjust for the expiration of the entire rent payment.

P15-8   (Recording transactions in journals and ledgers)
Using the information given in P15-6 and P15-7, record the transactions in general journal form. Then, post the journal entries to ledger T-accounts, like those shown in Table 15-11. (To help keep track of your postings, give each journal entry the same reference number or letter shown in the problems, and insert that number or letter to the left of the amount recorded in the T-accounts.)

P15-9   (Preparing a trial balance and financial statements)
From the ledger accounts prepared for P15-8, prepare a trial balance. Extend the trial balance to an eight-column work sheet like that shown in Table 15-16, and use the work sheet to prepare the following financial statements: (a) income statement, (b) statement of changes in owner's equity, and (c) balance sheet.

P15-10 (Preparing a closing entry)
Based on the answers you obtained in P15-9, prepare the closing entry.

P15-11 (Analyzing transactions on a work sheet)
Ted's Ambulette provides services to and from hospitals and nursing homes. Ted, who went into business recently, keeps records on a work sheet similar to that illustrated in the text. At the start of the new year, his work sheet shows these balances: Cash—$30,000; Accounts receivable—$15,000; Fuel and parts inventory—$8,000; Vehicles—$192,000; Accounts payable—$12,000; Loans payable—$180,000; Ted Elias, Capital—$53,000. (You will also need columns for Investments, Prepaid rent, Prepaid insurance, and Withholding tax payable.) These transactions occurred in the first month of the new year:
1. Ted leased a garage to store his vehicles and to make minor repairs. He paid $6,000 for 2 months' rent.
2. Ted bought accident insurance for a 2-year period, paying $12,000.
3. He received $13,000 from charge-account customers he had billed last year.
4. During the month he purchased $10,000 of fuel and repair parts on credit.
5. He received $50,000 during the month from customers who paid in cash.
6. At month-end, he sent out bills for $14,000 to charge-account customers.
7. He paid $12,000 to suppliers from whom he had purchased on account.
8. Ted's drivers and other employees earned $30,000. He paid them $28,000 and withheld $2,000 in taxes, which he will pay the government next month.
9. On the 15th of the month, Ted invested some of his cash in a 6-month $20,000 Treasury note.
10. During the month, Ted used $6,000 in fuel and repair parts from inventory.
11. Ted paid utility bills amounting to $3,000. He also received a utility bill for $1,000 that he had not paid at month-end.

Record the opening balances on a work sheet similar to that illustrated in the text, and then analyze these transactions on the work sheet.

P15-12 (Analyzing accrual transactions on a work sheet)

Analyze the following accrual-type events, and add them to the work sheet you prepared for P15-11.

1. Adjust for the expiration of 1 month's rent.
2. Adjust for the expiration of 1 month's accident insurance.
3. Adjust for the "using up" of the vehicles during the month. (Assume the vehicles have a useful life of 48 months from the beginning of the year.)
4. Accrue 1 month's interest owed on the $180,000 loan. The interest rate on the borrowing is 8 percent a year. (Add a column for Interest payable.)

P15-13 (Recording transactions in journals and ledgers)

Using the information given in P15-11 and P15-12, record the transactions in general journal form. Then post the journal entries to ledger T-accounts, like those shown in Table 15-11. (To help keep track of your postings, give each journal entry the same reference number or letter shown in the problems, and insert that number or letter to the left of the amount recorded in the T-accounts.)

P15-14 (Preparing a trial balance and financial statements)

From the ledger accounts prepared for P15-13, prepare a trial balance. Extend the trial balance to an eight-column work sheet like that shown in Table 15-16, and use the work sheet to prepare the following financial statements: (a) income statement, (b) statement of changes in owner's equity, and (c) balance sheet.

P15-15 (Preparing a closing entry)

Based on the answers you obtained in P15-14, prepare the closing entry.

P15-16 (Recording debits and credits)

Joseph DeLapa, DDS, opened his practice on June 1, 2013. He had the following transactions during the 3-month period June 1–August 31. Record the transactions in general journal form. Then, post the journal entries to general ledger T-accounts.

1. Dr. DeLapa invested $20,000 of his own cash in the business.
2. He borrowed $80,000 on June 1 from the Vista Bank to pay for dental equipment and provide working capital.
3. He rented office space, effective June 1, agreeing to a 5-year lease. He paid the landlord $8,000 to cover the 4-month period June 1–September 30.
4. He received an invoice from a contractor for $20,000 for work done in April and May to get the office space in condition to receive patients. (Note: Debit an asset account called Leasehold improvements.)
5. He purchased dental chairs and related equipment, on credit, at a cost of $56,000. The chairs and equipment were delivered and installed on June 1.
6. He purchased dental supplies on credit at a cost of $5,000.
7. During the 3 months ended August 31, Dr. DeLapa performed dental services and billed his patients a total of $96,000. He received cash for the entire amount.
8. He paid his dental hygienist and his receptionist a total of $21,000 for work through August 29.
9. He paid creditors a total of $78,000.

P15-17 (Preparing adjusting journal entries)

Prepare adjusting journal entries for the following events related to the transactions in P15-16, and post the journal entries to general ledger T-accounts. (Use the T-accounts set up for P15-16 where appropriate, and set up new T-accounts as needed.)

1. Accrue interest for 3 months on the bank loan in P15-16, transaction 2. Dr. DeLapa had to repay the $80,000 loan in five annual installments of $16,000, starting May 31, 2014, with interest at the rate of 6 percent per annum on the unpaid balance.
2. Adjust for the expiration of the prepaid rent in transaction 3.
3. Adjust for 3 months' amortization on the $20,000 leasehold improvement in transaction 4. The leasehold improvement should be amortized over the 5-year life of the lease.

4. Record depreciation for 3 months on the equipment purchased for $56,000 in transaction 5. The equipment has an estimated useful life of 7 years.

5. Dr. DeLapa took an inventory of the dental supplies purchased in transaction 6. The inventory totaled $4,100, the remainder having been consumed in providing dental care.

6. Accrue $700 for 2 days' salaries for Dr. DeLapa's employees.

P15-18 (Preparing a trial balance and financial statements)

From the ledger accounts prepared for P15-16 and P15-17, prepare a trial balance. Extend the trial balance to an eight-column work sheet like that shown in Table 15-16, and use the work sheet to prepare the following financial statements: (a) income statement, (b) statement of changes in owner's equity, and (c) balance sheet.

P15-19 (Accounts receivable and sales transactions; comprehensive problem)

Camp Bryn Mawr, a summer camp, started the year with cash of $40,000, land costing $300,000, and buildings and equipment costing $250,000. Because the camp had no liabilities, the assets were offset by the equity account F. Jonas, Capital, in the amount of $590,000. The following transactions occurred during the year:

1. Jonas sent bills in the amount of $150,000 to the parents of 75 campers.

2. Jonas purchased 80 camper packages (consisting of uniforms and supplies) on credit from a vendor. He received the packages and put them in inventory. He also received a bill for $4,800 (80 packages costing $60 a package) from the vendor.

3. When they arrived at the camp, each of the 75 campers received a camper package. Jonas sent bills in the amount of $6,750 to the parents, charging them $90 a package.

4. Jonas received cash in the amount of $148,750 from the parents, based on the bills sent out in transactions 1 and 3.

5. During the summer, Jonas paid employee salaries in the amount of $100,000 and food expenses of $8,000. (Assume all the food was consumed.)

6. Jonas paid the invoice for $4,800 for transaction 2.

7. Anticipating that several parents might not pay their bills, Jonas set up an allowance for uncollectible receivables in the amount of $4,000.

8. One of the parents, who owed $2,000, declared bankruptcy. Jonas wrote off the account as uncollectible.

9. Jonas made a provision for depreciation for the year, assuming that the buildings and equipment had a useful life of 20 years.

10. Jonas promised the camp director a bonus of $5,000, based on the excellent work she had done during the year. Jonas, therefore, accrued a liability for that amount.

Use the preceding information to do the following:

a. Prepare journal entries to record these transactions. (Among others, you will need accounts for Revenues—camper fees, Revenues—uniform sales, and Inventory—uniforms.)

b. Post the journal entries to ledger T-accounts.

c. From the ledger accounts, prepare a trial balance.

d. Using the trial balance, prepare an income statement, a statement of changes in owner's equity, and a balance sheet.

INDEX